WITHDRAWN
UTSA Libraries

Firm-Level Internationalization, Regionalism and Globalization

THE ACADEMY OF INTERNATIONAL BUSINESS
Published in Association with the UK Chapter of the Academy of International Business

Titles already published in the series:

International Business and Europe in Transition (Volume 1)
Edited by Fred Burton, Mo Yamin and Stephen Young

Internationalisation Strategies (Volume 2)
Edited by George Chryssochoidis, Carla Miller and Jeremy Clegg

The Strategy and Organization of International Business (Volume 3)
Edited by Peter Buckley, Fred Burton and Hafiz Mirza

Internationalization: Process, Context and Markets (Volume 4)
Edited by Graham Hooley, Ray Loveridge and David Wilson

International Business Organization (Volume 5)
Edited by Fred Burton, Malcolm Chapman and Adam Cross

International Business: Emerging Issues and Emerging Markets (Volume 6)
Edited by Carla C. J. M. Millar, Robert M. Grant and Chong Ju Choi

International Business: European Dimensions (Volume 7)
Edited by Michael D. Hughes and James H. Taggart

Multinationals in a New Era: International Strategy and Management (Volume 8)
Edited by James H. Taggart, Maureen Berry and Michael McDermott

International Business (Volume 9)
Edited by Frank McDonald, Heinz Tusselman and Colin Wheeler

Internationalization: Firm Strategies and Management (Volume 10)
Edited by Colin Wheeler, Frank McDonald and Irene Greaves

The Process of Internationalization (Volume 11)
Edited by Frank MacDonald, Michael Mayer and Trevor Buck

International Business in an Enlarging Europe (Volume 12)
Edited by Trevor Morrow, Sharon Loane, Jim Bell and Colin Wheeler

Managerial Issues in International Business (Volume 13)
Edited by Felicia M. Fai and Eleanor J. Morgan

Anxieties and Management Responses in International Business (Volume 14)
Edited by Rudolf Sinkovics and Mo Yamin

Corporate Governance and International Business (Volume 15)
Edited by Roger Strange and Gregory Jackson

Contemporary Challenges to International Business (Volume 16)
Edited by Kevin Ibeh and Sheena Davies

Resources, Efficiency and Globalisation (Volume 17)
Edited by Pavlos Dimitratos and Marian V. Jones

Firm-Level Internationalization, Regionalism and Globalization
Edited by Elaine Hutson, Rudolf R. Sinkovics and Jenny Berrill

Firm-Level Internationalization, Regionalism and Globalization

Edited by

Elaine Hutson, Rudolf R. Sinkovics and Jenny Berrill

Selection and editorial content © Elaine Hutson, Rudolf R. Sinkovics and Jenny Berrill 2011
Individual chapters © the contributors 2011
Foreword © Frank McDonald 2011

All rights reserved. No reproduction, copy or transmission of this publication may be made without written permission.

No portion of this publication may be reproduced, copied or transmitted save with written permission or in accordance with the provisions of the Copyright, Designs and Patents Act 1988, or under the terms of any licence permitting limited copying issued by the Copyright Licensing Agency, Saffron House, 6-10 Kirby Street, London EC1N 8TS.

Any person who does any unauthorized act in relation to this publication may be liable to criminal prosecution and civil claims for damages.

The authors have asserted their rights to be identified as the authors of this work in accordance with the Copyright, Designs and Patents Act 1988.

First published 2011 by
PALGRAVE MACMILLAN

Palgrave Macmillan in the UK is an imprint of Macmillan Publishers Limited, registered in England, company number 785998, of Houndmills, Basingstoke, Hampshire RG21 6XS.

Palgrave Macmillan in the US is a division of St Martin's Press LLC, 175 Fifth Avenue, New York, NY 10010.

Palgrave Macmillan is the global academic imprint of the above companies and has companies and representatives throughout the world.

Palgrave® and Macmillan® are registered trademarks in the United States, the United Kingdom, Europe and other countries.

ISBN 978–0–230–28997–0 hardback

This book is printed on paper suitable for recycling and made from fully managed and sustained forest sources. Logging, pulping and manufacturing processes are expected to conform to the environmental regulations of the country of origin.

A catalogue record for this book is available from the British Library.

A catalog record for this book is available from the Library of Congress.

10 9 8 7 6 5 4 3 2 1
20 19 18 17 16 15 14 13 12 11

Printed and bound in Great Britain by
CPI Antony Rowe, Chippenham and Eastbourne.

Contents

List of Illustrations	viii
Foreword	xi
Acknowledgements	xii
List of Contributors	xiii

Introduction   1
Jenny Berrill, Elaine Hutson and Rudolf R. Sinkovics

Part I   Regional and Global Perspectives

1. The Relation between Alliance Entrepreneurship, Alliance Capability and Foreign Market Performance – An Empirical Investigation   11
   Saba Khalid and Jorma Larimo

2. Foreign Direct Investment in Emerging Asia: Implications of the International Production Network   27
   Juthathip Jongwanich

3. From Federations to Global Factories: Assessing the Contribution of the Subsidiary Middle Manager in Today's MNE   48
   Dónal O'Brien, Pamela Sharkey-Scott and Pat Gibbons

4. Regional Multinational Enterprises and the International Financial Crisis   64
   Alan M. Rugman and Chang Hoon Oh

Part II   Outward FDI

5. The Persistence of Outward Foreign Direct Investment from German Manufacturing Industries   81
   Heinz-Josef Tüselmann, Frank McDonald, Martin T. Bohl, Svitlana Voronkova and Paul Windrum

6. Multinational Performance and Intellectual Property Rights: Evidence from 46 Countries   96
   Yong Yang and Pedro S. Martins

7. The Influence of Exports on Outward Foreign Direct Investment: The Case of India   113
   Rakhi Verma and Louis Brennan

8 Internationalization, Financial Incentives and Firm Growth: Evidence from Italy 126
Mariasole Bannò, Lucia Piscitello and Celeste Amorim Varum

Part III Entrepreneurial Firms: Internationalization and Performance

9 Contingency Factors in International Entrepreneurial Orientation – Performance Relations of Firms with Different Levels of Internationalization 143
Sanna Sundqvist, Olli Kuivalainen and John W. Cadogan

10 Forging the Link between Business Model and Value Chain Constructs in the Context of an Internationalizing Entrepreneurial Firm – A Case Study 163
Liisa-Maija Sainio, Sami Saarenketo, Niina Nummela and Taina Eriksson

11 Entrepreneurial Marketing Strategies During the Growth of International New Ventures 177
Johanna Hallbäck and Peter Gabrielsson

Part IV Human Resources, Leadership and Culture

12 Interpersonal Relationships in Transnational, Virtual Teams 201
Angelika Zimmermann

13 Intercultural Ethical Leadership Competence: Contrasting Ireland and Germany 216
Mary A. Keating, Gillian S. Martin and Christian J. Resick

14 The Role of Timing, Duration and Intensity of Training Programmes for Expatriate Adjustment: An Empirical Analysis 233
Markus G. Kittler

Part V Knowledge and Networks

15 Subsidiaries as Learning Engines: Understanding Middle Managers' Search for Knowledge as Micro-foundation 249
Esther Tippmann, Pamela Sharkey-Scott and Vincent Mangematin

16 Converging Themes: Networks, International Performance and the Telecoms Sector 263
Breda Kenny and John Fahy

17 The Link between Born Global Growth, Network Evolution and Firm Performance: A Theoretical Framework 292
Fabian Sepulveda and Mika Gabrielsson

Part VI International Joint Ventures

18 Conceptual, Operational and Methodological Considerations in
    Studying the Trust–Performance Relation: A Critical Review of
    Empirical Research in International Strategic Alliances   315
    Tahir Ali and Jorma Larimo

19 Asset Specificity, Asset Opacity and Ownership Structures in
    Domestic and Cross-Border Joint Ventures   345
    Sougand Golesorkhi and Mo Yamin

Part VII Corporate Governance and Organization

20 Economic Organization and Social Solidarity: *Keiretsu* as a
    Local/Global Concept   365
    Tomoko Oikawa

21 Institutional Determinants of Good Corporate Governance: The
    Case of Nigeria   379
    Emmanuel Adegbite and Chizu Nakajima

22 Socially Entrepreneurial Behaviour of Multinational Corporations:
    Are MNCs 'Social Entrepreneurs'?   397
    Misagh Tasavori and Rudolf R. Sinkovics

23 'Imported' Management Practices: The Disclosure of Individual
    Executive Compensation and Firm Performance   412
    Amon Chizema

Index   431

List of Illustrations

Tables

1.1	Descriptive statistics	19
1.2	Inter-construct correlations and the AVE (square roots) along the diagonal	20
1.3	PLS path analysis results (standardized beta coefficients and t-values)	21
2.1	Share of parts and components in world parts and components trade (per cent)	29
2.2	Share of parts and components in manufacturing trade (per cent)	30
2.3	FDI inflows by region and selected economies (billion US$), 1971–2007	31
2.4	The Granger causality test for emerging Asian economies, 1992–2007	33
2.5	Estimation results	42
4.1	The world's largest 500 companies by sector and region	66
4.2	The world's largest 500 companies by country	70
4.3	The world's largest 500 companies by developing country	72
4.4	Intra-regional assets (per cent) by sector and region	73
4.5	Performance (ROS) by sector and region	75
5.1	Results of unit root tests	89
5.2	Results of Zivot–Andrews unit root test	90
6.1	Descriptive statistics – multinational and domestic firms	101
6.2	Descriptive statistics – firms from developed versus developing countries	102
6.3	Descriptive statistics ($OSTS^{H'ipr}$ vs. $OSTS^{L'ipr}$)	103
6.4	Multinationality and performance: linear effects	107
6.5	Multinationality and performance: firms from developed countries	108
6.6	Multinationality and performance: firms from developing countries	109
7.1	Augmented Dickey–Fuller tests for unit roots	120
7.2	Cointegration tests	120
7.3	Granger causality tests for OFDI and exports based on VECM	121
8.1	Summary of studies addressing the effect of HCMs towards OFDI	128
8.2	Description of the variables and sources of data	133
8.3	Comparison between benefiting firms and non-benefiting firms	134
8.4	Treatment effect model – two-steps estimates	135

9.1	Invariance diagnostics	150
9.2	Construct correlations and scale properties	153
9.3	Fit measures for the main effect, fully unrestricted, fully restricted and final models	154
9.4	Fit measures for the fully unrestricted and the partially restricted models	155
9.5	Path coefficient and *t*-values	156
12.1	Influences between relationship aspects as indicated in the reviewed literature	203
12.2	Configuration examples	210
13.1	Mean culture scores for respondents from Ireland and Germany	218
13.2	Endorsement of ethical leadership among middle managers in Ireland and Germany	222
13.3	Ethical leadership themes between Irish and German managers	224
13.4	Attributes and behaviours attributed to integrity and leader integrity	225
14.1	Pearson correlations	238
14.2	Independent samples *t*-test (two-tailed)	240
15.1	Salience of middle managers' knowledge search aspects and level of organizational adaptation	256
16.1	Activities carried out by respondent firms	273
17.1	Focus areas of selected born globals literature	295
17.2	Comparative summary of IMP and strategic networks views	297
18.1	Sample location, relationship type, industries studied, data collection side, methodology and data analysis methods	317
18.2	The theoretical approaches, conceptualization, dimensions, levels and operationalization of trust	323
18.3	Performance measurement and performance effects of trust	330
18.4	Trust to performance relation across ISA geographical location, trust levels and alliance type	336
19.1	The Pearson correlation matrix for independent variables ($n=542$)	354
19.2	Descriptive statistics ($n=542$)	355
19.3	Results of the ordered logit analysis ($n=542$)	356
20.1	Summary of characteristics of the Japanese and English languages regarding self	374
21.1	A breakdown of the professional/disciplinary backgrounds of the survey respondents	383
21.2	A breakdown of survey respondents' institutional expertise	383
22.1	Examples of social entrepreneurship definitions	400
23.1	Examples of companies in the DAX 30, MDAX and SDAX listings	420
23.2	Descriptive statistics and correlations	422
23.3	Results of hierarchical regression analysis on firm performance (ROA)	424

Figures

1.1	Hypothesized relations	17
2.1	FDI and parts and components trade in emerging Asian economies	32
3.1	Floyd and Wooldridge (1992) typology of middle management involvement in strategy	55
3.2	Proposed extensions to the Floyd and Wooldridge (1992) typology	55
6.1	Distribution of multinational performance (ROS)	104
6.2	Distribution of multinationality (OSTS) and firm performance	104
6.3	Distribution of multinationality ($OSTS^{H'ipr}$ & $OSTS^{L'ipr}$) and firm performance	105
6.4	Scatterplot of the number of overseas subsidiaries in high- and low-IPR countries	106
7.1	Indian OFDI (1981–2006)	115
7.2	Indian exports (1981–2006)	116
10.1	The business model construct of the study	167
10.2	The business model of Syscon Ltd	170
11.1	Entrepreneurial marketing strategy dimensions in an INV	182
11.2	Conceptual framework on the development of entrepreneurial marketing strategies in an international new venture	184
16.1	Final model	275
17.1	Conceptual framework of BG network evolution and proposition development	301
21.1	Institutional determinants of corporate governance	392
22.1	Continuum of social entrepreneurship based on funding strategy	405
22.2	Social entrepreneurship definition	406
22.3	Corporate social entrepreneurship definition	408

Appendices

GLOBE Culture dimensions and definitions	229
CFA and constructs reliability	282

Foreword

The 37th Annual Conference of the Academy of International Business, United Kingdom and Ireland (UKI) Chapter was held for the first time in the Republic of Ireland on 8–10 April 2010 at the School of Business and the Institute for International Integration Studies at Trinity College Dublin. This book contains a selection of papers presented at the conference that highlight key issues in the theme of the conference – 'Regionalism and Globalization'. The book is the 18th volume in the Palgrave AIB UK and Ireland International Business series.

The importance of the conference theme was powerfully illustrated by the keynote addresses by Peter Buckley 'The Regional and Global Implications of the Rise of the Global Factory' and by Alan Rugman 'Has the World Financial Crisis Reinforced Regionalism at the Expense of Globalization'. The first section of this book explores directly many of the major issues in this important topic. The following sections of the book investigate this topic in the context of some of the key issues in international business.

The 37th Annual Conference attracted 170 delegates from 20 countries, with 38 different nationalities among the delegates. The delegates presented 101 papers at the conference and a further 40 papers were given in the Doctoral Colloquium. A special session held during the conference on research methods in international business reflected the commitment of the AIB UK and Ireland Chapter to encouraging the development of research in international business. The output of the Chapter, including this book, confirms the commitment of the Chapter to promote and develop international business research in the UK and Ireland and in the wider community of international business scholars. Please visit our website to explore the work of the Chapter and to find out how to become involved with the work of the Chapter: www.aib-uki.org.

Frank McDonald
Chair, Academy of International Business,
UK and Ireland Chapter

Acknowledgements

Many thanks to the School of Business and the Institute for International Integration Studies at Trinity College Dublin for hosting the 37th Annual Conference of the Academy of International Business, United Kingdom and Ireland (UKI) Chapter. Particular thanks to Colm Kearney (Conference Chair) and Anna Morgan Thomas (Doctoral Colloquium Convenor) and the associated staff and doctoral students at Trinity College Dublin.

List of Contributors

Emmanuel Adegbite is a lecturer in corporate governance at Newcastle Business School, UK. Emmanuel's research interests include comparative corporate governance systems, institutional configurations of corporate governance in varieties of capitalism, corporate governance in developing countries, corporate governance regulation, corporate social responsibility and business ethics. He has notable research outputs in these areas as well as numerous paper presentations at leading national and international conferences. Before joining Newcastle Business School, Emmanuel held a visiting appointment at Cass Business School, London, where he also received his PhD.

Tahir Ali is a PhD student at the University of Vaasa, Finland. He received his MSc degree in Economics and Business Administration from the University of Vaasa, and his research interests include international joint ventures, international strategic alliances and trust management issues.

Mariasole Bannò is a research fellow at the Department of Industrial and Mechanical Engineering at the University of Brescia, Italy. She graduated in Industrial Engineering in 2003 from the University of Brescia and defended her PhD thesis entitled 'Allocation, effects and effectiveness of public incentive programmes to firms' outward internationalisation' in 2009. Her research interests concern the outward and inward internationalization of firms and the evaluation of public policies.

Jenny Berrill is a lecturer in the School of Business Studies, Trinity College Dublin, Ireland. Her research interests are in the area of international finance and multinational companies (MNCs). She has published articles in the *Journal of Economics and Business* and *Research in International Business and Finance*.

Martin T. Bohl is Professor of Monetary Economics at the Westfälische Wilhelms-University Münster, Germany.

Louis Brennan is a professor at the School of Business and a research associate of the Institute for International Integration Studies at Trinity College Dublin, Ireland. He is Director of the Global Business Systems centre at Trinity College and is currently Chair of EU COST Action IS0905, encompassing researchers from 19 countries that are addressing the emergence of non-triad multinationals and their impact on Europe.

John W. Cadogan is Professor of Marketing at the Business School, Loughborough University, where he has held faculty positions since 2003. He researches issues in marketing strategy, international marketing and sales, and has published in a wide range of outlets on these topics, including in the *Journal of the Academy of Marketing Science, Journal of International Business Studies, International Journal of Research in Marketing, Journal of Business Research, British Journal of Management, Journal of International Marketing, Industrial Marketing Management,* and the *European Journal of Marketing,* among others. He has been editor of the *International Marketing Review* since 2007.

Amon Chizema is a senior lecturer in international business and strategy at Loughborough University, UK. His research interests include international corporate governance, the dynamics of institutions and economic development. Amon's research has been published in leading journals such as the *Journal of Management Studies, Journal of World Business, Corporate Governance: An International Review* and *International Business Review.* He has presented several papers at major conferences such as the Academy of International Business, Academy of Management and Society for the Advancement of Socio-Economics. He received his PhD in International Business from Loughborough University.

Taina Eriksson is a researcher in international business at the Turku School of Economics, University of Turku, Finland. She is currently working on her doctoral dissertation in which she examines dynamic capabilities in the context of internationalizing technology-intensive SMEs. She is also project coordinator in a research project on the value chain management of internationalizing software firms.

John Fahy currently holds the Chair in Marketing at the University of Limerick, Ireland. He has a distinguished track record of teaching and research in the fields of marketing and business strategy. In particular, he is known for his work in the area of marketing resources and capabilities and how these factors impact on organizational performance. He is a founding member of the MC21 group, which has conducted research on marketing resources and performance across 15 countries. Other current research interests include evolutionary perspectives on marketing and neuro-marketing. He is the author of 38 articles on marketing and strategy that have been published in journals such as the *Journal of Marketing, Journal of International Business Studies, Journal of Business Research, Journal of Marketing Management, European Journal of Marketing, International Business Review* and *Sloan Management Review.*

Mika Gabrielsson is Professor of International Business at the Aalto University School of Economics, Finland. He holds DSc and MSc degrees from Helsinki School of Economics (now Aalto University). His teaching covers areas such as internationalization of the firm and global marketing management, and his research interests include, among other topics, rapid globalization. He has been active in several research projects that have been funded by the Academy of Finland and the Finnish Funding Agency for Technology and Innovation, such as 'Born Globals' and 'Response to Globalization'. Mika has published over 140 articles in refereed international journals, edited books and conference proceedings. He is on the editorial board of *Industrial Marketing Management*. Before joining the academic world, he held several senior positions in purchasing and marketing in global high-tech companies.

Peter Gabrielsson, DSc, is Professor of International Marketing at the University of Vaasa, and adjunct professor of international business at Aalto University School of Economics, Finland. His teaching covers areas such as export and global marketing, and his research interests include the globalization process of firms, born globals, globalizing internationals and global marketing strategies. He is currently leading a large research project investigating born globals, funded by the Finnish funding agency of technology and innovation. He has published in journals such as the *International Business Review*, *International Marketing Review* and *Industrial Marketing Management*. He has long experience in senior management positions at Nokia and other global ICT firms.

Pat Gibbons was appointed Jefferson Smurfit Professor of Strategic Management at University College Dublin in 2003. He has a PhD in strategic planning and policy from the University of Pittsburgh. Before entering academia, Pat worked in a number of financial and corporate strategy roles with KPMG, Jefferson Smurfit Group, the Investment Bank of Ireland and An Post (the Irish Post Office). His current research interests revolve around control practices of MNCs, the impact of strategic planning systems on organizational behaviour and performance, and the application of social theory to strategic process research.

Sougand Golesorkhi is a senior lecturer at Manchester Metropolitan University Business School. Her research interest is mainly focused on the economics and financial analysis of cross-border joint ventures.

Johanna Hallbäck is a researcher at the Marketing and International Business unit of the University of Vaasa, where she is pursuing a doctoral degree in International Marketing. She is currently coordinating a large research project investigating born globals, funded by Tekes, the Finnish funding agency of technology and innovation. She has also worked as a lecturer in the fields of export marketing, internationalization, market research and case study research in international business. Her research interests lie in the interface of international business, entrepreneurship and marketing, taking a cross-disciplinary approach to researching small and new firms. She already has had academic articles and chapters in books published, and has presented papers at several conferences such as the Academy of International Business (AIB) and European International Business Academy (EIBA) meetings, and at the International Council for Small Business (ISCB) World Conference. She has received a best paper award at the Research in Entrepreneurship and Small Business (RENT) conference and been nominated for best paper awards at the ICSB World

Conference and at the Entrepreneurship, Innovation and Small Business (EISB) Conference.

Elaine Hutson is a lecturer in finance at University College Dublin. Her research interests are mainly in the sub-discipline of corporate finance, and include small business financing, mergers and acquisitions, and firm-level foreign exchange exposure. Her capital markets research interests include hedge funds performance and regulation, the characteristics of stock market returns, and the history of the managed funds industry. Her work has been published in international business (IBR and JIBS) and finance journals including the *Journal of International Business Studies, International Business Review, Journal of Empirical Finance, Journal of Banking and Finance, Journal of International Financial Markets, Institutions and Money, International Review of Financial Analysis, Journal of the Asia Pacific Economy* and *Venture Capital*.

Juthathip Jongwanich is an assistant professor at the School of Management, Asian Institute of Technology (AIT), Thailand. Before she joined the AIT, she worked as an economist at the Macroeconomics and Finance Research Division, Asian Development Bank. She is interested in issues relating to international economics and international macroeconomics.

Mary A. Keating is a senior lecturer in human resource management at Trinity College Dublin. She is a research associate of the International Institute for Integration Studies (IIIS) at Trinity, and a Fellow of the Salzburg Seminar. Her research interests are in the area of International HRM, cross-cultural management and leadership, and human resource management practice across sectors, particularly the healthcare sector, including the management of knowledge and professional workers in the sector.

Breda Kenny is a lecturer in marketing and entrepreneurship at the Tipperary Institute, Ireland. She obtained her PhD from the University of Limerick. Her research focuses on networking capability and international performance of high-tech SMEs. Breda's teaching interests are in the areas of international business, marketing and entrepreneurship. She is involved in numerous projects with industry, development agencies and the European Commission. Her work has appeared in such journals the as the *International Journal of Entrepreneurship and Innovation Management, Irish Journal of Management* and *Journal of Language for International Business*. Breda has extensive industry experience and is also co-founder and marketing director of Surecom NS Ltd.

Saba Khalid is Assistant Professor of International Marketing at the University of Vaasa, Finland. She completed her doctoral degree in 2009. Her research interests include strategies for market-based firm competence, international alliance learning, and management capabilities and their relation with export performance.

Markus G. Kittler is a lecturer in management at the Stirling Management School, University of Stirling, Scotland (UK). He received his PhD from the University of Erlangen-Nuremberg (Germany) and won the Neil Hood and Stephen Young prize for the most original new doctoral work at the AIB UKI conference in 2009. His main research interest is international business with a particular focus on IHRM issues. His research on expatriate management appeared in *The International Journal of Human Resources Management*, *Cross-Cultural Management* and *German Journal of Human Resource Research*.

Olli Kuivalainen, DSc (Econ.) is Professor of International Marketing at the School of Business, Lappeenranta University of Technology, Finland. His research interests are in the areas of international entrepreneurship, and strategic management, marketing and internationalization of knowledge-intensive firms, the focus especially being on firms operating in the domains of media and information and communication technologies. He has published articles in the *Journal of World Business*, *Journal of International Marketing*, *Technovation*, *International Journal of Production Economics* and *Journal of International Entrepreneurship*, among others.

Jorma Larimo is Professor of International Marketing at the University of Vaasa, Finland. He is the Vice Dean of the Business Faculty and the Director of the Finnish Graduate School in International Business (FIGSIB). His research interests include internationalization of SMEs, strategies and performance in international joint ventures and other forms of alliances, entry and establishment mode analysis, and entry and marketing strategies in Central and Eastern European countries. He is an active member of several academic associations, and his research has been published in several edited books and international journals, including the *Journal of Business Research*, *Journal of International Business Studies*, *Journal of International Marketing*, *Journal of World Business* and *Management International Review*.

Vincent Mangematin is a professor at Grenoble Ecole de Management (GEM), France. His research analyses the dynamics of knowledge creation and circulation in high-tech industries and the related strategies of organizations involved in knowledge production. He has published in several journals, including *Strategic Management Journal*, *Long Range Planning* and *Research Policy*.

Gillian S. Martin is a senior lecturer in business German at Trinity College Dublin. She is a Fellow of Trinity College Dublin and a research associate in the International Institute for Integration Studies (IIIS) at Trinity. Her main research interests are in intercultural communication and negotiation in organizational settings, with a particular focus on Germany and Ireland, cross-cultural comparative leadership, intercultural and intracultural doctor–patient communication in the area of diabetes care, and multidisciplinary, multicultural teamwork in healthcare settings.

Pedro S. Martins is Professor of Applied Economics at Queen Mary, University of London, and a Research Fellow of CEG-IST, Lisbon. After obtaining his PhD in Economics from the University of Warwick, he lectured at the University of St Andrews. Pedro Martins has published his research in several journals including the *Journal of Labour Economics*, *Journal of the European Economic Association*, *Labour Economics*, and *Economics Letters*.

Frank McDonald is Professor of International Business and Associate Dean of Research at University of Bradford School of Management, UK, and Chair of the Academy of International Business, UK and Ireland Chapter.

Chizu Nakajima is director of the Centre for Financial Regulation and Crime at Cass Business School, UK. She specializes in financial services law, international law, company law, corporate governance, corporate social responsibility, business ethics and the control of financial crime. Chizu is on the editorial board of a number of leading journals, including *The Company Lawyer*, *Journal of Financial Crime*, *Journal of Money Laundering Control* and *International Journal of Disclosure and Governance*, and has served for many years as co-director of the annual Cambridge International Symposium on Economic Crime. She has published widely on legal and ethical issues, including conflicts of interest in financial services and the control of financial crime and money laundering from an international comparative perspective, and has led numerous interdisciplinary research projects in these areas. Before joining Cass, Chizu worked for a number of financial institutions in the City. Chizu chairs the British Japanese Law Association and is a Fellow and Member of the Advisory Council of the Society for Advanced Legal Studies, a Freeman of the City of London and a Liveryman.

Niina Nummela is Professor of International Business at the Turku School of Economics, University of Turku, Finland. She has published in the area of international entrepreneurship, small business management, inter-firm co-operation, and research methods. She has contributed to the *Journal of World Business*, *Management International Review*, *European Journal of Marketing*, *International Small Business Journal*, and *Journal of Engineering and Technology Management*, among others.

Dónal O'Brien currently holds a research position in the School of Management at Dublin Institute of Technology. He is pursuing a PhD in strategy development in multinational subsidiaries. Prior educational qualifications include a degree in management and marketing, and a Master's in strategic management. Before working at DIT Dónal gained commercial experience in a number of sectors including banking, accounting, retail, and sports and leisure, and he has start-up business experience.

Chang Hoon Oh is an assistant professor of international business and strategy in the Faculty of Business at Brock University, Canada. His research interests centre on geographic and product diversification, non-market strategy of MNEs, and globalization versus regionalization. Dr Oh's research has appeared in the *Strategic Management Journal*, *Journal of International Business Studies* and *Global Environmental Change*, among others.

Tomoko Oikawa is an associate researcher with the Euro-Asia Centre at the University of Limerick, Ireland, and holds a PhD from the same university. Her main research interests are in modelling business groups in Asia in comparison with those in Europe, and in comparing technological structure in Japan with other Asian and European countries. She has a BA in history from Ochanomizu University and a BA in economics from Fukushima University in Japan, and an MA in women's studies from the University of Limerick.

Lucia Piscitello is Professor of International Institutions and Regulation at Politecnico di Milano. She has been Visiting Researcher at the Rutgers Business School (USA) and at the University of Reading (UK), where she is also an associate member of the Centre for International Business and Strategy. She holds a PhD in Industrial Engineering, awarded in 1998. Her research interests cover the economics and management of MNEs and the international aspects of technological change. Her recent studies focus particularly on the internationalization of R&D, spillovers and externalities stemming from FDI in infrastructure and service sectors, the relation between internationalization and skill upgrading, the relation between forms of internationalization, knowledge transfer and technological catching up through FDI. She has participated in various applied research projects promoted by the EC, the Italian National Research Council, and the Italian Ministry of Research, among others. She has published in the *Journal of International Business Studies*, *International Business Review*, *Industrial and Corporate Change*, *Cambridge Journal of Economics*, *Regional Studies*, *Structural Change and Economic Dynamics*, *Transnational Corporations*, *Journal of International Management*, *Management International Review*, *Revue d'Economie Industrielle*, among others.

Christian J. Resick is an assistant professor of Organizational Behavior and Management in the Management Department of LeBow College of Business, Drexel University. His research is aimed at understanding the psychological mechanisms linking people to their work environments, including cultures, climates, leaders and teammates, along with the implications for various aspects of organizational behaviour. A particular focus of his work examines the meaning, endorsement and enactment of ethical leadership across cultures.

Alan M. Rugman is Professor of International Business in the Henley Business School at the University of Reading. Previously, he held the L Leslie Waters Chair of International Business at the Kelley School of Business, Indiana University, 2001–2009. Professor Rugman's forty books include *Inside the Multinationals* (1981, reissued in 2006); *Multinationals and Transfer Pricing* (1985); *Global Corporate Strategy* and *Trade Policy* (1990); *Foreign Investment and North American Free Trade* (1994); *International Business*, 4th edition (2006); *Environmental Regulations and Corporate Strategy* (1999); *Multinationals as Flagship Firms* (2000); *The End of Globalization* (2000; 2001); *The Oxford Handbook of International Business* (2001, 2nd edition 2008); *The Regional Multinationals* (2005); and *Regional Aspects of Multinationality and Performance* (2007). Professor Rugman is a Fellow of the Academy of International Business and the Royal Society of Arts. He has served as a consultant to major companies, research institutes, government agencies, and as an advisor on trade, foreign investment and international competitiveness to two Canadian Prime Ministers. From 2004 to 2006, Professor Rugman served as President of the Academy of International Business (AIB).

Sami Saarenketo is Professor of International Marketing at the School of Business, Lappeenranta University of Technology, Finland. His primary areas of research interest are international marketing and entrepreneurship in technology-based small firms. He has published on these issues in the *Journal of World Business*, *International Business Review*, *European Business Review*, *European Journal of Marketing* and *Journal of International Entrepreneurship*, among others.

Liisa-Maija Sainio is Professor of International Marketing at the School of Business, Lappeenranta University of Technology, Finland. Her research interests include business models, different types of innovation and their effects on firm strategy, and customer knowledge processing. She has published in *Technological Forecasting and Social Change*, *R & D Management*, *Industrial Marketing Management* and *Technovation*, among others.

Fabian Sepulveda is a researcher and doctoral candidate at the Aalto University School of Economics in Finland. He holds a BSc in electrical engineering from North Carolina State University, and an MSc in Finance from Rotterdam School of Management. He has over 12 years of international experience in private industry, and his most recent positions were held in investment banking and management consulting in London. He is currently a researcher in the 'Born Globals' project financed by the Finnish funding agency for technology and innovation.

Pamela Sharkey-Scott is a research fellow at the College of Business, Dublin Institute of Technology, Ireland. She holds a PhD in strategic planning and entrepreneurship from University College, Dublin. Prior to entering academia, Pamela was a senior corporate banker, and has since been involved in several consulting projects. She teaches International Business and Supply Chain Management at both primary and postgraduate levels. She has published in several international journals, including the *Journal of International Management* and *Strategy and Leadership*.

Rudolf R. Sinkovics is Professor of International Business at Manchester Business School, UK, where he is currently head of the Comparative and International

Business Group and Director of the MBS-CIBER (Centre of International Business Research). His research centres on inter-organizational governance, the role of ICT in firm internationalization and research methods in international business. He received his PhD from Vienna University of Economics and Business Administration (WU-Wien), Austria. His work has been published in International Business and International Marketing journals. Born in Austria, he now lives and works in Manchester, UK.

Sanna Sundqvist is Professor in International Marketing at the School of Business, Lappeenranta University of Technology, Finland. She received her DSc in technology from LUT. Her research interests deal with export performance, diffusion of innovations and market orientation. She has published in the *Journal of Business Research*, the *Journal of the Academy of Marketing Science*, the *International Journal of Research in Marketing, Technological Forecasting and Social Change, Industrial Marketing Management* and *Journal of World Business*, among others.

Misagh Tasavori holds a master's degree from Sharif University of Technology, Tehran, Iran, and is currently a PhD candidate in comparative and international business at Manchester Business School. Her research focuses on social entrepreneurship and corporate social entrepreneurship within MNEs. She contributes actively to research projects in the MBS-CIBER. Born in Iran, she now lives and works in Manchester, UK.

Esther Tippmann is a funded PhD candidate at the School of Management, Dublin Institute of Technology, Ireland. Her research interests include knowledge processes in the multinational enterprise; more specifically subsidiary middle managers' knowledge engagements, their contribution to organizational learning and subsidiary evolution. Esther's work has been presented at several international conferences including the AIB-UKI, AoM and EGOS, and she was awarded the 'Michael Z Brooke Prize' for the Best Doctoral Paper at the AIB-UKI Conference, 2010.

Heinz-Josef Tüselmann is Professor of International Business and Director of the Centre for International Business and Innovation (CIBI) at Manchester Metropolitan University Business School, UK.

Celeste Amorim Varum is an assistant professor in the Department of Economics, Management and Industrial Engineering of the University of Aveiro, Portugal, and a researcher in the centre for Governance, Competitiveness and Public Policies (GOVCOPP). She has been a visiting researcher at the Politécnico di Milano and at the Joint Research Centre of the European Commission in Ispra/Italy. She holds a PhD in Economics and MSc in International Business and Economic Integration from the University of Reading, UK, and a degree in Economics from the University of Évora, Portugal. She has published several book chapters and articles in the areas of internationalization, innovation and firms' competitiveness, in several journals including the *International Business Review*, *European Journal of Development Research*, *Notas Económicas*, *Scientometrics* and *Futures*, among others.

Rakhi Verma is a PhD student in the School of Business at Trinity College Dublin, Ireland. Her research interests focus on FDI and in particular FDI from the fast-growing emerging economies. Rakhi holds an undergraduate degree in science and an MBA.

Svitlana Voronkova is a researcher at the Centre for European Economic Research (ZEW), Mannheim, Germany. Her research interests are in the area of international finance and emerging markets. In particular, Svitlana focuses on emerging markets of Central and Eastern Europe. She has published a number of articles on financial integration and institutional investors in several international finance journals, including *Journal of International Money and Finance*, *Journal of Business Finance and Accounting* and *International Review of Economics and Finance*.

Paul Windrum is Associate Professor in Strategy at Nottingham University Business School. His areas of research expertise are the strategic management of innovation, services (public and private sector), and health innovation. He is a visiting professor at the Max Planck Institute of Economics, Jena. Paul has worked on a number EU projects on services innovation, such as PUBLIN and ServPPIN. He is on the Editorial Board of the journal *Structural Change & Economic Dynamics* and has published in leading innovation journals such as *Research Policy*, *Industrial & Corporate Change*, *Technological Forecasting and Social Change* and *Journal of Evolutionary Economics*. He is co-editor of the book *Innovation in Public Services: Entrepreneurship, Creativity and Management* (2008).

Mo Yamin is Professor of International Business at Manchester Business School, UK. His research focuses on the role of subsidiaries within multinational companies, linkages of firms with local companies, and the impact of MNCs on economic development. He received his PhD in Economics from the University of Manchester.

Yong Yang is Research Fellow at Brunel Business School, working on a FP7 project funded by the European Commission. He received his PhD from Queen Mary, University of London, and holds an MSc in Business Management from the University of East Anglia. In September 2010, Yong Yang was appointed lecturer in international business and entrepreneurship at the University of Essex.

Angelika Zimmermann is a lecturer in international business and strategy at Loughborough University Business School, UK. Her research focuses on qualitative research in the areas of international virtual teams and international human resource management, with a current focus on China and India. Her research has been published in the *International Journal of Human Resource Management, International Studies of Management and Organization, International Journal of Cross Cultural Management* and *International Journal of Management Reviews*. Angelika has also worked as an internal consultant for intercultural support and training at the Robert Bosch Group, Germany.

Introduction

Jenny Berrill, Elaine Hutson and Rudolf R. Sinkovics

The current international business environment is characterized by two contradictory but at times mutually supplementary trends – regionalism and globalization. The enhanced integration of recent decades has led to increasingly global production, distribution and consumption systems, and to cultural and political ideologies expressed in global rather than country-specific contexts. This process is not unidirectional. Regionalization is part of the process of globalization, but it can also be a counter force to globalization as stakeholders act to protect their perceived interests. Partly in response to the global slowdown and partly in response to globalization, the regional actions of firms, governments, NGOs and other institutions form the complex landscape within which firms operate in the third millennium. Studies on these topics are now legion, provoking an extraordinary variety of interpretations, discussions and controversies which in turn have given rise to ever more new studies.

This collection continues the discussion. The 23 chapters included in this book are drawn from the 37th Academy of International Business (United Kingdom and Ireland Chapter) conference, held at Trinity College Dublin in April 2010 and chaired by Professor Colm Kearney. The chapters are laid out in seven parts, as follows: regional and global perspectives; outward FDI; entrepreneurial firms: internationalization and performance; human resources, leadership and culture; knowledge and networks; international joint ventures; and corporate governance and organization. Each of these chapters is briefly introduced below.

Part I   Regional and global perspectives

Part I contains four chapters on regional and global perspectives. In Chapter 1, Khalid and Larimo argue that value from alliance knowledge may be created not only through exploitation and augmentation of the existing knowledge base but also through entrepreneurial actions in accessing and integrating key strategic resources that exist in alliance relationships. Using a sample of 100 ICT sector firms mainly from Scandinavia and Asia Pacific, they find a positive and significant relation between alliance entrepreneurship, alliance capability and foreign market strategic goals. However, more significant support is received for the model indicating the relation between alliance entrepreneurship and alliance capability through moderating interaction effects of barriers to alliance knowledge transfer and firm-level learning orientation. In the context of foreign market entry, their study extends the notion of alliance capability, in combination with alliance entrepreneurship, to foreign market performance following market entry.

In Chapter 2, Jongwanich examines the determinants of FDI flows in emerging Asian economies, with an emphasis on the implication of the existing international production network in promoting inward FDI. She uses bilateral FDI data from 7 emerging (host) Asian economies and 61 home countries, both developed and developing, from 1994 to 2007. Using the gravity model, she shows that inward FDI in the region is primarily in the form of vertical FDI, and the existing international production network has become an important factor in promoting (vertical) FDI inflows. The establishment of service links and an attractive location for market accessibility to the main market core provide multinational enterprises (MNEs) with the advantage of producing at the local market, and importing necessary supplies (other parts and components) from other countries. The results imply that policies aimed at improving service links and market accessibility conditions in a regional and global context are becoming more beneficial for a host country in promoting FDI inflow than focusing on bilateral relationships.

In Chapter 3, O'Brien, Sharkey-Scott and Gibbons analyse the contribution of subsidiary middle managers to subsidiary strategy development. They present the findings of an in-depth case study exploring the role of subsidiary middle managers in developing strategy within a well-established and successful MNE. The evidence suggests that while the subsidiaries do engage in formal strategy development, the contribution of the middle managers to this process is predominantly in implementation. This is highlighted by the strong evidence for downward strategic influences, but O'Brien, Sharkey-Scott and Gibbons found limited evidence for the existence of the upward strategic influences of middle managers.

In Chapter 4, Rugman and Oh investigate the impact of the international financial crisis on MNE strategy. They find that the financial crisis has had an indirect impact on the strategies of MNEs, the primary effect being to make MNEs the national champions of their home governments. They claim, however, that this has an asymmetric impact. Emerging market MNEs continue to be strongly home country directed. In contrast, developed market MNEs are less centralized and hierarchical in their operations (with more autonomy to subsidiary managers in their networks). This suggests that developed market MNEs are likely to benefit more from international diversification than are emerging market MNEs. Rugman and Oh conclude that the international financial crisis has had complex repercussions on the strategies of MNEs, and that these repercussions vary across countries, in particular between Chinese and US MNEs.

Part II   Outward FDI

Part II contains four chapters on the topic of outward FDI. In Chapter 5, Tüselmann, McDonald, Bohl, Voronkova and Windrum conduct a longitudinal study examining German FDI outflows in ten mature manufacturing industries between 1976 and 2003, to investigate if there is evidence of industry-level shock persistence. Their results, using disaggregated industry-level data, confirm that outward German FDI is shock persistent, as had been suggested in studies using aggregate-level data on total German FDI and for the manufacturing sector as a whole. This study provides evidence that there is no industry-specific differential response to shocks, with the exception of the chemical industry. Their results do not imply broad support for the global factory thesis other than possibly for the chemical industry. They suggest that both the global factory and regionalist strategies need to take into account the national business systems of home countries and industry-specific factors.

In Chapter 6, Yang and Martins use firm-level data – over 16,000 multinationals from 46 countries from 1997 to 2006 – to examine the extent to which the performance of multinational firms varies with the level of intellectual property rights (IPR) of the host economy. They find that the positive relation between multinationality and performance is larger when firms invest in low-IPR countries. In other words, the benefits of investing abroad are larger when the subsidiary is in a low-IPR country compared to high-IPR country subsidiaries. They interpret these results as indicating that the potential of globalization, in particular by increasing investment in low-IPR countries (which are typically developing countries), has not yet been met by multinational firms.

In Chapter 7, Verma and Brennan investigate the relation between outward FDI and exports in India. They analyse the Granger causal relation based on a vector error correction model over the period 1981–2006, and find a unidirectional causality between exports and outward FDI from India. Verma and Brennan argue that more exports from India will lead to greater outward FDI from the home country. However, Indian outward FDI may not create additional exports. The findings suggest that the future growth of Indian companies will be influenced by the share that they can garner in the world market, not only by producing in the country and exporting, but also by investing overseas to become better integrated into the global economy and to compete with global companies.

In Chapter 8, Bannò, Piscitello and Amorim Varum highlight that home country measures to promote outward FDI receive little attention in the literature. They test the direct impact of a particular public incentive in Italy, whereby a public agency can invest directly in foreign ventures upon the firms' domestic growth. The analysis is conducted on data from 237 Italian firms that received an incentive to promote Italian companies' FDI outside the European Union in the period 1991–2007, versus a counterfactual sample of firms that internationalized in the same period without any incentive. They find positive effects of the financial incentive on the benefiting firm's growth, compared to the counterfactual sample of non-benefiting firms. Their results support the position that the influence of home country measures can be increased through tailor-made approaches (e.g. through regional and country targeting) on the formulation and administration of measures.

Part III Entrepreneurial firms: internationalization and performance

Part III contains three chapters relating to the internationalization and performance of entrepreneurial firms. In Chapter 9, Sundqvist, Kuivalainen and Cadogan extend the current literature by applying entrepreneurial orientation to international business. They apply structural equation modelling to survey data collected from Finland and New Zealand. Their results indicate that entrepreneurial behaviour is important for managers involved in international business. Sundqvist, Kuivalainen and Cadogan recommend that before engaging in proactive behaviour, competitive aggressiveness and venturesome risk-taking, managers should study their international market environments carefully as strong emphasis on entrepreneurial behaviour does not always contribute positively to profits – performance is contingent on environmental turbulence. Their findings also suggest that an excessively rapid global diversification strategy – the born global pathway – does not benefit from competitive aggressiveness or risk-taking when markets are changing, whereas this kind of entrepreneurial behaviour is advisable for internationalizing firms following a more traditional internationalization pathway.

In Chapter 10, Sainio, Saarenketo, Nummela and Eriksson focus on how value is created in the international entrepreneurial firm. They outline the role of a clearly framed business model in international entrepreneurial behaviour. The novelty of their approach is that both inward and outward internationalization processes are simultaneously examined, thus highlighting a holistic approach to internationalization. Their business model construct also facilitates the examination of both upstream and downstream value creation processes simultaneously, and thus evaluates the internationalization configuration from a new perspective. They use a case study approach to test the applicability of the business model concept for international entrepreneurship. They provide a detailed description of the networked inward and outward activities of the internationally operating firm, as well as an analytical tool for evaluating the status of the business model from the value creation perspective and anticipating future changes.

In Chapter 11, Hallbäck and Gabrielsson investigate how the marketing strategies of early and rapidly internationalizing firms evolve during their evolution from international new venture (INV) to global firm, and the factors that influence the development and performance of these strategies. A conceptual model and propositions for the development and performance of entrepreneurial marketing strategies in INVs are developed. They identify two dimensions of entrepreneurial marketing that are important for an INV: innovativeness of marketing strategies and adaptation of marketing strategies to customers and countries. To further develop the understanding of entrepreneurial marketing strategies in INVs, they derive key factors from the literature that influence their development: the turbulence, technical complexity and global diversity of the industry environment; the firm culture in terms of entrepreneurial and market orientation; the dynamic capabilities of the firm; and the global growth phase of the firm. Finally, the ability of the INV to balance the level of innovativeness and adaptation of its marketing strategies to fit with these external and internal conditions is regarded as critical for achieving higher marketing performance during INV growth.

Part IV Human resources, leadership and culture

Part IV contains three chapters in the area of human resources, leadership and culture. In Chapter 12, Zimmermann provides a review of the literature on transnational and virtual teams to highlight the distinctive characteristics of relationships within such teams. This review deviates from the prevalent linear input-process-output models of team functioning that follow classic system models. Instead, Zimmermann makes a first step towards a non-linear systems analysis and, through this, a configurational perspective on relationships in transnational teams. She demonstrates the need for a configurational perspective on interpersonal relationships in transnational teams and, based on previous research, suggests two examples of typical configuration.

In Chapter 13, Keating, Martin and Resick examine beliefs about ethical leadership held by managers in Ireland and Germany, and discuss the implications for creating intercultural ethical leadership competence. Managers from Ireland and Germany converged in their beliefs about the centrality of character/integrity for effective ethical leadership, confirming previous research. Comparative qualitative analysis suggests that differences exist in the meaning of ethical and unethical leadership as well as in the meaning of integrity for German and Irish managers. The study takes a first step towards achieving a better understanding of the cross-culturally endorsed and culturally specific expectations for ethics and ethical leadership in two societies from different cultural clusters and, with this, towards identifying a range of competencies that will enhance how leaders in these countries deal with ethical challenges.

In Chapter 14, Kittler analyses the role of timing, duration and intensity of expatriate training for expatriate adjustment. The study is designed to examine whether pre-departure or post-arrival training results in better adjustment of expatriates. His results show that the benefits of expatriate training programmes remain inconclusive. Overall, consistent with previous research, Kittler's findings suggest minor advantages of post-arrival training programmes as the more effective tool in helping staff to adjust to the work environment abroad. This study provides an indication of the effectiveness of training programmes for expatriates and offers a systematic approach to time-related variables.

Part V Knowledge and networks

Part V contains three chapters relating to knowledge and networks. In Chapter 15, Tippmann, Sharkey-Scott and Mangematin investigate how subsidiary middle managers search for knowledge when dealing with problems, and evaluate the outcomes in terms of generating organizational adaptation. They use multiple case studies of 3 ICT subsidiaries and 33 knowledge search processes.

Tippmann, Sharkey-Scott and Mangematin argue that middle managers' proactive and self-initiated search for knowledge is a micro-foundation of subsidiary learning. The findings contribute by offering a micro-perspective of how middle managers' actions generate organization-level outcomes, extending theory on knowledge flows and subsidiary learning.

In Chapter 16, Kenny and Fahy focus on SMEs in the telecommunications sector, to reveal a different perspective on internationalization, networking capability and on the industry itself. They note that the SME component of this sector does not seem to engage in inter-firm collaborations to the same extent as their larger counterparts. Kenny and Fahy examine the impact of network effects on firm performance in international markets, and find that stronger ties are more influential on international performance than weak ties. Similarly, network coordination and human capital resources are found to be positively and significantly associated with international performance. Strong ties, trust, network initiation and synergy-sensitive resources are all positively associated with international performance but are not significant. Weak ties, relational capability, network learning and information sharing are negatively associated with international performance.

In Chapter 17, Sepulveda and Gabrielsson investigate how born global networks evolve as firms grow. They analyse four elements of networks and tie them to born global performance: network content, management, centrality and evolution. They propose a theoretical framework of born global network evolution and advance propositions on network elements and firm performance: that as a born global's internal resources mature, the content it seeks from networks evolves from basic to strategic, the structure of its networks changes and its network centrality improves. Further, a born global's entrepreneurial behaviour prompts a calculative approach to network management; and networks provide opportunities, competitive advantages and risk management that are positively related to a born global's performance. Sepulveda and Gabrielsson suggest that their chapter forms the conceptual basis for future empirical studies.

Part VI International joint ventures

Part VI contains two chapters on the topic of international joint ventures. In Chapter 18, Ali and Larimo claim that trust is one of the most widely researched but least understood and most contentious areas of international business. They conduct a critical review of empirical research published between 1980 and 2009 on the performance effects of trust in international strategic alliances by evaluating the conceptualization and operationalization of core constructs of trust and performance along with the methodologies used. Their review of 29 selected studies suggest that (1) empirical research on the trust–performance relation is beset by differences in the conceptualization and operationalization of core constructs of trust and performance, and (2) while there are positive indirect links between trust and alliance performance, the direct positive trust–performance link proves more consistent.

In Chapter 19, Golesorkhi and Yamin, applying insights from transaction costs analysis, propose that the relative specificity and opacity of assets contributed by joint venture partners is significantly related to their equity share ownership. They employ data on the specificity and opacity of the assets contributed by partners to the joint venture to test hypotheses relating to share ownership in both domestic and international joint ventures. Golesorkhi and Yamin's results show a positive relation between the (relative) specificity of assets contributed to the international joint ventures by foreign partners and the likelihood of their owning a larger share of the international joint venture's equity. They also find that cultural distance between the 'home' and foreign partner negatively affects this relation.

Part VII Corporate governance and organization

Part VII contains four chapters on the topic of corporate governance and organization. In Chapter 20, Oikawa attempts to define and clarify the concept of *keiretsu*. She conjectures that *keiretsu* is essentially the principles of social solidarity based on the cultural system in Japan. In exploring the principles of *keiretsu* she uses a linguistic approach; in particular, structural linguistics known as the Sapir–Whorf hypotheses. She concludes that the principles of *keiretsu* are trust and dependence, which are the core values in Japanese society. This implies that *keiretsu* cannot be universal.

In Chapter 21, Adegbite and Nakajima argue that corporate governance models, especially in developing countries, are inapplicable if they are not institutionally based and explained. They provide empirical evidence on how the institutional theoretical framework of corporate governance applies to a particular national context – Nigeria. Adegbite and Nakajima illustrate two classes of institutional effects on corporate governance: those external to the firm (macro) and those internal (micro). The external institutional environments that profile a firm's corporate governance consist of the country's social, economic, political and legal environments, while those internal to the firm consist of the firm's/industry's values, culture, history and ethics. Their model represents an encompassing framework that provides illumination on certain institutional effects and relationships, thereby encapsulating the complex dynamics and realities of governance in modern-day corporations. It thus constitutes a useful context to analyse corporate governance structures – across diverse countries, cultures, belief systems, traditions, industries, scholarly orientations and disciplines.

In Chapter 22, Tasavori and Sinkovics examine the question of whether MNCs can be recognized as social entrepreneurs. Their analysis illustrates that social entrepreneurship may not be an appropriate term for the socially entrepreneurial behaviour of MNCs. However, as MNCs incorporate both economic and social missions simultaneously, they follow the lead of corporate social responsibility and corporate entrepreneurship scholars and suggest that the term 'corporate social entrepreneurship' be used for large organizations. Tasavori and Sinkovics seek to address the call for interdisciplinary research in the field of international business to understand the complex and multidimensional activities of MNCs in solving social problems.

In the final chapter, Chapter 23, Chizema shows that the disclosure of individual executive compensation is significantly positively associated with firm performance in German firms. This supports the argument that shareholder value is maximized by the disclosure of corporate information; pay disclosure may motivate directors to act in shareholders' interests by improving firm performance. He also finds that the relation between the disclosure of individual executive compensation and firm performance is more positive among firms that were early adopters of IAS/US GAAP and that have American Depository Receipts. Chizema finds some evidence that the association between the disclosure of individual executive compensation and firm performance is stronger in firms with larger management boards. The chapter further demonstrates that the adoption of good management innovations coming from different corporate governance systems may still be resisted by firms. The fact that firms may reject good practices raises the question of whether national corporate governance codes must be voluntary or mandatory. This study is one of the first to examine the effect of disclosing individual executive compensation on firm performance in a stakeholder-oriented governance system where there is concern about the inflow of shareholder-oriented governance practices.

Conclusion

While not exhaustive, this book provides some evidence on the theme of 'Firm-level Internationalization, Regionalism and Globalization'. This collection includes interesting conceptual and empirical work from colleagues affiliated with universities and organizations throughout the world, primarily Europe but also the United States and Asia. We hope that this edited text will provide useful ideas and stimulate further research that seeks to investigate the challenges that firm-level internationalization creates, and delve further into the area of regionalism and globalization in international business.

Part I
Regional and Global Perspectives

1
The Relation between Alliance Entrepreneurship, Alliance Capability and Foreign Market Performance – An Empirical Investigation

Saba Khalid and Jorma Larimo

Introduction

Small- and medium-sized entrepreneurial firms involved in manufacturing and marketing their own products act as small global factories (Buckley, 2009a) in a global network. They play multiple roles: they undertake original equipment manufacture (OEM); design, engineering and R&D for the product; and act as customers for contract manufacturers. Additionally, entrepreneurial firms deal with local market alliances in foreign countries to acquire market knowledge (Knight and Kim, 2009). Local market information is a key source of competitive advantage in foreign markets. Managing and learning from alliances adds to the complexity of the internationalization of these firms.

Buckley (2009a) suggests that mobilization of entrepreneurial abilities is one of the barriers that firms need to overcome in the face of increasing globalization. Entrepreneurial ability is linked to entrepreneurs being innovative in organizing invention, marketability and entry of product or service to the global marketplace. Information in this process enables entrepreneurs to combine their judgement with physical assets, thus enabling them to bear risks and mobilize capital. Further, the rise of the global factory demands new management skills, which include an entrepreneurial ability to optimally locate and control firm activities (Buckley, 2009b). Entrepreneurial actions in accessing external information and integrating internal competencies are critical in entrepreneurial decision-making. Buckley (2009b, p. 233) also asserts that 'the ability to coordinate external organizations into the strategy of the focal firm, to liaise with the external bodies and government and to cohere these strategies into a grand strategy – are at the heart of the skills necessary to organize a successful global factory.'

In this chapter, we link these fundamental assumptions of the global factory concerning entrepreneurial abilities with the domain of alliance entrepreneurship. The role of alliance entrepreneurship in organizing alliance knowledge with its effects on how alliance capability affects expansion after entry into foreign markets is not fully captured in prior studies. This is supported by Robson and

Katsikeas (2005), who state that parent firms' top management attitude towards alliances and creating alliance formation conditions has yet to receive emphasis in the collaborative strategy literature. Studies on how alliance capability influences new market entry strategy are, however, emerging (Ranft and Marsh, 2008; Schreiner et al., 2009; Yeoh, 2004).

To create value through the alliances, alliance capability (Annand and Khanna, 2000) development is top of the agenda for entrepreneurial firms. Entrepreneurial small- and medium-sized firms are likely to possess more inventive capabilities for value creation due to their size and the free flow of communication between employees (Alvarez and Barney, 2001). Specifically in market entry strategies, development of alliance capability enables firms to internalize external information, and to create value from alliance knowledge when the knowledge base of the firm is augmented with the knowledge existing in the alliance relationship (Meyer et al., 2009; Sarkar et al., 2001; Yeoh, 2004).

In line with the existing gap in the literature concerning alliance entrepreneurship, our study develops and tests empirically a model that focuses on the following three goals. *First*, we analyse the extent to which alliance entrepreneurship relates to information asymmetry between alliance and organizational knowledge in new market entry. *Second*, we examine to what extent alliance entrepreneurship affects alliance capability and foreign market performance; and *third*, we analyse to what extent alliance knowledge transfer barriers and learning orientation moderate the relation between alliance entrepreneurship and alliance capability, and foreign market performance. Finally we discuss the implications of alliance entrepreneurship in the context of the knowledge integration ability of the global factory and how alliance capability benefits SMEs in a global factory.

In the context of foreign market entry, our study extends the notion of alliance capability, in combination with alliance entrepreneurship, to foreign market performance following market entry. This contributes to the recent research that calls for more attention to the process issues involved in alliance capability and knowledge acquisition (Heimeriks, 2008; Ranft and Marsh, 2008) and the literature that explores the role of alliance entrepreneurship (Alvarez and Barney, 2001; Sarkar et al., 2001). Earlier research looks at alliance capability either as an individual phenomenon of learning through alliance knowledge acquisition (Annand and Khanna, 2000; Kale and Singh, 2007) or by integrating the firm-level processes of knowledge acquisition to alliance capability development (Heimeriks, 2008; Schreiner et al., 2009), and explores the initial conditions and constituent elements of alliance capability development. Schreiner et al. (2009) suggest paying more attention to exploring the constituent dimensions of alliance capability, specifically focusing on how these dimensions affect alliance outcome in post-formation phases. We focus on post-formation alliance value creation, and link alliance entrepreneurship, alliance capability and foreign market strategic goals.

In this study, alliances – as a form of inter-organizational relationship – are conceived on the basis of the degree to which participants are linked, or coupled (Barringer and Harrison, 2000). We follow the definition of Doz and Hamel

(1998): alliances are an arrangement between two or more firms that establish an exchange relationship but have no joint ownership involved. A buyer–supplier relationship could be one example of such loosely coupled alliances.

Theory and hypotheses

Alliance entrepreneurship

Shane and Venkataraman (2000) suggest that entrepreneurial opportunities are those situations in which new goods, services, raw materials and organizing methods can be introduced and sold at a cost greater than that of producing them. Shane (2000) argues that organization of knowledge from various sources to create unique resources can only result in developing opportunities when a flow of knowledge from external sources to the firm creates symmetries between external and internal information. The role of entrepreneurial ability in creating such symmetry is, however, critical when dealing with alliances. Information symmetry between partners is linked to increased opportunity identification when an internal combination of the firm-specific resources meets the requirements of the external environment. For example, if technical (R&D) and market planning teams (distributor partners) do not share a common vision, matching internal and external knowledge may not take place. Cohendet et al. (2000) also support the entrepreneurial function as a source of competitive advantage for firms, when entrepreneurs act to create an external environment by developing certain business relationships. Thus, through an entrepreneurial function, entrepreneurs create a link between the external and the internal environments by accessing and integrating trans-organizational key strategic resources and know-how (Sarkar et al., 2001).

Robson and Katsikeas (2005) mention that a parent firm's top management's general attitude towards alliances reflects not only the strength of the initiating force behind international strategic alliance formation and its ongoing investment efforts, but it also shapes relationship satisfaction. In line with these ideas, we conceptualize alliance entrepreneurship as entrepreneurial attitude targeted specifically in developing symmetry between alliance and the organizational knowledge base. Thus, the organization of activities to acquire and utilize alliance knowledge is a significant function for entrepreneurial firms. Entrepreneurial strategic orientation associated with forming access relationships into valuable complementary resources and know-how directs and limits firms' alliance relationships to key strategic resources to create value (Buckley, 2009a, 2009b). Therefore, entrepreneurs create opportunities in new markets by utilizing alliance knowledge through a complementary process of exploitation and augmentation of alliance knowledge. Thus, we propose,

Hypothesis 1: *In the post-alliance phase, alliance entrepreneurship is positively related to developing a common vision between alliance knowledge and firm activities.*

Alliance capability

Foreign market knowledge continues to be alliance knowledge within the relationship unless firms deliberately utilize and exploit alliance knowledge by expanding into foreign markets post-entry. We explore alliance entrepreneurship in two ways: *first*, the orientation of the firm's top management team and employees towards the building of an alliance knowledge-sharing environment at firm and at alliance levels, and *second*, entrepreneurial ability to manage alliance-based relationships. These two activities, collectively, have been treated as alliance capability (Annand and Khanna, 2000; Schreiner et al., 2009).

We examine the entrepreneurship literature and knowledge-based view to analyse how entrepreneurial activities that promote sharing and organizing alliance knowledge influence alliance capability and the ability for the firm to achieve the foreign market strategic goals. The efforts expended by entrepreneurs in organizing foreign market knowledge through alliance partners, in setting up an open and decentralized organizational environment, and in the sharing of knowledge organized from existing and new alliances, are subject to analysis. While the top management's efforts relate to providing the conditions for active search and the free flow of information within the firm, the export managers act as the front-line personnel who explore international opportunities. Top management's vision to support an open environment in the firm and to transfer and share knowledge is one factor that facilitates front-line export managers to perform the necessary activities to introduce and sell products and to develop procedural knowledge related to exports within the firm. This coincides with one of the main themes in entrepreneurship studies that concentrate on why, when and how opportunities for the creation of goods and services come into existence. Thus both top and front-line managers organize knowledge of the external and internal markets, particularly relevant to those activities that require managerial orientation and input. Thus, we propose,

Hypothesis 2: *In the post-alliance phase, alliance entrepreneurship is positively related to alliance capability.*

Alliance entrepreneurship and foreign market performance

The knowledge-based aspect explains a firm's success from the viewpoint of its ownership of difficult-to-imitate resource combinations, which enable a firm to conceive and implement strategies to improve competitive positions (Barney, 1991; Wernerfelt, 1984). Alliances as the means of accessing foreign market knowledge are a strategic issue for firms. A firm's alliance capability strengthens when it successfully manages to utilize alliance knowledge for fulfilment of both alliance and the firm's own strategic goals. Embedding the alliance knowledge into various value-creating activities (Zollo and Winter, 2002) either jointly or just by the parent firm may result in a greater degree of alliance capability. Organizational learning and knowledge-based studies also assume that capabilities arise when knowledge is utilized, deployed and combined to produce enhanced values and when organizational knowledge is embedded into various value-creating activities. Thus, firms must learn to deal with information acquisition, dissemination and transfer processes in order to sustain improved performance.

Alliance performance has been recognized as alliances out-compete others by a collective utilization of alliance knowledge that involves developing a broader set of capabilities with adaptation of organizational and technological systems at product levels (Mesquite et al., 2008). On this basis, we conceive firm performance as the fulfilment of foreign market strategic goals. However, buyer–supplier knowledge acquisition efforts must be taken into consideration as a collective acquisition of know-how pertaining to alliance-specific needs where partners actively participate; only then is it likely to affect alliance performance. From the knowledge-based perspective, a collective knowledge acquisition leads to tacit alliance-specific assets (Kogut and Zander, 1993; Simonin, 1997). As other firms are unable to access and replicate the alliance-specific knowledge, the alliance retains a competitive advantage compared to firms outside the alliance. The cumulative nature of knowledge leads to greater rates of learning and application into areas other than the alliance, thus influencing individual firms' performance. We propose,

Hypothesis 3: In the post-formation phase, alliance entrepreneurship is positively linked to the fulfilment of its strategic goals in the foreign market.

Barriers to alliance knowledge sharing

Following Grant (1991), who suggests that knowledge without the right organizational mechanisms to transfer it into productive use is relatively worthless for firms, we consider that the dynamic process of alliance knowledge acquisition and utilization requires specific external and internal knowledge management mechanisms. Entrepreneurial ability in organizing alliance knowledge may be affected by barriers to alliance knowledge transfer. This merits investigation into the effects of knowledge transfer barriers between the local and foreign firm in the post-formation phases of the alliance relationship.

As the alliance learning motives of the partnering firms are different, acquisition and dissemination of the alliance knowledge may in some cases turn out to be a more difficult process than the intra-firm dissemination of alliance knowledge. To achieve competence in market knowledge, its transference must occur in both dimensions; from local distributor to foreign firm and from foreign firm to within its departments (Buckley, 2009b). We conceptualize barriers to alliance knowledge transfer on the basis of situational context. In an alliance where the local partner provides strategic market knowledge, and the foreign firm internalizes it to utilize it in development of services and product, knowledge is originally located in a different setting from where it is transferred. Barriers to alliance knowledge acquisition are the constraints that prohibit a foreign firm's ability to acquire local market knowledge through the alliance, thereby influencing entrepreneurial ability to initiate, expand or sustain export marketing operations. Several scholars claim that all resource transfers are sticky or inert, as the complexity, ability to codify and tacitness of knowledge itself create barriers to knowledge transfer (Kogut and Zander, 1993; Szulanski, 1996). The knowledge evolution cycle (Zollo and Winter, 2002) also assumes that the ability of a firm to create new knowledge varies, as all firms differ in the degree to which the knowledge is articulated and codified.

The acquisition and utilization of knowledge requires firms to implement managerial processes to transfer and receive knowledge (Eisenhardt and Martin, 2000; Teece et al., 1997). The utilization of knowledge depends on the user firm's capabilities; specifically the integration and coordination of routines, which allow the user firm to reconfigure, reintegrate and transform its resources into new competencies and competitive advantages (Teece et al., 1997). Thus, firms may face problems in acquiring and accessing alliance knowledge if its knowledge transfer mechanisms are not developed.

Hypothesis 4: Barriers to alliance knowledge acquisition negatively moderate the relation between alliance entrepreneurship and alliance capability.

Learning orientation

Although alliance knowledge acquisition may turn out to be a major challenge when the learning orientation of the partnering firms is not at the same level, this may offer some incentives for the partnering firm to learn from the alliance. Previously existing organizational knowledge also acts as an incentive for entrepreneurs to acquire new knowledge as they match alliance knowledge to what is already known. This may help them to judge alliance knowledge and share experiences between partners. However, partnering firms may not have similar degrees of inter-firm knowledge acquisition and dissemination needs, as a mutual learning environment is the exception rather than the rule (Inkpen, 1998).

Earlier studies relate a firm's absorptive capacity (Cohen and Levinthal, 1990) and its transformative (Garud and Nayyar, 1994) or knowledge exploration and exploitation capacities to alliance knowledge acquisition as an indicator of the ability to learn. Khanna et al. (1998) suggest that in order to reach a similar level of learning as the alliance, entrepreneurs must pursue a continuous allocation of resources to learning mechanisms and aim to achieve common benefits from the alliance. As a binding factor between the partnering firms, this might require higher investment on developing inter-firm alliance knowledge acquisition mechanisms. However, it could depict a successful alliance beneficial to all of the partners. Firms would, therefore, develop formal mechanisms to share market information between partners, to earn mutual trust, to maximize knowledge sharing and to learn from the experience of the partner firms in the foreign market.

With increased alliance learning, partnering firms gain experience in leveraging and exploiting the alliance knowledge. As Inkpen (1998, p. 224) mentions 'alliances create the potential for firms to acquire knowledge associated with partner's skills and capabilities.' Thus, as alliance knowledge provides the opportunity for firms to upgrade and renew the existing organizational knowledge base of the

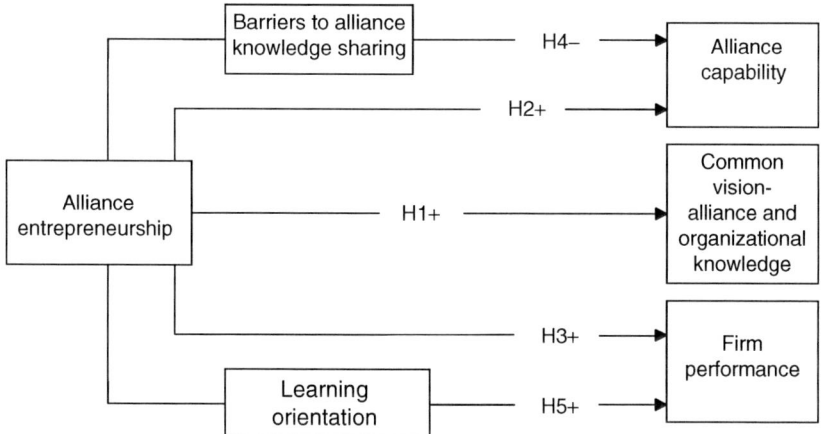

Figure 1.1 Hypothesized relations

firm, its utilization is critical to internalize it. If the alliance dies, the knowledge base is eroded.

Hypothesis 5: *The learning orientation of a firm positively moderates the relation between alliance entrepreneurship and foreign market performance.*

In line with the objectives of the study, Figure 1.1 summarizes the hypothesized relations. In the context of new market entry, the first three hypotheses indicate relations between alliance entrepreneurship and common vision, alliance capability and alliance performance. Hypotheses 4 and 5 indicate the moderating variables relation.

Research methodology

The target population of our study consisted of software development firms from the ICT sector, which sell their own software solutions in foreign countries. A contact list of 500 companies, mainly from Scandinavia (including Finland) and Asia Pacific, was drawn up from online yellow pages using a key word strategy. International sales and marketing managers, considering that they are in direct contact with local alliances, were chosen as target respondents. Based on our choice criteria of having a minimum of 2 years' experience of sales to foreign customers, having partnerships with resellers and/or some foreign technology partnerships with firms such as IBM, Microsoft, SAP or Oracle and having an international product developed by the firm, 300 usable contact firms were selected. In May 2006, a preliminary email describing the purpose of the survey was sent. A month later, the detailed questionnaire was sent through a research software programme. In the first attempt only 25 answers were received. Later on, direct contacts were made via phone calls, after which there was a continuous stream of responses. With reminder phone calls and further emails, a sample of 100 firms was achieved in January 2007, yielding a 33 per cent response rate.

Measures

All the questions were developed as multi-item options on a seven-point Likert scale. The respondents were instructed to choose one specific market and a specific post-formation alliance relationship in that market. Further, we instructed them to refer to alliance knowledge as the knowledge of customers' requirements and needs in that specific market acquired through the alliance relationship.

Operation of constructs

We adapted the three-item scale from Jaworski and Kohli (1993) and one from Heide and John (1992) to alliance entrepreneurship. The variables regarding alliance entrepreneurship concerned the behaviour of the entrepreneurs about knowledge sharing in the firms. In this question, particularly from the viewpoint of alliance knowledge, respondents were asked to what extent alliance knowledge-sharing behaviour of the top managers influenced the achievement of targeted sales in the foreign market.

Based on Schreiner et al. (2009), alliance capability reflects the knowledge/skills to address key issues that arise in managing any individual inter-firm collaboration after alliance formation. We considered post-formation alliance knowledge sharing as a specific area requiring managerial skills in distributor relationship. With this criterion, we adapted two items from Jaworski and Kohli (1993) and one from Maydeu-Olivares and Lado (2003). All of these items specifically relate to alliance knowledge sharing within the firm. Two items relate to alliance knowledge sharing between partners and were adapted from Lusch and Brown (1996) and Heide and Miner (1992). The learning orientation was conceived as a firm-level construct and was measured by adapting a three-item seven-point Likert scale from Calantone et al. (2002). Common vision in utilizing the alliance knowledge was also adapted from Jaworski and Kohli (1993). We specifically asked respondents to what extent the following activities lead to the development of a common vision between marketing and product development personnel.

Our review of the literature on alliance knowledge did not provide information on barriers to knowledge sharing between alliance partners. We therefore followed a pilot study with two software firms to generate some relevant items particularly suitable for the software industry. A thorough discussion of the barriers to alliance knowledge transfer at the firm and market levels was conducted. At the firm level, barriers were related to impediments hindering knowledge sharing within the firm, whereas alliance knowledge-sharing barriers at the market level concerned issues affecting alliance knowledge sharing and acquisition between partners. A list of several items was generated through this discussion. A pre-test to items finally selected from the discussion was carried out with two academics. Face-to-face meetings with managers were then held to pre-test the questionnaire. During the pre-testing procedure each respondent's comments were recorded.

Table 1.1 Descriptive statistics

	Minimum	Maximum	Mean	Std. Deviation
FONDTYEAR	1974	2006	1995	7.156
EXPYEAR	1985	2007	2001	3.772
PRDTDEVYEAR	Before 1984	2001–2006	1996–2000	0.907
INTLOPERTNCON	1	7	2.86	1.686
DURATION	1	36	6.50	5.075
NUMEXPCON	1	100	11.63	14.497
NUMEXPRDT	0	50	5.07	6.585
NUMINTLCLNT	0	100000	1537	10521
NUMINTLDIS	0	100	8.08	16.291
NUMINTLFT	0	15	2.43	2.835

Their understanding of each item was matched with the researcher's intended meaning. These questions were further re-tested through email exchanges with relevant managers. Later in the survey study, the respondents were asked to what extent these factors prolonged the time frame for the growth of sales in the foreign market.

Sample

Table 1.1 provides summary statistics for the sample. From the sample of total respondents ($N = 100$), 69 firms were founded between years 1995 and 2006. The number of employees for the export product ranged from 1 to 50 for 77.2 per cent of the respondent firms. The largest proportion of responding firms had their export operations in Scandinavian countries, then Europe, North America and South America.

Analysis and results

Measure validation

We followed structural equation modelling (SEM) approach for measuring and estimating our theoretical model with linear relations between variables. We selected PLS variance-based SEM due to the small sample size (the number of observations is slightly higher than the number of variables) and the epistemic view of data to theory.

We validated the measurement model by assessing internal consistency, convergent and discriminant validity (Hulland, 1999). In the reflective mode, all the indicators in the outer measurement model loaded with greater than 0.50 values on their respective latent variables indicated a high degree of individual item reliability. The cross-loadings of the latent variables in the measurement model indicated all the indicators loaded higher on their respective latent variables than the other blocks in the model. Internal consistency was further validated by the composite reliability, which for all the constructs was greater than the acceptable value of 0.7, especially for strategic goals to foreign market construct. These are summarized in Table 1.2.

Table 1.2 Inter-construct correlations and the AVE (square roots) along the diagonal

Latent variables/constructs	Composite reliability	AVE	ALLENT	ALLCAP	FMPER	BARKNTR	LERORN
Alliance entrepreneurship	0.71	0.46	0.67				
Alliance capability	0.77	0.53	0.43	0.72			
Foreign market performance	0.83	0.55	0.00	0.37	0.74		
Barriers to knowledge transfer	0.74	0.50	−0.19	−0.44	−0.32	0.70	
Learning orientation	0.93	0.83	0.43	0.47	0.31	0.38	0.91

The convergent validity of the reflective block of the model, the average variance extracted (AVE) (Fornell and Larcker, 1981), indicated three latent variables in the reflective mode of the model having a greater than 0.50 AVE (see Table 1.2). However, the alliance entrepreneurial construct was just slightly higher than the accepted value. Values higher than and equal to 0.5 indicate that the measurement errors account for relatively less variance in the indicators than the latent variables. Thus, the latent variables measured the real phenomenon with fewer measurement errors. For that reason, all the latent constructs were found to be sound and satisfactorily valid.

To assess the discriminant validity, we followed Fornell and Larcker (1981) and analysed the square roots of the AVEs of the latent variables (Chin, 1998). In our measurement model, the square roots of the AVEs of the latent constructs, higher than the correlation among any other latent variables, confirmed to the above-mentioned discriminant validity standards. It indicated more variance shared between the latent variable components and its block of indicators than with components of another latent variable representing a different block of indicators. Further, the values for AVE demonstrated that the latent independent variables of alliance entrepreneurship, alliance knowledge-sharing barriers, and learning orientation captured 46, 50 and 83 per cent variance from their indicators respectively. The latent dependent variables of alliance capability and foreign market performance captured 53 and 55 per cent respectively, indicating a strong to moderate prediction impact of the measurement model.

Structural model

We used the bootstrapping method of sampling and standard errors were calculated on the basis of 200 bootstrapping runs (Chin, 1998). As Table 1.3 indicates, the analysis of the structural model is conducted in two stages: the first stage analyses only the main effects without including the moderating variables (model I) and the second stage includes the moderating variables (model II).

In model I, our results indicate R-squareds of 0.14 and 0.20 for alliance capability and foreign market performance respectively. Our first hypotheses (H1), which

Table 1.3 PLS path analysis results (standardized beta coefficients and t-values)

Exogenous variables	PLS (model I)	PLS (model II)
H1 Alliance entrepreneurship – common vision	0.49(5.73)**	0.49(5.17)**
H2 Alliance entrepreneurship – alliance capability	0.34(2.47)*	0.18(1.15)*
H3 Alliance entrepreneurship – foreign performance	−0.19(1.10)	−0.00(0.17)
H4 Barriers to alliance knowledge × alliance entrepreneurship and alliance capability	–	0.31(0.59)**
H5 Learning orientation × alliance entrepreneurship and alliance capability	–	0.11(0.59)**
Construct R^2	Alliance capability = 0.14	Alliance capability = 0.30*
	Foreign market performance = 0.20	Foreign market performance = 0.30*

Notes: *, **, show significance at <0.01, 0.05 levels.

suggests a positive relation between alliance entrepreneurship and common vision between alliance and organizational knowledge, is upheld ($\beta = 0.49$; $t = 5.73$; $p < 0.05$). The relation between alliance entrepreneurship and alliance capability is significant at the 0.05 level ($\beta = 0.38$; $t = 2.95$; $p < 0.01$), which confirms H2. The third hypotheses (H3) concerning alliance entrepreneurship to foreign market performance is not supported ($\beta = -0.19$, $t = 1.10$).

Model II includes the moderating effects of barriers to alliance knowledge sharing and learning orientation (Hypotheses 4 and 5). Following Chin et al. (2003), the indicators to the predictor (alliance entrepreneurship and capability) and moderator (knowledge-sharing barriers and learning orientation) variable were mean-centred and multiplied to obtain the interaction effects. Table 1.3 indicates the change in the R-squared for alliance capability and foreign market performance moderated by barriers to alliance knowledge sharing and learning orientation. Tabachnick and Fidell (1996) suggest that the difference in R-squared indicates the effects of the interaction and relative comparison between the two models. The R-squared attributable to the moderating effects in model II depicted statistical significance at 0.01 and greater than the R-squared values for model I. This shows a greater effect of moderating variables in predicting the alliance capability and foreign market performance.

Discussion

Buckley and Ghauri (2004) point out that fundamental issues such as global versus local, centralized versus decentralized, standardized versus adapted in the global organization of firms require knowledge management. In managing such issues, entrepreneurs focus on managing knowledge flows and attempt to combine the organizational knowledge base and spatially fixed-local specific knowledge. They acknowledge that spatial issues are bound up with a whole set of temporal, organizational, strategic and process issues. Our study has focused on the integration of knowledge within a global factory in the context of SMEs, and viewed alliance capability as one mechanism to integrate knowledge from the global factory.

We consider that SMEs benefit from alliance capability in a global factory by managing information asymmetry between internal and external sources. This asymmetry could significantly affect entrepreneurial ability to benefit from alliance knowledge. Buckley and Ghauri (2004) further suggest that global sourcing requires obtaining the optimum combination of inputs from the variety of opportunities available in the global market. Our first hypothesis confirmed that in a global environment, alliance entrepreneurship is linked to creating a common vision between organizational and alliance knowledge which is differently spatially located. Creation of a common vision is the first step in bridging between the partners to create optimum benefits from the available knowledge. Our second hypothesis that alliance entrepreneurship is positively associated with alliance capability also confirms that alliance capability strengthens the inventive abilities of entrepreneurs. This is more certain when in the process of supplying new products, new production methods, market making and creating new forms of organization (Buckley, 2009a); entrepreneurs manage information flows and take opportunities.

Our third hypothesis, that alliance entrepreneurship is positively associated with foreign market performance, is not supported in our analysis. Following Grant and Baden-Fuller (2004), Spender (1992), and the global factory assumptions, we suggest a possible explanation: that alliance partners' motives in using alliance knowledge is directly related to whether entrepreneurs exploit the existing alliance knowledge base only or augment it by further exploration into complementary activities. Grant and Baden-Fuller (2004) mention that by engaging in a joint motive of mutual learning, partners could attain technological convergence or could learn from each other and diversify in dissimilar but complementary capabilities. Thus, we conclude that another area where global entrepreneurial abilities may benefit in achieving foreign market performance, in the context of foreign market entry and expansion, is the entrepreneurial orientation to manage alliance knowledge as a complementary process of knowledge exploitation and augmentation. Our lack of support to hypothesis 3 could further be attributed to the fact that we did not include an investigation of how alliance knowledge was utilized by the foreign firm in diversifying its activities. This is also in line with March's (1991) and Spender's (1992) views that a firm's knowledge management process deals with two distinct dimensions of activities: exploration, which increases a firm's stock of knowledge, and exploitation, through which firms deploy existing knowledge to create value. Therefore, alliance knowledge management, from the viewpoint of entering and expanding into foreign markets, could offer greater potential to create entrepreneurial profits and value creation as it encompasses exploitation as well as augmentation of the organizational knowledge base.

The second aim of our study was to analyse the extent to which firm-level alliance knowledge transfer barriers moderated the relation between alliance entrepreneurship and alliance capability. The moderating effect can be attributed to the link between knowledge sharing and coordination mechanisms. This importance can further be accredited to the orientation of the top management team in emphasizing the significance of knowledge sharing in the firm's risk-taking behaviour, experimenting with products and giving employees an authority to make decisions. All these factors contribute positively towards the learning ability of the firm and further assert the importance of firm- and market-level knowledge sharing. Schreiner et al. (2009) suggest alliance capability consists of the communication, coordination and bonding skills of a firm. By showing a positive relation between barriers to alliance knowledge transfer and alliance capability, our study confirms that alliance capability comprises these skills.

In our study, learning orientation was also seen to moderate the relation between alliance entrepreneurship and foreign market performance. This result is, however, inconsistent with previous research that considers learning processes as a higher-order dynamic capability (Kale and Singh, 2007; Schreiner et al., 2009) that enables firms to develop the first-order capability to manage alliances. However, by conceptualizing learning processes as moderator to foreign market performance, we extend prior research that learning orientation as a higher-order dynamic capability is also instrumental in post-formation alliance performance. This is an important finding of our study as it could explain why some learning alliances fail (Beamish and Delios, 2001) when partners fail to invest in the mutual learning process post-formation. The learning processes of a firm also enable it to deploy previous alliance know-how in building up and managing new alliances, and to leverage alliance knowledge in the inter-firm network of prior alliances in which they are embedded.

Limitations and future research directions

Although positioned within the global factory assumptions, our study focused only on information flows between alliance partners. However, information flows into and from production, distribution, advertising, R&D and market research are also emphasized as critical elements of the information structure of the global factory (Buckley, 2009a). We suggest greater attention in the global factory framework to information exchange and integration from external sources such as alliances. As research on alliance entrepreneurship is emerging, and relatively few empirical studies linking alliance entrepreneurship in the domain of alliance capability exist, we suggest more research on the topic. Specifically, we propose that future research should focus on other behavioural characteristics of entrepreneurs, such as personal motives and personal prior experience with alliances, as key factors in alliance entrepreneurship towards alliance capability.

Our study did not include the effect of prior experience in the alliance capability conceptualization. Schreiner et al. (2009) mention that the alliance literature predominantly focuses on greater prior experience in managing alliance relationships with alliance capability, and therefore new research must focus on exploring elements that constitute alliance capabilities rather than on conditions that lead to it. On this basis we suggest to managers dealing with alliances to focus on transferring prior as well as existing alliance knowledge to achieve post-alliance/entry gains. We further suggest that managers invest in learning processes – not only at the early stage of alliances, but as ongoing mechanisms to manage alliances.

References

Alvarez, S.A. and Barney, J.B. (2001) 'How do entrepreneurs organize firms under conditions of uncertainty', *Journal of Management*, 31(5), 776–93.

Annand, B.N. and Khanna, T. (2000) 'Do firms learn to create value? The case of alliances', *Strategic Management Journal*, 21(3), 295–315.

Barney, J.B. (1991) 'Firm resources and sustained competitive advantage', *Journal of Management*, 17(1), 99–120.

Barringer, B.R. and Harrison, J.S. (2000) 'Walking a tight rope: creating value through inter-organizational relationships', *Journal of Management*, 26(3), 367–403.

Beamish, P.W. and Delios, A. (2001) 'Survival and profitability: the roles of experience and intangible assets in foreign subsidiary performance', *Academy of Management Journal*, 44(5), 1028–38.

Buckley, P.J. (2009a) 'The impact of the global factory on economic development', *Journal of World Business*, 44(2), 131–43.

Buckley, P.J. (2009b) 'Internalisation thinking: from the multinational enterprise to the global factory', *International Business Review*, 18(3), 224–35.

Buckley, P.J. and Ghauri, P.N. (2004) 'Globalisation, economic geography and the strategy of the multinational enterprises', *Journal of International Business Studies*, 35(2), 81–98.

Calantone, R.J., Cavusgil, T.S. and Zhao, Y. (2002) 'Learning orientation, firm innovation capability, and firm performance', *Industrial Marketing Management*, 6(3), 515–24.

Chin, W.W. (1998) 'The partial least squares approach for structural equation modelling', in G.A. Marcoulides (ed.) *Modern Methods for Business Research*, 295–335 (Mahwah, NJ: Lawrence Erlbaum Associates).

Chin, W.W., Marcolin, B.L. and Newsted, P.R. (2003) 'A partial least squares latent variable modelling approach for measuring interaction effects: results from a Monte Carlo simulation study and an electronic-mail emotion/adoption study', *Information Systems Research*, 14(2), 189–217.

Cohen, W. and Levinthal, L. (1990) 'Absorptive capacity: a new perspective on learning and innovation', *Administrative Science Quarterly*, 35(1), 128–52.

Cohendet, P., Llerena, P. and Marengo, L. (2000) 'Is there a pilot in the evolutionary firm?' in N. Foss and V. Mahnke (eds) *Competence, Governance and Entrepreneurship*, 95–115 (Oxford: Oxford University Press).

Doz, Y. and Hamel, G. (1998) *Alliance Advantage: The Act of Creating Value through Partnering* (Boston, MA: Harvard Business School Press).

Eisenhardt, K.M. and Martin, J.A. (2000) 'Dynamic capabilities: What are they?', *Strategic Management Journal*, 21(11), 1105–21.

Fornell, C. and Larcker, D. (1981) 'Structural equation models with unobservable variables and measurement error', *Journal of Marketing Research*, 18(1), 39–50.

Garud, R. and Nayyar, P. (1994) 'Transformative capacity: continual structuring by inter-temporal technology transfer', *Strategic Management Journal*, 15(5), 365–85.

Grant, R.M. (1991) 'The resource-based theory of competitive advantage: implications for strategy formulation', *California Management Review*, 33(3), 114–35.

Grant, R.M. and Baden-Fuller, C. (2004) 'A knowledge accessing theory of strategic alliances', *Journal of Management Studies*, 41(1), 61–84.
Heide, J.B. and John, G. (1992) 'Do norms matter in marketing relationships?', *Journal of Marketing*, 56(1), 32–44.
Heide, J.B. and Miner, A.S. (1992) 'The shadow of the future: effects of anticipated interaction and frequency of control on buyer seller cooperation', *Academy of Management Journal*, 35(1), 265–91.
Heimeriks, K.H. (2008) *Developing Alliance Capabilities* (Palgrave Macmillan).
Hulland, J. (1999) 'Use of partial least squares (PLS) in strategic management research: a review of four recent studies', *Strategic Management Journal*, 20(2), 195–204.
Inkpen, A. (1998) 'Learning, knowledge acquisition, and strategic alliances', *European Management Journal*, 16(2), 223–9.
Jaworski, B.J. and Kohli, A.K. (1993) 'Market orientation: antecedents and consequences', *Journal of Marketing*, 57(3), 53–70.
Kale, P. and Singh, H. (2007) 'Building firm capabilities through learning: the role of alliance learning process in alliance capability and firm level alliance success', *Strategic Management Journal*, 28(10), 981–1000.
Khanna, T., Gulati, R. and Nohria, N. (1998) 'The dynamics of learning alliances: competition, cooperation, and relative scope', *Strategic Management Journal*, 19(3), 193–210.
Knight, G.A. and Kim, D. (2009) 'International business competence and the contemporary firm', *Journal of International Business Studies*, 40(2), 255–73.
Kogut, B. and Zander, U. (1993) 'Knowledge of the firm and the evolutionary theory of the multinational corporation', *Journal of International Business Studies*, 24(1), 625–45.
Lusch, R.F. and Brown, J.R. (1996) 'Interdependency, contracting, and relational behaviour in marketing channels', *Journal of Marketing*, 60(4), 19–38.
March, J.G. (1991) 'Exploration and exploitation in organizational learning', *Organization Science*, 2(1), 71–87.
Maydeu-Olivares, A. and Lado, N. (2003) 'Market orientation and business performance: a mediated model', *International Journal of Service Industry Management*, 14(3), 284–309.
Mesquite, L.F., Anand, J. and Brush, T.H. (2008) 'Comparing the resource-based and relational views: knowledge transfer and spillover in vertical alliances', *Strategic Management Journal*, 29(9), 913–41.
Meyer, K.E., Wright, M. and Pruthi, S. (2009) 'Managing knowledge in foreign entry strategies: a resource-based analysis', *Strategic Management Journal*, 30(5), 557–74.
Ranft, A.L. and Marsh, S.J. (2008) 'Accessing knowledge through acquisitions and alliances: an empirical examination of new market entry', *Journal of Management Issues*, 20(1), 51–67.
Robson, M.J. and Katsikeas, C.S. (2005) 'International strategic alliance relationship within the foreign investment decision process', *International Marketing Review*, 22(4), 399–419.
Sarkar, M.B., Echambadi, R. and Harrison, J. (2001) 'Alliance entrepreneurship and firm market performance', *Strategic Management Journal*, 22(6–7), 701–11.
Schreiner, M., Kale, P. and Corsten, D. (2009) 'What really is alliance management capability and how does it impact on alliance outcome and success?', *Strategic Management Journal*, 30(13), 1395–419.
Shane, S. (2000) 'Prior knowledge and the discovery of entrepreneurial opportunities', *Organizational Science*, 11(4), 448–69.
Shane, S. and Venkataraman, S. (2000) 'The promise of entrepreneurship as a field of research', *Academy of Management Review*, 25(1), 217–26.
Simonin, B.L. (1997) 'The importance of collaborative know-how: an empirical test of the learning organization', *Academy of Management Journal*, 40(5), 1150–74.
Spender, J.-C. (1992) 'Limits to learning from the West: how Western management advice may prove limited in Eastern Europe', *International Executive*, 34(5), 389–410.
Szulanski, G. (1996) 'Exploring internal stickiness: impediments to the transfer of best practice within the firm', *Strategic Management Journal*, 17, 27–44.

Tabachnick, B.G. and Fidell, L.S. (1996) *Using Multivariate Statistics*, 3rd edn (New York: Harper and Row).

Teece, D.J., Pisano, G. and Shuen, A. (1997) 'Dynamic capabilities and strategic management', *Strategic Management Journal*, 18(7), 509–33.

Wernerfelt, B. (1984) 'A resource-based view of the firm', *Strategic Management Journal*, 5(1), 171–80.

Yeoh, P.-L. (2004) 'International learning: antecedents and performance implications among newly internationalizing companies in an exporting context', *International Marketing Review*, 21(4/5), 511–35.

Zollo, M. and Winter, S.G. (2002) 'Deliberate learning and the evolution of dynamic capabilities', *Organization Science*, 13(3), 339–51.

2
Foreign Direct Investment in Emerging Asia: Implications of the International Production Network

Juthathip Jongwanich

Introduction

Since the early 1990s, international product fragmentation – the cross-border dispersion of component production/assembly within vertically integrated production processes – has become an important feature of the structural interdependence of the world economy. Rapid advances in production technology and technological innovations in transport and communication have allowed companies to 'unbundle' the stages of production so that different tasks can be performed in different places. These dynamics have resulted in a shift in the composition of trade towards intermediate (parts and components) goods. Although production sharing is now a global phenomenon, there is evidence that it is far more important for emerging Asian countries than elsewhere (Athukorala, 2008). The share of the parts and components trade in the region has generally increased substantially over the past two decades, although India still remains a minor player in global production networks. Multinational enterprises (MNEs) from the US, Europe, Japan and recently foreign investors from the East Asian newly industrialized economies (NIEs) have played a pivotal role in linking the countries in the region to regional and global production networks.

Foreign direct investment (FDI) inflows in emerging Asian economies over the past two decades have also risen noticeably. It increased to almost US$250 billion in 2007, from around US$10 billion in 1981–1990. The existence of these phenomena has raised the question of whether the increasing importance of international production network has an implication in promoting FDI inflows in the region. It is possible that the existing production network in a host country changes the strategy of MNEs in performing investment overseas. MNEs try to take advantage of the existing production network, including service links established in the host country/region, resulting in further promotion of FDI in that country/region. Vertical FDI, where home country firms relocate different parts of production to take advantage of factor endowment between countries, could also become more crucial and dominate traditional or horizontal FDI, where multi-plant firms roughly duplicate the same activities in multiple countries.

While FDI has been widely recognized as a growth-enhancing factor in investment-receiving (host) countries, a positive relation between these two variables could have an implication for policymakers in promoting and sustaining FDI inflows. In particular, a need to strengthen factors affecting the production network, especially service links such as logistical capability, availability of world-class operators, and technical and managerial skills (Barry and Bradley, 1997), could become a top priority in addition to the traditional determinants of FDI inflows such as income levels, natural resources and competitiveness (labour costs, real exchange rates). Although this issue is policy-relevant, there are few studies examining the phenomenon (e.g. Milner et al., 2004; Vogiatzoglou, 2007).

Previous studies either examine only one particular country or exclude developing countries. Furthermore, a number of relevant factors determining FDI are left out in these empirical studies. For example, Milner et al. (2004) examine the vertical integration of production and FDI between Japan and Thailand using firm-level information on Japanese multinational activity in Thailand over the period 1985–95. The paper examines vertical FDI towards the home country market by using the market size of Japan as a proxy variable for the vertical FDI. There are only four variables used as control variables: unskilled labour intensity in Thailand; transport costs; incentive of Thai government to foreign investors; and US preferential treatment under GSP. Vogiatzoglou (2007) examines the relation between vertical specialization and FDI in emerging Asian countries. However, in the study, only OECD countries are included as home countries while vertical specialization is proxied by the bilateral trade between home and host countries. Vertical FDI towards the third countries is not examined in the study.

To redress these weak points, this chapter uses bilateral FDI inflows in emerging Asian countries, and includes both developed and developing countries as investment exporting (home) countries. The gravity model is applied to bilateral FDI inflows and extended to include the implication of (existing) international production networks and other relevant FDI determinants.

International product fragmentation

The structure of production and trade in East and Southeast Asia has changed since the early 1990s. The cross-border dispersion of component production/assembly within vertically integrated production processes, or the so-called international product fragmentation, has dominated production and trade patterns in the region. Note that parts and components are calculated from the 5-digit Standard of International Trade Classification (SITC) data, United Nations Commodity Statistics Database (UNCOMTRADE). The lists of parts and components are extended from Athukorala (2006) and Jongwanich (2010). There are 319 items classified as parts and components in which 256 products are in SITC7 and 63 products are in SITC8.

The importance of the international production network in the region can be shown through a significant increase in parts and components trade, and this can be seen in Table 2.1. The proportion of parts and components trade from emerging Asian economies into the world market has increased substantially over

Table 2.1 Share of parts and components in world parts and components trade (per cent)

	Exports				Imports			
	1992	1995	2000	2007	1992	1995	2000	2007
World (US$ billion)	616.7	960.0	1653.8	3003.4	614.3	953.8	1647.4	2946.4
Developed countries	77.7	71.1	63.4	50.5	86.8	79.7	63.8	52.3
Developing countries	22.3	28.9	36.6	49.5	13.2	20.3	36.2	47.7
Asia	13.2	18.4	23.8	33.6	22.3	28.0	24.0	31.3
Emerging Asia*	13.2	18.3	23.9	34.0	22.0	27.8	23.9	31.1
East Asia	7.1	9.6	12.8	23.7	12.3	14.1	13.6	21.4
PRC	1.6	2.7	5.3	14.6	2.5	2.6	4.2	11.3
Hong Kong	1.4	1.0	1.1	0.8	3.9	5.0	4.4	5.7
Korea	1.8	3.2	3.9	4.9	3.4	3.7	2.8	2.5
Taiwan	2.5	2.7	2.6	3.8	2.5	2.8	2.2	1.9
Southeast Asia	6.0	8.5	10.8	9.5	9.3	13.2	10.0	8.8
Indonesia	0.1	0.2	0.4	0.5	0.9	0.9	0.3	0.3
Malaysia	1.5	2.4	3.8	3.0	2.3	3.4	2.7	2.2
Philippines	0.5	0.8	1.8	1.7	0.4	0.5	1.1	0.5
Singapore	3.1	4.0	3.4	2.4	4.1	6.3	4.3	4.1
Thailand	0.8	1.1	1.4	1.7	1.6	2.1	1.4	1.4
Vietnam	0.0	0.0	0.0	0.1	0.0	0.0	0.1	0.3
South Asia	0.4	0.3	0.2	0.4	0.7	0.7	0.4	1.1
India	0.1	0.1	0.2	0.4	0.4	0.5	0.4	0.9

Notes: * Emerging Asia comprises the PRC; Hong Kong; Korea; Taiwan; Indonesia; Malaysia; Philippines; Singapore; Thailand; Vietnam; and India.
Source: Compiled from UNCOMTRADE Database, downloaded November 2009.

the past two decades. Emerging Asia's share in world exports of parts and components increased from 13.2 per cent in 1992 to 34.0 per cent in 2007, while the share in world imports of these economies rose to 31.1 per cent in 2007 from 22.0 per cent in 1992. The international production network grew faster in emerging Asia than other developing countries. In 2007, emerging Asia's parts and components exports and imports accounted for 69 per cent and 65 per cent of total developing Asia's exports and imports, respectively. Countries in East and Southeast Asia stand out in emerging Asia for their heavy dependence on parts and components for trade dynamism.

The growing importance of the international production network in the region is also revealed by the higher proportion of parts and components in manufacturing trade. In terms of exports, the share of parts and components in total manufacturing in emerging Asia increased from 19.6 per cent in 1992 to 38.9 per cent in 2007. The share grew substantially in Southeast Asian countries, followed by East Asia. In the Philippines, for example, almost 82 per cent of total manufacturing exports in 2007 were parts and components, while parts and components accounted for more than 55 per cent of total manufacturing exports in Malaysia and Singapore. Among Southeast Asian countries, Indonesia and Vietnam have seen a slower progress in participating in global production sharing.

Parts and components are also important in developing Asia's import basket; these figures can be seen in Table 2.2. The share of parts and components in

30 *Regional and Global Perspectives*

Table 2.2 Share of parts and components in manufacturing trade (per cent)

	Exports				Imports			
	1992	1995	2000	2007	1992	1995	2000	2007
World (US$ billion)	23.1	26.2	34.4	31.8	23.2	26.2	34.5	31.5
Developed countries	24.3	26.7	34.1	28.5	27.4	30.7	32.9	27.1
Developing countries	19.8	25.0	35.0	36.1	n.a.	n.a.	37.6	38.3
Asia	19.2	25.8	36.8	38.0	30.7	36.0	44.2	47.4
Emerging Asia*	19.6	26.2	37.6	38.9	31.0	36.2	44.6	47.6
East Asia	14.7	20.6	29.9	35.8	27.3	30.4	39.0	46.4
PRC	8.7	13.4	23.7	32.0	23.5	23.9	40.6	49.0
Hong Kong	16.0	19.9	35.3	39.2	22.2	28.0	37.4	50.2
Korea	18.4	31.4	44.1	46.5	40.2	39.4	47.1	36.3
Taiwan	20.4	25.1	30.2	47.8	30.0	34.1	32.1	39.4
Southeast Asia	34.6	40.9	58.7	52.5	38.5	46.5	57.5	55.6
Indonesia	4.6	8.3	20.0	27.5	26.5	30.4	25.8	25.3
Malaysia	34.1	38.5	67.4	59.6	43.7	50.1	65.4	58.1
Philippines	37.3	51.0	77.3	81.6	29.2	30.2	64.4	52.7
Singapore	51.8	58.9	71.6	57.6	45.4	57.8	64.2	63.7
Thailand	23.0	29.9	42.7	44.4	31.5	35.0	49.4	40.2
Vietnam	n.a.	n.a.	11.7	13.9	n.a.	n.a.	18.4	20.9
South Asia	10.1	8.6	5.4	10.4	19.7	22.7	21.2	27.6
India	3.2	4.6	7.4	13.3	21.6	23.7	26.5	27.4

Notes: * Emerging Asia comprises the PRC; Hong Kong; Korea; Taiwan; Indonesia; Malaysia; Philippines; Singapore; Thailand; Vietnam; and India.
Source: Compiled from UNCOMTRADE Database, downloaded November 2009.

total manufacturing imports rose to 46.4 per cent from 27.3 per cent. Parts and component imports are limited in South Asia compared to East and Southeast Asia. Most of the parts and components trade is in machinery and transport equipment (SITC 7), especially ICT products, followed by basic (resource-based) manufacturing (SITC 6) and miscellaneous exports (SITC 8).

A comparison of the data on the share of parts and components in total exports and imports points to an important difference between the PRC and the other emerging Asian countries. In the PRC, parts and components account for a much larger share of imports than exports, whereas in the other emerging Asian countries the percentage share of parts and components exports tends to be higher than imports. These different trade patterns imply an increasingly important role being played by the PRC as a final product assembler using parts and components procured from countries in the region, with Southeast Asian countries among this group.

Foreign direct investment and international production networks

As can be seen in Table 2.3, total FDI inflows to developing Asia have increased substantially over the past three decades, and most of this – almost 70 per cent of global FDI flows – was contributed by developed countries, especially Europe and

Table 2.3 FDI inflows by region and selected economies (billion US$), 1971–2007

	1971–80	1981–90	1991–96	1997–99	2000–05	2006	2007
World	28	108	256	760	848	1,411	1,833
Developed economies	22	85	163	548	592	941	1,248
Developing economies	6	23	89	203	237	413	500
Asia	2	14	59	104	143	273	319
Emerging Asia*	2	10	55	99	125	203	241
East Asia	1	5	34	68	93	132	157
PRC	0	2	26	44	54	73	84
Hong Kong	0	2	6	17	29	45	60
Korea	0	0	1	6	6	5	3
Taiwan	0	1	1	2	2	7	8
South Asia	0	0	2	4	7	26	31
India	0	0	1	3	5	20	23
Southeast Asia	1	5	20	28	27	51	61
Indonesia	0	0	3	1	0	5	7
Malaysia	0	1	5	4	3	6	8
Philippines	0	0	1	1	1	3	3
Singapore	0	2	7	13	14	25	24
Thailand	0	1	2	6	5	9	10
Vietnam	0	0	1	2	1	2	7

Note: * Emerging Asia comprises the PRC; Hong Kong; Korea; Taiwan; Indonesia; Malaysia; Philippines; Singapore; Thailand; Vietnam; and India.
Source: UNCTAD/TNC database, downloaded April 2009.

the US. FDI inflows in emerging Asia increased from only US$10 billion in 1981–90 to US$241 billion in 2007, comprising almost 15 per cent of world FDI inflows in 2007, the highest recipient of inward FDI among developing regions. Inward FDI has increased dramatically in East Asia, especially the PRC, since the early 1990s. It rose from US$5 billion in 1981–90 to US$34 billion in 1991–6, and by 2007 was US$157 billion. Most of the FDI inflows to developing Asia went to the PRC, followed by Hong Kong. MNEs also invested substantially in Southeast Asia, especially in 1993–6 – a period during which the motivation of foreign investors shifted from FDI concentrated on import substitution to export-oriented production. Singapore, followed by Thailand and Malaysia, was the key FDI destination in Southeast Asia, while FDI inflows were relatively limited in the Philippines.

It is clear from examining Tables 2.1 and 2.3 that FDI inflows and trade in parts and components in emerging Asian countries are correlated. The growth rate of these two series, as shown in Figure 2.1, clearly reveal the co-movement of these two variables, with more volatility found in FDI inflows. The correlation coefficient of the growth rate of these two variables in emerging Asian countries is 0.62, with the highest correlation found in Southeast Asian countries, followed by East Asia. One implication of this is that an increase in trade in parts and components could *simultaneously* increase FDI inflows in the region. However, as clearly pointed out in the literature (Athukorala, 2006; Rangan and Lawrence,

32 *Regional and Global Perspectives*

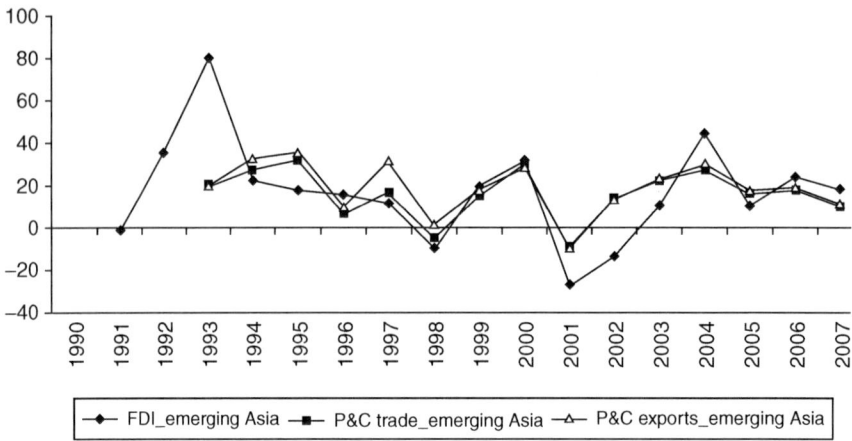

Figure 2.1 FDI and parts and components trade in emerging Asian economies
Notes: This figure plots growth rate of inward FDI, growth in parts and components (P&C) trade and growth in parts and components exports in emerging Asia.
Source: UNCTAD/TNC database, downloaded April 2009 and UNCOMTRADE Database, downloaded November 2009.

1999; Urata, 2001), production outsourcing practices were first employed by MNEs before leading to a tightening of the production network and a rise in the parts and components trade. Thus, FDI inflows tend to be a key factor in determining a rise in trade in parts and components, while changes in the parts and components trade should not simultaneously change the movements of FDI inflows. However, the existence of production outsourcing practices may have an implication for attracting FDI in the subsequent period, as firms are able to benefit from existing service links established in a host country or region.

Granger causality tests

This has implications for the quantitative analysis. If changes in trade in parts and components can simultaneously determine FDI inflows, system equations should be performed in examining FDI determinants and the implications on the international production network to avoid bias in the quantitative results. However, if the simultaneity of trade in parts and components and FDI inflows is rejected, it would be plausible to test the implications of the international production network on FDI determinants by applying the initial (existing) condition of the production network. The Granger causality test between FDI inflows and trade in parts and components is performed for emerging Asian countries and sub-regions in these countries during 1992–2007. After the late 1980s, FDI inflows went mainly into export-oriented production rather than production for import substitution, so the Granger causality test is also applied to test the relation between FDI inflows and exports in parts and components.

Table 2.4 reports the results of these causality tests. It is evident that for emerging Asian economies, the null hypothesis of 'FDI does not cause trade in parts and

Table 2.4 The Granger causality test for emerging Asian economies, 1992–2007

Null hypothesis	F-statistics
1. Emerging Asia	
1.1 Trade in parts and components	
Trade does not Granger cause FDI	2.747
FDI does not Granger cause trade	4.076*
1.2 Exports in parts and components	
Exports does not Granger cause FDI	2.313
FDI does not Granger cause exports	3.341**
2. East Asia	
2.1 Trade in parts and components	
Trade does not Granger cause FDI	2.339
FDI does not Granger cause trade	2.453
2.2 Exports in parts and components	
Exports does not Granger cause FDI	2.917
FDI does not Granger cause exports	4.150*
3. Southeast Asia	
3.1 Trade in parts and components	
Trade does not Granger cause FDI	0.255
FDI does not Granger cause trade	3.571*
3.2 Exports in parts and components	
Exports does not Granger cause FDI	0.486
FDI does not Granger cause exports	2.438
4. South Asia (India)	
4.1 Trade in parts and components	
Trade does not Granger cause FDI	5.464*
FDI does not Granger cause trade	2.380
4.2 Exports in parts and components	
Exports does not Granger cause FDI	3.696**
FDI does not Granger cause exports	0.160

Notes: * = 1 per cent significance, ** = 5 per cent significance.

components' is rejected at the 5 per cent level of significance, while we cannot statistically reject the null hypothesis of 'trade in parts and components does not cause FDI'. This result implies that FDI inflows tend to determine changes in trade in parts and components, but the reverse relation is not applicable. In other words, changes in trade in parts and components are unlikely to *simultaneously* determine changes in FDI inflows in emerging Asian countries. This evidence is also found when exports of parts and components are tested with FDI inflows.

If we consider sub-regions, there is also evidence for emerging Southeast Asian countries that changes in trade (exports) in parts and components were not able to significantly cause movement of FDI inflows. In contrast, FDI inflows significantly cause changes in trade (exports) in parts and components. The evidence from emerging South Asia – that is, India – is different from those found in the other two sub-regions. It seems that FDI inflows do not have a statistically significant effect on parts and components trade (exports), while trade (exports) of parts and components tends to influence FDI. The weak influence of FDI inflows on trade in parts and components could have emerged because the dramatic increase of FDI inflows in the late 2000s went mostly into the services sector, both financial and non-financial. Even though during the early 1990s FDI inflows mostly went into electrical equipment and transport industry, they contributed less to the parts and components trade (Table 2.2).

All in all, the causality results provide empirical support for the argument that for emerging Asia as a whole, except India, FDI tends to be a predetermined factor in promoting the international production network; that is, trade in parts and components in emerging Asia. In contrast, trade in parts and components do not *simultaneously* cause changes in FDI inflows in these economies. The results tend to imply that to examine the implication of international production network on FDI, the existence (initial condition) of production outsourcing practices tends to be more relevant. In addition, including India in our analysis may be problematic as evidence of the effects of trade on FDI is less clear in this country. Thus, in our empirical analysis the initial condition of production outsourcing practices is used to address this issue, and India is excluded from our country coverage. Note also that in our quantitative analysis, we allow for a simultaneous relation between FDI and production network (proxied by trade in parts and components) and include India in our analysis. However, the diagnostic tests when applying the initial condition of production network and excluding India are far better.

Analytical framework: Determinants of inward FDI and the implications for the international production network

FDI generally originates from the decision of MNEs to enter into international production and to relocate parts of their activities in a selected host country. There is still no single analytical framework to capture the whole range of motivations embedded in the investment profile of a country. Dunning (1981, 1986) developed the investment development path (IDP) model illustrating a positive relation between the level of a country's development and its investment profile. At the lowest level of development, firms do not have ownership advantages. Consequently, there is no outward foreign direct investment (OFDI) taking place, while inward foreign direct investment (IFDI) is limited. In the final stage, the net investment position of the country fluctuates around zero; that is, the magnitudes of IFDI and OFDI are similar. Based on this analytical framework, a stage of development – particularly an income level – is crucial in determining the investment profile of the country.

This model, however, cannot address the increased complexity in the motives underpinning FDI. There is evidence that the investment profile of countries at similar levels of development, especially in terms of income per capita, can be different. In addition, a number of developing countries, such as the PRC, India, Brazil and Mexico, which are classified as stage 1 or 2, began to engage in OFDI earlier than what was predicted by the IDP model. This implies that there are other crucial factors determining the investment profile of a country.

Based on the theoretical and empirical literature, motivations driving a foreign firm to invest in developing countries can be grouped into the following factors. First is natural resource-seeking FDI. Under this motivation, home country firms undertake OFDI to access immobile natural factor endowments in host countries, such as oil and minerals, so a country that has a high level of natural resource endowment is likely to attract inflows of resource-seeking MNEs. Recently, there is evidence that resource-rich countries, such as Malaysia, Indonesia, Laos and Cambodia have begun to attract 'resource-seeking' investors from the PRC because of the limited resource endowment in China and the rapid expansion of domestic demand for commodity products (Athukorala and Hill, 2008).

Second is market-seeking FDI. Firms undertake market-seeking FDI in response to opportunities inherent in host countries – in order to strengthen existing markets or to develop and explore new markets. In addition, a limited home country market pushes firms to invest in other countries. The impact of this on companies may be intensified by factors in other markets such as trade barriers and a lack of international linkage with customers in targeted markets. Third is efficiency-seeking FDI, whereby foreign investors seek lower cost locations for their production and operation activities. Increases in production costs in the home economy caused by rapid economic expansion and the scarcity of resources and inputs drive firms to invest in other countries with potential markets. A rise in labour costs as well as inflationary pressure which can affect all factor inputs are common factors in driving firms to invest overseas. The concept of efficiency-seeking FDI is, to some extent, similar to IDP. A country tends to lose its competitiveness when there has been a rapid expansion of economic growth and the economy is already developed. To maintain its competitiveness, firms seek to invest abroad.

It is noteworthy that in addition to low labour costs, human capital may be crucial in attracting efficiency-seeking FDI. Based on a new endogenous growth model, human capital is important in increasing the marginal productivity of capital and foreign investors may therefore take into account the level of a host country's human capital. This factor is particularly important for foreign firms who invest in capital-, knowledge- and technology-intensive activities, but less important for foreign firms who invest in labour-intensive activities.

In addition, institutions and the prevailing investment climate of the host countries are also crucial factors in attracting inward FDI (Buckley et al., 2007; Bénassy-Quéré et al., 2005). Culture proximity, for example, facilitates the development of international business and social networks that can help companies to internationalize in world markets. This informal channel could help firms in their home country to reduce transaction costs, especially business opportunity search costs, and to mitigate any risk perception of the company. Ethnic and family networks can constitute a firm-specific advantage and can compensate a company in the case of late entry into international markets, leading to a special ownership advantage (Li, 2003).

Government policies, including trade and investment, as well as capital and financial accounts, are crucial elements in the investment climate. While a high degree of openness to international market leads to well-established international links and distribution networks, MNEs – especially those engaging in export-oriented industries – are likely to invest in a country that has a high degree of trade, investment and financial account liberalization. The presence of a developed infrastructure is another element engendered in the investment climate that could have a positive impact on FDI attraction. It facilitates the production process and the distribution of produced goods, and reduces operating costs.

Macroeconomic stability – in monetary, fiscal and exchange rate policy – is another factor that favours the attraction of FDI. A sound macroeconomic environment decreases risks for foreign investment and exerts generally a positive effect on inward FDI. Depreciation of the real exchange rate in host countries may attract FDI through two key channels. Particularly those MNEs in export-oriented industries can benefit from the host country's real exchange rate depreciation, which leads to an improvement in the host country's international competitiveness. Meanwhile, imperfect information in financial markets can cause external financing to be more expensive than internal financing. Consequently, domestic currency depreciation can lead to cheaper transferring costs from home to host countries.

Implications of international product fragmentation (production network) on FDI

The existence of international product fragmentation is hypothesized to be another factor affecting inward FDI into developing Asia. It could further promote FDI, especially vertical FDI or export-platform FDI, where firms locate different stages of production in different places to take advantage of factor endowments between countries, since foreign investors could derive benefits from the existence of 'service links' in the country or region. This form of FDI occurs because of inter-country differences in factor endowments that provide incentives to locate skilled-labour-intensive activities in a relatively skilled-labour-abundant country and unskilled activities in a corresponding suitable national location (Helpman and Krugman, 1985).

There are two forms of vertical FDI that the existence of an international production network can further promote, namely (1) vertical FDI oriented towards the home market, and (2) vertical FDI oriented towards a third country. The former occurs when there is a bilateral vertical specialization-production link between the home and the host countries. In other words, the home country firms seek to exploit the abundance of resource endowment in the host country before shipping products back home. According to Milner et al. (2004), the size of the home market for parts and components, instead of the size of the host market, is critical in determining vertical FDI oriented towards the home market.

Vertical FDI oriented towards the third country occurs when the home country firm locates production (parts and components/intermediate products) in the host country before exporting products to third countries. The existence of service links, especially accessibility into the third countries, could further promote this form of FDI. Locations with good market accessibility to the main market core provide MNEs with the advantage of exporting products into the economic core, while producing at the local market, and importing necessary supplies from the core easier and cheaper (Kumar, 1998).

The empirical model

In order to examine the determinants of inward FDI in developing Asia, a gravity model is applied. The basic gravity model argues that market size of home (M_i) and host (M_j) countries and the distance between them ($Distance_{ij}$) are important determinants in the choice of location of foreign direct investment. The market size of the home (M_i) and host country (M_j) is proxied by real GDP per capita (constant 2000 US$). A positive relation between the market size of the host country (M_j) and FDI inflows – especially market-seeking FDI – is expected, while there is an ambiguous sign of market size in the home country (M_i). A large home country market size indicates a greater aggregate income and therefore a higher ability to invest abroad; however, a limited market size in the home country could also stimulate home country firms to seek other potential markets.

The sign of distance ($Distance_{ij}$) is also ambiguous. On the one hand, a greater distance between countries makes a foreign operation more difficult and expensive to supervise, thereby discouraging FDI. Particularly as geographical distance is also a proxy for cultural distance or barriers and information costs, a larger bilateral distance is expected to be a negative factor affecting inward FDI. However, while distance is positively related to trade costs, a greater distance may encourage firms to perform FDI instead of trade. Thus a positive relation between distance and FDI may be revealed, especially for horizontal FDI, where trade costs between home and host countries are crucial.

The basic gravity equation model is extended to include other factors in determining FDI. To examine the impact of the existence of international product fragmentation in promoting FDI (vertical FDI), two variables are included into the model. The first variable is the *initial* value of share of bilateral imports of parts and components between the home country *i* and the host country *j* in the total manufacturing imports of a country *i* ($BIMP_{ij}$) to capture the impact of (existing) international product fragmentation on vertical FDI oriented towards the home market. This is calculated via equation (2.1). It is plausible that multinational firms are more inclined to further invest in a country where they have information on the economic and production conditions of host country, which may be revealed through bilateral trade in parts and components between these two countries, and where the home country market for these products is large enough that economies of scale in production can be easily achieved and the fixed costs of inter-country transporting and transacting can be reduced (Milner et al., 2004).

$$\text{BIMP}_{ij,t} = \frac{\text{Imports}^{P\&C}_{ij,t-1}}{\text{Manufacturing imports}_{i,t-1}} \tag{2.1}$$

The second variable is the *initial* value of the total trade in parts and components in the total manufacturing trade in a country j, excluding bilateral imports of parts and components in a country i (IIT_{ij}). This is calculated as follows:

$$IIT_{ij,t} = \frac{\left(\text{Total Exports}^{P\&C}_{j,t-1} - \text{Exports}^{P\&C}_{ij,t-1}\right) + \left(\text{Total Imports}^{P\&C}_{j,t-1} - \text{Imports}^{P\&C}_{ij,t-1}\right)}{\text{Total Manufacturing Trade}_{j,t-1}} \quad (2.2)$$

This index is designed to capture the impact of (existing) international product fragmentation on vertical FDI in the third country. A high value of this index in the host country j reflects the high level of a host economy's market accessibility and the high quality of service links. This would help to further attract FDI since MNEs could benefit from existing service links and locations with developed market accessibility; that is, the inherent advantages of being able to export parts and components to the other potential markets and import the necessary supplies.

To capture resource-seeking FDI, the share of crude material (SITC2) and fuel (SITC3) exports of a host country j in total world crude and fuel exports (Res_j) is used to proxy the abundance of resources in the host country. A positive relation between Res_j and inward FDI in the host country j is expected, as MNEs are able to relocate their production to exploit natural resources and inputs in the host country. Labour costs (ULC_j) in the host country j, are included in the model to capture efficiency-seeking FDI. Labour costs are considered as wages (per month) in manufacturing sector. To capture the labour productivity of the host country, wage (per month) is adjusted by labour productivity, proxied by value-added (constant 2,000 US$) per worker. A negative result between these two variables and inward FDI in the host country j is expected – lower labour costs (as well as higher labour productivity) would attract more FDI.

Two real exchange rates are included in the model. The first is the bilateral real exchange rate between the home country i and the host country j (RER_{ij}) and the second is the real effective exchange rate in the host country j ($REER_j$). The former is intended to capture the cost of transferring capital between the two countries, while the latter is designed to reflect the incentive for MNEs in maintaining their competitiveness by relocating production plants. A positive relation between the real effective exchange rate in the host country j ($REER_j$) and inward FDI in developing Asia is expected, but the sign of bilateral RER (RER_{ij}) is uncertain. Although a real exchange rate depreciation of a host country's currency against the home country j (a depreciation of RER_{ij}) would reduce the transfer cost of capital and could promote inward FDI in the host country, depreciation could encourage a home country's firms to import instead of performing FDI. In contrast, any depreciation of the real effective exchange rate ($REER_j$) in the host country is likely to encourage FDI, especially export-oriented FDI, since exports from the host country become cheaper relative to its trading partners.

The investment climate in the host country j is proxied by macroeconomic stability, financial openness, developed infrastructure and trade policy openness – measured in terms of tariffs, non-tariff barriers, as well as Free Trade Agreements

(FTAs). Macroeconomic stability (MS_j) is the weighted average of money M2 growth, inflation, and standard deviation of inflation. Financial openness (FO_j) is intended to measure the level of international capital market controls, comprising foreign ownership/investment restrictions and capital controls. Infrastructure ($INFRA_j$) is proxied by the percentage of paved road to total road in the host country j. A positive relation between these variables and inward FDI in developing Asia is expected.

Tariff barriers (TB_j) are calculated as the weighted average of revenue from trade taxes (per cent of total trade), the mean tariff rate and the standard deviation in tariff rates, and non-tariff barriers (NTB_j) are the weighted average of non-tariff barriers and the compliance costs of importing and exporting. In addition to tariffs and non-tariff barriers, the model includes the dummy variables free trade agreements, regional trade agreements ($RTAs_j$) and bilateral trade agreements between the home country i and the host country j ($BTAs_{ij}$). In contrast to the other investment climate variables, the relation between trade policy openness, including FTAs, and FDI is uncertain, and depends on the type of FDI. As trade policy openness can reduce trade costs, firms with vertical FDI tend to benefit from the reduction of trade costs and therefore have an incentive to locate production plants in the host country. In contrast, there is less tariff-jumping incentive for horizontal FDI, so reduced costs will discourage firms from building plants with high sunk costs in the host country.

All in all, the empirical model for determinants of inward FDI in developing Asia is as follows:

$$\text{FDI}_{ij} = \beta_0 + \beta_1 M_i + \beta_2 M_j + \beta_3 \text{Distance}_{ij} + \beta_4 \text{BIMP}_{ij} + \beta_5 \text{ITT}_{ij} + \beta_6 \text{Res}_j$$
$$+ \beta_7 \text{ULC}_j + \beta_8 \text{RER}_{ij} + \beta_9 \text{REER}_j + \beta_{10} \text{MS}_j + \beta_{11} \text{FO}_j + \beta_{12} \text{INFRA}_j$$
$$+ \beta_{13} \text{TB}_j + \beta_{14} \text{NTB}_j + \beta_{15} \text{RTAs}_j + \beta_{16} \text{BTAs}_{ij} + v_{ij} \qquad (2.3)$$

where

FDI_{ij} is the real FDI flow from the source country i to the host country j (as a percentage of GDP)

M_i and M_j is the market size of the home country i and the host country j (real GDP per capita, constant 2000 US$)

$Distance_{ij}$ is the geographical distance between the source country i and the host country j (kilometres)

$BIMP_{ij}$ is the *initial* value of the share of bilateral imports of parts and components of the home country i from the host country j in total manufacturing imports of country i (per cent)

IIT_{jj} is the *initial* value of the total trade in parts and components in the total manufacturing trade in country j, excluding bilateral imports of parts and components in country i (per cent)

Res_j is the share of crude material (SITC2) and fuel (SITC3) exports of host country j in world total crude and fuel exports (per cent)

ULC_j is wages (per month) in the manufacturing sector (US$) adjusted by labour productivity, measured by value-added in the host country j (constant 2000 US$/worker)

RER_{ij} is the bilateral real exchange rate between the source country i and host country j (index: 2000 = 100)

$REER_j$ is the real effective exchange rate in the host country j (with its key trading partners) (index: 2000 = 100)

MS_j is the measure for macroeconomic stability (the weighted average of money [M2] growth, inflation, and the standard deviation of inflation) in host country j (index: 1–10, higher values indicate greater macroeconomic stability)

FO_j is the financial openness measure (foreign ownership and/or investment restriction and capital controls) in host country j (index: 1–10, higher values indicate greater financial openness (de jure measure))

$INFRA_j$ is the measure of infrastructure development (percentage of paved road to total road) in host country j (per cent)

TB_j is the measure of tariff barriers (revenue from trade taxes (per cent of total trade), mean tariff rate and the standard deviation of tariff rate) in host country j (index: 1–10, higher values indicate lower tariff barriers, i.e. greater trade openness)

NTB_j is the measure of non-tariff barriers (level of non-tariff barriers and compliance costs of importing and exporting) in host country j (index: 1–10, the higher the index, the lower the non-tariff barriers)

$RTAs_j$ is the dummy variables for participation by host country j in regional trade agreements. There are three dummy variables: (1) the Asia-Pacific Trade Agreement (APTA) (1 for country participating in APTA and 0 otherwise); (2) the ASEAN Free Trade Area (AFTA) (1 for ASEAN Free Trade Area and 0 otherwise); and (3) ASEAN-other non-member countries (*AFTAHub*) (1 for country outside ASEAN that signed the agreement with AFTA and 0 otherwise)

$BTAs_{ij}$ is the dummy variable for the presence of bilateral trade agreements signed between the home country i and host country j.

The bilateral FDI data are derived from the UNCTAD/TNC database for the period 1994–2007. Based on data availability, our emerging Asian economies sample consists of seven host economies: PRC, Hong Kong, Korea, Malaysia, Philippines, Singapore and Thailand. India is excluded from our analysis because of its lack of involvement in the international production network. There are 61 home countries, both developed and developing. The bilateral FDI data are deflated by CPI in the host country to get the real bilateral FDI flow.

Real GDP per capita (constant 2,000 US$), real GDP (constant 2,000 US$) and percentage of paved road to total road are obtained from the World Bank (World Development Indicators database). The data on nominal exchange rates and the consumer price indices for computing real exchange rates are from International Financial Statistics (IFS), International Monetary Fund (IMF). Trade data come from the United Nations Commodity Statistics Database (UNCOMTRADE). Parts and components are separable from final goods within the United Nations

Commodity Statistics Database (UNCOMTRADE) at the 5-digit Standard International Trade Classification (SITC). Employment data are from Key Indicators, Asian Development Bank and wages (per month) data of the manufacturing sector are from the International Office Database. Macroeconomic stability, trade and financial openness are from The Fraser Institute.

To examine the determinants of bilateral FDI flow in developing Asia, an unbalanced panel econometric procedure is applied for five non-overlapping, 3-year periods during 1994–2007 with 8 host countries and 61 home countries. Three-year periods are applied, instead of on a yearly basis, to reduce the business cycle fluctuations associated with data series. However, the data set contains a large number of missing variables for bilateral FDI and a small number of disinvestment (negative) figures. Excluding missing and negative observations, our panel data is reduced from 2,835 to 990 panel (unbalanced) observations. To deal with the issue of censored data, a Tobit model is applied (Stein and Daude, 2006; Loungani et al., 2002). The unit root test for panel data is first performed to ensure that there is no unit root for all dependent and independent variables. Because no unit root was found, the level of both dependent and independent variables can be used without concern regarding spurious regression.

Results

Table 2.5 reports estimation results based on the Tobit regression model. All variables in equation (2.3) are first included and the result is reported in column A. Variables that are statistically insignificant are then excluded and the result is reported in column B. To test whether firms from developed countries behave differently from those in developing countries, G3 dummy variables are introduced into equation (2.3). Column C reports all variables attached with G3 dummy variables and column D reports only variables that are statically significant. Attention is paid to column D throughout the rest of the chapter. Note that for all these three equations, the Huber/White methodology is applied for robust standard errors.

As it forms the key hypothesis of this chapter, we first examine the implication of the existing international production network in promoting FDI inflow in emerging Asia economies. The estimation result (column D) shows that the coefficients for $BIMP_{ij}$ and ITT_{ij} are positive and statistically significant. The statistical significance of $BIMP_{ij}$ reflects that the existence of international production networks could further promote FDI from home country i to exploit any abundance of resource endowment in the host country j and, subsequently, ship the products (parts and components) back to the home country. This result confirms that multinational firms are more inclined to further invest in a country where they already have information on economic and production conditions. We also found the statistical significance of G3 dummy variables corresponding to $BIMP_{ij}$. This tends to show that the existence of the production network is more crucial for MNEs from developed countries in promoting vertical FDI oriented to home market countries than those from developing countries.

Table 2.5 Estimation results

Variables	A	B	C	D
Intercept	−106.63 (−6.54)*	−100.33 (−7.47)*	−93.63 (−7.29)*	−93.55 (−7.21)*
Market size of home country (M_i)	1.17 (21.05)*	1.17 (21.20)*	0.93 (12.58)*	0.88 (12.33)*
Market size of host country (M_j)	13.34 (5.06)*	12.36 (5.37)*	9.84 (4.51)*	10.58 (4.78)*
Market size of host country ($M_j^{\wedge 2}$)	−0.87 (−5.49)*	−0.81 (−5.86)*	−0.66 (−4.95)*	−0.70 (−5.27)*
Distance ($Distance_{ij}$)	−0.30 (−2.38)*	−0.30 (−2.50)*	−0.76 (−4.79)*	−0.47 (−3.69)*
The *initial* value of the share of bilateral imports P&C of home country i from the host country j in total imports of country i ($BIMP_{ij}$)	0.75 (12.49)*	0.76 (12.71)*	0.48 (4.52)*	0.61 (6.49)*
The *initial* value of total trade in P&C in the total manufacturing trade in country j, excluding bilateral imports of parts and components in country i (IIT_{jj})	0.73 (0.39)			
The *initial* value of total trade in P&C ($IIT_{jj}^{\wedge 2}$)	2.06 (2.47)*	1.70 (10.02)*	1.60 (7.07)*	1.54 (9.13)*
Labour costs (ULC_j)	−0.32 (−0.13)			
Labour costs ($ULC_j^{\wedge 2}$)	−0.14 (−0.38)	−0.08 (−2.56)*	−0.05 (−1.27)	−0.08 (−2.56)*
Natural resources ($Res_j^{\wedge 2}$)	0.39 (1.96)**	0.38 (2.01)**	0.53 (2.11)**	0.41 (2.09)**
Bilateral RER (RER_{ij})	1.17 (2.44)*	1.10 (2.40)*	1.46 (2.30)**	0.80 (1.74)**
Real effective exchange rate ($REER_j$)	3.83 (3.70)*	3.65 (4.25)*	4.84 (4.69)*	4.95 (5.84)*
Infrastructure ($INFRA_j$)	1.13 (2.54)*	1.10 (2.78)*	1.35 (2.36)*	1.00 (2.60)*
Macroeconomic stability (MS_j)	1.17 (1.47)	0.89 (1.71)**	1.67 (2.19)**	1.59 (2.30)**
Financial openness (FO_j)	3.13 (7.70)*	3.06 (8.05)*	2.53 (4.71)*	2.92 (8.07)*
Tariff barriers (TB_j)	0.01 (0.01)			
Non-tariff barriers (NTB_j)	8.04 (8.03)*	7.96 (8.84)*	7.53 (6.54)*	7.21 (8.19)*
Asia-Pacific Trade Agreement (APTA)	0.72 (1.74)**	0.68 (1.66)**	0.61 (1.44)	
ASEAN Free Trade Area (AFTA)	0.03 (0.07)			

ASEAN-other non-member countries (*AFTAhub*)	0.61 (1.61)**	0.66 (1.78)**	1.16 (2.74)*	0.97 (2.36)*
Bilateral Trade Agreement (BTA$_{ij}$)	0.49 (1.53)			
(M_i)*dummyG3			1.59 (5.96)*	1.55 (6.12)*
(Distance$_{ij}$)*dummyG3			1.44 (6.14)*	
(BIMP$_{ij}$)*dummyG3			0.45 (3.74)*	0.24 (2.37)*
(IIT$_{jj}^{\wedge 2}$)*dummyG3			−0.09 (−0.40)	
(ULC$_j^{\wedge 2}$)*dummyG3			−0.03 (−0.66)	
(Res$_j^{\wedge 2}$)*dummyG3			−0.35 (−1.10)	−0.20 (−2.06)**
(RER$_{ij}$)*dummyG3			−2.06 (−2.50)*	
(REER$_j$)*dummyG3			−2.12 (−2.02)**	−2.52 (−4.25)*
(INFRA$_j$)*dummyG3			−0.47 (−0.63)	
(MS$_j$)*dummyG3			−1.53 (−1.81)**	−1.24 (−1.72)**
(FO$_j$)*dummyG3			0.03 (0.06)	
(NTB$_j$)*dummyG3			−1.16 (−0.99)	
No. Observations	990	990	990	990
S.E. of regression	2.04	2.03	1.94	1.96

Notes: All variables are in logarithms. * = 1 per cent significance and ** = 5 per cent significance.

The statistical significance of IIT_{ij} shows that the existence of the global production network could further promote vertical FDI oriented towards a third market in the host country *j*. The establishment of service links and good market accessibility to the main market core provides MNEs with the advantage of being able to export and import necessary supplies (other parts and components) from other countries. Interestingly, an exponential relation between IIT_{ij} and FDI is found in our analysis and the coefficient corresponding to this variable is higher than that corresponding to $BIMP_{ij}$, implying that the existence of the global production network could promote more vertical FDI towards the third market than vertical FDI towards the home market. Policies aiming to improve 'service links' and the 'market accessibility condition' in a global context would be more relevant in promoting FDI inflows in the region than focusing on bilateral relationships.

The market size of home (M_i) countries has a crucial effect on inward FDI in developing Asia. A 1 per cent increase in real GDP per capita in a home country leads to a 0.91 per cent increase in inward FDI in emerging Asian economies. Column D in Table 2.5 also shows that the behaviour of MNEs from developed countries is statistically different from those in developing countries; the G3 dummy variable corresponding to (M_i) is positive and statistically significant. A 1 per cent increase in GDP per capita with developed countries could lead to an FDI inflow into emerging Asian economies of 2.4 per cent. The positive impact of the market size of a home country confirms the IDP model – that the state of development in a country is crucial for the country in performing outward FDI.

The positive relation between the market size of the host country (M_j) and the level of inward FDI is also found in the estimation results. However, the market size of host countries per se seems to become less important when the income per capita of the country increases and reaches a certain level, which is around US$2,500 (constant 2000 prices). Among emerging Asian countries in our sample, this variable is more relevant for the PRC and Philippines, as income per capita in these two countries is lower than the threshold level. This variable seems to be less relevant for Hong Kong, Singapore and Korea, as per capita income in these countries is far higher than the threshold level – around US$35,000; US$30,000 and US$15,000 (constant 2000 prices) in 2007, respectively. In fact, these countries have already played a role in performing outward foreign direct investment.

The negative and statistical significance of the coefficient corresponding to distance reflects the fact that the greater distance between countries could increase the costs of investment, especially operational and supervisory costs. As this variable acts as a proxy for culture, this significant relation could also reflect barriers and information costs, especially in a situation of asymmetric information. Thus, the negative coefficient of distance tends to confirm that inward FDI in developing Asia is mostly in the form of vertical, instead of horizontal FDI.

While vertical FDI inflow is very important to emerging Asia, the host country's specific inherent factors, particularly labour costs (adjusted by labour productivity), bilateral real exchange rate (RER_{ij}) and real effective exchange rate ($REER_j$) are crucial in determining the extent of inward FDI. We find a negative relation between labour costs and inward FDI, confirming that the host countries that have a low level of labour costs tend to attract more the efficiency-seeking FDI and labour-intensive production activities. Athukorala and Hill (2008) point out that the dramatic increase in FDI inflows to the PRC over the past two decades could be attributed to the lower labour costs in the country. However, as the PRC has expended rapidly, there is evidence of a significant increase in wage rate. This has begun to erode the PRC attractiveness as the low-wage investment location and entices Chinese firms involved in labour-intensive manufacturing to relocate production to lower wage neighbours, such as in Cambodia and Vietnam. Note that while this variable is adjusted by labour productivity, this implies that upgrading skilled labour becomes an important element in maintaining FDI in the region when labour costs rise.

Both the bilateral (RER_{ij}) and real effective exchange rates ($REER_j$) are positive and significant. The significance of bilateral RER_{ij} confirms that costs of transferring capital are relevant in affecting FDI inflow to emerging Asian economies. The depreciation of a host country's currency (RER_{ij}), which leads to a cheaper cost of transferring capital, results in a higher level of FDI inflow. The depreciation of the real effective exchange rate ($REER_j$) in the host country against her trading partners could promote inward FDI in emerging Asia. This reflects the fact that most inward FDI in the region is dominated by export-oriented FDI, and currency competitiveness is a prime consideration for overseas investors in establishing a plant and export into a third market. Note that the statistically negative significance of G3 dummy variables associated with the real effective exchange rate ($REER_j$) reveals that MNEs from developed countries are less concerned about movements of the real exchange rate than MNEs from developing countries when investing in emerging Asian countries. The statistical insignificance of G3 dummy variables associated with the real exchange rate (RER_{ij}) implies that MNEs from developed and developing countries treat costs of transferring capital differently.

The investment climate in the host country is important in determining inward FDI. All measures reflecting the investment climate except tariff barriers are positive and significant. The insignificance of the tariff barrier variable could emerge from the fact that during the estimation period tariff rates in these economies declined noticeably, and a number of schemes introduced in host countries exempted foreign investors from tariffs. We found only one free trade agreement to be statistically significant in promoting FDI inflow in emerging economies – the ASEAN-other non-member countries (AFTAHub). Bilateral trade agreement (BTA_{ij}) is positive but insignificant, reflecting the fact that a region-wide trade agreement tends to be more effective in promoting FDI inflow than agreements at the bilateral level. This result is consistent with the findings above related to the implication of the global production network in which an improvement of service links and market accessibility in a region would benefit more from attracting FDI inflow than establishing a bilateral relationship.

Finally, we found statistical significance in the coefficient corresponding to the abundance of natural resources ($Resource_j$) in the host country. The non-linear (exponential) relation shows that the advantages in attracting FDI would fall more in a country that has a high level of resource abundance, all other things being equal. Based on our data, Malaysia has the highest ratio of crude material (SITC2) and fuel (SITC3) exports as a proportion of total world crude and fuel exports, followed by Singapore and PRC. Note that this motivation tends to be less important for MNEs from developed countries than those from developed countries as the G3 dummy variable associated with this variable is negative and statistically significant.

Conclusion and policy inferences

This chapter examines the determinants of FDI flow in emerging Asian economies with an emphasis on the implication of the existing international production network (international product fragmentation) in promoting inward FDI. The gravity model is applied with the bilateral FDI data, consisting of 7 emerging (host) Asian economies, namely the PRC, Hong Kong, Korea, Malaysia, Philippines, Singapore and Thailand, and 61 home countries, both developed and developing, during the period 1994–2007. The estimation result shows that inward FDI taking place in the region is mostly in the form of vertical FDI and the existing international production network has become an important factor in promoting (vertical) FDI inflow. Both vertical FDI oriented towards the home market (i.e. a bilateral vertical specialization-production link between the home country and the host country) and FDI oriented towards the third market (i.e. the home country firm locates production in the host country before exporting products to third countries) are promoted by the (existing) international production network, but the latter tends to dominate the former. The establishment of service links and an attractive location for market accessibility to the main market core provide MNEs with the advantage of producing at the local market, and importing necessary supplies (other parts and components) from other countries. The result implies that policies aiming to improve 'service links' and 'market accessibility condition' in a regional and global context would become more beneficial for a host country in promoting FDI inflow than focusing on a bilateral relationship.

Strengthening supply-side capacity and improving 'services links' and a 'good market accessibility condition' should be established as policy priorities in promoting inward FDI in the region. To strengthen 'services links' a policy leading towards reducing trade costs is crucial. This policy includes customs reform and improvement of infrastructure and logistical services, as well as increased legal certainty and strengthened governance in enforcing contracts to protect intellectual property rights. Improvements in the availability of world-class operators and technical and managerial skills are also critical in strengthening the production network.

The positive relation of the existing international production network reflects that a latecomer in the global production network could face disadvantages in attracting FDI inflows. Such a country needs to put more effort into improving its investment climate, including infrastructure, trade and investment policy, as well as human capital development, to attract and maintain FDI inflow. These are traditional factors, which are found to be statistically significant in promoting FDI in our quantitative analysis. Strengthening these factors could indirectly help a country enter into the global production network and further promote FDI flow.

Acknowledgements

The author would like to thank participants at the Trade and Industry Conference, held at Australian National University on 19–20 November 2009, and the 37th Academy of International Business (UK and Ireland Chapter) conference, held at Trinity College Dublin during 8–10 April 2010. In particular, the author would like to thank Professor Prema-Chandra Athukorala for his comments and suggestions.

References

Athukorala, P. (2006) 'Product fragmentation and trade patterns in East Asia', *Asian Economic Papers*, 4(3), 1–27.
Athuokorala, P. (2008) 'New patterns of trade and investment in Asia: implications for financial integration', paper presented to the conference on *Monetary and Financial Issues in Economic Integration in Asia*, organized by The School of Economics, University of Adelaide, Adelaide, August.
Athukorala, P.C. and Hill, H. (2008) 'Asian trade and investment: patterns and trends', paper presented to workshop at the Ninth GDN Conference, Brisbane, January.
Barry, F. and Bradley, J. (1997) 'FDI and trade: the Irish host-country experience', *Economic Journal*, 107(445), 1798–811.
Bénassy-Quéré, A., Fontagené, L. and Lahréche-Révil, A. (2005) 'How does FDI react to corporate taxation?', *International Tax and Public Finance*, 12(5), 583–603.
Buckley, P.J., Clegg, L.J., Cross, A.R., Liu, X., Voss, H. and Zheng, P. (2007) 'The determinants of Chinese outward foreign direct investment', *Journal of International Business Studies*, 38(4), 499–518.

Dunning, J.H. (1981) 'Explaining the international direct investment position of countries: towards a dynamic or development approach', *Weltwirtschaftliches Archiv*, 117(1), 30–64.

Dunning, J.H. (1986) 'The investment development cycle revisited', *Weltwirtschaftliches Archiv*, 122(4), 667–75.

Helpman, E. and Krugman, P. (1985) *Market Structure and Foreign Trade* (Cambridge, MA: MIT Press).

Jongwanich, J. (2010) 'Determinants of export performance in East and Southeast Asia', *World Economy*, 33(1), 20–41.

Kumar, N. (1998) 'Multinational enterprises, regional economic integration and export-platform production in the host countries: an empirical analysis for the US and Japanese corporations', *Weltwirtschaftliches Archiv*, 134(3), 450–83.

Li, P.P. (2003) 'Toward a geocentric theory of multinational evolution: the implications from the Asian TNCs as latercomers', *Asian Pacific Journal of Management*, 20(2), 217–42.

Loungani, P., Mody, A. and Razin, A. (2002) 'The global disconnect: the role of transactional distance and scale economies in gravity equations', *Scottish Journal of Political Economy*, 49(5), 526–43.

Milner, C., Reed, G. and Talerngsri, P. (2004) 'Foreign direct investment and vertical integration of production by Japanese multinationals in Thailand', *Journal of Comparative Economics*, 32(4), 805–21.

Rangan, S. and Lawrence, R.Z. (1999) *A Prism on Globalization: Corporate Responses to the Dollar* (Washington, DC: The Brookings Institution).

Stein, E. and Daude, C. (2006) 'Longitude matters: time zones and the location of foreign direct investment', *Journal of International Economics*, 71(1), 96–112.

Urata, S. (2001) 'Emergence of a FDI-trade nexus and economic growth in East Asia', in J.E. Stiglitz and S. Yusuf (eds) *Rethinking the East Asian Miracle*, 409–459 (New York: Oxford University Press).

Vogiatzoglou, K. (2007) 'Vertical specialization and new determinants of FDI: Evidence from South and East Asia', *Global Economic Review*, 36(3), 245–66.

3
From Federations to Global Factories: Assessing the Contribution of the Subsidiary Middle Manager in Today's MNE

Dónal O'Brien, Pamela Sharkey-Scott and Pat Gibbons

Introduction

The literature on the multinational enterprise (MNE) concentrates on a hierarchical parent and child relationship between corporate headquarters and their subsidiaries. Classical theories of MNE evolution (Dunning, 1979; Johanson and Vahlne, 1977; Vernon, 1966) outlined subsidiary development as a HQ-driven process. The view was taken that strategic thinking emanates from the centre of the organization and is then implemented by subsidiaries which act as instruments of the parent company's overall strategy (Delany, 2000). An alternative perspective suggests that subsidiaries are far more than simply implementers of their parent companies' will (Birkinshaw and Hood, 1998; Jarillo and Martinez, 1990; Rugman and Verbeke, 2001; White and Poynter, 1984; Williams, 2009).

Subsidiary units evolve over time, and through their own actions and initiatives have the potential to modify the power structures of the MNE and influence strategy 'from below' (Andersson et al., 2007). One outcome of this progression is that MNEs become federative rather than unitary organizations as the structures of power and control become dispersed throughout the MNE (Bartlett and Ghoshal, 1990). The control problem in the federative MNE is the result of the invisibility of subsidiary networks and the resultant knowledge deficit for headquarters. However, recent developments in the field suggest that the federative structure may no longer be relevant. Increased globalization and improvements in ICT have enabled MNEs to tackle the control problem by dividing the scope of subsidiary activities into significantly smaller pieces (Yamin and Sinkovics, 2009). The result is amplified headquarters control over dispersed value chains; a development that Buckley describes as the emergence of the 'global factory' (Buckley, 2009b).

In a federal structure, strategy development at the subsidiary level is a key routine of the subsidiary unit. However, as recent literature departs from this on the basis of increased headquarters control over strategy, what does this mean for subsidiaries? Despite its demonstrated importance (Birkinshaw et al., 2005; Frost, 2001; Taggart, 1998), subsidiary strategy development is an element of the internal functioning of subsidiaries – which has remained a neglected research area (Dörrenbächer and Geppert, 2009). Taking Floyd and Wooldridge's (1992, 1997) model of middle manager strategic influence as an initial starting point, the objective of this chapter is to study the contribution of subsidiary middle managers and to contribute to the underdeveloped literature on subsidiary strategy development at a time of change in MNEs.

We present the findings of an in-depth case study to explore the role of subsidiary middle managers in developing strategy within a well-established and successful MNE. First, we contribute by confirming anecdotal evidence that subsidiaries engage in formal strategy development. Second, the findings show that increased headquarters control over strategy has serious consequences for the overall contribution of the subsidiary middle manager. Besides its potential for theory development, this area is particularly relevant to practitioners on two levels. At the subsidiary level, the strategic contribution of the middle management levels is vital in protecting the subsidiary's long-term position within the MNE; and subsidiaries are recognized as sources of knowledge that can be diffused and utilized throughout the MNE network, helping to stimulate the continuous adaption and 'constant reinvention' required to compete in the global environment (Mudambi, 2008). Unlocking the potential of the subsidiary middle manager is an essential component to deliver on this promise.

Theoretical framework

There is a voluminous literature in international business that examines the organization of the firm across national borders (Buckley and Casson, 1976; Dunning, 1993). The economic geography literature has dealt exhaustively with questions regarding the location of economic activity, both in the regional and international context (Dicken, 2003; Fujita et al., 1999). In addition, extensive outsourcing-related literatures have highlighted the complex structures that exist in MNEs today (Buehler and Haucaup, 2006; Bunyaratavej et al., 2007; Doh, 2005). From an international business perspective, understanding this range of areas is becoming more important (Buckley and Ghauri, 2004), but there is little evidence of an interface between these literatures (Mudambi, 2008), particularly from a subsidiary perspective. A full review of these research areas is not possible within the scope of this chapter. Instead, we draw on these literatures to highlight the potential constraints resulting from recent developments in MNEs on subsidiary strategy development and the strategic influence of subsidiary middle managers.

From federations to global factories

Conceptualizing the MNE as a federative rather than a unitary organization was proposed by Bartlett and Ghoshal (1990). They contended that in the case of MNEs, 'fiat' is particularly limited not only because some of the subsidiaries are very distant and resource-rich, but more so because they control critical linkages with key actors in their local environments. The resulting subsidiary embeddedness has two related consequences with serious implications for the ability of headquarters to retain exclusive control over strategy (Yamin and Sinkovics, 2007). First, embeddedness generates knowledge-based resources through subsidiary linkages within networks (Andersson et al., 2002; Forsgren et al., 1999). Such resources are typically outside the control of MNE headquarters and increase a subsidiary's power and hence its scope for independent action and initiatives (Andersson et al., 2002, Birkinshaw and Ridderstråle, 1999; Mudambi and Navarra, 2004). Second, and perhaps more importantly, the networks in which the subsidiary is located are often invisible to corporate headquarters (Holm et al., 1995). As a consequence, knowledge deficit is created and related bounded rationality problems arise for headquarters in terms of the subsidiary's operating environment and resource base (Cantwell and Mudambi, 2005).

Andersson et al. (2007) contend that the vital element in the federative model is that it highlights how a subsidiary's own actions can influence the strategy of the MNE 'from below'. Consequently, the federative model proposes a landscape where subsidiaries have a number of strategic options to influence their own future and that of the overall MNE. Over the last two decades, resource-based theories adopting the federal perspective (Ghoshal and Bartlett, 1990) emphasize the role of subsidiary units as knowledge creators, supporting the premise that subsidiaries access power and influence within the MNE network (e.g. Birkinshaw, 1997; Bouquet and Birkinshaw, 2008; Delany, 2000). But in that time the evidence of MNEs actually operating as federations, as a result of a substantial number of subsidiaries gaining significant influence with the MNE, has been unclear. Hymer's (1970) earlier analysis suggests that the overall consideration determining the extent of multinationality remains the retention of control over corporate strategy by headquarters. Recent literature seems to confirm this proposition as evidence emerges of a retreat from the federative structure. MNE top management, enabled by changes in structure and developments in ICT, have begun dealing with the question of who controls strategy in the MNE.

The root of the control problem in the federative structure is the invisibility of subsidiary networks and the resultant knowledge deficit for headquarters. However, although MNE headquarters may experience a limit to their power in controlling distant subsidiaries, they retain power to structure the corporation in suitable ways to reduce its federative character (Yamin and Forsgren, 2006). There is evidence of this power in two important structural developments which may herald the 'demise of the federative MNE' (Yamin and Sinkovics, 2007, p. 326). First, subsidiary value chain scope is being dramatically reduced, driven by MNE top management's increased control over their network of subsidiaries. In the federative MNE, national subsidiaries play an important role in the organization. National responsiveness is widely regarded as a vital requirement for competitive advantage. This involves subsidiaries developing the local knowledge and organizational capabilities to coordinate a number of value-added activities to serve local demands effectively. But the national subsidiary is becoming an 'endangered species' (Birkinshaw, 2001). In the place of a national subsidiary, there is a series of discreet value-added activities, each of which reports through its own business unit or functional line. Buckley and Ghauri (2004) observed a similar phenomenon and contend that MNE strategies now revolve around the disintegration of the value chain. The managers of MNEs are increasingly able to segment their activities and to seek the optimal location for increasingly specialized slivers of activity (Buckley and Ghauri, 2004).

The second structural development comprises increased off-shoring and outsourcing of core activities. Off-shoring has the potential to undermine or reduce the value of firm-level advantages, especially those that are immobile or tied to core activities (Doh, 2005). The relevance of outsourcing to the demise of the federative structure is that, through outsourcing, the MNE centre shifts from invisible networks around subsidiaries to visible networks controlled by the centre itself. As a result, externalization actually helps to reduce the power of subsidiaries by shifting the balance of power in favour of control and planning by the MNE centre (Nolan et al., 2002; Strange and Newton, 2006).

The motivation for the establishment of subsidiaries has changed, and there is therefore a need to adopt a new approach to studying subsidiary development. Traditionally international business scholars assumed that the key strategic issue for the MNE was the handling of the tension between the imperative of global integration on the one hand and the need for national responsiveness on the other (Bartlett and Ghoshal, 1987). The need for responsiveness in part reflected an environment in which national governments had significantly more bargaining power in their dealings with MNEs than they generally do today; globalization has reduced the need for national responsiveness. Overall MNE strategies are moving towards greater global (or at least regional) integration, and their investment decisions are increasingly motivated by efficiency and strategic asset seeking. The growing liberalization of markets and greater mobility of firm-specific assets have become key influences on MNE strategies (Dunning, 2000, 2002; Dunning and Narula, 2004). The pattern of FDI flow is increasingly influenced by the reality that host countries fit into the strategic calculation of MNEs as sites for key resources or capabilities rather than markets. The more precise use of locational and ownership strategies by MNEs is the very essence of increasing globalization.

Subsidiaries are now fulfilling roles in global value chains which are strictly controlled by corporate headquarters (Gereffi et al., 2005; Sturgeon et al., 2008). Rather than operating as federations, Buckley predicts that MNEs will develop into 'global factories' (Buckley, 2009a). Global factories arise due to the MNEs' evolution into differentiated networks that only internalize those activities that it cannot more profitably outsource (Buckley and Ghauri, 2004). As a result, they are increasingly able to alter location and internalize decisions for activities which were previously locationally bound by being tied to other activities. Subsidiary embeddedness in networks is reduced and control predominantly resides at the top of the organization (Buckley, 2009a). From the subsidiary perspective, there is an important contribution to be made in studying the consequences of these recent developments on the internal functioning of the subsidiary. Taking the subsidiary middle manager as the unit of analysis, this chapter focuses on their input to subsidiary strategy development and how recent changes in the structure of the MNE are impacting on this role.

Subsidiary strategy development

Historically, the unit of analysis was the firm, and the role of subsidiaries in strategy development was largely overlooked. However, the modern multinational subsidiary is now conceptualized as competing in a complex competitive arena – with an internal environment of other subsidiaries, internal customers and suppliers, and an external environment consisting of customers, suppliers and competitors (Birkinshaw et al., 2005). This suggests that subsidiaries must develop different strategies to cope with the particular market in which they compete, but little research has been carried out on what strategy development takes place and who contributes to strategy development within the subsidiary (Dörrenbächer and Gammelgaard, 2006; Dörrenbächer and Geppert, 2009).

In previous research, middle-level managers have not been considered part of the strategy development process, except as providers of informational inputs and directors of implementation (Floyd and Wooldridge, 1997). However, contemporary theory suggests that middle managers attempt to influence the strategy development process (Hornsby et al., 2002); and that given their contribution in other areas of the organization, their potential role in this process should not be overlooked. As top management teams struggle to cope with increasingly complex and dispersed organizations (Wooldridge et al., 2008), strategic activity and decision-making has become more dispersed throughout the organization (Balogun and Johnson, 2004). Thus, the role of the middle manager in strategy development has become an important area of research.

Middle managers hold a unique position within the organization. The description of the 'linking' pin by Likert (1961) is used to define this unique position. Here, a superior in one group is a subordinate in the next, and so on throughout the organization. This is particularly relevant to MNEs where there may be numerous levels of management. As participants in multiple, vertically related groups, middle managers coordinate top and operating level activities, and they are involved in processes that have both upward and downward influences on strategy formulation.

Research question

If the federal structure exists, and subsidiaries develop their own strategy and influence MNE strategy 'from below', what is the role of the subsidiary middle manager in this process? However, if recent trends in the literature that suggest a retreat from federal structures towards global factories are correct, how does this affect the strategic contribution of subsidiary middle managers?

Methodology

Research design

The complex activities of middle managers in developing strategy are explored through a case study research design (Eisenhardt, 1989; Yin, 2003). Case studies are particularly appropriate when 'the phenomenon under study is not readily distinguishable from its context' (Yin, 2003, p. 4). This is certainly the situation when studying subsidiary middle managers, whose contribution to strategy development is often tied up in their daily interactions within different levels of the organization (Wooldridge et al., 2008). However, there are difficulties in conducting case research. First, there is the charge of having too small a sample; and second, there is the problem of non-representativeness. Despite these difficulties, Siggelkow (2007) proposes three important uses for case research: motivation, inspiration and illustration. In this chapter, the choice of case-based research is predominantly to motivate further research in a relatively underdeveloped area. By grounding the study in a real-life situation it is far more likely to promote discussion, and the conceptual contribution put forward in the chapter will be a great deal more relevant.

Selecting the case

In common with other investigations of the role of middle managers in organizations (Balogun and Johnson, 2004, 2005; Huy, 2002; Rouleau, 2005), we present the results of a study of a single organization. This organization was specifically selected to represent a mature and well-established provider of pharmaceutical products, operating in a relatively stable environment. The chosen setting is a world-leading healthcare MNE (Alpha) with its headquarters in the US and operations in more than 130 countries. The company is a broad-based healthcare company and has sales, manufacturing, research and development and distribution facilities around the world. The company's Irish operation was selected for this study as it consists of four subsidiaries, each with an individual history of existence in Ireland, and with very specific mandates in pharmaceuticals, nutrition, diagnostics or medical products. These subsidiaries provided a context in which a variety of types, levels and methods of strategy development could be observed. Its strong market position has supported the development of a range of innovative products and strategies (as appropriate to describe Alpha), but costs have recently become a primary consideration and several of the local activities have been outsourced. One of the reasons for Alpha's selection is its reputation for building subsidiary networks and encouraging subsidiary development.

Data collection

Initial analysis was carried out in a review of the company website, annual reports and press releases. Then semi-structured interviews of approximately 1 hour were organized with 12 middle managers across the 4 subsidiaries. The middle managers were identified by the general manager of each subsidiary. The results were recorded and transcribed, and contact summary sheets were drawn up summarizing main themes and recording initial impressions or interesting ideas (Miles and Huberman, 1994). Semi-structured interviews were chosen as the most appropriate collection tool to assess the opinions of middle managers on this process. The interview questions focused on how managers interacted with different levels of the organization in the strategy development process. Similar studies such as Birkinshaw (1997), which looked at the phenomenon of strategy development at the subsidiary level, also used the method of semi-structured interviews. To obtain the middle manager's perspective there was an emphasis on identifying middle managers with a clear understanding of the company's strategies. In a similar study of this phenomenon, Floyd and Wooldridge (1997) employed an operational definition of middle managers, as provided by Pugh et al. (1968): 'Middle managers are organisation members who link the activities of vertically related groups and who are responsible for at least sub-functional work flow, but not the work flow of the whole organisation.' This definition of middle managers is also employed in this research.

Data analysis

Given the exploratory nature of the research, NVIVO proved crucial in developing a rich and insightful case study. The data collected from the semi-structured interviews included a wide range of information on middle manager roles, interactions and strategic functions. Coding the data in NVIVO enabled cross-case analysis between the subsidiaries, which contextualized the findings and provided a more in-depth analysis.

Findings

Subsidiary strategy development

To analyse subsidiary strategy development, we examined which of the two perspectives of subsidiary strategy development set out by Birkinshaw (1997) best describes strategy development in each of the subsidiaries. The first perspective focuses on subsidiaries that are given a mandated strategic role by their parent company. The second perspective is based on subsidiaries with the competencies to develop strategy at the subsidiary management level. Birkinshaw (1997) suggested that the subsidiary mandated role perspective favoured corporate headquarters control, while the subsidiary strategy development perspective favoured higher levels of subsidiary influence. The primary research collected in this study tends to support the first of the perspectives identified by Birkinshaw (1997). In all the subsidiaries, strategic goals and objectives are set by the parent company, and although subsidiary management has certain influence within their mandate, the overall theme from the interviewees was that strategy is developed at corporate headquarters and passed down to the subsidiaries. One of the interviewees from Site D commented that

> We have very little visibility of the strategy which is developed at the corporate level; our main strategic input is to take the strategy given to us by corporate headquarters and break it down into achievable goals for the subsidiary.

Subsidiary middle management's strategic contribution

The findings sought to explore the contribution of subsidiary middle managers to strategy development, by considering the emergence of an updated model based on Floyd and Wooldridge's (1992) (see Figure 3.1) original typology. Based on the premise of upward and downward influences of middle managers, it

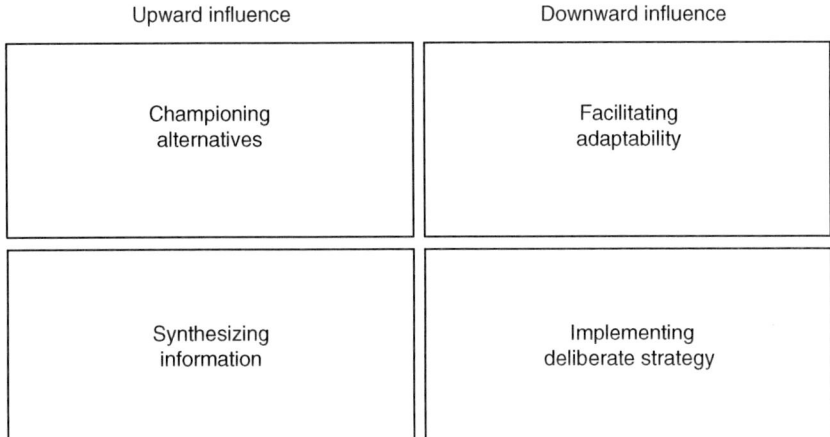

Figure 3.1 Floyd and Wooldridge (1992) typology of middle management involvement in strategy

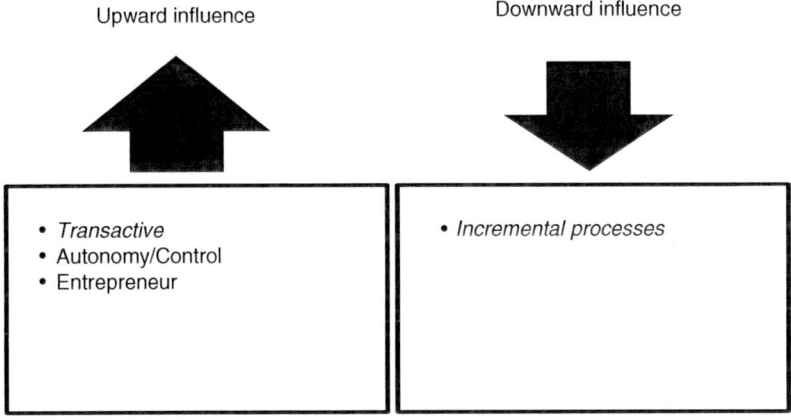

Figure 3.2 Proposed extensions to the Floyd and Wooldridge (1992) typology

provides a framework on which to study the strategic contribution of subsidiary middle managers. From a review of the literature on strategy development, and more specifically subsidiary strategy development, additional strategic roles were also highlighted (see Figure 3.2) for their potential significance in an updated model. It was expected that a number of these roles would emerge specific to the subsidiary middle manager.

Middle manager strategic influences (Floyd and Wooldridge, 1992)

Upward influences

Championing alternatives. From the primary research collected, there is limited evidence of this process taking place in the subsidiaries. In Site A, one of the interviewees contended that it was expected in the organization that middle management must 'be innovative and identify possible opportunities for the subsidiary'. The interviewee from Site C also proposed that 'middle managers always have the opportunity to bring their ideas to higher management', but he could not cite any examples of this process taking place. Although the process of championing alternatives was evident from some interviews, all of the interviewees emphasized that their overall strategic goals were always set out by corporate headquarters. Middle management would only suggest an alternative if it was going to aid the subsidiary in the accomplishment of headquarters' goals. As one interviewee in Site D put it 'our strategic goals are always based on cost effectiveness and quality as set by HQ. Our strategic inputs are limited to finding new ways to reduce costs or to improve quality.' In summary, only three of the twelve interviewees identified strongly with this strategic influence; overall there was a lack of conclusive evidence of it taking place.

Synthesizing information. There was evidence of this strategic role taking place at varying degrees in the subsidiaries. Each interviewee confirmed that top management relied on them for information on the internal and external processes of which they had particular knowledge. For example, in Site B one middle manager explained that 'due to the rapid change of technology and business processes in their business sector top management were very reliant on the information they received from the middle manager level.' The interviewees contended that the knowledge that staff holds in a highly technical business sector such as healthcare development is vital to organizations, and therefore how staff present it to top management can shape the strategy process. However, all of the interviewees identified some frustration in their lack of input in this process, and they could not cite any examples of how, through synthesizing information, they had been able to influence strategy 'from below' (Andersson et al., 2007).

Downward influences

Facilitating adaptability. The evidence collected in the research suggested that middle managers believed that facilitating learning was a strategic role for middle managers. In the healthcare sector, knowledge is a prime asset; and as technology and products change so rapidly, facilitating learning is a vital function in all of the companies. An interviewee in Site B proposed that 'technology is changing and new products are being developed so rapidly that if staff are not working with the new technologies for even a short period of time their knowledge becomes redundant.' This was a common theme in all of the interviews.

Implementing deliberate strategy. In all four subsidiaries, the interviewees identified their role in implementing strategy as one of their most important strategic roles. For example, in Site C, one interviewee stated that 'in their day-to-day work, middle managers influence strategy by passing it down through the organisation.' An interviewee from Site C described the most important strategic role of middle managers as the process of breaking down strategy from top level strategy into day-to-day work. In Site D, one interviewee stated that the main strategic input of middle managers was 'to map out the day-to-day work within the subsidiary'. The evidence collected from the primary research confirmed the importance of this strategic role as proposed by Floyd and Wooldridge (1992), and it emerged as the most identifiable strategic influence of middle managers in the subsidiaries.

Proposed extensions to Floyd and Woodridge's (1992) typology

Upward influences

Transactive. Partial evidence of the importance of a transactive mode between middle management and higher management levels, as proposed by Hart (1992), was apparent in a number of the subsidiaries. The interviewees identified the relationship between top management and middle management as having an influence on strategy development. One of the middle managers from Site A commented that 'as the personal relationship between top management and middle managers developed over time, so too did the input of middle management to strategy development.' Interviewees also noted that subsidiary top management placed considerable importance on building a culture of personal interaction between management levels. In some cases the middle managers suggested that their only chance of exerting an upward strategic influence was based on the personal relationship they had built up with higher-level management.

Autonomy/control. For middle managers to contribute to strategy it is accepted that there is a certain level of autonomy required to allow this process to take place (Burgelman, 1983). The middle managers identified a certain level of autonomy in their day-to-day activities, but a majority of interviewees contended that overall they were constrained by low levels of autonomy in the subsidiary. An interviewee in Site D compared the subsidiary to a previous place of employment, and commented that

> I worked in a company which gave high levels of autonomy to management levels within the company, but it is difficult to see that situation arising here to the same degree, as corporate headquarters will always favour a control relationship over the subsidiary rather than allowing higher levels of autonomy to management levels within the subsidiary.

Middle manager entrepreneur. There was little evidence of this role for middle managers proposed by Birkinshaw (1997). The interviewees did not see themselves as entrepreneurs. One of the interviewees in Site B thought that 'over time this role may emerge but it was difficult to see it developing at the moment.' Interestingly, the theme from the interviewees was that they did not identify entrepreneurial skills as a key competence for a middle manager.

Downward Influences

Incremental processes. There is evidence of this incremental dimension in the results of the primary research. Proposed by Bailey et al. (2000), this mode highlights how the uncertainty of the environment means middle managers must be constantly evaluating changes and opportunities in the environment. In all of the interviews there was evidence to show that middle managers believed that building their competencies and being vigilant to the changes in technology were important functions of their role. For example, one of the interviewees in Site D believed that he had very little strategic influence on top management, but he proposed that building his own competencies and those of the staff around him was one of the important factors driving strategy in the organization. Similarly, one interviewee in Site B contended that 'strategy could emerge from the skills and knowledge which were developed at the lower levels of the company.'

Summary

To summarize, the evidence suggests that while the subsidiaries do engage in strategy development, the contribution of the middle managers to this process is predominantly in implementation. This is highlighted by the strong evidence for the downward strategic influences proposed in the original typology, but there is limited evidence for the existence of the upward strategic influences of middle managers. This was also confirmed by findings for the proposed extensions to the updated typology.

Discussion

Subsidiary strategy development has been a neglected research area, which this chapter sought to address (Dörrenbächer and Geppert, 2009). The objective was to confirm that subsidiaries engage in strategy development and to study middle managers' perception of their role in this process. Although a key task of middle managers is implementing strategy, little research has examined the particular roles they play in this process and how their contribution is captured in formal and informal methods of strategy development (Balogun, 2003).

The findings confirm that subsidiaries do engage in strategy development, but subsidiary management's influence in this process is limited. What emerged from this case was that strategy predominantly flows from headquarters down through the subsidiary rather than subsidiaries influencing strategy 'from below' as the federative structure suggests (Andersson et al., 2007). This was highlighted by the central theme of the model (Floyd and Wooldridge, 1992) employed in this study – the distinction between middle manager upstream and downstream strategic influences. We found strong evidence of the downstream influences. All of the interviewees saw a major strategic role in their day-to-day activities. Implementing deliberate strategy and facilitating adaptability were strategic roles that all of the interviewees identified. There was also evidence of the incremental planning outlined by Bailey et al. (2000), and integrated into the model. Overall, middle managers in the subsidiaries strongly identified with downward strategic influences.

However, the evidence for the upward influences was less clear. There was limited evidence for the role of 'championing alternatives', and for the proposed extension of a 'transactive role', but overall the results showed a lack of evidence for the upward strategic influences of middle management. The levels of autonomy within the subsidiaries were low and middle management identified a high degree of headquarters control. One of the most striking examples of the lack of upward influence was the complete lack of evidence for the entrepreneurial role of subsidiary middle managers, which Birkinshaw (1995) identified as being an important source of value creation for the MNE.

The data from the four subsidiaries show very little confirmation for the federative structure proposed by Ghoshal and Bartlett (1990) and highlighted more recently by Andersson et al. (2007). An important element of the federative structure is the subsidiaries' ability to influence the MNE 'from below' (Andersson et al., 2007). The interviewees did not express the opinion that subsidiary management had such power within the network. Instead, headquarters control over subsidiary activities was one of the outstanding themes in the interviews. The interviewees highlighted the pressure they were under to meet headquarters targets, but they could not see many options in trying to change the power balance. Their main focus was on fulfilling their role as set by headquarters and not jeopardizing their position within the MNE.

The feedback from the interviewees suggests that the subsidiaries are more closely aligned to the 'global factory' concept proposed by Buckley (2004, 2009b). The subsidiaries fulfil very particular roles within dispersed value chains throughout the world. A number of the interviewees expressed the opinion that their main strategic input was to constantly improve on costs and efficiency. Outside of that they had very little input to strategy development. This was reflected in the strong evidence of middle managers' downward influences keeping the strategic goals set by headquarters 'cascading down' through the subsidiary. Control over strategy resides at headquarters, and subsidiary middle management's contribution to strategy is predominantly in implementation.

Implications

Organizations have become increasingly aware that middle managers play a pivotal role in developing new ideas, reshaping firm capabilities and affecting strategic renewal (Pappas and Wooldridge, 2007), but is this evident in today's MNEs? Not long ago the MNE was being held up as an organization with a particular competence for knowledge creation due to the potential within its network of diverse subsidiaries. But as the global factory emerges, resulting in knowledge and innovation being created in smaller pockets of the MNE, what does the future hold for the subsidiary middle manager? Are they destined to be implementers rather than creators?

Limitations of the study

Like all research, the study presented in this chapter suffers from a number of important limitations that must be kept in mind when interpreting the results. The preliminary nature of the study led to a number of important restrictions. This particular study used a small number of subsidiaries in one case organization in a limited geographical area. Hence, there is a need to conduct extensive research across different industries and geographical regions before any generalizations can be drawn. Additionally, the research used only a qualitative approach to collect data; a study employing both qualitative and quantitative approaches would provide a more in-depth analysis on this topic.

Other areas for future research

The findings from this study represent an exciting and valuable contribution to our knowledge of an under-researched area – the strategic roles of middle managers in the strategy development process of multinational subsidiaries. One of the major contributions of an exploratory study of this kind is to highlight opportunities for further research. In particular, the proposed extensions to the model outlined in the study would benefit from longitudinal analysis. To seek further justification of the validity of this model a more thorough research process should be undertaken.

References

Andersson, U., Forsgren, M. and Holm, U. (2002) 'The strategic impact of external networks: subsidiary performance and competence development in the multinational corporation', *Strategic Management Journal*, 23(11), 979–96.

Andersson, U., Forsgren, M. and Holm, U. (2007) 'Balancing subsidiary influence in the federative MNC: a business network view', *Journal of International Business Studies*, 38(5), 802–18.

Bailey, A., Johnson, G. and Daniels, K. (2000) 'Validation of a multi-dimensional measure of strategy development process', *British Journal of Management*, 11(2), 151–62.

Balogun, J. (2003) 'From blaming the middle to harnessing its potential: creating change intermediaries', *British Journal of Management*, 14(1), 69–83.

Balogun, J. and Johnson, G. (2004) 'Organizational restructuring and middle manager sensemaking', *Academy of Management Journal*, 47(4), 523–49.

Balogun, J. and Johnson, G. (2005) 'From intended strategies to unintended outcomes: the impact of change recipient sensemaking', *Organization Studies*, 26(11), 1573–601.

Bartlett, C.A. and Ghoshal, S. (1987) 'Managing across borders: new strategic requirements', *Sloan Management Review*, 28(4), 7–17.

Bartlett, C.A. and Ghoshal, S. (1990) 'The multinational corporation as an inter-organisational network', *Academy of Management Review*, 15(4), 603–25.

Birkinshaw, J. (1995) 'Encouraging entrepreneurial activity in multinational corporations', *Business Horizons*, 38(3), 32–8.

Birkinshaw, J. (1997) 'Entrepreneurship in multinational corporations: the characteristics of subsidiary initiatives', *Strategic Management Journal*, 18(3), 207–29.

Birkinshaw, J. (2001) 'Strategy and management in MNE subsidiaries', in A. Rugman and T.L. Brewer (eds) *The Oxford Handbook of International Business* (New York: Oxford University Press).

Birkinshaw, J. and Hood, N. (1998) 'Multinational subsidiary evolution: capability and charter change in foreign-owned subsidiary companies', *Academy of Management Review*, 23(4), 773–95.

Birkinshaw, J. and Ridderstråle, J. (1999) 'Fighting the corporate immune system: a process study of subsidiary initiatives in multinational corporations', *International Business Review*, 8(2), 149–80.

Birkinshaw, J., Hood, N. and Young, S. (2005) 'Subsidiary entrepreneurship, internal and external competitive forces, and subsidiary performance', *International Business Review*, 14(2), 227–48.

Bouquet, C. and Birkinshaw, J. (2008) 'Weight versus voice: how foreign subsidiaries gain attention from corporate headquarters', *Academy of Management Journal*, 51(3), 577–601.
Buckley, P.J. (2004) 'Government policy responses to strategic rent seeking transnational firms', *Transnational Corporations*, 5(2), 1–17.
Buckley, P.J. (2009a) 'The impact of the global factory on economic development', *Journal of World Business*, 44(2), 131–43.
Buckley, P.J. (2009b) 'Internalisation thinking: from the multinational enterprise to the global factory', *International Business Review*, 18(3), 224–35.
Buckley, P.J. and Casson, M.C. (1976) *The Future of the Multinational Enterprise* (London: Macmillan).
Buckley, P.J. and Ghauri, P.N. (2004) 'Globalisation, economic geography and the strategy of multinational enterprises', *Journal of International Business Studies*, 35(2), 81–98.
Buehler, S. and Haucaup, J. (2006) 'Strategic outsourcing revisited', *Journal of Economic Behaviour and Organisation*, 61(3), 325–38.
Bunyaratavej, K., Hahn, E. and Doh, J. (2007) 'International off-shoring of services: a parity study', *Journal of International Management*, 13(1), 7–21.
Burgelman, R.A. (1983) 'A model of interaction of strategic behaviour, corporate context, and the concept of strategy', *Academy of Management Review*, 8(1), 61–70.
Cantwell, J. and Mudambi, R. (2005) 'MNE competence creating subsidiary mandates', *Strategic Management Journal*, 26(12), 1109–28.
Delany, E. (2000) 'Strategic development of the multinational subsidiary through subsidiary initiative-taking', *Long Range Planning*, 33(2), 220–44.
Dicken, P. (2003) *Global Shift: Reshaping the Global Economic Map in the 21st Century* (Thousand Oaks, CA: Sage Publications).
Doh, J.P. (2005) 'Offshore outsourcing: implications for international business and strategic management theory and practice', *Journal of Management Studies*, 42(3), 695–704.
Dörrenbächer, C. and Gammelgaard, J. (2006) 'Subsidiary role development: the effect of micro-political headquarters-subsidiary negotiations on the product, market and value-added scope of foreign-owned subsidiaries', *Journal of International Management*, 12(3), 266–83.
Dörrenbächer, C. and Geppert, M. (2009) 'A micro-political perspective on subsidiary initiative-taking: evidence from German-owned subsidiaries in France', *European Management Journal*, 27(2), 100–12.
Dunning, J.H. (1979) 'Explaining changing patterns of international production: in defence of the eclectic theory', *Oxford Bulletin of Economics and Statistics*, 41(4), 269–95.
Dunning, J.H. (1993) *Multinational Enterprises and the Global Economy* (New York: Addisson Wesley).
Dunning, J.H. (2000) 'The eclectic paradigm as an envelope for economic and business theories of MNE activity', *International Business Review*, 9(2), 163–90.
Dunning, J.H. (2002) *Regions, Globalization, and the Knowledge-Based Economy* (Oxford: Oxford University Press).
Dunning, J.H. and Narula, R. (2004) *Multinationals and Industrial Competitiveness: A New Agenda* (Cheltenham: Edward Elgar).
Eisenhardt, K.M. (1989) 'Building theory from case study research', *Academy of Management Review*, 14(4), 532–50.
Floyd, S.W. and Wooldridge, B. (1992) 'Middle management involvement in strategy and its association with strategic type', *Strategic Management Journal*, 13(S1), 153–68.
Floyd, S.W. and Wooldridge, B. (1997) 'Middle managements strategic influence and organisational performance', *Journal of Management Studies*, 34(3), 465–85.
Forsgren, M., Pedersen, T. and Foss, N.J. (1999) 'Accounting for the strengths of MNC subsidiaries: the case of foreign owned firms in Denmark', *International Business Review*, 8(2), 191–6.

Frost, T. (2001) 'The geographic sources of foreign subsidiaries' innovations', *Strategic Management Journal*, 22(2), 101–23.
Fujita, M., Krugman, P. and Venables, A. (1999) *The Spatial Economy: Cities, Regions and International Trade* (Boston: The MIT Press).
Gereffi, G., Humphrey, J. and Sturgeon, T. (2005) 'The governance of global value chains', *Review of International Political Economy*, 12(1), 78–104.
Ghoshal, S. and Bartlett, C.A. (1990) 'The multinational corporation as an interorganizational network', *Academy of Management Review*, 15(4), 603–25.
Hart, S. (1992) 'An integrated framework for strategy making processes', *Academy of Management Review*, 17, 327–51.
Holm, U., Johanson, J. and Thilenius, P. (1995) 'Headquarters knowledge of subsidiary network contexts in the multinational corporation', *International Studies of Management and Organization*, 2(1/2), 97–120.
Hornsby, J., Kuratko, D. and Shaker, Z. (2002) 'Middle managers' perception of the internal environment for corporate entrepreneurship: assessing the measurement scale', *Journal of Business Venturing*, 17(3), 253–73.
Huy, Q.N. (2002) 'Emotional balancing of organizational continuity and radical change: the contribution of middle managers', *Administrative Science Quarterly*, 47(1), 31–69.
Hymer, S.H. (1970) 'The efficiency (contradictions) of multinational corporations', *The American Economic Review: Papers and Proceedings*, 60(2), 441–8.
Jarillo, J. and Martinez, J. (1990) 'Different roles for subsidiaries: the case of multinational corporations in Spain', *Strategic Management Journal*, 11(7), 501–12.
Johanson, J. and Vahlne, J. (1977) 'The internationalization process of the firm, a model of knowledge development and increasing foreign market commitments', *Journal of International Business Studies*, 8(1), 23–32.
Likert, R. (1961) *New Patterns of Management* (New York: McGraw Hill).
Miles, M. and Huberman, M. (1994) *Qualitative Data Analysis: An Expanded Sourcebook* (London: Sage).
Mudambi, R. (2008) 'Location, control and innovation in knowledge intensive industries', *Journal of Economic Geography*, 8(5), 699–725.
Mudambi, R. and Navarra, P. (2004) 'Is knowledge power? Knowledge flows, subsidiary power and rent-seeking within MNCs', *Journal of International Business Studies*, 35(5), 385–406.
Nolan, P., Sutherland, D. and Zhang, J. (2002) 'The challenge of the global business revolution', *Contributions to Political Economy*, 21(1), 91–110.
Pappas, J. and Wooldridge, B. (2007) 'Middle managers' divergent strategic activity: an investigation of multiple measures of network centrality', *Journal of Management Studies*, 44(3), 323–41.
Pugh, D., Hickson, D., Hinings, D. and Turner, C. (1968) 'Dimensions of organisational structure', *Administrative Science Quarterly*, 13(1), 65–91.
Rouleau, L. (2005) 'Micro-practices of strategic sense-making and sense-giving: how middle managers interpret and sell change every day', *Journal of Management Studies*, 42(7), 1413–41.
Rugman, A. and Verbeke, A. (2001) 'Subsidiary specific advantages in multinational enterprises', *Strategic Management Journal*, 22(3), 237–50.
Siggelkow, N. (2007) 'Persuasion with case studies', *Academy of Management Journal*, 50(1), 20–4.
Strange, R. and Newton, J. (2006) 'Stephen Hymer and the externalization of production', *International Business Review*, 15(2), 180–93.
Sturgeon, T., Van Biesebroek, J. and Gereffi, G. (2008) 'Value chains, networks and clusters: reframing the global automotive industry', *Journal of Economic Geography*, 8(3), 297–321.
Taggart, J. (1998) 'Strategy shifts in multinational subsidiaries', *Strategic Management Journal*, 19(7), 663–81.

Vernon, R. (1966) 'International investment and international trade in the product cycle', *Quarterly Journal of Economics*, 80(2), 190–207.
White, R. and Poynter, T. (1984) 'Strategies for foreign-owned subsidiaries in Canada', *Business Quarterly*, 49(2), 59–69.
Williams, C. (2009) 'Subsidiary-level determinants of global initiatives in multinational corporations', *Journal of International Management*, 15(1), 92–104.
Wooldridge, B., Floyd, S. and Schmid, T. (2008) 'A middle-manager perspective: current contributions, synthesis and future research', *Journal of Management*, 34(6), 1190–221.
Yamin, M. and Forsgren, M. (2006) 'Hymer's analysis of the multinational organization: power retention and the demise of the federative MNE', *International Business Review*, 15(2), 166–79.
Yamin, M. and Sinkovics, R. (2007) 'ICT and the MNE reorganisation: the paradox of control', *Critical Perspectives on International Business*, 3(4), 322–36.
Yamin, M. and Sinkovics, R. (2009) 'Infrastructure or foreign direct investment?: an examination of the implications of MNE strategy for economic development', *Journal of World Business*, 44(2), 144–57.
Yin, R.K. (2003) *Case Study Research: Design and Methods*, 3rd edn (London: Sage).

4
Regional Multinational Enterprises and the International Financial Crisis

Alan M. Rugman and Chang Hoon Oh

Introduction

It is shown here that theoretical analysis of multinational enterprises (MNEs) has not been changed by the international financial crisis of 2008. Indeed, the financial crisis is mainly explained by failures of macroeconomic policy and the associated global imbalance of foreign exchange reserves and financial assets, in particular between China and the US. In other words, it is portfolio (financial) investment that has been misaligned rather than the foreign direct investment (FDI) undertaken by MNEs. While MNEs operate mainly regionally, not globally, and also benefit from regional international diversification, they have themselves been adversely affected by the financial crisis, and flows of FDI have fallen substantially. This may be a short-term effect since there should be few long-term effects of the financial crisis on MNE strategy.

The international financial crisis of 2008 has mainly affected MNEs because of changes in government policies. Our main theme is that government policies put in place to mitigate the macroeconomic impact of the crisis have protectionist elements (in the form of subsidies). The impact of such strong government support, in a strategic sense, is to make MNEs into national champions. However, there is an uneven, even asymmetrical, impact of government support on MNEs. In general, the new MNEs from emerging economies (in particular from China) serve as well-known agents for their home government strategy, which is to improve national competitiveness. In contrast, Western MNEs from North America and Europe are less dependent on their home governments and are today indirect national champions.

We explore the relationship between government policy and the strategic positioning of MNEs. Traditionally, this linkage has been examined at a microeconomic level, usually with industry-level analysis of the ways in which home government support for specific sectors can lead to an improvement in the international competitiveness of leading firms in each sector. For example, Porter (1990) examines the international competitiveness of nations based upon the exports and outward FDI of leading firms using a broadly sectoral level of analysis. In contrast to this type of research, today we need new analysis at firm level to understand the ways in which macroeconomic policy initiatives (in the form of bailouts and other subsidies) have led to possible changes in the strategies of MNEs.

Our principal finding is that the effect of the financial crisis varies across regions; macroeconomic imbalances in the form of a large trade surplus and huge foreign exchange reserves in Asia, in particular in China, led to the rapid growth of Asian state-owned MNEs. In contrast, Western MNEs are likely to expand at a much slower rate as their competitive advantages are firm-specific and only indirectly affected through government support. In summary, Chinese MNEs are likely to benefit more from the world financial crisis than will US MNEs. However, this asymmetric macroeconomic impact of the crisis needs to be analysed within the microeconomic framework of MNE strategy, and the reality that most MNE activity is home-region based (Rugman, 2005). Here, Western MNEs can realize the benefits of intra-regional international diversification, especially if they focus upon entry to the markets of North America and Europe. In contrast, Chinese MNEs will go through a stage of FDI in the US and Africa (for market-seeking and natural resource-seeking reasons respectively) but will not benefit as much from international diversification. These regional differences affect the world industry structure in the way that emerging economies position themselves in manufacturing and service sectors.

The international financial crisis and MNEs

The world financial crisis of 2008 was characterized by a temporary breakdown in the banking systems of the US and some leading European countries. The underlying cause was the failure of large banks in these Western countries to correctly value mortgage-based securities in a situation where derivative instruments led to a system-wide underpricing of risk.

In more traditional macroeconomic terms, in the US there was an excessive amount of consumption (C) and government spending (G), and a lack of investment (I). This excess aggregate demand, whereby $C+G$ exceeded I, was facilitated through sustained inflows of financial capital, especially from China. With the off-shoring of US (indeed, world) manufacturing to China there was a persistent surplus in China's balance of trade such that its excess savings (S) were recycled into the purchase of US treasury bonds. The US current account deficit was offset by these inflows of Chinese financial capital. As these inflows of financial capital went into US government bonds for a decade or more, there was a sustained increase in G and C, but without an increase in I. In turn, the increase in C led to a housing boom in the US while the increase in G helped to maintain US hegemonic imperialism. The long-run solution to the US-driven part of the world financial crisis will be to reduce US C and G with an increase in I. This Keynesian explanation of the underlying macroeconomic policy considerations behind the world financial crisis omits any culpability of MNEs as direct instruments in the crisis. However, MNEs, especially banking MNEs, may have played an indirect role.

Table 4.1 The world's largest 500 companies by sector and region

	2000				2008			
	Manuf.	Services	Financial	Total	Manuf.	Services	Financial	Total
N. America	77	86	39	202	69 (−8)	62 (−24)	29 (−10)	160 (−42)
Europe	59	49	48	156	82 (+23)	58 (+9)	46 (−2)	186 (+30)
Asia Pacific	61	51	25	137	80 (+19)	41 (−10)	24 (−1)	145 (+8)
Rest of world	2	0	3	5	6 (+4)	0 (+0)	3 (+0)	9 (+4)
Total	199	186	115	500	237 (+38)	161 (−25)	102 (−13)	500

Note: Values in parentheses are changes in number of firms from 2000.

The indirect role of MNEs in the world financial crisis arises from the fact that there were 102 financial institutions in the list of the world's 500 largest companies for 2008 – see Table 4.1. Of these, 57 are multinational banks which operate within the regulatory and institutional context of the triad regions of North America, Europe and Asia. Somewhat paradoxically, the Asian banks were not involved in the financial crisis, partly because many of them are state-owned, particularly in China. In general, Asian governments, striving to avoid another Asian financial crisis, used their banks to store foreign exchange reserves and improved their financial heath. In particular, China accrued huge amounts of US dollar-based securities, as did other Asian countries such as Korea and Singapore. This reinforced the global financial imbalance over the last 10 years. More recycling of dollar-denominated debt would be useful, although the means to this end is not our main concern.

Here, our focus is upon analysis of the strategies of MNEs as they respond to the world financial crisis and, in particular, interact with governments. The bailouts of banks and the auto sector in the US essentially act as a new form of subsidy, leading to a new form of protection and a renewal of competitive pressures between MNEs from North America, Europe and Asia.

In the rest of this chapter we examine the nature of MNE strategy in this new financial environment. We link this to an analysis of the extent to which MNEs now use their networks of subsidiaries as a source of competitive advantage and so, indirectly, realize the benefits of intra-regional international diversification. We find that most MNEs, especially those from China and other emerging economies, are centralized hierarchies, rather than networks. In this situation, MNEs still benefit from international real asset diversification across their home region and have a more stable stream of sales and assets over time than do large firms concentrated in their home country alone, as first shown by Rugman (1976). These 'fallout' financial benefits to MNEs of real asset intra-regional diversification are the results of micro-level MNE strategic decisions about mode of entry and are independent of the financial crisis. Thus, we argue that home country bailouts basically serve as protectionist subsidies and reinforce triad-based rivalry between the world's largest MNEs.

MNEs as regional networks

As a link to understanding the strategy of MNEs, we first need to recognize that the traditional model of MNEs examines the extent to which country-specific advantages (CSAs) and firm-specific advantages (FSAs) interact to explain patterns of FDI and performance. This CSA/FSA framework was first developed in Rugman (1981), and refined by Rugman and Verbeke (1992) and serves as a basic framework used to analyse international business strategy (see, e.g. Birkinshaw et al., 1998; Boddewyn et al., 1986; Rugman, 2009). Within this framework, MNEs can be identified within the eclectic paradigm as either market-seekers, natural resource-seekers, efficiency-seekers or asset-seekers (Dunning, 1981). This serves to link location factors (CSAs) in the home and host nations with firm-level factors involving issues of ownership and internalization.

Traditionally, MNEs are recognized as developing FSAs based upon an internal knowledge advantage. Early internalization theory by Buckley and Casson (1976), Rugman (1981) and Hennart (1982) used transaction cost economics to explain FSAs in knowledge due to the ability of the MNE to exchange intermediate products across its internal network. The organizational structure of the MNE was assumed to be the traditional centralized and hierarchical M-form organization analysed by 2009 Nobel Prize winner Oliver Williamson (1975). Such MNEs could spread their FSAs, developed in association with home country costs, to foreign markets through FDI and other modes of entry. This led to the development of non-location-bound FSAs (NLB FSAs) (see Rugman and Verbeke, 1992).

It was only with the development of the economic integration and national responsiveness framework popularized by Bartlett and Goshal (1989) that the role of subsidiaries in creating capabilities (FSAs) became a subject of interest. In their restatement of the integration/responsiveness matrix, Rugman and Verbeke (1992) stylized the development of subsidiary capabilities as being location-bound FSAs (LB FSAs). Subsequently, a huge literature has developed which examines the nature, extent and rationale for such subsidiary initiatives; this literature is summarized in Rugman and Verbeke (2001), Birkinshaw (2000) and Birkinshaw and Pedersen (2009).

Scholars in management, using theories of organization behaviour and business policy, have attempted to define and assess the nature and extent of subsidiary capabilities and initiatives (Birkinshaw and Pedersen, 2009). Virtually this entire research stream analyses the MNE as a business network. Subsidiaries interact with each other and the parent firm as network actors. Using such network thinking it is conceptually possible that LB FSAs can be converted into NLB FSAs. For example, the best practice of a subsidiary can become generic to the entire network of the MNE. There may also be ways in which subsidiaries develop complementary assets such that their recombination can generate new NLB FSAs (Verbeke, 2009).

The problem with this network approach to MNEs is that the empirical evidence suggests that the parent firm rarely concedes strategic decision-making ability to its subsidiaries. In other words, most MNEs remain centralized, hierarchical

M-form organizations. Earlier studies had shown that most large US MNEs were centralized until the 1990s. It is well known that Japanese MNEs exist in a home culture of hierarchy (Westney, 2001). A few European-based MNEs may appear to pursue strategies of national responsiveness, but these are often the result of a policy of mergers and acquisitions in which firms taken over are initially left alone to continue with their operations in countries unfamiliar to the purchaser. In general, European MNEs do not have a strategy to develop NLB FSAs across such networks; indeed, such MNE networks are not true networks in the sense of management scholarship.

Over the last decade a set of some 90 MNEs from emerging economies has entered the list of the world's largest 500 firms. It is well known that MNEs from China, Korea, Singapore and other Asian countries (including India) are very hierarchical and centralized in their strategic decision-making (e.g. Chen, 2004; Whitley, 1990). Finally, MNEs from Brazil and Russia are generally in natural resource sectors, which also tend to be project specific and tightly controlled through centralized financing, budgets and marketing (Ramamurti and Singh, 2008).

In summary, it is apparent that the great majority of the world's 500 largest firms retain their traditional focus upon centralized decision-making within hierarchical organizational structures. The need for such centralized budgeting and company-wide strategy has been reinforced by the world financial crisis of 2008. To an increasing extent, national governments are interacting with the top management teams of parent firms in allocating state funds to revive faltering financial institutions and manufacturing firms. Thus the revival of home country CSAs, in the form of such financial subsidies, challenges network thinking as applied to regional MNEs. Ownership and control of the parent firm leads to alliances with home country governments and a revival of triad-based rivalry between MNEs from North America, Europe and Asia. This will reinforce the intra-regional nature of MNE activity and strategy, as demonstrated in Rugman and Verbeke (2004). We now link this thinking on the network nature of regional MNEs to the older (and rediscovered) literature of international diversification, which is a financial aspect of MNEs often neglected in the modern treatment of MNE strategy.

Regional multinationals and international diversification

A recently neglected aspect of MNEs is that they engage in real asset international financial diversification. Since an MNE is defined as a business with affiliates (subsidiaries) in different countries, it can stabilize its overall earnings by offsetting downturns at home with export sales abroad in more buoyant markets. As first applied to MNEs in Rugman (1976, 1979), the principles of international diversification suggest that MNEs can partially offset idiosyncratic country-specific business cycles through their operations across borders. In other words, MNEs are bundles of real assets offering a more stable stream of sales and revenues over time when compared with purely domestic firms of similar size and in similar industries.

Put less technically, MNEs can arbitrage the differences in changes in GDP across the countries in which they operate. In the recent context of a global financial crisis, the principles of international diversification indicate that MNEs are less affected by the financial crisis than are domestic firms. In other words, although financial markets are mainly global, the real asset (goods) markets in which MNEs operate are not perfectly integrated. Indeed, recent research shows that MNEs operate mainly within the broad region of their home triad market (see Rugman and Verbeke, 2004).

The regional nature of business means that MNEs are partially insulated from a global financial crisis. In particular, a US-led collapse in financial institutions has less impact on European and Asian MNEs which average over 75 per cent of their sales and assets in their home regions. Provided that the business cycles of North America, Europe and Asia are not perfectly positively correlated, there remain benefits of both inter-regional and intra-regional international diversification for MNEs; the following data support this point.

The regional nature of the world's 500 largest firms in 2008 was shown earlier in Table 4.1. It reports the number of MNEs in the broad triad as 186 in Europe; 160 in North America (NAFTA); and 145 in Asia Pacific, as of 2008. Since 2000, European firms have increased in number by 30; North American have fallen by 42 and those from Asia Pacific have increased by 8 firms (notably due to an increase of Chinese and Indian firms and decrease of Japanese firms).

Table 4.1 also reports that in 2008 there were 237 MNEs in manufacturing and 161 in services and of these there are 102 in financial services. Between 2000 and 2008, the manufacturing set actually increased by 38 firms (from 199 to 237), while services and financial services decreased by 25 (from 186 to 161) and 13 (from 115 to 102) respectively. The service and financial sectors show a different trend from the manufacturing sector. Although the outsourcing in service has been a discernible trend (Walsh and Deery, 2006), the service sector declined significantly while the manufacturing sector increased. The financial sector also showed a slight decreasing trend, but mainly because of US banks.

The fall of US and Japanese multinationals

The most notable change in the world economic system between 2000 and 2008 is the relative decline of US and Japanese MNEs. They have lost their market position to developing country MNEs. Table 4.2 reports the number of MNEs by key countries; that is, those with more than ten MNEs listed in the Global 500 in 2008. The number of US and Japanese MNEs has dropped dramatically, from 185 to 142 for the US and from 104 to 68 for Japan (with a decline across three types of sector).

Among developed country MNEs, only European MNEs (except for the UK) showed an increase; Germany, France, Switzerland, Netherlands, Italy and Spain have more MNEs in 2008 than in 2000. It is possible that European MNEs have benefited from the enlargement of the European Union (Fratianni and Oh,

Table 4.2 The world's largest 500 companies by country

	2000				2008			
	Manuf.	Services	Financial	Total	Manuf.	Services	Financial	Total
US	73	80	32	185	60 (−13)	59 (−21)	23 (−9)	142 (−43)
Japan	50	36	18	104	35 (−15)	23 (−13)	10 (−8)	68 (−36)
France	14	16	7	37	16 (+2)	16 (+0)	8 (+1)	40 (+3)
Germany	11	12	11	34	15 (+4)	14 (+2)	10 (−1)	39 (+5)
UK	10	11	12	33	11 (+1)	11 (+0)	7 (−5)	29 (−4)
Canada	3	5	7	15	7 (+4)	1 (−4)	6 (−1)	14 (−1)
China	2	6	4	12	18 (+16)	12 (+6)	7 (+3)	37 (+25)
Korea	5	5	1	11	10 (+5)	3 (−2)	1 (+0)	14 (+3)
Switzerland	4	2	5	11	7 (+3)	2 (+0)	4 (−1)	13 (+2)
Netherlands	3	2	4	9	4 (+1)	4 (+2)	2 (−2)	10 (+1)
Italy	3	2	3	8	3 (+0)	3 (+1)	4 (+1)	10 (+2)
Spain	2	2	2	6	6 (+4)	3 (+1)	3 (+1)	12 (+6)

Note: See note in Table 4.1.

2009). These benefits include a much larger home market, stabilizing the business cycle and currency exchange fluctuations, and a subsidy from the integrated bureaucracy of the European Union.

The rise of developing countries' multinationals

Table 4.3 reports that only 9 developing countries had any MNEs in the list for 2000, but 15 countries had MNEs in the 2008 list, thus the entries of developing countries' MNEs more than doubled from 7 per cent (34 out of 500) to 18 per cent (91 out of 500). The BRIC countries (Brazil, Russia, India and China) all increased their MNEs but also MNEs from other developing countries such as Taiwan, Israel, Poland, Saudi Arabia, Thailand and Turkey entered the list in 2008. In addition, other mature developing countries such as South Korea, Mexico and Singapore continued to increase their positions.

The growth of developing countries' MNEs does not show a flat world but it balances the distribution of MNEs across three regions and within each region of the triad. In Asia Pacific, Japan is no longer leading the regional economy, as now South Korea, China and India have many more MNEs to accompany Japan. However, these Asian MNEs' activities are, in general, limited within their home region. Except for a few globally operating MNEs such as Samsung Electronics, Hyundai Motors, Cemex, Flextronics, Tata Group, Hutchison Whampoa and Hon Hai Precision Industry, most MNEs in developing countries are national champions and at most regional champions, as shown in Rugman and Oh (2008).

Asymmetry in international strategy

In Table 4.4 we show the share of intra-regional assets (home region assets divided by total assets in percentages). Table 4.4 demonstrates that MNEs from North America and Asia Pacific have reduced their assets in their home region by 6.7 per cent points and 1.8 per cent points respectively. In other words, these MNEs expanded into foreign regions of the triad although they retained 75 per cent of their assets in their home region. These MNEs likely benefited from diversification but possibly suffered from the liability of inter-regional foreignness, which includes a financial crisis. In contrast, European MNEs increased their assets in Europe by 6.3 per cent points and had about 73 per cent of assets in Europe. In other words, these European MNEs focused more on their home region. Again, these European MNEs likely benefited from the integration of the EU, but did not engage in further inter-regional diversification.

Looking at sectoral differences, MNEs in the financial sector focused on their home region of the triad, while manufacturing and services MNEs, except for European MNEs, expanded into foreign regions. The financial sector in developing countries is still protected by their governments, and these countries have their own national champions. Thus foreign financial MNEs had a hard time entering the developing countries. The international financial crisis, at least indirectly, affected financial MNEs and reduced their risky assets in foreign regions.

The data indicate that the world's largest firms are operating on a regional, not a global, basis. Thus they benefit from regional international diversification, rather than being globally interdependent. In turn, this suggests that the world

Table 4.3 The world's largest 500 companies by developing country

	2000				2008			
	Manuf.	Services	Financial	Total	Manuf.	Services	Financial	Total
China	2	6	4	12	18(+16)	12(+6)	7(+3)	37(+25)
Korea	5	5	1	11	10(+5)	3(−2)	1(+0)	14(+3)
Brazil	1	0	2	3	3(+2)	0(+0)	3(+1)	6(+3)
Mexico	1	1	0	2	2(+1)	2(+1)	0(+0)	4(+2)
Russia	1	1	0	2	6(+5)	1(+0)	1(+1)	8(+6)
India	1	0	0	1	6(+5)	0(+0)	1(+1)	7(+6)
Malaysia	1	0	0	1	1(+0)	0(+0)	0(+0)	1(+0)
Singapore	1	0	0	1	2(+1)	0(+0)	0(+0)	2(+1)
Venezuela	1	0	0	1	1(+0)	0(+0)	0(+0)	1(+0)
Taiwan	0	0	0	0	5(+5)	0(+0)	1(+1)	6(+6)
Israel	0	0	0	0	1(+1)	0(+0)	0(+0)	1(+1)
Poland	0	0	0	0	1(+1)	0(+0)	0(+0)	1(+1)
Saudi Arabia	0	0	0	0	1(+1)	0(+0)	0(+0)	1(+1)
Thailand	0	0	0	0	1(+1)	0(+0)	0(+0)	1(+1)
Turkey	0	0	0	0	1(+1)	0(+0)	0(+0)	1(+1)
Total	14	13	7	34	59(+45)	18(+5)	14(+7)	91(+57)

Note: See note in Table 4.1.

Table 4.4 Intra-regional assets (per cent) by sector and region

	2000				2008			
	Manuf.	Services	Financial	Total	Manuf.	Services	Financial	Total
N. America	71.1	89.6	87.8	82.0	64.6 (−6.5)	82.4 (−7.2)	89.0 (+1.2)	75.3 (−6.7)
Europe	55.3	80.5	74.1	66.9	63.5 (+8.2)	80.9 (+0.4)	80.1 (+6.0)	73.2 (+6.3)
Asia Pacific	81.8	86.1	81.0	83.3	76.2 (−5.6)	84.9 (−1.2)	91.4 (+10.4)	81.5 (−1.8)
Total	70.6	87.0	80.3	78.5	67.7 (−2.9)	82.4 (−4.6)	85.1 (+4.8)	76.1 (−2.4)

Note: See note in Table 4.1. 286 and 334 firms' information used for 2000 and for 2007 respectively.

financial crisis has regional stabilizers. If so, then MNEs need to continue to ignore globalization rhetoric and, instead, focus on a strategy of deeper home region-based integration and international diversification.

Asymmetry in performance

In Table 4.5, we use return on sales (ROS) in order to measure performance. The profitability of large MNEs dramatically decreased about 50 per cent (from 0.066 to 0.031) on average. The decrease of profitability of North American MNEs was the greatest, and that of European MNEs, the lowest. All three industries decreased their profitability: the average ROS was decreased by 26 per cent (from 0.066 to 0.049) for manufacturing MNEs, by 53 per cent (from 0.064 to 0.030) for service MNEs and by 111 per cent for financial MNEs on average.

A close look gives us a better idea about the effect of the financial crisis. Both North American and European manufacturing MNEs slightly increased their profitability, and their service MNEs showed positive profitability. Only North American and European financial MNEs showed negative profitability in 2008. In particular the decline in profitability of financial MNEs in North America is noticeable (from 0.077 to –0.060). Thus the financial crisis somewhat directly affects the profitability of financial MNEs but indirectly affects the other MNEs in manufacturing and service sectors.

MNEs in Asia Pacific showed a decline in profitability in all three types of sector. We presume that the decline in profitability of MNEs in Asia Pacific resulted from the emergence of Chinese and Indian MNEs that are state-owned, or formerly were state-owned, firms. These MNEs are, in general, inefficient in operation as they are protected by national government policies. The profitability of these MNEs is indirectly affected by the financial crisis in the US, where they do not have sizeable operations, but directly affected by domestic market conditions and government policies. We discuss this in the next section.

MNEs and government policy

This analysis yields a new insight into the relation between MNEs and governments. In his analysis of *The competitive advantage of nations*, Porter (1990) demonstrated that the home government often viewed its MNEs as national champions, generating national competitive advantage and transmitting this throughout the world. This thinking built upon earlier analysis of the bargaining between MNEs and governments by Ray Vernon (1971), in which he demonstrated the multinational spread of US technological advantages through the worldwide networks of US MNEs. In both approaches US MNEs are viewed as national champions – they are the commercial instruments for the extension of US economic hegemony. In this pre-network analysis, MNEs operate as centralized and hierarchical institutions; the subsidiaries in host economies dance to the tune of head office.

The world financial crisis has served to reinforce this home country dominance over the network activities of MNEs. In particular, the large bailouts of firms in

Table 4.5 Performance (ROS) by sector and region

	2000				2008			
	Manuf.	Services	Financial	Total	Manuf.	Services	Financial	Total
N. America	0.057	0.071	0.077	0.066	0.063 (+0.006)	0.024 (−0.047)	−0.060 (−0.137)	0.026 (−0.040)
Europe	0.061	0.071	0.068	0.066	0.064 (+0.003)	0.037 (−0.034)	−0.017 (−0.085)	0.036 (−0.030)
Asia Pacific	0.083	0.046	0.129	0.064	0.014 (−0.069)	0.030 (−0.016)	0.060 (−0.069)	0.026 (−0.038)
Total	0.066	0.064	0.070	0.066	0.049 (−0.017)	0.030 (−0.034)	−0.008 (−0.078)	0.031 (−0.035)

Note: See note in Table 4.1.

the US banking, auto and related sectors have reinforced the importance of head office in the home country. The coordination of international macroeconomic policy by the G20 members led to the explicit treatment of MNEs as players in the home country economic policies of these countries. The autonomy of host country subsidiaries has been eroded such that bailouts and other types of government regulation are negotiated by head office rather than by subsidiary managers. This has led to a situation in which the decentralized national responsiveness strategies for MNEs advocated by Bartlett and Ghoshal (1989) have largely become redundant as MNEs have reverted to their role as national champions, as in the 1970s and 1980s. This trend in Western MNEs has been reinforced by the rise of large MNEs from China and other emerging economies.

Taken together, the home country and home government bargaining of Western MNEs, along with the rise of Chinese and other Asian MNEs, has led to a scenario in which many more MNEs have become the instruments of home government economic policy. In this area of international political economy the overriding tension remains between the US and China. The large Chinese surplus in its balance of trade with the US gives China a huge financial surplus which continues to be reinvested in the US. Within this macroeconomic environment, Chinese MNEs operate as champions of Chinese international economic policy.

In contrast, US MNEs are still following efficiency-based strategies of competitive advantage in which government support is an indirect attribute. In other words, US MNEs are secondary instruments of US international economic policy, especially in comparison with the more directed and focused Chinese MNEs. Thus there is a type of rivalry between US and Chinese MNEs, but it is related asymmetrically to their linkages with their respective home governments. The relation is weaker for US than Chinese MNEs.

As an offset to the asymmetric disadvantage, the benefits of international diversification apply more strongly to US MNEs than to Chinese ones. US MNEs have a 50-year lead in establishing foreign subsidiaries and in developing their networks of such affiliates. They enjoy the benefits of a more stable stream of earnings over time given their international sales and assets spread across the world, albeit with a home region bias. In contrast, Chinese MNEs are newer, focused upon natural resource-seeking (and possibly market-seeking) activities. They lack skills in systems integration and coordination, such that subsidiaries are generally bereft of managerial skills (Rugman and Doh, 2008). This suggests that US MNEs will align their business strategies with those of the US government on a more temporary basis than will Chinese MNEs align their strategies with the US government. Chinese MNEs will help China recycle its huge financial surplus, inevitably increasing the economic power of China and Chinese MNEs relative to the US and US MNEs.

In terms of sustainability it is difficult to speculate about the impact of the financial crisis upon the role of MNEs as agents of sustainable development. Using stakeholder theory it is apparent that leading Western MNEs have long adopted the basic criteria of corporate social responsibility. When these MNEs go abroad as indirect national champions they spread the virtues of corporate social responsibility through their network best practices. In general, the networks of Western MNEs exhibit virtues of sustainable development. In contrast, MNEs from emerging economies are likely to be blunt instruments of home country policy and are more concerned with market entry and growth. To the extent that the world financial crisis favours emerging economy MNEs at the expense of Western MNEs, there will be an overall negative impact on sustainable development.

There will be increased rivalry between Chinese and US MNEs. In acting as national champions, Chinese MNEs will find that regulations affecting the natural environment will act as entry barriers. The European and North American markets will become more difficult for the centralized and hierarchical Asian MNEs. This may lead to a stronger regional effect in which Chinese MNEs find themselves more confined to Asia and Africa, while North American and European MNEs focus more on inter-regional activity and somewhat reduce the proportion of their activity in Asia.

Conclusions

In this chapter we have examined the impact of the international financial crisis on MNE strategy. We examined the macroeconomic nature of the financial crisis and found that it has had an indirect impact on the strategies of MNEs. (This is not to deny that flows of foreign direct investment have decreased, but this is not the focus of this chapter.) The main impact of the world financial crisis is to make MNEs the national champions of their home governments. But this has an asymmetric impact. Emerging economies' MNEs continue to be strongly home country directed; clearly, they are instruments of Chinese economic policy. In contrast, developed economies' MNEs are somewhat less centralized and hierarchical in their operations (with more autonomy to subsidiary managers in their networks). This suggests that developed economies' MNEs are likely to benefit more from international diversification than are emerging economies' MNEs. We conclude that the world financial crisis has complex repercussions on the strategies of MNEs, and that these repercussions vary across countries, in particular between Chinese and US MNEs.

References

Bartlett, C. and Goshal, S. (1989) *Managing across borders: The transnational solution* (Boston, MA: Harvard Business School Press).
Birkinshaw, J. (2000) *Entrepreneurship in the global firm* (London: Sage).
Birkinshaw, J. and Pedersen, T. (2009) 'Strategy and management in MNE subsidiaries', in A.M. Rugman (ed.) *The Oxford handbook of international business*, 367–88 (Oxford: Oxford University Press).
Birkinshaw, J., Hood, N. and Jonsson, S. (1998) 'Building firm-specific advantages in multinational corporations: The role of subsidiary initiative', *Strategic Management Journal*, 19(3), 221–41.

Boddewyn, J.J., Halbrich, M.B. and Perry, A.C. (1986) 'Service multinationals: conceptualization, measurement, and theory', *Journal of International Business Studies*, 17(3), 41–57.

Buckley, P.J. and Casson, M. (1976) *The future of the multinational enterprise* (London: Macmillan/New York: Holmes and Meier).

Chen, M. (2004) *Asian management systems* (London: Thomson Learning).

Dunning, J.H. (1981) *Explaining international production* (London: Unwin).

Fratianni, M. and Oh, C.H. (2009) 'Expanding RTAs, trade flows, and the multinational enterprise', *Journal of International Business Studies*, 40(7), 1206–27.

Hennart, J-F. (1982) *A theory of multinational enterprise* (Ann Arbor, MI: University of Michigan Press).

Porter, M.E. (1990) *The competitive advantage of nations* (New York: Macmillan).

Ramamurti, R. and Singh, J. (2008) *Emerging multinationals from emerging markets* (Cambridge, UK: Cambridge University Press).

Rugman, A.M. (1976) 'Risk reduction by international diversification', *Journal of International Business Studies*, 7(2), 75–80.

Rugman, A.M. (1979) *International diversification and the multinational enterprise* (Lexington, MA: D.C. Heath).

Rugman, A.M. (1981) *Inside the multinationals* (New York: Columbia University Press).

Rugman, A.M. (2005) *The regional multinationals, MNEs and 'global' strategic management* (Cambridge: Cambridge University Press).

Rugman, A.M. (2009) *Rugman reviews international business* (Basingstoke: Palgrave Macmillan).

Rugman, A.M. and Doh, J. (2008) *Multinationals and development* (New Haven and London: Yale University Press).

Rugman, A.M. and Oh, C.H. (2008) 'The international competitiveness of Asian firms', *Journal of Strategy and Management*, 1(1), 57–71.

Rugman, A.M. and Verbeke, A. (1992), 'A note on the transnational solution and the transaction cost theory of multinational strategic management', *Journal of International Business Studies*, 23(4), 761–72.

Rugman, A.M. and Verbeke, A. (2001) 'Subsidiary-specific advantages in multinational enterprises', *Strategic Management Journal*, 22(3), 237–50.

Rugman, A.M. and Verbeke, A. (2004) 'A perspective on the regional and global strategies of multinational enterprises', *Journal of International Business Studies*, 35(1), 3–18.

Verbeke, A. (2009) *International business strategy* (Cambridge: Cambridge University Press).

Vernon, R. (1971) *Sovereignty at bay* (New York: Basic Books).

Walsh, J. and Deery, S. (2006) 'Refashioning organizational boundaries: outsourcing customer service work', *Journal of Management Studies*, 43(3), 557–82.

Westney, E. (2001) 'Japan', in A.M. Rugman (ed.) *Oxford handbook of international business*, 623–47 (Oxford: Oxford University Press).

Whitley, R.D. (1990) 'Eastern Asian enterprise structures and the comparative analysis of forms of business organization', *Organization Studies*, 11(1), 47–74.

Williamson, O.E. (1975) *Markets and hierarchies* (New York: Basic Books).

Part II
Outward FDI

5
The Persistence of Outward Foreign Direct Investment from German Manufacturing Industries

Heinz-Josef Tüselmann, Frank McDonald, Martin T. Bohl, Svitlana Voronkova and Paul Windrum

Introduction

The longitudinal properties of outward FDI and multinational company (MNC) strategies and activities have been extensively investigated by international business scholars (Buckley et al., 2007; Butler and Domingo, 1998; Liu et al., 2005). There has, however, been less investigation of the role of outward FDI in the debates about regionalism and globalization (Buckley, 2009a; Rugman, 2003; Rugman and Verbeke, 2004). In principle, if significant numbers of MNCs are developing 'global factory'-type strategies, this should be accompanied by marked changes in outward FDI that lead to step changes in trend FDI flows as firms engage in substantial new off-shoring operations and complex foreign investments to reap the benefits from the increasing opportunities to internationalize their activities (Buckley, 2009b; Buckley and Ghauri, 2004). An alternative view is that internationalization is primarily a regional process, whereby MNCs conduct most of their activities in the major economic regions of the world, and that this has not changed significantly despite growing trade and capital liberalization (Rugman 2003, 2005; Rugman and Hodgetts, 2001). Thus although new areas such as China and India are increasingly part of the global economy and have become major regional areas, this process does not lead to large-scale changes in the underlying determinants of FDI. In this view, outward FDI trends are likely to be stable in the long run in which shocks to the system do not disturb long-run trends.

The characteristics of national business systems affect FDI; consequently these factors require consideration in any investigation of the trend of outward FDI. Recently, there has been increasing attention paid to incorporating comparative institutional literature, such as the varieties of capitalism (Hall and Soskice, 2001) and national business systems (Whitley, 1999) literatures, into the analytical frameworks of the international business domain, as epitomized in special issues in the *Journal of International Business Studies* (2008, Vol. 30, No. 4) and *International Business Review* (2002, Vol. 11, No. 6). In this context, German FDI has played a central role in public, economic and policy debates in Germany on the importance of institutional factors for economic activities (Deutscher Bundestag, 2001; *Financial Times*, 2004; Franz, 2001). A common thread in the critique of the German model of capitalism has been that in the coordinated market economy institutional setting, German public policy and the high degree of coordination in policy decision-making constrain economic actors from adjusting swiftly to rapid changes in external environments and exogenous shocks, thereby leading to a path-dependent and slower rate of adjustment in companies' extra-institutional environment, leading to a severe misalignment of companies' needs because of constraints arising from the national institutional setting (Berthold and Stettes, 2001; Witt and Lewin, 2007). Institutional systems are therefore likely to affect the trend of German outward FDI.

In the light of the above background, a longitudinal study to test whether the outward FDI of German manufacturing industries has been shock persistent can provide statistical evidence to inform the wider international business debates, including the debates on global factory and regional strategy. The focus of this chapter is on the existence of structural breaks connected to shocks that impact on outward FDI from manufacturing industries. Tests are made to check for structural breaks for data on outward German FDI stock in the period 1976–2003. The study focuses on mature manufacturing industries because there are long-run data available for these industries that permits robust tests of shock persistency. If shock effects do impact outward FDI, there should be a persistent effect on the total stock of FDI.

This chapter examines German FDI outflows in ten mature manufacturing industries to assess if there is evidence of industry-level shock persistence. Industry-specific factors are often neglected in studies on the impact of exogenous shocks on FDI. There have been studies on total and manufacturing FDI (Agarwal et al., 1991; Lipsey, 1999, 2001), but there have been no studies that investigate industry effects. In this connection, there is an increasing appreciation that aggregate FDI figures may mask an industry-specific differential impact and associated FDI responses, which in turn necessitates a disaggregated, industry-level analysis. A growing body of literature highlights the importance of industry-specific characteristics for FDI. These factors include the degree of global exposure, capital intensity, the degree of product differentiation and the technology intensity of industries (Agarwal, 1997; Dunning, 2000a; UNCTAD, 2000).

Background

The German economy was buffeted by a variety of exogenous shocks in the period 1976–2003, including fundamental structural changes. Notable here are German reunification in October 1990, followed by the collapse of communism in bordering eastern European countries in the early 1990s and the extension of the EU to include former communist states. The German economy also experienced economic and monetary shocks in this period. These included crises and eventual collapse of the currency 'snake' in 1979, the subsequent creation of the EMS in the same year, the crises of EMS in 1992 and 1993, and the end of Deutschmark and introduction of the Euro in 1999. The period covered by the data also includes the enlargement of the EU from 9 to 15 members, the implementation of the Single European Market programme, and extensive privatization programmes in Germany and among many of her main trade partners. In the 1990s trading and FDI significantly increased with the Asian tigers and later the reforms in China led to significant changes to trade and investment levels with China. These economic and monetary shocks led to considerable incentives for the development and rationalization of many German industries. There were also a number of technology shocks in this period. New technologies, particularly new IT, were introduced that led to restructuring of the international activities of firms (Dunning, 2000b), and the reconfiguration of national and international supply chains (Tavares and Young, 2006). Shocks caused by oil price increases were also experienced; notably the 1979 oil crisis that occurred in the wake of the revolution in Iran.

The level and development of German manufacturing FDI stocks exhibit several distinctive regional and sector patterns. With regard to the former, outward manufacturing FDI stocks have been traditionally focused on Western industrialized countries and have become increasingly concentrated in these countries, accounting for nearly 84 per cent of German FDI stocks in 2003, compared to 75 per cent in 1976 (Deutsche Bundesbank, 1978, 2005). Furthermore, a handful of these countries account for a large share of German FDI as it has become increasingly concentrated in these host destinations, albeit with varying growth rates and changing shares within this country group. Over 65 per cent of German manufacturing FDI stock was concentrated in the US, Belgium, UK, France and the Netherlands (in descending order) by the end of 2003. This compares to 48 per cent in 1976 (Deutsche Bundesbank, 1978, 2005). The industry pattern of German manufacturing FDI displays a similar and growing concentration. Germany's four large export industries dominated German manufacturing FDI. The motor vehicle, chemical, mechanical engineering and electrical engineering industries accounted for over 65 per cent of all German manufacturing outward stock in 1976, and this figure had risen to 84 per cent by the end of 2003 (Deutsche Bundesbank, 1978, 2005). The chemical and motor vehicle industries accounted for the bulk of these investments with their combined share of all German manufacturing outward stocks amounting to nearly 50 per cent in 1976 and 67 per cent in 2003 (Deutsche Bundesbank, 1978, 2005). The increasing concentration of German manufacturing FDI in these two industries is largely accounted for by the motor vehicle industry, whose share of all German manufacturing outward stock increased from about 15 per cent in 1976 to 46 per cent in 2003, whereas the share of the chemical industry dropped from over 33 per cent in 1976 to 21 per cent in 2003 (Deutsche Bundesbank, 1978, 2005). In all, German manufacturing FDI stock has traditionally been focused on a handful of host countries and industries, with this concentration become gradually more pronounced over the years. Furthermore, there is some empirical evidence, at the aggregate level, that suggests inertia and shock persistence of German FDI in general, and of the manufacturing sector in particular (Agarwal et al., 1991; Hubert and Pain, 2002; Jost and Nunnenkamp, 2002).

The issue of shocks on outward FDI complements other research that has explored the stability of FDI flows. There have been studies on the relative stability of inward FDI to developing countries, compared with other financial flows and portfolio investments, observed, for example, during the Latin American debt crisis of the 1980s, the Mexican currency crisis of 1994–5, and the financial crises of 1997–8 in East Asia (Lipsey, 1999, 2001). These studies found that inward flows of FDI were not as volatile as other forms of inward financial investment in these countries during these particular periods. A theoretical explanation for this relative stability, based on transaction costs, has been put forward by Goldstein and Razin (2003). What has not been considered sufficiently is whether shocks have affected the level of outward FDI at the industry level. German FDI is of particular interest in this regard because Germany is not only the third-largest source of outward FDI in terms of global stock (UNCTAD, 2006), but the development of German FDI, and in particular manufacturing FDI, is often ascribed country-of-origin-specific patterns in responding to changes in global and host country investment conditions (Agarwal et al., 1991; Jungnickel and Shams, 2001).

Another literature that is of interest is that on hysteresis related to sunk costs (Baldwin, 1989; Dixit, 1989; Krugman, 1989). Roberts and Tybout (1997) examined the decisions by Colombian manufacturing plants in four key sectors for the period 1981–9. They found that exports increased following an initial shock that led to a favourable change in the exchange rate. They further discovered that decisions to export remain persistent even when the exchange rate returned to its previous PPP value. This is explained by Roberts and Tybout (1997) in terms of the lumpiness of the decision to export. FDI decisions are also lumpy because of the high sunk costs associated with this type of investment. This view on the lumpiness of FDI is challenged by those that argue that the financial sophistication of MNCs makes FDI similar to portfolio investment (Albuquerque, 2003; Hausmann and Fernandez-Arias, 2000). Thus, the ability of MNCs to finance and re-finance FDI from a multitude of sources, in terms of countries and types of financial instruments, reduces the lumpiness of FDI (Fernandez-Arias and Hausmann, 2001).

The studies on the stability of FDI suggest that it is more stable than portfolio investment (Mallampally and Sauvant, 1999; Nunnenkamp, 2001). This view is supported by the literature on transaction and sunk costs on exports, which imply that FDI has similarities to exports and that FDI is lumpy (Baldwin, 1989; Krugman, 1989; Roberts and Tybout, 1997). This literature suggests that FDI is likely to be shock persistent because the underlying drivers of FDI are stable due to high transaction and sunk costs, and therefore such investment is subject to shocks that alter the underlying drivers. However, other literature suggests that the financial sophistication of MNCs reduces the transaction and sunk costs of FDI thereby making FDI similar to portfolio investment (Albuquerque, 2003; Hausmann and Fernandez-Arias, 2000). In this view, FDI would not be shock persistent.

Econometric methods

Augmented Dickey–Fuller and Kwiatkowski unit root tests

The theoretical predictions discussed above can be analysed empirically with the help of unit root tests. With this econometric technique it can be decided whether a time-series belongs to the group of trend stationary or difference stationary time-series. In case a time-series contains a deterministic linear time trend, the variable can be characterized as a trend stationary process. Fluctuations around the linear trend are considered to be mostly temporary, and due to the transitory character of shocks, deviations return completely to the trend. In contrast, random walk processes can be characterized as difference stationary time-series. The important property of these time-series is that shocks have a permanent character. When the time-series is shocked it never completely returns to its trend. Hence, unit root processes exhibit the shock persistence (Kennedy, 2003).

We apply the augmented Dickey and Fuller (1979, 1981) test and the approach proposed by Kwiatkowski et al. (1992), hereafter ADF and KPSS test. The ADF test is implemented using the regression:

$$\Delta y_t = \alpha_0 + \alpha_1 y_{t-1} + \alpha_2 t + \sum_{i=1}^{l} \gamma_i \Delta y_{t-i} + \varepsilon_t \tag{5.1}$$

Δ denotes the first difference operator, y_t the time-series under investigation, t a linear time trend and ε_t the error term. The ADF test analyses the null hypothesis of a unit root in the (log) level of the time-series: $H_0 : \alpha_1 = 0$, versus the alternative hypothesis of trend stationarity. The critical values are MacKinnon's (1991) response surface estimates. The lag length l is determined by implementing the general-to-specific procedure suggested by Hall (1994) starting with the lag $l = 3$.

In contrast to the ADF test, the KPSS test investigates the null hypothesis of trend stationarity against the alternative of a unit root. Let $\hat{u}_t$, $t = 1, 2, \ldots, T$, the estimated residuals from the regression:

$$y_t = \beta_0 + \beta_1 t + u_t \tag{5.2}$$

The KPSS test statistic is defined as:

$$LM = \sum_{t=1}^{T} S_t^2 / \hat{s}_{Tl}^2, \tag{5.3}$$

where $S_t = \sum_{i=1}^{t} \hat{u}_t$, $t = 1, 2, \ldots, T$ and

$$\hat{s}_{Tl}^2 = T^{-1} \sum_{t=1}^{T} \hat{u}_t^2 + 2T^{-1} \sum_{\tau=1}^{l} \left(1 - \frac{\tau}{l+1}\right) \sum_{t=\tau+1}^{T} \hat{u}_t \hat{u}_{t-\tau} \tag{5.4}$$

where *l* is a truncation lag. Sephton (1995) provides response surface estimates of approximate critical values for the *LM* test statistic. The maximum truncation lag is set to $l=2$.

Due to the different null hypotheses of the ADF and the KPSS test, we can implement a simple confirmatory analysis to confirm our conclusions about unit root (Choi, 1994; Kwiatkowski et al., 1992; Maddala and Kim, 1995). It is generally agreed that using both tests gives the most reliable results (Amano and van Norden, 1992). If the ADF test cannot reject the null hypothesis of a unit root in the log level of the time-series and the KPSS test rejects the null hypothesis of trend stationarity, we have found confirmation for the difference stationarity and the persistence of shocks in the FDI time-series.

Zivot and Andrews unit root test

Occurrence of an exogenous shock may have permanent effect on the level of variables. In statistical terms, this may result in under-rejection of the null hypothesis of a unit root (Perron, 1990; Zivot and Andrews, 1992), when a trend stationary process with a break in its parameters is erroneously concluded to be a unit root (non-stationary) process. The likelihood of occurrence of a structural break increases with the data span. Since our data set covers 28 years, we perform an additional unit root test suggested by Zivot and Andrews (1992) that assumes a trend stationary process with a break under alternative hypothesis. Related work includes studies by Rappoport (1990) and Banerjee et al. (1990). However, it is not the purpose of this chapter to exploit the variety of unit root tests available, and we choose the Zivot and Andrews test based on its popularity in empirical financial research. The advantage of this test over the one of Perron (1990) is that the break point is endogenous; that is, it is estimated from the data rather then assumed based on the history of macroeconomic effects. This feature of the Zivot–Andrews test avoids a potentially erroneous assumption regarding the date of the break.

The Zivot–Andrews unit root test is formulated as follows. Under the null hypothesis of a unit root, the time-series is assumed to follow a process given by:

$$y_t = \mu + y_{t-1} + u_t \tag{5.5}$$

Under the alternative hypothesis, the series is assumed to follow a trend stationary process with a structural break in parameters. Since the break may occur both in intercept and slope of the data, Zivot and Andrews suggest three model specifications under the alternative hypothesis:

$$y_t = \mu^A + \theta^A DU_t(\lambda) + \beta^A t + \alpha^A y_{t-1} + \sum_{j=1}^{k} c_j^A \Delta y_{t-j} + u_t \tag{5.6}$$

$$y_t = \mu^B + \beta^B t + \gamma^B DT(\lambda) + \alpha^B y_{t-1} + \sum_{j=1}^{k} c_j^B \Delta y_{t-j} + u_t \quad (5.7)$$

$$y_t = \mu^C + \theta^C DU_t(\lambda) + \beta^C t + \gamma^C DT(\lambda) + \alpha^C y_{t-1} + \sum_{j=1}^{k} c_j^C \Delta y_{t-j} + u_t \quad (5.8)$$

where $\lambda = T_B/T$ is the estimated time of the break (measured as a fraction of a sample), $DU_t(\lambda) = 1$ if $t > T_B$ and 0 otherwise; $DB_t(\lambda) = t - T_B$ if $t > T_B$ and 0 otherwise, and k is the lag length. Dummy variables DU_t and DT_t model break in intercept and slope, respectively.

The estimation of an endogenous timing of the break λ is performed by running a series of regressions with a different date T_B. Namely, T_B is set to all the sample dates and regressions equations (5.6)–(5.8) are estimated with all possible break points. For practical purposes, however, T_B is assumed to belong to the interval $[0.1T; 0.9T]$. As a result, a series of t-statistics for the α^i coefficient is obtained, where $i = A, B, C$. The ultimate test statistic for a given model specification is the one constituting the strongest evidence against the null hypothesis; that is, the smallest statistic in this series:

$$t_{\alpha^i}[\lambda_{\inf}^i] = \inf_{\lambda \in [0.1T; 0.9T]} t_{\alpha^i}(\lambda) \quad (5.9)$$

The asymptotic distribution and critical values for the statistic (5.9) for the models A, B and C are provided in Zivot and Andrews (1992).

Data

We use data on German outward FDI measured across industries. The annual data on the stock of German industrial FDI was extracted from the Deutsche Bundesbank publications *Kapitalverflechtung mit dem Ausland*, for the period 1976–2003. Prior to 1995, the Bundesbank defined industries using the German industrial classification. After 1995 it adopted the European Union NACE (Rev. 1) industrial classification (Deutsche Bundesbank, 1997).

The identification of industry in official Bundesbank data uses the two-digit NACE classification. For the purpose of consistent identification for the duration of the sample, the FDI data prior to 1995 have been reclassified using the NACE (Rev. 1) classification. However, for a number of industries such re-classification was not possible and some industries had to be amalgamated in order to achieve consistency to the pre-1995 classification scheme. The final sample includes the following ten manufacturing industries (NACE codes in brackets):

1. Food and Beverages (15)
2. Textiles (17)
3. Clothing and Leather (18, 19)
4. Wood, Paper, Publishing Printing (20, 21, 22)

5. Chemicals (24)
6. Rubber and Plastics (25)
7. Glass, Ceramics and Cement (26)
8. Metals and Metal Products (27, 28)
9. Machinery and Equipment (29)
10. Motor Vehicles (34)

The time-series for tobacco was not included in the calculations because of missing values. The sample accounted for 88 per cent of all German manufacturing outward stock in 2003 (77 per cent in 1976) (Deutsche Bundesbank, 1978, 2005). With the exception of the pharmaceutical industry, which is contained in the two-digit chemical industry, the sample consists of mature industries. The Bundesbank does not provide industry data for FDI stocks at the three-digit NACE code; therefore it was not possible to separate out this high-tech industry (based on the OECD categorization of technology intensity of industries (OECD, 1997)).

In the Deutsche Bundesbank publications, the FDI data prior to 1999 is reported in millions of Deutschmarks and in millions of Euro afterwards. The data were therefore converted into Euro using the fixed exchange rate between Euro and Deutschmark as provided by the European Central Bank (http://www.ecb.int/home/html/index.en.html). To account for the impact of inflation on FDI valuation, the data have been deflated using the German consumer and producer price indices (CPI and PPI respectively). The data on CPI and PPI have been extracted from the Deutsche Bundesbank *Monatsbericht*.

Empirical results and discussion

Table 5.1, below, contains the empirical findings on the unit root tests for the FDI time-series deflated by the producer price index. (In addition to the producer price index we used the consumer price index to deflate the time-series. The findings (not reported but available on request) are qualitatively the same.) For all time-series, the ADF tests cannot reject the null hypothesis of a unit root. The findings of the KPSS tests are broadly in line with this result. With only a few exceptions the KPSS tests reject the null of trend stationarity. Hence, the empirical evidence on the stochastic properties of German FDI time is in favour of the shock persistence property.

The findings of the Zivot–Andrews unit root test – that assumes stationarity with a structural break under the alternative hypothesis – are presented in Table 5.2. For all the series of industrial FDI, apart from the chemical industry, the null hypothesis of a unit root cannot be rejected. This result is generally in line with the findings of both the ADF and KPSS tests. It provides additional evidence in favour of the persistence of shocks in the FDI series and this evidence is robust to the possible presence of structural break of the parameters of the underlying process.

The results provide support for the view that German FDI displays shock persistency that was suggested in studies on total German FDI and for the

Table 5.1 Results of unit root tests

	ADF		KPSS		
	τ_τ	l	$l = 1$	$l = 2$	$l = 3$
Food and beverages	−2.50	0	0.31***	0.21**	0.17**
Clothing and leather	−2.60	0	0.34***	0.22***	0.17**
Pulp, paper and paper products; publishing and printing	1.01	0	0.59***	0.34***	0.25***
Rubber and plastic products	−2.86	2	0.19**	0.11	0.08
Non-metallic mineral products: glass, ceramics and so on.	−2.34	0	0.28***	0.17**	0.13*
Metals and metal products	−2.23	0	0.39***	0.24***	0.19**
Machinery and equipment	−1.30	0	0.45***	0.28***	0.23***
Vehicles and vehicle parts	−1.50	0	0.38***	0.21**	0.15**
Textiles	0.42	0	0.47***	0.27***	0.20**
Chemicals	−0.38	2	0.47***	0.30***	0.25***
Manufacturing industry	−1.92	0	0.21**	0.13*	0.10

Notes: ***, **, * denote significance at 1, 5 and 10 per cent respectively. τ_τ denotes the value of the ADF test statistics; l denotes the number of lags used for estimation of equations (5.1) and (5.4). Critical values for the ADF tests are from MacKinnon (1991) and for the KPSS tests are from Sephton (1995).

manufacturing sector as a whole (Agarwal et al., 1991; Hubert and Pain, 1999; Jost and Nunnenkamp, 2002). This study provides evidence that there is no industry-specific differential response to shocks in the period 1976–2003, with the exception of the chemical industry. Mature German manufacturing industries, apart from the chemical industry and other manufacturing industries that could not be included in this sample, constitute two-thirds of all German manufacturing FDI stock (Deutsche Bundesbank, 2005). This study therefore confirms, for mature German industries, the general impression of existing aggregate level studies that outward German FDI is shock persistent.

The results do not provide support for the view that in general the trend of FDI outflows is less prone to shocks than other types of investments. The results therefore challenge, at least for most German mature manufacturing industries, studies that support the view that FDI is not shock persistent (Aizenman and Marion, 2004; Albuquerque, 2003; Desai et al., 2004; Fernandez-Arias and Hausmann, 2001; Firoozi, 1997; Frankel and Rose, 1996; Levchenko and Mauro, 2006). The findings support the view that high transaction and sunk costs lead to lumpy FDI which is prone to shock persistency. However, the German chemical industry does not seem to be shock persistent. This could be due to a number of industry-specific factors and/or a combination of such factors.

Table 5.2 Results of Zivot–Andrews unit root test

Industry	Minimum t-statistics	Lag (k)	Estimated date of the break ($\hat{\lambda}$)
Food and beverages	−3.31	0	1999
Clothing and leather	−3.69	0	1994
Pulp, paper and paper products; publishing and printing	−2.18	2	1998
Rubber and plastic products	−3.64	0	1995
Non-metallic mineral products: glass, ceramics and so on	−2.86	0	1992
Metals and metal products	−4.83	0	1986
Machinery and equipment	−3.52	0	1986
Vehicles and vehicle parts	−4.78	2	1995
Textiles	−2.09	0	1999
Chemicals	−5.19*	2	1994

Notes: The table reports test statistics for Zivot and Andrews (1992) unit root test. The null hypothesis of a unit root is tested against the alternative of stationarity with a structural break of unknown timing. Zivot and Andrews (1992) allow three model specifications: break in intercept only, break in a trend and break in both intercept and trend. We estimated all three model specifications. Reported results are for model allowing for the break in both intercept and a trend, since this model is least restrictive:

$y_t = \mu + \theta DU_t(\lambda) + \beta t + \gamma DT(\lambda) + \alpha y_{t-1} + \sum_{j=1}^{k} c_j \Delta y_{t-j} + \varepsilon_t$, where DU and DT are dummy variables modelling break and λ is the assumed date of the break. The number of lags k is chosen based on the values of the relevant t-statistic. * denotes significance at the 5 per cent level.

Studies on outward German investment have shown that fundamental structural changes induced by the Single European Market programme and the collapse of communism in Central and Eastern Europe have been most frequent in the chemical industry (Hubert and Pain, 2002). Furthermore, the chemical industry at the two-digit NACE code includes different types of industries at the three-digit NACE codes in terms of technology intensity and risk exposure – such as bulk chemicals, petrochemicals and pharmaceuticals. It may therefore be possible that non-shock persistency of the chemical FDI may be accounted for by certain industries within the chemical sector. The petrochemical industry can be expected to have been particularly affected by oil crises, monetary shocks and currency crises. The high-tech pharmaceutical industry will have been particularly affected by technological shocks. In periods of rapid technological advances, liberal market economies such as the US – with innovation systems that encourage rapid innovations – are thought to become attractive locations for German pharmaceutical MNCs (and other German MNCs in high-tech industries). This is relative to the German location, where the innovation system is thought to lend itself better to incremental innovations – which have underpinned the competitive advantages of German MNCs in the medium and medium-high-tech industries (Hall and Sosckice, 2001; Hall and Gingerich, 2009).

Indeed, studies highlight the increased significance of outward FDI of German pharmaceutical companies to the US since the mid-1990s, in terms of both the lead market function of the US pharmaceutical market and the attractiveness of the US R&D environment for this industry (Belitz, 2002; Klodt, 2001). One possible scenario could be that the non-shock persistency of the chemical sector time-series is accounted for by high-tech industries, while the mature industries in the chemical sector may well have been shock persistent, but with the effect of the former being of a magnitude that induced non-shock persistency for the aggregate chemical sector. However, the limitations of the data prevented tests from being performed at the three-digit NACE code for the chemical sector and on other German industries including service industries and some of the other newer and more high-technology industries.

Moreover, it is possible that the nature of German MNCs and the characteristics of German financial institutions limit the ability of German MNCs to adopt the kind of sophisticated financial arrangements that would make FDI more like portfolio investment. It is, however, difficult to imagine that German MNCs' behaviour is very different from MNCs that are based in other countries. However, to investigate these issues and the issues in the preceding paragraph further, as well as providing further tests of the conflicting views on the shock persistency of FDI, requires more disaggregated industry data and data from a variety of countries.

Concluding remarks

Although the German economy was buffeted by several shocks in the period 1976–2003, including fundamental structural change, the disaggregated industry-level study confirmed for mature German manufacturing industries the general impression of existing aggregate-level studies that outward German FDI is shock persistent. The results do not imply broad support for the global factory thesis other than possibly for the chemical industry. The nature of German business systems combined with the dominance of traditional manufacturing industries in German FDI appears to weaken the drivers of the global factory strategy. If there is a move towards global factory strategies in German MNCs it appears to have had little effect thus far on the trend of their outward FDI. It is possible that German industries outside of the traditional manufacturing sector are more affected by the drivers of the global factory strategy. The results imply broad support for the regionalist strategy proposed by Rugman, in that German outward FDI for the traditional manufacturing sector is generally stable in the face of widespread and often radical shocks in the global economy. The focus of outward German FDI in the US and Europe also lends some support to the Rugman thesis. However, it is possible that the regionalist strategy thesis is not supported for non-manufacturing industries in Germany, and the German chemical industry appears to have been affected by global shocks. Moreover, MNCs that are centred in different national business systems may react differently to global shocks. It is therefore not clear if the regionalist strategy is dominant regardless of the business systems in home countries and of industry. In general, the results suggest that both the global factory and regionalist strategies need to take into account the national business systems of home countries and industry-specific factors.

An important issue for future research is whether the relation between business systems and the FDI strategies of companies works well in times of crisis and rapid change in relation to newer high-tech manufacturing industries and knowledge-intensive service industries. However, due to limitations in official German FDI data, this question cannot be answered by the data available for this study. If the non-shock persistency in the chemical sector was attributable to factors in the high-tech pharmaceutical sector within the chemical industry, rather than the other medium-tech sectors within this industry, this would imply that the global factory thesis is supported – but only for certain industries outside the traditional medium-tech manufacturing. This inference about the global factory thesis would be strengthened if other high-tech industries, or sectors within industries, also displayed non-shock persistency. Furthermore, it is possible that the shock persistency of outward FDI flows is influenced by particular national business systems, implying that the global factory thesis is affected by the institutional systems of host countries.

To shed more light on the shock persistency of FDI and to substantiate the issues raised in this chapter requires further longitudinal studies based on more fine-grained industry classifications and firm-level data in combination with the regional distribution of FDI outward stocks. However, in the light of publicly available data limitations for time-series analyses, such studies will be difficult to undertake. Furthermore, comparative longitudinal investigations along the lines of this study that include other major FDI home countries as well as incorporating institutional variables that adequately proxy national business models and their dynamics pose numerous data and conceptual research challenges. Nevertheless, such research would enhance our understanding of the links between institutional systems, industry and MNC FDI strategies, and would help to develop and refine the global factory and regionalization views of MNC strategy.

References

Agarwal, J. (1997) 'European integration and German FDI: implications for domestic investment and Central European economies', *National Institute Economic Review*, 160, 87–99.

Agarwal, J., Gubitz, A. and Nunnenkamp, P. (1991) 'Foreign investment in developing countries – the case of Germany', *Kieler Studien 238* (Kiel: Institute of World Economics).

Aizenman, J. and Marion, N. (2004) 'International reserve holdings with sovereign risk and costly tax collection', *Economic Journal*, 114(497), 569–91.

Albuquerque, R. (2003) 'The composition of international capital flows: risk sharing through foreign direct investment', *Journal of International Economics*, 61(2), 353–83.

Amano, R.A. and van Norden, S. (1992) 'Unit root tests and the burden of proof', *Bank of Canada Working Paper*, No. 92–7.

Baldwin, R. (1989) 'Hysteresis in import prices; the beachhead effect', *American Economic Review*, 78(4), 773–85.

Banerjee, A., Dolado, J. and Galbraith, J. (1990) *Recursive Tests for Unit Roots and Structural Breaks in Long Annual GNP Series*, Unpublished Manuscript, University of Florida, Department of Economics.

Belitz, H. (2002) 'Deutschland als Forschungsstandort multinationaler Unternehmen', *Deutsches Institut für Wirtschaftsforschung: DIW Wochenbericht*, 16, 24–30.

Berthold, N. and Stettes, O. (2001) 'Der Flächentarifvertrag – vom Wegbereiter des Wirtschaftswunders zum Verursacher der Beschäftigunsmisere', in W. Zohlnhofer (ed.) *Tarifautonomie auf dem Prüfstand* (Berlin: Sigma).
Buckley, P. (2009a) 'The impact of the global factory on economic development', *Journal of World Business*, 44(2), 131–43.
Buckley, P. (2009b) 'International thinking: from the multinational enterprise to the global factory', *International Business Review*, 18(3), 224–35.
Buckley, P. and Ghauri, P. (2004) 'Globalisation, economic geography and the strategy of multinational enterprises', *Journal of International Business Studies*, 35(2), 81–98.
Buckley, P., Clegg, J., Cross, A., Liu, X., Voss, H. and Zheng, P. (2007) 'The determinants of Chinese outward foreign direct investment', *Journal of International Business Studies*, 38(3), 499–518.
Butler, K. and Domingo, C. (1998) 'A note on political risk and the required return on foreign investment', *Journal of International Business Studies*, 29(3), 392–401.
Choi, I. (1994) 'Residual-based tests for the null of stationary with application to US macroeconomic time series', *Econometric Theory*, 10(3/4), 720–46.
Desai, M.A., Foley, C.F. and Hines, J.R. (2004) 'A multinational perspective on capital structure choice and internal capital markets', *Journal of Finance*, 59(6), 2451–88.
Deutsche Bundesbank (1978) *Kapitalverpflechtung mit dem Ausland* (Frankfurt a.M.).
Deutsche Bundesbank (1997) Bestimmungsgründe grenzüberschreitender Direktinvestitionen, *Montatsberich August* (Frankfurt a.M.).
Deutsche Bundesbank (2005) *Kapitalverpflechtung mit dem Ausland* (Frankfurt a.M.).
Deutscher Bundestag (2001) 14 Wahlperiode, Drucksache 14/5741 of 02 April 2001 (Berlin).
Dickey, D. and Fuller, W. (1979) 'Distribution of estimators for autoregressive time series with a unit root', *Journal of the American Statistical Association*, 74(366), 427–31.
Dickey, D. and Fuller, W. (1981) 'The likelihood ratio statistics for autoregressive time series with a unit root', *Econometrica*, 49(4), 1057–72.
Dixit, A. (1989) 'Entry and exit decisions under uncertainty', *Journal of Political Economy*, 97(3), 620–38.
Dunning, J. (2000a) *Regions, Globalization, and the Knowledge Economy* (Oxford: Oxford University Press).
Dunning, J. (2000b) 'The eclectic paradigm as an envelope for economic and business theories of MNE activity', *International Business Review*, 9(2), 163–90.
Fernandez-Arias, E. and Hausmann, R. (2001) 'Is foreign direct investment a safer form of financing?', *Emerging Markets Review*, 2(1), 34–49.
Financial Times (2004) 'How a Rhineland behemoth changed course', 22 November, 18.
Firoozi, F. (1997) 'Multinationals FDI and uncertainty: an exposition', *Journal of Multinational Financial Management*, 7(3), 265–73.
Frankel, J. and Rose, A. (1996) 'Currency crashes in emerging markets: an empirical treatment', *Journal of International Economics*, 41(3/4), 351–66.
Franz, W. (2001) 'Das betriebsverfassungsgesetz ist komplett überflüssig', *Handelsblatt*, 26 December, 5.
Goldstein, I. and Razin, A. (2003) 'An information-based trade off between foreign direct investment and foreign portfolio investment: volatility, transparency, and welfare', *NBER Working Papers*, No. 9426.
Hall, A. (1994) 'Testing for a unit root in time series with pre-test data-based model selection', *Journal of Business and Economics Statistics*, 12, 461–70.
Hall, P. and Gingerich, D. (2009) 'Varieties of capitalism and institutional complementarities in the political economy: an empirical analysis', *British Journal of Political Science*, 39(3), 449–82.
Hall, P. and Soskice, D. (eds) (2001) *Varieties of Capitalism: The Institutional Foundations of Comparative Advantage* (Oxford: Oxford University Press).
Hausmann, R. and Fernandez-Arias, E. (2000) 'Foreign direct investment: good cholesterol?', Paper presented at Seminar *The New Wave of Capital Inflows: Sea Changes or Just Another*

Tide, Annual Meeting of the Board of Governors, Inter-American Development Bank and Inter-American Investment Corporation.

Hubert, F. and Pain, N. (1999) 'Innovation and the regional and industrial pattern of German foreign direct investment', in R. Barrell and N. Pain (eds) *Investment, Innovation and the Diffusion of Technology in Europe*, 168–94 (Cambridge, MA: University Press).

Hubert, F. and Pain, N. (2002) 'Fiscal incentives, European integration and the location of foreign direct investment', *NIESR Discussion Papers* (London: National Institute of Economic and Social Research).

Jost, T. and Nunnenkamp, P. (2002) 'Bestimmungsgründe deutscher direktinvestitionen in entwicklungs-und reformländern – hat sich wirklich was verändert?' *Kieler Arbeitspapier, 1124* (Kiel: Institut für Weltwirtschaft).

Jungnickel, R. and Shams, R. (2001) 'The internationalization of the German firms', in Z. Vodusek (ed.) *Foreign Direct Investment in Latin America: The Role of European Investors* (Washington, DC: Inter-American Investment Bank).

Kennedy, P. (2003) *A Guide to Econometrics*, 5th edn (Cambridge, MA: MIT Press).

Klodt, H. (2001) 'Direktinvestitionen, fusionen und strukturwandel', *Kieler Arbeitspapiere* (Kiel: Institut für Weltwirtschaft).

Krugman, P. (1989) *Exchange Rate Instability* (Cambridge, MA: MIT Press).

Kwiatkowski, D., Phillips, P., Schmidt, P. and Yongcheol, S. (1992) 'Testing the null hypothesis of stationarity against the alternative of a unit root', *Journal of Econometrics*, 54(1–3), 159–78.

Levchenko, A. and Mauro, P. (2006) 'Do some forms of financial flows help protect from sudden stops?', *IMF Working Paper*, WP/06/2002, Washington DC.

Lipsey, R. (1999) 'The role of foreign direct investment in international capital flows', *NBER Working Paper*, No. 7094.

Lipsey, R. (2001) 'Foreign direct investors in three financial crises', *NBER Working Papers*, No. 8084.

Liu, X., Buck, T. and Shu, C. (2005) 'Chinese economic development, the next stage: outward FDI?', *International Business Review*, 14(1), 97–115.

MacKinnon, J. (1991) 'Critical values for cointegration tests', in R.F. Engle and C.W.J. Granger (eds) *Long-Run Economic Relationships* (Oxford: Oxford University Press).

Maddala, G. and Kim, I.M. (1995) *Unit Root, Cointegration and Structural Change* (Cambridge: Cambridge University Press).

Mallampally, P. and Sauvant, K. (1999) 'Foreign direct investment in developing countries', *IMF Finance & Development*, (32), 1259–67.

Nunnenkamp, P. (2001) 'Foreign direct investment in developing countries: what policy-makers should not do and what economists don't know', *Kiel Institute for World Economics Discussion Papers*, No. 380.

OECD (1997) *Internationalisation of Industrial R&D: Patterns and Trends* (Paris: OECD).

Perron, P. (1990) 'Testing for a unit root in a time series with a changing mean', *Journal of Business and Economic Statistics*, 8(2), 153–62.

Rappoport, P. (1990) *Testing for the Frequency of Permanent Shifts in Time Series*, Unpublished Manuscript, Rutgers University, Department of Economics.

Roberts, M.J. and Tybout, J.R. (1997) 'The decision to export in Colombia: an empirical model of entry with sunk costs', *The American Economic Review*, 87(4), 545–64.

Rugman, A. (2003) 'Regional strategy and the demise of globalization', *Journal of International Management*, 9(4), 409–17.

Rugman, A. (2005) 'A further comment on the myth of globalization', *Journal of International Management*, 11(3), 441–5.

Rugman, A. and Hodgetts, R. (2001) 'The end of global strategy', *European Management Journal*, 19(4), 333–43.

Rugman, A. and Verbeke, A. (2004) 'A perspective on regional and global strategies of multinational enterprises', *Journal of International Business Studies*, 35(1), 3–18.

Sephton, P.S. (1995) 'Response surface estimates of the KPSS stationarity test', *Economics Letters*, 47(3–4), 255–61.
Tavares, A. and Young, S. (2006) 'Sourcing patterns of foreign-owned multinational subsidiaries in Europe', *Regional Studies*, 40(6), 583–99.
UNCTAD (2000) *World Investment Report 2000* (Geneva and New York: United Nations).
UNCTAD (2006) *World Investment Report 2006* (Geneva and New York: United Nations).
Whitley, R. (1999) *Divergent Capitalisms: The Social Structuring and Change of Business Systems* (Oxford: Oxford University Press).
Witt, M. and Lewin, A. (2007) 'Outward foreign direct investment as escape response to home country institutional constraints', *Journal of International Business Studies*, 38(4), 579–94.
Zivot, E. and Andrews, D. (1992) 'Further evidence on the great crash, the oil-price shock, and the unit-root hypothesis', *Journal of Business and Economic Statistics*, 10(3), 251–70.

6
Multinational Performance and Intellectual Property Rights: Evidence from 46 Countries

Yong Yang and Pedro S. Martins

Introduction

From a theoretical viewpoint, multinationality can play an important role in enhancing a firm's profitability. For instance, multinationality allows firms to exploit economies of scale and scope, while internalizing their tangible and intangible assets (Buckley and Casson, 1976; Dunning, 1988; Rugman, 1986). Moreover, many empirical studies have presented corroborating evidence of a positive link between multinationality and performance, in particular when drawing on firm-level data (Goerzen and Beamish, 2003; Pangarkar, 2008; Tallman and Li, 1996).

Although these studies have made important contributions, one shortcoming of this literature is that it has generally disregarded the role of differences across investment destinations, opting instead for an aggregate view of overseas investment. This view may have been appropriate until the 1980s, when the geographical range of FDI investments was relatively narrow. However, more recently, such location choices may have become particularly important as globalization has been opening up new destinations for FDI.

One important aspect in this context is that new FDI destinations in developing countries typically exhibit considerable heterogeneity in several variables regarded as important in determining the success of any foreign venture. Examples of these variables include infrastructure, political stability and transportation costs. In this context, an important question for academics and practitioners alike is whether performance gains from FDI differ with respect to the location choice made by multinational firms. In this chapter, we focus specifically on the role of the host country's level of intellectual property rights (IPR). In particular, we want to know if the returns to investment in high-IPR countries differ from the returns to investment in low-IPR countries. This goal is feasible given our access to and analysis of an impressive data set, which includes information about more than 16,000 multinational firms with headquarters in 46 countries.

Countries with a high ratio of R&D to GDP or a high proportion of scientists and engineers in the labour force have markedly stronger IPR. The situation is different in those developing countries that tend to be keen on encouraging low-cost imitation. Until these countries move into a middle income range – with greater domestic inventiveness and absorptive capability – they will tend to exhibit low IPR because they have little intellectual property to protect (World Bank, 2001).

Multinational firms may prefer to locate their overseas investment in high-IPR countries in order to minimize the risk of imitation and knowledge dissipation. While there is a high risk of technology imitation in countries with low IPR, multinational firms may benefit from higher returns when they invest in these low-IPR countries, for instance through economies of scale from internalizing their intangible assets. This entails a theoretical trade-off between benefits and costs of low-IPR host country investment.

In our empirical evidence, we find a clear positive relation between multinationality and firm performance, which is consistent with findings in Tallman and Li (1996), Goerzen and Beamish (2003), Pangarkar (2008) and Yang and Martins (2010). However, we also find that investment in low-IPR countries is associated with larger effects on performance. We interpret these results as indicating that while IPR would be key from the point of view of multinationals exploiting their (intellectual and other) assets abroad, low-IPR locations probably offer other production advantages that more than compensate for the low-IPR risk. Alternatively – or complementarily – low-IPR locations may face absorption constraints such that in practice the risk of losing ownership advantages is not significant enough.

Literature review

Earlier theories of foreign direct investment (Hymer, 1960; Vernon, 1966) leading to the internalization/eclectic paradigm (Buckley and Casson ,1976; Dunning and Lundan, 2008) offered a general framework for the extent and pattern of international trade and foreign investment, based in part on the role of transaction costs. According to those views, multinational firms have opportunities to share their core competitive advantages among different geographic markets through the internalization of intangible assets. These theories can explain the emergence and growth of multinational firms. Related approaches include resource-based views, which are based on the concept of ownership advantage (Penrose, 1959). These views postulate that resources are the source of competitive advantages if they are valuable, rare and difficult to imitate. Resources include all assets, capabilities, organizational processes, information and human competences controlled by a firm that enable the firm to improve its effectiveness and efficiency.

Other theories include those about learning (Johanson and Vahlne, 1977), which predict increasing resource commitments to foreign markets over time as a result of the accumulation of organizational experience. In this case, internationalization is seen as the product of a series of incremental decisions and additional resources committed to foreign markets which affect the firm's perceived opportunities and risks. Moreover, economic theory predicts that the level of engagement with international business is strongly related to the efficiency of the firm. For instance, while the most productive firms will tend to export and/or invest in foreign plants, their least productive counterparts may only serve the domestic market (Melitz, 2003).

At the same time, international business may generate significant feedback effects in terms of enhanced productivity for those firms that do not restrict their operations to their home markets. A large literature has tested empirically this multinationality-performance (MP) relationship. In particular, several studies have examined the MP link by drawing on firm-level data, which allows one to control for a number of potential biases present in more aggregated data. However, this more recent firm-level literature has not yet produced a solid set of stylized facts, as suggested by surveys (Li, 2007) and meta-analysis (Yang and Driffield, forthcoming), even if these gaps may be explained in part by methodological and data set differences.

Our contribution

This chapter, which follows from our companion piece Yang and Martins (2010), departs from the empirical studies presented above in two major respects. First, we argue that the location choices of overseas investment – in particular the high/low IPR of the host country – may be a crucial aspect to explain the performance of multinational firms. Although strong IPR of the host countries can stimulate greater FDI inflows, countries with low IPR are likely to display a relatively low technology capability and large potential market, which are crucial factors for multinational firms to internalize their intangibles. Therefore, we believe these two types of countries should not be lumped together when assessing the effects of international expansion upon firm performance.

The second contribution made in this chapter concerns the analysis of a much wider range of multinational headquarter countries than in prior research. All previous studies consider only a single country (typically the US) or, alternatively, a small set of countries (again, the exception is Yang and Martins, 2010). This relatively small range of countries may raise questions concerning the representativeness of the evidence. In this context, our chapter makes an original contribution: we exploit comparable data for a very large number of firms (16,533 in total), covering almost all economic sectors from 46 countries, including many OECD countries and also some of the largest developing nations.

Data

Our analysis draws on Orbis, a data set that includes detailed accounting and financial information for the largest firms across the world. The data are collected and made available by Bureau van Dijk, a large international consultancy firm. According to Bureau van Dijk, the information in Orbis is sourced from different providers, all of which are experts in their regions, providing detailed descriptive information, in particular about the company financial status (see Yang and Martins (2010) for more details). The records of each company include information on whether the company has ownership stakes in its subsidiaries (defined as a minimum 25.01 per cent share control over its overseas subsidiary) and the subsidiary location. Therefore, we are able to calculate the ratio of subsidiaries in foreign countries in relation to its total number of subsidiaries – the measure of the extent of multinationality of a firm that we use in this chapter. The financial and operational information of the firms in our data is generally available for the period 1997–2006, but multinationality information is available only for the latest year in the data, which in most cases is 2006.

We consider firms that have information available on expenditure on investment, employees, assets, firm age, return on sales (ROS) and number of subsidiaries (including overseas subsidiaries). Firms without at least one of these variables are excluded from our sample. As all monetary measures are reported in home currencies, we convert them to Euro using exchange rates retrieved from the IMF.

Given access restrictions related to the cost of the data, we focused our analysis on the largest countries in the world and the largest firms in each country. In the data set that we consider, firms' home countries are therefore concentrated in the US, the European Union and some developing countries. There are significant numbers of firms based in France, Germany, Italy, Japan, the UK, the US and Taiwan. Moreover, we also find that the pattern of firm location is broadly consistent with typical patterns of investment.

Key variables

The main variables considered in this study are the following:

> *Firm Performance*: Several performance measures have been used in the MP literature, including accounting-based variables (return on assets, return on sales, etc.), market-based variables (Tobin's q, risk-adjusted returns, and so on), innovations, patents and technical efficiency. Accounting- and market-based variables became predominant in the last decade. In this chapter, multinational performance is measured using (consolidated) ROS, an accounting-based variable defined as after-tax profits divided by total sales.
>
> *Multinationality*: The most common aggregate multinationality measure used in the literature is the foreign sales to total sales ratio (FSTS). However, one problem with this variable is that the level of the firm's sales in foreign countries typically does not exclude intermediate goods exported from the home country and resold by its overseas subsidiaries, resulting in possible bias. Our chapter uses instead another common multinationality measurement, the ratio of the number of overseas subsidiaries in relation to all subsidiaries (OSTS), although a potential problem with the use of this kind of measure is assuming all subsidiaries are equally important, without taking into account such factors as their size and activity, which are not available in our data. We obtain this variable by exploiting the availability in our data set of information on whether the company has an ownership stake in its subsidiaries. We also draw on information about the subsidiary location to separate domestic from overseas subsidiaries.

However, as mentioned above, neither OSTS nor other typical measures of international involvement capture any differentiated effects from location choice upon performance. In particular, the costs and benefits associated with various country environments may vary widely. Our chapter remedies this by taking different location choices for overseas investment into consideration (Berry, 2006; Pantzalis, 2001; Qian et al. 2008). Specifically, we split the location of investments into high-IPR and low-IPR countries, using the latest World Bank definition.

In our data, countries with IPR levels higher (lower) than the average IPR across countries are defined as high- (low) IPR countries. High-IPR countries include the members of G8, most of the EU, Argentina, Australia, Bolivia, Botswana, Brazil, Chile, China, Colombia, Ecuador, El Salvador, Hong Kong, Iceland, India, Israel, Jordan, South Korea, Malaysia, Mexico, Morocco, New Zealand, Norway, Panama, Philippines, Singapore, South Africa, Switzerland, Trinidad and Tobago, Turkey and Ukraine. In contrast, low-IPR countries include Algeria, Angola, Bangladesh, Benin, Burkina Faso, Burundi, Cameroon, Central African Republic, Chad, Congo, Costa Rica, Côte d'Ivoire, Dominican Republic, Egypt, Ethiopia, Fiji, Gabon, Ghana, Grenada, Guatemala, Guyana, Haiti, Honduras, Indonesia, Iran, Iraq, Jamaica, Kenya, Liberia, Madagascar, Malawi, Mali, Mauritania, Mauritius, Mozambique, Nepal, Nicaragua, Niger, Nigeria, Pakistan, Papua New Guinea, Paraguay, Peru, Rwanda, Saudi Arabia, Senegal, Sierra Leone, Somalia, Sri Lanka, Sudan, Swaziland, Syrian Arab Republic, Tanzania, Thailand, Togo, Tunisia, Uganda, Venezuela, Vietnam, Zambia and Zimbabwe. We obtain Park and Ginarte's IPR index from the CEPII Distances Dataset.

We then measure the level of multinationality of each firm in three complementary ways: OSTS, the ratio of the number of overseas subsidiaries in relation to the firm's total subsidiaries; $OSTS^{H'ipr}$, the ratio of the number of subsidiaries in high-IPR countries relative to the firm's total subsidiaries; and $OSTS^{L'ipr}$, the ratio of the number of subsidiaries in low-IPR countries relative to the firm's total subsidiaries.

Intangible assets: According to the theoretical background described above, overseas subsidiaries can have opportunities to internalize the (intangible) assets of their multinational parents. Moreover, such assets may also facilitate the bargaining with host governments, in terms of subsidies, tax breaks or other concessions, given the potential for technological spillovers and other benefits to the host economy. (Worker mobility is one possible channel for such spillovers – see Martins, forthcoming.) While expenditures in R&D are typically used as a proxy for intangible assets (Allen and Pantzalis, 1996; Berry, 2006; Li et al. 2007; Lu and Beamish, 2004), we do not have this variable for most firms in our data set. We instead use the level of investment expenditure as a proxy for R&D expenditures. We also consider firm size as a proxy for the physical and financial resources of a firm, measured by the log of total assets (Pantzalis, 2001) and the log of the number of employees (Elango, 2004; Qian et al., 2008).

Other controls: We control for a number of other variables that may also influence firm performance and be correlated with multinationality, including firm age, ownership structure and business cycle (year) effects. Firm age is measured using information on the starting year of its operations (Qian et al., 2008), and ownership structure is controlled for by calculating the ratio of shares owned by foreign shareholders in relation to total shares (Pantzalis, 2001). We also control for industry (two-digit codes) and country effects.

Descriptive statistics

Table 6.1, below, presents summary statistics from our data set. It contains 38,294 firms, of which 21,761 are domestic and 16,533 are multinational (defined here as firms with at least one foreign subsidiary). The right panel of the table presents the descriptive statistics for firms with at least one subsidiary in an overseas country (multinational firms), and the left panel contains domestic firms.

The right panel of Table 6.1 shows that, on average, a multinational firm in our data has 20.8 subsidiaries, of which 9.9 are located overseas. Around 8.5 subsidiaries are located in high-IPR countries, while the remaining 1.4 are located in low-IPR countries. Fifty-eight per cent of the multinational subsidiaries are located

Table 6.1 Descriptive statistics – multinational and domestic firms

	Domestic firms			Multinational firms		
	Mean	Std. Dev.	Obs	Mean	Std. Dev.	Obs
Sales	433.78	6560.55	21760	1233.11	10652.29	16531
Return on sales	0.072	0.10	21761	0.084	0.10	16533
Subsidiaries	5.52	17.19	21761	20.82	51.92	16533
Dev	0.72	0.44	21761	0.75	0.43	16533
Overseas subsidiaries	0	0	21761	9.91	28.74	16533
$OS^{H'ipr}$	0	0	21761	6.98	22.16	16533
$OS^{L'ipr}$	0	0	21761	2.92	8.98	16533
OSTS	0	0	21761	0.58	0.32	16533
$OSTS^{H'ipr}$	0	0	21761	0.38	0.34	16533
$OSTS^{L'ipr}$	0	0	21761	0.20	0.28	16533
Firm age	27.91	27.51	21761	36.35	34.14	16533
Investment	26.051	153.90	21761	115.55	615.67	16533
Employment	1464.70	5592.15	21761	4808.10	24471.92	16533
Total assets	497.68	6980.73	21761	1372.64	11423.60	16533
Foreign ownership	8.52	25.95	21761	12.24	26.95	16533
Sector	47.96	20.57	21761	43.51	19.86	16533

Notes: All monetary variables are denominated in € millions. 'Multinational firms' are firms with at least one subsidiary in an overseas market; these comprise the sample for our subsequent analysis. 'All firms' are firms with at least one subsidiary. 'Subsidiaries' refers to the total number of subsidiaries; 'overseas subsidiaries' refers to the number of subsidiaries in foreign countries; 'dev' is the ratio of firms from developed countries in relation to total firms; $OS^{H'ipr}(OS^{L'ipr})$ is the number of subsidiaries in high- (low) IPR countries; OSTS refers to the ratio of number of overseas subsidiaries to total subsidiaries; and $OSTS^{H'ipr}$ ($OSTS^{L'ipr}$) is the ratio of subsidiaries in high- (low) IPR countries to total subsidiaries.

in overseas markets (OSTS); 38 per cent in high-IPR economies (OSTS$^{H'ipr}$), and 20 per cent in low-IPR countries (OSTS$^{L'ipr}$).

Multinational firms appear to be more productive than domestic firms. For instance, the average return on sales for multinational firms is 0.084, while for domestic firms it is 0.072. Multinational firms are also older (36 vs. 28 years); invest more (€116 vs. €26 million); are more capital intensive (€1,373 vs. €498 million); and have larger workforces (4,808 vs. 1,465 employees).

As we are also interested in highlighting any differences between multinationals based in developed and developing countries, we present a comparison of those two groups in Table 6.2, below. We find that a majority of multinational firms are headquartered in developed countries – 12,356 in developed and 4,177 in developing countries. The developed-country multinationals appear to be more productive than those in developing countries. For instance, the average return on sales for developed-country and developing-country multinational firms is 0.089 and 0.069 respectively.

Most overseas subsidiaries are located in high-IPR countries. On average, a developed-country multinational firm in our data set has 11.14 overseas subsidiaries, of which 9.74 are located in high-IPR countries. A developing-country

Table 6.2 Descriptive statistics – firms from developed versus developing countries

	Developed country firms			Developing country firms		
	Mean	Std. Dev.	Obs	Mean	Std. Dev.	Obs
Sales	1460.49	12203.67	12354	585.26	3245.90	4177
Return on sales	0.089	0.10	12356	0.069	0.09	4177
Subsidiaries	23.55	57.94	12356	12.74	25.51	4177
Overseas subsidiaries	11.14	31.74	12356	6.26	16.44	4177
Dev	1	0	12356	0	0	4177
OS$^{H'ipr}$	9.74	28.84	12356	4.89	14.96	4177
OS$^{L'ipr}$	1.40	4.71	12356	1.37	2.91	4177
OSTS	0.58	0.33	12356	0.56	0.32	4177
OSTS$^{H'ipr}$	0.47	0.35	12356	0.37	0.35	4177
OSTS$^{L'ipr}$	0.11	0.23	12356	0.19	0.28	4177
Firm age	39.15	35.93	12356	28.06	26.54	4177
Investment	141.01	735.25	12356	46.86	278.92	4177
Employment	5554.82	26900.51	12356	2599.22	14945.52	4177
Total assets	1635.86	13042.37	12356	612.74	3740.84	4177
Foreign ownership	13.06	26.75	12356	9.81	27.41	4177
Sector	44.30	20.01	12356	41.14	19.24	4177

Notes: All monetary variables are denominated in € millions. 'Subsidiaries' refers to the total number of subsidiaries; 'overseas subsidiaries' refers to the number of subsidiaries in foreign countries; 'dev' is the ratio of firms from developed countries in relation to total firms; OS$^{H'ipr}$ (OS$^{L'ipr}$) is the number of subsidiaries in high- (low) IPR countries; OSTS refers to the ratio of number of overseas subsidiaries to total subsidiaries; and OSTS$^{H'ipr}$(OSTS)$^{L'ipr}$ is the ratio of subsidiaries in high- (low) IPR countries to total subsidiaries.

Table 6.3 Descriptive statistics ($OSTS^{H'ipr}$ vs. $OSTS^{L'ipr}$)

	$OSTS^{H'ipr} \geq OSTS^{L'ipr}$			$OSTS^{H'ipr} < OSTS^{L'ipr}$		
	Mean	Std. Dev.	Obs	Mean	Std. Dev.	Obs
Sales	1337.82	6362.06	13235	843.88	20239.95	3296
Return on sales	0.084	0.10	13237	0.083	0.10	3296
Subsidiaries	23.49	56.16	13237	10.06	26.67	3296
Dev	0.78	0.41	13237	0.62	0.49	3296
Overseas subsidiaries	11.53	31.71	13237	3.36	7.16	3296
$OS^{H'ipr}$	10.49	28.83	13237	0.55	2.81	3296
$OS^{L'ipr}$	1.04	4.17	13237	2.81	4.65	3296
OSTS	0.58	0.32	13237	0.53	0.32	3296
$OSTS^{H'ipr}$	0.55	0.32	13237	0.03	0.08	3296
$OSTS^{L'ipr}$	0.03	0.08	13237	0.50	0.32	3296
Firm age	38.81	36.02	13237	26.46	22.69	3296
Investment	134.61	713.98	13237	47.39	283.21	3296
Employment	5342.45	26157.19	13237	2662.09	15829.00	3296
Total assets	1473.58	7619.98	13237	990.99	20569.90	3296
Foreign ownership	13.58	28.01	13237	6.84	21.41	3296
Sector	44.37	20.11	13237	40.02	18.46	3296

Notes: All monetary variables are denominated in € millions. 'Subsidiaries' refers to the total number of subsidiaries; 'overseas subsidiaries' refers to the number of subsidiaries in foreign countries; 'dev' is the ratio of firms from developed countries in relation to total firms; $OSTS^{H'ipr}(OS^{L'ipr})$ is the number of subsidiaries in high (low) IPR countries; OSTS refers to the ratio of number of overseas subsidiaries to total subsidiaries; and $OSTS^{H'ipr}(OSTS^{L'ipr})$ is the ratio of subsidiaries in high (low) IPR countries to total subsidiaries.

multinational firm has only 6.26 overseas subsidiaries, a majority – 4.89 – are located in high-IPR countries.

We next separate our sample of multinational firms by overseas investment location choice. Table 6.3, above, presents summary statistics for these two groups of firm. The left panel presents statistics for 13,237 multinational firms with more investment in high-IPR countries ($OSTS^{H'ipr} > OSTS^{L'ipr}$), and the right panel contains 3,296 multinationals with more investment in low-IPR countries ($OSTS^{H'ipr} < OSTS^{L'ipr}$). Firms with more investment in high-IPR countries have higher sales (€1,338 vs. €844 million); are older (39 vs. 26 years); invest more (€135 vs. €47 million); are more capital intensive (€1,474 vs. €991 million), and employ more people (5,342 vs. 2,662 employees). There is, however, no difference in profitability between these two groups of firms as measured by their returns on sales (0.084 vs. 0.083).

We present the distribution of return on sales across countries in Figure 6.1, below. For most of our sample firms, return on sales falls between 0 and 0.2. In Figure 6.2 we depict the distribution of multinationality (OSTS) across countries and the mean firm performance for each level of multinationality. This figure provides some (moderate) evidence of a positive relation between firm performance and multinationality. However, when breaking down our measure

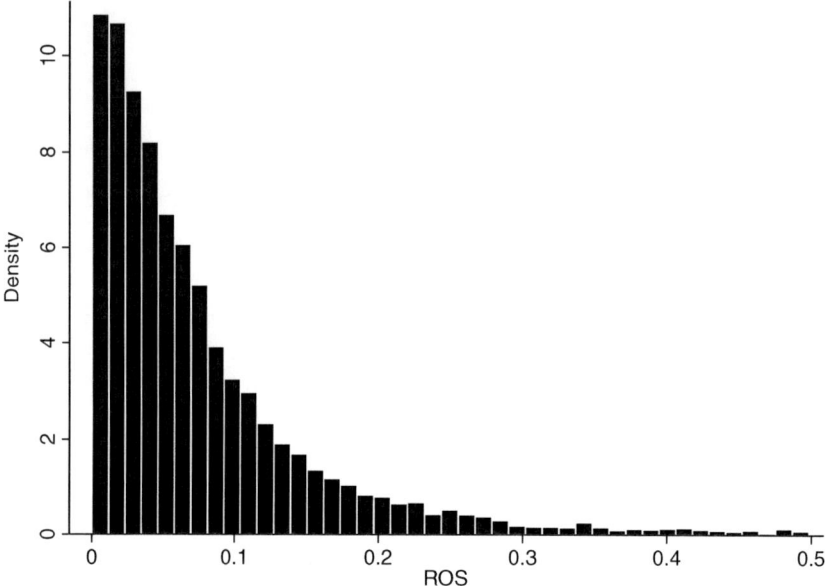

Figure 6.1 Distribution of multinational performance (ROS)
Note: ROS is return on sales.

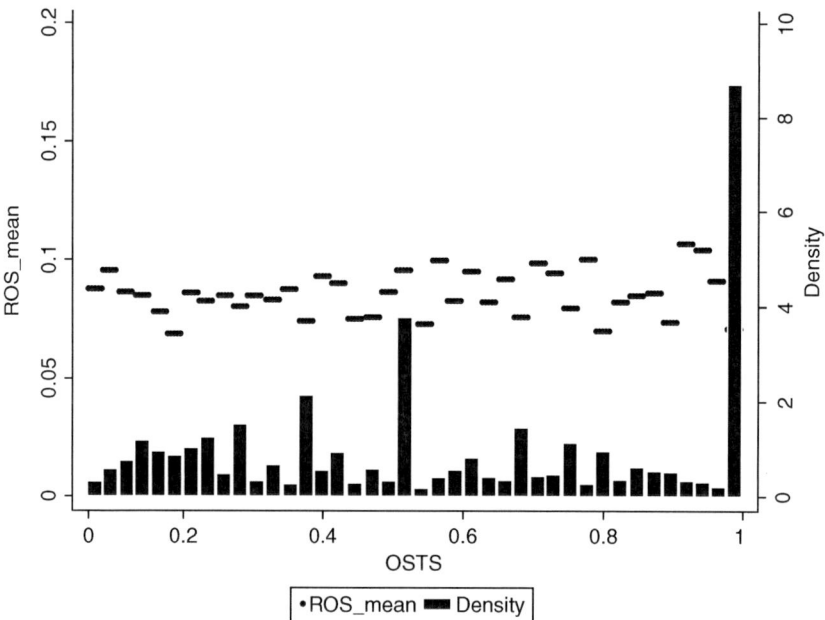

Figure 6.2 Distribution of multinationality (OSTS) and firm performance
Notes: In this figure, we depict the distribution of multinationality as measured by OSTS (Density) and the mean firm performance (ROS) for each level of multinationality OSTS is the ratio of number of overseas subsidiaries in relation to its total subsidiaries. All countries are weighted equally.

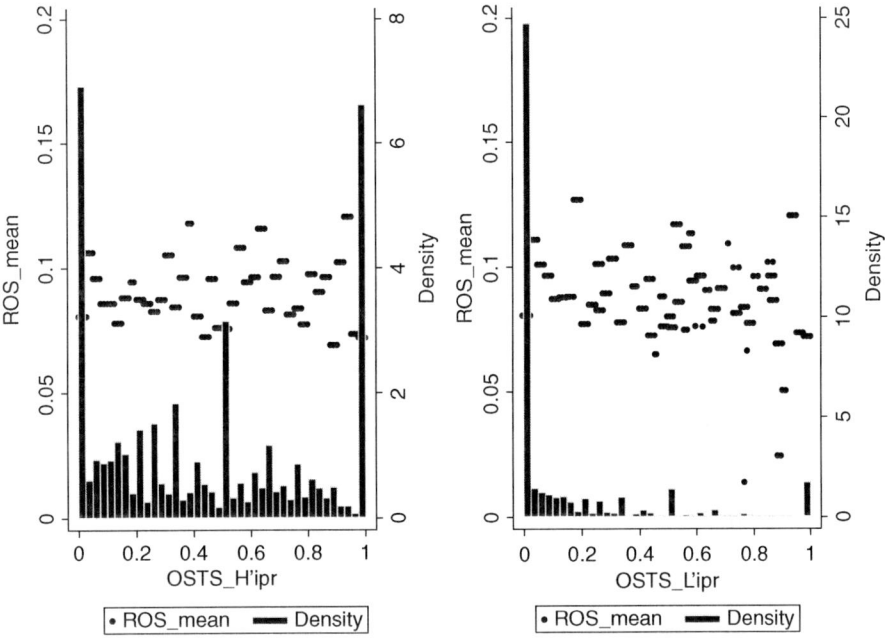

Figure 6.3 Distribution of multinationality (OSTS$^{H'ipr}$ & OSTS$^{L'ipr}$) and firm performance

Notes: OSTS$^{H'ipr}$ is the ratio of number of subsidiaries in high-IPR countries relative to total subsidiaries, and OSTS$^{L'ipr}$ is the ratio of number of subsidiaries in low-IPR countries relative to total subsidiaries.

of multinationality (OSTS) into its two components according to our definition (OSTS$^{H'ipr}$ and OSTS$^{L'ipr}$), as seen in Figure 6.3, above, there does not appear to be a clear pattern.

We also present a scatter-plot of the number of overseas subsidiaries in developed countries (OS$^{H'ipr}$) and developing countries (OS$^{L'ipr}$) in Figure 6.4. Here we find some evidence of a trade-off between the two variables, although most multinationals in our data set exhibit small numbers of high- and – especially – low-IPR country subsidiaries.

Results

We estimate the relation between multinationality and firm performance using the following equation:

$$Y_{it} = \beta_1 \text{OSTS}_{it}^{H'ipr} + \beta_2 \text{OSTS}_{it}^{L'ipr} + \lambda X_{it} + \gamma_t + e_{it} \quad (6.1)$$

where Y_{it} is the return on sales of firm i in year t; OSTS$_{it}$ refers to the ratio of number of foreign subsidiaries in relation to total subsidiaries over the same period; and OSTS$_{it}^{H'ipr}$ $\left(\text{OSTS}_{it}^{L'ipr}\right)$ is the ratio of number of overseas subsidiaries in high- (low) IPR countries in relation to total subsidiaries, that is, OSTS$_{it}$ = OSTS$_{it}^{H'ipr}$ + OSTS$_{it}^{L'ipr}$.

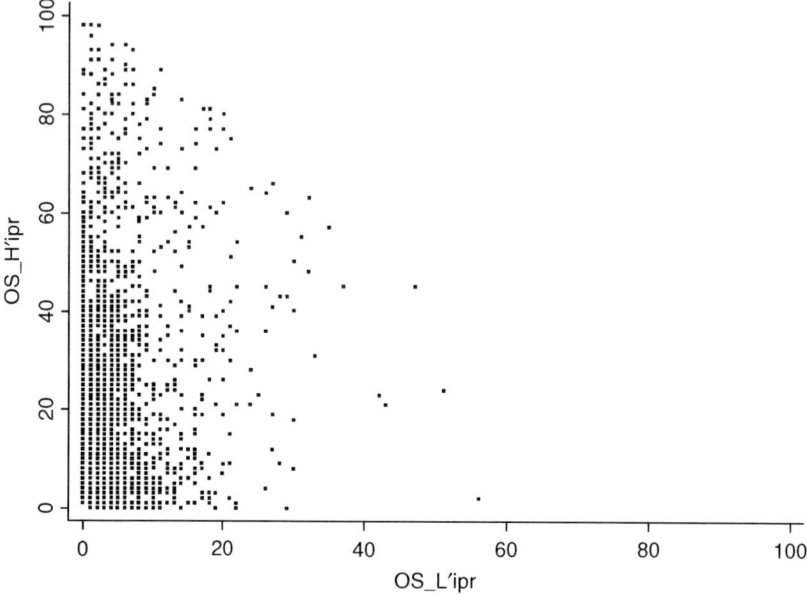

Figure 6.4 Scatterplot of the number of overseas subsidiaries in high- and low-IPR countries
Notes: The horizontal axis is the number of overseas subsidiaries in low-IPR countries, and the vertical axis presents the number of overseas subsidiaries in high-IPR countries.

The equation also includes control variables, including intangible assets, firm age, ownership structure, industry and country effects (X_{it}) and business cycle effects (γ_t). The key parameters are β_1 and β_2, which indicate the average change in performance attributed to changes in the overseas presence in high and low IPR countries, respectively. (For completeness, we also present results based on Yang and Martins (2010), in which the following version of the equation above is estimated: $Y_{it} = \beta OSTS_{it} + \lambda X_{it} + \gamma_t + e_{it}$.)

Table 6.4 reports our main estimates. The results presented in column 1 exclude any measure of multinationality. As can be seen, our control variables have the expected signs and size. For example, investment, assets and foreign ownership have a positive sign and are highly significant, suggesting that higher levels of these variables are associated with better firm performance. Moreover, these signs are largely unchanged across subsequent specifications in columns 2 to 5, when controls for different types of subsidiaries are included.

Importantly, we document a positive and significant relation between multinationality (as substituted by OSTS) and firm performance (Yang and Martins, 2010). The result in column 2 indicates that a 10 percentage-point increase in the ratio of overseas subsidiaries with respect to total subsidiaries translates into an increase of return on sales of 0.0013. Although this point estimate is small, it compares with a mean return on sales of 0.084, suggesting a significant economic effect. However, when we separate the estimation of the high and low IPR countries subsidiaries ratio (columns 3 and 4), we find that the high-IPR

Table 6.4 Multinationality and performance: linear effects

	(1)	(2)	(3)	(4)	(5)
OSTS		0.013***			
		(0.003)			
OSTS$^{H'ipr}$			0.007***		0.011***
			(0.003)		(0.003)
OSTS$^{L'ipr}$				0.017***	0.023***
				(0.004)	(0.004)
Investment	0.006***	0.006***	0.006***	0.006***	0.006***
	(0.0004)	(0.0004)	(0.0004)	(0.0004)	(0.0004)
Employment	−0.024***	−0.024***	−0.024***	−.024***	−.024***
	(0.0007)	(0.0007)	(0.0007)	(0.0007)	(0.0007)
Total assets	0.024***	0.024***	0.024***	0.024***	0.025***
	(0.0008)	(0.0008)	(0.0008)	(0.0008)	(0.0008)
Firm age	−0.00004	0.0004	0.0001	0.0001	0.0004
	(0.0008)	(0.0008)	(0.0008)	(0.0008)	(0.0008)
Foreign ownership	0.00009***	0.00009***	0.00009***	0.00009***	0.00009***
	(0.00003)	(0.00003)	(0.00003)	(0.00003)	(0.00003)
Const.	−0.333***	−0.349***	−0.339***	−0.340***	−0.351***
	(0.028)	(0.028)	(0.028)	(0.028)	(0.028)
Obs.	16533	16533	16533	16533	16533
R^2	0.187	0.189	0.188	0.188	0.189

Notes: The dependent variable is return on sales. OSTS refers to the ratio of number of overseas subsidiaries relative to total subsidiaries; OSTS$^{H'ipr}$(OSTS$^{L'ipr}$) is the ratio of subsidiaries in high- (low) IPR countries to total subsidiaries. 'Firm Age', 'Investment', 'Employment' and 'Total Assets' are in logarithms. All columns above include a full set of fixed effects, including sector, region and year dummies. Values in parentheses are standard errors. Significance levels: *: 0.10; **: 0.05; ***: 0.01.

subsidiaries ratio coefficient is 0.007 (and significant at the 1 per cent level), but the low-IPR subsidiaries ratio coefficient is more than twice as large, at 0.017 (and also is significant at the 1 per cent level). Finally, in column 5 we control both for high- and low-IPR subsidiaries ratios, following the specification of equation (6.1). We find that controlling for the low-IPR subsidiaries ratio increases the size of the high-IPR coefficient (0.011, significant at the 1 per cent level). Similarly, when controlling for high-IPR subsidiaries ratio, the low-IPR countries coefficient increases (0.023).

From this set of results, we conclude that the relation between multinationality and performance appears to be positive. When separating the sample between overseas subsidiaries in high- and low-IPR countries, we find the return from overseas subsidiaries in low-IPR countries appears to be much larger than that from subsidiaries in high-IPR countries.

Robustness

To check the robustness of our previous results, we now conduct estimates under different specifications. In particular, we split our sample by the developed/developing status of the home country of the multinational. Our interest

Table 6.5 Multinationality and performance: firms from developed countries

	(1)	(2)	(3)	(4)	(5)
OSTS		0.015***			
		(0.003)			
OSTS$^{H'ipr}$			0.008**		0.012***
			(0.003)		(0.003)
OSTS$^{L'ipr}$				0.024***	0.030***
				(0.005)	(0.006)
Investment	0.006***	0.006***	0.006***	0.006***	0.006***
	(0.0005)	(0.0005)	(0.0005)	(0.0005)	(0.0005)
Employment	−.025***	−0.025***	−0.025***	−0.025***	−0.025***
	(0.0008)	(0.0008)	(0.0008)	(0.0008)	(0.0008)
Total assets	0.025***	0.026***	0.025***	0.026***	0.026***
	(0.0009)	(0.0009)	(0.0009)	(0.0009)	(0.0009)
Firm age	−0.0003	0.0001	−.0002	−0.00007	0.0002
	(0.001)	(0.001)	(0.001)	(0.001)	(0.001)
Foreign ownership	0.00006*	0.00005	0.00006*	0.00006*	0.00005
	(0.00003)	(0.00003)	(0.00003)	(0.00003)	(0.00003)
Const.	−0.357***	−0.379***	−0.365***	−0.365***	−0.381***
	(0.037)	(0.037)	(0.037)	(0.037)	(0.037)
Obs.	12356	12356	12356	12356	12356
R^2	0.189	0.19	0.189	0.19	0.191

Notes: The dependent variable is return on sales. OSTS refers to the ratio of number of overseas subsidiaries relative to total subsidiaries; OSTS$^{H'ipr}$(OSTS$^{L'ipr}$) is the ratio of subsidiaries in high (low) IPR countries to total subsidiaries. 'Firm Age', 'Investment', 'Employment' and 'Total Assets' are in logarithms. All columns above include a full set of fixed effects, including sector, region and year dummies. Values in parentheses are standard errors. Significance levels: *: 0.10; **: 0.05; ***: 0.01.

in this decomposition follows from the evidence of an increasing number of multinationals emerging from developing countries, contrasting with the focus in the literature on multinationals based in the US (and, to a lesser extent, other developed countries). Table 6.5, above, presents our results with the sample comprising multinationals based in developed countries only. We find, similarly to the results for all firms, a positive effect from foreign presence; in particular the presence in low-IPR countries. In column 5, when controlling both for high- and low-IPR subsidiaries, we find that the low-IPR countries' coefficient is again much bigger than the high-IPR subsidiaries' coefficient (0.030 vs. 0.012). All coefficients are significant at the 1 per cent level.

Next we consider only those multinationals that have their headquarters in developing countries; our results can be found in Table 6.6. As expected, the number of observations in this analysis falls considerably, with possible implications in terms of the statistical significance of the results. Again we find a positive effect from overseas expansion on multinational performance: the OSTS coefficient in column 2 is 0.009 and significant at the 5 per cent level. However, when decomposing the effects by either developed or developing subsidiaries, we find that both coefficients are again positive but none are significant at standard

Table 6.6 Multinationality and performance: firms from developing countries

	(1)	(2)	(3)	(4)	(5)
OSTS		0.009**			
		(0.004)			
OSTS$^{H'ipr}$			0.006		0.009*
			(0.004)		(0.005)
OSTS$^{L'ipr}$				0.006	0.011
				(0.006)	(0.007)
Investment	0.005***	0.005***	0.005***	0.006***	0.005***
	(0.0007)	(0.0007)	(0.0008)	(0.0008)	(0.0008)
Employment	−0.018***	−0.018***	−0.018***	−0.018***	−0.018***
	(0.001)	(0.001)	(0.001)	(0.001)	(0.001)
Total assets	0.019***	0.019***	0.019***	0.019***	0.019***
	(0.001)	(0.001)	(0.001)	(0.001)	(0.001)
Firm age	0.001	0.002	0.002	0.002	0.002
	(0.002)	(0.002)	(0.002)	(0.002)	(0.002)
Foreign ownership	0.0002***	0.0002***	0.0002***	0.0002***	0.0002***
	(0.00005)	(0.00005)	(0.00005)	(0.00005)	(0.00005)
Const.	−0.214***	−0.223***	−0.216***	−0.217***	−0.224***
	(0.044)	(0.044)	(0.044)	(0.044)	(0.044)
Obs.	4177	4177	4177	4177	4177
R^2	0.17	0.171	0.17	0.17	0.171

Notes: The dependent variable is return on sales. OSTS refers to the ratio of number of overseas subsidiaries relative to total subsidiaries; OSTS$^{H'ipr}$(OSTS$^{L'ipr}$) is the ratio of subsidiaries in high (low) IPR countries to total subsidiaries. 'Firm Age', 'Investment', 'Employment' and 'Total Assets' are in logarithms. All columns above include a full set of fixed effects, including sector, region and year dummies. Values in parentheses are standard errors. Significance levels: *: 0.10; **: 0.05; ***: 0.01.

levels. Finally, when controlling simultaneously for foreign penetration in both developed and developing countries, the latter coefficients are larger, but not significant.

Conclusions

The literature on the relation between multinationality and performance is almost exclusively based on data from particular home countries (typically the US) and a period of time focused on the 1990s. More importantly, the literature typically does not distinguish between host economies. In this paper, we have distinguished between host economies by their level of IPR. The extent to which a firm's intellectual property is protected by the host country is potentially of great importance to a multinational's performance.

In this chapter, we have examined a large sample of over 16,000 multinationals from 46 countries over the period 1997–2006. Our central finding is that the positive relation between multinationality and performance is larger when firms invest in low-IPR countries. In other words, our estimates show that the effect of investing abroad is stronger when the subsidiary is in a low-IPR-country compared to high-IPR-country subsidiaries. We interpret these results – which corroborate our earlier findings (Yang and Martins, 2010) – as indicating that the potential of globalization, in particular by increasing investment in low-IPR countries (which are typically developing countries), has not yet been met by multinational firms. Geographical diversification into low-IPR countries may be an important source of competitive advantage that deserves more serious consideration from business leaders and academics alike. Moreover, the most promising expansion strategies may involve setting up subsidiaries in several developing countries rather than just a small number of such countries. This can be rationalized by taking into account not only the many obstacles in low-IPR (developing) countries, but also the similarities of such obstacles across developing countries and the consequent economies of scale of a more ambitious international investment approach.

One limitation to our study is the cross-sectional nature of our data set. This prevents us from relating the changes in multinationality within firms to the changes in their performance over time, holding constant time-invariant factors that may affect both multinationality and firm performance. Stronger IPR enforcement lowers the costs of enforcing contracts (e.g. monitoring and litigation costs), mitigating the cost of technology transfer (Contractor, 1980). Since multinational enterprises dominate the production of technology, stricter IPR in host countries would improve multinational performance given the returns they obtain from technology licensing in those locations.

In contrast, firms may prefer to locate subsidiaries in countries that are clearly technologically inferior so as to protect themselves against ready imitation, for such countries' overseas subsidiaries are less sensitive to IPR protection. Zhao (2006) also shows that IPR distance is less relevant in inter-organisational transfer of technological knowledge, and firms can choose to locate development activities in weak IPR locations so as to minimize the risk of knowledge dissipation. However, the literature pays little attention to the relation between changes in IPR and changes in internationalization practices. We are trying to get information on the location of subsidiaries across years, which would allow us to analyse the role of IPR changes in the host country on multinational performance.

Given the emphasis that IB theory places on the location advantage, and more recently to technology and/or innovation in particular, it is perhaps surprising that the literature pays so little attention to the possibility of reverse causality. Our estimates also do not rule out some form of reverse causality or sample selection: for instance, perhaps only sufficiently profitable multinationals can afford to establish subsidiaries in low-IPR countries. We leave these topics for future research.

Acknowledgements

We thank comments from an anonymous referee. We also thank Elaine Hutson and conference participants at AIB-UKI (Dublin). We are responsible for all errors.

References

Allen, L. and Pantzalis, C. (1996) 'Valuation of the operating flexibility of multinational corporations', *Journal of International Business Studies*, 27(4), 633–53.

Berry, H. (2006) 'Shareholder valuation of foreign investment and expansion', *Strategic Management Journal*, 27(12), 1123–40.

Buckley, P.J. and Casson, M. (1976) *The Future of the Multinational Enterprise* (New York: Palgrave MacMillan).

Contractor, F.J. (1980) 'The composition of licensing fees and arrangements as a function of economic development of technology recipient nations', *Journal of International Business Studies*, 11(3), 47–63.

Dunning, J.H. (1988) 'The theory of international production', *International Trade Journal*, 31(1), 21–46.

Dunning, J.H. and Lundan, M. (2008) *Multinational Enterprises and the Global Economy* (Cheltenham, UK/Northampton, USA: Edward Elgar Publishing).

Elango, B. (2004) 'Geographic scope of operations by multinational companies: an exploratory study of regional and global strategies', *European Management Journal*, 22(4), 431–41.

Goerzen, A. and Beamish, P.W. (2003) 'Geographic scope and multinational enterprise performance', *Strategic Management Journal*, 24(13), 1289–306.

Hymer, S. (1960) *The International Operations of National Firms: A Study of Direct Foreign Investment* (Cambridge MA: MIT Press).

Johanson, J. and Vahlne, J.E. (1977) 'The internationalization process of the firm – a model of knowledge development and increasing foreign market commitments', *Journal of International Business Studies*, 8(1), 23–32.

Li, L. (2007) 'Multinationality and performance: a synthetic review and research agenda', *International Journal of Management Reviews*, 9(2), 117–39.

Li, L., Qian, M.G. and Qian, M.Z. (2007) 'Product diversification, multinationality, and country involvement: what is the optimal combination?', *Journal of Global Marketing*, 20(4), 5–23.

Lu, J.W. and Beamish, P.W. (2004) 'International diversification and firm performance: the S-curve hypothesis', *The Academy of Management Journal*, 47(4), 598–609.

Martins, P.S. (forthcoming) 'Paying more to hire the best? Foreign firms, wages and worker mobility', *Economic Inquiry*.

Melitz, J.M. (2003) 'The impact of trade on intra-industry reallocations and aggregate industry productivity', *Econometrica*, 71(6), 1695–725.

Pangarkar, N. (2008) 'Internationalization and performance of small- and medium-sized enterprises', *Journal of World Business*, 43(4), 475–85.

Pantzalis, C. (2001) 'Does location matter? An empirical analysis of geographic scope and MNC market valuation', *Journal of International Business Studies*, 32(1), 133–55.

Penrose, E.T. (1959) *The Theory of the Growth of the Firm* (Oxford: Basil Blackwell).

Qian, G.M., Li, L., Li, J. and Qian, Z.M. (2008) 'Regional diversification and firm performance', *Journal of International Business Studies*, 39(2), 197–214.

Rugman, A.M. (1986) 'New theories of the multinational enterprise: an assessment of internalization theory', *Bulletin of Economic Research*, 38(2), 101–18.

Tallman, S. and Li, J. (1996) 'Effects of international diversity and product diversity on the performance of multinational firms', *Academy of Management Journal*, 39(1), 179–96.

Vernon, R. (1966) 'International investment and international trade in the product cycle', *Quarterly Journal of Economics*, 80(2), 190–207.

World Bank (2001) 'Intellectual property: balancing incentives with competitive access', in Richard Newfarmer, Uri Dadush and Nicholas Stern (eds) *Global Economic Prospects*, 129–50 (Washington, DC: World Bank).

Yang, Y and Driffield, N (forthcoming) 'Multinationality-performance relationship: A meta-analysis', *Management International Review*, forthcoming.

Yang, Y. and Martins, P.S. (2010) 'Firm performance and the geography of FDI: evidence from 46 countries', *Working Paper 30, Queen Mary Centre for Globalisation Research*.

Zhao, M.Y. (2006) 'Conducting R&D in countries with weak intellectual property rights protection', *Management Science*, 52(8), 1185–99.

7
The Influence of Exports on Outward Foreign Direct Investment: The Case of India

Rakhi Verma and Louis Brennan

Introduction

The past decade has witnessed increasing internationalization of developing countries' economic activities, and this has become a permanent, sizeable and rising feature of the world economy. This phenomenon has taken place in the context of a progressive liberalization of international economic relations, which has led to a spectacular increase in both goods and services exchange as well as capital movements (Kumar, 2007; Pradhan, 2007a). India has recently embarked on the path of globalization through outward investment. At the same time, India's exports have grown much faster than GDP over the past few decades (Sharma, 2000). In nominal terms, Indian outward foreign direct investment (OFDI) increased about 160-fold, from US$80 million to $12.9 billion between 1981 and 2006, and exports rose during the same period 14-fold, from $8 billion to $120 billion. The conceptual models of foreign direct investment (FDI) and international trade have traditionally been developed separately (UNCTAD, 1996). The integration of FDI and trade theories is still in its infancy, and research on their possible linkages is sparse.

Before addressing the scope of this chapter and the methodology used, it is important to highlight the importance of this study. A country's OFDI–exports relation may depend on industry or sector type, but there is a need to explain the OFDI–exports relation on a macroeconomic level using aggregate data. Such an analysis allows cross-country studies; an important issue is whether OFDI from countries pursuing export-oriented policies grows faster than those not pursuing such policies. An understanding of the linkages between OFDI and exports will help governments harmonize their policies for growth and development.

Our aim in this chapter is to analyse the empirical relation between OFDI and exports for India at the macroeconomic level by means of Granger-causality tests in a cointegration framework. Using this approach, the existence of a long-run relation among two or more non-stationary processes is tested by examining the stability of deviations from the relation using the coefficients estimated by fitting static regressions.

Overview of Indian OFDI and exports

Outward foreign direct investment

The first policy guidelines came into existence in 1969, and they heralded a restrictive regime for Indian OFDI activities. The concept of 'two waves' has been described for Indian OFDI. The first wave (1970–91) was entirely different from the second wave (1991 onwards) in terms of both the policy objectives of the Indian government and the strategies adopted by Indian firms to invest abroad. In the first phase, the goal of the Indian government was to use OFDI as a tool of 'south-south cooperation' (Pradhan, 2007a). The approval procedure for OFDI was cumbersome, and the policy towards home companies investing abroad was restrictive – there were restrictions, for example, on the extent of ownership participation, cash transfer against overseas investment, and exports of secondhand and reconditioned machinery for OFDI. It should be noted, however, that during the first wave the Indian government's policy was to promote its OFDI abroad, specifically for exporting purposes. Exports of home-made machinery and equipment against OFDI were provided, with normal fiscal benefits granted to commodity exports under the trade policy, such as grants of import replenishment licences, cash compensatory support for exports, deferred payment facilities, tax exemption for dividend receipts, and technical and other service payments received from abroad.

In the second wave of Indian OFDI, the basic objective of OFDI policy shifted from 'south-south cooperation' to the strategic objective of 'global competitiveness'. Policymakers realized that OFDI, rather than merely supporting exports, is a strategic tool that can help Indian firms to acquire new technologies, skills and other competitive assets urgently required for survival and growth in a globalizing world economy. Since the start of the second phase in 1991, India has expanded the geographical scope of bilateral investment agreements (BITs) to a large number of countries. BITs provide reciprocal encouragement and facilitation for bilateral investment flows between two countries, and contain a legal framework for investment protection. The rapid growth of the Indian economy in the last decade has bolstered the confidence of domestic enterprises to cross borders with relatively aggressive investments, resulting in a spate of acquisitions (Gubbi et al., 2009).

Export performance

From independence until the early 1960s, the growth of Indian exports was stagnant (Cohen, 1964). Two notable developments have taken place in India's export sector since the 1970s. First, exports have grown much faster than its GDP. Second, there has been a substantial change in India's export mix. Several factors appear to have contributed to these developments, namely the real depreciation of the exchange rate, liberalization in investment policy (especially from the early 1980s) and the provision of export subsidies to reduce the anti-export bias created by the import substitution policy. Export subsidies, which took many forms such as duty draw-back, subsidized credit and direct subsidies, helped reduce the bias against exports. Joshi and Little (1994) attributed a considerable part of the success in export expansion during the second half of the 1980s to the management of the real exchange rate. After 1986, Indian exports grew considerably faster than world trade and as fast as exports from comparable developing countries (Joshi and Little, 1994). A sharp devaluation of the Indian rupee after the early 1990s further strengthened export growth, despite some slowdown in exports during the macroeconomic crisis of the early 1990s and the 1997–8 Asian crisis.

While India's manufacturing exports lag far behind those of other Asian countries (both in quantity and quality), India is performing very well in services exports. India's share in world exports of services doubled from 0.6 per cent in 1990 to 1.2 per cent in 2001, while exports of goods rose only from 0.5 per cent to 0.7 per cent. The rapid growth of the services sector in the domestic economy has thus been associated with an increase in competitiveness in world markets.

Historically, one of the important policy objectives of promoting Indian OFDI was that it should serve as a vehicle for promoting exports with minimal adverse effect on foreign exchange reserves (Pradhan, 2007b). In the first wave, the Indian government's OFDI policies insisted that overseas investment had to be non-cash – such as exports of home-made machinery, equipment and technical know-how – and only a small cash remittance was permitted for meeting preliminary expenses related to the setting up of the overseas unit. Indian equity participation in overseas projects was therefore intended to exploit the potential export benefits of Indian OFDI. In the second wave, resort was increasingly made to OFDI as a means of developing trade-supporting networks abroad. The creation of customer care and service centres abroad ensured timely after-sales services to global customers and improved exports from the home country (Pradhan, 2007b). Particularly since 2001, Indian firms are investing overseas for many other reasons – not just for export promotion.

Figures 7.1 and 7.2 depict the quantity in US dollars of Indian OFDI and exports respectively, for the period 1981–2006. It is clear that Indian exports and OFDI began to grow rapidly (but at different magnitudes) at about the same

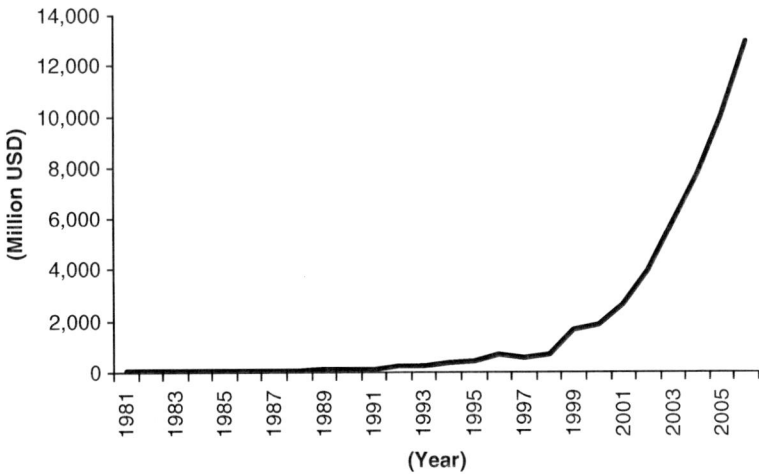

Figure 7.1 Indian OFDI (1981–2006)

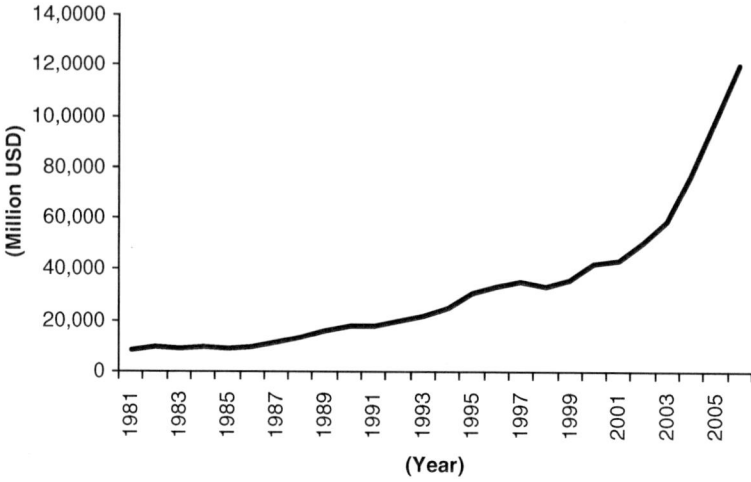

Figure 7.2 Indian exports (1981–2006)

time – around the mid-1990s. The effect of this accelerated internationalization on growth and domestic employment in the Indian economy depends, among other factors, on the relation between FDI and exports (Pfaffermayr, 1994). One major potential impact of OFDI is the trade effect, particularly on the exports of the home country. Theoretical arguments for the relation between FDI and trade have suggested that the two complement one another or are substitutes.

In relation to the substitute-complementary issue, the causal relationship between trade and FDI is complicated, and depends on the types of trade and FDI being considered. Studies suggest that empirical investigations in assessing true FDI–trade relation are warranted (Liu et al., 2001). However, despite the growth experienced by both exports and OFDI in recent years, the relation between them has not been extensively explored (Bajo and Montero, 2001). Taking the Indian economy as a case study, this chapter attempts to understand how exports affect OFDI.

Literature review

In the international economics and business literature, the following two aspects of possible linkages between OFDI and exports are discussed: (1) whether OFDI is a substitute for, or a complement to, exports; and (2) whether OFDI causes exports, or the other way round. The theoretical literature on both international trade and the behaviour of multinational firms does not give a clear indication as to whether foreign production is a substitute for, or a complement to, international trade (Pain and Wakelin, 1998). Overseas investment is postulated to follow the initial exploration of overseas markets through exports in the product cycle theory (Vernon, 1966). OFDI for building trade-supporting infrastructure abroad, like distribution networks, customer care centres and service centres, could help to improve exports of the final product. The overseas investments boom during the 1990s by developing country enterprises (such as Indian enterprises) was motivated to support and assist export markets with a local presence, develop marketing networks and provide after-sales services (Kumar, 1998).

The Uppsala model suggests that the internationalization process of the firm is most closely associated with its exports (Johanson and Vahlne, 1977, 1990, 1992; Johanson and Wiedersheim-Paul, 1975). The model distinguishes four different modes of entering an international market, where the successive stages represent higher degrees of international involvement.

Step 1: No regular export activities.
Step 2: Export via independent representatives (agents).
Step 3: Establishment of an overseas sales subsidiary.
Step 4: Overseas production/manufacturing units.

Markusen (1984) shows that OFDI and exports can be complementary, provided that the basis for trade is something other than differences in factor endowments. Helpman (1984) and Helpman and Krugman (1985) illustrate that the degree of specialization is a positive function of relative factor endowments. If differences in factor endowments are not substantial, a capital-abundant country will produce capital-intensive differentiated goods at home and exchange them for the labour-intensive homogeneous goods from a labour-abundant country. However, if there are substantial differences in factor endowments, the capital-abundant country tends to export headquarters' services such as R&D into the labour-abundant country in exchange for finished varieties of a differentiated good and a homogeneous good, rather than simply exporting the differentiated good. Thus, FDI generates complementary trade flows from the labour-intensive country. In addition, parent firms may export intermediate inputs to their subsidiaries if vertical integration is involved. A positive relation between OFDI and exports has also been mentioned by Wagner (1991).

A two-stage least squares estimation by Veugelers (1991) shows a significant impact of FDI flows between OECD countries on their exports. Petri (1994) argues that the relation is not predictable because the trade impact of FDI can be influenced by a range of factors such as firm strategies, motivation for FDI and government policies. Lin (1995) estimates exports and imports equations augmented with several FDI variables for Taiwan vis-à-vis four ASEAN countries (Indonesia, Malaysia, the Philippines and Thailand), and finds a positive and significant effect for OFDI on exports. Pfaffermayr (1996) argues that OFDI and exports can have common determinants such as capital, labour, skill and R&D intensities. Within this endogenous framework, Pfaffermayr (1996) estimates a simultaneous equations system using time-series and cross-sectional industry-level data from Austrian manufacturing and finds a significant complementary relation between FDI and exports in the 1980s and early 1990s.

Another theory states that the impact on trade depends on the type of FDI it stimulates (Markusen et al., 1996; Markusen, 1998). If FDI is vertical – where multinational firms geographically split stages of production – it is likely to stimulate trade. However, if FDI is horizontal – where multinational firms produce final goods in multiple locations – it is likely to substitute for trade. Dunning (1998) suggests that the relation between trade and FDI is conditional on the kind of trade and FDI being considered and the conditions under which each takes place.

While some attention has been paid to the substitution-complement relations, explicit testing for causality between FDI and trade is rare, the exceptions being Pfaffermayr (1996) and Liu et al. (2001). The causality relation between India's exports and its OFDI has not been investigated so far, although there are few studies that have attempted to understand the importance of exports for OFDI. For example, Lall (1986) surveyed 162 Indian enterprises, including 24 foreign investors, during 1977–9 and revealed that impediments to exports provided an incentive for OFDI. Dasgupta and Siddharthan (1985) and Agarwal (1985) found interdependence between Indian exports and OFDI during late 1970s and early 1980s in sectors comprising largely standardized goods and with relatively low skill and technological content. Similar analysis was reported by Pradhan (2007a, 2007b), in which he applied data from 3,951 manufacturing firms during 1990 and 2000. Since the study covered only manufacturing firms, it does not provide any comprehensive conclusions on the export–OFDI relation on a macroeconomic level.

Data and methodology

Our analysis is based on annual data covering OFDI stocks and exports from 1981 to 2006. Both of the variables are in log form. The two variables are identified as follows:

EX: Total exports in year i
OFDI: Outward foreign direct investment stocks in year i.

The earlier published data on investment projects abroad and at home understates the true magnitude of Indian investments for several reasons. Some existing foreign investment projects have not been properly registered, subsidiaries were generally left out, and the measurement of the size of the investment has been inadequate (Morris, 1987). As a consequence of these shortcomings, the Indian government revised (starting in November 2002) its computation of FDI figures in line with the best international practice and based on the recommendations of a committee set up to examine the issue. This led to a substantial improvement in FDI numbers (Jha, 2003). The UNCTAD data – which corrects for this problem – is therefore used here for the chosen period.

The reason for the 1981 start date is mainly because at that time the Indian Prime Minister Rajiv Gandhi introduced an outward-orientated industrialization policy, and India began to open its economy to the rest of the world. Although the Indian economy became truly open only after 1991, the period of the 1980s cannot be ignored for two reasons. First, the growth of Indian exports during this time was immense; exports increased twofold between 1981 and 90 and 1991 and 2000. Second, policymakers introduced OFDI in the 1980s as an export promotion tool, so it is likely that some outward investment was undertaken then in order to benefit from the extra facilities provided by the Indian government to exporters. The potentially important influence of government intervention on OFDI is necessarily omitted as the Indian government has consistently encouraged FDI and trade, particularly exports, during the sample period 1981–2006.

For the time-series data, the first step is to test the stationarity property of the variables. It is well known that standard regression techniques may produce spurious results if the variables under consideration contain unit roots and are non-stationary. In spurious regressions, the results suggest that there are statistically significant relations among the variables when in fact they merely reflect a contemporaneous correlation, not a causal relation. Studies on domestic investment, foreign investment and business cycles suggest that macroeconomic variables may be cointegrated (King et al., 1991; Love and Lage-Hidalgo, 2000). Therefore, it is important to test whether the variables under the study are cointegrated and have a long-run relation. Augmented Dickey–Fuller (ADF) tests are applied to detect the integration order of the variables, and cointegration is tested using the Johansen and Juselius (1990) procedure in which two tests are conducted based on the maximal Eigenvalue and trace test; and the maximum likelihood method is used to test for the presence of a cointegrating relation between the economic variables.

To investigate the causality between OFDI and exports we perform a simple Granger causality test, augmented with an appropriate error-correction term (ECT) derived from the long-run cointegrating relation of OFDI and exports. The concept of causality was initially defined by Granger (1969) in a Vector autoregressive (VAR) representation. However, the standard VAR which is derived from difference data are mis-specified if the variables are cointegrated because the ECTs are excluded (MacDonald and Kearney, 1987). In a bivariate framework, the Granger causality tests are performed by the following two equations:

$$x_t = \alpha_0 + \sum_{i=1}^{k} \alpha_i y_{t-i} + \text{ECT}_{t-1} + \varepsilon_t \tag{7.1}$$

$$y_t = \gamma_0 + \sum_{i=1}^{k} \gamma_i x_{t-i} + \text{ECT}_{t-1} + \sqrt{t} \tag{7.2}$$

In equation (7.1), H_0: $\alpha_i = 0$ for $i = 1, \ldots, k$ and H_1: $\alpha_i \neq 0$ for at least one i, and in equation (7.2), H_0: $\gamma_i = 0$ for $i = 1, \ldots, k$ and H_1: $\gamma_i \neq 0$ for at least one i.

The variable 'y' Granger causes variable 'x' if the null hypothesis (H_0) in equation (7.1) is rejected. Similarly, the variable 'x' Granger causes variable 'y' if H_0 in equation (7.2) is rejected. The variable 'x' is exports and 'y' is OFDI, where as α and γ represent short-run influences on dependent variable and ECT is derived from long-run cointegrating relation.

Results

Prior to testing for a causality relation between the time-series, it is necessary to establish that they are integrated of the same order. First, the ADF test for unit roots in both the variables was performed for levels and first differences of the natural log values. Both the variables under consideration are not stationary in their levels, but become stationary when they are first differenced. The results, with both level and first differenced data, are presented in Table 7.1.

Henceforth, the first differenced data for both variables will be used. Once the absence of a unit root was confirmed, we performed the Johansen cointegration test. It is well documented in the econometric literature that a crucial factor in using the Johansen procedure is the lag length. Cheung and Lai (1993) also point to the importance of proper lag specifications in estimating cointegrated systems. Though questions about optimal lags are raised in the literature, the issue of the best statistical method to use in determining the optimal lags in Granger causality tests is unsolved (Amoateng and Amoako-Adu, 1996).

Cheung and Lai (1993) suggested that for autoregressive processes, standard lag selection criteria such as the Akaike's information criterion (AIC) can be used for choosing the right lag order for Johansen's tests. AIC has been found to be a better criterion than the other criteria in the case of small samples (Liew, 2004). In examining the cointegration between exports and imports in Malaysia, Baharumshah et al. (2003) confirmed a two-lag length of VAR for the Johansen tests based on the AIC. Following these studies, we found a seven-lag length appropriate for our study. The results of the cointegration test are presented in Table 7.2.

We find that the two variables are cointegrated with rank 1 and have a long-run relation. The evidence of cointegration between variables rules out the possibility

Table 7.1 Augmented Dickey–Fuller tests for unit roots

Variables	Specification	Lag	Level		First difference	
				p-value		p-value
L_OFDI	Constant	0	1.483	0.999	−5.442	0.001
	Constant	1	1.884	1.000	−3.544	0.007
	Constant and trend	2	−1.750	0.723	−3.519	0.037
L_EX	Constant	3	1.121	0.998	−3.112	0.026
	Constant with trend	3	−2.055	0.571	−3.430	0.047

Notes: Null hypothesis: log OFDI and log exports contain a unit root.

Table 7.2 Cointegration tests

Null	Eigenvalue	Trace test	p-value	Lmax test	p-value
Rank = 0	0.9937	99.397	0.000	91.103	0.000
Rank ≤ 1	0.3692	8.2934	0.004	8.293	0.004

Table 7.3 Granger causality tests for OFDI and exports based on VECM

Test for causality of	By	Lag	t-statistic	p-value
L_OFDI	L_EX	1	4.967	0.008
		2	5.449	0.006
		3	4.324	0.012
		4	3.870	0.018
		5	5.073	0.007
		6	5.931	0.004
ECT			−5.844	0.004
L_EX	L_OFDI	1	0.110	0.918
		2	−0.211	0.843
		3	0.455	0.673
		4	1.181	0.303
		5	1.339	0.252
		6	0.581	0.592
ECT			−1.264	0.275

of Granger non-causality, although it does not say anything about the direction of causality. In this case, the application of a vector error correction model (VECM) will allow the direction of the causality to be determined while at the same time allow us to differentiate between short-run and long-run influences.

The results derived from these methods are presented in Table 7.3, which shows a clear pattern emerging for the causal link between exports and OFDI. The first null hypothesis – that Indian OFDI does not cause exports from the home country – cannot be rejected at any lag. Indian OFDI growth therefore does not cause the growth in exports from India, either in the short-run or the long-run.

The second null hypothesis – that Indian exports do not cause OFDI from the home country – is rejected at all lags. The evidence shows that in both the short-run and the long-run, the growth of Indian exports causes growth in OFDI. However, we find positive as well as negative t-statistics in various lags while performing causality tests for OFDI and exports. The estimations therefore do not point to any clear-cut conclusion on Indian exports being a substitute for, or complementary to, OFDI.

Conclusion

This chapter examines causal linkages between Indian OFDI and exports based on a time-series data over 1981–2006. The analyses suggest that there is unidirectional causal relation between Indian exports and its OFDI. The empirical results indicate that more exports from India will lead to greater OFDI. In terms of causality, the existing literature suggests that many firms follow the traditional step-by-step sequence of servicing foreign markets: they trade in a foreign market in the first instance because trade is easier and less risky than FDI. After learning more about the economic, political and social conditions and gaining more experience, home country firms may establish production subsidiaries in the foreign market. However, foreign subsidiaries may eventually begin to export (Johanson and Vahlne, 1992; Nicholas, 1982; UNCTAD, 1996). Thus, there can be a two-way causal link: trade will first cause FDI and FDI may eventually cause trade. Kumar (2006) suggested that during the 1990s Indian OFDI was clearly concentrated in the countries that are key destinations for Indian exports. During 1990–2001, Indian outward investments were undertaken by exporters to support their exporting activity with local presence, develop a marketing network and provide after-sales service (Kumar, 2006). However, our analysis shows that growth in OFDI does not lead to growth in exports. The results of this study also contradict the findings of Pradhan (2007a, 2007b) that Indian OFDI promotes exports.

Two reasons can be attributed for Indian OFDI having no effect on its exports. First, it has been suggested that the demand for Indian exports increases when its export prices fall in relation to world prices, and is not affected even by inward FDI (Sharma, 2000). Thus, we can say that at a macroeconomic level, export prices mainly drive Indian exports rather than inward and outward FDI. Second, at the microeconomic level, firm-specific factors such as the type of technology and the skill intensity of the workforce play an important role in Indian exports (Lal, 2004), and overall, some credence can be given to an Indian export-led strategy in the last three decades. The findings in this study also suggest that the motivation for overseas investment has been more than just export promotion for Indian firms. Several studies support this conclusion (Gubbi et al., 2009; Kumar, 2007; Pradhan, 2007a, 2007b). Exports were the predominant means towards globalization. Now, the scenario has changed. There is a growing realization that the future growth of Indian companies will be influenced by the share that they can garner in the world market – not only by producing in the country and exporting, but also by acquiring overseas assets, including intangibles like brands and goodwill, to establish an overseas presence and to upgrade their competitive strength in overseas markets (Gopinath, 2007).

Compared to other empirical research, we do not find a clear support for a single theoretical model such as the 'substitute' or the 'complementary' model of exports and stocks of OFDI. But it has also been argued that OFDI can substitute and complement exports depending upon the type of FDI – vertical or horizontal (Markusen et al., 1996). Further theoretical and empirical analysis is needed in order to achieve a better understanding of the substitute-complementary relation of Indian exports and OFDI.

Because of the data limitations, this research was carried out at the macro-level only. It would be desirable to carry out causality tests at the industry or firm level, given that the FDI–trade linkage can be industry- and even firm-specific. Despite this limitation, the results are policy-relevant and are of central importance to development planning and strategies. Our study adds to the growing stream of research on emerging economy firms by empirically testing some of the recently proposed theoretical arguments related to their internationalization paths. While there is a large body of research examining international expansion of these firms through acquisitions, joint ventures and strategic alliances, exports as a mode of internationalization for emerging economy firms are not well understood. Our study contributes important insights to the internationalization literature of India, as well as complementing some of the findings in the literature on trade and FDI. We hope future research will build upon these findings.

Acknowledgements

This work was supported by the Trinity Postgraduate Research Studentship to Rakhi Verma.

References

Agarwal, J.P. (1985) *Pros and Cons of Third World Multinationals: A Case Study of India* (Tubingen: Kieler Studien), p.195.

Amoateng, K. and Amoako-Adu, B. (1996) 'Economic growth, export and external debt causality: the case of African countries', *Applied Economics*, 28(1), 21–7.

Bajo, O. and Montero, M. (2001) 'Foreign direct investment and trade: a causality analysis', *Open Economies Review*, 12(3), 305–23.

Baharumshah, A.Z., Lau, E. and Fountas, S. (2003) 'On the sustainability of current account deficits: evidence from four ASEAN countries', *Journal of Asian Economics*, 14(3), 465–87.

Cheung, Y.W. and Lai, K.S. (1993) 'Finite-sample sizes of Johansen's likelihood ratio tests for cointegration', *Oxford Bulletin of Economics and Statistics*, 55(3), 313–25.

Cohen, B.I. (1964) 'The stagnation of Indian exports, 1951–1961', *The Quarterly Journal of Economics*, 78(4), 604–20.

Dasgupta, A. and Siddharthan, N. (1985) 'Industrial distribution of Indian exports and joint ventures abroad', *Development and Change*, 16(1), 159–74.

Dunning, J.H. (1998) 'The European internal market program and inbound foreign direct investment', in J.H. Dunning (ed.) *Globalization, Trade and Foreign Direct Investment*, 49–115 (Oxford: Elsevier).

Granger, C.W.J. (1969) 'Investigating causal relations by econometric models and cross-spectral methods', *Econometrica*, 37(3), 424–38.

Gopinath, S. (2007) 'Overseas investments by Indian companies – evolution of policy and trends', *International Conference on Indian Cross-Border Presence/Acquisitions*, Mumbai, www.rbi.org.in/scripts/BS_SpeechesView.aspx?Id=320, date accessed 3 October 2009.

Gubbi, S.R., Aulakh, P.S., Ray, S., Sarkar, M.B. and Chittoor, R. (2009) 'Do international acquisitions by emerging-economy firms create shareholder value? The case of Indian firms', *Journal of International Business Studies*, 41(3), 397–418.

Helpman, E. (1984) 'A simple theory of international trade with multinational corporations', *Journal of Political Economy*, 92(3), 451–71.

Helpman, E. and Krugman, P.R. (1985), *Market Structure and Foreign Trade* (Cambridge: MIT Press).

Jha, R. (2003) 'Recent trends in FDI flows and prospects for India', *Working Paper*, Australian National University, Australia, 18 August.

Johanson, J. and Vahlne J.E. (1977) 'The internationalization process of the firm – a model of knowledge development and increasing foreign market commitments', *Journal of International Business Studies*, 8(1), 23–31.

Johanson, J. and Vahlne J.E. (1990) 'The mechanism of internationalization', *International Marketing Review*, 7(4), 11–24.

Johanson, J. and Vahlne, J.E. (1992) 'Management of foreign market entry', *Scandinavian International Business Review*, 1(3), 9–27.

Johanson, J. and Wiedersheim-Paul, F. (1975) 'The internationalization of the firms: four Swedish cases', *Journal of Management Studies*, 12(3), 305–22.

Johansen, S. and Juselius, K. (1990) 'Maximum likelihood estimation and inference on cointegration with applications to the demand for money', *Oxford Bulletin of Economics and statistics*, 52(2), 169–210.

Joshi, V. and Little, I.M.D. (1994) *India: Macroeconomics and Political Economy 1964–1991* (Washington, DC: World Bank).

King, R.G., Plosser, C.I., Stock, J.H. and Waston, M.W. (1991) 'Stochastic trends and economic fluctuation', *American Economic Review*, 81(4), 819–40.

Kumar, N. (1998) 'Emerging outward foreign direct investment from Asian developing countries: prospects and implications', in N. Kumar (ed.) *Globalization, Foreign Direct Investment and Technology Transfers*, 177–94 (London: Routledge).

Kumar, N. (2006) 'Emerging multinationals: trends, patterns and determinants of outward investment by Indian enterprises', *Research and Information System for Developing Countries*, New Delhi.

Kumar, N. (2007) 'Emerging TNCs: trends, patterns and determinants of outward FDI by Indian enterprises', *Transnational Corporations*, 16(1), 1–26.

Lal, K. (2004) 'E-business and export behavior: evidence from Indian firms', *World Development*, 32(3), 505–17.

Lall, R.B. (1986) *Multinationals from the Third World: Indian Firms Investing Abroad* (Delhi: Oxford University Press).

Liew, V.K.S. (2004) 'Which lag length selection criteria should we employ?', *Economics Bulletin*, 3(33), 1–9.

Lin, A.L. (1995) 'Trade effects of foreign direct investment: evidence for Taiwan with four ASEAN countries', *Review of World Economics*, 131(4), 737–47.

Liu, X., Wang, C. and Wei, Y. (2001) 'Casual links between foreign direct investment and trade in China', *China Economic Review*, 12(2–3), 190–202.

Love, J.H. and Lage-Hidalgo, F. (2000) 'Analysing the determinants of US direct investment in Mexico', *Applied Economics*, 32(10), 1259–67.

MacDonald, R. and Kearney, C. (1987) 'On the specification of Granger-causality tests using the cointegration methodology', *Economics Letters*, 25(2), 149–53.

Markusen, J.R. (1984) 'Multinationals, multi-plant economies, and the gains from trade', *Journal of International Economics*, 16(3–4), 205–26.

Markusen, J.R. (1998) 'Multinational firms, location and trade', *World Economy*, 21(6), 733–56.

Markusen, J.R., Venables, A.J., Konan, D.E. and Zhang, K.H. (1996) 'A unified treatment of horizontal direct investment, vertical direct investment, and the pattern of trade in goods and services', *NBER Working Paper No. W5696*.

Morris, S. (1987) 'Trends in foreign direct investment from India (1950–1982)', *Economic and Political Weekly*, 22(45), 1909–18.

Nicholas, S.J. (1982) 'British multinational investment before 1939', *Journal of European Economic History*, 11(3), 605–30.

Pain, N. and Wakelin, K. (1998) 'Export performance and the role of foreign direct investment', *The Manchester School of Economic and Social Studies Supplement*, 66, 62–8.

Petri, P.A. (1994) 'The regional clustering of foreign direct investment and trade', *Transnational Corporations*, 3(2), 1–24.

Pradhan, J.P. (2007a) 'Growth of Indian multinationals in the world economy: implications for development', *Working Paper No. 04*, Institute for Studies in Industrial Development, New Delhi.

Pradhan, J.P. (2007b) 'How do Indian multinationals affect exports from home country', *Working Paper No. 07*, Institute for Studies in Industrial Development, New Delhi.

Pfaffermayr, M. (1994) 'Foreign direct investment and exports: a time series approach', *Applied Economics*, 26(4), 337–51.

Pfaffermayr, M. (1996) 'Foreign outward direct investment and exports in Austrian manufacturing: substitutes or complements?', *Weltwirtschaftliches Archiv*, 132(3), 501–52.

Sharma, K. (2000) 'Export growth in India: has FDI played a role?', *Working Paper No. 86*, Economic Growth Center Yale University.
United Nations Conference on Trade and Development (UNCTAD) (1996), World Investment Report, United Nations, New York and Geneva.
Vernon, R. (1966) 'International investment and international trade in the product life cycle', *Quarterly Journal of Economics*, 80(2), 190–207.
Veugelers, R. (1991) 'Locational determinants and ranking of host countries: an empirical assessment', *Kyklos*, 44(3), 363–82.
Wagner, J. (1991) *Die bundesrepublikanische Industrie auf dem Weltmarkt* (Berlin: Duncker & Humblot).

8
Internationalization, Financial Incentives and Firm Growth: Evidence from Italy

Mariasole Bannò, Lucia Piscitello and Celeste Amorim Varum

Introduction

Internationalization has become increasingly important for the survival, growth and long-term viability of business organizations (Lu and Beamish, 2004; Shapiro, 1982; Wright and Ricks, 1994). An environment that supports firms' internationalization and growth is indispensable for the success of domestic firms. From a national standpoint, the engagement of more companies in international business is regarded as an effective way of coping with the trade deficit problems and loss of competitiveness experienced by many developed and developing countries (Kokko, 2006).

While in the past most policy schemes were directed at export promotion, in the last decade a variety of home country measures (HCMs) have been launched by several governments to encourage internationalization through foreign investment towards other countries of the home region and to countries in other regions. The perceived benefits of foreign direct investment (FDI) for home economies are now seen as far outweighing its drawbacks, but policymakers are increasingly concerned with the role and effectiveness of such policy schemes (Lou et al., 2009; Sarmah, 2003; UNCTAD, 2001). Most research on policies towards internationalization does not focus on FDI but on other types of international activities, such as exports. In the field of outward foreign direct investment (OFDI), the roles of the regulatory stance and formal policy of the capital-exporting country to promote OFDI have been largely neglected (Brewer, 1993; Globerman and Shapiro, 1999; Sarmah, 2003; Te Velde, 2007; UNCTAD, 2001). In addition, the pace of internationalization differs across firms and markets, challenging policymakers (Buckley and Ghauri, 2004).

This chapter aims at filling this gap by providing an empirical analysis on the efficiency of an Italian financial incentive towards OFDI. Italian HCMs include a panoply of financial supports: government grants to cover part of the capital for production or marketing investment costs and participation in international tenders; subsidized loans; loan guarantees; publicly funded venture capital participation; and government insurance at preferential rates. The largest portion of financial incentives is granted by central government; nevertheless, a fraction of the annual budget is allocated by regional administrations. All of these measures have been in place for more than 10 years, while most regional interventions were set up in the last few years.

In this chapter we aim to test the direct impact of a particular public incentive, whereby a public agency can invest directly in foreign ventures upon the firms' domestic growth. The analysis is conducted on data from 237 Italian firms that received an incentive to promote Italian companies' FDI outside the European Union in the period 1991–2007, versus a counterfactual sample of firms that internationalized their activity in the same period without any incentive. This is one of the first attempts to develop a rigorous evaluation of a policy for firms' outward internationalization, exploiting the availability of detailed information on the functioning of the programme of incentives. We contribute to the ongoing discussion of the effects of these policies on firm performance. An investigation of the role of financial incentives may refine our conceptual understanding of the internationalization–performance link.

Internationalization, HCMs and firm performance

In this section we discuss the rationale for formal policies towards OFDI, and in particular the potential role of financial incentives. As in Globerman and Shapiro (1999), we consider formal foreign investment policies and distinguish them from other policies that might affect FDI directed primarily at other targets, such as competition and labour policies, competition and innovation policies. Public policies directed at inward FDI may also directly or indirectly affect outward flows. Economic theory suggests various rationales for governments to subsidize firms – particularly for SMEs. In this section, we discuss how access to public financial support for internationalization may have a positive impact on firms' performance and growth. The research hypothesis derives from insights from the literature on financial constraints and internationalization, and from the research on effects of public policy on firm performance.

The rationale for HCMs to promote OFDI

Information provision and technical assistance, financial support, investment insurance schemes, fiscal benefits, measures related to trade and to the transfer of technology encompass the major types of HCMs that have been used by governments to promote or otherwise influence OFDI flows (Sarmah, 2003; Te Velde, 2007). Taking as a basic principle that internationalization is good for home country welfare (Kokko, 2006) by contributing to the growth, survival and long-term competitiveness of firms, HCMs are launched to mitigate information and coordination failures in the international investment process that deter investments and increase the costs of internationalization by firms. Costs can accrue due to political and economic uncertainty and unanticipated changes to the business environment. Increased costs also stem from higher information-processing demands and transaction costs at intra-company level, which are highly influenced by a company's geographic spread, international experience, cultural diversity, and organizational structure.

The promotion of internationalization seeks to reduce economic and political risks, overcome uncertainties, and alleviate any shortfalls in resources and capabilities in a company embarking on the internationalization process or seeking to invest in an environment that is distant in geographical, cultural and institutional terms. HCMs may also be directed to provide support for economic fundamentals and governance structures in host countries required for successful investment projects (Sarmah, 2003; Te Velde, 2007). A large group of studies discusses the effects of broad shifts in formal OFDI policy (e.g. Aggarwal and Agmon, 1990; Buckley et al., 2007; Globerman and Shapiro, 1999; Kumar, 2007; Pradhan, 2004; Shapiro and Globerman, 2003). From these studies the consensus is that government may serve as both a constraint on and an enabling mechanism for OFDI, but several aspects moderate the efficiency of the policy.

There is a second group of studies that discusses particular HCMs to promote OFDI, and these are summarized in Table 8.1. Although being markedly positive regarding the effects of HCMs, this literature suggests that the effectiveness of HCMs is likely to depend on a number of variables. HCMs may not be able to boost

Table 8.1 Summary of studies addressing the effect of HCMs towards OFDI

Study	Nature of research	Home country	Data/years of coverage	HCMs or other HC policies affecting OFDI	Results
Duran and Ubeda (2001)	Empirical	Spain	Questionnaires, 127 firms, end of the 1990s	Exhibitions and international missions	+ With international experience
Maeseneire and Claeys (2007)	Empirical	Belgium	32 Belgian SMEs	FDI finance	+ Role of public financial support to
Sarmah (2003)	Appreciative	Various to developing		HCMs	+
Svetličič (2007)	Empirical	Slovenia	FDI flows, since the 1950s	OFDI policy stages	+
Svetličič, Jaklic and Burger (2007)	Empirical	Selected 5 CE countries	180 questionnaires	Policy towards SMEs	+ Suggestions for change
Te Velde (2007)	Appreciative	UK to developing	Last 4 decades	HCMs	Partly effective
UNCTAD (2001)	Appreciative	Developed to developing	Last decades	HCMs	Effective

successful OFDI if domestic investors lack the capabilities to invest abroad. Size is also relevant as larger firms are more likely to venture abroad than smaller firms because they often have better access to market information and possess financial strength, allowing them to bear greater risks. The degree of internationalization of the company seems also to have a positive effect on the probability and success of OFDI being undertaken (Duran and Ubeda, 2001).

Together with firm structural characteristics, the effectiveness of HCMs and the probability of success in internationalization processes may also depend on industry, motive for investment, and home and host-country economic conditions. The government's intervention and influence may be more important for projects with natural resource-seeking, strategic asset-seeking and diversification motives, but less so for market-seeking and efficiency-seeking projects (see Lou et al., 2009 on Chinese OFDI; OECD, 2008). Otherwise, HCMs could play a role mainly in directing OFDI into developing countries that are usually capital-scarce, while FDI is attracted to industrial countries due to their opportunity for high returns (Sarmah, 2003; Te Velde, 2007; UNCTAD, 2001). Hence, these conditions and the firm's structural characteristics, industry, international experience, motives for investment and destination country should be taken into account when examining the effects of HCMs.

There are as yet only two empirical studies addressing the effectiveness of stimulating additional OFDI (Duran and Ubeda, 2001; Maeseneire and Claeys, 2007). Duran and Ubeda (2001) analysed the efficiency of Expotecnia, a programme of fairs showing products in various countries with a view to increasing exports and direct investment, launched in the 1980s by the Spanish Institute for Foreign Trade. While the role of financial incentives to internationalization is an ongoing topic, little or no research exists on whether and to what extent financial incentives affect the relation between internationalization and firm performance; the exception being Maeseneire and Claeys (2007), who empirically examine the role of public incentives to OFDI. As a result, little is known about how home country financial incentives influence the scope and deployment of FDI, and how it improves firm performance.

It must be noted that successful government intervention implies that the related social benefits exceed the financial and administrative costs. It is important that public incentive schemes be evaluated and, if necessary, modified (Lenihan et al., 2007; Mosselman and Prince, 2004). Evaluating the return from OFDI is particularly important; Ishida and Matsushima (2008) demonstrate that any form of government intervention to encourage OFDI can be beneficial only up to a point because excessive OFDI may result in welfare losses in the home country.

Financial incentives to FDI and growth

A number of studies document the lack of capital available to finance international activities, in particular among SMEs (European Commission, 2003). Maeseneire and Claeys (2007) argue that many of the issues that firms face in attracting capital for FDI are equivalent to those experienced by firms for financing R&D – volatile returns, asymmetric information and a lack of collateral – which make it difficult to access debt for international expansion. In their empirical study they confirm the existence of financing constraints experienced by SMEs for their foreign investments, which may severely harm firm survival and growth potential (Maeseneire and Claeys, 2007).

In the context of internationalization through exports, Banerjee and Newman (2004) argue that financial subsidies help correct allocative distortions created by poor credit markets, and therefore can boost internationalization. In particular, loans and equity participation for investment projects in foreign countries may improve the profitability of projects and reduce uncertainties and costs for foreign investors (Kline, 2003; Sarmah, 2003; Te Velde, 2007; UNCTAD, 2001) that result from an unfamiliar context and the 'liability of foreignness' (Zaheer, 1995).

In the context of industrial policy for promoting domestic investments, the literature is not unanimous in demonstrating the efficiency of financial incentives in improving the employment and turnover of assisted firms (see, e.g., Bergström, 2000; Skuras and Tzelepis, 2004; Wallsten, 2000; and for FDI Brewer and Young, 1997; Guisinger, 1992; Lim, 2005; Markusen and Nesse, 2007; Oxelheim and Ghauri, 2004). There is scarce evidence on the role and effectiveness of financial incentives for OFDI. In Maeseneire and Claeys (2007), many firms reported that without government support, some of their FDI projects would not have been executed. Maeseneire and Claeys (2007) also reported that with additional financial resources, SMEs felt that they could more fully realize their growth potential – both at home and abroad. Based on these arguments, we expect incentives to benefit firms. The access to public financial support may alleviate the financing constraints that firms face in exploring and selecting from a range of foreign investment alternatives, and therefore it may have a substantial positive impact on their performance and growth. In this chapter, we test the direct impact of public incentives for OFDI on the firm's growth.

Methodology

For public policy evaluation it is important to observe the counterfactual conditions, in order to answer the question as to whether the observed outcomes result from the particular public policy and not from other determinants (Marschak, 1953). Because it is impossible to determine exactly what would have happened in the absence of the incentive, we need a methodology that allows us to identify the causal relation between the incentive and the outcome, controlling for other possible determinants of the outcome (Bartik and Bingham, 1997), and accounting for possible selection bias (Heckman, 1979). Selection bias can be caused by *self-selection* and *agency selection*. In the former case, firms that apply for the incentive may not be representative of the total population of eligible firms; in the latter, the agency accepts only the applications that meet the selection criteria. To overcome validity problems and selection bias, it is necessary to impute an appropriate counterfactual outcome for the sample of benefiting firms (Moffit, 1991). A variety of different approaches that do not require experimental data have been proposed, but the most common method compares a group of benefiting firms, usually called the treatment group, with a group of non-benefiting firms – the control group (for a review of non-experimental methods, see Blundell and Costa Dias, 2000).

In this study we use the treatment effect model, which is a two-stage selection model. The first step aims to account for selection and self-selection bias and the second step evaluates the impact of the incentive on the outcome. Two regressions are estimated simultaneously (Lee, 2005): the first is a probit regression, predicting the probability of receiving the incentive; the second is a linear regression for the outcome (i.e. the firm's growth) as a function of the treatment variable (the incentive), controlling for other observable explanatory variables. Theoretically, the solution is to propose and estimate a model of the selection and self-selection decision; that is, to define an incentive assignment equation where x_i is the set of exogenous covariates that affect the incentive assignment and that could explain different attitudes between benefiting and non-benefiting firms. In particular, the model assumes that D_i^*, the probability of receiving the incentive, is a linear function of the observed covariates x_i and the random component ε_i. We assume that the incentive assignment is determined by:

$$D_i^* = \beta x_i + \varepsilon_i \qquad (8.1)$$

The endogenous binary variable D_i is modelled as the outcome of the unobservable latent variable D_i^*, and the observed decision is:

$$D_i = 1, \quad \text{if} \quad D_i^* > 0$$
$$D_i = 0, \quad \text{if} \quad D_i^* \leq 0$$

The second step is made of a linear regression for the outcome y_i (firm growth) as a function of the treatment variable D_i (the incentive), controlling for other observable explanatory variables,

$$y_i = \delta w_i + \gamma D_i + u_i \qquad (8.2)$$

where w_i is the set of exogenous control variables that can influence the response.

The empirical analysis

Data

Simest is the institution dedicated to support and promote Italian companies' international growth outside the European Union. It was set up as a limited company in 1990 and, controlled by the Ministry of International Trade and Commerce, it manages all major public financial instruments supporting outward internationalization. In this chapter we focus on Law 100/1990, according to which Simest can invest directly in foreign ventures and acquire up to 25 per cent of the Italian foreign affiliate's equity. The duration of equity shares is in principle up to a maximum of eight years, within which the pre-agreed reacquisition of

Simest shares with partner firms is established. Although Simest can, in principle, evaluate investment proposals from any company, its business is primarily with SME investment in Eastern Europe. Simest also acquires interests in foreign firms that are active in the same business sector as the home firm proposing the project; no sector is excluded. To the end of 2006, Simest had acquired shareholdings in 469 Italian foreign affiliates, subscribed to 150 capital increases for a total of €412 million, and sold 253 shareholdings for a total of €193.4 million. The data set for the empirical analysis combines three sources: Simest's balance sheets, which provide information on assignments of incentives to Italian firms during 1991–2006; the database Reprint, which provides a census of outward and inward FDI in Italy (from 1986); and AIDA (Bureau van Dijk), which provides balance sheet data for Italian firms. Complete information is available for 237 benefiting firms and for 307 non-benefiting firms (the control group).

The model and the variables

We adopt a traditional treatment effects model (Lee, 2005), which allows us to assess whether public support affects the growth of benefiting versus non-benefiting firms. Our dependent variables for the first and second stage estimations respectively are:

(1) *D_incentive*, which is a dummy variable that equals 1 if the firm has received the incentive, and zero otherwise; and
(2) *Firm_growth*, which is measured by the rate of growth of the Italian parent company's turnover between t_{0-1} and t_{0+2} where t_0 is the year of the foreign initiative.

The full set of variables and their sources are summarized in Table 8.2. The explanatory variables for the first stage include the firm's structural characteristics and its financial constraints, and two features relating to the project: country destination and the project's size. The structural characteristics include size and age, which have traditionally been considered as a proxy for managerial skills, thus affecting the firm's ability to obtain external resources (Blanes and Busom, 2004; González et al., 2005). We use annual turnover as a proxy for size (*Log_sales*); and age (*Firm_age*) is measured in number of years. We expect larger and older firms to be more likely to obtain the incentive. Previous experience in international markets may also increase the likelihood of the firm to both apply and obtain the incentive, so we include the variable *Int_experience*, which is the number of the firm's previous outward investments. As the effective cost of going abroad may vary across firms as a result of differences in the availability and cost of finance, we include as a proxy for financial constraint the ratio between a firm's bank debt and its turnover (*BanksD_sales*). We expect a positive relation between variables substituting the existence of firms' financial constraints and the likelihood of obtaining the incentive.

In the process of project selection, Simest evaluates each firm's success. We therefore include return on investment (*ROI*) as a measure of the firm's profitability, and

Table 8.2 Description of the variables and sources of data

Variable	Description	Source
Dependent variables		
Firm_growth	Turnover of the Italian firm between t_{0-1} and t_{0+2}	AIDA
D_incentive	Dummy variable taking the value of 1 if the firms obtained the incentive in t_0, and zero otherwise	Simest
Independent variables		
Firm's structural variable and firm's financial constraint		
Log_sales	Logarithm of annual turnover (thousands €) in t_{0-1}	AIDA
Firm_age	Age of the firm (years) in t_{0-1}	Reprint
Int_experience	Number of previous outward foreign direct investments	AIDA
ROI	Return on Investment (percentage) in t_{0-1}	Reprint
North	Dummy variable taking value of 1 when the firm is in North Italy, and zero otherwise	AIDA
BanksD_sales	Ratio between Banks debt and turnover in t_{0-1}	
FDI project characteristics		
East_Europe	Dummy variable taking value of 1 when the FDI destination country is Eastern Europe, and zero otherwise	Reprint
North_America	Dummy variable taking value of 1 when the FDI destination country is North America, and zero otherwise	Reprint
Greenfield	Dummy variable taking the value of 1 if the foreign affiliate is Greenfield, and zero otherwise	Reprint
Majority	Dummy variable taking the value of 1 if the foreign affiliate is majority-owned in t_{0-1}, and zero otherwise	Reprint
Empl_affiliate	Number of employees of foreign affiliates, in t_{0-1}	Reprint
Sales_affiliate	Turnover of foreign affiliates, in t_{0-1}	Reprint

we expect a positive relation between profitability and the likelihood of obtaining the incentive. Although Simest can, in principle, evaluate proposals for all types of foreign investments, these measures are mainly directed towards promoting larger investments in Eastern Europe. We include the size of the foreign affiliate created (*Sales_affiliate*) and a dummy for the destination of the investment (*East_Europe*).

The second stage of the analysis estimates the effect of the incentive on firm growth (*Firm_growth*), which is a continuous, fully observable variable. Previously, we discussed that the ability of HCMs to promote OFDI seems to be dependent on several factors (see Te Velde, 2007), such as the firm's international experience (*Int_experience*) and its financial constraints (*BanksD_sales*). We also include firm-level control variables that according to the literature may affect firm growth: size (*Log_sales*) and firm age, as well as profitability (*ROI*). We use dummies representing the nature of the project (greenfield vs. acquisition; *Greenfield*), the share held by the Italian parent company in the foreign affiliate (majority vs. minority; *Majority*), and the size of the foreign affiliate measured

Table 8.3 Comparison between benefiting firms and non-benefiting firms

	Benefiting firms (237)	Non-benefiting firms (307)	Significance
Dependent variables			
Firm_growth[a]	2.9	0.8	**
Independent variables			
Firm's structural variable and firm's financial constraint			
Sales[a]	90.6	33.4	***
Firm_age[b]	33	33	n.s.
Int_experience[b]	9	2	***
ROI[a]	7.53	8.82	*
North[c]	74%	76%	n.s.
BanksD_sales[a]	27.44	19.32	***
FDI Project characteristics			
East_Europe[c]	46%	55%	**
North_America[c]	7%	9%	n.s.
Greenfield[c]	73%	67%	n.s.
Majority[c]	91%	84%	**
Empl_affiliate[b]	121.10	53.77	***
Sales_affiliate[a]	10.01	4.92	***

[a] t-test between the two categories (mean).
[b] Mann–Whitney test between the two categories (median).
[c] Proportion test between the two categories (percentage).
* Significance at the 10 per cent level.
** Significance at the 5 per cent.
*** Significance at the 1 per cent level.

by number of employees (*Empl_affiliate*). Finally, we control for possible differences in opportunities in the destination countries (*East_Europe* or *North_America*), as well as in the home region of the firm in Italy (north vs. south of Italy; *North*) and industry sectors of the parent company. Table 8.3 reports the average values of the variables and the significant differences for the two groups of firms. The correlation analysis reveals acceptable correlation indexes between the examined variables.

Econometric findings

The results of the empirical estimates for the treatment model are reported in Table 8.4. It is worth noting that the correlation between the error terms of the two equations (the coefficient rho) is significantly different from zero (at $p < 0.01$), and so it confirms that both the firm and the project characteristics affect incentive assignment and the latent outcome; therefore, in estimating the effects of the incentive a selection bias arises.

As far as the selection model is concerned, our results confirm that both the parent company's characteristics and the FDI features explain the likelihood of receiving the incentive. Larger firms with previous international experience are more likely to get the incentive (both *Log_sales* and *Int_experience* are positive

Table 8.4 Treatment effect model – two-steps estimates

	Coef.	Std. error
Dependent variable: Firm_growth		
D_incentive	12.05***	3.03
Firm's structural variable and firm's financial constraint		
Log_sales	−7.99***	1.05
Firm_age	−0.00	0.00
Int_experience	0.06	0.07
ROI	0.06	0.07
North	−1.77	1.26
BanksD_sales	−0.05*	0.03
Industry dummies	Yes	
FDI project characteristics		
East_Europe	−2.53**	1.23
North_America	4.78**	2.10
Greenfield	2.81	1.79
Majority	0.02	0.79
Empl_affiliate	0.02***	0.00
Cons	53.16***	7.48
Dependent variable: D_incentive		
Log_sales	0.24**	0.11
Firm_age	−0.00	0.00
Int_experience	0.27***	0.04
ROI	−0.01	0.01
BanksD_sales	0.01**	0.00
Sales_affiliate	0.02**	0.01
East_Europe	0.13	0.13
Cons	−2.92***	0.78
Lambda	−6.87	1.94
Rho	−0.54	
Sigma	12.78	

* Significance at the 10 per cent level.
** Significance at the 5 per cent.
*** Significance at the 1 per cent level.

and significant at $p < 0.05$ and $p < 0.01$, respectively). Likewise, our results support the idea that market imperfections give rise to financial constraints and make firms more likely to apply for (and to get) public funding (*BanksD_sales* is positive and significant at $p < 0.05$). Interestingly, notwithstanding the selection procedure should a priori favour initiatives to Eastern European countries, the relevant dummy (*East_Europe*) does not come out significantly different from zero, while the affiliate size does contribute positively to the incentive assignment (*Sales_affiliate* is significant at $p < 0.01$).

The results for second stage valuation equation confirm the positive and highly significant effect (at $p < 0.01$) of the financial incentive on firms' growth.

However, smaller and less indebted companies grow more rapidly (*Log_sales* and *BanksD_sales* are negative and significant at $p < 0.01$ and $p < 0.10$, respectively) while all the other firms' specificities do not seem to impact on growth. On the contrary, the parent's growth crucially depends on the characteristics of the foreign initiative: indeed, the estimated coefficients confirm that FDI size contributes positively to the firm growth (*Empl_affiliate* is significant at $p < 0.01$), as well as the FDI's localization in developed countries (*North_America* is positive and significant at $p < 0.05$).

Conclusions

In the past, many governments viewed OFDI as an undesirable transfer of capital and jobs to other countries. In the 1990s and 2000s, they began to look at it as a way to build globally competitive firms, to accelerate the development of high-value activities and productivity, to bring about technological transformation, and to better allocate home resources. Governments should therefore not only try to attract FDI, but should also do more to facilitate outflows of FDI. The differential pace of internationalization across firms and markets presents a number of challenges to policymakers in local, national and regional governments, and in international institutions (Buckley and Ghauri, 2004). Simply encouraging OFDI through macroeconomic policies may be inefficient. Despite the fact that many countries make use of several measures to promote OFDI, HCMs are much less discussed than other factors affecting FDI, and their effectiveness and efficiency have also seldom been studied in detail. There is ample scope for further research on measuring and assessing the effectiveness of home country policy measures towards OFDI.

We have analysed a specific measure implemented in Italy, and found positive effects of the financial incentive on the benefiting firm's growth, compared to the counterfactual sample of non-benefiting firms. The government's involvement in OFDI may have helped to reduce capital market failures and the uncertainty and risk associated with investing in unfamiliar host countries (Te Velde, 2007), which is more critical for smaller companies with less financial and management resources to spend for research and analysis prior to embarking into a foreign market (Wright et al., 2007).

Policy measures in the home country may well be more important than non-policy ones due to the ease with which home governments can quickly alter them. On the other hand, non-policy determinants may take many years to modify. Obviously, the policy effects also depend on the relative cross-national options, in addition to the different motivations for FDI, as stressed by Brewer (1993) and Kokko (2006). Our results support the position that the influence of HCMs can be increased through tailor-made approaches (e.g. through regional and country targeting) on the formulation and administration of measures.

To the best of our knowledge, this chapter is the first systematic evaluation of public incentives addressing firms' outward internationalization. The agenda for future research is rich. The specification of the model presented in this chapter should be improved by introducing better measures of certain phenomena. *First*, a better understanding of the selection and self-selection process would benefit from the possibility of accessing data on firms whose applications were not selected for the incentive. *Second*, firms' internationalization processes could be modelled taking into account motivations underlying each FDI initiative, although that would require additional data gathering using surveys and questionnaires. The effects of the subsidies could be tested under different firm specificities. These factors may affect the success of the promotion programmes and must be taken into consideration for policymaking. *Finally*, the effects of public incentives may be also evaluated as far as their indirect impact (associated to externalities and spillovers) is concerned, for example on social welfare. Moreover, our results concern a single type of incentive addressing firms' internationalization, while a comparative analysis of alternative mechanisms would provide useful suggestions to policymakers for the design of appropriate tools, and the improvement of existing ones.

Acknowledgements

We acknowledge the support from the Italian Ministry of Education (FIRB, Project RISC – RBNE039XKA). Celeste Amorim Varum acknowledges the Sabbatical Grant from the Portuguese Fundação para a Ciência e Tecnologia (FCT) [SFRH/S=BSAB/920/2009].

References

Aggarwal, R. and Agmon, T. (1990) 'The international success of developing country firms: role of government-directed comparative advantage', *Management International Review*, 30(2), 163–80.

Banerjee, A. and Newman, A. (2004) *Inequality, Growth and Trade Policy*, Working paper, MIT.

Bartik, T.J. and Bingham, R.D. (1997) 'Can economic development programs be evaluated?', in R.D. Bingham and R. Mier (eds) *Dilemmas of Urban Economic Development: Issue in Theory and Practice*, 246–77 (Thousand Oaks, CA: Sage Publications).

Bergström, F. (2000) 'Capital subsidies and the performance of firms', *Small Business Economics*, 14(3), 183–93.

Blanes, J.V. and Busom, I. (2004) 'Who participates in R&D subsidy programs? The case of Spanish manufacturing firms', *Research Policy*, 33(10), 1459–76.

Blundell, R. and Costa Dias, M. (2000) 'Evaluation methods for non-experimental data', *Fiscal Studies*, 21(4), 427–68.

Brewer, T. (1993) 'Government policies, market imperfections and foreign direct investment', *Journal of International Business Studies*, 24(1), 101–20.

Brewer, T.L. and Young, S. (1997) 'Investment incentives and the international agenda', *The World Econ*omy, 20(2), 175–98.

Buckley, P., Clegg, J., Cross, A.R., Liu, X., Voss, H. and Zheng, P. (2007) 'The determinants of Chinese outward foreign direct investment', *Journal of International Business Studies*, 38(4), 499–518.

Buckley, P.J. and Ghauri, P.N. (2004) 'Globalisation, economic geography and the strategy of multinational enterprises', *Journal of International Business Studies*, 35(2), 81–98.

Duran, J.J. and Ubeda, F. (2001) 'The efficiency of government promotion for outward FDI: the intention to invest abroad', *Multinational Business Review*, 9(2), 24–32.

European Commission (2003) 'Observatory of European SMEs', *Internationalisation of SMEs*.

Globerman, S. and Shapiro, D. (1999) 'The impact of government policies on foreign direct investment: the Canadian experience', *Journal of International Business Studies*, 30(3), 513–32.

González, X., Jaumandreu, J. and Pazó, C. (2005) 'Barriers to innovation and subsidy effectiveness', *RAND Journal of Economics*, 36(4), 930–50.

Guisinger, S. (1992) 'Rhetoric and reality in international business: a note on the effectiveness of incentives', *Transnational Corporations*, 1(2), 111–23.

Heckman, J.J. (1979) 'Sample selection bias as a specification error', *Econometrica*, 47(1), 153–61.

Ishida, J. and Matsushima, N. (2008) *Outward Foreign Direct Investment in a Unionized Oligopoly: Welfare and Policy Implications*, OSIPP Discussion Paper No. 08E005.

Kline, J.M. (2003) 'Enhancing the development dimension of home country measures', in UNCTAD (ed.) *The Development Dimension of FDI: Policy and Rule Making Perspectives* (New York and Geneva: United Nations), 101–14.

Kokko, A. (2006) *The Home Country Effects of FDI in Developed Economies*, EIJS Working Paper Series 225, The European Institute of Japanese Studies.

Kumar, N. (2007) 'Emerging TNCs: trends, patterns and determinants of outward FDI by Indian enterprises', *Transnational Corporations*, 16(1), 1–26.

Lee, M.J. (2005) *Micro-Econometrics for Policy, Program, and Treatment Effects* (New York: Oxford University Press).

Lenihan, H., Hart, M. and Roper, S. (2007) 'Introduction to the special issue on industrial policy evaluation: theoretical foundations and empirical innovations: new wine in new bottles', *International Review of Applied Economics*, 21(3), 313–19.

Lim, S.H. (2005) 'Foreign investment impact and incentive: a strategic approach to the relationship between the objectives of foreign investment policy and their promotion', *International Business Review*, 14(1), 61–76.

Lou, Y., Xue, Q. and Han, B. (2009) 'How emerging market governments promote outward FDI: experience from China', *Journal of World Business*, 45(1), 68–79.

Lu, J. and Beamish, P. (2004) 'International diversification and firm performance: the S-curve hypothesis', *Academy of Management Journal*, 47(4), 598–609.

Maeseneire, W. and Claeys, T. (2007) *SMEs, FDI and financial constraints*, Vlerick Leuven Gent Management School Working Paper Series 2007/25.

Markusen, A. and Nesse, K. (2007) 'Institutional and political determinants of incentive competition: reassessing causes, outcomes, remedies', in A. Markusen (ed.) *Reining in the Competition for Capital: International Perspective*, 1–41 (Kalamazoo Michigan: Upjohn Institute for Employment Research).

Marschak, J. (1953) 'Economic measurements for policy and prediction', in W.C. Hood and T.C. Koopmans (eds) *Studies in Econometric Method*, Cowles Commission for Research in Economics, Monograph no.14 (New York: Wiley).

Moffit, R. (1991) 'Program evaluation with non-experimental data', *Evaluation Review*, 15(3), 291–314.

Mosselman, M. and Prince, Y. (2004) *Review of Methods to Measure the Effectiveness of State Aid to SMEs*, Final Report to the European Commission (Brussels: EIM Business and Policy Research).

OECD (2008) 'China's outward direct investment', *OECD Investment Policy Reviews: China 2008*, Chapter 3 (Paris: OECD).

Oxelheim, L. and Ghauri, P. (2004) *European Union and the Race for Foreign Direct Investment in Europe* (Oxford: Elsevier).

Pradhan, J. (2004) 'The determinants of outward foreign direct investment: a firm-level analysis of Indian manufacturing', *Oxford Development Studies*, 32(4), 619–39.

Sarmah, P. (2003) *Home Country Measures and FDI: Implications for Host Country Development*. Centre for Competition, Investment and Economic Regulation Monographs on Investment and Competition Policy (CUTS), 13, 0316.

Shapiro, A. (1982) *Multinational Financial Management* (Boston: Allyn and Bacon).
Shapiro, D. and Globerman, S. (2003) 'Foreign investment policies and capital inflows in Canada: a sectoral analysis', *Journal of Business Research*, 56(10), 779–90.
Skuras, D. and Tzelepis, D. (2004) 'The effects of regional capital subsidies on firm performance: an empirical study', *Journal of Small Business and Enterprise Development*, 11(1), 121–9.
Te Velde (2007) 'Understanding developed country efforts to promote foreign direct investment to developing countries: the example of the United Kingdom', *Transnational Corporations*, 16(3), 83–104.
United Nations Conference on Trade and Development (UNCTAD) (2001) *Home Country Measures*, UNCTAD International Investment Agreements Issues Paper Series (Geneva: United Nations Publication).
Wallsten, S.J. (2000) 'The effects of government-industry R&D programs on private R&D: the case of the small business innovation research program', *RAND Journal of Economics*, 31(1), 82–100.
Wright, W. and Ricks, A. (1994) 'Trends in international business research: twenty-five years later', *Journal of International Business*, 25(4), 687–701.
Wright, M., Westhead, P. and Ucbasaran, D. (2007) 'Internationalization of small and medium-sized enterprises (SMEs) and international entrepreneurship: a critique and policy implications', *Regional Studies*, 41(7), 1013–30.
Zaheer, S. (1995) 'Overcoming the liability of foreignness', *Academy of Management Journal*, 38(2), 341–63.

Part III

Entrepreneurial Firms: Internationalization and Performance

9
Contingency Factors in International Entrepreneurial Orientation – Performance Relations of Firms with Different Levels of Internationalization

Sanna Sundqvist, Olli Kuivalainen and John W. Cadogan

Introduction

In the early stages of firms' internationalization, where firms in many cases are seeking to establish themselves and where new international firms are exploiting new opportunities created by globalization, the entrepreneurial aspects of internationalization come to the fore (Mathews and Zander, 2007). Many firms regard entrepreneurial behaviour as essential if they are to survive in a world that tends to be driven by change (Balabanis and Katsikea, 2003; Wiklund and Shepherd, 2005). One of the key concepts used to measure entrepreneurial activities in firms is entrepreneurial orientation (EO), which can be defined as the decision-making styles, processes and methods that inform a firm's entrepreneurial activities (Lumpkin and Dess, 1996).

The research community has so far studied the role of EO in the international context to a lesser extent (see, e.g., the review conducted by Keupp and Gassmann, 2009, and the meta-analysis of the EO by Rauch et al., 2009). Consequently, there is limited research that focuses on the role of entrepreneurship and its linkage to strategy and performance in international markets. However, in some studies it has been found that EO has a direct effect or is an important driver behind several parameters of international performance (Balabanis and Katsikea, 2003; Knight, 2001; Knight and Cavusgil, 2004; Zahra et al., 1997). In some cases, various dimensions of EO or international entrepreneurial orientation (IEO) have been shown to have different effects on performance (Kuivalainen et al., 2007; Voss et al., 2005). In this chapter, we follow the conceptualizations suggested by Lumpkin and Dess (1996) in the entrepreneurial research literature and McDougall and Oviatt (2000) in international entrepreneurship research, and define IEO of a firm as *capabilities which reflect proactive and innovative methods, risk-taking attitudes, autonomous actions and emphasize outperforming rivals aiming at the discovery, enactment, evaluation and exploitation of opportunities across national borders.*

The purpose of this chapter is to study how dimensions of IEO affect international performance and how this relation differs between firms possessing different levels of degree of internationalization (DOI). Differing DOI among firms can be seen as different international profiles, that is, the scale and scope and timing of internationalization of the firms differ; and the firms also operate in different competitive international environments. The present study aims to extend the works of Zahra and Garvis (2000), Lumpkin and Dess (2001) and Wiklund and Shepherd (2005) by studying IEO and applying EO to international business, examining the effects of different dimensions of IEO on the firm's international performance, and extending the research of the role of moderating effects on the relation between entrepreneurial orientation and firm performance. To address the research questions, structural equation modelling is applied to survey data collected from Finland and New Zealand.

Conceptual framework and hypotheses

Entrepreneurial orientation/international entrepreneurial orientation

EO is one of the central concepts in entrepreneurship research. EO is seen as an internal capability or resource, which is one driver of a firm's business strategy (Ekeledo and Sivakumar, 2004; Jantunen et al., 2005; McDougall et al., 1994). In line with this, in this chapter we see EO as a strategic orientation of the firm (Wiklund and Shepherd, 2003, 2005), and consider entrepreneurial activities as firm-level resources or capabilities which further affect a firm's performance and thus competitive advantage in the long run.

EO and/or IEO is normally presented having either three or five dimensions. The five dimensions of EO/IEO presented in the literature characterize different elements of the construct. Briefly, the *innovativeness* of the firm is seen in its propensity for new idea generation, experimentation and R&D activities resulting in new products and processes (Lumpkin and Dess, 1996). *Autonomy* refers to independent actions carried through either by an individual or team aimed at bringing forth a business concept or idea and carrying it to action and completion (Lumpkin and Dess, 2001). *Risk-taking* represents managers' willingness to pursue opportunities that carry a reasonable risk of costly failure. This would also mean that a firm would be willing to invest resources in projects even if there were a high potential for failure (Miller and Friesen, 1982). *Proactiveness* refers to a posture of anticipating and acting on future wants and needs in the market; this would enable a firm to gain a first mover advantage vis-à-vis its competitors (Lumpkin and Dess, 1996). *Competitive aggressiveness* reflects the intensity of a firm's operations in its attempt to outperform rivals within the industry. The characteristics of this type of behaviour can be seen in how a firm responds to competitors' actions (Lumpkin and Dess, 2001). In the case of IEO, the dimensions are seen as similar to the EO dimensions, but they are related to firms' international activities – that is, its operations in international markets.

Several recent research studies indicate that the dimensions of EO often vary independently rather than co-vary (Kropp et al., 2006; Voss et al., 2005). Similar results have also been found regarding IEO (Kuivalainen et al., 2007). It may be that an entrepreneurial approach for a firm means that there is a high demand for resources, and as this kind of approach is risk-oriented (Covin and Covin, 1990; Covin and Slevin, 1989), it may not be possible – or even necessary – for firms operating in demanding and turbulent international markets to possess all five dimensions of IEO. Differences regarding the existence and effect of various dimensions may even be more striking in the case of IEO as internationalization is often more risky and resource-demanding than domestic entrepreneurial actions.

Explaining internationalization: pathways and degree of internationalization of the firm

There are multiple efforts to explain internationalization (Jones and Coviello, 2005). These include, for example, traditional behavioural internationalization models (see Johanson and Vahlne, 1977, 1990, 2009 for their internationalization process model), foreign direct investment/economics-based models (Buckley and Casson, 1976) and, most recently, international new ventures/born globals and born-again globals (Bell et al., 2001; Knight and Cavusgil, 2004; Oviatt and McDougall, 1994). Due to the size constraints of this chapter, these approaches are not discussed at length; however, it is important for us to point out that in line with Mathews and Zander (2007, p. 398), we view the 'firm's internationalization not through a strict sequence of "stages", nor as a result of comparative static advantages, but through pathways that reflect entrepreneurial observation and strategic action'. Consequently, an international path, pattern or pathway is the term we can use to describe 'stereotypical' internationalization processes or behaviours which can be distinguished from each other (regarding terminology of paths and patterns: see, e.g. Bell et al., 2003; Crick and Spence, 2005; Jones and Coviello, 2005; Kuivalainen et al., 2007).

Selecting an internationalization pathway or pattern is the preliminary or general phase of defining the strategic principles and actions for achieving growth and internationalization in each firm's own context and it is naturally dependent on the firm's internal resources and capabilities as well as opportunities and challenges in the external environment. The outcomes of this decision can eventually be seen as a degree of internationalization (DOI) of the firm. A firm's DOI is a multifaceted construct (Sullivan, 1994), incorporating two core elements of a firm's strategy for international activities: scale and scope (Tallman and Li, 1996). In the case of exporting firms, the scale of the firm's export operations refers to the quantity of exporting business conducted relative to overall operations (Contractor, 2007; Sullivan, 1994;), whereas scope of exporting activities refers to the range of geographic regions and/or countries in which the firm is operating (Ayal and Zif, 1979; Rugman and Verbeke, 2004; Tallman and Li, 1996). These two aspects of internationalization highlight the concept of a firm's international diversification strategy (Tallman and Li, 1996), and together they determine a firm's DOI, with exporters that have greater scale and scope being seen as more international (Kuivalainen et al., 2007). A few common criteria with which so-called bornglobal firms (i.e. firms which internationalize rapidly and intensively after the firm has been founded) have been separated from the rest include, for example, the foreign to total sales ratio being more than 25 per cent (scale indicator; Knight and Cavusgil, 2004) and a large number of countries or continents in which the firm does business (scope indicator; Oviatt and McDougall (1994) write about 'multiple countries').

Furthermore, Jones and Coviello (2005, p. 292) note that 'internationalization may be captured as patterns of behaviour, formed by an accumulation of evidence manifest as events at specific reference points in time.' Consequently, there is a third element of DOI which has to be taken into consideration: time. Time can be seen as a 'hidden' dimension in the internationalization 'fingerprint' with which we are able to study the actual internationalization pathway instead of static DOI (Kutschker et al., 1997). The basic tenet of born globals is that their internationalization patterns or pathways are differentiated by the pace and the DOI in relation to their more traditionally internationalizing counterparts (Knight and Cavusgil, 1996, 2004; Moen, 2002). Consequently, time can be used to distinguish between internationalizing firms – into groups such as born globals or true born globals (Kuivalainen et al., 2007), or traditionally internationalizing firms. Overall, by utilizing the three dimensions of internationalization discussed above, we can determine if there are differences in internationalization behaviour, and in the most optimal situation we can analyse, for example, possible differences in antecedents (such as IEO and environmental turbulence), and outcomes of internationalization (such as performance) between the various pathways; or in other words, the internationalization profiles of the firms.

International entrepreneurial orientation and performance

There are several studies in which firms possessing high EO have been found to outperform their counterparts with lower EO (Wiklund and Shepherd, 2005; Zahra and Covin, 1995). In most of the extant studies, however, unidimensional EO/IEO measures have been used. Although there are fewer studies focusing on five-dimensional EO/IEO (with exceptions such as Jambulingam et al., 2005), there is no reason to expect that multi-dimensional EO/IEO could not be seen as having a positive effect on performance based on similar arguments presented in the unidimensional entrepreneurial literature stream (Wiklund and Shepherd, 2005). This positive relation is supported widely in the extant conceptual literature and also in recent empirical studies. For example, Dess et al. (1997) conclude that successful operations (in uncertain and complex environments) often demand a strong entrepreneurial stance in strategy-making. Some existing results are contradictory, however: Smart and Conant (1994) were not able to find a significant relation between EO and performance. Also Lumpkin and Dess (2001, p. 430) have noted '...that entrepreneurial processes involve complex phenomena that may not always be associated with strong performance'. EO has also been shown to have non-significant relations with aspects of business success under certain conditions, and perhaps to have negative relations with dimensions of business success under other conditions.

Myers et al. (2007) note that the search for fit between organizational and environmental structures can be seen as a core concept within normative models of strategic formulation. In the context of internationalization, the contingency perspective can be based on the idea that a firm's internationalization process is dependent on various contextual factors (Jones, 1999; Li et al., 2004). Consequently, its international performance is determined by the extent to which a firm's behaviour matches or fits its internal or external context.

Effect of DOI

One interesting area of study that we emphasize here is the need for fit between the firm's strategic orientations, such as EO/IEO to its DOI. It is important to remember that firms that change their DOI are not just changing an internal aspect of the firm's strategy. Internationalization brings with it environmental complexity, and for this reason McDougall and Oviatt (1996, p. 27) conclude that DOI 'is an important environmental contingency... in addition to increased logistical costs, entrepreneurs and managers may need to learn something about foreign laws, language, culture, and competitors'. Furthermore, the management, exporting and marketing competencies and skills that provide the exporter with competitive advantage in its domestic and current international markets may not be the same as those that create advantage in new export markets (Cadogan et al., 2009; McDougall and Oviatt, 1996). Thus, when firms expand internationally and increase their DOI, they must learn how to change and adapt their international strategies 'to be congruent with their new environment[s]' (McDougall and Oviatt, 1996, p. 27).

An increase in DOI – for example, further geographical diversification – may also lead to the situation where limited managerial, organizational and financial resources are distributed too thinly across markets: a firm is not capable of managing its international growth. This stretch of resources could reduce the ability of firms and managers to respond to, for example, the various marketing requirements of foreign markets. Furthermore, for firms selling to many diverse foreign markets, the costs incurred in collecting and interpreting market intelligence will inevitably be greater than for firms selling to a few, similar markets with lower psychic distance (Ellis, 2007; Liesch and Knight, 1999). It may be that lack of market information prevents a firm from being proactive, innovative and competitively aggressive in international markets. Interestingly, Rugman and Verbeke (2004, 2008) have recently argued that most of the large multinational enterprises (MNEs) are either single- or bi-regional, and not really multinational (i.e. operating with the same volume in triad markets) when measured by the spread of their sales and assets. Consequently, their argument is that MNEs, although they would like to possess a transnational strategy (Bartlett and Ghoshal, 2000), do not seem to be that successful; more often the reality is that assets and sales tend to be concentrated in geographic space, and in this case the transnational approach may make an MNE too complicated to manage internally (Rugman and Verbeke, 2008). The problems of being global or multinational can affect both SMEs and MNEs.

Overall, we expect, however, that there is a positive relation between all the dimensions of IEO and international performance. Nevertheless, as the findings of Lumpkin and Dess' (2001) study on US firms suggest that different dimensions of EO may have different effects on firm performance, we study and test the performance outcomes of various IEO sub-dimensions separately in order to identify distinct and unique relations between aspects of IEO and international performance. This approach is supported also by Zahra (1993) who noted that different entrepreneurship activities may vary in their association with company profitability. Hence, we hypothesize:

Hypothesis 1: *IEO has a positive effect on international performance.*

However, we expect that the magnitude and direction of the dimensions may differ, and thus a multi-dimensional approach to IEO is adopted; and that it differs between the 'internationalization profiles', so analyses are conducted separately for three different groups of firms with different levels of DOI.

Effect of environmental turbulence

In many studies dynamism (i.e. the rate and unpredictability of change in the industry, e.g. regarding technologies utilized or rapid changes in customer behaviour) and hostility (i.e. an unfavourable business climate with high levels of competitive intensity and uncertainty) are seen as important dimensions of the external environment (Miller and Friesen, 1982; Zahra et al., 1997). The possible turbulence of the environment can be measured by studying the different environments in which the firm operates. It is acknowledged that the relationship between entrepreneurial activities and performance is context-specific (Lumpkin and Dess, 1996). Lyon et al. (2000) further note that the relationship between entrepreneurial behaviour and firm performance may be contingent rather than direct. There are some empirical studies that have examined the moderating effects of environmental variables on the EO–performance relation (Covin and Slevin, 1989; Lumpkin and Dess, 2001). From an international business perspective, environment is believed to have a prevalent influence on organizational behaviour, and thus it has been proposed that firms should attain alignment with environmental conditions in order to realize superior performance abroad (Romanelli and Tushman, 1986). While studies have found that EO is an important driver behind several parameters of international performance (Balabanis and Katsikea, 2003; Knight, 2001; Knight and Cavusgil, 2004; Zahra et al.,1997), researchers have yet to identify environmental conditions that make different IEO dimensions more or less important in determining international business success.

The research on the role of the international environment on international entrepreneurship is scarce. The few existing empirical studies (see Zahra and Garvis, 2000; Zahra et al., 1997) on the topic have treated entrepreneurship as unidimensional, and thus the effect of environment on the relations between individual dimensions of IEO and international performance is a largely unexplored issue. Zahra and Garvis (2000) investigated directly the moderating effect of international environmental conditions on the international performance of entrepreneurial activities, and found that hostility of the international environment positively moderates the relation between international entrepreneurship and performance. Their results also showed diminishing returns to aggressive pursuit of entrepreneurial activities abroad under hostile environments (Zahra and Garvis, 2000). Environmental turbulence seems to have an effect on the relation between IEO and international performance; but there is clearly need for further information regarding the magnitude of this effect. We test this relation. The two focal sub-concepts used in this chapter are market dynamism (such as changes in export demand and customers' preferences and needs) and technological turbulence (such as changes and opportunities in the market, stemming from technological development). Hence, we hypothesize that environmental turbulence has an effect on the relation between IEO dimensions and international performance:

Hypothesis 2: *The relation between IEO and international performance is moderated by (a) market dynamism, and (b) technological turbulence.*

Methodology

Data collection

Data were obtained via separate mail surveys from two sources – New Zealand and Finnish exporters. The New Zealand sampling frame comprised *Profile Direct's* entire listing of 1,022 New Zealand exporting firms with 50 or more employees, and *Kompass Finland's* entire database of 1,205 exporting firms with 50 or more employees was used for the Finnish sampling. From the New Zealand sampling frame, 853 firms were selected randomly for contact, whereas all Finnish firms in the sample frame were contacted. The target contact in both samples was the export marketing manager, the marketing manager, the CEO or else the person that a firm representative said would know most about the firm's exporting operations. Firms were contacted by telephone to determine eligibility and to elicit cooperation in this study, and those agreeing to participate were mailed a questionnaire and a cover letter explaining the study. Of the original 853 New Zealand firms, 438 of the company names provided on the database were found to be ineligible since the firms had never exported, did no longer export, or were listed more than once. Of the remaining 415 eligible firms, 45 declined to participate, stating time constraints or company policy as reasons. Usable responses from 292 New Zealand exporting firms were obtained, a response rate of 70 per cent. Of the contacts listed on the Finnish database, 237 of the 1,205 listed names proved to be ineligible, leaving a total of 968 eligible contacts. Of these, 21 declined to participate and 783 usable responses were returned, a response rate of 81 per cent. A comparison of early and late respondents indicated that non-response bias was not a problem in either sample (Armstrong and Overton, 1977). The high response rates achieved also provided support for response equivalence.

Measurement items

IEO

The Jambulingam et al. (2005) scale was mainly applied here as it offers several multi-item measures for each dimension separately and (as shown in Table 9.1), comparison of reliabilities reported by previous studies focusing on sub-dimensions of EO reveals that the Jambulingam et al. (2005) study reported the highest alphas for the sub-dimensions. We first used the Jambulingam et al. (2005) 'proactiveness' scale, adapted for the international business context and extended to identify which managers seized the opportunities in anticipation of future market conditions. A three-item nine-point Likert scale was applied. Our 'innovativeness' scale was based on the scale of Jambulingam et al. (2005). All three scale items were modified to capture the international aspects of innovativeness, and innovativeness was measured with nine-point Likert scale items. We then assessed the degree to which managers took risks using items drawn from the Jambulingam et al. (2005) 'risk-taking' scale, again adapted to gauge the role of risk-taking as part of the firm's internationalization strategy. Our risk-taking scale thus consisted of three nine-point Likert scale items. The 'competitive aggressiveness' measure was based on items from Narver and Slater's (1990) competitor orientation scale and Jaworski and Kohli's (1993) market responsiveness scale. The scale consisted of four seven-point Likert scale items. Our 'autonomy' scale was based on the Jambulingam et al. (2005) autonomy scale items and adapted to the international context. We measured autonomy with five seven-point Likert scale items.

Market dynamism

According to Merz and Sauber (1995), environmental turbulence can be defined in terms of dynamism (i.e. unpredictable environmental changes), hostility (i.e. environmental threats to the firm's vitality), and heterogeneity (i.e. diversity of the firm's environment). Market dynamism was measured as perceived by the export managers. Measures were adapted from Cadogan et al. (2002), who used measures initially developed by Jaworski and Kohli (1993), and subsequently modified them for use in an export setting. The 'market dynamism' scale, measured with five-item seven-point Likert scale, captures changes in export customer preferences and needs, as well as customer demand and market growth.

Table 9.1 Invariance diagnostics

	χ^2 *(df)*	$\Delta\chi^2$ (Δdf)	RMSEA	CAIC	NNFI	CFI	GFI
Configural invariance	488.466 (353)		0.027	1688.314	0.98	0.98	0.97
Metric invariance	549.363 (366)	60.897 (13)	0.031	1645.913	0.98	0.98	0.97
Partial metric invariance	500.216 (363)	11.75 (10)	0.027	1620.604	0.98	0.98	0.97
Factor invariance	517.703 (371)	17.487 (8)	0.028	1574.523	0.98	0.98	0.97

Note: RMSEA = root mean square error of approximation; CAIC = consistent Akaike information criterion; NNFI = non-normed fit index; CFI = comparative fit index; GFI = goodness-of-fit index.

Technology turbulence

As it has been proposed that perceived characteristics of the environment significantly influence entrepreneurship activities (Zahra, 1993), we measured environmental turbulence by assessing technological turbulence as perceived by managers. Measures were adapted from Cadogan et al. (2002). Our scale of 'technological turbulence' captures changes and opportunities occurring in the firm's export markets as a result of technology. We measured technological turbulence with a four-item seven-point Likert scale.

International profiles

There is a need for multiple criteria (like scale and scope of internationalization, see, e.g. Ayal and Zif, 1979; Yeoh, 2004; and time) to study the phase of internationalization. Thus, firms in our samples were classified into three groups based on their scale, scope and rapidness of internationalization.

Scale of internationalization

Foreign sales as a percentage of total sales, among the other turnover measures, are mostly performance-related financial measures of the scale of DOI (Sullivan, 1994), and thus scale of internationalization was measured with export ratio (export sales as a percentage of total sales). We used the cut-off criterion of 25 per cent (see Knight and Cavusgil, 1996, 2004; Madsen et al., 2000; Moen, 2002). Although this is an arbitrary figure, it gives us an idea of how important international activities are for a firm, and by using this figure we can also compare our results with a number of earlier studies.

Scope of internationalization

In terms of market scope, the number of continents (Rugman, 2001) can be used as a proxy for market scope, and was thus adopted here. We asked managers in which of the following continents they had international operations: Australia and Pacific, Asia and Middle East, Europe, and America. Firms were labelled as truly global if they operated at least in three continents.

Time of internationalization

Madsen et al. (2000) and Knight and Cavusgil (2004) define born globals as firms that start export activities within 3 years of establishment. Thus, if companies had internationalized within 3 years, they were labelled rapid firms.

Firm types across scale, scope and time

Based on the three measures mentioned above, we classified firms in our sample into four groups, and labelled groups as follows: (1) *truly born globals* ($N = 250$), which internationalized within 3 years of their establishment, whose export ratio was at least 25 per cent, and who operated in at least three continents; (2) *global firms* ($N = 446$), which had either an export ratio above 25 per cent or operated in several continents; (3) *international firms* ($N = 295$), which were active in international markets, but their export ratio was below 25 per cent; and (4) *apparently born globals* ($N = 60$), which internationalized within 3 years of their establishment, and either had high export ratio (above 25 per cent) or operated in more than three continents. Based on the low number of firms in each group, we dropped 'apparently born globals' from further analyses.

Export performance

We assessed export performance by measuring aspects of the firm's profits: the firm's degree of satisfaction with its export profits over the last 3 years; the firm's degree of satisfaction with its market share in its export markets (this scale item was later deleted based on CFA results); and an overall assessment of the profitability of the firm's exporting operations during the last financial year. A three-item ten-point Likert scale was applied.

Assessment of measures

Initial purification of the scales was undertaken using exploratory factor analysis. To establish the cross-national applicability and external validity of the instruments, it was necessary to confirm that the scales have measurement equivalence/invariance across the countries. Configural, metric and factor variance invariances were tested with established procedures (Steenkamp and Baumgartner, 1998) for our eight latent variables: proactiveness, innovativeness, risk-taking, competitive aggressiveness, autonomy, market dynamism, technological turbulence and export profit performance. To evaluate measurement scales the following fit criteria were used: $\Delta \chi^2$ (Δ df), RMSEA, CAIC, NNFI and CFI (Steenkamp and Baumgartner, 1998). Table 9.1 shows that for configural invariance model, χ^2 was not significant ($\chi^2(353) = 488.466$, $p < 0.001$), but all other fit indices – RMSEA $= 0.027$, NNFI $= 0.98$ and CFI $= 0.98$ – were excellent. These results indicate that our scales exhibit acceptable configural invariance across the New Zealand and Finland samples.

Metric invariance tests for equal scale intervals or metrics across countries: this is tested by constraining the factor loadings of the baseline model to be the same across countries. As shown in Table 9.1, although there was a significant increase in χ^2 between the models of configural and metric invariance ($\Delta \chi^2(13) = 60.897$, $p < 0.001$), the χ^2/df for the model change from configural to metric invariance (χ^2/df $= 4.68$) and the other fit indices were still acceptable. However, as the $\Delta \chi^2$ was significant, partial metric invariance tests – which are suggested as a compromise between full measurement invariance and a lack of measurement invariance (Steenkamp and Baumgartner, 1998) – were conducted at the next phase. The measurement invariances suggested that three items were not invariant. Partial metric invariance was achieved by letting LISREL analyse these loadings separately for the New Zealand and Finland sample. Our partial metric invariance model shows an acceptable fit: $\Delta \chi^2(10) = 11.750$, RMSEA $= 0.027$, NNFI $= 0.98$ and CFI $= 0.98$ (Table 9.1).

Table 9.2 Construct correlations and scale properties

	1	2	3	4	5	6	7	8
1. Proactiveness								
2. Risk-taking	0.32							
3. Competitive aggressiveness	0.39	0.16						
4. Innovativeness	0.72	0.37	0.36					
5. Autonomy	−0.16	−0.02	−0.15	−0.12				
6. Market dynamism	0.20	0.15	0.07	0.22	−0.02			
7. Technological turbulence	0.12	0.12	0.10	0.19	−0.01	0.25		
8. Profit performance	0.31	0.06	0.24	0.30	−0.19	0.02	0.10	
Construct reliability (CR)	0.82	0.84	0.76	0.89	0.72	0.76	0.87	0.80
Average variance extracted (AVE)	0.70	0.73	0.51	0.80	0.48	0.46	0.69	0.68

Factor invariance was tested by constraining the correlations between latent variables to equality across countries. Our results (Table 9.1) again show acceptable fit for the model: $\Delta\chi^2(8) = 17.487$, RMSEA $= 0.028$, NNFI $= 0.98$ and CFI $= 0.98$. These invariance tests indicate that in general, New Zealand and Finland exporters hold the same factor structures for the eight latent variables in our model, and this result further supports combining the data sets.

Unidimensionality of the measures was assessed using CFA. Our confirmatory factor analysis indicated acceptable fit (χ^2 (df) $= 250.095$ (162); $p < 0.001$; RMSEA $= 0.024$; GFI $= 0.99$; NNFI $= 0.99$; CFI $= 0.98$). After the CFA, because of the model complexity, single indicants were constructed for the following multi-item scales: proactiveness, innovativeness, risk-taking, competitive aggressiveness, autonomy, market dynamism and technology turbulence, by averaging across the items (Bagozzi and Heatherton, 1994).

Table 9.2, above, shows the correlation coefficients for the summated scales and details the construct reliability and the average variance extracted (AVE) for each scale. All scales returned construct reliabilities in excess of 0.60, and with some exceptions the scales also returned an AVE greater than 0.50 (Bagozzi and Yi, 1988). In order to test the moderator effects, multiplicative product terms were calculated for interaction terms. These terms were orthogonalized using the procedure by Little et al. (2006).

Analysis and results

The modelling was undertaken using LISREL 8.30 (Jöreskog and Sörbom, 1996) with the maximum likelihood (ML) estimation procedure. Modelling was done using a series of nested models for each group. First, a main effects model was estimated across the groups, with the error variance of each latent variable set at $[(1 - \alpha) \sigma^2]$ (where α is the construct reliability from the sample and σ^2 is the standard deviation of the construct in the sample). As can be seen from Table 9.3, below, the model fit was good: χ^2 (162) $= 260.095$ ($p < 0.001$), RMSEA $= 0.024$, GFI $= 0.98$, NNFI $= 0.99$ and CFI $= 0.99$.

Table 9.3 Fit measures for the main effect, fully unrestricted, fully restricted and final models

Model	χ^2 (df)	RMSEA	CAIC	NNFI	CFI	GFI
Measurement model	260.095 (162)	0.024	–	0.99	0.99	0.98
Main effects	132.023 (81)	0.044	–	0.96	0.97	0.95
Fully unconstrained	899.198 (397)	0.062	2263.921	0.87	0.90	0.89
Fully constrained	703.931 (343)	0.057	2494.636	0.89	0.92	0.90
Final	877.152 (391)	0.062	2289.206	0.87	0.90	0.89

A fully unrestricted model – in which the factor loadings were constrained to be equal across the clusters while the path coefficients were allowed to vary – was then estimated. Following this, a fully restricted model was estimated with each path coefficient constrained invariant across the country samples.

Comparing the fully unrestricted and the fully restricted models provided information concerning the invariance of the model relationships (Singh, 1995). First, the increase in χ^2 resulting from constraining path coefficients invariant across the clusters was significant at $\alpha = 0.001\,\text{df}(54) = 195.267$. Furthermore, RMSEA decreased while the GFI, NNFI and CFI increased. Thus there is some evidence to suggest that the relationships specified are not invariant across the clusters. Additional analysis was therefore undertaken to determine whether an improvement in model fit could be obtained by relaxing some of the path invariance constraints.

Following Singh's (1995, p. 607) recommendation, we estimated a series of '"partially restricted" models that restrict path coefficients one-at-a-time to be equal' across the three clusters. For each partially restricted model, the test statistic and fit indices were examined relative to the fully constrained model (see Table 9.4). The results of this process identified four paths which, when allowed to vary across the clusters, improved the model fit. The path estimates and *t*-values for the 'final' model are provided in Table 9.5, and the fit measures appear in Table 9.3. The final model provided an acceptable fit: $\chi^2(391) = 877.152\,(p < 0.001)$, RMSEA $= 0.062$, GFI $= 0.90$, NNFI $= 0.87$ and CFI $= 0.90$. Thus, in many ways the final model represents an improvement on the fully constrained model. We can see from Table 9.3 that the final model is significantly better than the fully unconstrained model ($\Delta\chi^2(6) = 22.046$).

Findings and discussion

As can be seen in Table 9.5, the hypothesized constructs do a relatively good job at predicting the dependent variable: profit performance (the squared multiple correlation was 0.12). IEO was significantly related to profit performance. However, not all of the five dimensions contributed positively to profits: the relations between risk-taking and profits and autonomy and profits were significant but negative. One possible explanation for the unexpected negative relation between risk-taking

Table 9.4 Fit measures for the fully unrestricted and the partially restricted models

Influence held invariant	Model χ^2 (df)	$\Delta\chi^2$ (Δdf)	RMSEA	CAIC	NNFI	CFI	GFI	Invariance supported
None – fully constrained model	899.198 (397)		0.062	2263.921	0.87	0.90	0.89	
Proactiveness ⇨ profit performance	894.094 (395)	5.104 (2)	0.062	2274.594	0.87	0.90	0.89	Yes
Risk-taking ⇨ profit performance	894.784 (395)	4.414 (2)	0.062	2275.284	0.86	0.90	0.89	Yes
Competitive aggressiveness ⇨ profit performance	891.135 (395)	8.063 (2)[a]	0.062	2271.635	0.87	0.90	0.89	No
Innovativeness ⇨ profit performance	893.841 (395)	5.357 (2)	0.062	2274.341	0.87	0.90	0.89	Yes
Autonomy ⇨ profit performance	897.099 (395)	2.099 (2)	0.062	2277.6	0.86	0.90	0.89	Yes
Market dynamism ⇨ profit performance	896.366 (395)	2.832 (2)	0.062	2276.866	0.87	0.90	0.89	Yes
Technological turbulence ⇨ profit performance	894.919 (395)	4.279 (2)	0.062	2275.42	0.86	0.90	0.89	Yes
Proactiveness × market dynamism ⇨ profit performance	893.837 (395)	5.361 (2)	0.062	2274.337	0.87	0.90	0.89	Yes
Risk-taking × market dynamism ⇨ profit performance	891.631 (395)	7.567 (2)[a]	0.062	2272.131	0.87	0.90	0.89	No
Competitive aggressiveness × market dynamism ⇨ profit performance	898.161 (395)	1.037 (2)	0.063	2278.662	0.86	0.90	0.89	Yes
Innovativeness × market dynamism ⇨ profit performance	894.131 (395)	5.067 (2)	0.062	2274.631	0.87	0.90	0.89	Yes
Autonomy × market dynamism ⇨ profit performance	896.699 (395)	2.499 (2)	0.062	2277.199	0.86	0.90	0.89	Yes
Proactiveness × technology turbulence ⇨ profit performance	896.882 (395)	2.316 (2)	0.062	2277.382	0.86	0.90	0.89	Yes
Risk-taking × technology turbulence ⇨ profit performance	897.423 (395)	1.775 (2)	0.063	2277.923	0.86	0.90	0.89	Yes
Competitive aggressiveness × technology turbulence ⇨ profit performance	899.292 (395)	−0.094 (2)	0.063	2279.792	0.86	0.90	0.89	Yes
Innovativeness × technology turbulence ⇨ profit performance	898.687 (395)	0.511 (2)	0.063	2279.187	0.86	0.90	0.89	Yes
Autonomy × technology turbulence ⇨ profit performance	890.909 (395)	8.289 (2)[a]	0.062	2271.409	0.87	0.90	0.89	No

Only one path held invariant at a time.
[a] Significant at $p < 0.05$.

Table 9.5 Path coefficient and t-values

	Standardized parameter estimates				t-values			
	Not global players	Global firms	Truly BGs	All groups	Not global players	Global firms	Truly BGs	All groups
Proactiveness				0.104				1.981**
Risk-taking				−0.054				−1.626*
Competitive aggressiveness	0.285	0.13	0.07	0.173	4.445***	2.510***	1.051	3.314***
Innovativeness				−0.121				−3.645***
Autonomy				−0.074				−2.135**
Market dynamism				0.047				1.460*
Technological turbulence				−0.165				−2.505***
Proactiveness × market dynamism	0.152	−0.007	0.004	0.035	2.565***	−0.144	0.068	0.860
Risk-taking × market dynamism				0.143				2.166**
Competitive aggressiveness × market dynamism				0.000				−0.008
Innovativeness × market dynamism				0.004				0.074
Autonomy × market dynamism				−0.030				−0.849
Proactiveness × technology turbulence				−0.006				−0.167
Risk-taking × technology turbulence				0.023				0.399
Competitive aggressiveness × technology turbulence								
Innovativeness × technology turbulence								
Autonomy × technology turbulence	−0.189	−0.04	−0.019		−3.142***	−0.829	−0.298	

Squared multiple correlations for structural equation = 0.12 for all groups
Squared multiple correlations for structural equation = 0.23 for Not global players
Squared multiple correlations for structural equation = 0.16 for Global firms
Squared multiple correlations for structural equation = 0.13 for Truly BGs

Note: In order to determine whether variance explained in performance was equal across the three groups, the final model was re-run so that variance was freed across the groups. Model fit statistics χ^2 (389) = 868.275 ($p < 0.001$), RMSEA = 0.06, GFI = 0.89, NNFI = 0.87 and CFI = 0.90. The change in chi-square was significant at $p = 0.05$ ($\Delta \chi^2$ (2) = 8.877).
*$p < 0.10$; **$p < 0.05$; ***$p < 0.01$.

and profits may arise from our research setting. It may be that the results from various risky investments that export managers engage in materialize as profits only in the long run, and consequently the hypothesized causal relation is not captured without a longitudinal research setting. Another possible explanation is that the negative relation between risk-taking and profit performance in international markets results from the costs of operating in international markets being higher than the operating costs of local counterparts (Zahra and Garvis, 2000). This result clearly calls for more research as we do not have detailed information about the type of risks taken (i.e. to what extent risks relate to marketing strategies, new product development, investments decisions, partner selection and so on).

Autonomy refers to independent actions aimed at bringing forth a business concept or idea (Lumpkin and Dess, 2001). In general, autonomy is seen to be beneficial for a firm as it encourages innovation, and increases the competitiveness and effectiveness of a firm (Brock, 2003; Burgelman, 2001). However, Covin et al. (2006) have noted that firms that are overly dependent on participation in decision-making and require consensus to be reached before launching entrepreneurial initiatives may suffer financially (Covin et al., 2006). Thus, it seems that for international and global firms operating in multiple markets, consensus and autonomy are not necessarily suitable approaches as they make decision-making rigid and slow.

We have also found that the importance of certain variables on export profit performance appears to differ along the firm's international profile (DOI), particularly the role of competitive aggressiveness. Competitive aggressiveness contributed positively to profit performance for international and global firms, but not for truly born global firms. Truly born global firms were those which had internationalized within 3 years of their establishment, whose export ratio was at least 25 per cent, and which operated in at least three continents. Taking the broad scope and scale of truly born globals' international activities, it may be that their relative standing in international markets does not require a more aggressive competitor strategy. It may be that competitive aggressiveness is important in creating the international market presence and increasing sales but is not crucial in the later stages in internationalization pathways where the focus has shifted on keeping the position. Consequently, the focus of entrepreneurial strategies may then shift from exploration (finding new customers and winning them from competitors) to exploitation (serving existing customers better). Additionally, born global firms are often referred to follow the niche strategy in which competitive aggressiveness may not be relevant due to the nature of markets served.

We also controlled for the direct paths between environmental variables and profit performance, and found that both market dynamism and technology turbulence are significant predictors of profit performance. Under high levels of market dynamism, all firms' profit performance diminished. Indeed, if firms are finding that markets are becoming more turbulent and unpredictable, rather than responding to these conditions in an entrepreneurial way they may find that realizing their real options in a different way is more profitable. Technology turbulence, on the other hand, contributed positively to profit performance.

We also proposed some moderating effects. First, it was hypothesized that IEO's relationship with international performance differs along the market dynamism (H2a). This hypothesis is supported: proactiveness, risk-taking and innovativeness were found to be significant moderators. For firms operating in markets characterized by high levels of market dynamism, proactiveness actually leads to lower profits, and this holds for all groups. Market dynamism refers to changes in customer preferences and needs as well as international customer demand and market growth. It appears that in situations in which firms are operating in multiple markets – where customer needs are uncertain and rapidly changing – it becomes impossible to act in anticipation of market needs. An analogy can be derived from high-technology markets and industry evolution/technological cycles (Anderson and Tushman, 1991) where each technological discontinuity inaugurates a technology cycle. The breakthrough initiates an era of ferment, characterized with several competing designs, each embodying the fundamental breakthrough advance in a different way – thus creating thus customer FUD – fear, uncertainty, doubt. The design competition culminates in the appearance of a 'dominant design' which will become a market standard. According to Anderson and Tushman (1991) the winner of the design competition is seldom at the industry's performance frontier. On the other hand, in the same situation (i.e. under high levels of market dynamism), innovativeness seems to enhance profit performance across all types of international firms. Innovativeness was defined as a firm's propensity for new idea generation, experimentation and R&D activities (Lumpkin and Dess, 1996). Thus, we argue that in turbulent markets characterized with varying customer needs, entrepreneurial firms should rely on exploration strategies. Market-driving behaviour has also been suggested as key for non-international firms (Weerawardena and O'Cass, 2004).

The risk-taking dimension of IEO has a significant and positive effect on profit performance among international firms. Interestingly, the relation between risk-taking and profit performance becomes negative for firms operating in global markets, whereas for born globals the relation is positive (although not significant). Hence, for firms that are developing new markets and looking for new customers, risk-taking is beneficial, but for firms with global operations this may not be the case. It was also hypothesized that the IEO's relation with international performance differs with technology turbulence (H2b). Only limited support was found for H2b, as only one of the hypothesized moderators returned significant values. The results imply that for firms operating in markets characterized with high levels of technology turbulence, autonomy reduced international profits. This is especially true for international, but not for global, firms.

Managerial implications and further research

It is evident that our results indicate that entrepreneurial behaviour is important for managers involved in international business. However, they also imply that before engaging in proactive behaviour, competitive aggressiveness and venturesome risk-taking, managers should study their international market environments carefully and truly understand the nature of these turbulent markets, as strong emphasis on entrepreneurial behaviour does not always contribute positively to profits; performance is contingent on environmental turbulence. It also seems that excessive rapid global diversification strategy – the born global pathway – does not benefit from competitive aggressiveness or risk-taking when markets are changing, whereas this kind of entrepreneurial behaviour is advisable for internationalizing firms following a more traditional internationalization pathway. This may be because many truly born global firms are global niche operators who, in the most optimal situation, know their target customers well. If there is a need for competitive aggressiveness or if the market is extremely dynamic it naturally hinders the profits of such operators. Negative results regarding the autonomy dimension show that our results are partly in line with Zahra and Garvis (2000), who found that increases in international corporate entrepreneurship activity leads to negative returns in multiple foreign markets, and explained the negative returns by the difficulties firms can experience in managing complex foreign operations and by the costliness of coordinating, directing, and managing the venture.

To conclude, our study provides some new insights regarding the IEO–international performance relation. More research is needed, however, and we especially would like to encourage longitudinal studies focusing on the relation between actual internationalization pathways, IEO behaviour and performance.

References

Anderson, P. and Tushman M.L. (1991) 'Managing through cycles of technological change', *Research and Technology Management*, 34(3), 26–31.
Armstrong, J.S. and Overton, T.S. (1977) 'Estimating non-response bias in mail surveys', *Journal of Marketing Research*, 14(3), 396–402.
Ayal, I. and Zif, J. (1979) 'Marketing expansion strategies in multinational marketing', *Journal of Marketing*, 43(2), 84–94.
Bagozzi, R.P. and Heatherton, T.F. (1994) 'A general approach to representing multifaceted personality constructs: application to state self-esteem', *Structural Equation Modeling*, 1(1), 35–67.
Bagozzi, R.P. and Yi, Y. (1988) 'On the evaluation of structural equation models', *Journal of the Academy of Marketing Science*, 16(1), 74–94.
Balabanis, G.I. and Katsikea, E.S. (2003) 'Being an entrepreneurial exporter: does it pay?', *International Business Review*, 12(2), 233–52.
Bartlett, C.A. and Ghoshal, S. (2000) *Transnational Management. Text, Cases, and Readings in Cross-Border Management*, 3rd edn (Singapore: McGraw Hill).
Bell, J., McNaughton, R. and Young, S. (2001) ' "Born-again global" firms – an extension to the "born global" phenomenon', *Journal of International Management*, 7(3), 173–89.
Bell, J., McNaughton, R., Young, S. and Crick, D. (2003) 'Towards an integrative model of small firm internationalization', *Journal of International Entrepreneurship*, 1(4), 339–62.
Brock, D.M. (2003) 'Autonomy of individuals and organizations: towards a strategy research agenda', *International Journal of Business and Economics*, 2(1), 57–73.
Buckley, P.J. and Casson, M.C. (1976) *The Future of Multinational Enterprises* (New York: Holmes and Meier Publishers).
Burgelman, R.A. (2001) *Strategy is Destiny: How Strategy-making shapes a Company's Future* (New York: Free Press).

Cadogan, J.W., Diamantopoulos, A. and Siguaw, J.A. (2002) 'Export market-oriented activities: their antecedents and performance consequences', *Journal of International Business Studies*, 33(3), 615–26.

Cadogan, J.W., Kuivalainen, O. and Sundqvist, S. (2009) 'Export market-oriented behavior and export performance: quadratic and moderating effects under differing degrees of market dynamism and internationalization', *Journal of International Marketing*, 17(4), 71–89.

Contractor, F.J. (2007) 'Is international business good for companies? The evolutionary or multi-stage theory of internationalization vs. the transaction cost perspective', *Management International Review*, 47(3), 453–75.

Covin, J.G. and Covin, T.J. (1990) 'Competitive aggressiveness, environmental context, and small firm performance', *Entrepreneurship Theory and Practice*, 14(4), 35–50.

Covin, J.G., Green, K.M. and Slevin, D.P. (2006) 'Strategic process effects on the entrepreneurial orientation-sales growth rate relationship', *Entrepreneurship Theory and Practice*, 30(1), 57–81.

Covin, J.G. and Slevin, D.P. (1989) 'Strategic management of small firms in hostile and benign environments', *Strategic Management Journal*, 10(1), 75–87.

Crick, D. and Spence, M. (2005) 'The internationalization of "high performing" UK high-tech SMEs: a study of planned and unplanned strategies', *International Business Review*, 14(2), 167–85.

Dess, G.G., Lumpkin, G.T. and Covin, J. (1997) 'Entrepreneurial strategy making and firm performance: test of contingency and configurational models', *Strategic Management Journal*, 18(9), 677–95.

Ekeledo, I. and Sivakumar, K. (2004) 'International market entry mode strategies of manufacturing firms and service firms', *International Marketing Review*, 21(1), 68–101.

Ellis, P.D. (2007) 'Distance, dependence and diversity of markets: effects on market orientation', *Journal of International Business Studies*, 38(3), 374–86.

Jambulingam, T., Kathuria, R. and Doucette, W.R. (2005) 'Entrepreneurial orientation as a basis for classification within a service industry: the case of retail pharmacy industry', *Journal of Operations Management*, 23(1), 23–42.

Jantunen, A., Puumalainen, K., Saarenketo, S. and Kyläheiko, K. (2005) 'Entrepreneurial orientation, dynamic capabilities, and international performance', *Journal of International Entrepreneurship*, 3(3), 222–43.

Jaworski, B.J. and Kohli, A.K. (1993) 'Market orientation: antecedent and consequences', *Journal of Marketing*, 57(3), 53–70.

Johanson, J. and Vahlne, J.-E. (1977) 'The internationalization process of the firm: a model of knowledge development and increasing foreign market commitments', *Journal of International Business Studies*, 8(1), 23–32.

Johanson, J. and Vahlne, J.-E. (1990) 'The mechanism of internationalization', *International Marketing Review*, 7(4), 11–24.

Johanson, J. and Vahlne, J.-E. (2009) 'The Uppsala internationalization process model revisited: from liability of foreignness to liability of outsidership', *Journal of International Business Studies*, 40(9), 1411–31.

Jones, M.V. (1999) 'The internationalization of small high-technology firms', *Journal of International Marketing*, 7(4), 15–41.

Jones, M.V. and Coviello, N.E. (2005) 'Internationalization: conceptualising an entrepreneurial process of behaviour in time,' *Journal of International Business Studies*, 36(3), 284–303.

Jöreskog, K.G. and Sörbom, D. (1996) *LISREL 8: User's Reference Guide* (Chicago: Scientific Software International).

Keupp, M.M. and Gassmann, O. (2009) 'The past and the future of international entrepreneurship: a review and suggestions for developing the field', *Journal of Management*, 35(3), 600–33.

Knight, G.A. (2001) 'Entrepreneurship and strategy in the international SME', *Journal of International Management*, 7(3), 155–71.
Knight, G.A. and Cavusgil, S.T. (1996) 'The born global firm: a challenge to traditional internationalization theory', *Advances in International Marketing*, 8, 11–26.
Knight, G.A. and Cavusgil, S.T. (2004) 'Innovation, organizational capabilities, and the born-global firm', *Journal of International Business Studies*, 35(2), 124–41.
Kropp, F., Lindsay, N.J. and Shoham, A. (2006) 'Entrepreneurial, market, and learning orientations and international entrepreneurial business venture performance in South African firms', *International Marketing Review*, 23(5), 504–23.
Kuivalainen, O., Sundqvist, S. and Servais, P. (2007) 'Firms' degree of born-globalness, international entrepreneurial orientation and export performance', *Journal of World Business*, 42(3), 253–67.
Kutschker, M., Bäurle, I. and Schmid, S. (1997) 'International evolution, international episodes, and international epochs – implications for managing internationalization', *Management International Review*, 37(Special issue 2), 101–24.
Li, L., Li, D. and Dalgic, T. (2004) 'Internationalization process of small and medium-sized enterprises: toward a hybrid model of experiential learning and planning', *Management International Review*, 44(1), 93–116.
Liesch, P.W. and Knight, G.A. (1999) 'Information internalization and hurdle rates in small and medium enterprise internationalization', *Journal of International Business Studies*, 30(2), 383–94.
Little, T.D., Bovaird, J.A. and Widaman, K.F. (2006) 'On the merits of orthogonalizing powered and product terms: implications for modeling interactions among latent variables', *Structural Equation Modeling*, 13(4), 497–51.
Lumpkin, G.T. and Dess, G.G. (1996) 'Clarifying the entrepreneurial orientation construct and linking it to performance', *Academy of Management Review*, 21(1), 135–72.
Lumpkin, G.T. and Dess, G.G. (2001) 'Linking two dimensions of entrepreneurial orientation to firm performance: the moderating role of environment and industry life cycle', *Journal of Business Venturing*, 16(5), 429–51.
Lyon, D.W., Lumpkin, G.T. and Dess, G.G. (2000) 'Enhancing entrepreneurial orientation research: operationalizing and measuring a key strategic decision making process', *Journal of Management*, 26(5), 1055–85.
Madsen, T.K., Rasmussen, E.S. and Servais, P. (2000) 'Differences and similarities between born globals and other types of exporters', *Advances in International Marketing*, 10, 247–65.
Mathews, J.A. and Zander, I. (2007) 'The international entrepreneurial dynamics of accelerated internationalization', *Journal of International Business Studies*, 38(3), 387–403.
McDougall, P.P. and Oviatt, B.M. (1996) 'New venture internationalization, strategic change, and performance: a follow-up study', *Journal of Business Venturing*, 11(1), 23–40.
McDougall, P.P. and Oviatt, B.M. (2000) 'International entrepreneurship: the intersection of two research paths', *Academy of Management Journal*, 43(5), 902–8.
McDougall, P.P., Shane, S. and Oviatt, B.M. (1994) 'Explaining the formation of international new ventures: the limits of theories from international business research', *Journal of Business Venturing*, 9(6), 469–87.
Merz, G.R. and Sauber, M.H. (1995) 'Profiles of managerial activities in small firms', *Strategic Management Journal*, 16(7), 551–64.
Miller, D. and Friesen, P.H. (1982) 'Innovation in conservative and entrepreneurial firms: two models of strategic momentum', *Strategic Management Journal*, 3(1), 1–25.
Moen, Ø. (2002) 'The born globals – a new generation of small European exporters', *International Marketing Review*, 19(2/3), 156–75.
Myers, M.B., Droge, C. and Cheung, M.S. (2007) 'The fit of home to foreign market environment: an exploratory study of the relationship of congruence to performance', *Journal of World Business*, 42(2), 170–83.

Narver, J.C. and Slater, S.F. (1990) 'The effect of market orientation on business profitability', *Journal of Marketing*, 54(4), 20–35.

Oviatt, B.M. and McDougall, P.P. (1994) 'Toward a theory of international new ventures', *Journal of International Business Studies*, 25(1), 45–64.

Rauch, A., Wiklund, J., Lumpkin, G.T. and Frese, M. (2009) 'Entrepreneurial orientation and business performance: an assessment of past research and suggestions for the future', *Entrepreneurship Theory and Practice*, 33(3), 761–87.

Romanelli, E. and Tushman, M.L. (1986) 'Inertia, environments, and strategic choice: a quasi-experimental design for comparative-longitudinal research', *Management Science*, 32(5), 608–21.

Rugman, A.M. (2001) 'The myth of global strategy', *International Marketing Review*, 18(6), 583–8.

Rugman, A.M. and Verbeke, A. (2004) 'A perspective on regional and global strategies of multinational enterprises', *Journal of International Business Studies*, 35(1), 3–18.

Rugman, A.M. and Verbeke, A. (2008) 'A new perspective on the regional and global strategies of multinational services', *Management International Review*, 48(4), 397–411.

Singh, J. (1995) 'Measurement issues in cross-national research', *Journal of International Business Studies*, 26(3), 597–619.

Smart, D.T. and Conant, J.S. (1994) 'Entrepreneurial orientation, distinctive marketing competencies and organizational performance', *Journal of Applied Business Research*, 10(3), 28–38.

Steenkamp, J.-B.E.M. and Baumgartner, H. (1998) 'Assessing measurement invariance in cross-national consumer research', *Journal of Consumer Research*, 25(1), 78–90.

Sullivan, D. (1994) 'Measuring the degree of internationalization of a firm', *Journal of International Business Studies*, 25(2), 325–42.

Tallman, S. and Li, J. (1996) 'Effects of international diversity and product diversity on the performance of multinational firms', *Academy of Management Journal*, 39(1), 179–96.

Voss, Z.G., Voss, G.B. and Moorman, C. (2005) 'An empirical examination of the complex relationships between entrepreneurial orientation and stakeholder support', *European Journal of Marketing*, 39(9/19), 1132–50.

Weerawardena, J. and O'Cass, A. (2004) 'Exploring the characteristics of the market-driven firms and antecedents to sustained competitive advantage', *Industrial Marketing Management*, 33(5), 419–28.

Wiklund, J. and Shepherd, D. (2003) 'Knowledge-based resources, entrepreneurial orientation, and the performance of small and medium-sized businesses', *Strategic Management Journal*, 24(3), 1307–14.

Wiklund, J. and Shepherd, D. (2005) 'Entrepreneurial orientation and small business performance: a configurational approach', *Journal of Business Venturing*, 20(1), 71–91.

Yeoh, P.-L. (2004) 'International learning: antecedents and performance implications among newly internationalizing companies in an exporting context', *International Marketing Review*, 21(4/5), 511–35.

Zahra, S.A. (1993) 'Environment, corporate entrepreneurship, and financial performance: a taxonomic approach', *Journal of Business Venturing*, 8(4), 319–40.

Zahra, S.A. and Covin, J.G. (1995) 'Contextual influence on the corporate entrepreneurship – performance relationship: a longitudinal analysis', *Journal of Business Venturing*, 10(1), 43–58.

Zahra, S.A. and Garvis, D.M. (2000) 'International corporate entrepreneurship and firm performance: the moderating effect of international environment hostility', *Journal of Business Venturing*, 15(5/6), 469–92.

Zahra, S.A., Neubaum, D.O. and Huse, M. (1997) 'The effect of the environment on export performance among telecommunications new ventures', *Entrepreneurship Theory and Practice*, 22(1), 25–46.

10
Forging the Link between Business Model and Value Chain Constructs in the Context of an Internationalizing Entrepreneurial Firm – A Case Study

Liisa-Maija Sainio, Sami Saarenketo, Niina Nummela and Taina Eriksson

Introduction

Expansion to international markets requires changes in company strategy in order for it to fit into the novel environment (Calof and Beamish, 1995; Lam and White, 1999; McDougall and Oviatt, 1996). However, prior research on international entrepreneurship (IE) provides only a limited understanding of how companies change during internationalization (Nummela et al., 2006), and how this internal change is reflected in their value chain. The concept of the value chain seems to be central in IE research, which emphasizes that successful internationalization is based on controlling, not necessarily owning, value-creating assets and knowledge located in different parts of the globe (Oviatt and McDougall, 1994). Internationally entrepreneurial firms move their assets globally in order to stay competitive. Consequently, the value chain of these companies is often disintegrated and globally dispersed, and the company itself resembles a 'global factory' that reflects the combination of the innovation, distribution and production of goods and services worldwide (Buckley, 2009; Buckley and Ghauri, 2004). We do not assert, however, that all the value chain activities of entrepreneurial firms need to spread globally. For example, due to a global specialization in many industries, such as information and communications technology (ICT), some value chain activities never diffuse to all the continents of the 'triad', but locate more on a regional basis (e.g. sourcing and production in China and India). Therefore it might also be more efficient for a company to pursue regional rather than global strategy (Rugman and Verbeke, 2004).

Given these controversial developments within the global versus regional continuum, it is rather surprising that past research has so far mostly ignored the viewpoint of the value chain in explaining the evolution of internationalizing entrepreneurial firms (Axinn and Matthyssens, 2001; Zahra and George, 2002). The goal of this chapter is to explore how value is created in an internationalizing entrepreneurial firm. This chapter examines the relatively recent concept of business model in the context of international entrepreneurship by forging the links between business model and value chain constructs. While the role of business model has been discussed in the strategy and innovation literature, it has not been that explicitly pronounced in the domain of international entrepreneurship. We argue that the business model construct is a viable tool in understanding how exploitation of international opportunities and value creation across companies can be organized in practice. In line with Styles and Seymour (2006, p. 134), we define international entrepreneurship as *the behavioural processes associated with the creation and exchange of value through the identification and exploitation of opportunities that cross national borders.* The creation of value across borders seems to be one of the cornerstones in international entrepreneurship, and this study focuses on exploring how value is created in the international entrepreneurial firm. The output of the chapter is a detailed description of the networked inward and outward activities of the internationally operating firm, as well as an analytical tool for evaluating the status of the business model from the value creation perspective and anticipating future changes.

Theoretical discussion

Perspectives on the business model construct

Literature on business models has developed during the past two decades in various fields, providing several definitions that reflect fundamental theoretical differences in business model and strategy conceptualization. Recently there have been numerous efforts to conceptualize a business model (Tikkanen et al., 2005; Zott and Amit, 2010), to link it with the firm's strategy (Chesbrough, 2010; Teece, 2010) and to examine it as a dynamic phenomenon (Doz and Kosonen, 2010; McGrath, 2010). However, the use of the concept is still quite heterogeneous and no consensus of its definition yet exists. First, there are definitions that follow Porterian value chain thinking; streams (Mahadevan, 2000) or flows (Timmers, 2000) of the firm are used to describe the functions or activities of an organization in a meaningful way. Second, definitions may reflect the resource-based view of the firm (Penrose, 1959). These definitions are strongly asset- (Boulton et al., 2000) or resource-based (Hamel, 2000). Third, in the more recent literature on business models, the concept is referred to as a *design* or *architecture* with the notion of value creation at its core. For instance, Smith et al. (2010, p. 450) define business model as 'the design by which an organization converts a given set of strategic choices into value, and uses a particular organizational architecture in order to create and capture that value'. There are also differences in the width of the definition: the revenue model or earnings logic may be the narrowest content of the business-model concept, while at the other extreme, business model incorporates all possible functions into the definition (Chesbrough and Rosenbloom, 2002; Slywotzky, 1996). In this chapter, we adopt the definition of Zott and Amit (2008), who define business model as a structural template describing the organization of a focal firm's transactions with all of its external constituents in factor and product markets. This definition focuses on inter-firm transactions, but builds on the resource-based view; the focus of interest is on the value-adding exchange in the transactions and the essential resources of the focal firm that are needed to enable the exchanges.

The concept of business model is a representation of management thinking and practice, which helps the decision-makers to see, understand and run their activities in a distinct and specific way (Chararbaghi et al., 2003, p. 373). In particular, although a business model is always described from the viewpoint of an individual firm, the concept itself is not restricted inside the company's boundaries. On the contrary, a business model describes how the organization is linked to external shareholders, and how it engages in economic exchanges with them to create value for all exchange partners (Zott and Amit, 2007). Thus, the focus of organization design has shifted from the administrative structure of the firm to the structural organization of its exchanges with external stakeholders and value creation (Zott and Amit, 2008).

Another aspect highlighting the linkage between the concept of business model and international entrepreneurship is the identification, evaluation and exploitation of opportunities – an emerging theme in the international entrepreneurship literature (Dimitratos and Jones, 2005). Particularly the latter phase – exploitation – has so far attracted only limited interest in the literature (Zahra, 2005). In our opinion, the business model would serve as a viable framework in understanding how the exploitation of international opportunities and value creation across companies can be organized in practice. After all, entrepreneurs' primary driver for international activities is value creation through cross-border resource combinations (Autio, 2005), and it is evident that international entrepreneurs exchange and co-create value (tangible or intangible, actual or symbolic) with a variety of different actors, including suppliers, customers, society, financiers (Styles and Seymour, 2006) and even competitors (Bengtsson and Kock, 1999).

Surprisingly, the business model and value creation in international entrepreneurial firms have not been explicitly linked in the prior literature. Therefore, this chapter presents a contribution to the international entrepreneurship literature by forging the links between IE, value creation and business model concept. Previous business model literature largely concentrates on the firm-internal viewpoint. We argue that, especially in the context of international entrepreneurial firms, value creation must be examined in the interfaces of the firm. Thus, our business model concept serves as a tool for understanding the kinds of exchange and value that each partner gives and receives in the company interface.

Presentation of the theoretical framework

The starting point in our analysis of the links between business model, value chains and international entrepreneurship is that an opportunity equals a possibility to create and capture value. As Zahra (2005) describes, entrepreneurial actions define the core of the venture's ability to develop ways to create value beyond established competitors. Thus, the ventures gain access to resources through cooperation agreements, such as partnerships, both up- and downstream. These inter-organizational networks form an important source of competitive advantage in international entrepreneurship (Keupp and Gassmann, 2009; Rialp et al., 2005), and it is a central challenge to decision-makers in these firms to manage them. Governing the supplier and partner networks plays a key role in the success of an individual firm's business model (Westerlund, 2009). In the context of international entrepreneurship, the value creation of the firm is based on cross-border combination of valuable resources, and the firm needs to internationalize in order to create value, not just seek markets for its outputs (Autio, 2005). Therefore, the business model should be able to identify where and how international new ventures create value (Zahra, 2005).

In this study, we build our business model concept based on Zott and Amit's (2008) description of business model as a 'structure and governance of a firm's boundary-spanning direct exchanges'. This view concentrates on the direct exchanges between suppliers, partners and customers, but does not include the whole value chain participating in the end-customer value creation. This viewpoint is especially suitable for international context, since it enables the examination of the value creation process as the core of the business model, instead of trying to describe all the functions or assets of the company, which often leads to descriptive business models without any dynamics. Zott and Amit (2007) also argue that one of the central design tasks of entrepreneurs is to define the ways in which their business interacts with suppliers, customers and partners. From the perspective of the international entrepreneurial firm, it is essential to define the central resources and capabilities that enable the transactions with up- and downstream partners, and the incentives for the transactions which make the firm an attractive buyer or seller from the partner's perspective. Previously, there have been few studies in the field of international business and entrepreneurship taking the holistic approach (including both upstream and downstream activities) in the analysis of the internationalization configuration of the firms (Fletcher, 2001; Knudsen and Servais, 2007; Servais et al., 2006, are exceptions).

Interfaces of value-creating transactions

The firm must manage direct value-creating transactions in three separate interfaces: customers, suppliers and partners (see Figure 10.1). The arrows in the figure describe the value-creating exchange in each interface, and the resulting ties and dependency between the actors. Although in international markets the customer interface may be managed through sales partners, the actual product/service is still in direct contact with the customer, and this is the most critical point in value creation. Therefore it is central to examine the nature of this exchange in terms of what is actually offered to the customer, and how that offering stands out from that of competitors. Additionally, the type of relationship with the customer is of importance – whether the firm is able to raise the customer's switching costs and create a customer lock-in (Javalgi et al., 2005).

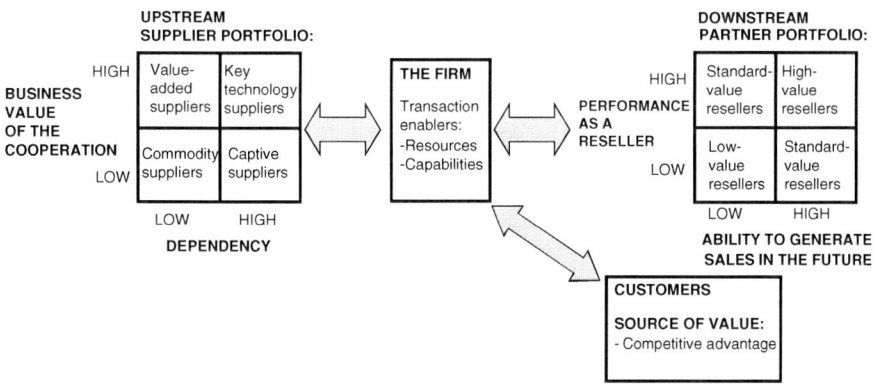

Figure 10.1 The business model construct of the study

Partner categorization

Value may be created with both upstream and downstream partners. The nature of these partnerships defines how value creation is managed. Stronger ties with partners imply higher levels of cooperation and trust, but also a higher level of strategic vulnerability (Cook and Emerson, 1978). The relationship between partners can also be evaluated in terms of power and dependency – the state of closeness that evolves between partners as a result of collaboration (Håkansson, 1982). As firms are concentrating on their core competencies, they are externalizing value activities and creating strong supplier partnerships with stronger ties and dependency. When key supplier relationships become more and more strategic in nature, the firm should be able to evaluate the value creation potential of the available and existing suppliers (Möller and Törrönen, 2003). This highlights the fact that all partners are not equal in the business model of an international entrepreneurial firm, and thus a classification of partners is necessary. For this purpose, we use the portfolio approach (see Krapfel et al., 1991 for the use of portfolio approach in categorizing relationships). Here we apply a classification that has been developed for internationally operating software firms (Ruokonen et al., 2008). Accordingly, upstream partners, such as suppliers, may be classified into four groups in terms of dependency and value created; and downstream partners, such as sales partners, in terms of current and future sales performance (Figure 10.1). This kind of classification allows the key decision-makers to evaluate which parts of the value chain offer most potential for value creation in the future and which require revision. The latter is particularly significant, as the change related to identification and exploitation of opportunities is bound to be reflected in the value chain.

Value creation potential

Exploitation of international opportunities requires collaboration with reliable partners who expect that the focal firm actually offers an incentive to its partner;

why – besides monetary compensation – does this partner want to interact with the firm, and how could this relationship be strengthened? Thus, the value creation analysis of the business model construct must be twofold: supplier incentive versus supplier value to the firm, and partner incentive versus partner value to the firm. In order to evaluate a supplier's value creation potential, Möller and Törrönen (2003) propose that it consists of three functions: efficiency (e.g. profit or volume), effectiveness (providing solutions with more value to customers) and network (access to other suppliers, getting market information or market signals). From the supplier's perspective, the incentive for the relationship is determined by the willingness and ability of transaction partners to provide sufficient demand for current and expected future outputs compared with the availability and cost of establishing relationships with alternative partners (Krapfel et al., 1991).

An internationalizing entrepreneurial firm must be able to leverage its foreign distributor's (downstream partner's) competencies to maximize its performance outcomes abroad and overcome uncertainty and risk of foreign markets (Knight and Cavusgil, 2004). In addition, since resources are limited, the focal firm should be able to leverage its learning process from different markets related to partner management to seek efficiency in managing the partner portfolio. Therefore, the value of using partners is evident for an entrepreneurial firm: to tap to their market knowledge, to gain access to new markets and to grow. On the other hand, the sales partner incentive may relate to product or service novelty that increases their own competitive advantage (Narula and Hagedoorn, 1999).

On the other hand, it can be expected that international expansion requires changes of actors in the value chain and also changes in the relationships with current actors and their roles. Value creation is also a central element in this process, as building long-term relationships requires that both parties gain value from it. The dynamism emerges from changing actors, changing levels of dependency and a changing logic of value creation. As the relationships change, the firm-internal resources and capabilities to manage these changes must also adapt to be able to govern and support these value-creating transactions (Möller and Svahn, 2003).

Methodology and data collection

In order to test the applicability of the business model concept for international entrepreneurship, we take a case-study approach. In order to minimize the effects of external and situational factors, we limit our analysis to a single company, chosen with theoretical sampling. Theoretical sampling is carried out with a view to choosing cases that are likely to replicate or extend the emergent theory (Eisenhardt, 1989, p. 537). The theoretical criteria also have to be kept in mind; that is, how well they fit the conceptual categories and what their explanatory power is (Eisenhardt, 1989; Smith, 1991). In the case selection, we set out to find a company that would be characterized by the following: (1) a business model with boundary-spanning exchange relationships both upstream and downstream of the value chain; (2) the utilization of these partner relationships and networks in internationalization; (3) both sourcing and sales activities carried out in several target countries; and (4) enough experience in internationalization to enable the activities to be thoroughly analysed. The case company Syscon Ltd fulfils these requirements. Syscon Ltd is a provider of complex ICT systems mainly to public sector organizations. It was founded in 1996, and currently holds an 85 per cent market share in its home market for its main product. For the reasons of confidentiality, the name of the company has been changed.

In gathering the data, we pursued the principles of data collection established by Eisenhardt (1989) and Yin (1994), and used multiple sources of evidence. The data collection consisted of both individual interviews and group interview sessions with the key managers of the company. In order to be able to devise the company's business model, background knowledge was needed about the product concept, the history of internationalization, the way public sector customers buy the solution and how customer value is created. In addition, in order to categorize upstream suppliers and downstream sales partners, knowledge was needed on those actors. We had the opportunity to interview some of the key persons several times between October 2008 and August 2009. Finally, one larger group interview session with four key informants, concentrating on the business model concept, was conducted in August 2009. In all of the interviews, a set of open-ended questions was used. The interview duration ranged from 25 to 180 minutes, and they were recorded and subsequently transcribed. We complemented the interview materials with secondary sources of information (such as brochures, customer magazines, presentations and internet) in order to improve the reliability and validity of the findings derived from the interviews.

The business model of Syscon Ltd

The goal of the empirical case study was to apply our framework to describe the business model of the chosen internationalizing entrepreneurial firm in order to see what it reveals concerning value creation in the chosen interfaces: customers, upstream suppliers and downstream partners. In addition, we wanted to examine what kinds of changes in value creation appear concerning the key resources and capabilities of Syscon Ltd, and derive conclusions of the applicability and benefits of the framework.

Customer value and customer lock-in at Syscon Ltd

The value of the product from the customer perspective depends on who is considered to be the customer. The product enables more security and efficiency in customer care in customer interface; in addition, from the perspective of the public organization decision-maker, it provides measurable cost savings and easy maintenance. The product provides unique advantages compared to competitors, such as customer-specific tailoring and scalability. Product uniqueness means that the customers need to be educated about the benefits of the product; the level of knowledge differs considerably between target markets. The core product is very standardized, but tailoring is done based on the required interfaces and also the number of units in use and the way they are interconnected. Currently the product is the only IP-based solution for its purpose in the market, which saves the extra cabling costs in the customer organizations. The customer lock-in is very strong: *'If we get 3–4 units* (inside one organization), *then it is too late for the poor customer to change.'* The organization gets more benefit from the system if it expands to more units inside one organization. Since the customers represent public organizations with public tendering requirements, it is essential to be in contact with customers very early and educate the potential customer about the unique characteristics and benefits of the solution. *'We must work as much as possible before the bid is defined, because if they specify a simpler system, we have lost the deal.'* Although export sales are officially in the hands of partners, the Syscon sales managers are also constantly on the move, visiting the customers. Since the company is relatively small, they can react to new customer needs flexibly and adapt the product better than their larger competitors.

Upstream suppliers

Syscon exploited international opportunities early as they made a strategic decision to outsource the production before downstream internationalization began. Both the software and hardware production are outsourced, largely to international suppliers. Currently the firm has 15 suppliers, with one-third of them in Europe, one-third in Asia and the rest national. When examining the value formation in upstream suppliers, the current suppliers were categorized with regard to dependency and business value of the cooperation (see Figure 10.2). The size of the circle in Figure 10.2 refers to the volume of purchases from the supplier category in question. The largest volume of purchases comes from key contract manufacturers with high dependency and high business value. There is also a relatively large amount of bulk components from commodity suppliers. For the section of value-added suppliers, the firm representatives categorized third-party product purchases that require a low level of integration. These parts provide value for the final product but the dependency of these suppliers was considered rather low. On the other hand, there were also some captive suppliers providing products

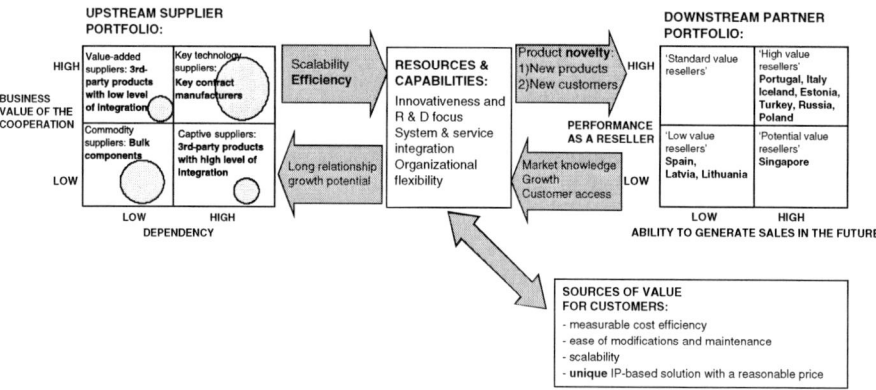

Figure 10.2 The business model of Syscon Ltd

with high levels of required integration. This group was considered to be problematic, since the business value is low but the integration is time-consuming. The firm is currently reorganizing its supplier portfolio. They have realized that they need to reduce the number of suppliers to make transactions more efficient, have more negotiating power through bigger purchases and concentrate on suppliers with potential for large volumes as international growth continues. Thus, they are clearly seeking efficiency (Möller and Törrönen, 2003) in their value formation upstream, with fewer partners. The incentive for suppliers to form long-term relationships with the company is to take advantage of this growing new venture with larger volumes. This concentration will imply stronger ties and higher dependency on fewer suppliers.

Downstream sales partners

The company's internationalization activities downstream are more recent than upstream. The impetus for international sales has come from a saturated home market, where the firm holds the market leader position. The growth strategy is aggressive: the goal is that by 2012, 50 per cent of the revenue comes from international markets. The firm offers only one of their products internationally – the IP-based infrastructure solution for public organizations. The firm has had a very strict policy in partner selection; the potential partner has to be a systems integrator that appreciates new technologies and has advanced IT knowledge. In addition, the partner must be benefit- instead of price-centred and of a suitable size so that it is easy to form good working relations with the contact persons.

Finally, the partner must be making direct sales to the final customer. At present the company has one sales partner in each target country. Therefore, the downstream partner categorization was made at country level. The firm representatives categorized the resellers based on their subjective evaluation on their current and expected future performance. The vast majority of target countries were categorized as 'high-value resellers', as they have very promising and active partners with big deals in Portugal, Italy, Iceland, Estonia, Turkey, Russia and Poland. High-value resellers are defined as partners that generate the most sales and are able to achieve (and increase) sales in the future (Ruokonen et al., 2008). Moreover, these 'core partners' are able to offer a complete chain of customer service functions: pre-sales, sales, consultancy, implementation, technical support and after-sales (Varis et al., 2005). The countries that are now placed in the category of low-value resellers represent small markets with challenges in public sector financing. Currently no countries were positioned as standard value resellers, and only the partner in Singapore was considered as having strong future potential but low current performance.

Partner performance is evaluated on a monthly basis, in terms of closed deals, customer sales calls and offers made. Every partner is visited six times a year to ensure smooth cooperation. The firm has seen the value of the first installation as a reference in new markets: *'It is essential in every market, and the partner definitely utilizes it in their marketing efforts.'* The dependency on sales partners was considered to be on a high level: the partners have the local market and public sector customer knowledge. In addition, changing partners requires a lot of effort, although at the moment finding new partners is easy since the product is unique. Product uniqueness was considered the basis for the partners' choice of working with Syscon, and thus the source of value. There were two reasons why the Syscon solution was beneficial for the partners' product portfolio: it either enabled new sales to their existing customer base, or it enabled the partner to access new customer groups.

Since the internationalization process is in its first stages and the company's resources are limited, they are currently approaching new markets with a probe-and-learn strategy. If a market opens up properly, that market will be getting most of their resources, as the company representative describes: *'Next autumn we will make the sale to the first unit in Italy, and if the system starts to rock, we will focus all our resources to that market so that this market will grow as fast as possible.'*

Key resources and capabilities and changes in value creation

As the case description indicates, Syscon is an international entrepreneurial firm which has succeeded in its strategy formation and concentration on its core competencies. The analysis has revealed that the key resources and capabilities from the perspective of value formation are innovativeness and focus on R&D, system and service integration, and organizational flexibility. Concentration on R&D and the aggressive outsourcing of all production has worked well, although now the company seeks further efficiency in their upstream supplier portfolio. Related to outsourcing, Syscon has also shifted its in-house capabilities to software, integration and services instead of hardware sales, and aims to change its pricing structures accordingly. Previously their internationalization emphasis was on supplier side (see, e.g. an 'international sourcer' in Knudsen and Servais's (2007) typology of internationalization configuration), but now there is a clear strategic focus and concentration of resources on downstream internationalization. This new emphasis puts demands for stronger efficiency and scalability of volumes upstream, thus creating dynamism in the business model. Figure 10.2 shows the application of the developed framework for the business model of Syscon Ltd with both upstream and downstream partner categorizations, key resources and capabilities and value exchange between partners.

The company wants to keep strong ties to sales partners: *'We want to be a partner that is close.'* Due to the very technical and complex nature of the product offering, sales support requires many technical resources, especially in the partner-training phase. Syscon is also present in the first sales calls in foreign markets, and gives sales training. We expect that the desire for closeness will be a future challenge for the company. Limited resources push the company to use sales partners, so there is no direct interface with the customers. Additionally, with further international expansion the number of partners is bound to increase. As a result, considerable pressure will be put on development of value chain management capabilities as well as partner portfolio management.

The business model of Syscon faces multiple internal and external pressures. At present Syscon is enjoying the position of having the most innovative product in the market. Eventually, competitors will follow. How should the business model adapt to the competitor pressures? Again, examining the value formation may give some indications: first, from customer perspective, increasing options will put pressure on pricing, but also on new product features such as new options for integration or new types of additional services to create added value. Second, sales partners may need stronger incentives to stay loyal to the focal firm and its products; the firm should therefore pay even more attention to partner satisfaction in terms of both monetary and other incentives. Third, competition for top-quality suppliers may become fiercer. The company should be able to leverage its previous learning experiences from partner management and integrate those experiences already to the market choice and partner-scanning phase, so that it may maximize its efficiency in partner management.

Conclusions

Our research complements previous studies on international entrepreneurship and provides a useful addition to the literature by outlining the role of a clearly framed business model in international entrepreneurial behaviour. The novelty of the approach is that inward and outward internationalization processes (Korhonen et al., 1996) are simultaneously examined, thus highlighting a holistic approach to internationalization (as suggested by Fletcher, 2001). Additionally, our business model construct provides a way to examine both upstream and downstream value creation processes simultaneously, and thus evaluate the internationalization configuration (Knudsen and Servais, 2007) from a new perspective. Our case company is an example of a successful 'global start-up strategy' (Oviatt and McDougall, 1994) as the firm actively pursues both international sourcing and selling, and is able to manage this 'global factory'.

Even though the importance of business models for value creation has been highlighted, the explicit connection to cross-border activities with suppliers, customers and competitors has remained an untouched field of scholarly inquiry. As customer value is increasingly created through collaboration with partners and suppliers, there is a growing need for integration between the units responsible for these critical cross-boundary relationships, and managing these value processes (Piercy, 2009). The development of this value-based business model construct in international entrepreneurship suggests that there is a need for an inter-disciplinary approach. For instance, IE scholars should examine the incentives for international upstream suppliers more closely by building on the supply management literature.

To conclude, firms exist to create value. An international entrepreneurial firm is faced with resource constraints, so their value creation must be boundary-spanning. We believe that the presented business model concept enables an internationalizing entrepreneurial firm to examine the totality of its operation from the value creation perspective, so that the situation of both upstream and downstream activities and their interaction may be strategically analysed.

References

Autio, E. (2005) 'Creative tension: the significance of Ben Oviatt's and Patricia McDougalls's article "Toward a theory of international new ventures" ', *Journal of International Business Studies*, 36(1), 9–19.

Axinn, C.N. and Matthyssens, P. (2001) 'Limits of internationalization theories in an unlimited world', *International Marketing Review*, 19(5), 436–49.

Bengtsson, M. and Kock, S. (1999) 'Cooperation and competition in relationships between competitors in business networks', *Journal of Business and Industrial Marketing*, 14(3), 178–94.

Boulton, R., Libert, B. and Samek, S. (2000) 'A business model for the new economy', *Journal of Business Strategy*, 21(4), 29–35.

Buckley, P.J. (2009) 'The impact of the global factory on economic development', *Journal of World Business*, 44(2), 131–43.

Buckley, P.J. and Ghauri, P.N. (2004) 'Globalisation, economic geography and the strategy of multinational enterprises', *Journal of International Business Studies*, 35(3), 81–98.

Calof, J.L. and Beamish, P.W. (1995) 'Adapting to foreign markets: explaining internationalization', *International Business Review*, 4(2), 115–31.

Chararbaghi, K., Fendt, C. and Willis, R. (2003) 'Meaning, legitimacy and impact of business models in fast-moving environments', *Management Decision*, 41(4), 372–82.

Chesbrough, H. (2010) 'Business model innovation: opportunities and barriers', *Long Range Planning*, 43(2/3), 354–63.

Chesbrough, H. and Rosenbloom, R. (2002) 'The role of the business model in capturing value from innovation: evidence from Xerox corporation's technology spin-off companies', *Industrial and Corporate Change*, 11(3), 529–55.

Cook, K. and Emerson, R.M. (1978) 'Power, equity and commitment in exchange networks', *American Sociological Review*, 43(5), 721–39.

Dimitratos, P. and Jones, M. (2005) 'Future directions for international entrepreneurship research', *International Business Review*, 14(2), 119–28.

Doz, Y. and Kosonen, M. (2010) 'Embedding strategic agility – a leadership agenda for accelerating business model renewal', *Long Range Planning*, 43(2/3), 370–82.

Eisenhardt, K.M. (1989) 'Building theories from case study research', *Academy of Management Review*, 14(4), 532–50.

Fletcher, R. (2001) 'A holistic approach to internationalisation', *International Business Review*, 10(1), 25–49.

Hamel, G. (2000) *Leading the Revolution* (Boston, MA: Harvard Business School Press).

Håkansson, H. (1982) (ed.) *International Marketing and Purchasing of Industrial Goods. An Interaction Approach* (Chichester, UK: John Wiley and Sons).

Javalgi, R.G., Radulovich, L.P., Pendleton, G. and Scherer, R.F. (2005) 'Sustainable competitive advantage of internet firms: a strategic framework and implications for global marketers', *International Marketing Review*, 22(6), 658–72.

Keupp, M. and Gassmann, O. (2009) 'The past and the future of international entrepreneurship: a review and suggestions for developing the field', *Journal of Management*, 35(3), 600–33.

Knight, G.A. and Cavusgil, S.T. (2004) 'Innovation, organizational capabilities, and the born-global firm', *Journal of International Business Studies*, 35(2), 124–41.

Knudsen, M.P. and Servais, P. (2007) 'Analyzing internationalization configurations of SME's: the purchaser's perspective', *Journal of Purchasing and Supply Management*, 13(2), 137–51.

Korhonen, H., Luostarinen, R. and Welch, L. (1996) 'Internationalization of SMEs: inward-outward patterns and government policy', *Management International Review*, 36(4), 315–29.

Krapfel, R.E., Salmond, D. and Spekman, R. (1991) 'A strategic approach to managing buyer-seller relationships', *European Journal of Marketing*, 25(9), 22–37.
Lam, L.W. and White, L.P. (1999) 'An adaptive choice model of the internationalisation process', *International Journal of Organizational Analysis*, 7(2), 105–34.
Mahadevan, B. (2000) 'Business models for internet-based e-commerce: an anatomy', *California Management Review*, 42(4), 55–69.
McDougall, P.P. and Oviatt, B.M. (1996) 'New venture internationalization, strategic change, and performance: a follow-up study', *Journal of Business Venturing*, 11(1), 23–40.
McGrath, R.G. (2010) 'Business models: a discovery driven approach', *Long Range Planning*, 43(2/3), 247–61.
Möller, K.E. and Svahn, S. (2003) 'Managing strategic nets – a capability perspective', *Marketing Theory*, 3(2), 209–34.
Möller, K.E. and Törrönen, P. (2003) 'Business suppliers' value creation potential: a capability-based analysis', *Industrial Marketing Management*, 32(2), 109–18.
Narula, R. and Hagedoorn, J. (1999) 'Innovating through strategic alliances: moving towards international partnerships and contractual agreements', *Technovation*, 19(5), 283–94.
Nummela, N., Loane, S. and Bell, J. (2006) 'Change in SME internationalisation: an Irish perspective', *Journal of Small Business and Enterprise Development*, 13(4), 562–83.
Oviatt, B.M. and McDougall, P.P. (1994) 'Toward a theory of international new ventures', *Journal of International Business Studies*, 25(1), 45–64.
Penrose, E. (1959) *The Theory of the Growth of the Firm* (Oxford University Press: Oxford).
Piercy, N.F. (2009) 'Strategic relationships between boundary-spanning functions: aligning customer relationship management with supplier relationship management', *Industrial Marketing Management*, 33(8), 857–64.
Rialp, A., Rialp, J. and Knight, G.A. (2005) 'The phenomenon of early internationalizing firms: what do we know after a decade (1993–2003) of scientific inquiry?', *International Business Review*, 14(2), 147–66.
Rugman, A.M. and Verbeke, A. (2004) 'A perspective on regional and global strategies of multinational enterprises', *Journal of International Business Studies*, 35(1), 3–18.
Ruokonen, M., Hätönen, J., Lindqvist, J., Jantunen, S., Marjakoski, E. and Hurmelinna-Laukkanen, P. (2008) 'Global network management – ideas and tools for ICT firms to thrive in international network environment', Technology Business Research Center, Lappeenranta University of Technology and Turku School of Economics. Available at: http://tbrc-community.lut.fi/vcm/publication/downloadable-documents.
Servais, P., Zucchella, A. and Palamara, G. (2006) 'International entrepreneurship and sourcing: international value chain of small firms', *Journal of Euromarketing*, 16(1/2), 105–17.
Slywotzky, A. (1996) *Value Migration* (Boston: Harvard Business School Press).
Smith, C. (1991) 'The Case-Study: A vital yet misunderstood research method for management', in N.C. Smith and P. Dainty (eds) *The Management Research Handbook*, 145–58 (London: Routledge).
Smith, W., Binns, A. and Tushman, M. (2010) 'Complex business models: managing strategic paradoxes simultaneously', *Long Range Planning*, 43(2/3), 448–61.
Styles, C. and Seymour, R.G. (2006) 'Opportunities for marketing researchers in international entrepreneurship', *International Marketing Review*, 23(2), 126–45.
Teece, D. (2010) 'Business models, business strategy and innovation', *Long Range Planning*, 43(2/3), 172–94.
Tikkanen, H., Lamberg, J-A., Parvinen, P. and Kallunki, J-P. (2005) 'Managerial cognition, action, and the business model of the firm', *Management Decisions*, 43(6), 789–809.
Timmers, P. (2000) *Electronic Commerce: Strategies and Models for Business-to-Business Trading* (Chichester: John Wiley and Sons Ltd).
Varis, J., Kuivalainen, O. and Saarenketo, S. (2005) 'Partner selection for international marketing and distribution in corporate new ventures', *Journal of International Entrepreneurship*, 3(1), 19–36.

Westerlund, M. (2009) 'The role of network governance in business model performance', Helsinki School of Economics, Working papers, W-472, October.

Yin, R.K. (1994) *Case Study Research – Design and Methods* (Thousand Oaks, CA: Sage Publications).

Zahra, S.A. (2005) 'A theory of international new ventures: a decade of research', *Journal of International Business Studies*, 36(1), 20–8.

Zahra, S.A. and George, G. (2002) 'International entrepreneurship: the current status of the field and future research agenda', in M. Hitt, D. Ireland, D. Sexton and M. Camp (eds) *Strategic Entrepreneurship: Creating an Integrated Mindset*, 255–88 (Cambridge, MA: Blackwell).

Zott, C. and Amit, R. (2007) 'Business model design and the performance of entrepreneurial firms', *Organization Science*, 18(2), 181–99.

Zott, C. and Amit, R. (2008) 'The fit between product market strategy and business model: implications for firm performance', *Strategic Management Journal*, 29(1), 1–26.

Zott, C. and Amit, R. (2010) 'Business model design: an activity system perspective', *Long Range Planning*, 43(2/3), 216–26.

11
Entrepreneurial Marketing Strategies During the Growth of International New Ventures

Johanna Hallbäck and Peter Gabrielsson

Introduction

The traditional marketing approach views marketing as a managerial process, and it emerged mainly from the focus on large, established companies (Kotler, 1997). Although the definition of marketing evolves and new approaches are being established researchers have, during the past two decades, pointed out that marketing theories may not be adequate for understanding smaller, younger and entrepreneurial firms (Carson and Cromie, 1989; Carson and Gilmore, 2000; Coviello et al., 2000; Hills et al., 2008). In dealing with these latter firms, researchers have emphasized the interplay of marketing and entrepreneurship and adopted a concept of entrepreneurial marketing (Bjerke and Hultman, 2002; Hills and LaForge, 1992; Hills et al., 2008; Morris et al., 2002). Entrepreneurial marketing can be seen as an umbrella concept for many of the emergent and innovative perspectives on marketing (Morris et al., 2002). It is positioned in the interface of entrepreneurship and marketing fields and is an approach for marketing under conditions such as environmental turbulence, complexity and diminishing resources (Hill et al., 2008; Moffit and Chiagouris, 2008; Morris et al., 2002). Although the international business environment as a context is certainly a turbulent and complex one especially for smaller, resource-constrained firms, research on entrepreneurial marketing in the international business of these types of firms is rather scarce.

Similarly, in the international business field, internationalization has traditionally been researched from the perspective of either older firms or large multinational corporations, and it has been viewed as an incremental, risk-averse process involving a varying number of stages (Bilkey and Tesar, 1977; Cavusgil, 1980; Johanson and Vahlne, 1977; Johanson and Wiedersheim-Paul, 1975; Luostarinen, 1979). Inspired by the increased interest over the last 20 years about early, rapid and entrepreneurial internationalization of new and small ventures, the research field of international entrepreneurship (IE) has emerged (Keupp and Gassmann, 2009; McDougall, 1989; Zahra, 2005). IE has been described as the intersection of two research traditions, international business and entrepreneurship (Dana et al., 1999; McDougall and Oviatt, 2000), and defined as 'the discovery, enactment, evaluation, and exploitation of opportunities – across national borders – to create future goods and services' (Oviatt and McDougall, 2005a, p. 540). International new ventures (INVs) have been an important topic in IE and there is now a significant body of research in this area (Keupp and Gassmann, 2009); however, the scope of IE has gradually broadened (Chandra and Coviello, 2010; McDougall and Oviatt, 2000; Oviatt and McDougall, 2005a, 2005b; Zahra, 2005). While the research conducted in the past two decades has offered important insights into the characteristics and behaviour of INVs, their marketing strategies have received less attention, and research in this area is still in a nascent stage (Keupp and Gassmann, 2009; Rialp et al., 2005; Styles and Seymour, 2006). The rapid internationalization of INVs, together with the trends towards regionalism and globalization, influence the marketing of these ventures – making it a challenging task to perform.

Consequently, this study focuses on the marketing strategies of early and rapidly internationalizing firms during their evolution from INV to a global firm. The research question of the study is: how do entrepreneurial marketing strategies evolve during the growth of INVs, and what factors influence the development and performance of these strategies? To address this question, three objectives have been formulated: (1) to identify the dimensions of the entrepreneurial marketing strategies of INVs; (2) to understand how the entrepreneurial marketing strategies develop during global growth of INVs and what factors influence this development; and (3) to discuss the relation between entrepreneurial marketing strategies and the marketing performance in INVs.

The study aims to bring new knowledge to the field of IE, and it draws on three research traditions: marketing, entrepreneurship and international business. The concept of entrepreneurial marketing (Hills et al., 2008; Morris et al., 2002) is adopted to examine the interface between marketing and entrepreneurial firms, while recent developments in the IE field are included to allow a focus on INVs.

Literature review and entrepreneurial marketing dimensions

Earlier research on marketing in IE and INVs

Research on rapidly internationalizing firms over the past 20 years has contributed to the establishment of the research stream of international entrepreneurship (Dana et al., 1999; McDougall and Oviatt, 2000). Whereas the emphasis in IE studies has been on empirical research, the theoretical frameworks adopted are still widely fragmented or in some cases undefined (Keupp and Gassmann, 2009; Rialp et al., 2005). Researchers have taken different theoretical approaches to study the phenomenon of early, rapid and entrepreneurial internationalization, such as networking (Coviello and Munro, 1995, 1997; Loan and Bell, 2006; Sharma and Blomstermo, 2003), market strategies (e.g. Burgel and Murray, 2000; Shrader et al., 2000), the entrepreneurial view (Jones and Coviello, 2005; Knight, 2000), the resource-based view (Bloodgood et al., 1996), and the knowledge- and learning-based view (e.g. Autio et al., 2000; Yli-Renko et al., 2002; Zahra et al., 2000). The development of INV research and IE field has been challenged by the heterogeneity of conceptual as well as operational definitions of early internationalizing firms. This heterogeneity is parallel to the various concepts that researchers have used to refer to these firms, such as global start-ups (Oviatt and McDougall, 1995), born globals (Harveston et al., 2000; Knight and Cavusgil, 2004; Rennie, 1993) and infant multinationals (Lindqvist, 1991). The concept of the INV was introduced in the end of 1980s (McDougall, 1989) and has since been widely adopted (Zahra, 2005). In this study we adopt the definition of Oviatt and McDougall (1994, p. 49); an INV is 'a business organization that, from inception, seeks to derive significant competitive advantage from the use of resources and the sale of outputs in multiple countries'.

Despite the vast interest in INVs, research on their marketing activities has been limited and has lacked sound theoretical grounding (Keupp and Gassmann, 2009; Rialp et al., 2005; Styles and Seymour, 2006). While some research has touched on the marketing strategy elements, these have less often been the core focus of the studies. Researchers have studied market expansion strategies, such as market selection pattern, operation modes and distribution methods abroad (Burgel and Murray, 2000; McNaughton, 2003; Melen and Nordman, 2009; Moen and Servais, 2002; Shrader et al., 2000; Zahra et al., 2000); and they have also discussed the role of niche marketing in INVs (Knight, 1997; Madsen and Servais, 1997; Zucchella and Palamara, 2007). INV researchers that have adopted a network or relationship approach have studied the INV's role in the international expansion, growth and success; however, fewer studies have discussed the networks and relationships specifically from the marketing strategy viewpoint. In their study of high-technology entrepreneurial firms, Coviello and Munro (1995) found that while marketing responsibilities related to sales, market and competitor analysis, pricing and promotion decisions, as well as customer education were shared with network partners, product development decisions and activities were not. The more focused research on marketing strategies has investigated the issues of branding (Gabrielsson, 2005), product strategies in terms of product portfolio development (Laanti et al., 2007) and product uniqueness and quality (Knight and Cavusgil, 2004; Knight et al., 2004).

It has been argued that the international market orientation, especially customer focus and responsiveness, is characteristic of INVs (Moen, 2002) and potentially influential to their general marketing competence, product quality and differentiation preferences (Knight et al., 2004). Foreign distributors' roles in the marketing of INVs have been discussed in brief (Knight and Cavusgil, 2004; Knight et al., 2004). Yet another area of interest has been the role of the internet in the marketing strategies of INVs, and a few studies have investigated its use in product development, marketing communication, sales, distribution, customer service, market intelligence and competitor analysis (Loane, 2006; Servais et al., 2007). Decision-making relating to strategic standardization and adaptation has received limited attention in the INV research area. Early research suggests that INVs need clear-cut decisions about whether to follow highly adapted and custom-made or highly standardized strategy (Madsen and Servais, 1997). It has been argued that in the information and communication technology (ICT) industry INVs use more standardized marketing strategies than traditionally internationalizing or globalizing firms in order to manage rapid expansion into global markets (Gabrielsson and Gabrielsson, 2003).

The entrepreneurship–marketing interface: entrepreneurial marketing

Entrepreneurial marketing research has evolved since the 1980s and it is becoming one of the key issues in mainstream marketing. Scholars have expressed increasing interest first in the overlap between conventional marketing theories and entrepreneurship, and second in the implications that the adoption of entrepreneurial marketing has for management, competencies and resources required, as well as the practical applications of these to managers and educators (Collinson and Shaw, 2001). In these studies, entrepreneurial marketing has most often been applied to marketing by small firms when they behave entrepreneurially (Bjerke and Hultman, 2002) or innovatively (Carson et al., 1995). Entrepreneurial marketing is indeed encountered more often in small than in large firms (Collinson and Shaw, 2001), since established firms face stronger internal barriers to the entrepreneurial approach to marketing (Carson et al., 1995). However, entrepreneurial marketing is not restricted to small firms, but is also important to large firms because it allows them to discover, assess and exploit entrepreneurial opportunities more effectively and to gain competitive advantage (Collinson and Shaw, 2001; Miles and Darroch, 2006).

There is no consensus in the literature about the definition or the dimensions of entrepreneurial marketing. The concept has been used rather loosely and inconsistently; it has been associated with creative marketing activities in small and resource-constrained firms and also with the unplanned, non-linear, visionary marketing actions of the entrepreneur (Morris et al., 2002). It can be seen to reflect such marketing perspectives as expeditionary (Hamel and Prahalad, 1991), guerrilla (Levinson, 1993), disruptive (Dru, 1996), radical (Hill and Rifkin, 1999), counterintuitive (Clancy and Krieg, 2000), customer-centric (Sheth et al., 2000), buzz (Kelly, 2007; Rosen, 2001) and convergence marketing (Wind and Mahajan, 2002). In essence, entrepreneurial marketing encompasses two research traditions: entrepreneurship and marketing, and it has been argued that the key areas of interface between these two are change (Carson et al., 1995), and the opportunistic nature and innovativeness in the management approach (Collinson and Shaw, 2001). First, entrepreneurial marketing refers to change in the process of market management that challenges established market conventions (Chaston, 2000). Second, entrepreneurial marketing is said to be much more opportunity-driven than traditional administrative marketing (Hills et al., 2008). Third, the concept integrates marketing with the innovativeness central to entrepreneurship (Schumpeter, 1934) in that the focal point of entrepreneurial marketing can be seen as *innovative value creation* (Morris et al., 2002). The literature review suggests that entrepreneurial marketing has distinctive features related to opportunity identification, customer interaction, resource leveraging and risk management (Bjerke and Hultman, 2002; Hills et al., 2008; Moffit and Chiagouris, 2008; Morris et al., 2002). The underlying character of solutions in these marketing strategies is innovativeness in creating value for customers.

The characteristics associated with entrepreneurial marketing coincide in many ways with the 'blue ocean strategy' (Kim and Mauborgne, 2004, 2005). Instead of focusing on competition as the benchmark, the firm extends the focus beyond conventional boundaries of competition and makes competitors irrelevant by creating unknown and uncontested market space – blue ocean – and thereby a leap in value for both buyers and the firm itself (Kim and Mauborgne, 2004). A shift in strategic focus may be pursued by thinking across substitute industries or across strategic groups within the firm's industry, by redefining the buyer groups of the industry (to include the chain of purchasers, users and influencers that are involved in the purchase decision), by looking across complementary product and service offerings (to define how value is created and affected by them), by thinking beyond the prevailing functional-emotional orientation of the firm industry's appeal to buyers, or by shaping (rather than adapting to) external environmental trends over time (Kim and Mauborgne, 1999). All these alternative approaches to marketing provide opportunities for value innovation; that is, to create new value curves for the offering.

Entrepreneurial marketing strategy dimensions in the context of INVs

Despite some research on the entrepreneurship/marketing interface in international SMEs (Knight, 2000), there is a paucity of IE and INV research that studies the development of marketing strategies and adopts the entrepreneurial marketing approach to their theoretical background (Kocak and Abimbola, 2009). In this study, we define entrepreneurial marketing strategy in an INV as *an unconventional approach to marketing that challenges the established market conventions and includes an innovative approach to value creation and adaptation of these strategies to international markets*. The entrepreneurial marketing strategies in an INV are viewed through two dimensions: (a) innovativeness of marketing strategies, and (b) adaptation of marketing strategies to countries and customers.

The first dimension is derived from the entrepreneurial marketing literature, where the innovativeness of marketing solutions in creating customer value has been identified as a key component of entrepreneurial marketing (Carson et al., 1995; Morris et al., 2002). Although innovativeness has been included in the studies of INVs or small internationalizing firms, they have tended to investigate it on the entrepreneur or firm culture level (Dimitratos and Plakoyiannaki, 2003), often under the term entrepreneurial orientation (Knight, 2000, 2001; Knight and Cavusgil, 2004; Kropp et al., 2006; also the definition of international entrepreneurship by McDougall and Oviatt, 2000). Few of the studies on international SMEs (Knight, 2000) or INVs (Knight and Cavusgil, 2004, 2005) have examined whether entrepreneurial orientation, and thus innovativeness in firm culture, is related to increased strategic competence and use of generic business strategies (differentiation, cost leadership, marketing leadership or quality focus). However, they have been inadequate and imprecise in elaborating further the manifestation of innovativeness on the level of the marketing strategies of INVs.

Integrating the concept of entrepreneurial marketing to the INV context implies that careful consideration has to be given to acknowledging the important features of international business. One such feature is the adaptation and standardization of marketing strategies; a firm entering multiple markets is always faced with the necessity of deciding whether and how to adapt to the individual countries or customers (Cavusgil et al., 1993; Jain, 1989). The importance of this topic is evidenced by the vast literature committed to the adaptation/standardization debate over the past 40 years in the field of international marketing (Buzzell, 1968; Levitt, 1983; Ryans et al., 2003; Theodosiou and Leonidou, 2003). The issue, however, has had little attention in the INV context, suggesting that this is an interesting dimension to be elaborated in this study. Consequently, the second dimension of INV entrepreneurial marketing indicates that within the elements of marketing strategies, an INV can decide how much to follow the same practice with different countries or customers, and how much to adapt the marketing solutions. This is not an either/or decision in which the firm selects an entirely standardized or adapted marketing strategy; instead, it is about the degree and manner of adaptation/standardization along different elements of the strategy (Ryans et al., 2003).

Combining these two dimensions creates four alternative marketing strategies for an INV, as depicted in Figure 11.1. Traditional marketing strategy refers to incremental rather than radical innovativeness, and to a strategic approach that is strongly based on conventional marketing management thinking and on a process involving analysis, marketing planning and control (Kotler, 1997), which is often managed by a separate marketing department. The decision-making concerning the marketing mix elements – the four Ps (Kotler, 1997; McCarthy, 1960) or the seven Ps (Booms and Bitner, 1981) – is based on secondary and primary marketing research in order to focus the firm's resources and decisions according

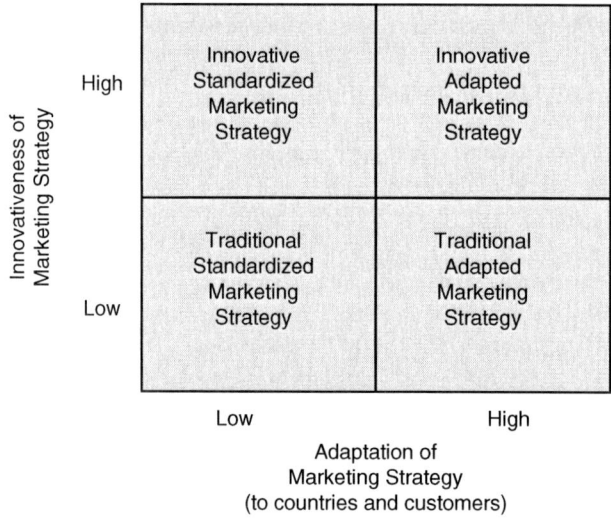

Figure 11.1 Entrepreneurial marketing strategy dimensions in an INV

to the market needs and special features of the international environment (such as the economic, political, legal, cultural and financial environments) (Albaum et al., 2005; Czinkota and Ronkainen, 1995; Kotler, 1997). Development from domestic markets to a global marketing strategy evolves step-wise from exports in individual countries to more advanced international marketing activities such as foreign direct investment (FDI) (Czinkota and Ronkainen, 1995). The elements of traditional strategy can be more standardized across countries and customers or then adopted so that they meet the requirements of different customers or countries, resulting in two alternative strategies for an INV as shown in the two lower quadrants of Figure 11.1.

Value creation through innovative marketing strategies resides in adopting a long-term orientation to opportunity recognition and exploitation through continuously redefining the product and market context (Hills et al., 2008; Morris et al., 2002). Marketing is seen as the guiding organizational philosophy rather than as a function or responsibility of a separate marketing department or individual, and the management of marketing strategies is characterized by intuition, informality and speedy decision-making (Collinson and Shaw, 2001). The value-creation strategies are designed around innovative solutions to achieve customer intimacy (Morris et al., 2002) in the global markets and breaking the value/cost trade-off by simultaneous pursuit of differentiation *and* low cost (Kim and Mauborgne, 2004).

Although an innovative marketer is perhaps less inclined to view marketing strategies through the marketing mix elements emphasized in the traditional marketing literature, the execution of innovative strategies implicitly indicates an unconventional approach to product planning and development, pricing, distribution and/or promotion. As an example, promotion may be targeted to a future customer group not yet discovered by the competitor, or the promotional information may be delivered with an unusual attention-evoking message content and by using alternative, customer-involving channels for delivering the message (Chaston, 2000). Promotion has an important role in the purchase decision process, and by creating rather than meeting demand, the innovative marketers can use promotion to influence the purchase process before or during the customer's need recognition phase. Furthermore, innovative distribution may serve as a means of increasing customer intimacy and creating competitive entry barriers (Chaston, 2000; Rangan et al., 1993). This may indicate unbundling the traditional channel functions of information communication, sales negotiation, order-taking, physical distribution and after-sales service, and use of hybrid channel strategies in which the tasks are reorganized on the basis of the special competence of channel partners in the customer interface (Rangan et al., 1993).

Innovative pricing involves breaking the conventions held by the industry or customers regarding price determination and the price–quality relation. An entrepreneurial marketer aims to change customer attitudes towards the prevailing price, search for ways to utilize illogical customer behaviour with regard to price, and exploit customers' distrust of current suppliers ('high quality cannot be provided with low price') by introducing an unprecedented and distinct pricing policy to integrate low pricing and product quality differentiation (Chaston, 2000). An INV with highly innovative marketing strategies also has to decide whether and to what extent some or all of the strategy elements are adapted country-wise or customer-wise. Although the degree of adaptation is likely to vary between the marketing strategy elements and activities, in its entirety the decisions will indicate either a more standardized or a more adapted innovative marketing strategy, as described in the upper quadrants of Figure 11.1.

Conceptual framework and propositions

A conceptual model of the development and influence mechanisms

The conceptual model of the entrepreneurial marketing strategies and the factors influencing their development and performance are presented in Figure 11.2. Here the entrepreneurial marketing strategies are viewed through the two dimensions presented in the previous section; that is, the innovativeness of marketing strategies and the adaptation of marketing strategies to countries and customers. The marketing strategies are seen as varying and developing along these dimensions as the INVs grow and globalize, and the manifestation of the variance and development may be understood as a result of the different internal characteristics and environmental conditions of INVs.

The industry environment is expected to affect the entrepreneurial marketing strategies of INVs. Industry environment refers to environmental turbulence, hostility, diversity, technical complexity and restrictiveness that form constraints, contingencies, opportunities and problems for a firm (Khandwalla, 1977). Whether the customer is a business organization or a consumer is also

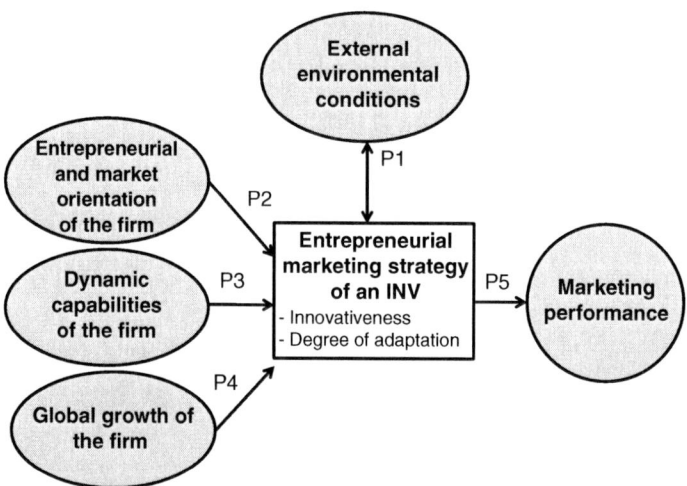

Figure 11.2 Conceptual framework on the development of entrepreneurial marketing strategies in an international new venture

an important environmental feature. In general, consumer markets have been regarded as more suitable for adaptation than industrial markets (Jain, 1989). However, later research has indicated that business-to-business customers often require high customization. The environment causes pressure on the firm, and marketing activities are attempts to influence the environment, to insulate the firm from its unfavourable aspects, or to exert pressure back on the environment (Khandwalla, 1977). The 'contingency theories' argue that the properties of the environment cause differences in the strategies and structures of organizations (Khandwalla, 1977). The contingency perspective on organization strategy stresses the importance of strategic fit and coalignment with environmental conditions in order to achieve higher performance (Ginsberg and Venkatraman, 1985; Katsikeas et al., 2006; Venkatraman, 1989).

The internal firm characteristics influencing the development of entrepreneurial marketing strategies include firm culture and dynamic capabilities. Previous research has argued that entrepreneurial marketing strategies are influenced by firm culture, especially by entrepreneurial orientation and market orientation (Morris et al., 2002). Entrepreneurial orientation refers to strategy-making processes that encompass many aspects of the organization's culture, shared value system and corporate vision (Lumpkin and Dess, 1996) and 'provide organizations with a basis for entrepreneurial decisions and actions' (Rauch et al., 2009, p. 762). Market orientation has been defined as the organization culture that 'most effectively and efficiently creates the necessary behaviours for the creation of superior value for buyers and, thus, continuous superior performance for the business' (Narver and Slater, 1990, p. 21). The two orientations may also interact in the forming of appropriate marketing strategies and performance (Blesa and Ripollès, 2003; Matsuno et al., 2002). Indeed, tying the core values of entrepreneurial orientation – proactiveness, innovativeness and risk-taking (Covin and Slevin, 1989, 1991; Lumpkin and Dess, 1996; Miller, 1983) – to elements of market orientation such as customer orientation, competitor focus and interfunctional coordination (Narver and Slater, 1990) might be central to the creation of entrepreneurial marketing strategies in INVs.

The marketing strategies available for the INV are expected to be dependent on the nature of its resources, especially the dynamic capabilities of the firm (Hamel and Prahalad, 1993; Teece et al., 1997). Traditionally, firm resources have been related to tangible and intangible assets which are tied semi-permanently to the firm, taking a variety of forms such as knowledge, skilled personnel, brand equity, machinery, capital and organizational procedures (Wernerfelt, 1984). Regardless of the resource type, a sustained competitive advantage is supported by resources that are rare and valuable in improving firm effectiveness and efficiency, but also imperfectly imitable and non-substitutable by alternative resources (Barney, 1991). In an environment of rapid change, the dynamic capability perspective emphasizes the importance of a firm's ability to integrate, build and reconfigure internal and external competencies; competitive advantage is seen to rest on a firm's distinctive coordinating and combining processes, and to be shaped by the firm's asset position and the evolution paths it has developed (Teece et al.,

1997). To achieve less resource-intensive ways of competing, capability to leverage resources becomes critical (Hamel and Prahalad, 1993). Indeed, the earlier literature suggests that INVs do not necessarily have to own their resources in order to achieve rapid international growth. Value creation can be obtained by alternative governance structures such as licensing, franchising and, most evidently, networking (Oviatt and McDougall, 1994) and resource leveraging. In addition to the resources owned by an INV, global growth is strengthened first by domestic partners and later by global networks (Laanti et al., 2007). Access to resources by other means than ownership also brings the risk of leakage. While the conditions of a new venture often necessitate acceptance of this risk, it is likely that INVs tend to increase ownership of resources as they become more established.

Global growth is expected to influence the evolution of marketing strategies (Douglas and Craig, 1989). The growth of firms and their different stages have been studied in the management literature (Greiner, 1998). In general, it has been suggested that small business growth evolves stage-wise, where in the early phases, management is likely to be entrepreneurial and in later phases more managerial, administrative and professional (Bjerke and Hultman, 2002; Scott and Bruce, 1987). Global growth has also been investigated in the INV literature, where the main focus has been on international sales growth and rapid foreign expansion to new countries (Autio et al., 2000; McDougall and Oviatt, 1996; Oviatt and McDougall, 2005a). Although INVs tend to exhibit rapid parallel expansion into many foreign countries, it has been suggested that their global growth evolves through phases (Gabrielsson et al., 2008). The INVs might also differ in their expansion patterns, being either more regional, such as European-focused, or global (Hallbäck and Larimo, 2006; Rugman and Verbeke, 2004). The firm's global growth phase and growth management approach are likely to induce different marketing strategies depending on the current phase of the firm's growth. In INVs, global growth has been found to relate to the product strategies and adaptation level of product, branding and distribution channel strategies (Gabrielsson and Gabrielsson, 2003; Laanti et al., 2007).

Instead of overall firm performance, this study focuses on the intermediate consequences for the performance of entrepreneurial marketing strategies in an INV. As such, despite the vast literature committed to the topic, previous research has found mixed or insignificant results on the relation between marketing standardization or adaptation with firm performance, essentially due to their inappropriate level and depth of analysis and focus on direct relationships between adaptation and performance (Katsikeas et al., 2006; Theodosiou and Leonidou, 2003). Researchers have pointed out that instead of focusing on performance only from the firm's standpoint, the outcomes should also be viewed in terms of value-added to the customer (Ryans et al., 2003). Assessing the marketing-related outcomes offers an appropriate means to include these performance viewpoints. In order to understand the role of marketing in the firm's overall performance, the marketing-related outcomes of marketing strategies have to be identified (Townsend et al., 2004). The outcomes are likely to include features such as market share, new product introduction rate, and sales growth (indirectly) (Townsend et al., 2004), and also desirability and growth of the customer base as well as customer satisfaction and loyalty-related factors (Morris et al., 2002). These marketing-related outcomes of marketing strategy have been found to increase financial performance (such as profitability, return on investment and cash flow). Earlier research also suggests that instead of focusing on the direct relation between marketing strategy and performance, the analysis should acknowledge the coalignment of the strategy with environmental and firm contingencies (Katsikeas et al., 2006). In the next subsection, a more detailed discussion of the expected relations between the concepts of the model is provided, followed by the development of five theoretical propositions.

Propositions

A highly turbulent environment entails both growth opportunities and uncertainties, and this is expected to influence the marketing strategies (Khandwalla, 1977). Turbulence is related to industry life cycle; in the fermentation phase of technology development, innovative marketing strategies are particularly necessary, while in the era of incremental change, cost economies are more important and therefore the marketing strategies become more standardized and innovativeness is more incremental (Anderson and Tushman, 1990). The technical complexity and restrictiveness in the industry is reflected by the need for information of high technical sophistication to meet the requirements of different parts of the industry value chain. Highly complex technical requirements in the industry that vary between countries and customers foster innovative solutions in marketing and greater adaptation of the strategies used. Industry diversity may be understood in terms of heterogeneity in customer and market characteristics and needs. It is important for the firm to understand how global the industry is and to match this globalization potential with its strategy (Yip, 1989). The more homogeneous the customers' needs, the existence of global customers and channels, and the higher the economies of scale and learning advantages, the more suitable are standardized marketing strategies (Yip, 1989).

When these are less present in the industry, adapted marketing strategies are expected to prevail (Jain, 1989; Yip, 1989). While the globalization of markets increases the possibilities for global standardization, the parallel trend of regionalism, for example the integration of European Union, diminishes country-specific differences but increases the importance of regional market needs (Buckley and Ghauri, 2004). Industry diversity also relates to the emergence of narrow niche segments in the markets, which in turn are likely to make more room for small firms to create innovative solutions in its marketing strategies. The small firm with limited resources is especially sensitive to changes in the external environment. However, entrepreneurial marketing could be a significant means to create change and extend the firm's influence over the environment (Zeithaml and Zeithaml, 1984). In sum, the external business environment, generally characterized by high turbulence, complexity and diversity, increases the need for firms to adapt and be flexible in approaching customers and competitors, yet at the same time to be highly innovative in their marketing strategies (Achrol, 1991). Thus, it may be postulated as follows:

Proposition 1 *The greater the turbulence, technical complexity and global diversity of the INV's industry environment, the greater the innovativeness of marketing strategies and adaptation of these to customers and countries.*

The entrepreneurial orientation – the firm's culture that is based on the values of proactiveness, innovativeness and risk-taking – is expected to influence the development and exploitation of more innovative marketing strategies. A proactive firm culture might enhance marketing strategies that constantly employ new market positions based on the latent needs of the customers and created demand as well as experiment with new marketing tactics (Kim and Mauborgne, 2004; Morris et al., 2002). Innovativeness in firm culture is also expected to be reflected in marketing strategies through, for example, continuous redefining of the product and market context, strategically managing a portfolio of innovations, and highly inventive approaches to new products and service development (Morris et al., 2002). Innovative marketing strategies break the value/cost trade-off by eliminating and reducing the factors an industry competes on and raising and creating elements never offered by the industry (Kim and Mauborgne, 2004). The proclivity for risk-taking in the firm is likely to be reflected at the strategic level, in that the firm is willing to commit resources and invest in new products as well as untested marketing tactics with higher likelihood of failure (Morris et al., 2002). Risk perception is inversely related to familiarity and experience, and in comparison with new and small firms, the financially oriented senior managers of more established, larger firms are likely to perceive radical changes in marketing as extremely risky and prefer calm behaviour to sustain steady increase in profits (Chaston, 2000). Going further, earlier research has shown that market orientation, as it relates to customer responsiveness, may have diminishing effects on innovativeness (Narver et al., 2004). At the same time, market orientation is likely to increase the adaptation of marketing strategies as it enhances strategies that employ customer-responsive interaction and value creation. In entering different country markets or regions, responsiveness to the specific needs of local customers might be needed and thereby an increased market orientation might raise the level of adaptation of the marketing strategies. Thus, the following is proposed:

Proposition 2 a) *The greater the entrepreneurial orientation of the INV, the more innovative is the marketing strategy.* **b)** *The greater the market orientation of the INV, the greater is the adaptation of marketing strategy to customers and countries.*

In the traditional view, the resources of the firm determine the product-market activities that are optimal for the firm (Wernerfelt, 1984). Resources are important for the internationalization of small and new ventures, such as increasing the speed and degree of their international sales (Zahra et al., 2003). In INVs especially, the dynamic capabilities are related to innovativeness of marketing strategies – the firm's ability to access a variety of resources and competencies either by ownership or by resource-leveraging (Hamel and Prahalad, 1993) and to reconfigure, build and integrate them into competencies to deliver offerings of superior value yet produced at low relative costs (Hunt and Morgan 1996; Teece et al., 1997). INVs are characterized by scarce resources, implying that they need effective leveraging of resources through cooperation and networking or by effective bundling of resources to overcome this restriction (Hamel and Prahalad, 1993; Zahra et al., 2003). The expertise of INV management is also a crucial source in forming dynamic capabilities that foster an innovative approach to marketing strategies (Read et al., 2009). It is postulated as follows:

Proposition 3 *The more dynamic capabilities owned or leveraged through external sources, the greater the innovativeness of INV marketing strategies.*

The marketing of an INV might be expected to change as the firm grows; it is likely that instead of maintaining an entrepreneurial or traditional marketing approach, a firm will shift between entrepreneurial and traditional, more formalized strategic and integrated marketing as it evolves (Moffit and Chiagouris, 2008; Morris et al., 2002). This is related to the mechanism of growth, which as such may differ over time. While entrepreneurial growth involves creating new business ventures, managerial growth is more characterized by expanding market coverage with the current venture (Bjerke and Hultman, 2002; Scott and Bruce, 1987). In the early phase of an INV, the need for entrepreneurial growth is likely to prevail, thereby triggering innovative marketing strategies to focus on new markets, products, value co-creation and value chain cooperation as well as higher adaptation of strategies to establish initial market position and customer segments. In the phase of rapid parallel expansion to new country markets, the growth is more managerial in nature and requires effective management of the marketing process of the existing products as well as aligning the operations and using country- and customer-based standardization during expansion. However, in a fast growing INV, the elements of both growth mechanisms may co-exist and are likely to impact upon the dimensions of the INV's entrepreneurial marketing strategies. It is proposed that:

Proposition 4 a) *In the early phase of the INV's global growth cycle more innovative marketing strategies and customer or/and country adaptation are employed.* ***b)*** *In the latter phase of the INV's global growth cycle, effective management of marketing strategies is emphasized and both customer and country standardization are utilized.*

Entrepreneurial marketing may be expected to influence both the financial and non-financial outcomes of the firm. It is expected to particularly influence elements of marketing performance, such as market share, new product introduction rate, and achieving a fast-growing desirable, satisfied and loyal customer base (Morris et al., 2002). However, the consequences for performance of innovative marketing strategies and their adaptation are likely to be context-dependent

(Katsikeas et al., 2006). Marketing performance is likely to result from the appropriateness of the level of marketing strategy innovativeness and adaptation within the external environmental context. Similarly, marketing strategies have to be aligned with the firm's culture and capabilities to ensure more effective implementation of the strategies (Townsend et al., 2004) and thereby higher performance. The level of innovativeness of marketing strategies and adaptation that best fits the current growth phase of the firm is likely to have a positive effect on the marketing performance of an INV (Calantone et al., 2006; Kim and Mauborgne, 2004).

Proposition 5 *The entrepreneurial marketing strategies that are balanced with the external environmental conditions, entrepreneurial and market orientation, dynamic capabilities and global growth phase of the INV are expected to contribute to higher marketing performance.*

Conclusions

International new ventures have received much attention during the last 20 years (Keupp and Gassmann, 2009; McDougall, 1989; Rialp et al., 2005). The development of marketing strategies during firm globalization has also been of interest to researchers (Douglas and Craig, 1989; Gabrielsson and Gabrielsson, 2004). Nevertheless, the development of INV marketing strategies during their global growth has seldom been studied. Especially uncommon are studies that adopt the entrepreneurial marketing and adaptation point of view to understand the development of their marketing strategies during growth. Researchers have recently called for understanding the INV evolution process over time (Jones and Coviello, 2005; Zahra, 2005) and the current study attempts to shed light on this issue by focusing on the development of INVs' marketing strategies.

In this study, a conceptual model and five propositions of the development and performance of entrepreneurial marketing strategies in INVs were developed. For this purpose, we identified two dimensions of entrepreneurial marketing that are important for an INV: innovativeness of marketing strategies and adaptation of marketing strategies to customers and countries, thus indicating a typology of four alternative marketing strategies for an INV. Based on earlier research on the marketing/entrepreneurship and international business/entrepreneurship interface, the study elaborated on the possible manifestations of innovativeness in marketing strategies that an INV may utilize, and the role of adaptation in these strategies as the firm evolves. To further develop the understanding of entrepreneurial marketing strategies in INVs, we derived key factors from the literature that influence their development: the turbulence, technical complexity and global diversity of the industry environment; the firm culture in terms of entrepreneurial and market orientation; the dynamic capabilities of the firm; and the global growth phase of the firm. Finally, the ability of the INV to balance the level of innovativeness and adaptation of its marketing strategies to fit with these external and internal conditions is regarded as critical for achieving higher marketing performance during INV growth.

The theoretical contribution of this study belongs first in the paradigm of international entrepreneurship. By integrating the literature on entrepreneurship, marketing and international business, this chapter has theoretically contributed to the understanding of the entrepreneurial marketing strategies in the context of INVs. The approach adopted also brings new knowledge to the entrepreneurial marketing literature (Morris et al., 2002) by discussing entrepreneurial marketing in INVs and elaborating the influences of global context to entrepreneurial marketing strategies. While the INV literature has discussed growth (Autio et al., 2000; Bloodgood et al., 1996; Gabrielsson et al., 2008; Sapienza et al., 2006) and the performance consequences of international expansion and growth (McDougall and Oviatt, 1996; Zahra et al., 2000), how marketing strategy evolves as INVs grow has been investigated only to a limited extent.

Recognizing the importance of innovative marketing strategies for INVs with limited resources but with huge global market opportunities is an important contribution. In addition, this chapter has integrated the adaptation viewpoint to INV marketing strategies and added knowledge to the adaptation-standardization literature, which has not discussed in depth the adaptation-standardization from this particular firm point of view. The study contributes to the standardization-adaptation debate (Buzzell, 1968; Cavusgil et al., 1993; Jain, 1989; Theodosiou and Leonidou, 2003) by presenting a view emphasizing the importance of understanding that the global growth phase of an INV exerts an effect behind the adaptation decision. The INV may need adaptation in the early phase of growth, while the importance of standardizing strategies may increase in a later phase – a notion that has received very limited theoretical or empirical research attention. Regarding performance, earlier research stresses the importance of strategy fit with conditions of the firm in order to achieve higher performance (Katsikeas et al., 2006). However, marketing performance has received less attention in the INV context, particularly the role of strategy alignment with external and internal conditions in the forming of marketing performance. In this chapter, it is posited that in developing marketing strategies, INVs should carefully consider the conditions related to the industry environment, internal firm culture, dynamic capabilities and global growth phase of the firm in order to achieve higher marketing performance. Based on these notions, the study has aimed to offer managerial contribution by discussing what type of marketing strategies INVs could emphasize during growth and global expansion.

As this study was limited to theoretical elaboration and proposition development, it is suggested that the conceptual framework and propositions should be empirically examined and developed further. Both qualitative and quantitative studies of different types of INVs are needed to enhance understanding of the topic. In future studies we particularly encourage the use of either longitudinal or cross-sectional approaches, since it is important to understand the development of marketing strategies during the INV growth as well as to capture the manifestation of marketing strategies in different phases of the global expansion and the marketing performance consequences of the strategies used. Finally, the interrelations between the influencing factors – the external and internal conditions of an INV – and the role of these interrelations in the development of entrepreneurial marketing strategies deserve attention in future research.

Acknowledgements

This research is part of the 'Born Globals – Growth Stages and Survival' cooperation project between the University of Vaasa, Aalto University School of Economics and six partner firms. We would like to thank the financiers of the project: the LIITO-program of the Finnish Funding Agency for Technology and Innovation (Tekes), and the partner firms.

References

Achrol, R.S. (1991) 'Evolution of the marketing organization: new forms for turbulent environments', *Journal of Marketing*, 55(4), 77–93.

Albaum, G., Duerr, E. and Strandskov, J. (2005) *International Marketing and Export Management*, (Harlow: Prentice Hall).

Anderson, P. and Tushman, M.L. (1990) 'Technological discontinuities and dominant designs: a cyclical model of technological change', *Administrative Science Quarterly*, 35, 604–33.

Autio, E., Sapienza, H.J. and Almeida, J.G. (2000) 'Effects of age at entry, knowledge intensity, and imitability on international growth', *Academy of Management Journal*, 43(5), 909–24.

Barney, J. (1991) 'Firm resources and sustained competitive advantage', *Journal of Management*, 17(1), 99–120.

Bilkey, W.J. and Tesar, G. (1977) 'The export behaviour of smaller-sized Wisconsin manufacturing firms', *Journal of International Business Studies*, 8(1), 93–8.

Bjerke, B. and Hultman, C.M. (2002) *Entrepreneurial Marketing. The Growth of Small Firms in the New Economic Era* (Cheltenham: Edward Elgar Publishing).

Blesa, A. and Ripolles, M. (2003) 'The role of market orientation in the relationship between entrepreneurial proactiveness and performance', *Journal of Entrepreneurship*, 12(1), 1–19.

Bloodgood, J.M., Sapienza, H.J. and Almeida, J.G. (1996) 'The internationalization of new high-potential U.S. ventures: antecedents and outcomes', *Entrepreneurship Theory and Practice*, 20(4), 61–76.

Booms, B.H. and Bitner, M.J. (1981) 'Marketing strategies and organization structure for service firms', in J.H. Donnelly and W.R. George (eds) *Marketing of Services*, 47–51 (Chicago, IL: American Marketing Association).

Buckley, P.J. and Ghauri, P.N. (2004) 'Globalisation, economic geography and the strategy of multinational enterprises', *Journal of International Business Studies*, 35(2), 81–98.

Burgel, O. and Murray, G.C. (2000) 'The international market entry choices of start-up companies in high-technology industries', *Journal of International Marketing*, 8(2), 33–62.

Buzzell, R.D. (1968) 'Can you standardize multinational marketing', *Harvard Business Review*, 46(6), 102–13.

Calantone, R., Kim, D., Schmidt, J.B. and Cavusgil, T.S. (2006) 'The influence of internal and external firm factors on international product adaptation strategy and export performance: a three-country comparison', *Journal of Business Research*, 59(2), 176–85.

Carson, D. and Cromie, S. (1989) 'Marketing planning in small enterprises: a model and some empirical evidence', *Journal of Marketing Management*, 5(1), 33–49.

Carson, D., Cromie, S., McGowan, P. and Hill, J. (1995) *Marketing and Entrepreneurship in SMEs – An Innovative Approach* (London: Prentice Hall).

Carson, D. and Gilmore, A. (2000) 'Marketing at the interface: not "what?" but "how?"', *Journal of Marketing Theory and Practice*, 8(2), 1–7.

Cavusgil, S.T. (1980) 'On the internationalization process of firms', *European Research*, 8(6), 273–81.

Cavusgil, S.T., Zou, S. and Naidu, G.M. (1993) 'Product and promotion adaptation in export ventures: an empirical investigation', *Journal of International Business Studies*, 24(3), 479–506.

Chandra, Y. and Coviello, N. (2010) 'Broadening the concept of international entrepreneurship: consumers as international entrepreneurs', *Journal of World Business*, 45(3), 228–36.

Chaston, I. (2000) *Entrepreneurial Marketing: Competing by Challenging Conventions* (London: MacMillan Press Ltd.).

Clancy, K.J. and Krieg, P.C. (2000) *Counterintuitive Marketing: Achieve Great Results Using Uncommon Sense* (New York: The Free Press).

Collinson, E. and Shaw, E. (2001) 'Entrepreneurial marketing – a historical perspective on development and practice', *Management Decision*, 39(9), 761–6.

Coviello, N.E., Brodie, R.J. and Munro, H.J. (2000) 'An investigation of marketing practice by firm size', *Journal of Business Venturing*, 15(5–6), 523–45.

Coviello, N. and Munro, H. (1995) 'Growing the entrepreneurial firm: networking for international market development', *European Journal of Marketing*, 29(7), 49–57.

Coviello, N. and Munro, H. (1997) 'Network relationships and the internationalisation process of small software firms', *International Business Review*, 6(4), 361–86.

Covin, J.G. and Slevin, D.P. (1989) 'Strategic management of small firms in hostile and benign environments', *Strategic Management Journal*, 10(1), 75–87.

Covin, J.G. and Slevin, D.P. (1991) 'A conceptual model of entrepreneurship as firm behaviour', *Entrepreneurship Theory and Practice*, 16(1), 7–25.

Czinkota, M.R. and Ronkainen, I.A. (1995) *International Marketing* (Fort Worth, TX: Dryden Press).

Dana, L.P., Etemad, H. and Wright, R.W. (1999) 'Theoretical foundations of international entrepreneurship', in A.M. Rugman and R.W. Wright (eds) *Research in Global Strategic Management. International Entrepreneurship: Globalisation of Emerging Businesses*, 3–22 (Greenwich, CT: JAI Press Inc.).

Dimitratos, P. and Plakoyiannaki, E. (2003) 'Theoretical foundations of an international entrepreneurial culture', *Journal of International Entrepreneurship*, 1(2), 187–215.

Douglas, S.P. and Craig, S.C. (1989) 'Evolution of global marketing strategy: scale, scope and synergy', *Columbia Journal of World Business*, 24(3), 47–59.

Dru, J-M. (1996) *Disruption Over-tuning Conventions and Shaking Up the Marketplace* (New York: John Wiley & Sons).

Gabrielsson, M. (2005) 'Branding strategies of born globals', *Journal of International Entrepreneurship*, 3(3), 199–222.

Gabrielsson, M. and Gabrielsson, P. (2003) 'Global marketing strategies of born globals and globalising internationals in the ICT field', *Journal of Euromarketing*, 12(3/4), 123–45.

Gabrielsson, P. and Gabrielsson, M. (2004) 'Globalizing internationals: business portfolio and marketing strategies in the ICT field', *International Business Review*, 13(6), 661–84.

Gabrielsson, M., Kirpalani, M.V.H., Dimitratos, P., Sohlberg, C.A. and Zucchella, A. (2008) 'Born globals: propositions to help advance the theory', *International Business Review*, 17(4), 385–401.

Ginsberg, A. and Venkatraman, N. (1985) 'Contingency perspective of organizational strategy: a critical review of the empirical research', *Academy of Management Review*, 10(3), 421–34.

Greiner, L.E. (1998) 'Evolution and revolution as organizations grow', *Harvard Business Review*, 76(3), 55–67.

Hallbäck, J. and Larimo, J. (2006) 'Variety in international new ventures – typological analysis and beyond', *Journal of Euromarketing*, 16(1/2), 37–57.

Hamel, G. and Prahalad, C.K. (1991) 'Corporate imagination expeditionary marketing', *Harvard Business Review*, 69(4), 81–92.

Hamel, G. and Prahalad, C.K. (1993) 'Strategy as stretch and leverage', *Harvard Business Review*, 71(2), 75–84.

Harveston, P.D., Kedia, B.L. and Davis, P.S. (2000) 'Internationalization of born global and gradual globalizing firms: the impact of the manager', *Advances in Competitiveness Research*, 8(1), 92–9.

Hill, S. and Rifkin, G. (1999) *Radical Marketing: From Harvard to Harley, Lessons from Ten that Broke the Rules and Made it Big* (New York: Harper Collins).

Hills, G.E., Hultman, C.M. and Miles, M.P. (2008) 'The evolution and development of entrepreneurial marketing', *Journal of Small Business Management*, 46(1), 99–112.

Hills, G.E. and LaForge, R.W. (1992) 'Research at the marketing interface to advance entrepreneurship theory', *Entrepreneurship Theory and Practice*, 16(3), 33–59.

Hunt, S.D. and Morgan, R.M. (1996) 'The resource-advantage theory of competition: dynamics, path dependencies, and evolutionary dimensions', *Journal of Marketing*, 60(4), 107–14.

Jain, S.C. (1989) 'Standardization of international marketing strategy: some research hypotheses', *Journal of Marketing*, 53(1), 70–9.

Johanson, J. and Vahlne, J-E. (1977) 'The internationalization process of the firm – a model of knowledge development and increasing foreign market commitments', *Journal of International Business Studies*, 8(1), 23–32.

Johanson, J. and Wiedersheim-Paul, F. (1975) 'The internationalization of the firm – four Swedish cases', *Journal of Management Studies*, 12(3), 305–22.

Jones, M.V. and Coviello, N.E. (2005) 'Internationalisation: conceptualising an entrepreneurial process of behaviour in time', *Journal of International Business Studies*, 36(3), 284–303.

Katsikeas, C.S., Samiee, S. and Theodosiou, M. (2006) 'Strategy fit and performance consequences of international marketing standardization', *Strategic Management Journal*, 27(9), 867–90.

Kelly, L. (2007) *Beyond Buzz: The Next Generation of Word-of-Mouth Marketing* (New York: Amacom).

Keupp, M.M. and Gassmann, O. (2009) 'The past and future of international entrepreneurship: a review and suggestions for developing the field', *Journal of Management*, 35(3), 600–33.

Khandwalla, P.N. (1977) *The Design of Organizations* (New York: Harcourt Brace Jovanovich).

Kim, W.C. and Mauborgne, R. (1999) 'Creating new market space – a systematic approach to value innovation can help companies break free from the competitive pack', *Harvard Business Review*, 77(1), 83–93.

Kim, W.C. and Mauborgne, R. (2004) 'Blue ocean strategy', *Harvard Business Review*, 82(10), 76–84.

Kim, W.C. and Mauborgne, R. (2005) 'Blue ocean strategy: from theory to practice', *California Management Review*, 47(3), 105–21.

Knight, G.A. (1997) *Emerging Paradigm for International Marketing: The Born Global Firm* (Dissertation, Michigan State University).

Knight, G.A. (2000) 'Entrepreneurship and marketing strategy: the SME under globalization', *Journal of International Marketing*, 8(2), 12–32.

Knight, G.A. (2001) 'Entrepreneurship and strategy in the international SME', *Journal of International Management*, 7(3), 155–71.

Knight, G.A. and Cavusgil, T.S. (2004) 'Innovation, organizational capabilities, and the born-global firm', *Journal of International Business Studies*, 35(2), 124–41.

Knight, G.A. and Cavusgil, T.S. (2005) 'A taxanomy of born-global firms', *Management International Review*, 45(3), 15–35.

Knight, G.A., Madsen, T.K. and Servais, P. (2004) 'An inquiry into born-global firms in Europe and the USA', *International Marketing Review*, 21(6), 645–65.
Kocak, A. and Abimbola, T. (2009) 'The effects of entrepreneurial marketing on born global performance', *International Marketing Review*, 26(4/5), 439–52.
Kotler, P. (1997) *Marketing Management: Analysis, Planning, Implementation and Control* (Upper Saddle River, NJ: Prentice Hall).
Kropp, F., Lindsay, N.J. and Shoham, A. (2006) 'Entrepreneurial, market, and learning orientations and international entrepreneurial business venture performance in South African firms', *International Marketing Review*, 23(5), 504–23.
Laanti, R., Gabrielsson, M. and Gabrielsson, P. (2007) 'The globalization strategies of business-to-business born global firms in the wireless technology industry', *Industrial Marketing Management*, 36(8), 1104–17.
Levinson, C. (1993) *Guerrilla Marketing: Secrets for Making Big Profits from Your Small Business* (Boston: Haoughton Mifflin Company).
Levitt, T. (1983) 'The globalisation of markets', *Harvard Business Review*, 61(3), 99–102.
Lindqvist, M. (1991) *Infant Multinationals: The Internationalization of Young, Technology-Based Swedish Firms* (Dissertation, Stockholm School of Economics).
Loane, S. (2006) 'The role of internet in the internationalization of small and medium sized companies', *Journal of International Entrepreneurship*, 3(4), 263–77.
Loane, S. and Bell, J. (2006) 'Rapid internationalisation among entrepreneurial firms in Australia, Canada, Ireland and New Zealand; an extension to the network approach', *International Marketing Review*, 23(5), 467–85.
Lumpkin, G.T. and Dess, G.G. (1996) 'Clarifying the entrepreneurial orientation construct and linking it to performance', *Academy of Management Review*, 21(1), 135–72.
Luostarinen, R. (1979) *Internationalization of the Firm* (Dissertation, Helsinki School of Economics).
Madsen, T.K. and Servais, P. (1997) 'The internationalization of born globals: an evolutionary process?', *International Business Review*, 6(6), 561–83.
Matsuno, K., Mentzer, J.T. and Özsomer, A. (2002) 'The effects of entrepreneurial proclivity and market orientation on business performance', *Journal of Marketing*, 66(3), 18–32.
McCarthy, J.E. (1960) *Basic Marketing: A Managerial Approach* (Homewood, IL: Richard D. Irwin).
McDougall, P.P. (1989) 'International versus domestic entrepreneurship: new venture strategic behavior and industry structure', *Journal of Business Venturing*, 4(6), 387–400.
McDougall, P.P. and Oviatt, B.M. (1996) 'New venture internationalization, strategic change, and performance: a follow-up study', *Journal of Business Venturing*, 11(1), 23–40.
McDougall, P.P. and Oviatt, B.M. (2000) 'International entrepreneurship: the intersection of two research paths', *Academy of Management Journal*, 43(5), 902–6.
McNaughton, R. (2003) 'The number of export markets that a firm serves: process models versus the born-global phenomenon', *Journal of International Entrepreneurship*, 1(3), 297–311.
Melen, S. and Nordman, E.R. (2009) 'The internationalisation modes of born globals: a longitudinal study', *European Management Journal*, 27(4), 243–54.
Miles, M.P. and Darroch, J. (2006) 'Large firms, entrepreneurial marketing processes, and the cycle of competitive advantage', *European Journal of Marketing*, 40(5/6), 485–501.
Miller, D. (1983) 'The correlates of entrepreneurship in three types of firms', *Management Science*, 29(7), 770–91.
Moen, Ø. (2002) 'The born globals – a new generation of small European exporters', *International Marketing Review*, 19(2), 156–75.
Moen, Ø. and Servais, P. (2002) 'Born global or gradual global? Examining the export behavior of small and medium-sized enterprises', *Journal of International Marketing*, 10(3), 49–72.

Moffit, T. and Chiagouris, L. (2008) 'What would Richard Branson do? Entrepreneurial marketing can lead a company to victory in the marketplace', *Marketing Management*, 17(3), 59–62.

Morris, M.H., Schindehutte, M. and LaForge, R.W. (2002) 'Entrepreneurial marketing: a construct for integrating emerging entrepreneurship and marketing perspectives', *Journal of Marketing Theory and Practice*, 10(4), 1–19.

Narver, J.C. and Slater, S.F. (1990) 'The effect of a market orientation on business profitability', *Journal of Marketing*, 54(4), 20–35.

Narver, J.C., Slater, S.F. and MacLachlan, D.L. (2004) 'Responsive and proactive market orientation and new-product success', *Journal of Product Innovation Management*, 21(5), 334–47.

Oviatt, B.M. and McDougall, P.P. (1994) 'Toward a theory of international new ventures', *Journal of International Business Studies*, 25(1), 45–64.

Oviatt, B.M. and McDougall, P.P. (1995) 'Global start-ups: entrepreneurs on a worldwide stage', *Academy of Management Journal*, 9(2), 30–43.

Oviatt, B.M. and McDougall, P.P. (2005a) 'Defining international entrepreneurship and modeling the speed of internationalization', *Entrepreneurship Theory and Practice*, 29(5), 537–53.

Oviatt, B.M. and McDougall, P.P. (2005b) 'The internationalization of entrepreneurship', *Journal of International Business Studies*, 36(1), 2–8.

Rangan, K.V., Corey, R.E. and Cespedes, F. (1993) 'Transaction cost theory: inferences from clinical field research on downstream vertical integration', *Organisation Science*, 4(3), 454–77.

Rauch, A., Wiklund, J., Lumpkin, G.T. and Frese, M. (2009) 'Entrepreneurial orientation and business performance: an assessment of past research and suggestions for future', *Entrepreneurship Theory and Practice*, 33(3), 761–87.

Read, S., Dew, N., Sarasvathy, S.D., Song, M. and Wiltbank, R. (2009) 'Marketing under uncertainty: the logic of an effectual approach', *Journal of Marketing*, 73(3), 1–18.

Rennie, M.W. (1993) 'Global competitiveness: born global', *McKinsey Quarterly*, 4, 45–52.

Rialp, A., Rialp, J. and Knight, G.A. (2005) 'The phenomenon of early internationalizing firms: what do we know after a decade (1993–2003) of scientific inquiry?', *International Business Review*, 14(2), 147–66.

Rosen, E. (2001) *The Anatomy of Buzz: How to Create Word-of-Mouth Marketing* (London: HarperCollinsBusiness).

Rugman, A.M. and Verbeke, A. (2004) 'A perspective on regional and global strategies of multinational enterprises', *Journal of International Business Studies*, 35(1), 3–18.

Ryans, J.K., Griffith, D.A. and White, S.D. (2003) 'Standardization/adaptation of international marketing strategy – necessary conditions for the advancement of knowledge', *International Marketing Review*, 20(6), 588–603.

Sapienza, H.J., Autio, E., George, G. and Zahra, S.A. (2006) 'A capabilities perspective on the effects of early internationalization of firm survival and growth', *Academy of Management Review*, 31(4), 914–33.

Schumpeter, J.A. (1934) *The Theory of Economic Development* (Cambridge, MA: Harvard University Press).

Scott, M. and Bruce, R. (1987) 'Five stages of growth in small business', *Long Range Planning*, 20(3), 45–52.

Servais, P., Madsen, T.K. and Rasmussen, E.S. (2007) 'Small manufacturing firms' involvement in international e-business activities', *Advances in International Marketing*, 17, 297–317.

Sharma, D.D. and Blomstermo, A. (2003) 'The internationalization process of born globals: a network view', *International Business Review*, 12(6), 739–53.

Sheth, J.N., Sisodia, R.S. and Sharma, A. (2000) 'The antecedents and consequences of customer-centric marketing', *Journal of Academy of Marketing Science*, 28(1), 55–66.

Shrader, R.C., Oviatt, B.M. and McDougall, P.P. (2000) 'How new ventures exploit trade-offs among international risk factors: lessons for the accelerated internationalization of the 21st century', *Academy of Management Journal*, 43(6), 1227–47.

Styles, C. and Seymour, R.G. (2006) 'Opportunities for marketing researchers in international entrepreneurship', *International Marketing Review*, 23(2), 126–45.

Teece, D.J., Pisano, G. and Shuen, A. (1997) 'Dynamic capabilities and strategic management', *Strategic Management Journal*, 18(7), 509–33.

Theodosiou, M. and Leonidou, L.C. (2003) 'Standardization versus adaptation of international marketing strategy: an integrative assessment of the empirical research', *International Business Review*, 12(2), 141–71.

Townsend, J.D., Yeniyurt, S., Deligonul, S.Z. and Cavusgil, T.S. (2004) 'Exploring the marketing program antecedents of performance in a global company', *Journal of International Marketing*, 12(4), 1–24.

Venkatraman, N. (1989) 'The concept of fit in strategy research: toward verbal and statistical correspondence', *Academy of Management Review*, 14(3), 423–44.

Wernerfelt, B. (1984) 'A resource-based view of the firm', *Strategic Management Journal*, 5(2), 171–80.

Wind, Y. and Mahajan, V. (2002) 'Convergence marketing', *Journal of Interactive Marketing*, 16(2), 64–79.

Yip, G. (1989) 'Global strategy…in a world of nations?', *Sloan Management Review*, 31(1), 29–41.

Yli-Renko, H., Autio, E. and Tontti, V. (2002) 'Social capital, knowledge, and the international growth of technology-based new firms', *International Business Review*, 11(3), 279–304.

Zahra, S.A. (2005) 'A theory of international new ventures: a decade of research', *Journal of International Business Studies*, 36(1), 20–8.

Zahra, S.A., Ireland, R.D. and Hitt, M.A. (2000) 'International expansion by new venture firms: international diversity, mode of market entry, technological learning, and performance', *Academy of Management Journal*, 43(5), 925–50.

Zahra, S.A., Matherne, B.P. and Carleton, J.M. (2003) 'Technological resource leveraging and the internationalisation of new ventures', *Journal of International Entrepreneurship*, 1(2), 163–86.

Zeithaml, C.P. and Zeithaml, V.A. (1984) 'Environmental management: revising the marketing perspective', *Journal of Marketing*, 48(2), 46–53.

Zucchella, A. and Palamara, G. (2007) 'Niche strategy and export performance', *Advances in International Marketing*, 17(1), 63–87.

Part IV
Human Resources, Leadership and Culture

12
Interpersonal Relationships in Transnational, Virtual Teams

Angelika Zimmermann

Introduction

Transnational, virtual teams play a key role for international organizations in achieving local responsiveness as well as global integration. Team members in different countries can contribute their local knowledge and ideas to a transnational team, whilst team members located at headquarters ensure that the firm's global requirements are met. Transnational teams are, therefore, able to create organizational knowledge that can be applied on a global scale. Over the last decade, research on transnational teams (TNTs) has grown from a small, specialist area into a major stream of interest covering several disciplines. TNTs have been investigated by social psychologists as well as experts on international business and information systems. This has led to the first literature reviews (Berg, 2006; Connaughton and Shuffler, 2007; Podsiadlowski, 2002; Stahl et al., 2007) and an edited book on the subject (Shapiro et al., 2005). Given that TNTs are often geographically dispersed, many TNT studies include issues of virtual collaboration. Due to the importance of transnational, virtual teams for international organizations, many researchers have focused on what makes these teams effective.

What is to date missing is a comprehensive overview of the most significant relationship aspects in TNTs and their interconnections. The objective of this chapter is to provide a selective literature review that is able to sketch such a broad picture from what has been examined so far. It focuses on the transnational and virtual team literature to highlight the distinctive characteristics of relationships in transnational, virtual teams. Previous research will be integrated to identify suggested interrelations between different relationship aspects. Thereby, this review will deviate from the prevalent linear Input-Process-Output models of team functioning that follow classic system models (Hackman and Oldham, 1980; McGrath, 1984). Instead, it will make a first step towards a non-linear systems analysis and, through this, a configurational perspective on relationships in TNTs.

The non-linear systems approach claims that social systems tend to consist of a multitude of elements that influence each other reciprocally, making it impossible to clearly distinguish cause and effect (see Mendenhall, 1999, for a review). The configurational perspective, in turn, has been developed in organizational theory (Miller, 1990; 1996). It posits that organizational reality cannot be explained by unidirectional, causal relationships between isolated variables, but only in terms of variable configurations; that is, 'multidimensional constellations of conceptually distinct characteristics that commonly occur together' (Meyer et al., 1993, p. 1175). The effect of single variables depends on their interaction with the multitude of other variables in a configuration.

Methods of the review

In this chapter the term 'team' is used broadly to designate a group of people working on a common task. The term 'transnational, virtual teams' was chosen to designate research that focuses on transnational – or international, multinational, multicultural, cross-cultural or global – teams that are at the same time virtual; that is, geographically dispersed and collaborating with the help of electronic communication media. The label 'transnational' is here regarded as more generic than 'multinational' or 'multicultural', because it comprises teams composed of either many or only two nationalities, and it includes diversity of nationality, rather than only cultural diversity. All of these terms were used for a web-based literature search. Both empirical and conceptual papers and book chapters were included when they made a significant contribution to the leading questions. Table 12.1 provides an overview matrix of the relationship aspects and their influences on each other as indicated by the reviewed literature.

Relationship aspects prominent in the literature will be presented in the sequence shown in Table 12.1. I first discuss aspects classified as 'cognitive', including team identity, sub-group formation, shared understanding, and trust. I then turn to behavioral aspects in terms of communication, knowledge creation, and conflicts, before describing the affective aspect 'interpersonal affect'. Throughout, I summarize what has been said about the function of these aspects, both with regard to team performance and their influence on other relationship aspects, particularly those discussed in this review. The next focus will be on cultural diversity and virtuality as the two characteristics of the team structure that have been discussed most frequently and with regard to all relationship aspects. It is demonstrated how they make effective relationships more important but at the same time often harder to achieve in TNTs. However, diversity and virtuality can also have certain positive effects on relationship aspects. As the discussion progresses, I will outline how each newly introduced relationship aspect relies on those mentioned before. This will demonstrate that diversity and virtuality have a further, indirect influence on relationship aspects through these interconnections. When discussed in the literature, it is further explained how each relationship aspect relates to a number of other factors. Within the team structure, many suggestions have been made regarding team leadership, shared goals, and task interdependence. Only a few insights have been developed regarding the influence of the organizational context, in particular sub-unit interdependence and localization–integration strategies, as well as socio-political context factors. To draw conclusions, I highlight the main insights regarding non-linear

Table 12.1 Influences between relationship aspects as indicated in the reviewed literature

	Team identity	Sub-group formation	Shared understanding	Trust	Communication	Knowledge creation	Conflicts	Interpersonal affect
Team identity	–							
Sub-group formation	A,B	–						
Shared understanding	B		–					
Trust	A	A	A	–				
Communication	A,B	A	A,B	A,B	–			
Knowledge creation	A	A	A,B	A,B	A	–		
Conflicts	A,B	A	A,B	A	A,B	B	–	
Interpersonal affect		A,B	A	A,B	A		A,B	–

Notes: A denotes aspect on the top is reported to influence aspect on the left, and B denotes aspect on the left is reported to influence aspect on the top.

systems and configurations, develop configuration examples, and make a number of suggestions for future research.

Cognitive aspects of relationships in TNTs

Team identity

Team identity has been claimed to be a key facet of social capital (Nahapiet and Ghoshal, 1998, p. 244) and is therefore a crucial aspect of relationships in TNTs. Team identity is commonly explained on the basis of social categorization and social identity theory. Social categorization theory posits that people form their initial impressions of each other according to social categories (Turner, 1987). Social identity theory, in turn, suggests that individuals identify with a group (their 'ingroup') on the basis of their perceived degree of similarity with others, which in turn depends on their social categorization of self and others (Tajfel, 1982).

A TNT can have a stronger or weaker team identity; that is, stronger or weaker social identification of team members with the team as their ingroup. Team identity has been linked to many other relationship aspects. It has been suggested to increase TNT members' mutual trust (Henttonen and Blomqvist, 2005; Maznevski et al., 2006; Zakaria et al., 2004), to motivate members to contribute their knowledge to the TNT (Fulk et al., 2005) and thus to create intellectual capital (Nahapiet and Ghoshal, 1998). Hinds and Mortensen (2005) found that team identity moderates the effect of geographic distribution on interpersonal conflicts in TNTs.

A strong team identity appears to be more difficult to achieve in TNTs compared to mono-national teams. The main factors within the team structure are cultural differences and virtuality. For example, Shapiro et al. (2002) suggest that limited socio-emotional understanding due to cultural differences makes it more difficult to achieve team identity, whilst also making it more relevant. They further reason that team identity formation is restrained by virtuality and reliance on electronic communication media, leading to a lack of visibility of team members' faces and of personal, informal bonding.

Sub-group formation

Sub-groups in teams are typically understood to form along 'fault lines', that is, hypothetical dividing lines which split a group into sub-groups according to members' shared core attributes (Lau and Murnighan, 1998, p. 328). In TNTs, nationality characteristics are likely to be the salient attributes that form the basis of sub-group identities (Gibson and Grubb, 2005). Multinational group members are therefore likely to categorize members of other nationalities as part of 'outgroups' and evaluate them less positively than in-group members (Gibson and Grubb 2005, p. 72).

When examining the relation of sub-group formation with other relationship aspects, it becomes apparent that sub-group formation may have either negative or positive effects. Early and Mosakowski (2000) found that strong fault lines in TNTs were related to low levels of team identity, communication problems and relational conflict. In the same vein, Cramton (2001) reports that polarized groups withheld information from each other, which implies limited knowledge creation. Accordingly, Cramton and Hinds (2005) suggest that sub-group formation in international teams can lead to ethnocentrism, which entails negative evaluation of the other sub-group, and relationships marked by competition and conflict.

However, sub-groups are not always detrimental for team functioning and may even have positive effects on other relationship aspects (see Panteli and Davison, 2005; Stahl et al., 2007). Gibson and Vermeulen (2003) demonstrated that when sub-groups were moderately strong, that is, a moderate number of characteristics were shared within the sub-group (e.g. nationality), but a number of other characteristics were shared with members of other sub-groups (e.g. profession), the team maintained an 'inclusive atmosphere' and sub-groups stimulated team learning, a form of knowledge creation.

The effect of sub-groups on team functioning seems to depend on various factors within the team structure, such as the prevalence of superordinate, shared team goals, acting as a bridging mechanism in TNTs that strengthens team identity (Earley and Gardner, 2005; Earley and Gibson, 2002; Mcdonough and Cedrone, 2000). Moreover, the team leader can take an important role in stressing similarities of group members across national sub-groups, and in emphasizing shared group goals (Davison and Ward, 1999).

Shared understanding

It is essential for TNTs to achieve a shared understanding of various team and situation features, given its effect on other relationship aspects. For example, Shapiro et al. (2002) claim that limited socio-emotional understanding will weaken team identity. Shared communication codes, language, narratives (Baba et al., 2004) are seen to be necessary for exchanging information and thereby creating knowledge. Kittler (2010) provides in-depth evidence of the importance of shared understanding for intercultural communication. Hinds and Mortensen (2005) found that shared context moderates the effect on team member distribution of task-related conflict. Team members' perception of a shared understanding can further create positive affect and trust (Klimoski and Mohammed, 1994). According to Sutanto et al. (2005), a shared, organized knowledge structure enhances not only social interactions but also the task performance of a TNT.

As with team identity, TNTs are likely to face greater difficulties in achieving a shared understanding than mono-national teams, due to structural characteristics. Both cultural differences and physical distance tend to create a divergence of team members' perceptions of team and situation aspects (Gibbs, 2009; Govindarajan and Gupta, 2001). Shared understanding in TNTs is dependent on further structural characteristics, including team leaders who can, for example, design common goals (Earley and Mosakowski, 2000).

Trust

Trust has received wide attention in the TNT literature. Trust is usually defined on a cognitive level, for example as a 'willingness to be vulnerable to another party irrespective of the trustor's ability to monitor or control that party' (Rousseau et al., 1998; cited in Earley and Gardner, 2005, p. 11). Trust amongst TNT members is important for many other relationship aspects. Gibson and Gibbs (2006) demonstrate that trust supports innovation – and hence knowledge creation – in TNTs, by helping to create a safe communication climate where team members are willing to express their ideas openly.

However, building trust is more difficult in TNTs compared to collocated, mononational teams and may therefore take longer to develop (Gluesing and Gibson, 2004; Hambrick et al., 1998). Cultural and geographical distance can lead to negative sub-group processes, including mistrust towards out-group members (Gibson and Manuel, 2003). A number of additional factors of the team structure influence trust in TNTs. Team leaders can facilitate the development of trust (Davison and Ward, 1999; Govindarajan and Gupta, 2001). Gibson and Manuel (2003) suggest that trust increases with higher interdependence of team members' tasks, outcomes and resources, amongst others. Interdependence is seen to entail more frequent interactions, resulting in greater familiarity, thereby making it easier to judge each others' trustworthiness. Earley and Gardner (2005) further claim that interdependence can be increased by shared goals. Organizational factors of trust in TNTs have not received explicit attention.

Behavioral aspects of relationships in TNTs

Communication

Communication has a crucial impact on various relationship aspects in TNTs. TNT members need to communicate in order to develop a shared understanding about their expectations, rules and so on (Earley and Mosakowski, 2000, p. 36). As mentioned, communication is also important for building trust. It serves to obtain information about each other, thereby decreasing uncertainties and providing evidence for each others' trustworthiness. Moreover, unsolicited communication can demonstrate benevolence (Jarvenpaa et al., 1998). Not surprisingly, successful information sharing is necessary for creating knowledge. Moreover, spontaneous, informal communication was found to reduce interpersonal and task conflicts in global virtual teams (Hinds and Mortensen, 2005).

Communication, like other relationship aspects, has been suggested to be more difficult and at the same time more crucial in TNTs compared to mono-national, collocated teams. TNT members' different cultural contexts can lead to disparities in communication codes, leading to misunderstanding (Adler, 1997; Erez and Earley, 1993; Hambrick et al., 1998; Kittler, 2010). At the same time, communication is particularly important in TNTs for getting to know one another's communication norms and values (DiStefano and Maznevski, 2000; Maznevski, 1994). The virtual team structure places further obvious constraints on communication. Virtual communication relies on non-synchronous and less rich media which provide fewer contextual cues and less immediate feedback than face-to-face communication. However, Connaughton and Shuffler (2007) point out that not just the amount of communication may be relevant for TNT functioning, but also its process in relation to its content. Maznevski and Chudoba (2000) demonstrate that successful TNTs used strong, regular patterns of communication, matching communication function with form, and adhering to face-to-face meetings at regular intervals.

Team leaders can take an important role in facilitating the appropriate form and frequency of communication through team building and creating shared goals (Davison and Ward, 1999; Govindarajan and Gupta, 2001), as well as designing task interdependence. Kumar et al. (2005) highlight that companies can circumvent barriers to communication in globally distributed teams by applying organizational strategies that serve to control interdependence between different subsidiaries. Moreover, Puck et al. (2006) suggest that a strong organizational culture may overrule cultural restraints to open communication, particularly if English is used as a corporate language.

Knowledge creation

Knowledge creation has received considerable attention as a desirable process and outcome of TNT work. It is often equated with team learning. For instance, Zellmer-Bruhn and Gibson (2006, p. 501) define team learning as the collective acquisition, combination, creation and sharing of knowledge by teams. The importance of knowledge creation or team learning becomes apparent when considering its effect on other relationship aspects. Team learning regarding existing and new norms is required for creating a shared understanding. Successful knowledge creation is also likely to strengthen team members' trust in the team's competence.

Like the other relationship aspects in TNTs, knowledge creation and innovation are influenced by the cultural diversity and virtuality of TNT members. This influence can be positive, and some authors therefore stress that differences of culture and context should not be equalled out (Earley and Gibson, 2002; Janssens and Brett, 2006) but embraced (Gibson and Grubb, 2005). However, diversity and dispersion can also pose challenges to knowledge creation in TNTs. An important analysis by Fulk et al. (2005) emphasizes that individuals have a tendency to respond to immediate local needs for knowledge sharing before the needs of the dispersed TNT. Fulk et al. suggest that identification with the team is an important motivator, because it leads team members to value the collective benefit provided by the distributed knowledge commons.

Knowledge creation can be influenced by the same factors that affect other relationship aspects, both indirectly, through the ties with these aspects, and directly. Fulk et al. (2005) point out that the development of a transactive memory system relies on interdependence between team members (which would include interdependence of tasks and sub-units). Zellmer-Bruhn and Gibson (2006) demonstrate that the organizational strategies of local responsiveness versus global integration affect learning in TNTs. They explain that local responsiveness provides local offices with more independence, which is necessary for initiating new processes and products. Moreover, local responsiveness requires several functions (such as

R&D) to be located at the subsidiary. This leads to interdependence with other subsidiaries and the need to share perspectives.

Conflicts

TNT research has examined task and relationship conflict and, to a lesser extent, process conflict (Mortensen and Hinds, 2001; Stahl et al., 2007). Relationship conflict has consistently been associated with process losses and decreased performance. This can be explained by the effect of conflicts on other relationship aspects. For example, Earley and Mosakowski (2000) demonstrated that affective conflicts were associated with less effective team identity and communication in TNTs. Task conflict can, in contrast, have either positive or negative effects, depending on the nature of the task. Constructive conflicts between contrasting views may be necessary to create a shared understanding (Tuckman, 1987). Constructive arguments concerning task-related disagreements are seen to lead to more information sharing, which is part of communication (De Dreu and Weingart, 2003), and to knowledge creation (Earley and Gibson, 2002). A number of researchers have addressed the question of whether TNTs face more conflicts than collocated, mono-national teams. Cultural differences and virtuality are again the main distinguishing factors. There are many reasons why cultural differences could increase conflicts in TNTs, but results are inconclusive. Members of different cultures hold different views on what justifies conflict, what can be classified as a conflict, and on appropriate ways of dealing with conflicts (Davison and Ekelund, 2004). Von Glinow et al. (2004) therefore suggest that emotional conflict is more likely and harder to solve in multicultural teams. Moreover, Kankanhalli et al. (2007) demonstrated that cultural diversity contributed to both task and relationship conflict.

Conflicts in TNTs are influenced by many of the previously examined factors. Relationship conflicts may be less detrimental when task interdependence is low (Kankahalli et al., 2007). Team leaders can take a role in monitoring conflict (Davison and Ekelund, 2004). They can control information exchange by using temporal coordination mechanisms to ensure conflicts are recognized and dealt with at an early stage (Montoya-Weiss et al., 2001). Shared goals, in turn, can help foster team identity and may thereby reduce conflicts (Earley and Mosakowski, 2000). The effect of the organizational context has not been investigated explicitly.

Interpersonal affect

Interpersonal affect in TNT can be defined as the positive or negative feelings that team members hold towards each other, which includes like and dislike (Joshi et al., 2002) as well as attraction, attachment and affection (Jarvenpaa and Leidner, 1999). Interpersonal affect is influential for many other relationship aspects. Interpersonal attraction due to trait similarity is a reason for identifying with a sub-group (Adler, 1997). Positive affect (positive feelings that team members hold towards each other), as well as conveying attraction and affection by taking the initiative to respond to each other, may fuel a propensity to trust in

TNTs (Earley and Mosakowsk,i 2000, p. 27; Jarvenpaa and Leidner, 1999, p. 811). Negative affect, including tension, dislike and annoyance, are defining symptoms of affective conflict (Mortensen and Hinds, 2001), making it hard to distinguish whether negative affect causes, or results from, affective conflict.

Positive affective ties may be more difficult to achieve in conditions of cultural diversity and virtuality. Adler (1997) suggests that multinational team members are likely to be less attracted to members of the national out-group and will therefore develop more dislike. Both cultural differences and virtual collaboration may also inhibit positive affect indirectly, through their influence on other relationship aspects.

Whilst factors within the TNT structure and the organizational context have not been examined with regard to interpersonal affect, Jelinek and Wilson (2005) and Hambrick et al. (1998) point out that features of the socio-political context, namely the historical and current relationships (for example, animosities) between countries may cause a certain affect (such as tension) between individuals, regardless of their cultural distance.

Discussion

This review has provided an overview of the examined complex interrelations between relationship aspects in TNTs. The matrix in Table 12.1 aims to clarify this picture. Importantly, the matrix confined to the suggestions made in the literature and can therefore only provide an indication of existing interrelations. In the reviewed literature, influences in one direction or the other were suggested for the majority of combinations of aspects. Moreover, mutual influences with other aspects were shown for team identity (mutual influence with three other aspects), sub-group formation (with two other aspects), shared understanding (with three other aspects), trust (with three other aspects), communication (with four other aspects), knowledge creation (with two other aspects), conflicts (with four other aspects), and interpersonal affect (with two other aspects). Many more interrelations are likely to exist.

By demonstrating complex interrelations and several mutual influences between an integrated set of relationship aspects, this review has followed the approaches of non-linear systems and configurations. As mentioned in the introduction, the non-linear systems view claims that social systems tend to consist of a multitude of elements that influence each other reciprocally, making it impossible to clearly distinguish cause and effect (Mendenhall, 1999). In the review, certain influences between different relationship aspects had to be isolated in order to allow for a clearer analysis, rather than analysing more complex interaction effects. It was thereby possible to suggest certain cause and effect relations theoretically. However, the array of mutual influences suggests that in practice it may not be possible to distinguish cause and effect.

It is possible, however, to suggest typical factor-relationship configurations under consideration of the more frequently examined factors, that is, factors within the team structure. These are cultural diversity, virtuality, task

Table 12.2 Configuration examples

Configuration 1: Commitment and tight coupling

Factors	Relationship aspects	
Strong cultural differences	Team identity	Strong
High level of virtuality	Subgroup formation	Moderate, supports team learning
High task interdependence		
Strong integrative leadership	Role expectations	Highly clear
Strong shared goals	Shared understanding	High
High interdependence between organisational units	Trust	High
	Communication	Highly effective
Emphasis on organisational integration	Knowledge creation, innovation	High across subgroups
	Contribution of effort	High
	Conflicts	Constructive
	Interpersonal affect	Highly developed
	Satisfaction	High

Configuration 2: Commitment and loose coupling

Factors	Relationship aspects	
Strong cultural differences	Team identity	Strong
High level of virtuality	Subgroup formation	Strong, supports learning within organisational subunits
Low task interdependence		
Weak integrative leadership		
Strong shared goals	Role expectations	Less clear
Weak interdependence between organisational units	Shared understanding	Lower
	Trust	Possibly lower
Emphasis on localisation	Communication	Sufficiently effective
	Knowledge creation, innovation	High within local subunit Sufficient exchange between subgroups
	Contribution of effort	High
	Conflicts	Constructive
	Interpersonal affect	Less developed
	Satisfaction	High

interdependence, team leadership and shared goals. Based on a synthesis of the reviewed research, two possible configurations are suggested, and these are summarized in Table 12.2. These two configurations were chosen to demonstrate that positive relationships can be achieved by different constellations of relationship aspects, depending on the overall configuration of factors and relationship aspects. The focus is thus on the ambiguous effects outlined in the literature, and on the options of localization versus globalization.

Configuration 1 is characterized by the orchestrating theme of 'commitment and tight coupling'. Relationships in this configuration are positive, because the potential negative effects of strong cultural differences and virtuality are reduced despite high task interdependence, through integrative team leadership and using shared goals. Configuration 2 follows the orchestrating theme of 'commitment and loose coupling'. Cultural differences and virtuality are strong, and integrative leadership is weak. Nevertheless, the TNT's relationships function well, because the team has strong shared goals, and relationships are less relevant due to low task interdependence. Configuration 1 is more typical in a firm that stresses global integration, with tight coupling of team members across different nations. In contrast, configuration 2 is more commonly found when firms aim to localize their operations, entailing smaller task interdependence between members of different countries.

Sub-group formation is moderate in configuration 1 and supports team learning, as the integrative leader fosters an inclusive atmosphere (Gibson and Vermeulen, 2003) and a strong team identity. In configuration 2, sub-groups are strong but the shared goals support a strong team identity and thereby help circumvent the potential negative effects of sub-groups, even though integrative leadership is weak. The sub-groups can thus arrive at sufficiently effective communication with each other and avoid relational conflicts (Earley and Mosakowski, 2000). Team learning will occur rather within the local sub-groups than the whole team (Zellmer-Bruhn and Gibson, 2006).

In configuration 1, the close cooperation and frequent communication required by task interdependence, as well as the integrative leader, will help achieve a shared understanding of roles and norms, leading to effective communication and high levels of trust. In configuration 2, shared understanding may be weaker, leading to less effective communication and possibly lower trust (see Kumar et al., 2005), which can impede knowledge creation. However, the shared goals and strong team identity will motivate team members to exchange sufficient knowledge between sub-groups where necessary. Conflicts are likely to be constructive in both configurations, given the strong team identity and shared goals. In configuration 1, the high levels trust and shared understanding will additionally serve to solve conflicts, whilst relationship conflicts will be less detrimental in configuration 2, given the low task interdependence (Kankahalli et al., 2007). Interpersonal affect, positive and negative, is likely to be more developed in configuration 1, due to weaker sub-groups, stronger communication and understanding, and better personal acquaintance through close cooperation with interdependent tasks. This will further affect trust, knowledge creation and conflicts.

From these two examples, several other configurations can be inferred, such as a configuration of strong cultural diversity and virtuality in combination with weak leadership and goals as well as high interdependence, likely to trigger several negative relationship dynamics. Interestingly, the second configuration example accords with Gibbs' (2009) finding that 'dialectical tensions' in a global software team were not detrimental to team interactions, as long as the tensions were managed and negotiated well. Configuration 2 suggests that, instead of aiming at the highest possible degree of integration, it is possible to achieve effective interpersonal relationships despite strong sub-groups, less clear role expectations, and incomplete shared understanding. This also accords with findings by Zimmermann and Sparrow (2007), who demonstrate that TNTs worked effectively by balancing integration and differentiation of interaction styles and work practices.

Conclusions and implications

This review aimed to demonstrate the need for a configurational perspective on interpersonal relationships in TNTs. On the basis of previous research, two examples of typical configuration were suggested. To further pursue this perspective, future research should include a broad array of relationship aspects and factors. It could thereby systematically identify more comprehensive configurations of both relationship aspects and factors, and their association with each other. This would not render former IPO models invalid, but would demonstrate the degree to which they simplify the complex, larger picture. IPO models risk missing crucial interaction effects, but they allow for a simplification that helps examine the mechanisms of influences between certain relationship aspects in more depth. Results from such analyses can be used to inform more holistic, but typically less detailed, configuration research. For practitioners, such an overview of relationship and factor configurations could provide valuable recommendations on sets of strategic and management practices that can support positive relationship configurations under particular structural and organizational conditions. Focusing only on a few variables in isolation may not help achieve effective TNT relationships, given their interactions with other elements of the configuration.

To conduct such research on typical configurations, it would be necessary to include a broad range of relationship aspects across a number of different team structures and organizational contexts, and in different socio-political environments. In-depth, qualitative case research would be the most suitable to explore this complex social phenomenon, allowing for rich descriptions and explanations of various relationship configurations and their dependence on configurations of factors in specific team structures, organizational contexts, and socio-political contexts. Comparative, multiple case studies of different teams and companies would be particularly useful for highlighting the structural and context influences. Real-life organizations are the suitable context for revealing existing configurations. Field experiments, in turn, which do not eliminate the rich real-life context, could be set up to systematically investigate configurations and consolidate previous findings. Such cross-level research implies that data should be collected at the level of individuals (for example, through interviews) as well as teams (observation of team meetings and email correspondence) and the organization (analysis of strategy documents and organizational charts). Longitudinal research would be preferable, as relationship aspects may develop and influence each other over time. This would also allow for examining whether incremental changes will at some point lead to a qualitative change and a switch from one configuration to another, as suggested by configuration theorists (Meyer et al., 1993; Miller, 1990).

References

Adler, N.J. (1997) *International Dimensions of Organizational Behavior*, 3rd edn (Cincinnati: South-Western College Publishing).

Baba, M.L., Gluesing, J., Ratner, H. and Wagner, K.H. (2004) 'The contexts of knowing: natural history of a globally distributed team', *Journal of Organizational Behavior*, 25(5), 547–87.

Berg, N. (2006) 'Globale teams: eine kritische analyse des gegenwaertigen forschungsstandes', *Zeitschrift fuer Personalforschung*, 20(3), 215–32.

Connaughton, S.L. and Shuffler, M. (2007) 'Multinational and multicultural teams. A review and future agenda', *Small Group Research*, 38(3), 387–412.

Cramton, C.D. (2001) 'The mutual knowledge problem and its consequences for dispersed collaboration', *Organization Science*, 12(3), 346–71.

Cramton, C.D. and Hinds, P. (2005) 'Subgroup dynamics in internationally distributed teams. Ethnocentrism or cross-national learning?', *Research in Organizational Behavior*, 26, 231–63.

Davison, S.C. and Ekelund, B.Z. (2004) 'Effective team process for global teams', in H.W. Lane, M.L. Maznevski, M.L. Mendenhall and J. McNett (eds) *Handbook of Global Management. A Guide to Managing Complexity*, 227–49 (Oxford: Blackwell).

Davison, S.C. and Ward, K. (1999) *Leading International Teams* (London: McGraw Hill).

De Dreu, C.K. and Weingart, L.R. (2003) 'Task versus relationship conflict and team effectiveness. A meta-analysis', *Journal of Applied Psychology*, 88(4), 741–9.

DiStefano, J. and Maznevski, M.L. (2000) 'Creating value with diverse teams in global management', *Organizational Dynamics*, 29(1), 45–63.

Earley, P.C. and Gardner, H.K. (2005) 'Internal dynamics and cultural intelligence in multinational teams', in D.L. Shapiro, M.A. Von Glinow and J.L. Cheng (eds) *Managing Multinational Teams: Global Perspectives*, 1–32 (Oxford: Elsevier/JAI Press).

Earley, C. and Gibson, C.B. (2002) *Multinational Work Teams. A New Perspective* (Mahwah, NJ: L.Erlbaum).

Earley, P.C. and Mosakowski, E. (2000) 'Creating hybrid team cultures: an empirical test of transnational team functioning', *Academy of Management Journal*, 43(1), 26–49.

Erez, M. and Earley, P.C. (1993) *Culture, Self-identity and Work* (New York: Oxford University Press).

Fulk, J., Monge, P. and Hollingshead, A.B. (2005) 'Knowledge resource sharing in dispersed multinational teams: three theoretical lenses', in D.L. Shapiro, M.A. Von Glinow, and J.L. Cheng (eds) *Managing Multinational Teams: Global Perspectives*, 155–88 (Oxford: Elsevier/JAI Press).

Gibbs, J.L. (2009) 'Dialectics in a global software team: negotiating tensions across time, space, and culture', *Human Relations*, 62(6), 905–35.

Gibson, C.B. and Gibbs, J.L. (2006) 'Unpacking the concept of virtuality: the effects of geographic dispersion, electronic dependence, dynamic structure, and national diversity on team innovation', *Administrative Science Quarterly*, 51(3), 451–95.

Gibson, C.B. and Grubb, A.R. (2005) 'Turning the tide in multinational teams' in D.L. Shapiro, M.A. Von Glinow and J.L. Cheng (eds) *Managing Multinational Teams: Global Perspective*, 69–96 (Oxford: Elsevier/JAI Press).

Gibson, C.B. and Manuel, J.A. (2003) 'Building Trust', in C.B. Gibson and S.G. Cohen (eds) *Virtual Teams that Work*, 59–86 (San Francisco, Jossey-Bass).

Gibson, C.B. and Vermeulen, F. (2003) 'A healthy divide: subgroups as a stimulus for team learning behavior', *Administrative Science Quarterly*, 48(2), 202–39.

Gluesing, J.C. and Gibson, C.B. (2004) 'Designing and forming global teams', in H.W. Lane, M.L. Maznevski, M.L. Mendenhall and J. McNett (eds) *Handbook of Global Management. A Guide to Managing Complexity*, 199–226 (Oxford: Blackwell).

Govindarajan, V. and Gupta, A.K. (2001) 'Building an effective global business team', *MIT Sloan Management Review*, 42(4), 63–71.

Hackman, J.R. and Oldham, G.R. (1980) *Work Redesign* (Reading, MA: Addison-Wesley).
Hambrick, D.C., Davison, S.C., Snell, S.A. and Snow, C.C. (1998) 'When groups consist of multiple nationalities: towards a new understanding of the implications', *Organization Studies*, 19(2), 181–205.
Henttonen, K. and Blomqvist, K. (2005) 'Managing distance in a global virtual team: the evolution of trust through technology-mediated relational communication', *Strategic Change*, 14(2), 107–19.
Hinds, P.J. and Mortensen, M. (2005) 'Understanding conflict in geographically distributed teams: the moderating effect of shared identity, shared context, and spontaneous communication', *Organization Science*, 16(3), 290–307.
Janssens, M. and Brett, J.M. (2006) 'Cultural intelligence in global teams. A fusion model of collaboration', *Group and Organization Management*, 31(1), 124–53.
Jarvenpaa, S.L. and Leidner, D.E. (1999) 'Communication and trust in global virtual teams', *Organization Science*, 10(6), 791–815.
Jarvenpaa, S.L., Knoll, D.E. and Leidner, D.E. (1998) 'Is anybody out there? The implications of trust in global virtual teams', *Journal of Management Information Systems*, 14(4), 29–64.
Jelinek, M. and Wilson, J. (2005) 'Macro influences on multicultural teams: a multi-level view', in D.L. Shapiro, M.A. Von Glinow and J.L. Cheng (eds) *Managing Multinational Teams: Global Perspectives*, 209–32 (Oxford: Elsevier/JAI Press).
Joshi, A., Labianca, G. and Caligiuri, P. (2002) 'Getting along long distance: understanding conflict in a multinational team through network analysis', *Journal of World Business*, 37(4), 227–84.
Kankanhalli, A., Tan, B. and Wei, K.K. (2007) 'Conflict and performance in global virtual teams', *Journal of Management Information Systems*, 23(3), 237–74.
Kittler, M. (2010) 'Understanding misunderstanding in intercultural communication. Theoretical approach and empirical analysis', *PhD-Thesis*, University of Erlangen-Nuremberg.
Klimoski, R. and Mohammed, S. (1994) 'Team mental model: construct or metaphor?', *Journal of Management*, 20(2), 403–37.
Kumar, K., Van Fenema, P.C. and Von Glinow, M.A. (2005) 'Intense collaboration in globally distributed work teams: evolving patterns of dependencies and coordination', in D.L. Shapiro, M.A. Von Glinow and J.L. Cheng (eds) *Managing Multinational Teams: Global Perspectives*, 125–54 (Oxford: Elsevier/JAI Press).
Lau, D.C. and Murnighan, J.K. (1998) 'Demographic diversity and faultiness: the compositional dynamics of organizational groups', *The Academy of Management Review*, 23, 325–40.
Maznevski, M.L. (1994) 'Understanding our differences: performance in decision-making groups with diverse members', *Human Relations*, 47(5), 531–52.
Maznevki, M.L and Chudoba, K. (2000) 'Bridging space over time: global virtual team dynamics and effectiveness', *Organization Science*, 11(5), 473–92.
Maznevski, M.L., Davison, S.C. and Jonsen, K. (2006) 'Global virtual team dynamics and effectiveness' in G.K. Stahl and I. Bjorkman (eds) *Handbook of Research in International Human Resource Management*, 364–84 (Cheltenham: Edward Elgar).
McDonough, E.F. and Cedrone, D. (2000) 'Meeting the challenge of dispersed team management', *Research Technology Management*, July-August, 12–7.
McGrath, J.E. (1984) *Groups: Interaction and Performance* (Englewood Cliffs, NJ: Prentice-Hall).
Mendenhall, M.E. (1999) 'On the need for a paradigmatic integration in international human resource management', *Management International Review*, 39(3), 65–87.
Meyer, A.D., Tsui, A.S. and Hinings, C.R. (1993) 'Configurational approaches to organizational analysis', *Academy of Management Journal*, 36(6), 1175–95.
Miller, D. (1990) 'Organizational configurations: cohesion, change, and prediction', *Human Relations*, 43(8), 771–89.
Miller, D. (1996) 'Configurations revisited', *Strategic Management Journal*, 17(7), 505–12.

Montoya-Weiss, M.M., Massey, A.P. and Song, M. (2001) 'Getting it together: temporal coordination and conflict management in global virtual teams', *Academy of Management Journal*, 44(6), 1251–62.

Mortensen, M. and Hinds, P.J. (2001) 'Conflict and shared identity in geographically distributed teams', *International Journal of Conflict Management*, 12(3), 212–38.

Nahapiet, J. and Ghoshal, S. (1998) 'Social capital, intellectual capital, and the organizational advantage', *The Academy of Management Review*, 23(2), 242–266.

Panteli, N. and Davison, R. (2005) 'The role of subgroups in the communication patterns of global virtual teams', *IEEE Transactions on Professional Communication*, 48(2), 191–200.

Podsiadlowski, A. (2002) 'Multicultural workgoups: a differentiated view on group heterogeneity with regard to design and type of diversity', *Zeitschrift fuer Sozialpsychologie*, 33(4), 241–59.

Puck, J., Rygl, D. and Kittler, M. (2006) 'Cultural antecedents and performance consequences of open communication and knowledge transfer in multicultural process-innovation teams', *Journal of Organisational Transformation & Social Change*, 3(2), 223–41.

Rousseau, D.M., Sitkin, S.B., Burt, R.S. and Camerer, C. (1998) 'Not so different after all: a cross-discipline view of trust', *Academy of Management Review*, 23(3), 393–404.

Shapiro, D.L., Furst, S.A., Spreitzer, G.M. and Von Glinow, M.A. (2002) 'Transnational teams in the electronic age: are team identity and high performance at risk?' *Journal of Organizational Behavior*, 23, 455–67.

Shapiro, D.L., Von Glinow, M.A. and Cheng, J.L. (2005) *Managing Multinational Teams: Global Perspectives* (Oxford: Elsevier/JAI Press).

Stahl, G., Maznevski, M.L., Voigt, A. and Jonsen, K. (2007) 'Unravelling the diversity-performance link in multicultural teams: meta-analysis of studies on the impact of cultural diversity in teams', *INSEAD Faculty and Research Working Paper*, 36/OB.

Sutanto, J., Phang, C.W., Kuan, H.H., Kankahalli, A. and Tan, B.C. (2005) 'Vicious and virtuous cycles in global virtual team role coordination', *Proceedings of the 38th Hawaii International Conference on System Sciences*.

Tajfel, H.H. (1982) *Social Identity and Intergroup Relations* (Cambridge, UK: Cambridge University Press).

Tuckman, B. (1987) 'Developmental sequence in small groups', *Psychological Bulletin*, 63, 384–99.

Turner, J.C. (1987) *Rediscovering the Social Group: A Self-Categorization Theory* (Oxford: Blackwell).

Von Glinow, M.A., Shapiro, D.L. and Brett, J.M. (2004) 'Can we talk, and should we? Managing emotional conflict in multicultural teams', *Academy of Management Review*, 29(4), 578–92.

Zakaria, N., Amelinckx, A. and Wilemon, D. (2004) 'Working together apart? Building a knowledge-sharing culture for global virtual teams', *Creativity and Innovation Management*, 13(1), 15–29.

Zellmer-Bruhn, M. and Gibson, C. (2006) 'Multinational organization context: implications for team learning and performance', *Academy of Management Journal*, 49(3), 501–18.

Zimmermann, A. and Sparrow, P.R. (2007) 'Mutual adjustment processes in international teams: lessons for the study of expatriation', *International Studies in Management and Organization*, 37(3), 65–88.

13
Intercultural Ethical Leadership Competence: Contrasting Ireland and Germany

Mary A. Keating, Gillian S. Martin and Christian J. Resick

Introduction

In recent years, several studies have examined the meaning and importance of ethical leadership for organizational success (Brown and Treviño, 2006; De Hoogh and Den Hartog, 2008; Gini, 1997; Resick et al., 2006; Treviño et al., 2003). However, there have been few attempts to clarify the attributes and actions that are important for building ethical leadership competence across cultures. By contrast, the leadership literature has made great progress in identifying the personal attributes and situational factors that might impact positively on managers' intercultural competence (Bolten, 2001; Dickson et al., 2003; Hatzer and Layes, 2003; Kim, 1991). Whilst there is some blurring in the usage of terms such as 'cross-cultural' and 'intercultural' in the literature, the latter has more recently been employed by scholars from a range of disciplines to refer to the creation of a 'mediated' culture or 'third space', which is negotiated by the participants in a particular encounter. The emphasis is more clearly on the process of interaction and negotiation between members of different cultures: the third culture, according to Casrnir (1999, p. 108) represents an 'expression of mutuality, one which can be understood, supported and defended by all who shared in its development. Not only that, a system of values or ethics could result whose very emergence-process could be identified as being ethical.'

The focus on interaction increases the relevance of relationship building and, with this, 'involves understanding and accepting as valid, multiple perspectives and multiple voices in co-creating what the participants believe to be important and ethical' (Clark and Matze, 1999, p. 129). Clearly, any interaction between members of different cultures involves non-negotiable issues, including those of an ethical nature (French, 2007). Equally, acceptance of the validity of multiple perspectives raises significant questions in respect of the concept of ethical relativism, which claims 'that there is no culture-free, universal morality and therefore no way of ranking moral views and practices as more or less right, at least across cultures' (Guirdham, 2005, p. 216). For example, views about the ethical appropriateness of activities such as whistle-blowing, price-fixing and profit maximization tend to differ across cultures (Schneider and Barsoux, 2003). At the same time, some ethical standards such as honesty, the protection of society, customer and employee rights, integrity, constraints on violence and deceit, and upholding contracts, laws and treaties (Bok, 1989; Schneider and Barsoux, 2003) may be universally accepted as ethical values. Yet, critically, Gudykunst and Kim (2003) point out that whilst general agreement on these values may exist across cultures, their practice differs.

Not surprisingly, Guirdham, (2005, p. 17) has argued that 'ethical issues are among the most problematic in intercultural work.' Jackson (2001) has observed that in spite of the increasingly multinational nature of the workplace, there is a lack of empirical study of cross-cultural differences and explanation of these differences in managerial ethics. Reviews of the behavioural ethics and ethical leadership research have also called for a better understanding of the universally supported and culturally specific expectations for ethics and ethical leadership (see Brown and Treviño, 2006; Treviño et al., 2006).

This chapter examines beliefs about ethical leadership held by managers in Ireland and Germany – two countries with a long history of cross-national partnerships and strategic alliances amongst their business communities (Keating et al., 2004), and discusses the implications for creating intercultural ethical leadership competence. First, we ask whether managers from Ireland and Germany differ in their endorsement of key components of ethical leadership. Second, we examine whether managers from these countries attribute different characteristics and behaviours to ethical leadership and leader integrity. Third, we examine the implications of these similarities and differences for developing intercultural ethical leadership competence. The chapter begins by elaborating key findings from the literatures on cross-cultural leadership, business ethics, and ethical leadership, with a particular emphasis on Germany and Ireland, before presenting the empirical study, which forms the basis of our research.

Societal culture, leadership and ethics

Societal culture

The shared values, expectations and practices that define a society's culture provide a frame of reference for making social judgements (Heine et al., 2002), including beliefs about ethical decision-making styles (Jackson, 2001). Thus, we anticipate that the societal cultural values held by citizens of Ireland and Germany will shape their perceptions of ethical leadership. Findings from the Global Leadership and Organizational Behavior Effectiveness study (Project GLOBE), which collected data from middle managers in three indigenous industries in 62 countries during the mid-1990s, provide some insights into the practices and values associated with the culture of Irish and German society (House and Javidan, 2004; House et al., 2004). Across nine dimensions of societal culture, which are summarized in the Appendix, the GLOBE findings revealed different cultural profiles, both in terms of common practices and behaviours (*as is* scales) and values (*as should be* scales) in Irish and German society (Keating et al., 2004). The society-level mean scores on each dimension are summarized in Table 13.1.

Table 13.1 Mean culture scores for respondents from Ireland and Germany

	Former West Germany		Former East Germany		Ireland	
	Mean score	Rank	Mean score	Rank	Mean score	Rank
Practices/As Is						
Uncertainty avoidance	5.22	4	5.16	6	4.30	22
Future orientation	4.27	12	3.95	25	3.98	22
Power distance	5.25	29	5.54	13	5.15	36
Institutional collectivism	3.79	54	3.56	59	4.63	9
Humane orientation	3.18	61	3.40	56	4.96	3
Performance orientation	4.25	21	4.09	33	4.36	16
In-group collectivism	4.02	55	4.52	46	5.14	39
Gender egalitarianism	3.10	44	3.06	47	3.21	39
Assertiveness	4.55	10	4.73	4	3.92	41
Values/As Should Be						
Uncertainty avoidance	3.32	59	3.94	52	4.02	49
Future orientation	4.85	57	5.23	42	5.22	43
Power distance	2.54	44	2.69	33	2.71	30
Institutional collectivism	4.82	28	4.68	34	4.59	35
Humane orientation	5.46	30	5.44	33	5.47	29
Performance orientation	6.01	29	6.09	22	5.98	30
In-group collectivism	5.18	55	5.22	53	5.74	28
Gender egalitarianism	4.89	15	4.90	14	5.14	3
Assertiveness	3.09	55	3.23	52	3.99	19

Notes: Responses range from 1 (low) to 7 (high).
Source: Based on data from House et al. (2004).

There is evidence of a substantial amount of divergence in cultural practices between Ireland and Germany on these dimensions: assertiveness, uncertainty avoidance, institutional collectivism and humane orientation. For values, the scores suggest a higher degree of convergence between the two countries, with managers in Ireland and Germany espousing higher levels of future orientation, humane orientation, performance orientation, gender egalitarianism and in-group collectivism, and lower levels of power distance and uncertainty avoidance. (The scores from managers from both former West and East Germany were strikingly similar (Brodbeck and Frese, 2007).) On the basis of dominant societal practices and value orientations, GLOBE researchers assigned Ireland to an Anglo culture cluster, together with Great Britain, the US, Canada, Australia and New Zealand, and Germany to a Germanic-Europe cluster, along with Austria and (German-speaking) Switzerland (Ashkanasy et al., 2002; Gupta and Hanges, 2004). Whilst members of societies grouped in the same cluster endorse similar types of leader characteristics (Dorfman et al., 2004), clusters provide universal classifications for which we must seek culturally specific explanations. This is important to bear in mind when identifying the components of intercultural ethical leadership competence within and across clusters.

Culture and leadership

Cultural norms and values, observed leader behaviours, follower values and goals, and the demands of the task place constraints on the types of leader behaviours and characteristics that are endorsed in a given situation (Lord et al., 2001). Cross-cultural leadership research has found that whilst some aspects of leadership appear to be universally endorsed as important for effective leadership, many beliefs about leadership vary systematically and considerably across societal cultures (Den Hartog et al., 1999; Dickson et al., 2003; Gerstner and Day, 1994).

The GLOBE findings provide evidence of variation in endorsed leadership prototypes in Germany and Ireland. Charismatic/value-based, team-oriented leadership and participative leadership are positively endorsed in the two countries, whilst there is significant divergence in respect of humane and autonomous leadership. Germany's ranking for humane leadership is within the lowest quartile of GLOBE-sampled countries, whilst its ranking for autonomous leadership is in the highest quartile. In contrast, Irish managers rank autonomous leadership lower and humane leadership much higher than German managers. In Ireland, the endorsed leadership profile can be explained with reference to higher levels of humane orientation and collectivism in Irish society, alongside lower uncertainty avoidance. In Germany, the endorsed leadership prototypes correlate with higher levels of individualism, assertiveness and uncertainty avoidance, and lower levels of humane orientation (Martin et al., 2004).

Culture and business ethics

Differences in cultural values are also associated with expectations regarding moral behaviour and issues of a moral or ethical nature (Jackson, 2001) and ethical leadership beliefs (Resick et al., 2006). In light of the underlying variation in their societal cultural profiles and variation in the endorsement of particular leadership styles, we suggest that ethical leadership will be differently understood in Germany and Ireland.

Throughout history, philosophers have debated the proper criteria for determining ethical behaviour: the Anglo-Saxon approach to business ethics is rooted in utilitarianism, which holds that the moral worth of actions is determined by their consequences and implies an instrumental, functionalist approach. In contrast, the German 'Wirtschaftsethik' is influenced by Kantian philosophy which holds that people should be treated as ends and never as means to the ends of others; it emphasizes individual interests based on the moral responsibility of the individual and the relation between the individual and the firm (Palazzo, 2002; Steinmann and Löhr, 1992). The stronger focus on consensual ethics in Germany means that decisions lie not with the individual, but with the moral community (van Luijk, 1990).

Interest in business ethics in Germany can be traced back to the early 1980s (Steinmann and Löhr, 1992), although more recent corporate scandals, for example in VW and Infineon, have served to heighten public interest in the practice of ethics and ethical leadership in organizations. A study by Ulrich et al. (1996), which sought to ascertain if the trend towards formalized models of business ethics was spilling over to Germany and Switzerland, revealed increased recognition of the need for business ethics, but reluctance to institute formal programmes. Rather, CEOs pointed to the continued existence of a traditional company ethos highlighting that ethical behaviour in Germany continues to be understood as going beyond mere compliance and, therefore, cannot be legislated for (Palazzo, 2002). These sentiments reflect a broader scepticism of formal codes of conduct in European corporations and, along with this, slower practices in adopting such codes of conduct (Robertson and Schlegelmilch, 1993).

There have been few empirical studies of business ethics in Ireland. The first comparative study was undertaken by Alderson and Kakabadse (1994). More recent studies include those of Hoven Stohs and Brannick (1999) and O'Dwyer and Madden (2006). Historically, there has existed an assumption that managers automatically draw on the moral teachings of the Catholic Church when seeking guidance on ethical issues (Murphy, 1995). Fogarty et al. (1984) reported within the context of the European Values Survey that 'Irish people [...] seem more likely than others in Europe to see wrong-doing in legalistic terms: clear boundaries, sin if one goes over them, but otherwise not very strong sensitivity to right and wrong' (p. 14). This legalistic view of boundaries in Ireland may be rooted in attitudes to sin and shaped more by what is forbidden and allowed than by an ethical concept of morality based on 'internalized concepts of right and wrong' (Lee, 1989, p. 111). Evidence presented since the revelation of widespread corporate misdoing in the early 1990s across a range of sectors has exposed a culture of non-compliance or superficial compliance in respect of commercial life (Murphy, 1995), a practice which may not be out of line with the Catholic heritage of forgiving the sinner, which fosters 'an understanding approach to rule breaking' (Duncan, 1994, p. 452).

Having observed that different value systems in Germany and Ireland shape expectations of effective leadership and the understanding of business ethics, we now examine differences in their endorsement of key components of ethical leadership and the behaviours, attributes and situations that managers in Ireland and Germany view as indicative of ethical leadership. Our objective is to identify both generic and culturally specific expectations for ethical leadership in the two countries as a means of informing the construction of intercultural ethical leadership competence.

Endorsement of ethical leadership

Defining ethical leadership

Ethical leadership involves the leaders' use of social power in their actions, decisions and influence tactics in ways that are truthful and accountable, respectful of the rights and dignity of others, and promote group success (Bass and Steidlmeier, 1999; Brown and Treviño, 2006; Ciulla, 2004; De Hoogh and Den Hartog, 2008; Gini, 1997; Kanungo and Mendonca, 1996; Petrick and Quinn, 1997; Resick et al., 2006; Treviño et al., 2003). Brown et al. (2005) have presented the most widely used conceptualization of ethical leadership from social learning and transactional perspectives. They define ethical leadership as the 'demonstration of normatively appropriate conduct through personal actions and interpersonal relationships, and the promotion of such conduct to followers through two-way communication, reinforcement, and decision-making' (p. 120).

To date, there have been few studies examining ethical leadership across cultures. Resick et al. (2006) defined four dimensions of ethical leadership and examined the endorsement of these dimensions across cultures, using data from Project GLOBE. The four dimensions included in their study were character/integrity, altruism, collective motivation and encouragement. They examined convergence and divergence in the endorsement of these four dimensions across culture clusters. The results indicate that character/integrity, collective motivation, and encouragement were universally endorsed as important for effective leadership, although considerable variation existed in the degree of endorsement. Across cultures, altruism tended to be viewed more neutrally to slightly positively. This chapter builds on this research by comparing the endorsement of these four dimensions of ethical leadership by middle managers from Ireland and Germany.

Comparing ethical leadership endorsement

The leadership scales developed by the GLOBE researchers contained 112 attributes or behavioural descriptors (e.g. autocratic; benevolent; visionary) measuring 21 dimensions of leadership (Hanges and Dickson, 2004). Middle managers rated each descriptor on a seven-point scale ranging from one (this behaviour or characteristic greatly inhibits a person from being an outstanding leader) to seven (this behaviour or characteristic contributes greatly to a person being an outstanding leader). Ethical leadership was not included among the leadership dimensions originally included in the GLOBE study. Resick et al. (2006) used a combination of Q-sort and factor analysis methodologies to derive a fifteen-item, four-factor ethical leadership measure. They argued that while these four dimensions do not capture all aspects of ethical leadership (e.g. having a broad ethical awareness or managing ethical accountability), they provide a useful starting point for examining beliefs about ethical leadership across cultures.

The comparison in the current study is based on responses from Ireland ($n = 156$), the former West Germany ($n = 411$) and the former East Germany ($n = 43$). First, we conducted a multivariate analysis of variance (MANOVA) to determine if middle managers from Ireland and Germany (former West and former East) differed in the overall degree of endorsement across the four dimensions. We then conducted a series of four one-way analyses of variance (ANOVA) and Tukey HSD post hoc tests to examine specific differences on each dimension.

Table 13.2 summarizes the mean level of endorsement for each of the four ethical leadership dimensions from middle managers in Ireland, the former

Table 13.2 Endorsement of ethical leadership among middle managers in Ireland and Germany

Country	Character/ integrity	Altruism	Encouragement	Collective motivation
Ireland				
Mean	6.19	4.68	6.30	6.29
Range	3.75–7.00	2.00–6.75	4.00–7.00	2.00–7.00
Germany – former West				
Mean	6.12	4.09	6.12	5.99
Range	2.50–7.00	1.50–7.00	2.00–7.00	4.00–7.00
Germany – former East				
Mean	6.11	4.24	5.97	5.91
Range	3.50–7.00	2.00–6.00	4.50–7.00	4.40–6.60
Analysis of variance (ANOVA)				
F	0.40	24.06*	4.65*	18.87*
df	2,608	2,608	2,608	2,608
R^2	0.00	0.07	0.05	0.06

Notes: Ireland $N = 156$; Germany – Former West $N = 411$; Germany – Former East $N = 43$.
Responses range from 1 (*greatly inhibits a person from being an outstanding leader*) to 7 (*contributes greatly to a person being an outstanding leader*). * denotes $p \leq 0.01$.

West Germany and the former East Germany. Results of the MANOVA analysis indicated that there was an overall difference in the degree of endorsement of the four ethical leadership dimensions. (Wilks Lambda $= 0.874$, $F = 10.53$, $p \leq 0.01$, $\eta^2 = 0.07$). We then conducted four one-way analyses of variance to establish whether differences existed between the middle managers on each dimension.

As can be seen in Table 13.2, the results from the ANOVA tests indicated that statistically significant differences existed between Irish and German managers along three of the four dimensions. The greatest differences were found for altruism ($F = 24.06$, $p \leq 0.01$), with society explaining approximately seven per cent of the variance in the scores. Tukey HSD analyses indicated that the mean level of endorsement among Irish managers ($M = 4.68$) was slightly but significantly higher than the mean level of endorsement among managers from the former West Germany ($M = 4.09$) and the former East Germany ($M = 4.24$). Similar differences were found for encouragement ($F = 4.65$, $p \leq 0.01$), with society explaining approximately 5 per cent of the variance in the scores. The mean level of endorsement among middle managers from Ireland ($M = 6.30$) was again slightly but significantly higher then the mean level of endorsement among middle managers from the former West Germany ($M = 6.12$) and the former East Germany ($M = 5.97$). For collective motivation an overall difference in scores was found between the societies ($F = 18.87$, $p \leq 0.01$), with society explaining approximately 6 per cent of the score variance. The follow-up analyses indicated that the mean level of endorsement among Irish managers ($M = 6.29$) was again slightly but significantly higher than the mean level of endorsement among managers from the former West Germany ($M = 5.99$) and former East Germany ($M = 5.91$). Irish and German middle managers did not differ in their endorsement of character/integrity ($F = 0.40$, ns).

In summary, the results show that middle managers from Ireland and Germany converged in their beliefs about the importance of character/integrity for effective leadership. Similarly, both Irish and German middle managers held more neutral views about the importance of altruism, though the degree of endorsement was slightly higher among Irish middle managers. The strong endorsement of encouragement and collective motivation by Irish middle managers may be explained with reference to the strong sense of institutional collectivism and team orientation that characterizes Irish society (Martin et al., 2004). Alderson and Kakabadse's (1994) study of attitudes towards business ethics amongst Irish senior managers found that they tend to view their role as culture creators to be critical in diffusing ethical conduct throughout their organizations. Leading by example is seen as important for setting ethical standards: hence the importance of two of the behaviours constituting collective motivation, 'communicative' and 'motive arouser'. The slightly weaker endorsement of collective motivation and encouragement by German middle managers may be explained in part by wider spans of control and a greater focus on autonomy in German organizations (Glunk et al., 1997; Maurice et al., 1980), which correspond with higher levels of individualism. Greater autonomy requires that professionals at all organizational levels work with a 'degree of self-discipline and self-programming' (Warner and Campbell, 1993, p. 99) relying less on management for motivation, encouragement or ethical guidance, as ethics are viewed as a private matter (Löhnert, 1998; Palazzo, 2002).

Whereas these findings provide some indication of the importance assigned to several elements of ethical leadership among Irish and German middle managers, they fail to provide insights into the cultural nuances that may exist regarding the meaning of ethical leadership. We therefore report the findings of a qualitative study that explores, at the emic level, the culture-specific behaviours and characteristics of ethical leadership in Ireland and Germany.

The meaning of ethical leadership in Ireland and Germany

In this section we review a subset of the findings from a larger qualitative study of beliefs about ethical leadership across six societies (Germany, the US, Ireland, Taiwan, Hong Kong, China) and three cultural clusters (Anglo, Confucian Asian, Germanic Europe) (see Resick et al., 2010). In brief, managers were sent an open response questionnaire, which addressed the meaning of ethical and unethical leadership. Respondents were asked to describe a situation where a leader demonstrated (a) ethical and (b) unethical leadership and to list characteristics and behaviours they associate with (a) ethical and (b) unethical leadership. As leader character/integrity was highly endorsed by both Irish and German middle managers from the analysis of Project GLOBE data, we specifically asked Irish and German managers to reflect on the meaning of leader integrity. Although integrity is an important element of business ethics across cultures, it is not necessarily conceived in the same way (Audi and Murphy, 2006).

A full description of the methodology and results of the qualitative study are found in Resick et al. (2010). The results discussed in this chapter will focus on ethical leadership and integrity. They are based on the responses of 51 managers from Ireland and Germany. Managers from Ireland ($n = 28$), were predominantly male (81 per cent), with a mean age of 43 years, had 5 or more years of managerial experience (85 per cent), and represented senior (77 per cent), middle (15 per cent) and front-line (8 per cent) levels of management. Managers from Germany ($n = 23$) were also predominantly male (65 per cent) with a mean age of 44 years, having five or more years of work experience (78 per cent), and represented senior (43 per cent), middle (26 per cent) and front-line (26 per cent) levels of management (with 5 per cent not responding). Questionnaires were distributed in German to the German managers and their responses were translated into English.

The manifest content of the manager responses was analysed through a series of inductive iterative cycles. Six ethical leadership themes were identified across societies. The themes include *accountability* (personal accountability, managing accountability), *consideration and respect for others* (treating others with dignity and respect), *fairness and non-discriminatory treatment* (making fair, just and objective decisions), *character* (honesty, trustworthiness, integrity), *collective orientation – organization and social* (protecting the interests of the firm and society), and *openness and flexibility* (being a good communicator and listener).

Table 13.3 compares the findings from Irish and German managers. Irish managers' responses appeared to focus on leader characteristics; for example, the most commonly provided responses aligned with character (79.3 per cent) and accountability (51.7 per cent). In contrast, German managers' responses focused somewhat more on leaders' use of their social power and treatment of others.

Table 13.3 Ethical leadership themes between Irish and German managers

Theme	Ireland (%)	Germany (%)
Accountability	51.7	31.8
Consideration and respect for others	34.5	72.7
Fairness and non-discriminatory treatment	27.6	45.5
Character	79.3	50.0
Collective orientation – organizational and social	37.9	63.6
Openness and flexibility	37.9	18.2

Notes: Adapted from Resick et al. (2010).

For example, the most commonly provided responses reflected consideration and respect for others (72.7 per cent) and collective orientation – organizational and social (63.6 per cent).

In addition, we asked managers from Ireland and Germany three questions aimed specifically at understanding the meaning of integrity: (a) How would you define integrity?, (b) Which behaviours and personal characteristics do you associate most closely with leader integrity?, and (c) Please describe a situation where you consider a leader to have acted with integrity. We conducted an indicative analysis of the responses through a series of iterative cycles and identified five themes across managers. The first theme, *authenticity*, involved leading with transparency, openness, sincerity, being upright and incorruptible, living one's values, and consistency between words and actions. The second theme, *honest*, included honesty and trustworthiness. The third theme, *just*, involved having a sense of justice, being loyal, fair in actions and decisions, and considerate to others. The fourth theme, *law abiding*, included adhering to laws, norms and standards. The fifth theme, *strong personal moral code*, involved having a strong set of personal values or morals, and being principled. Table 13.4 summarizes the responses of Irish and German managers.

Respondents from both Ireland and Germany unanimously indicated that leading with integrity involves *authenticity*. Responses from Irish managers also aligned closely with the *honesty* theme (80.8 per cent), again reflecting a focus on the person. German managers' responses were somewhat more diverse with the next most common responses aligning with *just* (60.9 per cent) and *honest* (47.8 per cent). Interestingly, *law abiding* was viewed as an attribute of leader integrity by several German managers (17.4 per cent), whereas none of the Irish managers provided responses aligning with this theme.

Moral positions in Ireland would appear to be closely linked to individual persons, although there is simultaneously a need for external regulation. The fact that Irish managers stress accountability and compliance may be seen as a means of filling the gap created by the decline in the moral authority of the Catholic Church and as a reaction to the culture of collusion and clientelism that has existed in Irish society: such in-group loyalty is compatible with high levels of both in-group and institutional collectivism. It also resonates with Fogarty et al.'s (1984) view of the more legalistic view of boundaries and contrasts with the German perspective that

Table 13.4 Attributes and behaviours attributed to integrity and leader integrity

Theme	Ireland (%)	Germany (%)
Authenticity	100.0	100.0
Honest	80.8	47.8
Just	42.3	60.9
Law abiding	0.0	17.4
Strong personal moral code	42.3	34.8

Notes: Ireland $N = 26$ and Germany $N = 23$.

ethical leadership would appear to extend beyond compliance (Palazzo, 2002). The German responses suggest a stronger focus on personal values and how managers use their position of authority as opposed to external regulation, which, in turn, corresponds with stronger endorsement of autonomous leadership in Germany (Martin et al., 2004) and, with this, stronger individualism within German society.

The importance for German managers of *consideration and respect for others* as an attribute of ethical leadership is compatible with their understanding of integrity and the emphasis on the *just* theme. It corresponds with the Kantian focus on the moral responsibility of the individual and the view that people should not be treated as a means to the ends of others (Palazzo, 2002; Steinmann and Löhr, 1992). The term 'Gemeinschaftsindividualismus' or community-oriented individualism (Löhnert, 1998) encapsulates the focus on individual autonomy and the institutionalized consideration and respect for others, which is compatible with lower levels of interpersonal humane orientation in German society.

The findings from the qualitative research suggest areas of convergence and divergence in the meaning of ethical leadership and integrity for German and Irish managers. Understanding these cultural contingencies in terms of both how ethical leadership is conceived and practised provides a basis for identifying the competencies, which might equip leaders to deal effectively with the challenges of leading ethically across national borders. We now examine the implications of these findings for building intercultural ethical leadership competence.

Conclusions and implications for intercultural ethical competence

In this section, we extrapolate from our findings to identify the kinds of competencies that will enable business leaders who work across Irish and German national boundaries to lead in an appropriate and effective way (Smith et al., 1998) when faced with ethical challenges or dilemmas.

Intercultural competencies

We suggest that cultural understanding of similarities and differences in the common practices and shared values espoused within a society provides an important baseline competence for leading ethically across cultures. Studies such as GLOBE can support Irish and German leaders in acquiring the culture-specific knowledge that facilitates the comparison of societal cultures along particular dimensions. In Germany and Ireland, cultural explanations for ethical behaviour might be sought inter alia in divergent assumptions about autonomy and individualism-collectivism. In itself, however, the acquisition of knowledge is an insufficient predictor of success in handling ethical dilemmas across cultures: it merely provides a necessary conceptual framework which allows the leader to understand the basis of cultural diversity and similarity and, with this, the culturally specific assumptions underlying particular behaviours.

A leader's ability to apply this knowledge appropriately and effectively requires the development of a second competence, namely critical cultural awareness. Byram (1997) defines critical cultural awareness as a 'rational and explicit standpoint from which to evaluate' (p. 54). Through critical reflection, German and Irish leaders can evaluate and interpret their own value system and that of the other culture and, in this way, establish a better basis for making ethical judgements and decisions. Critical cultural awareness involves a high level of self-awareness and self-regulation, which Goleman (1998) includes as two of the five components of emotional intelligence. The development of critical cultural awareness is supported by the ability to suspend judgement, tolerance of (moral) ambiguity and openness on the part of the leader. However, alongside these cognitive abilities, there is also an affective dimension, which includes empathy and sensitivity to other cultures.

Chen and Starosta (1996) distinguish between intercultural awareness and intercultural sensitivity: the former referring to the cognitive and the latter to the affective aspect of intercultural encounters. Intercultural moral sensitivity, which involves the capacity to evaluate and react sensitively to culturally specific expectations for moral behaviour, is a third important competence. Bennett's (1993) developmental model of intercultural sensitivity suggests that there is a learning process that allows an individual to move from an ethnocentric to an ethnorelative perspective. Intercultural moral sensitivity requires empathy. It can enable a German or Irish leader to appreciate the importance of the distinctive culture-bound behavioural aspects of ethical leadership and integrity and to react appropriately.

Cultural understanding, critical cultural awareness and intercultural moral sensitivity underpin what is arguably the central pillar or overarching meta-competence in leading ethically across cultures: intercultural mediation competence. As Goleman (1998) has noted, 'Cross-cultural dialogue can easily lead to miscues and misunderstandings. Empathy is an antidote. People who have studied it are attuned to subtleties in body language; they can hear the message beneath the words being spoken' (p. 101). Resolving ethical challenges involves dialogue. The interculturally competent ethical leader must be capable of drawing on his/her cognitive and affective abilities to mediate between different cultural identifications. Byram (1997) emphasizes that intercultural competence focuses on 'establishing and maintaining relationships instead of merely communicating messages or exchanging information' (p. 3). As the relational dimension of leadership becomes more critical (Clark and Matze, 1999), German and Irish leaders who seek to resolve an ethical dilemma must understand and be sensitive to how different culture-bound expectations about communication, for example, assertiveness with its implications for directness and indirectness and tolerance of ambiguity with its implications for explicitness and implicitness (Martin, 2001), will impact the actual process of mediation.

Ethical leadership competencies

Morrison (2006) has contended that leaders must have high levels of integrity to effectively address ethical dilemmas across cultures. Other commentators have identified integrity as a universal ethical standard (Schneider and Barsoux, 2003). Our quantitative study demonstrates endorsement of character/integrity in

Germany and Ireland. However, the findings of our qualitative study suggest that the understanding of leader integrity may be more nuanced and, thus, it may be enacted differently. While the foundation of integrity in both countries appears to be authenticity, this manifests itself in Ireland as a strong set of personal values with a focus on honesty and in Germany as an emphasis on just behaviour towards others.

This divergence is also apparent in the differential emphasis placed by German and Irish managers on the ethical leadership themes. Irish managers focused on the person, emphasizing honesty, integrity and accountability; German managers emphasized social relations and the responsible use of social power to protect the interests of the organization and society. Thus, the German leader collaborating with Irish counterparts would do well to understand the importance of framing decisions in terms of a strong personal value system and accountability. The Irish leader in Germany may want to stress consideration and respect for others and actively avoid any appearance of acting in self-interest so as to promote the perception by German colleagues and subordinates of being an ethical leader. This is, of course, not to suggest that leaders engaging in business across cultural boundaries should abandon their core values; rather they can engage in pro-social impression management, which has been shown to relate positively with attributions of charismatic leadership (Sosik et al., 2002).

When faced with a cultural or ethical dilemma, it is frequently the case that members of one culture use their own cultural and ethical value systems as an absolute standard against which to measure the behaviour of members of the other culture or they adopt the norms of the other culture. Both perspectives are, according to Barnlund (1980), inherently ethnocentric as they involve the subordination of the ethical premises of one or the other culture. The contrasting notion of ethical relativism claims that as there is no culture-free, universal morality, there is no way of ranking moral practices as more or less right across cultures. Arguments against ethical relativism include the assertion that obvious differences in moral beliefs and practices do not prove that they are all right (see Brinkmann, 2002). The concept of a meta-ethic proposed by Barnlund (1980) seeks to set ethical standards which embrace the perspectives of both cultures rather than using the frames of reference of one or other culture. By contrast, Donaldson and Dunfee (1994) advocate the development of hypernorms, which refer to fundamental principles of ethical behaviour that are universally endorsed. Regardless of whether one advocates the development of a 'negotiated' or 'generic' ethic or what Brinkmann (2002) calls an 'intercultural moral consensus', we suggest that the process of intercultural mediation will be facilitated through cultural understanding, critical cultural awareness and intercultural moral sensitivity.

In sum, our study, by including an emic perspective, has provided insights into leader behaviours and attributes that, although existing across cultures, are likely to be differentially attended to in Germany and Ireland. The data do not provide answers to questions about the comparative abundance or scarcity of these ethical leadership behaviours and characteristics in the two countries; however, they underline the extent to which they are 'top of mind'. Further, when there are discrepant perceptions of the ethicality of a given leader between Irish and German colleagues, our data provide some guidance as to the differing criteria likely to be used in the evaluation by the group members from the two cultures. In this way, the study takes a first step towards achieving a better understanding of the cross-culturally endorsed and culturally specific expectations for ethics and ethical leadership in two societies from different cultural clusters and, with this, towards identifying a range of competencies that will enhance how leaders in these countries deal with ethical challenges.

Appendix GLOBE Culture dimensions and definitions

Dimension	Definition
Power distance	The degree to which members of a society expect power to be distributed equally
Uncertainty avoidance	The extent to which a society relies on social norms, rules and procedures to alleviate unpredictability of future events
Humane orientation	The degree to which a society encourages and rewards individuals for being fair, altruistic, generous, caring and kind to others
Institutional collectivism	The degree to which societal institutional practices encourage and reward collective distribution of resources and collective action
In-group collectivism	The degree to which individuals express pride, loyalty and cohesiveness in their families
Assertiveness	The degree to which individuals are assertive, dominant and demanding in their relationships with others
Gender egalitarianism	The degree to which a society minimizes gender inequality
Future orientation	The extent to which a society encourages future-oriented behaviours such as delaying gratification, planning and investing in the future
Performance orientation	The degree to which a society encourages and rewards group members for performance improvement and excellence

Source: House et al. (2004).

References

Alderson, S. and Kakabadse, A. (1994) 'Business ethics and Irish management: a cross-cultural study', *European Management Journal*, 12(4), 432–41.
Ashkanasy, N., Trevor-Roberts, E. and Earnshaw, L. (2002) 'The Anglo cluster: legacy of the British Empire', *Journal of World Business*, 37(1), 28–39.
Audi, R. and Murphy, P.E. (2006) 'The many faces of integrity', *Business Ethics Quarterly*, 16(1), 3–21.
Barnlund, D. (1980) 'The cross-cultural arena: an ethical void', in N. Asuncion-Lande (ed.) *Ethical Perspectives and Critical Issues in Intercultural Communication*, 8–13 (Falls Church, VA: Speech Communication Association).

Bass, B.M. and Steidlmeier, P. (1999) 'Ethics, character, and authentic transformational leadership behavior', *The Leadership Quarterly*, 10(2), 181–217.
Bennett, M.J. (1993) 'Towards ethnorelativism: a developmental model of intercultural sensitivity', in R. M. Paige (ed.) *Education for the Intercultural Experience*, 2nd edn, 21–71 (Yarmouth, ME: Intercultural Press).
Bok, S. (1989) *A Strategy for Peace* (New York: Pantheon).
Bolten, J. (2001) *Interkulturelle Kompetenz* (Erfurt: Landeszentrale für politische Bildung).
Brinkmann, J. (2002) 'Business ethics and intercultural communication: exploring the overlap between two academic fields', *Intercultural Communication*, 5, available at http://www/immi.se/intercultural/nr5/abstract5.htm#brinkmann (accessed 1 September 2008).
Brodbeck, F.C. and Frese, M. (2007) 'Societal culture and leadership in Germany: at the interface between East and West', in J. Chhokar, F.C. Brodbeck and R.J. House (eds) *Culture and Leadership across the World: The GLOBE Book of In-depth Studies of 25 Societies*, 147–214 (Mahwah, NJ: Lawrence Erlbaum).
Brown, M.E. and Treviño, L.K. (2006) 'Ethical leadership: a review and future directions', *The Leadership Quarterly*, 17, 595–616.
Brown, M.E., Treviño, L.K. and Harrison, D.A. (2005) 'Ethical leadership: a social learning perspective for construct development and testing', *Organizational Behavior and Human Decision Processes*, 97, 117–34.
Byram, M. (1997) *Teaching and Assessing Intercultural Communicative Competence* (Clevedon: Multilingual Matters).
Casrnir, F.L. (1999) 'Foundations for the study of intercultural communication based on a third-culture building model', *International Journal of Intercultural Relations*, 23(1), 91–116.
Chen, G.M. and Starosta, W.J. (1996) 'Intercultural communication competence: a synthesis', *Communication Yearbook*, 19, 353–84.
Ciulla, J. (2004) *Is Good Leadership Contrary to Human Nature?* Presentation at the Gallup Leadership Institute Summit, Omaha, NE.
Clark, B. and Matze, M. (1999) 'A core of global leadership: relational competence', in W.H. Mobley, M. Gessner and V. Arnold (eds) *Advances in Global Leadership*, 1, 127–61 (Stamford, CT: JAI Press).
De Hoogh, A.H.B. and Den Hartog, D. (2008) 'Ethical and despotic leadership, relationships with leader's social responsibility, top management team effectiveness and subordinates optimism: a multi-level study', *The Leadership Quarterly*, 19, 297–311.
Den Hartog, D., House, R. J., Hanges, P.J., Ruiz-Quintanilla, S.A., Dorfman, P.W. and GLOBE (1999) 'Culture-specific and cross-culturally-generalizable implicit leadership theories: are attributes of charismatic/transformational leadership universally endorsed?', *The Leadership Quarterly*, 10(2), 219–56.
Dickson, M.W., Den Hartog, D.N. and Mitchelson, J.K. (2003) 'Research on leadership in a cross-cultural context: making progress and raising new questions', *The Leadership Quarterly*, 14, 729–68.
Donaldson, T. and Dunfee, T.W. (1994) 'Towards a unified conception of business ethics: integrative social contracts theory', *Academy of Management Review*, 19, 252–84.
Dorfman, P.W., Hanges, P.J. and Brodbeck, F.C. (2004) 'Leadership and cultural variation: the identification of culturally endorsed leadership profiles', in R.J. House, P.J. Hanges, M. Javidan, P.W. Dorfman and V. Gupta (eds) *Culture, Leadership, and Organizations: The GLOBE Study of 62 Societies*, 669–719 (Thousand Oaks, CA: Sage).
Duncan, W. (1994) 'Law and the Irish psyche: the conflict between aspiration and experience', *Irish Journal of Psychology*, 15(2/3), 448–55.
Fogarty, M.P., Ryan, L. and Lee, J.J. (1984) *Irish Values and Attitudes: The Irish Report of the European Value Systems Study* (Dublin: Dominican Publications).
French, R. (2007) *Cross-Cultural Management in Work Organisations* (London: CIPD).
Gerstner, C.R. and Day, D.V. (1994) 'Cross-cultural comparison of leadership prototypes', *The Leadership Quarterly*, 5, 121–34.

Gini, A. (1997) 'Moral leadership: an overview', *Journal of Business Ethics*, 16(3), 323–30.
Glunk, U., Wilderom, C. and Ogilvie, R. (1997) 'Finding the key to German-style management', *International Studies of Management and Organisation*, 26(3), 93–108.
Goleman, D. (1998) 'What makes a leader?', *Harvard Business Review*, 76(6), 92–102.
Gudykunst, W.B. and Kim, Y.Y. (2003) *Communicating with Strangers*, 4th edn (New York: McGraw Hill).
Guirdham, M. (2005) *Communicating Across Cultures at Work* (Basingstoke: Palgrave).
Gupta, V. and Hanges, P.J. (2004) 'Regional and climate clustering of societal cultures', in R.J. House, P.J. Hanges, M. Javidan, P.W. Dorfman and V. Gupta (eds) *Culture, Leadership, and Organizations: The GLOBE study of 62 Societies*, 95–101 (Thousand Oaks, CA: Sage).
Hanges, P.J. and Dickson, M.W. (2004) 'The development and validation of the GLOBE culture and leadership scales', in R.J. House, P.J. Hanges, M. Javidan, P.W. Dorfman and V. Gupta (eds) *Culture, Leadership, and Organizations: The GLOBE study of 62 Societies*, 122–151 (Thousand Oaks, CA: Sage).
Hatzer, B. and Layes, G. (2003) 'Interkulturelle handlungskompetenz', in A. Thomas, E-U. Kinast and S. Schroll-Machl (eds) *Handbuch Interkulturelle Kommunikation und Kooperation, Band 1: Grundlagen und Praxisfelder*, 138–48 (Göttingen: Vandenhoek and Ruprecht).
Heine, S.J., Lehman, D.R., Peng, K. and Greenholtz, J. (2002) 'What's wrong with cross-cultural comparisons of subjective Likert scales?: The reference-group effect', *Journal of Personality and Social Psychology*, 82(6), 903–18.
House, R.J., Hanges, P.J., Javidan, M., Dorfman, P.W. and Gupta, V. (2004) *Culture, Leadership, and Organizations: The GLOBE Study of 62 Societies* (Thousand Oaks, CA: Sage).
House, R.J. and Javidan, M. (2004) 'Overview of GLOBE', in R.J. House, P.J. Hanges, M. Javidan, P.W. Dorfman and V. Gupta (eds) *Culture, Leadership, and Organizations: The GLOBE Study of 62 Societies*, 9–26 (Thousand Oaks, CA: Sage).
Hoven Stohs, J. and Brannick, T. (1999) 'Codes and conduct: predictors of Irish managers' ethical reasoning', *Journal of Business Ethics*, 22(4), 311–26.
Jackson, T. (2001) 'Cultural values and management ethics: a 10-nation study', *Human Relations*, 54(10), 1267–302.
Kanungo, R.N. and Mendonca, M. (1996) *Ethical Dimensions of Leadership* (Thousand Oaks, CA: Sage).
Keating, M., Martin, G.S. and Brodbeck, F.C. (2004) 'Cross-cultural difference: a comparison of societal culture in Ireland and Germany', in M.A. Keating and G.S. Martin (eds) *Managing Cross-Cultural Business Relations: The Irish-German Experience*, 1–35 (Dublin: Blackhall).
Kim, Y.Y. (1991) 'Intercultural communication competence', in S. Ting Toomey and F. Korzenny (eds) *Cross-Cultural Interpersonal Communication* (Newbury Park, CA: Sage).
Lee, J.J. (1989) *Ireland 1912–1985, Politics and Society* (Cambridge: Cambridge University Press).
Lord, R.G., Brown, D.J., Harvey, J.L. and Hall, R.J. (2001) 'Contextual constraints on prototype generation and their multilevel consequences for leadership perceptions', *The Leadership Quarterly*, 12, 311–38.
Löhnert, B. (1998) 'Die kulturellen Grundlagen amerikanischer Unternehmensethikprogramme', in P. Ulrich and J. Wieland (eds) *Unternehmensethik in der Praxis*, 91–118 (Bern, Stuttgart, Vienna: Haupt).
Martin, G.S. (2001) *German-Irish Sales Negotiation: Theory, Practice and Pedagogical Implications* (Frankfurt: Peter Lang).
Martin, G.S., Keating, M. and Brodbeck, F. (2004) 'Organisational leadership in Ireland and Germany', in M.A. Keating and G.S. Martin (eds) *Managing Cross-Cultural Business Relations: The Irish-German Experience*, 41–69 (Dublin: Blackhall).
Maurice, M., Sorge, A. and Warner, M. (1980) 'Societal differences in organizing manufacturing units: a comparison of France, West Germany and Great Britain', *Organization Studies*, 1(1), 59–86.

Morrison, A. (2006) 'Ethical standards and global leadership', in W.H. Mobley and E. Weldon (eds) *Advances in Global Leadership*, 4, 165–79 (Stamford, CT: JAI Press).

Murphy, P.E. (1995) 'Top managers' views on corporate ethics', *Irish Marketing Review*, 8, 61–72.

O'Dwyer, B. and Madden, G. (2006) 'Ethical codes of conduct in Irish companies: a survey of code content and enforcement procedures', *Journal of Business Ethics*, 63(3), 217–36.

Palazzo, B. (2002) 'US-American and German business ethics: an intercultural comparison', *Journal of Business Ethics*, 41(3), 195–216.

Petrick, J.A. and Quinn, J.F. (1997) *Management Ethics: Integrity at Work* (Thousand Oaks, CA: Sage).

Resick, C.J., Hanges, P.J., Dickson, M.W. and Mitchelson, J.K. (2006) 'A cross-cultural examination of the endorsement of ethical leadership', *Journal of Business Ethics*, 63(4), 345–59.

Resick, C.J., Martin, G.S., Keating, M., Dickson, M.W., Kwan, H.K. and Peng, C. (2011) 'What ethical leadership means to me: Asian, American, and European perspectives', *Journal of Business Ethics*, doi: 10.1007, (Springer).

Robertson, D.C. and Schlegelmilch, B.B. (1993) 'Corporate institutionalization of ethics in the United States and Great Britain', *Journal of Business Ethics*, 12(4), 301–12.

Schneider, S. and Barsoux, J.L. (2003) *Managing across Cultures*, 2nd edn (Harlow: Pearson).

Sosik, J.J., Avolio, B.J. and Jung, D.I. (2002) 'Beneath the mask: examining the relationship of self-presentation attributes and impression management of charismatic leadership', *The Leadership Quarterly*, 13, 217–42.

Smith, S.L., Paige, R.M. and Steglitz, L. (1998) 'Theoretical foundations of intercultural training and applications to the teaching of culture', in D.L. Lange, C.A. Klee, R.M. Paige and Y.A. Yershova (eds) *Culture as the Core: Interdisciplinary Perspectives on Culture Teaching and Learning in the Language Curriculum* (Centre for Advanced Research on Language Acquisition, Working Paper Series: University of Minnesota).

Steinmann, H. and Löhr, A. (1992) 'A survey of business ethics in Germany', *Business Ethics: A European Review*, 1, 139–41.

Treviño, L.K., Brown, M. and Hartman, L.P. (2003) 'A qualitative investigation of perceived executive ethical leadership: perceptions from inside and outside the executive suite', *Human Relations*, 56(1), 5–37.

Treviño, L.K., Weaver, G.R. and Reynolds, S.J. (2006) 'Behavioral ethics in organizations: a review', *Journal of Management*, 32(6), 951–90.

Ulrich, P., Lunau, Y. and Weber, T. (1996) 'Ethikmassnahmen in der Unternehmenspraxis. Zum Stand der Wahrnehmung und Institutionalisierung von Unternehmensethik in schweizerischen und deutschen Firmen', Ergebnisse einer Befragung, *Beiträge und Berichte des Instituts für Wirtschaftsethik*, 37 (St Gallen: Universität St. Gallen).

Van Luijk, H.J.L. (1990) 'Recent developments in European business ethics', *Journal of Business Ethics*, 9(7), 537–44.

Warner, M. and Campbell, A. (1993) 'German management', in D.J. Hickson (ed.) *Management in Western Europe: Society, Culture and Organization in Twelve Nations*, 89–108 (Berlin: de Gruyter).

14
The Role of Timing, Duration and Intensity of Training Programmes for Expatriate Adjustment: An Empirical Analysis

Markus G. Kittler

Introduction

Individuals working outside their home country are a persistent phenomenon beyond the current discussion on regionalism versus globalization. For instance, in the notion of the global factory where increasingly important headquarters 'need to manage spatially dispersed and organisationally diffuse units' (Buckley, 2010, p. 81) expatriates might remain a desirable staffing option at various levels within the subsidiaries. A subsequent phenomenon is the challenge of expatriate adjustment in the host country. In order to support adjustment abroad, expatriates could be prepared for assignments pre-departure, and provided with supportive measures in the host country. However, as training programmes generally come with a cost, their effectiveness needs to be assessed and appropriate configurations have to be identified.

Regarding programme effectiveness, previous studies have led to heterogeneous results. For instance, Morris and Robie (2001) or Waxin and Panaccio (2005) support the assumed effectiveness of training programmes for adjustment, while other studies did not find empirical support (Kealey and Protheroe, 1996; Puck et al., 2008). The diverse results indicate that the relation between training and adjustment may be subject to type and extent of training measures. With regard to timing, existing literature has discussed pre-departure (PRDT) versus post-arrival training (POAT), and recommends a combination of these options (Selmer, 2001; Selmer et al., 1998). A particular lack of research is identified for the relation between the duration and intensity of training programmes and expatriate adjustment (Cole, 2008; Puck et al., 2008).

In line with Shapiro (1995), who describes time as the critical resource in the design and delivery of training, we assume that the success of training programmes can be argued to increase when timing, length and rigour of preparation are appropriately chosen to correspond with expatriates' needs. Furthermore, based on the implications of earlier work by Grove and Torbiorn (1985) it was suggested that expatriates' training should be timed to coincide with expatriates' motivation to learn (Selmer, 2001). In consequence, the objective of this chapter is to analyse the relation between three major components of time (timing/duration/intensity) and their association with the adjustment of expatriates.

Timing, duration and intensity of training programmes and adjustment

Expatriate training programmes have been defined as any method or set of methods which is intended to improve an individual's ability to cope, work and interact efficiently in a foreign country (Brewster and Pickard, 1994; Harris and Brewster, 1999; Kealey and Protheroe, 1996; Tung, 1981). Previous literature stresses the importance of training that contains elements that prepare for intercultural encounters – so-called cross-cultural training (CCT). It has been suggested that pre-departure CCT is vital for the preparation and adjustment of expatriate managers (Black and Mendenhall, 1989, 1990; Deshpande and Viswesvaran, 1992; Mendenhall et al, 2004; Tung, 1982).

Despite the important role that is attributed to expatriates in large multinational corporations (MNCs), there is often a lack of time for systematic preparation. For instance, Black and Mendenhall (1990) found that only 30 per cent of the assignees sent on international assignments with a length of 1–5 years had been provided with PRDT. In the case of small- and medium-sized companies (SMEs) and internationally mobile individuals, a lack of training can be argued to be the result of limited resources/funding (Kittler, 2003). Another reason for the missing investment in training could be seen in a negative perception of the effectiveness of training and negative experiences of previously trained individuals (Baumgarten, 1995; Katz and Seifer, 1996; Welch, 1994). Possible reasons – in turn – could be that the negative perception relates to ineffective training that might (apart from inappropriate training content) result from inappropriate timing, duration or intensity of the training measures utilized.

The timing of training programmes

The timing of training seems to be an essential component in the adjustment puzzle. The literature suggests that designated expatriates should be trained when they are most motivated to learn (Grove and Torbiorn, 1985; Torbiorn, 1994). Timing in the context of this chapter is defined as the time when the training measures take place. Individuals can be trained prior to their departure to the foreign culture (PRDT), after their arrival in the foreign culture (POAT), or be exposed to a combination of these two options. Because of the different timing, the methods of delivery vary for both options. A major reason for this variation is that PRDT often takes place in the home country, while POAT measures tend to take place on-site in the host country. In the same line of reasoning, PRDT and POAT are argued to differ in the context and eventually the rigour of the programme delivered (Mendenhall and Stahl, 2000).

In contrast to PRDT, POAT allows expatriates to acquire *and* apply cultural knowledge, skills and appropriate professional behaviour within the same environment. Bird et al. (1999) point out that the non-customized nature of PRDT and the high failure rates demonstrated by premature return have led to the conclusion that real-time POAT is more efficient than PRDT. Additionally, while the general aim of CCTs is to reduce or avoid potential mistakes (Ivancic and Hesketh, 1995), Sitkin (1992) proposed that in some cases making errors, and examining different ways to solve these, leads to knowledge enhancement. Thus, hypothesis 1 is as follows:

Hypothesis 1: *Post-arrival training is associated with better expatriate adjustment than pre-departure training.*

The duration of training programmes

A research question of practical significance relates to the duration of a traditional training programme (Thacker and Blanchard, 2006). Duration can be understood as an interval 'in which some phenomenon exists in a steady state, is stable, or is unchanging' (George and Jones, 2000, p. 662). The duration of training may vary from brief orientations of 1 day to intensive preparation for several days to a couple of weeks (Caligiuri et al., 2001; Gudykunst et al., 1996). Existing literature on training duration concludes that most MNCs often provide a very short training period (Baumgarten, 1995; Celaya and Swift, 2006) and that there is often a tension between company management and trainers regarding training length (Tsang, 1999; Weber and Antal, 2001). It was found recently that the lack of time and short-term decisions are the main reasons for training failure (Longnecker and Fink, 2006).

While there is no satisfactory stock of previous research focusing on the efficient length of expatriate training and its impact on the outcome and subsequent adjustment (Kanaya et al., 2005), the phenomenon seems well addressed for training in general. A meta-analysis by Taylor et al. (2005) has confirmed the positive relation between longer training programmes and greater skill enhancement. For example, Lee and Klein (2002) or Holladay and Quinones (2003) suggest that a longer training time would ensure better variability of practice skills and create self-efficacy. In contrast, when too little time is spent on preparation, the effects are poor work performance, inability to adjust and premature return (Osman-Gani and Toh, 1995) or cultural stereotyping (Gertsen, 1990). Thus, hypothesis 2 is as follows:

Hypothesis 2: *There is positive relation between training duration and expatriate adjustment.*

The intensity of training programmes

Training intensity is argued to be another essential time-related component of training programmes. As Briggs and Harwood (1982) have found, the more intensive an expatriate training is, the fewer the problems with adjustment, poor performance and efficiency failure. Therefore, choosing the relevant training intensity is a significant part of an individual's training programme and should be determined by the difference in the type of job and the cultural distance between the host and home country (Osman-Gani, 2000).

Previous literature has also attempted to clarify levels of intensity. The extent of low-intensity programmes ranged between 4 and 20 hours. In contrast, high-intensity programmes varied between 60 and 180 hours (Black and Mendenhall, 1989, 1990; Black et al., 1991, 1992). The cross-cultural literature suggests that a higher training intensity allows expatriates to better apply learned skills and behaviour in practice. This would also lead to better adjustment abroad. Thus, Hypothesis 3 is as follows:

Hypothesis 3: *There is a positive relation between training intensity and expatriate adjustment.*

Method

The empirical study was launched in June 2009 asking potential respondents (who had previously been identified via international company directories) to confirm their voluntary participation in the study. The data collection then took place in July/August 2009. The potential participants were approached with an email questionnaire that included questions on expatriate adjustment and the timing, duration and intensity of training attended. A week after the questionnaire was sent, participants were encouraged to take part in the research with a reminder email.

Sample

Overall, 272 usable surveys were returned. In the survey, targeted participants were allocated on almost all continents, with the majority of them in Asia (59.6 per cent). Europe (23.9 per cent), North America (10.7 per cent), Australia and Oceania (4.0 per cent) and Africa (1.8 per cent) were also represented. The average age of participants was 34.6 years, with males (72.7 per cent) making up almost three-quarters of respondents. The observation that female expatriates are still a minority is in line with other studies on expatriate adjustment (for example, Puck et al., 2008). The expatriates spend an average of 28 months in the host country and had on average 11 months of previous international experience. Only 11.8 per cent of respondents had participated solely in a PRDT, 25.4 per cent had solely received POAT, 31.2 per cent had attended both PRDT and POAT, and 31.6 per cent of the respondents had not received any training at all.

Measurements

As the questionnaire was particularly but not exclusively addressed to Chinese expatriates abroad, the questionnaires were translated into Mandarin by bilingual Chinese native speakers. A committee approach and back-translation were employed to ensure consistency between the English and the Chinese version (Brislin, 1970; Cha et al., 2007). Some (minor) errors or ambiguities were identified and corrected by the committee.

A dependent variable in this study is *expatriate adjustment*, which was measured using the 14-item scale of Black et al. (1991). This construct has been tested by many previous studies and is widely accepted (Bhaskar-Shrinivas et al., 2005;

Hechanova et al., 2003; Shaffer et al, 1999). The three dimensions *general adjustment* (GEN_ADJ, Cronbach's $\alpha = 0.82$), *interaction adjustment* (INT_ADJ. 0.88) and *work adjustment* (WORK_ADJ, 0.92) are measured with multiple items using a seven-point Likert scale of response, ranging from $1 =$ not adjusted at all to $7 =$ completely adjusted. Additionally, the variable AVER_ADJ was computed as the median adjustment value for all 14 items.

The time-related variables are timing, duration and intensity. For H1, the questions were designed to find out about the timing of the training, that is, whether PRDT or POAT were attended. In order to measure the *timing* of training, respondents were given fixed yes/no answers to choose from. Regarding H2, *duration* of the total training period was determined by direct questions regarding the duration of received PRDT or POAT, measured in months and weeks (Altonji and Spletzer, 1991). The expatriates that received PRDT or POAT were also asked to indicate *intensity* (H3) via two dimensions consisting of the average length of the daily training unit and the weekly frequency, that is, how many training units they attended per week.

Demographic *control variables* measured via direct questions are age, gender, marital status and the time spent in the foreign country (Gregersen and Black, 1992; Selmer, 2002). Communication and language skills which are considered as vital factors for expatriate adjustment were included using a modified scale of Takeuchi et al. (2002).

Results

The data were analysed using the statistical software package PASW version 17 (SPSS) for conducting *t*-tests and correlation analyses. This chapter presents the analysis of the association of timing of PRDT and POAT on all three dimensions of adjustment – GEN_ADJ, INT_ADJ and WORK_ADJ – as well as on average adjustment (AVERADJ). Hypothesis 1 suggested that POAT led to better adjustment than PRDT. In order to distinguish between the impacts of PRDT and POAT, this analysis was conducted using the sub-samples of expatriates who participated in *either* PRDT *or* POAT; 32 of the 272 respondents received only PRDT, and 68 received only POAT.

The results indicate that the impact of PRDT and POAT on expatriates' adjustment do not differ significantly for AVERADJ (PRDT: 5.139; POAT: 5.302), and there are also no significant differences for GEN_ADJ (5.250; 524) and INT_ADJ (4.859; 4.985). However, there is a significant difference for WORK_ADJ (5.229; 5.936). These findings suggest a greater impact of POAT on WORK_ADJ compared to PRDT. The mean difference is -0.707 at a significant level of $p = 0.02$. Consequently, H1 is partially supported.

Hypothesis 2 suggests a positive relation between total duration of the training period and expatriate adjustment. The results show a mean length of PRDT of 4.5 weeks with a minimum of 1 week and a maximum of 3 months. In comparison, the average POAT duration was 6.9 weeks, with a minimum of 1 week and maximum of 2 years. A Pearson two-tailed correlation was used to test the relation, and the full correlation matrix appears as Table 14.1. The results for PRDT duration

Table 14.1 Pearson correlations

		1	2	3	4	5	6	7	8	9
AVER_ADJ 1	Pearson Corr. Sig. (two-tailed) N									
GEN_ADJ 2	Pearson Corr. Sig. (two-tailed) N	0.837** 0.000 247								
INT_ADJ 3	Pearson Corr. Sig. (two-tailed) N	0.853** 0.000 247	0.597** 0.000 250							
WORK_ADJ 4	Pearson Corr. Sig. (two-tailed) N	0.819** 0.000 247	0.552** 0.000 254	0.505** 0.000 249						
PRDT_LENG 5	Pearson Corr. Sig. (two-tailed) N	−0.028 0.771 109	−0.089 0.346 115	−0.027 0.780 111	0.053 0.576 113					
PRDT_FREQ 6	Pearson Corr. Sig. (two-tailed) N	−0.179 0.065 107	−0.163 0.085 113	−0.091 0.348 109	−0.212* 0.026 111	−0.057 0.547 112				
PRDT_DUR 7	Pearson Corr. Sig. (two-tailed) N	0.001 0.996 107	−0.068 0.474 113	0.080 0.411 109	0.004 0.970 111	0.070 0.462 112	0.046 0.629 112			
POAT_LENG 8	Pearson Corr. Sig. (two-tailed) N	0.255** 0.002 139	0.161 0.051 147	0.174* 0.039 141	0.270** 0.001 145	0.424** 0.000 83	−0.089 0.428 82	−0.085 0.449 82		
POAT_FREQ 9	Pearson Corr. Sig. (two-tailed) N	0.103 0.236 134	0.102 0.229 142	0.068 0.432 136	0.082 0.333 140	0.178 0.112 81	0.261* 0.018 82	0.013 0.905 82	0.409** 0.000 142	
POAT_DUR 10	Pearson Corr. Sig. (two-tailed) N	0.116 0.178 135	0.166* 0.047 143	0.072 0.401 137	0.049 0.561 141	0.137 0.221 82	−0.022 0.844 83	0.060 0.590 83	−0.077 0.365 141	0.014 0.872 140

** Correlation is significant at the 0.01 level (two-tailed).
* Correlation is significant at the 0.05 level (two-tailed).

do not show a statistically significant association with any of the three adjustment dimensions. For the total duration of the POAT measure and its association with expatriate adjustment, the only significant relation is between POAT_DUR and GEN_ADJ (0.166; $p = 0.047$). Hence, H2 is not supported for PRDT, and is only partially supported for POAT.

Hypothesis 3 proposed a positive relation between training intensity and expatriate adjustment. Intensity does not show any statistically significant relation with the adjustment variables, so it was divided into its two components: frequency and length of the individual training units. The average PRDT length was 2 hours and 12 minutes and the average POAT length was 2 hours and 30 minutes. For both types of training, the participants attended an average of two units per week. With regard to training length, there is no significant relation identified for PRDT_LENG and adjustment at all. In contrast, the relation between POAT_LENG and the adjustment dimensions is significant, with the exception of GEN_ADJ (0.161, $p=0.051$), which slightly exceeds the standard significance level of $p < 0.05$. For INT_ADJ (0.174, $p = 0.039$) and WORK_ADJ (0.270, $p = 0.01$) as well as AVER_ADJ (0.255, $p = 0.02$), significant associations with POAT_LENG are found. Regarding training frequency, no significant relation between POAT_FREQ and the adjustment dimensions was found. The only significant relation for weekly training frequency is for PRDT_FREQ and WORK_ADJ ($-.212$, $p = 0.026$). However, as the coefficient is negative, the result for PRDT_FREQ and WORK_ADJ is contradictory to our hypothesis. In consequence, H3 is only partially supported.

The results for the control variables show no association between age, previous international experience and all three types of adjustment. An independent two-tailed *t*-test revealed that women were slightly better adjusted to interact with host country nationals and to the work environment abroad than men. Moreover, the study points to the importance of language skills, mainly in relation to INT_ADJ.

Discussion

Regarding Hypothesis 1, we find that POAT led to a significantly better degree of adjustment compared to PRDT only for the dimension of work adjustment. Comparing the results for PRDT and POAT and their influence on adjustment, we do not find any significant difference for general and interaction adjustment (see Table 14.2). This means that while the two types of training occur in physically distant places, their effect results in similar enhancement of the general and interaction adjustment of expatriates. However, training or support that would help expatriates to adjust to the working environment abroad is better delivered post-arrival. Thus, additional 'real-time' POAT or mentorship associated with issues as they arise is considered an effective mechanism to facilitate work adjustment. This finding has also been advocated in studies by Oddou (1991) and Florkowski and Fogel (1999). A related observation was made by Zimmermann and Sparrow (2007) who point to the important role of a mutual context in order to overcome work-related differences in teams.

Table 14.2 Independent samples *t*-test (two-tailed)

	Means PRDT	Means POAT	Mean difference	*p*-value	Std. error of difference	95 per cent Confidence interval of the difference	
						Lower	Upper
GEN_ADJ1	5.250	5.240	0.011	0.958	0.200	−0.386	0.407
INT_ADJ1	4.859	4.986	−0.126	0.607	0.244	−0.610	0.358
WORK_ADJ1	5.229	5.936	−0.707	0.002	0.219	−1.141	−0.273
AVER_ADJ	5.139	5.302	−0.163	0.377	0.184	−0.527	0.201

Furthermore, it has been suggested that local staff might be able to better support expatriates; not only as a result of expertise on culture, norms and behaviour (Osman-Gani, 2000), but also on local business practice and the specific job requirements abroad. Such local colleagues in a mentoring role could be argued to better cover job-specific challenges and thus improve the performance and job satisfaction of expatriates – which is strongly related to work adjustment in the host country. In addition, it has previously been suggested that training of expatriates should be conducted in time to coincide with the psychological receptivity and motivation to learn (Selmer et al, 1998). Therefore, since expatriates are preoccupied before departure, they might not be able to focus sufficiently on the training delivered pre-departure.

Hypothesis 2, which proposes a positive impact of training duration on expatriate adjustment, is not supported for PRDT and only partially supported for POAT. The results show average training times of 4.5 weeks (PRDT) and 6.9 weeks (POAT). In comparison, the figures from the literature suggest that training programmes often vary from brief day orientations to a couple of weeks (Caligiuri et al., 2001; Gudykunst et al., 1996). Thus, the training provided to the participants in this study was longer than the average duration found in previous studies. However, there is no positive correlation found between the length of PRDT-programmes and any of the three adjustment dimensions. A possible interpretation is that companies that provide an extended PRDT assume that their assignees would be effective as soon as they arrive abroad. However, even if the training received is deemed to be long enough, participants in that period might focus on other pre-departure issues and would not concentrate fully on learning.

The potential support for POAT and adjustment could result from a U-shaped relation. As Mendenhall (1999) suggests, the POAT should be delivered over an appropriate period of time. An adequate duration is necessary to support adjustment to the general, inter-actional and work environment in the host country. In consequence, protracted training periods might not only become less efficient, but also less effective with a detrimental effect on adjustment. A higher degree of sensitivity related to cultural adjustment resulting from intensive training participation might lead to a different perception of adjustment, which is likely to bias the self-reported perception of adjustment as compared to individuals who received little or no training.

Hypothesis 3 suggests a positive correlation between training intensity and adjustment, and the results support this hypothesis for POAT, but not for PRDT. This finding is in line with previous research indicating that intensive training programmes result in better adjustment and job satisfaction among expatriates (Eschbach et al., 2001). A possible explanation for the finding of a significant relation between POAT and adjustment is that this timing option contains measures that occur simultaneously with the practical applicability of the acquired skills. This may result in a more efficient adjustment to the host country environment. Moreover, the 'on-site' support is very likely to be provided by colleagues and experienced expatriates in the host country. This indicates a likelihood of better adjustment if the training intensity is sufficient. In contrast, a PRDT might not provide assignees with a satisfactory level of practical orientation since it is less likely to focus on their precise needs.

From the discussion above, it follows that MNCs investing in the training of their employees should focus on an appropriate intensity of POAT programmes as well as the content of these programmes. Therefore, a sequential type of training that considers the 'psychological receptivity' of expatriates and the variation of training duration and intensity seems advisable (Selmer et al., 1998). Such training would start with PRDT elements for the preparation of expatriates in advance of the move, and continue the learning process abroad, so that the development of new skills and behaviour in each training period is increased progressively.

In addition to the findings for the three hypotheses of this chapter, language and communication skills are identified as a significant factor in expatriate adjustment. These findings are in line with existing literature which shows that language proficiency enhances interaction adjustment (Nicholson and Imaizumi, 1993). In addition, Caligiuri et al. (2001) have suggested that language fluency leads to more realistic expectations regarding the host country environment – which are argued to support adjustment. Furthermore, practising the foreign language improves the expatriates' ability to communicate and interact with individuals from the host country. A lack of language training and acquired skills in turn would lead to 'ex-communication' where individuals are excluded from communications due to their inability to interact (Fantini, 1995). As the language skills are likely to become essential upon arrival in the host country (Zander, 2005), it might be worth while considering the language issue far more in PRDT than at present. In addition, it is suggested that language programmes have to be more rigorous when the assignment period is longer and when the interaction with host-country nationals is likely to be more intensive.

Conclusion

This chapter has analysed the role of timing, duration and intensity of expatriate training for expatriate adjustment. The study was designed to examine whether PRDT or POAT would result in better adjustment of expatriates. In addition, duration and intensity of training programmes were tested as factors that might affect the process of adaptation abroad. The findings did not fully support the hypotheses advanced, and the benefits of expatriate training programmes seem to remain inconclusive. Overall, the study suggests minor advantages of POAT programmes. This outcome is consistent with previous research (Black et al., 1999; Mendenhall, 1999).

The chapter has several limitations which need to be considered when interpreting the findings. The sample consists of a variety of home and host countries. However, the majority of the expatriates from the sample originated from Asia with China as the dominant home country. Future research should ensure that the results of this study would be applicable to managers from different countries. As for most work published on expatriate adjustment, this study is based on self-reported, cross-sectional data. A further limitation is related to the number of expatriates attending PRDT, which is smaller than those with POAT. This might mean that the possibility of detecting significant relations is lower (Hair et al., 1995). A similar constraint is applicable between the samples of expatriates with no training at all and the group that has received both PRDT and POAT. Furthermore, a more sophisticated statistical approach might provide additional insight.

Despite these limitations, this study provides an indication of the effectiveness of training programmes for expatriates and offers a systematic approach to time-related variables. POAT is considered the most effective tool in helping staff to adjust to the work environment abroad. Further research should shed more light on time-related antecedents of adjustment. Scholars should focus their research on different lengths and rigour of training measures in order to find the most efficient levels of duration and intensity for PRDT and POAT. As work adjustment is most strongly associated with time-related measures of expatriate training programmes in this study, further research might take a closer look at the different modes of work adjustment (Zimmermann et al., 2003) in order to provide additional insights.

References

Altonji, J.G. and Spletzer, J.R. (1991) 'Worker characteristics, job characteristics, and the receipt of on-the-job training', *Industrial and Labour Relations Review*, 45(1), 58–79.

Baumgarten, K.E.E. (1995) 'Training and development of international staff', in A.W.K. Harzing and J. van Ruysseveldt (eds) *International Human Resource Management*, 205–28 (London: Sage Publications,).

Bhaskar-Shrivinas, P., Harrison, D.A., Shaffer, M.A. and Luk, D.M. (2005) 'Input-based and time-based models of international adjustment: meta-analytic evidence and theoretical extensions', *Academy of Management Journal*, 48(2), 257–81.

Bird, A., Osland, J.S., Mendenhall, M. and Schneider, S.C. (1999) 'Adapting and adjusting to other cultures: what we know but not always tell', *Journal of Management Inquiry*, 8(2), 152–65.

Black, S.J., Gregersen, H. and Mendenhall, M (1992) *Global Assignments: Successfully Expatriating and Repatriating International Managers* (San Francisco: Jossey-Bass).

Black, J.S., Gregersen, H., Mendenhall, M. and Stroh, L.K. (1999) *Globalizing People through International Assignments* (New York: Addison-Wesley Longman).

Black, J.S. and Mendenhall, M. (1989) 'Selecting cross-cultural training methods: a practical yet theory based approach', *Human Resource Management*, 28(4), 511–40.

Black, J.S. and Mendenhall, M. (1990) 'Cross-cultural training effectiveness: a review and a theoretical framework for future research', *Academy of Management Review*, 15(1), 113–36.

Black, J.S., Mendenhall, M. and Oddou, G. (1991) 'Toward a comprehensive method of international adjustment: an integration of multiple theoretical perspectives', *Academy of Management Review*, 16(2), 291–317.

Brewster, C. and Pickard, J. (1994) 'Evaluating expatriate training', *International Studies of Management and Organization*, 24(3), 18–35.

Briggs, N.E. and Harwood, G.R. (1982) 'Training personnel in multinational business: an inoculation approach', *International Journal of Intercultural Relations*, 6(4), 341–54.

Brislin, R.W. (1970) 'Back-translation for cross-cultural research', *Journal of Cross-Cultural Psychology*, 1(3), 185–216.

Buckley, P.J. (2010) 'The role of headquarters in the global factor', in U. Andersson and U. Holm (eds) *Managing the Contemporary Multinational – the Role of Headquarters*, 60–84 (Cheltenham, UK: Edward Elgar).

Caligiuri, P., Phillips, J., Lazarova, M., Tarique, I. and Burgi, P. (2001) 'The theory of met expectations applied to expatriate adjustment: the role of cross-cultural training', *International Journal of Human Resource Management*, 12(3), 357–72.

Celaya, L. and Swift, J.S (2006) 'Pre-departure cultural training: US managers in Mexico', *Cross-Cultural Management: An International Journal*, 13(3), 230–43.

Cha, E-S., Kevin, H.K. and Erlen, J.A. (2007) 'Translation of scales in cross-cultural research: issues and techniques', *Journal of Advanced Nursing*, 58(4), 386–95.

Cole, N. (2008) 'How long should a training program be? A field study of "rules-of-thumb"', *Journal of Workplace Learning*, 20(1), 54–70.

Deshpande, S.P. and Viswesvaran, C. (1992) 'Is cross-cultural training of expatriate managers effective? A meta-analysis', *International Journal of Intercultural Relations*, 16, 295–310.

Eschbach, D., Parlker, G. and Stoeberl, P. (2001) 'American repatraite employees' retrospective assessments of the effects of cross-cultural training on their adaptation to international assignments', *International Journal of Human Resource Management*, 12(2), 270–87.

Fantini, A.E. (1995) 'Introduction—language, culture and world view: exploring the nexus', *International Journal of Intercultural Relations*, 19(2), 143–53.

Florkowski, G.W. and Fogel, D.S. (1999) 'Expatriate adjustment and commitment: the role of host-unit treatment', *International Journal of Human Resource Management*, 10(5), 783–807.

George, J.M. and Jones, G.R. (2000) 'The role of time in theory and theory building', *Journal of Management*, 26(4), 657–84.

Gertsen, M.C. (1990) 'Intercultural competence and expatriates', *International Journal of Human Resources*, 1(3), 341–62.

Gregersen, H. and Black, S. (1992) 'Antecedents of commitment to the parent company and commitment to the local operation for American personnel on international assignment', *Academy of Management Journal*, 35(1), 1–26.

Grove, C.L. and Torbiorn, I. (1985) 'A new conceptualization of intercultural adjustment and the goals of training', *International Journal of Intercultural Relations*, 9(2), 205–33.

Gudykunst, W.B., Guzley, R.M. and Hammer, M.R. (1996) 'Designing intercultural training', in D. Landis and R.S. Bhagat (eds) *Handbook of Intercultural Training*, 61–80 (Thousand Oaks, CA: Sage).

Hair, J.F.Jr, Anderson, R.E., Tatham, R.L. and Black, W.C. (1995) *Multivariate Data Analysis with Readings*, 4th edn (Upper Saddle River, NJ: Prentice-Hall).

Harris, H. and Brewster, C. (1999) 'An integrative framework for pre-departure preparation', in C. Brewster and H. Harris (eds) *International HRM: Contemporary Issues in Europe*, 223–40 (London: Routledge).

Hechanova, R., Beehr, T. and Christiansen, T. (2003) 'Antecedents and consequences of employees' adjustment to overseas assignment: a meta-analytic review', *Applied Psychology: An International Review*, 52(2), 213–36.

Holladay, C.L. and Quinones, M.A. (2003) 'Practice variability and transfer of training: the role of self-efficacy generality', *Journal of Applied Psychology*, 88(6), 1094–103.

Ivancic, K. and Hesketh, B. (1995) 'Making the best of errors during training', *Training Research Journal*, 1, 103–25.

Kanaya, T., Light, D. and Culp, K.M. (2005) 'Factors influencing outcomes from a technology-focused professional development program', *Journal of Research on Technology in Education*, 37(3), 313–29.

Katz, J. and Seifer, D. (1996) 'It's a different world out there: planning for expatriate success through selection, pre-departure training and on-site socialization', *Human Resource Planning*, 19(2), 32–47.

Kealey, D.J. and Protheroe, D.R. (1996) 'The effectiveness of cross-cultural training for expatriates: an assessment of the literature on the issue', *International Journal of Intercultural Relations*, 20(2), 141–65.

Kittler, M.G. (2003) 'Besondere herausforderung der schnellen internationalisierung für die personalbedarfsplanung und -deckung von kleinen und mittleren unternehmen', in D. Holtbrügge (ed.) *Die Internationalisierung von kleinen und mittleren Unternehmungen*. 171–93 (Stuttgart: Ibidem).

Lee, S. and Klein, H.J. (2002) 'Relationships between conscientiousness, self-efficacy, self-deception, and learning over time', *Journal of Applied Psychology*, 87(6), 1175–82.

Longnecker, C.O. and Fink, L.S. (2006) 'Closing the management skills gap: a call for action', *Development and Learning in Organizations*, 20(1), 16–9.

Mendenhall, M. (1999) 'On the need for paradigmatic integration in international human resource management', *Management International Review*, 39(3), 65–87.

Mendenhall, M. and Stahl, G. (2000) 'Expatriate training and development: where do we go from here?', *Human Resource Management*, 39(2/3), 251–65.

Mendenhall, M.E., Stahl, G.K., Ehnert, I., Oddou, G., Osland, S. and Kuhlmann, T.M. (2004) 'Evaluation studies of cross-cultural training programs. A review of the literature from 1988 to 2000', in D. Landis, M. Bennett and M.J. Bennett (eds) *Handbook of Intercultural Training*, 129–43 (Thousand Oaks, CA: Sage).

Morris, M.A. and Robie, C. (2001) 'A meta analysis of the effects of cross-cultural training on expatriate performance and adjustment', *International Journal of Training and Development*, 5(2), 112–25.

Nicholson, N. and Imaizumi, A. (1993) 'The adjustment of Japanese expatriates living and working in Britain', *British Journal of Management*, 4(2), 119–34.

Oddou, G.R. (1991) 'Managing your expatriates: what the successful firms do?', *Human Resource Planning*, 14(4), 301–8.

Osman-Gani, A.M. (2000) 'Developing expatriates for the Asia-Pacific region: a comparative analysis of multinational enterprise managers from five countries across three continents', *Human Resource Development Quarterly*, 11(3), 216–36.

Osman-Gani, A.M. and Toh, T.S. (1995) 'Developing managers for overseas assignments in the Pacific Rim: a study of international HRD issues in Singapore', in E.F. Holton (ed.) *Proceedings of the Annual Conference of the Academy of Human Resource Development* (Baton Rouge: Academy of Human Resource Development).

Puck, J.F., Kittler, M.G. and Wright, C. (2008) 'Does it really work? Re-assessing the impact of pre-departure cross-cultural training on expatriate adjustment', *The International Journal of Human Resource Management*, 19(2), 2182–97.

Selmer, J. (2001) 'The preference for pre-departure or post-arrival cross-cultural training', *Journal of Managerial Psychology*, 16(1), 50–8.

Selmer, J. (2002) 'Practice makes perfect? International experience and expatriate adjustment', *Management International Review*, 42(1), 71–87.

Selmer, J., Torbiorn, I. and Leon, C. (1998) 'Sequential cross-cultural training for expatriate business managers: pre-departure and post-arrival', *The International Journal of Human Resource Management*, 9(5), 831–40.

Shaffer, M.A., Harrison, D.A. and Gilley, K.M. (1999) 'Dimension, determinants, and differences in the expatriate adjustment process', *Journal of International Business Studies*, 30(3), 557–81.

Shapiro, L.T. (1995) *Training Effectiveness Handbook: A High-Results System for Design, Delivery and Evaluation* (New York: McGraw-Hill).

Sitkin, S.B. (1992) 'Learning through failure: the strategy of small doses', in B.M. Staw and L.L. Cummings (eds) *Research in Organizational Behaviour*, 484–91 (Greenwich, CT: JAI Press).

Takeuchi, R., Yun, S. and Russel, J.E. (2002) 'Antecedents and consequences of the perceived adjustment of Japanese expatriates in USA', *International Journal of Human Resource Management*, 13(8), 1224–44.

Taylor, P.J., Russ-Eft, D.F. and Chan, D.W.L. (2005) 'A meta-analytic review of behaviour modelling training', *Journal of Applied Psychology*, 90(4), 692–709.

Thacker, J.W. and Blanchard, P.N. (2006) *Effective Training* (Toronto: Pearson Prentice-Hall).

Torbiorn, I. (1994) 'Operative and strategic use of expatriates in new organizations and market structures', *International Studies of Management and Organization*, 24(3), 5–17.

Tsang, M.C. (1999) 'The cost of vocational training', *International Journal of Manpower*, 18(1/2), 63–89.

Tung, R.L. (1981) 'Selection and training of personnel for overseas assignments', *Columbia Journal of World Business*, 16(10), 68–78.

Tung, R.L. (1982) 'Selection and training procedures of US, European and Japanese multinationals', *California Management Review*, 25(1), 57–71.

Waxin, M-F. and Panaccio, A. (2005) 'Cross-cultural training to facilitate expatriate adjustment: it works!', *Personnel Review*, 34(1), 51–67.

Weber, C. and Antal, A.B. (2001) 'The role of time in organizational learning', in M. Dierkes, A.B. Antal, J. Child and I. Nonaka (eds) *Handbook of Organizational Learning and Knowledge*, 351–68 (Oxford: Oxford University Press).

Welch, D. (1994) 'Determinants of international human resource management approaches and activities: a suggested framework', *Journal of Management Studies*, 31(2), 139–64.

Zander, L. (2005) 'Communication and country clusters', *International Studies of Management and Organization*, 35(1), 83–103.

Zimmermann, A., Holman, D. and Sparrow, P. (2003) 'Unravelling adjustment mechanisms: adjustment of German expatriates to intercultural interactions, work, and living conditions in the People's Republic of China', *Intercultural Journal of Cross Cultural Management*, 3(1), 45–66.

Zimmermann, A. and Sparrow, P. (2007) 'Mutual adjustment processes in international teams: lessons for the study of expatriation', *International Studies of Management and Organization*, 37(3), 65–88.

Part V
Knowledge and Networks

15
Subsidiaries as Learning Engines: Understanding Middle Managers' Search for Knowledge as Micro-foundation

Esther Tippmann, Pamela Sharkey-Scott and Vincent Mangematin

Introduction

Knowledge refers to know-how, expertise or best practice, and – in contrast to information such as financial or operational data – knowledge equates to a skill, a routine or to external market data of strategic value (Gupta and Govindarajan 1991, 2000), and can be tacit or codified (Polanyi, 1966). Research on MNC knowledge flows has seen a great level of academic interest that has largely been driven by the recognition that knowledge is a critical factor in creating competitive success (Grant, 1996). Especially in the MNC, the knowledge-based advantage hinges on the capacity to effectively and efficiently reuse and integrate dispersed knowledge sources (Kogut and Zander, 1992; Nahapiet and Ghoshal, 1998). Considering that MNC activities are becoming increasingly fine-sliced, creating structurally highly complex organizations (Buckley, 2009; Buckley and Ghauri, 2004) to manage the even greater distribution of knowledge for re-use and learning may pose additional challenges.

Much research on MNC knowledge flows has concentrated on the organizational conditions that promote learning outcomes through the more efficient reuse of existing knowledge (Gupta and Govindarajan, 2000; Szulanski, 1996). These studies established, for example, that the motivation of the subsidiary to learn (Björkman et al., 2004; Gupta and Govindarajan, 2000), expectation of reciprocated knowledge transfers (Monteiro et al., 2008; Schulz, 2003), frequency of inter-unit communication (Monteiro et al., 2008), integration mechanisms (Gupta and Govindarajan, 2000; Szulanski, 1996; Tsai, 2002), the absorptive capacity of the subsidiary (Szulanski,1996) as well as subsidiary age (Monteiro et al., 2008) and subsidiary size (Gupta and Govindarajan, 2000; Tsai, 2002) affect the level and direction of knowledge flows. Although these studies provide valuable insights into the macro-level knowledge flow patterns in MNCs, their antecedents and consequences, this stream of research could not explore in detail the black box of knowledge flows. The knowledge flows were primarily studied at an aggregate, subsidiary level, leaving the question of how individuals at a micro-level engage in these processes less explored.

Our study departs from this predominant research stream by investigating the actual aspects of individuals' knowledge search. The term *knowledge search* incorporates all activities of 'looking for and identifying' knowledge (Hansen 1999, p. 83), and is driven by an actual demand for knowledge (Gray and Meister, 2004). It is a distinct phase preceding knowledge transfer (Hansen et al., 2005). Working within a context of increasingly fine-sliced activities, examining individual actors' actual search for distributed knowledge may provide valuable insights into if and how they mobilize the varied, increasingly specialized and distributed knowledge pockets of the MNC.

Invigorating interest in individual-level knowledge search, this study focuses on subsidiary middle managers because of their pivotal role in driving knowledge processes. Being centrally embedded in the organization's common knowledge exchanges allows middle managers to search for and integrate dynamically knowledge from front-line employees, management peers and top management (Nonaka, 1994). While they maintain a strategic view of the organization, middle managers also lead processes of competence modification that are critical for organizations to overcome inertial forces (Floyd and Lane, 2000; Floyd and Wooldridge, 1999). Overall, it is increasingly acknowledged that middle managers play a strategic role in organizations (Balogun and Johnson, 2004; Wooldridge et al., 2008).

Drawing on several calls for more understanding of the micro-foundations of organizational learning processes, especially how individual actions lead to organization-level learning (Felin and Foss, 2005, 2009; Felin and Hesterly, 2007; Friedman, 2001), we contribute by investigating how subsidiary middle managers search for knowledge to deal with non-routine problems (Nelson and Winter, 1982) that occurred within their focal unit and by evaluating the outcomes of their actions. The findings reveal subsidiary middle managers' active role in initiating knowledge inflows. We argue that dismissing the role played by the individuals' actual knowledge search overlooks the micro-foundations of MNC knowledge inflows: how are knowledge inflows initiated and how do they unfold? Finding that subsidiary middle managers' knowledge search leads to the adaptation and development of routines, we argue that micro-level knowledge search actions are an antecedent to achieving organizational learning outcomes – an important mechanism in understanding how subsidiaries contribute to MNC knowledge development (Birkinshaw et al., 1998; Rugman and Verbeke, 2001).

Theoretical background

Middle managers occupy a central position in organizations because of their immediate access to top management and front-line operations. They also regularly interact laterally with management peers. Studying middle managers' knowledge inflows, it has been found that they often use these lateral and vertical links to gather knowledge (Mom et al., 2007). Although middle managers benefit from this advantageous access to knowledge, our study had to take into consideration the particular context of MNC operations.

As the MNC constitutes an internally differentiated network of knowledge (Ghoshal and Bartlett, 1990), subsidiary middle managers work under the condition of high knowledge dispersion where knowledge is distributed among many different locations, units and functions. The structure and inter-dependencies of international operations determine where similar or related knowledge is located. In this context, the subsidiary may only possess a limited pool of knowledge colocated at the same site. The size and scope of subsidiary mandates are indicative of the knowledge stock that is located at the focal subsidiary (Gupta and Govindarajan, 2000; van Wijk et al., 2008). To mobilize relevant knowledge that could be located outside the focal operations, subsidiary middle managers' knowledge search may have to span distance.

Previous empirical studies on knowledge inflows to subsidiaries found that geographic distance between sites hinders the exchange of knowledge (Hansen and Løvås, 2004; Monteiro et al., 2008). If knowledge is colocated, the physical closeness permits more frequent, spontaneous and richer interpersonal communication that serves as a channel for knowledge search. To understand exactly how knowledge is searched, the study of spatial distance reaches its explanatory limits when investigating the cognitive processes of accessing knowledge. In particular, the transfer of tacit knowledge can only be partially explained by geographic proximity since even in physically close settings tacit knowledge is sticky and, as such, knowledge transfer is difficult (Szulanski, 1996). Thus, it is suggested that proximity is multi-dimensional (Boschma, 2005; Torre and Rallet, 2005).

Another dimension of proximity is cognitive closeness, which means that both actors possess a close stock of knowledge or overlap in their knowledge. Indeed, humans tend to search cognitively close in that they largely follow the path of previous knowledge accumulation (Cyert and March, 1963; Gavetti and Levinthal, 2000). Cognitive proximity facilitates the absorption of new knowledge (Cohen and Levinthal, 1990) because it enhances the communication between actors that knowledge is more easily understood, interpreted and processed. While cognitively distant search means entering the territory of dissimilar knowledge and dealing with search challenges, it can reward the middle managers with locating different and novel knowledge. This is an important aspect for generating new learning (Boschma, 2005; Noteboom, 2000).

When searching for a solution to deal with unusual managerial challenges, it has been observed that managers prefer replicating existing solutions that have demonstrated their viability previously (Menon and Pfeffer, 2003; Spender, 1989). Middle managers tend to implement satisfying solutions that remedy the problem rather than creating new solutions. Yet, the novelty of many challenges may mean that a solution is not readily available, necessitating that the middle managers use the search for knowledge to generate new learning.

When dealing with problems, the managers' task is to engage in an effective search for a solution (Nickerson and Zenger, 2004). As the search for knowledge requires resources, its effectiveness should be assessed in relation to its envisaged outcomes (Haas and Hansen, 2005, 2007). It is found, for example, that individuals whose job requires high intellectual demands, including a lot of variation and non-routine tasks, benefit most from sourcing additional knowledge (Gray and Meister, 2004). Also, knowledge search should be aligned to the degree of novelty and innovativeness of the potential solution (Gray and Meister, 2006).

In summary, the literature demonstrates the value of adopting a micro-perspective to understand organizational knowledge processes, especially to focus on middle managers. But to date there have been few empirical studies that investigate how subsidiary middle managers contribute towards knowledge inflows and MNC learning. To address these issues, our research questions are: How do middle managers search for knowledge; and what are the learning outcomes of their search?

Methods

Research design and setting

Being interested in gaining an in-depth understanding of the issues, a case study was considered to be the most appropriate research design. We use multiple-case studies to obtain more robust findings; compared to a single case study research design, the emerging theory is more accurate and theoretically transferable (Eisenhardt, 1989; Yin, 2003). The research setting is subsidiaries of three MNCs in the ICT industry. We focus on a single industry in order to reduce extraneous variation. The ICT industry was chosen because it offered two advantages. First, it is a dynamic industry (Brown and Eisenhardt, 1997), where environmental change poses non-routine problems that middle managers have to deal with. Second, it is a knowledge-intensive industry, making it particularly interesting for the study of knowledge processes.

We selected three subsidiaries by the principle of theoretical variation for in-depth analysis. All subsidiaries were wholly owned by their parent organizations. Although our sample MNCs were more successful than their direct competitors, they nonetheless exhibited considerable variation in their organizational variables, adding variance to the sample. At the corporate level, the companies differed in their number of subsidiaries, as an indicator of the fragmentation of organizational knowledge in general. The chosen subsidiaries varied in size, indicating different levels of knowledge stock at the focal unit (Gupta and Govindarajan, 2000; van Wijk et al., 2008), and number and kind of mandates – a sign of the concentration and scope of knowledge at the focal unit (Gupta and Govindarajan, 1991; Hansen and Løvås, 2004; van Wijk et al., 2008). In addition, the structure of international operations ranged from pan-regional to global responsibilities, with some selected units being regional or even global headquarters with higher autonomy while other units were part of a tightly coupled internal network of operations with less autonomy (Gupta and Govindarajan, 2000; Hansen and Løvås, 2004).

After securing access to the case organizations, we were able to characterize middle management. We adopted a broad definition of middle managers, including various mid-level professionals who all had access to top management

(Wooldridge et al., 2008). While most middle managers were in line management roles, with people and performance management as their main tasks, importantly their positions usually required them to drive improvements.

The three cases under review are Gamma, Epsilon and Sigma. These are pseudonyms. The specific details of the MNCs and subsidiaries are disguised to preserve anonymity, as are the names and details of respondents, organizational units, specific products and services, and geographical origins and locations. Our first case organization, Gamma, nourished a particularly strong innovation culture with continuous technological improvement at the heart of its vision, with costs a secondary consideration. The Gamma subsidiary that was part of this study hosted various business functions, and we were granted extensive access to a sales unit. The global sales activities were organized by region, and Gamma replicated its business processes globally, which were largely automated through software applications.

Epsilon, our second case organization, was highly committed to technology leadership. The mandate of the Epsilon subsidiary comprised mainly R&D activities, and we collected data from a development unit that had global responsibilities for a certain product, endowing this unit with considerable autonomy.

The third case, Sigma, pursued a strategy that centered on innovation-driven growth. The subsidiary that we examined hosted a range of different mandates, and we included the largest units: services and support, and sales, in this study. Sigma's middle managers often operated in tightly, globally integrated operations. Access to the firms was negotiated with the subsidiary senior management. We promised confidentiality to encourage openness of informants and to facilitate extensive access (Huber and Power, 1985; Miller et al., 1997) to archival and other data.

Data collection and analysis

We used multiple data collection techniques – study of secondary sources, interviews with middle managers, interviews with senior-level informants, and study of archive materials – to allow for internal triangulation in order to counteract the possibility of investigator, source and respondent bias (Jick, 1979). The complete data set comprised over 2,400 pages of information. We conducted 26 semi-structured interviews with subsidiary middle managers, ranging from 45 to 75 minutes duration. These yielded 33 cases of knowledge search processes, which constitute our unit of analysis for the micro-level data. The interviews gathered material on the detailed aspects relating to knowledge search activities for *specific* non-routine problems (Nelson and Winter, 1982) – situations of high and often uncertain knowledge needs. We enquired about a specific situation to reduce retrospective bias (Golden, 1992; Huber and Power, 1985; Miller et al., 1997). All interviews were recorded and transcribed verbatim. In the five interviews with senior-level managers, we explored subsidiary strategy and outcomes of the knowledge search processes in more detail. The archival data that we had access to was particularly important to triangulate the assessment of the outcomes of middle managers' knowledge search.

The analysis was conducted using NVivo (Sinkovics et al., 2008; Weitzman, 2000), and involved three main steps: micro-level knowledge search, search outcomes, and cross-subsidiary comparison. First, to analyse the micro-level knowledge search, we used the middle managers' description of the search process as the unit of analysis. For the purpose of this chapter, the analysis proceeded more deductively, coding middle managers' knowledge search under three broad themes: knowledge search intensity, proximity, and nature of knowledge searched. Second, we examined the outcomes of the middle managers' knowledge search. Our data suggested that the outcomes often impacted on the operational practices of the middle managers' unit. Thus, we based this assessment on two interrelated evaluations: (1) the extent to which learning outcomes became part of the organizational memory rather than remaining individual, and (2) if the learning outcomes represented an adaptation or development of routines – the evolutionary theory's notion of capability change (Zollo and Winter, 2002). Finally, the cross-organization analysis was assisted by compiling tabular information across cases (Miles and Huberman, 1994; Yin, 2003). This analysis related the salience of the search aspects to the organizational learning outcomes, in order to understand in more detail why middle managers in certain case subsidiaries were more or less successful in achieving organizational adaptation. Overall, multiple measures were employed to strengthen the trustworthiness of the qualitative data and analysis (Lincoln and Guba, 1985). These included multiple iterations of data analysis, triangulation, protecting the confidentiality of responses, and confirming the validity of the independent case analyses with respondents, including feedback in the subsequent cross-organization analysis.

Findings

This section summarizes the findings of the middle managers' micro-level knowledge search and outcomes of these efforts. For illustrative purposes, we present the assessment of the outcomes first, before outlining the micro-level knowledge search as well as the examination of how middle managers' actions related to the observed outcomes.

Subsidiary level learning outcomes: success in achieving organizational adaptation

In this section we report our assessment of the ability of the middle managers to generate organizational adaptation with the help of their problem-driven knowledge search processes. We found that in many cases the outcomes contributed at the meso-level of the organizational knowledge structure – the level of routines. Here, organizational learning occurred if novel insights became part of the organization's normal work practices. A typical result was that the middle managers' efforts accumulated in an existing routine to become adapted to the novel context of the particular challenge. One middle manager, for example, expressed: 'We looked at the old model that was there. We looked at where it needs to be improved' (Epsilon, middle manager 8). In these cases of routine adaptation, the existing practice served as a 'basic structure' (Gamma, middle manager 3) that the middle manager could 'tweak to what we needed' (Sigma, middle manager 10). In other cases, the middle managers developed a new working practice. Then, knowledge search aided in locating diverse knowledge pieces that were flexibly integrated into a new knowledge structure that became part of the unit's normal operations. A Gamma middle manager explained: 'And we have started to create specialist roles and new role career paths within Gamma to do this type of work' (Gamma, middle manager 8).

To evaluate the success of achieving organizational adaptation, we compared across the three case subsidiaries how often the results of the subsidiary middle managers' knowledge search represented an adaptation or development of routines. Importantly, this assessment showed heterogeneity. In Gamma, which was the most successful, many non-routine problems stipulated knowledge search processes that resulted in organizational adaptation. In the other two case organizations, middle managers were less successful in generating organizational adaptation as only about half of the knowledge search engagements led to the adaptation or development of routines.

Micro-foundation: middle managers' knowledge search

This section describes and explains how the subsidiary middle managers, at a micro-level, searched for distributed knowledge to help solve the initial non-routine problem. The middle managers engaged in a search process that can be described by (1) the nature of the knowledge sought, (2) the distance of the sources searched, and (3) the intensity of the search efforts.

Nature of knowledge sought

Initially, many middle managers searched for a best practice – an existing solution that they could leverage in their unit to solve the non-routine challenge: 'And I said: look, we have got this problem, have you heard of any good tools at Sigma?' (Sigma, middle manager 10). Such a best practice comprised a solution that had demonstrated its effectiveness in a different context, and the middle manager expected that the core could be meaningfully replicated. In many cases, however, it was insufficient to simply implement an existing solution because no suitable best practice could be located or adaptations needed to be undertaken. Then, the middle managers usually searched for tacit knowledge to gain further insights for crafting a solution. This tacit knowledge included peers' advice and experience: 'clarify things with him because he has been in the role much longer' (Epsilon, middle manager 5). It also incorporated the competence and skill of particular expert units: 'Different profiles, different skill sets. If you look at it, we tend to be more process and project management, trouble shooting orientated, and customer service; whereas the other unit has more a sales profile... They have really helped us' (Gamma, middle manager 6). Only in rare cases did the middle managers search for codified and external knowledge.

Distance of sources searched

The middle managers usually started their search for knowledge within their focal unit, where geographic proximity facilitated inter-personal interaction with the team or management peers. This search was not only geographically proximate; it was also characterized by cognitive closeness because the middle managers targeted knowledge sources similar to their own expertise. They then approached sister units, usually global management peers, for additional insights: 'The understanding of the situation was that I had to reach out to my peers in the US' (Sigma, middle manager 8). This search spanned geographic distance, yet remained close in terms of cognitive proximity. In other instances, the middle manager assessed that solving the non-routine problem would benefit from mobilizing dissimilar knowledge of related, but different units. This search spanned cognitive distance. In some cases, such dissimilar knowledge was co-located, allowing the middle manager to target cognitively distant knowledge in geographic proximity. We found, however, that subsidiary middle managers, in their search for specialist expertise, also approached geographically distant locations: 'We heavily used a mergers and acquisitions team based out of Canada' (Sigma, middle manager 6). In these cases, the subsidiary middle managers actively tackled search challenges on two dimensions because geographic dispersion and cognitive dissimilarity had to be dealt with simultaneously.

Intensity of the search efforts

The number of knowledge sources targeted varied between the different cases. If the middle managers were able to locate a working solution that was suitable for immediate replication early in the process, the intensity was lower. Overall, it was found that some subsidiary middle managers were very active and self-motivated, engaging in an intensive search. Other middle managers, however, were more hesitant in their search, approaching only a few, mainly known contacts. An overview of the findings, comparing the salience of the different search aspects across the three subsidiaries, is provided in Table 15.1.

Table 15.1 Salience of middle managers' knowledge search aspects and level of organizational adaptation

	Gamma	Sigma	Epsilon
Achieving organizational adaptation	More successful	Less successful	Less successful
Middle managers' knowledge search			
Intensity	High	Moderate	Low
Proximity of search			
Geographic proximate & cognitive proximate	High	Moderate	High
Geographic proximate & cognitive distant	High	High	Low
Geographic distant & cognitive proximate	High	Low	Low
Geographic distant & cognitive distant	Moderate	Moderate	Low
Nature of knowledge searched			
Tacit knowledge	Very high	High	High
Routine	Moderate	Low	Moderate
Codified knowledge	Low	Low	Low

Discussion

The objective of this study was to understand how subsidiary middle managers search for knowledge and the level of organizational adaptation generated. Using a micro-perspective to analyse the data, we have been able to unravel the detailed aspects of the knowledge search, delineating clearly how different micro-level activities in their combination and interaction constitute the knowledge search process. By doing so, we examine the black box of knowledge inflows, an area that is usually studied at an aggregate, subsidiary level. We also respond to recent assessments of the organizational knowledge literature (Felin and Foss, 2005, 2009; Friedman, 2001) in which micro-perspectives, such as the actions of individuals and how these actions contribute towards organizational-level learning, were highlighted as an important theoretical gap.

In the discussion below, we outline the implications of the cross-case comparative findings for developing a broader theory of middle managers' knowledge search, paying particular attention to subsidiary-level learning outcomes. Thereby, we link explicitly the observed heterogeneity in achieving subsidiary-level adaptations to the middle managers' search for knowledge.

Lifting the black box of knowledge inflows

MNCs exist because of their superior ability compared to markets to transfer knowledge internally (Buckley and Casson, 1976; Kogut and Zander, 1993). Thus, a substantial amount of research has examined how MNCs leverage knowledge. The focus of much previous research was on examining the level, antecedents and consequences of knowledge flows in and out of subsidiaries from a top management perspective (van Wijk et al., 2008), leaving under-explored the social elements of how these inflows are stipulated and unfold within subsidiaries.

Examining how middle managers search for knowledge to deal with unusual situations that occurred within their subsidiary unit, we observed that middle management plays an important role in initiating these knowledge inflows. We have found, for example, that subsidiary middle managers searched the distributed units of the corporation in a self-motivated manner. A typical feature of their search efforts was the aim to locate best practices, a superior or working solution, for reuse in their focal unit. Importantly, the subsidiary middle managers proactively initiated these knowledge inflows themselves, drawing attention to human agency in MNC learning (Saka-Helmhout, 2009). Thus, to further advance our understanding of knowledge inflows into subsidiaries means to more fully embrace the contribution subsidiary middle managers make in leveraging knowledge, for example, to improve the performance of their focal operations, which is the case in this study. This finding also suggests the need to re-examine who actually drives knowledge inflows into subsidiaries. While previous literature, often implicitly, assumed that HQ or subsidiary top management directs knowledge inflows, our data imply that subsidiary middle managers also drive these processes. Being intimately familiar with everyday operations, middle managers are in a better position than their more removed top management counterparts, to assess what kind of business process can solve business challenges. Middle managers then lead the search for knowledge which may occur outside of subsidiary top management's or HQ's direct visibility or control.

Middle managers' knowledge search as micro-foundation of subsidiary learning

The design of our study allowed a more detailed understanding of the outcomes of the subsidiary middle managers' knowledge search. Similar to previous studies (Menon and Pfeffer, 2003; Spender, 1989), our data suggests that middle managers initially try to locate an existing best practice that they can readily implement. Yet the complexity of most challenges often required the middle managers to mobilize multiple and diverse knowledge sources that they used to adapt or develop routines. This finding suggests that middle managers' search for knowledge in response to non-routine problem is a micro-foundation of organizational learning.

Similar to theoretical arguments by Felin and Foss (2009) that intentionality in response to rare events is a fruitful avenue for unravelling how routines actually emerge, our data imply that the subsidiary middle managers' deliberate actions in their search for knowledge represented an individual, micro-level antecedent to learning. The middle managers' active response in embracing the enhancement or development of new business processes and their choice to search for additional knowledge are indicative of how their actions can drive subsidiary learning.

To further understand what kind of knowledge search actions lead to organizational adaptation, we compared the salience of the different aspects of subsidiary middle managers' knowledge search across the three case organizations. The data suggest that middle managers who search more intensively and cross the boundaries of geographic and cognitive distance are more often able to adapt or create new routines. In these cases, the middle managers dynamically integrated varied knowledge components – an action that has been demonstrated to improve solution results (Okhuysen and Eisenhardt, 2002). The search of diverse knowledge sources has also the potential to introduce dialectical attributes to finding the solution. This is an important determinant of how effectively issues can be solved because it leads to a more critical evaluation of possible solutions (Nutt, 1984; Schweiger et al., 1989; Schwenk, 1989).

Implications for subsidiary management practice

Our finding that subsidiary middle managers' knowledge search is a driver of knowledge inflows and indeed subsidiary learning, has important implications for subsidiary management practice. Top management need to be aware that their prime task is to determine the direction of and provide an internal environment for capability development. Yet, the real actions of capability development unfold at lower levels where individuals like subsidiary middle managers actively engage in solution-finding processes that result in the modification of business processes. It is also important to realize that much of this activity occurs outside of top management's direct influence and control, but largely through lateral and team interactions. For top management, this means that subsidiary middle managers need to be made aware of the intended path of capability evolution to enable them to attune their solution-finding efforts accordingly.

The findings of this study also have implications for subsidiary middle managers. They need to realize that their knowledge search not only tackles an immediate challenge, but has much broader, indeed strategic, implications for the capacity of the MNC to leverage and develop its knowledge base. To this end, subsidiary middle managers need to be willing to tackle the challenges of knowledge dispersion – to search spatially distant, but more importantly dissimilar knowledge to increase the chances of locating and creating novel insights.

Limitations and future research

As is typical in case study research, questions arise to the extent to which the findings are transferrable to other contexts. We have employed certain measures to increase transferability. By replicating the study in three case organizations, more robust findings were yielded (Eisenhardt, 1989). Second, we studied a phenomenon – knowledge search by middle managers in response to non-routine problems – that, we believe, likewise occurs in other subsidiaries. However, further research could establish the generalizability to other organizational and industry contexts.

Another area that may warrant further research is examining more closely how the nature of the non-routine problem influences the middle managers' knowledge search. It may be worthwhile to differentiate between non-routine problems based on their degree of novelty: new to the organization or new to the industry (Spender, 1989). Further, our study investigated searches when knowledge needs are high – providing only limited suggestions for other situations. By adopting a micro-perspective and using the knowledge search process as a unit of analysis to uncover the actual search actions, future research could benefit by analysing explicitly individual-level factors of the middle manager, such as level of previous experience and education, as possible antecedents of particular knowledge search patterns.

Conclusion

The study reported in this chapter was an initial effort towards improving our understanding of micro-foundations of subsidiary knowledge inflows and subsidiary learning. Examining the knowledge search by subsidiary middle managers revealed their critical role in generating organizational adaptation through flexible knowledge integration. Middle managers' knowledge search that actively tackles search challenges of distant searches, and targets a variety of similar and dissimilar knowledge sources, seems more conducive for achieving organizational learning outcomes. Overall, our results emphasize individuals' search engagements, representing a novel approach to understanding the black box of subsidiary knowledge inflows and subsidiary learning.

Acknowledgements

We would like to thank DIT for the financial support of this study. We are also grateful for valuable comments from four anonymous reviewers of the AIB-UKI 2010 conference.

References

Balogun, J. and Johnson, G. (2004) 'Organizational restructuring and middle manager sensemaking', *Academy of Management Journal*, 47(4), 523–49.
Birkinshaw, J., Hood, N. and Jonsson, S. (1998), 'Building firm-specific advantages in multinational corporations: the role of subsidiary initiative', *Strategic Management Journal*, 19(3), 221–41.
Björkman, I., Barner-Rasmussen, W. and Li, L. (2004) 'Managing knowledge transfer in MNCs: the impact of headquarters control mechanisms', *Journal of International Business Studies*, 35(5), 443–55.
Boschma, R. (2005) 'Proximity and innovation: a critical assessment', *Regional Studies*, 39(1), 61–74.
Brown, S.L. and Eisenhardt, K.M. (1997) 'The art of continuous change: linking complexity theory and time-paced evolution in relentlessly shifting organizations', *Administrative Science Quarterly*, 42(1), 1–34.
Buckley, P.J. (2009) 'Internalisation thinking: from the multinational enterprise to the global factory', *International Business Review*, 18(3), 224–35.
Buckley, P.J. and Casson, M. (1976) *The Future of the Multinational Enterprise* (London: MacMillan).
Buckley, P.J. and Ghauri, P.N. (2004) 'Globalisation, economic geography and the strategy of multinational enterprises', *Journal of International Business Studies*, 35(2), 81–98.
Cohen, W.M. and Levinthal, D.A. (1990) 'Absorptive capacity: a new perspective on learning and innovation', *Administrative Science Quarterly*, 35(1), 128–52.
Cyert, R.M. and March, J.G. (1963) *Behavioral Theory of the Firm* (Englewood Cliffs, NJ: Prentice Hall Inc).
Eisenhardt, K.M. (1989) 'Building theory from case study research', *Academy of Management Review*, 14(4), 532–50.
Felin, T. and Foss, N.J. (2005) 'Strategic organization: a field in search of micro-foundations', *Strategic Organization*, 3(4), 441–55.
Felin, T. and Foss, N.J. (2009) 'Organizational routines and capabilities: historical drift and a course-correction toward microfoundations', *Scandinavian Journal of Management*, 25(2), 157–67.
Felin, T. and Hesterly, W.S. (2007) 'The knowledge-based view, nested heterogeneity, and new value creation: philosophical considerations on the locus of knowledge', *Academy of Management Review*, 32(1), 195–218.
Floyd, S.W. and Lane, P.J. (2000) 'Strategizing throughout the organization: managing role conflicts in strategic renewal', *Academy of Management Review*, 25(1), 154–77.
Floyd, S.W. and Wooldridge, B. (1999) 'Knowledge creation and social networks in corporate entrepreneurship: the renewal of organizational capability', *Entrepreneurship: Theory and Practice*, 23(3), 123–43.
Friedman, V.J. (2001) 'The individual as agent of organizational learning', in D. Meinolf, A.B. Antal, J. Child and I. Nonaka (eds) *Handbook of Organizational Learning*, 398–414 (Oxford: Oxford University Press).
Gavetti, G. and Levinthal, D. (2000) 'Looking forward and looking backward: cognitive and experiential search', *Administrative Science Quarterly*, 45(1), 113–37.
Ghoshal, S. and Bartlett, C.A. (1990) 'The multinational corporation as an interorganizational network', *Academy of Management Review*, 15(4), 625–6.

Golden, B.R. (1992) 'Research notes. The past is the present – or is it? The use of retrospective accounts as indicators of past strategy', *Academy of Management Journal*, 35(4), 848–60.
Grant, R.M. (1996) 'Toward a knowledge-based theory of the firm', *Strategic Management Journal*, 17(2), 109–22.
Gray, P.H. and Meister, D.B. (2004) 'Knowledge sourcing effectiveness', *Management Science*, 50(6), 821–34.
Gray, P.H. and Meister, D.B. (2006) 'Knowledge sourcing methods', *Information and Management*, 43(2), 142–56.
Gupta, A.K. and Govindarajan, V. (1991) 'Knowledge flows and the structure of control within multinational corporations', *Academy of Management Review*, 16(4), 768–92.
Gupta, A.K. and Govindarajan, V. (2000) 'Knowledge flows within multinational corporations', *Strategic Management Journal*, 21(4), 473–96.
Haas, M.R. and Hansen, M.T. (2005) 'When using knowledge can hurt performance: the value of organizational capabilities in a management consulting company', *Strategic Management Journal*, 26(1), 1–24.
Haas, M.R. and Hansen, M.T. (2007) 'Different knowledge, different benefits: toward a productivity perspective on knowledge sharing in organizations', *Strategic Management Journal*, 28(11), 1133–53.
Hansen, M.T. (1999) 'The search-transfer problem: the role of weak ties in sharing knowledge across organization subunits', *Administrative Science Quarterly*, 44(1), 82–111.
Hansen, M.T. and Løvås, B. (2004) 'How do multinationals leverage technological competencies? Moving from single to interdependent explanations', *Strategic Management Journal*, 25(8/9), 801–22.
Hansen, M.T., Mors, M.L. and Løvås, B. (2005) 'Knowledge sharing in organizations: multiple networks, multiple phases', *Academy of Management Journal*, 48(5), 776–93.
Huber, G.P. and Power, D.J. (1985) 'Retrospective reports of strategic-level managers: guidelines for increasing their accuracy', *Strategic Management Journal*, 6(2), 171–80.
Jick, T.D. (1979) 'Mixing qualitative and quantitative methods: triangulation in action', *Administrative Science Quarterly*, 24(4), 602–11.
Kogut, B. and Zander, U. (1992) 'Knowledge of the firm, combinative capabilities, and the replication of technology', *Organization Science*, 3(3), 383–97.
Kogut, B. and Zander, U. (1993) 'Knowledge of the firm and the evolutionary theory of the multinational corporation', *Journal of International Business Studies*, 24(4), 625–45.
Lincoln, Y.S. and Guba, E.G. (1985) *Naturalistic Inquiry* (Beverly Hills, CA: Sage).
Menon, T. and Pfeffer, J. (2003) 'Valuing internal vs. external knowledge: explaining the preference for outsiders', *Management Science*, 49(4), 497–513.
Miles, M.B. and Huberman, M.A. (1994) *Qualitative Data Analysis: An Expanded Sourcebook* (London: Sage).
Miller, C.C., Cardinal, L.B. and Glick, W.H. (1997) 'Retrospective reports in organizational research: a reexamination of recent evidence', *Academy of Management Journal*, 40(1), 189–204.
Mom, T., Van Den Bosch, F. and Volberda, H.W. (2007) 'Investigating managers' exploration and exploitation activities: the influence of top-down, bottom-up, and horizontal knowledge inflows', *Journal of Management Studies*, 44(6), 910–31.
Monteiro, F., Arvidsson, N. and Birkinshaw, J. (2008) 'Knowledge flows within multinational corporations: explaining subsidiary isolation and its performance implications', *Organization Science*, 19(1), 90–107.
Nahapiet, J. and Ghoshal, S. (1998) 'Social capital, intellectual capital, and the organizational advantage', *Academy of Management Review*, 23(2), 242–66.
Nelson, R.R. and Winter, S.G. (1982) *An Evolutionary Theory of Economic Change* (London: The Belknap Press of Harvard University Press).
Nickerson, J.A. and Zenger, T.R. (2004) 'A knowledge-based theory of the firm–the problem-solving perspective', *Organization Science*, 15(6), 617–32.

Nonaka, I. (1994) 'A dynamic theory of organizational knowledge creation', *Organization Science*, 5(1), 14–37.
Noteboom, B. (2000) 'Learning by interaction: absorptive capacity, cognitive distance and governance', *Journal of Management and Governance*, 4(1–2), 69–92.
Nutt, P.C. (1984) 'Types of organizational decision processes', *Administrative Science Quarterly*, 29(3), 414–50.
Okhuysen, G.A. and Eisenhardt, K.M. (2002) 'Integrating knowledge in groups: how formal interventions enable flexibility', *Organization Science*, 13(4), 370–86.
Polanyi, M. (1966) *The Tacit Dimension* (Garden City, New York: Doubleday and Co).
Rugman, A.M. and Verbeke, A. (2001) 'Subsidiary-specific advantages in multinational enterprises', *Strategic Management Journal*, 22(3), 237–51.
Saka-Helmhout, A. (2009) 'Agency-based view of learning within the multinational corporation', *Management Learning*, 40(3), 259–74.
Schulz, M. (2003) 'Pathways of relevance: exploring inflows of knowledge into subunits of multinational corporations', *Organization Science*, 14(4), 440–59.
Schweiger, D.M., Sandberg, W.R. and Rechner, P.L. (1989) 'Experiential effects of dialectical inquiry, devil's advocacy and consensus approaches to strategic decision making', *Academy of Management Journal*, 32(4), 745–72.
Schwenk, C. (1989) 'Research notes and communications: a meta-analysis on the comparative effectiveness of devil's advocacy and dialectical inquiry', *Strategic Management Journal*, 10(3), 303–6.
Sinkovics, R.R., Penz, E. and Ghauri, P.N. (2008) 'Enhancing the trustworthiness of qualitative research in international business', *Management International Review*, 48(6), 689–713.
Spender, J-C. (1989) *Industry Recipes: An Enquiry into the Nature and Sources of Managerial Judgment* (Oxford: Blackwell).
Szulanski, G. (1996) 'Exploring internal stickiness: impediments to the transfer of best practice within the firm', *Strategic Management Journal*, 17(2), 27–43.
Torre, A. and Rallet, A. (2005) 'Proximity and localization', *Regional Studies*, 39(1), 47–59.
Tsai, W. (2002) 'Social structure of "coopetition" within a multiunit organization: coordination, competition, and intraorganizational knowledge sharing', *Organization Science*, 13(2), 179–90.
Van Wijk, R., Jansen, J. and Lyles, M.A. (2008) 'Inter- and intra-organizational knowledge transfer: a meta-analytic review and assessment of its antecedents and consequences', *Journal of Management Studies*, 45(4), 830–53.
Weitzman, E.A. (2000) 'Software and qualitative research', in N.K. Denzin and Y.S. Lincoln (eds) *Handbook of Qualitative Research*, 803–20 (London: Sage).
Wooldridge, B., Schmid, T. and Floyd, S.W. (2008) 'The middle management perspective on strategy process: contributions, synthesis, and future research', *Journal of Management*, 34(6), 1190–221.
Yin, R.K. (2003) *Case Study Research: Design and Methods* (London: Sage).
Zollo, M. and Winter, S.G. (2002) 'Deliberate learning and the evolution of dynamic capabilities', *Organization Science*, 13(3), 339–51.

16
Converging Themes: Networks, International Performance and the Telecoms Sector

Breda Kenny and John Fahy

Introduction

The concept of the global factory sees the multinational enterprise (MNE) becoming much more like differentiated networks (Buckley and Ghauri, 2004). MNEs choose location and ownership policies so as to maximize profits, and this does not always involve internalizing their activities (Buckley, 2010). This is evident in the global telecommunications industry, where firms operating in the fast-changing telecommunications network environment need to build a large user base of new activities and businesses as quickly as possible to create or to sustain competitive advantages. Subcontracting and outsourcing have been associated with the decentralization of the organization to a new organizational form, often conceptualized as the network enterprise (Castells, 1998). The *managed services* model – which covers the end-to-end technology stack from network infrastructure right through to business applications – has developed significantly over the last 15 years in response to this trend in outsourcing, with the market in Ireland alone valued at €765 million in 2008 (Corrigan, 2008). Managed services have emerged in response to demand from businesses that increasingly recognize that outsourcing non-core business and IT activities enables them to focus on their strategic activities and on their customers, helping to keep costs low and stay ahead of the competition. Critical to this view of the global factory and regional business networks is the role played by small firms (Rugman and D'Cruz, 2000). These small firms, or high-technology SMEs (HTSMEs), are an integral part of the regional business networks, as they are suppliers, customers and, in some cases, competitors of MNEs.

By focusing on SMEs in the telecommunications sector, this study reveals a different perspective on internationalization, networking capability and indeed on the industry itself. Contrary to the overview of the industry provided by previous research (Kranenburg et al., 2008), the SME component of this sector does not seem to engage in inter-firm collaborations to the same extent as their larger counterparts. In fact, prior research in telecommunications has a tendency to focus on the large players such as mobile operators, leaving the small firm dimension under-researched. In relation to networking capability, smaller firms are more likely to be locked in and subject to inertia in networks due to their liabilities, whereas larger firms (MNEs/flagship firms) may often be better established within the network and can possibly exercise more power over smaller firms (Rugman and D'Cruz, 2000).

Research on business networks to date has focused on antecedents of network formation and relationships or relational content among firms, rather than outcomes or consequences of such relationships and networks (Kapasuwan, 2006; Werner, 2002). Several researchers have therefore suggested that there is an increasing need for business research to shift focus from traditional dyadic relationships to the larger business context of network relationships in order to understand firms' behaviour and performance (Achrol, 1997; Gulati, 1998; Rowley, 1997).

As observed in the literature, internationalizing SMEs overcome their resource constraints through network relationships. However, networking activity has not been conceptualized and measured as a competitive capability that contributes to SME internationalization (Loxton and Weerawardena, 2006). Still, detailed studies of what actually constitutes a networking capability are almost non-existent (Kale et al., 2002; Walter et al., 2006). This chapter aims to address a major gap in the literature by examining the impact of network effects on firm performance in international markets. To date most of the attention has been on the nature and structure of networks rather than on how these in turn impact on the performance of individual network members.

A capabilities model of network international performance

In this chapter a framework for the impact of networks on international performance is presented by building on the emerging literature on the dynamic capabilities view of the firm (Helfat and Peteraf, 2003; Teece et al., 1997). Dynamic capabilities are the organizational and strategic routines by which managers alter their firms' resource base through acquiring, shedding, integrating and recombining resources to generate new value-creating strategies (Eisenhardt and Martin, 2000). Dynamic capabilities include, but are not limited to, these routines. Moreover, not all processes are part of the dynamic capabilities of a firm, as some aim to enable firms to perform ongoing tasks or maintain the status quo (Loane et al., 2009). Thus, the defining characteristic underpinning dynamic capabilities is that they facilitate change (Helfat, 2007). It should also be recognized that the capacity to replenish social capital is itself a dynamic capability because it leads to the modification of the firm's resource base, of which network relationships ought to be recognized as an integral part (Døving and Gooderham, 2008; Loane and Bell, 2006).

The development of networking capabilities allows firms to facilitate change, identify opportunities and to respond quickly to them through relationships with other firms and organizations. Weerawardena et al. (2007) drew on the dynamic capabilities view of competitive strategy and the organizational learning literature to derive a novel conceptualization of accelerated internationalization in the born global firm. These authors contend that the building of dynamic capabilities involves processes that are knowledge-based and are instrumental in knowledge creation, integration and configuration. Whilst market-based learning is important, enabling the firm to learn what the market needs, the firm must also acquire knowledge from other sources to develop leading-edge innovative products and services that will fulfil these needs. This requires all sources of learning be recognized in the effort to explain the accelerated internationalization of a firm. It could well be argued that HTSMEs in the telecoms sector are in a unique position to take advantage of customer requirements, market knowledge and competitive intelligence, through the use of advanced technologies and applications. Consistent with this literature, this chapter views capabilities in terms of intricate configurations of resources and operating routines.

Extant research on firm capabilities has focused primarily on the link between capabilities and performance-related outcomes (Clark and Fujimoto, 1991; Henderson and Cockburn, 1994; Lieberman et al., 1990). However, far less attention has been paid to the sources of firm capabilities. The research that has been conducted in this area has focused on sources internal to the firm. McEvily and Zaheer (1999) maintain that there are important *external* sources of capabilities that firms draw upon to varying degrees (Galaskiewicz and Zaheer, 1999). They propose that these 'network resources' (Gulati, 1999) enable and constrain firms' abilities to acquire competitive capabilities through differential exposure to information and opportunities. This study focuses on the human capital, synergy sensitive resource and information sharing aspect of these network resources, and provides additional insight into the possible outcomes of deploying these resources. Networking capability for this study comprises network characteristics, network operation and network resources. Network characteristics include strong and weak ties (operationalized as foreign market entry mode), relational capability and trust. Network operation comprises network initiation, network coordination and network learning.

Research hypotheses

Strength of ties

The strength of ties literature is primarily concerned with the nature of the relational bond between two or more social actors (Granovetter, 1973; Uzzi, 1997). Tie strength researchers typically classify the relation between social actors as being linked by either a strong tie or a weak one (Rindfleisch and Moorman, 2001).

Rowley et al. (2000) conceptualize strong and weak ties as separate constructs, different in kind rather than degree based on Contractor and Lorange's (1988) original ordinal scale. They categorize equity alliances, joint ventures and non-equity cooperative (R&D) ventures as strong ties, while defining marketing agreements and licensing and patent agreements as weak ties, thereby capturing the strength of inter-firm relationships on the basis of the partners' typical levels of interaction in, and resource commitment to, each alliance type. As referred to earlier, networks allow firms to access foreign markets; therefore the categorization of strong and weak ties outlined above can be extended to include entry modes. Internationalization 'mode' refers to the organizational structure used to enter and penetrate a foreign market and includes indirect exporting (i.e. via domestic intermediary); direct exporting; exporting via foreign intermediary; sales and/or manufacturing joint venture; sales and/or manufacturing subsidiary; and licensing and franchising (Calof and Beamish, 1995). In terms of the firm's commitment of resources, exporting modes are lower-commitment modes, while foreign joint ventures and subsidiaries are higher-commitment modes.

In the literature, strong ties are shown to provide organizations with two primary advantages. First, strong ties are associated with the exchange of high-quality information and tacit knowledge (Uzzi, 1997). Based on a deeper understanding of a partner's operations, tacit knowledge is more readily transferred across organizational boundaries, which are blurred by close contact (Hagg and Johanson, 1983). Second, strong ties serve as part of the social control mechanism, which governs partnership behaviours. Firms enter strategic alliances with competitors to gain access to external resources, share risks and cost, or pool complementary skills (Kogut, 1988).

On the other hand, Granovetter (1973) argued that weak ties are conduits across which an actor can access novel information. A weak tie can be beneficial because it is more likely to embed an actor in (or provide access to) divergent regions of the network rather than to a densely connected set of actors (Granovetter, 1973).

The substantial support for the benefits derived from both strong and weak ties suggests that neither type is unconditionally preferred. Indeed, strong and weak ties have different qualities, which are advantageous for different purposes. In the context of international trade, it can be argued that strong ties are more beneficial than weak ties since they allow for greater volume of resources to move between actors (Podolny, 2001), have greater motivation to be of assistance and are typically more easily available (Granovetter, 1983), are more willing to take the time to carefully explain, detail or listen to novel or complex ideas (Granovetter, 1985; Uzzi, 1997; Moran, 2005). Thus:

Hypothesis 1a: There is a positive relation between strong ties and international performance.

Hypothesis 1b: There is a positive relation between weak ties and international performance.

Hypothesis 1c: The relation with international performance is stronger in strong ties than in weak ties.

Network relationships

Relational embeddedness refers to the degree of reciprocity and closeness among firms. Past research indicates that a high level of relational embeddedness in network relationships can enhance the level of access and transfer of fine-grained information and, more importantly, tacit knowledge and know-how among firms within the network (Gulati, 1998; Lorenzoni and Lipparini, 1999). Past research has operationalized relational embeddedness (Bonner et al., 2005; Rindfleisch and Moorman, 2001), relational skills (Walter et al., 2006), relational competence (Loxton and Weerewardena, 2006) and relational capital (Dyer and Singh, 1998; Gulati, 1995; Kale et al., 2002; Madhok, 1995) using similar constructs. Relational skills, also referred to as social competence (Baron and Markman, 2003), includes such aspects as communication ability, extraversion, conflict management skills, empathy, emotional stability, self reflection, sense of justice and cooperativeness (Marshall et al., 2003; Ritter and Gemünden, 2003). Social qualifications in a cross-cultural setting are of special interest; skills such as cultural awareness and foreign language competency are important for interpersonal interaction in the international trade arena (Kenny and Sheikh, 2000).

This chapter focuses on relational capability, which essentially is a measure of the quality of the relationship and is an amalgam of each of the terms mentioned above. The background literature consequently leads to the development of the following hypothesis:

Hypothesis 2: *The higher the level of relational capability of a firm within the network, the greater the impact on international performance.*

Trust

Trust between partners is often cited as a critical element of network exchange that in turn enhances the quality of the resource flows (Lorenzoni and Lipparini, 1999). A number of scholars have asserted that these distinctive elements of network governance can create cost advantages in comparison to coordination through market or bureaucratic mechanisms (Jarillo, 1988). In particular, mutual trust as a governance mechanism is based on the belief in the other partner's reliability in terms of fulfilment of obligation in an exchange (Pruitt, 1981). Trust allows both parties to assume that each will take actions that are predictable and mutually acceptable (Powell, 1990; Uzzi, 1997).

The focus here is on relational or interpersonal trust (Rousseau et al., 1998). Such trust is constructed through personal interactions and experiences with the other party. Conditions for this form of trust include the assessed integrity of the contact, their competence in ongoing exchanges, and their predictability through the alignment of goals and values (Rowley et al., 2000). What has been considered in previous research is network structure (i.e. closure) as a substitute for trust and not the trust associated with interpersonal relations. Trust, then, is often left unmeasured or else its presence is assumed to be associated with a certain structural form (Moran, 2005), such as strong ties or relational embeddedness. One exception to this is Wincent (2005), who measured trust in the context of networking width and depth inside the SME network and found trust to be related to corporate entrepreneurship. To the extent that trust is an important element and is engendered through interpersonal experiences (Granovetter, 1985; Rowley et al., 2000; Uzzi, 1997), Moran (2005) contends that it is important to measure it and determine its value, independent of structural characteristics of the network. Therefore, it can be argued that in a network, firms that trust their partners are more likely to engage, combine resources and trade together to enhance performance in international markets. Hence:

Hypothesis 3: *The higher the level of trust between partners in a network, the greater the impact on international performance.*

Network initiation

Initiation is based on the premise that inter-organizational relationships do not start on their own (Ritter and Gemünden, 2003); they are the result of specific investments. Typical activities to identify potential partners are visits to trade shows, monitoring industry-related journals and exploiting hints from existing partners. Network initiation involves a degree of network sensing. Network sensing is defined as the degree to which a firm actively seeks information on new alliance partnership opportunities (Bonner et al., 2005). Because opportunities for competitive advantage can be found through network relationships (Achrol, 1997; Burt, 1992), firms are constantly in search of new network partners, especially those that can provide unique and complementary resources. An active network sensing firm can be valuable to others seeking new partners by providing them access to valuable opportunities and reducing their search costs. In the context of this study, the focus is on network partners; therefore, similar to Walter et al. (2006), partner knowledge is organized and structured information about a firm's upstream and downstream partners (suppliers and customers) and competitors. Therefore, it can be argued that if a firm is actively engaged in seeking out partners, information and resources within the network, and initiates appropriate relationship development, it will have a greater chance of opening up opportunities that will lead to enhanced performance outcomes in international markets. Hence;

Hypothesis 4: *The more effective the level of network initiation capability the firm has, the greater the effect on its international performance.*

Coordination

Coordination implies that organizations involved in networks need to synchronize their activities so that their activities are in tune with one another (Mohr and Nevin, 1990). Such coordination includes the establishment and use of formal roles and procedures and the utilization of constructive conflict resolution mechanisms (Helfert and Vith, 1999).

Networks of firms also require strategic and coordinative planning. McNaughton and Bell (2001) stressed that exchanges in a network are not organized by market forces; rather they are structured by patterns of trust and opportunity. Coordination within a network, therefore, lends itself to partner integration. Partner integration refers to the degree to which the firm actively engages in coordinating activities and strategies and in the sharing of knowledge across alliance partners (Bonner et al., 2005). Effective integration across partners is critical for the productive use of a partner's resources through knowledge transfer. A critical aspect of any relationship is the potential for conflict between the alliance partners and how they deal with them (Kale et al., 2000). Conflict often exists in any alliance relationship on account of the inherent dependencies involved in such interactions. Given that a certain amount of conflict is expected, how such conflict is managed and coordinated is important (Borys and Jemison, 1989), as the impact of conflict resolution on the relationship can be productive or destructive (Deutsch, 1969).

Accordingly, it is reasonable to argue that a firm that actively coordinates activities across its partners is likely to have access to valuable resources and therefore becomes desired by other partners (Bonner et al., 2005), which in turn may lead to enhanced performance outcomes. Thus:

Hypothesis 5: *The greater the firm's network coordination capability, the greater the effect on international performance.*

Learning

Competition is increasingly knowledge based as firms strive to learn and develop capabilities faster than their rivals (D'Aveni, 1994; Teece and Pisano, 1994). However, the time between the identification of a problem and its arrival may not allow the firm to internally develop the knowledge and capabilities needed to respond effectively (Dierickx and Cool, 1989). Through 'learning alliances' firms can speed capability development and minimize their exposure to technological uncertainties by acquiring and exploiting knowledge developed by others (Grant and Baden-Fuller, 1995). This construct is similar to the notion of absorptive capacity, which refers to a firm's fundamental learning processes: its ability to identify, assimilate and exploit knowledge from the environment (Cohen and Levinthal, 1989; Lane and Koka, 2006). Lane and Lubatkin (1998) argue that the understanding of learning alliances has been limited to *how* they should be structured and managed, and that far less is known about *with whom* a learning alliance should be formed. Network learning, therefore, refers to the degree to which the organization engages in alliance learning activities, including the dissemination of lessons within the firm (Sinkula et al., 1997). It helps firms interpret and internalize the information and knowledge that it transfers and adapts (Sinkula et al., 1997). The information sharing aspect will be dealt with in a separate section. A firm that exhibits a strong network learning capability processes information and knowledge about past relationships, which can be effectively transferred to others for use in future relationships (Mohr and Spekman, 1994; Sinkula et al., 1997). In addition, firms that emphasize network learning practices should be in a good position to effectively use this information to select valuable partners and to manage effective linkages with those partners (Gulati, 1999; Powell, 1990). Accordingly, it can be argued that a firm that effectively learns from its network encounters will be more efficient in selecting and managing network activities that ultimately lead to performance outcomes in international trade. Hence:

Hypothesis 6: *The more effective a firm is in network learning, the greater the effect on international performance.*

Network resources

The issue under discussion here pertains to the human capital resources available for international expansion, namely, those resources that the firm can access and use to facilitate its international expansion efforts within the network. Entrepreneurs with more diverse levels of human capital are purported to have the ability to develop relevant skills and contacts and are able to tap into dense resource and information networks (Westhead et al., 2001). Wernerfelt (1984) argues that firms trying to establish an international presence must look for the unique resources they may possess. More specifically, the coordination of overseas operations, which must consider substantial variations in time zones, organizational structures and business environments, will severely tax even the most effective multinational corporations (Prahalad and Hamel, 1990). Hsu and Pereira (2008) demonstrated a positive relation between available resources and internationalization.

The management of these resources and the execution of the network management tasks is a complex process and, as such, it requires various types of qualifications (Jackson et al., 1991). According to Ritter and Gemünden (2003) a distinction can be made between specialist and social qualifications. The social aspect of these qualifications is dealt with under relational capability. Specialist qualifications include those that are necessary to handle 'the technical side' of relationships: technical skills are critical to understanding partners in terms of their technical needs, requirements and capabilities. Economic skills are required to define inputs and set prices. Knowledge about the other actors is an important resource. This knowledge includes information about the operations of partners, their personnel and resources, which are important for understanding their behaviour and the development of the network. In addition, experiential knowledge resulting from interactions with external partners is crucial. Such knowledge can be used to anticipate and evaluate critical situations and to select appropriate action (Helfert, 1998). It is experiential knowledge that reduces the firm's perception of market uncertainty or risk, which, in turn, impacts on commitment to international markets. Johanson and Vahlne (1977) argued that it is the need to acquire experiential knowledge that leads the firm to take small, incremental steps to open up new markets. Since then, a number of empirical studies have demonstrated that a firm is able to acquire relevant international knowledge from its relationships (Chetty and Ericksson, 2002).

With regard to specific industry knowledge, Westhead et al. (2001) found that specific industry knowledge and previous experience in selling goods and services abroad were strong predictors of the ability of the firm to be exporters (Westhead et al., 2001). The internationalization and network theory thus suggests that the human resources category (Grant, 1991) warrants investigation in terms of how this specific resource grouping enables an SME to maximize its network opportunities to enhance performance in international trade.

Hypothesis 7: *There is a positive relation between a firm's network human capital resources and international performance.*

Synergy sensitive resources

With a network orientation, a firm seeks complementary resources of its partners while maintaining internal unique resources necessary to attain the firm's strategic goals (Overby and Min, 2001). Another way firms can generate relational rents is by leveraging the complementary resource endowments of an alliance partner (Dyer and Singh, 1998). In some instances, a firm's ability to generate rents from its resources may require that these resources be utilized in conjunction with the complementary resources of another firm. Complementary resource endowments have been the focus of much prior discussion on the formation and management of alliances and have been discussed widely as a key factor driving returns from alliances (Teece, 1987).

In assessing the extent to which alliance partners can benefit by combining complementary resources, it is worthwhile to think about what proportion of the potential partner's strategic resources is synergy sensitive with the firm's resources (Dyer and Singh, 1998). As the proportion of synergy-sensitive resources in the potential partner increases, so do the potential benefits by combining the complementary resources. The notion of synergy-sensitive resources can be operationalized with reference to the concept of knowledge redundancy, which is broadly viewed as the degree of overlap in the knowledge base between two or more social actors (Burt, 1992; Rindfleisch and Moorman, 2001), partner fit – complementarity and compatibility (Dyer and Singh, 1998; Kale et al., 2000), and resource integration (Li and Lin, 2006). Complementarity between alliance partners refers to the lack of similarity or overlap between their core business and capabilities – the lower the similarity, the greater the complementarity (Mowery et al., 1996). Harrigan (1988) showed that ventures and partnerships are more likely to succeed when partners possess complementary missions and resource capabilities. Complementarity ensures that both partners bring different but valuable capabilities to the relationship (Kale et al., 2000). Researchers have also argued that compatibility of partners is an important aspect of fit that affects alliance outcomes (Kale et al., 2000). Compatibility in terms of resources is the key issue here and, in particular, how the combined resources of network partners are integrated to provide performance outcomes in terms of international trade. Hence:

Hypothesis 8: *The higher the level of synergy-sensitive resources within a network, the higher the impact on international performance.*

Information sharing

Assimilating and disseminating up-to-date information on partners, their resources and agreements with them to all involved departments, help to avoid redundant process and miscommunication and improve the detection of synergies between partners (Cohen and Levinthal, 1989). It has been stressed that impulses for the variation of existing capabilities often originate from outside the focal organization (Cohen and Levinthal, 1989, Lane and Lubatkin, 1998). These external sources can, for example, be seen in generally accessible information such as journals, seminars and consultants.

Penrose (1959) first recognized the role of knowledge in business management, stressing that knowledge is the important resource for the growth of the firm. However, knowledge is difficult to transfer and communicate across organizational boundaries (Li and Lin, 2006). Inkpen and Crossan (1995) point out that for learning strategies to be viable, firms must overcome the ambiguity associated with their partners' skills. Abrahamson and Rosenkopf (1993) suggest that firms often lack channels for sharing rich or reliable information with one another because they are unwilling to share such information in the first place. Burt (1982) and Baker (1992) have shown that the distinct social structural patterns in exchange relations within markets shape the flow of information. Moreover, a network of embedded ties accumulated over time can become the basis of a rich information exchange network that enables firms to learn about new alliance opportunities with reliable partners (Gulati, 1995; Powell et al., 1996). Gulati (1999) conceptualized the informational advantages bestowed by networks of inter-firm ties as a network resource. Moller and Torronen (2003) refer to network information potential as the degree to which market and other information can be obtained through working relationships with suppliers and customers. A number of empirical studies have demonstrated that a firm is able to acquire relevant international information from its relationships (Chetty and Ericksson, 2002; Holm et al., 1996). It is the contention of this study that the firm's network represents a source of information, either directly or indirectly, which can be capitalized upon in terms of the internationalization of the firm and thus improves international performance. Therefore:

Hypothesis 9: *The greater the level of information sharing within the network, the greater the impact on international performance.*

International performance

A review of the measures of international performance in the literature highlights the need to distinguish the factors that need to be considered in selecting appropriate measures. Griffin and Page (1993) argued that the multi-dimensionality of performance is not under discussion, but rather which performance measures to use. International performance in particular is a complex phenomenon, and the choice of individual export performance measures depends on contextual factors that are research method-specific, export business-specific, and target audience-specific (Katsikeas et al., 2000). To address these concerns, a balance of objective measures such as a company's marketplace and financial performance (Narver and Slater, 1990) with subjective measures such as levels of customer satisfaction (Walter et al., 2006) are deemed more appropriate for this higher-order construct (Weerawardena and Loxton, 2006).

Unit of analysis and data collection

For the current study, the population comprised all companies in the telecommunications, internet and related industries in Ireland. In order to compile a relevant sampling frame, data from the Central Statistics Office (CSO) and The Commission for Communications Regulation (ComReg), *Business and Finance* (an Irish business magazine) and Dun and Bradstreet were used. The focus was on a single industry in one country to control for industry- and country-specific factors affecting international performance. This study was based on a mail survey of 458 SMEs (with more than 3 and fewer than 250 employees) drawn from this population. The overall response rate was 40.39 per cent with a usable response rate of 33.64 per cent, and the unit of analysis was the firm. Table 16.1 provides an overview of the activities carried out by respondent firms.

Common method bias

Harman's single factor test was performed to test for the presence of common method variance bias. All variables were entered into an unrotated principal components analysis. The results of the analysis indicated 19 items with eigenvalues greater than one, and no single factor accounted for more than 33.7 per cent of the covariation. Only one variable accounted for 18 per cent of the variance. The

Table 16.1 Activities carried out by respondent firms

Main activity categories	Additional activities carried out by respondent firms
• Computer consultancy • Computer services miscellaneous • Computing and bureau services • Data communications • Internet services and web design • Telecommunications • Telephone cost management	• Systems integration/telephony integration services • Structured cabling • Solutions provider • Computer software/warehouse software/financial software services/software development services • Sales and maintenance • Multi-channel TV provider/Cable TV • Programme management • Engineering services • Translation and localization • Brand building and design/content provider/creator • Research • Online game publishing • E-commerce • Provision of IT infrastructure • Data centre • Cable communications

results indicate that common method variance, though probably present to some degree, does not affect the results.

Scale validation

The Appendix displays the results obtained from the estimation of the CFA model. An inspection of these results shows that all items loaded on their specified constructs. Convergent validity is evidenced by the large and significant ($t < 1.96$, $p < 0.05$) loadings on the items on respective constructs (Shoham, 1998). As far as the reliability is concerned, Appendix presents the results of the composite reliability (CR) and the average variance extracted (AVE). The values for the CR ranged from 0.65 to 0.91, which exceeds Bagozzi and Yi's (1988) recommended minimum level of 0.60. In terms of AVE, one of the ten constructs exceeded the 0.50 guideline and eight of the constructs are between 0.40 and 0.49. The low AVE on strong and weak ties should be examined in the context of the use of foreign entry mode as a new way of operationalizing the construct and as Ping (2007) suggests – a new measure in a new model tested for the first time. In general, for all constructs the indicators are considered sufficient and adequate in terms of how the measurement model is specified.

Results

Since the proposed measurement model was consistent with the data, the hypothesized structural model was estimated using LISREL 8.80. Before advancing to the estimation of the structural model, composite variables were created to deal with the issue of small sample size. The single factor method was used for this study, as according to Landis et al. (2000), it is the most frequently reported method in the literature and its purpose is to distil the original set of items to a reduced number of indicators that are empirically balanced measures of the constructs. Figure 16.1 shows the parameter estimates, t-values and the fit statistics for this structural model.

The overall chi-square for the structural model exhibited in Figure 16.1 is 699.55 with 472 degrees of freedom, and with three fit indices (CFI, IFI and RMSEA) above the guideline limits indicating a good fit between the hypothesized model and the observed data. Thus in general, the model fits the data; the next step is therefore to examine the parameter estimates. Estimated parameters with an absolute t-value greater than 1.96 indicate a significance path at the $p < 0.05$ level, and those with an absolute t value over 2.576 represent a significance path at the $p < 0.01$ level.

The hypothesis stating that stronger ties are more influential on international performance than weak ties is supported. Similarly, network coordination and human capital resources are found to be positively and significantly associated with international performance. Strong ties, trust, network initiation and synergy-sensitive resources are all positively associated with international performance but are not significant. Weak ties, relational capability, network learning and information sharing are negatively associated with international performance. Regarding the antecedents to international performance in this study, the R^2 value of 0.63 is

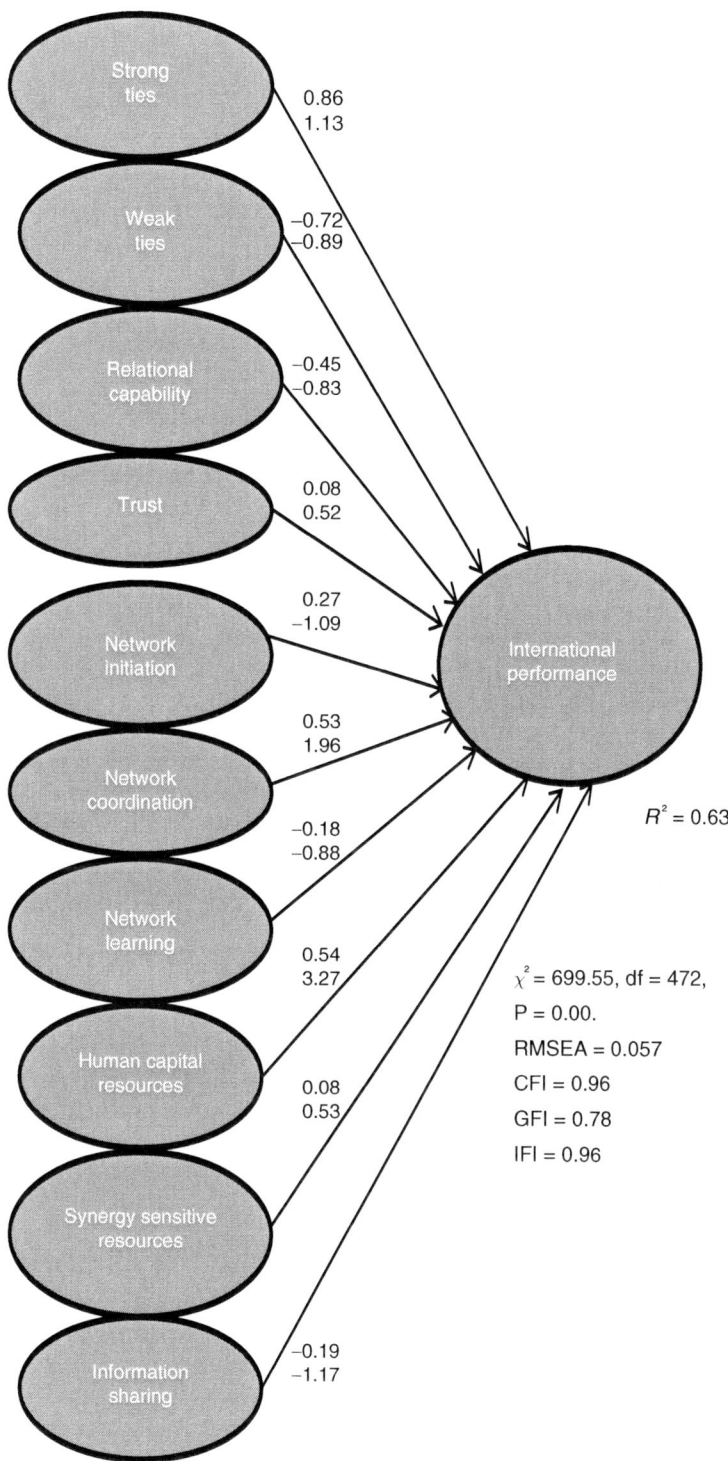

Figure 16.1 Final model
Note: Standardized parameter estimates above the line and *t*-values below the line.

respectable, indicating that a substantial proportion of variance of international performance is indeed predicted by the predictors considered.

Discussion

The lack of support for the hypotheses in relation to strong and weak ties and performance may not be surprising when considering the costs associated with building and maintaining ties. These relationship resources can be a liability because there is a downside pertaining to the risks involved and the investment in time and costs associated with forming, monitoring and sustaining social capital (Yli-Renko et al., 2002). Similar to the support for hypothesis 1c, Choo and Mazarol (2001) found that small firms using licensing, franchising, manufacturing and acquisition (similar to strong ties in this study) as principal market entry modes outperformed firms that were using direct exporting, strategic alliances, foreign distributor, independent overseas agent and joint venture (similar to weak ties in this study). These results are consistent with other studies that have attempted to assess the relation between performance and entry mode of multinationals (Li and Guisinger, 1991; Simmonds, 1990; Woodcock et al., 1994). On the choice of entry mode for high-technology firms, Burgel and Murray (2000) found that a high degree of required product/service customization leads to the exclusion of intermediaries during the international sales process. Given that the HTSMEs in this sample are predominantly in the services sector (see Table 16.1 for a complete list of activities carried out), and given the inseparable nature of services, these firms may tend to deal directly with their own customers in domestic as well as foreign markets.

Hypothesis 2 proposed a positive relation between relational capability and international performance. The results revealed a negative and a non-significant relation between these two variables. This finding is similar to the views of Sullivan-Mort and Weerawardena (2006), whose research on networking capability in high-tech born globals found that networking activity may not be the panacea for all 'ills' of small firms. Instead they comment that networking activity must take the form of a competitive capability complemented by entrepreneurial opportunity-seeking behaviour. Their research findings also identified a negative aspect of networks which they refer to as 'network rigidity'. Involvement in networks may limit strategic options, as opportunities must then be pursued within the network boundaries.

Hypothesis 3 posited a positive relation between trust and international performance. A positive relation between these variables did emerge; however, it was not significant at the 95 per cent confidence interval. This finding is consistent with Aulakh et al. (1996) and Wincent (2005) who did not find a significant relation between trust and performance. Both studies suggest that trust may be better understood as part of the culture of the firm and specifically, in the case of Aulakh et al. (1996), as the macro-cultural environment that surrounds the partnerships.

While some studies have found that trust improves performance (Cullen et al., 2000; Zhang et al., 2003), others have revealed the absence of a significant direct link between trust and performance (Sarkar et al., 2001; Fryxell et al., 2002), and still another (Lyles et al., 1999) reports a negative relation with performance. Similar findings from Grayson and Amber (1999) found that trust's effect on performance is lower for long-term versus short-term relationships. Selnes and Sallis (2003) found a negative interaction effect of trust and relationship learning on performance, leading to less information exchange, fewer meetings, less evaluation of the relationship and less adjusting to end-user performance.

Hite (2003) sees trust as the cornerstone of relationally embedded ties, as this study did not find support for the hypothesis relating relational capability to international performance. It is perhaps not too surprising that the relation between trust and international performance was not supported. However, the lack of a significant direct relation between trust and international performance should not trivialize the role of trust-building in inter-organizational partnerships. Trust may have other consequences, such as efficiency and longevity of the partnership, which were not explicitly considered in this study.

Network operation

Drawing on the growth stages theory of network development outlined by Batonda and Perry (2003), the initiation construct (Hypothesis 4) could be seen as being as part of the 'searching process'. The activities in this initial stage of the network development process are seen as phase one by a range of authors (Heide, 1994; Kanter, 1994; Wilson, 1995). Looking through this lens may lend some explanation to the lack of support for the relation between network initiation and international performance. If network initiation is seen as a stage in the process as distinct from an element of overall networking capability, then subsequent factors or variables will have a bearing on the international performance relation. Also, Batonda and Perry (2003) point out that the outcome of the stages model (including phase one) seem to be influenced by the interaction between economic actors and individuals in the network as well as external persons such as the network broker. It is also evident that sometimes foreign market opportunities are discovered completely by chance, with no clear initiating role attributable to the buyer, seller or third party (Ellis, 2000). Furthermore, Ellis (2000) contends that it is appropriate to treat the trade fair (which is referred to in this construct in this study) as a special kind of initiation scenario. Empirical support for this assertion is provided by Reid (1983, p. 154) who, based on his study of information search strategies used by exporters, found participation in international trade fairs to be 'more likely than any other information search activity to be of use to the export decision-maker'.

The finding that network coordination (Hypothesis 5) is positively related to international performance in this study is consistent with previous research findings on the role of the alliance or coordination function. This is also consistent with Katsikeas et al. (2009), who recognize that international exchange is most productive when the resources and capabilities of trading partners are coordinated and fully matched to the work requirements inherent in importing products to foreign markets (Crowston, 1997). Yet achieving optimal coordination is particularly difficult in international transactions, as the resources required for successful exchange are scattered across the employee-actors of the export and import firms (Zaheer et al., 1998). Fink et al. (2008) contended that international cooperation of SMEs require this kind of behavioural coordination for their long-term and highly complex transactions. The ability of an enterprise to deal with behavioural uncertainty within cooperation, and to resourcefully keep in check the danger of opportunistic behaviour on the part of the cooperation partner, influences the utility it derives from the cooperation relationship (Jarillo, 1988).

The relation between network learning capability and international performance is not supported in the findings of this research. This finding is consistent with those of Bonner et al. (2005), and a plausible explanation might be that a firm's network learning activities go largely unnoticed by managers in other firms because they are more internal and implicit and, as a result, have little influence on its perceived position with a relationship network. To the extent that the network learning activities are internal and unnoticeable by managers, they may not be acknowledged as an antecedent of the firm's own networking capability by managers. Furthermore, Nahapiet and Ghoshal (1998) argued that some aspects of social capital can hinder interaction and thus constrain rather than enhance learning. They argue that though social norms and identity have a positive effect on group performance, these attributes can also hinder the group's receptiveness to new information and to seek other methods of doing things.

Theory (for instance Giddens, 1994; Granovetter, 1973) and practice (Floren and Tell, 2004) support the notion that trust is the major prerequisite for learning in groups. Floren and Tell (2004) focused on the emergent nature of learning in groups or networks and in their research trust has proven to be an essential element supporting the learning process in networks. As the relation between trust and international performance is not supported in this study, given the argument that trust is a prerequisite to learning, it may come as no surprise that the relation between network learning and international performance is thus not supported.

Additional interesting insights can be gained from the results of the three hypotheses under the network operations heading. First, a positive but non-significant relation between network initiation and international performance, a positive and significant relation between network coordination and international performance, and a negative and non-significant relation between network learning and international performance. This range of findings could support Bonner et al.'s (2005) similar notion that performing, simultaneously, elements of network initiation, coordination and learning at high levels tends to strain the competencies and resources of an organization. This is consistent with the literature on resource-constrained small businesses. Therefore, managers have to carefully decide which strategic direction they should pursue. Should the firm create value for partners by being well informed about the breadth of opportunities, or should it strive to become an excellent coordinator of activities across multiple networks?

Network resources

A limited number of studies in the international entrepreneurship literature have focused on the firm's resource base, particularly in technology intensive sectors, and their potential impact on international performance (Coviello and McAuley, 1999). Furthermore, the internationalization literature has traditionally tended to examine small firms as a homogenous sector characterized by resource shortages, which act as inhibitors to geographical diversification (Buckley, 1989). The findings of this study paint a different picture of these HTSMEs: the picture is of small firms using their human capital – experience and industry knowledge – to enhance their international performance. However, creating synergy among network partners and effective information exchange is not a priority for these firms.

Resources that are not internal to the firm may be purchased in the market (Chetty and Wilson, 2003). However, Hart et al. (1995) concluded from their empirical study that some resources, especially industry-specific knowledge and reputation resources, are not readily tradable or accessible in the marketplace. Lavie (2007) contends that ties to prominent partners with abundant marketing and financial resources enhance market performance, whereas technology and human network resources fall short of creating value. Previous research in the semiconductor and software sectors reveals a difference in the nature and degree of complementarity of network resources (Stuart, 2000). Research on network resource combinations of small biotech firms by Tolstoy and Agndal (2010) suggests that resource limitations prompt firms to seek out resources available in their networks and combine these resources to exploit opportunities to enter new markets and to sell new products in existing markets. The findings in this research may be unique to the telecommunications industry, and further research in a cross-sectoral setting would shed more light on this issue.

The telecommunications industry

Moller and Svahn (2006) provided a typology of business networks based on their value creation characteristics. One particular type they refer to is the 'emerging new business net'. This typology is of relevance here in the context of the telecommunication and internet firms under investigation. Moller and Svahn (2006) argued that these firms aim at creating networks and nets through which new technologies, products or business concepts can be commercialized. This action is future-oriented in the sense that the economic value potential of these nets is generally fully realized only in the future. If the action is future-oriented, so too are the performance (and international performance) outcomes of these collaborative actions.

These future-oriented nets may require radical changes in existing value systems and in the creation of new value activities. For example, emerging mobile services are generally created through business nets involving a telecom operator, several 'middleware-type' software producers, and content and service providers. Emerging value systems involve complex collaboration and learning processes (e.g. the Symbian and Bluetooth coalitions), and an inter-organizational relationship formation that is difficult to specify in advance. Uncertainty and ambiguity related to value activities and to actors and their capabilities are inherent features of this landscape, exemplified by the converging information, communication, and e-content fields (Amit and Zott, 2001; Doz et al., 2001; Eisenhardt and Martin, 2000).

In emerging value systems, actors are facing great uncertainty of the relative value of new knowledge. For example, which technological modes like UMTS, CDMA and PDC in the third and even the fourth generation mobile telephones will become dominant designs in which markets? Moller and Svahn (2006) proposed that an impending hub firm should have specific resources and knowledge that make it an attractive mobilizer for potential partners. The more important these resources are perceived to be for the emergence of the new business field, the more power they accrue for their holder. The hub firm should also be able to create an organizational forum for sharing the work and responsibilities between the actors, to establish coordination mechanisms for network cooperation, and to instil a network identity (Gadde and Håkansson, 2001; Kale et al., 2002). The concept of the hub firm with agenda setting and mobilizing capabilities mentioned above has parallels with Rugman and D'Cruz's (2000) flagship firm in their framework of the flagship/five partners model. The five partners consist of a flagship firm (usually an MNE), key suppliers, key customers, competitors and the non-business infrastructure. As mentioned earlier, small businesses are an integral part of the business network conceptualized in this flagship model. Rugman and D'Cruz (2000) look specifically at the high technology and deregulation issues of the telecommunications sector in Canada and France.

Limitations and further research

This study examined the networking capabilities and international performance of SMEs only. It did not capture the role of large businesses in the sector (e.g. mobile operators or flagship firms), which in many cases are the main customers of these SMEs. In fact, Loane and Bell (2009) acknowledge that the role played by a firm's clients in supplying resources, including knowledge, has been under-investigated, particularly from an international entrepreneurship stance. The role of regulators, government agencies or other bodies that have control over the infrastructure, networks such as 3G and 4G, awarding licences, contracts and spectrum allocation was also not captured. Decisions and actions taken at this level in the industry (e.g. awarding of a mobile licence, or privatizing telecoms businesses) could have far-reaching effects for an SME's domestic as well as international business activities. Future research could address this issue in more detail.

The empirical data was collected from April to May 2008. Since then, this dynamic industry has experienced several structural changes in addition to those caused by the downturn in the world economy affecting all aspects of business and society, resulting in a number of companies in this industry going into liquidation.

A survey conducted in this sector after 2008 may reveal a very different set of results than those presented here.

This study measured the direct effects of constructs of networking capability on international performance. However, the literature provides additional evidence that the key to understanding how networking affects performance is to examine the factors that moderate the relation. Building on Brazeal and Herbert's (1999) model of the entrepreneurial process, Jones and Coviello's (2005) and Jones and Young's (2009) model, and the results of this study, a simple, descriptive model of internationalization as process-linked events consisting of networking capability leading to mode and country choice in a dynamic process of resource commitment and change is proposed as a means of further extending this research. Similar to the Jones and Coviello (2005) model, the mode is positioned as a formal event linking post and antecedent processes. This model differs from earlier iterations in that it incorporates initiation capability and human capital resources followed by trust as antecedents. The decision/action elements of this model comprise mode of entry/tie type, learning, coordination and relational capability. The post or decision/action elements include resource combination, information sharing and the relevant outcome variable – international performance in this case. Viewing internationalization in this way enables both event (entry mode and networking capability) and temporal process (internationalization) perspectives to be considered (Van de Ven and Engleman, 2004). This model would need to be validated on a new sample of companies.

Conclusion

This study makes a solid contribution to the international business literature by providing evidence of a collaboration–performance relation. The results therefore resonate with calls for research on the linkages between networks and firm performance. Past research has failed to examine networking activity in a unifying framework incorporating antecedent factors and performance outcomes. Furthermore, while much is known about the role of networking as a response to perceived uncertainty and its impact on firm performance in general, and in SMEs' performance in domestic settings, the relation between networking and international performance is under-researched. Consistent with some of the previous limited research on the topic, there is limited evidence of a direct relation between the two in this study.

These findings have important practical and policy implications. The effects of networks on internationalization should be analysed in terms of whether the potential strengths of networks match the requirements for foreign business development of HTSMEs. Networks and networking have resource implications. Thus, it is necessary to identify and review the resources that are critical to the international performance of their firms and develop and implement business strategies building on those resources in order to enhance the likelihood of international success. Against the background of this research, caution is advised against taking a one-size-fits-all view of networks, and also to allow for the possibility that firms may need support with networking before a network may reap the desired outcomes.

Appendix CFA and constructs reliability

Construct and items	Standardized loadings	Regression weights	*t*-values
Group 1			
Weak ties (CR = 0.77, AVE = 0.30)			
Direct importing	0.41	0.17	4.71
Indirect exporting via agent	0.60	0.36	7.37
Indirect exporting via distributor	0.61	0.37	7.53
Direct exporting	0.56	0.31	5.79
Exporting via foreign intermediary	0.57	0.33	6.97
Marketing agreements	0.63	0.39	7.79
Patenting agreements	0.52	0.27	5.17
Informal partnering arrangements	0.45	0.20	5.29
Strong ties (CR = 0.65, AVE = 0.25)			
Sales or manufacturing joint ventures	0.40	0.16	4.49
Equity alliances	0.54	0.30	5.38
Non-equity R and D alliances	0.64	0.42	7.79
Sales or manufacturing subsidiary	0.61	0.37	7.26
Licensing	0.34	0.12	3.86
Franchising	0.36	0.13	3.99
Relational capability (CR = 0.83, AVE = 0.47)			
Stay together during adversity/challenge	0.53	0.28	6.57
Feel indebted to our partners for what they have done for us	0.36	0.13	4.35
Expect that we will be working with our partners far into the future	0.63	0.40	8.23
Have close, personal interaction between the partners at multiple levels	0.73	0.53	9.83
See the value in mutual respect between the partners at multiple levels	0.86	0.73	12.54
Nurture mutually beneficial relationships	0.85	0.73	12.44
Trust (CR = 0.79, AVE = 0.47)			
They are very competent in the areas in which we interact	0.42	0.19	5.22
They have the ability to contribute to cooperative projects	0.52	0.27	6.35
We trust they would act in our companies' best interest	0.83	0.69	11.37
They share our overall goals and values	0.84	0.71	11.59
They are generally honest and truthful in the information provided	0.61	0.37	7.60
Group 2			
Initiation (CR = 0.87, AVE = 0.47)			
Inform ourselves of their respective markets	0.70	0.49	9.30
Inform ourselves of their products/services	0.52	0.39	8.02
Determine their strengths and weaknesses	0.79	0.62	11.10
Inform ourselves of their strategies and potentials	0.82	0.68	11.81

Judge in advance which possible partners we can pursue projects with	0.73	0.53	9.87
Seek opportunities to complement our capabilities and resources	0.57	0.47	8.61
Routinely gather information about prospective partners from various forums	0.52	0.27	5.46
Coordination (CR = 0.82, AVE = 0.44)			
We analyse what we would like and desire to achieve with which partner	0.55	0.31	5.35
We appoint coordinators who are responsible for the relationships with our partners	0.60	0.36	7.53
We discuss regularly with our partners how we can support each other in our success	0.78	0.60	10.54
We try to formalize our network relationships	0.78	0.61	10.74
The partners engage in joint problem-solving while resolving conflicts	0.57	0.45	8.66
Great emphasis is placed on dealing with cultural obstacles while resolving conflicts	0.54	0.30	5.71
Learning (CR = 0.83, AVE-0.40)			
We ensure that strategic decisions within our firm are informed by our networking activities	0.58	0.34	7.24
We value employee feedback for strengthening networking relations	0.56	0.31	6.86
We conduct periodic reviews to understand what we are doing	0.74	0.54	9.84
We periodically collect and analyse field experiences from our networks	0.71	0.50	9.29
We modify our network-related procedures as we learn from experience	0.72	0.52	9.58
Resources such as network manuals are developed	0.53	0.40	8.06
Company managers attend training programmes on network management	0.47	0.22	5.57
The company provides opportunities for on-the-job network training	0.51	0.26	5.20
Group 3			
Human capital resources (CR = 0.91, AVE = 0.68)			
We have the necessary management expertise to assess foreign market potential	0.80	0.63	11.44
We have the expertise to manage our network relationships	0.55	0.30	7.01
We have the industry knowledge to pursue foreign markets	0.88	0.78	13.51
We have technical expertise to assess foreign market potential	0.85	0.72	12.66
We have international experience in doing business in new markets	0.85	0.73	12.70
We have international experience in cooperating with other firms	0.82	0.68	12.06
Synergy-sensitive resources (CR = 0.83, AVE = 0.47)			
Network relationship allow efficient use of our firms resources	0.92	0.85	14.59

Appendix (Continued)

Construct and items	Standardized loadings	Regression weights	t-values
Network relationships lead to sound economic use of our firm	0.93	0.87	14.94
Network relationships allow effective use of our firms' knowledge base	0.86	0.73	12.89
There is high complementarity between the resources/capabilities	0.75	0.56	10.55
There is high similarity/overlap between the core capabilities of each partner	0.34	0.12	4.21
The management and operating styles of our network partners are compatible	0.43	0.19	5.40
We strive to achieve synergy through working together	0.55	0.43	8.76
Information sharing (CR = 0.86, AVE = 0.48)			
We share proprietary business information	0.54	0.41	8.27
We exchange internal management information timely for each other	0.73	0.53	9.87
We share information about competitors and environments	0.55	0.42	8.40
We share internal decisions with the partners that might be affected	0.81	0.66	11.45
Information is available and accessible in a format that can be easily utilized	0.73	0.54	9.91
We have processes to systematically transfer knowledge	0.56	0.32	7.08
Information is often spontaneously exchanged	0.74	0.55	10.1
Performance (CR = 0.88, AVE = 0.49)			
The international market share of your number 1 product/service	0.69	0.48	9.45
Your international sales growth over the last 3 years	0.91	0.82	14.18
Your average return on investment	0.33	0.11	4.00
Your total turnover	0.30	0.09	3.64
Your international turnover	0.93	0.90	15.45
Your total pre-tax profitability	0.27	0.075	3.33
Your international pre-tax profitability	0.90	0.91	13.99
Customer satisfaction in international markets	0.70	0.49	9.57
Customer retention in international markets	0.74	0.54	10.53

References

Abrahamson, E. and Rosenkopf, L. (1993) 'Institutional and competitive bandwagons: using mathematical modeling as a tool to explain innovation diffusion', *Academy of Management Review*, 18(3), 487–517.

Achrol, R.S. (1997) 'Changes in the theory of inter-organisational relations in marketing: toward a network paradigm', *Journal of the Academy of Marketing Science*, 25(1), 56–71.

Amit, R. and Zott, C. (2001) 'Value creation in e-business', *Strategic Management Journal*, 22(6/7), 493–520.

Aulakh, P.A., Kotabe, M. and Sahay, A. (1996) 'Trust and performance in cross-border marketing partnerships: a behavioral approach', *Journal of International Business Studies*, 27(5), 1005–32.

Bagozzi, R.P. and Yi, Y. (1988) 'On the evaluation of structural equation models', *Journal of Academy of Marketing Sciences*, 16(1), 74–94.

Baker, W.E. (1992) 'The network organisation in theory and practice', in N. Nohria and R.G. Eccles (eds) *Networks and Organisations: Structure, Form and Action* (Boston, MA: Harvard Business School Press).

Baron, M.A. and Markman, G.D. (2003) 'Beyond social capital: the role of entrepreneurs' social competence in their financial success', *Journal of Business Venturing*, 18(1), 41–60.

Batonda, G. and Perry, C. (2003) 'Approaches to relationship development processes in interfirm networks', *European Journal of Marketing*, 37(10), 1457–84.

Bonner, J.M., Kim, D. and Cavusgil, S.T. (2005) 'Self perceived strategic network identity and its effects on market performance in alliance relationships', *Journal of Business Research*, 58(10), 1371–80.

Borys, B. and Jemison, D. (1989) 'Hybrid arrangements as strategic alliances: theoretical issues in organisational combinations', *Academy of Management Review*, 14(2), 234–49.

Brazeal, D.V. and Herbert, J.F. (1999) 'The Genesis of Entrepreneurship', *Entrepreneurship Theory and Practice*, 23(3), 29–45.

Buckley, P.J. (1989) 'Foreign direct investment by small and medium sized enterprises: the theoretical background', *Small Business Economics*, 1(2), 89–100.

Buckley, P.J. (2010) 'The role of headquarters in the global factory', in U. Andersson and U. Holm (eds) *Managing the Contemporary Multinational the Role of Headquarters*, 60–84 (Cheltenham: Edward Elgar).

Buckley, P.J. and Ghauri, P.N. (2004) 'Globalisation, economic geography and the strategy of multinational enterprises', *Journal of International Business Studies*, 35(2), 81–98.

Burgel, O. and Murray, G.C. (2000) 'The international market entry choices of start-up companies in high-technology industries', *Journal of International Marketing*, 8(2), 30–63.

Burt, R.S. (1982) *Toward a Structural Theory of Action* (New York, Academic Press).

Burt, R.S. (1992) 'The social structure of competition', in N. Nohria and R.G. Eccles (eds) *Network and Organisations: Structure, Form, and Actions* (Boston, MA: Harvard Business School Press).

Calof, J. and Beamish, P.W. (1995) 'Adapting to foreign markets: explaining internationalisation', *International Business Review*, 4(2), 115–31.

Castells, M. (1998) *End of Millenium* (Oxford: Blackwell).

Chetty, S.K. and Eriksson, K. (2002) 'Mutual commitment and experiential knowledge in mature international business relationship', *International Business Review*, 11(3), 305–24.

Chetty, S.K. and Wilson, H. (2003) 'Collaborating with competitors to acquire resources', *International Business Review*, 12(1), 61–81.

Choo, S. and Mazzarol, T. (2001) 'An impact of performance of foreign market entry choices by small and medium sized enterprises', *Journal of Enterprising Culture*, 9(3), 291–312.

Clark, K. and Fujimoto, T. (1991) *Product Development in the World Automobile Industry* (Boston MA: Harvard Business School Press).

Cohen, W.M. and Levinthal, D.A. (1989) 'Innovation and learning: the two faces of R&D', *Economic Journal*, 99(397), 569–96.

Contractor, F.J. and Lorange, P. (1988) *Cooperative Strategies in International Business* (Lexingtion MA; Lexington Books).

Corrigan, D. (2008) Embracing the Future of IT, Managed Services, *Sunday Business Post Supplement*, May 11.

Coviello, N.E. and McAuley, A. (1999) 'Internationalisation and the smaller firm: a review of contemporary empirical research', *Management International Review*, 39(3), 223–56.

Crowston, K. (1997) 'A coordination theory approach to organisational process design', *Organisation Science*, 8(2), 157–75.
Cullen, J.B., Johnson, J.L. and Sakano, T. (2000) 'Success through commitment and trust: the soft side of strategic alliance management', *Journal of World Business*, 35(3), 223–40.
D'Aveni, R.A. (1994) *Hypercompetition: Managing the Dynamics of Strategic Manoeuvring* (New York: Free Press).
Deutsch, M. (1969) 'Conflicts: productive and destructive', *Journal of Social Issues*, 25(1), 7–41.
Dierickx, I. and Cool, K. (1989) 'Asset stock accumulation and sustainability of competitive advantage', *Management Science*, 35(12), 1504–11.
Døving, E. and Gooderham, P.N. (2008) 'Dynamic capabilities as antecedents of the scope of related diversification: the case of small firm accountancy practices', *Strategic Management Journal*, 29(8), 841–57.
Doz, Y.L., Santos, J. and Williamson, P. (2001) *From Global to Meta-national: How Companies Win in the Knowledge Economy* (Boston, MA: Harvard Business School Press).
Dyer, J.H. and Singh, H. (1998) 'The relational view: cooperative strategy and sources of competitive advantage', *Academy of Management Review*, 23(4), 532–50.
Eisenhardt, K. and Martin, L. (2000) 'Dynamic capabilities: what are they?', *Strategic Management Journal*, 21(10/11), 1105–21.
Ellis, P. (2000) 'Social ties and foreign market entry', *Journal of International Business Studies*, 31(3), 443–69.
Fink, M., Harms, R. and Kraus, S. (2008) 'Cooperative internationalisation of SMEs: self-commitment as a success factor for international entrepreneurship', *European Management Journal*, 26(6), 429–40.
Floren, H. and Tell, J. (2004) 'The emergent prerequisites of managerial learning in small firm networks', *The Leadership and Organisation Development Journal*, 25(3), 292–307.
Fryxell, G.E., Dooley, R.S. and Vryza, M. (2002) 'After the ink dries: the interaction of trust and control in US-based international joint ventures', *Journal of Management* Studies, 39(6), 865–86.
Gadde, L.E. and Håkansson, H. (2001) *Supply Network Strategies* (Chichester: Wiley).
Galaskiewicz, J. and Zaheer, A. (1999) 'Networks of competitive advantage', in S. Andrews and D. Knoke (eds) *Research in the Sociology of Organisations*, 237–61 (Stanford, CT: JAI Press).
Giddens, A. (1994) 'Living in a post traditional society', in U. Beck, A. Giddnes and S. Lash (eds) *Reflexive Modernization* (Oxford: Blackwell Publishers).
Granovetter, M.S. (1973) 'The strength of weak ties', *American Journal of Sociology*, 78(6), 1360–80.
Granovetter, M.S. (1983) 'The strength of weak ties: a network theory revisited', in C. Randall (ed.) *Sociological Theory*, 210–33 (San Fransisco, CA: Jossey Bass).
Granovetter, M.S. (1985) 'Economic action and social structure: the problem of embedded edition', *American Journal of Sociology*, 91(3), 481–510.
Grant, R.M. (1991) 'The resource based theory of competitive advantage: implications for strategy formulation', *Californian Management Review*, 33(3), 114–35.
Grant, R.M. and Baden-Fuller, C. (1995) 'A knowledge based theory of inter-firm collaboration', *Academy of Management Best Paper Proceedings*, 17–21.
Grayson, K. and Ambler, T. (1999) 'The dark side of long-term relationships in marketing services', *Journal of Marketing* Research, 36(1), 132–41.
Griffin, A. and Page, A.L. (1993) 'An interim report on measuring product development success and failure', *Journal of Product Innovation Management*, 10(4), 291–308.
Gulati, R. (1995) 'Does familiarity breed trust? The implications of repeated ties for contractual choice in alliances', *Academy of Management Journal*, 38(1), 85–112.
Gulati, R. (1998) 'Alliances and networks', *Strategic Management Journal*, 19(4), 293–317.
Gulati, R. (1999) 'Network location and learning: the influence of network resources and firm capabilities on alliance formation', *Strategic Management Journal*, 20(5), 397–420.

Hagg, I. and Johanson, J. (1983) *Firms in Networks: A New View of Competitive Power* (Stockholm: Business and Social Research Institute).
Harrigan, K.R. (1988) 'Strategic alliance and partner asymmetries', *Management International Review*, 28(2), 53–72.
Hart, M., Stevenson, H. and Dial, J. (1995) 'Entrepreneurship: a definition', in W. Bygrave, B. Bird, S. Birley, N. Churchill, M. Hay, R. Keeley and W. Wetzel (eds) *Frontiers of Entrepreneurship Research* (Babson Park, MA: Babson College).
Heide, J.B. (1994) 'Inter-organisational governance in marketing channels', *Journal of Marketing*, 58(1), 71–85.
Helfat, C. (2007) 'Relational capabilities: drivers and implications', in C.E. Helfat, S. Finkelstein, W. Mitchell, M. Peteraf, H. Singh, D.J. Teece and S.G. Winter (eds) *Dynamic Capabilities: Strategic Change in Organisations*, 65–80 (Oxford, UK: Blackwell).
Helfat, C.E. and Peteraf, M. (2003) 'The dynamic resource based view: capability lifecycles', *Strategic Management Journal*, 24(10), 997–1010.
Helfert, G. (1998) *Teams in Relationship Marketing: Design von Effektiven Kundenbeziehungsteams* (Wiesbaden: Galber).
Helfert, G. and Vith, K. (1999) 'Relationship marketing teams: improving the utilization of customer relationship potentials through a high team design quality', *Industrial Marketing Management*, 28(5), 553–64.
Henderson, R. and Cockburn, I. (1994) 'Measuring competence? Exploring firm effects in pharmaceutical research', *Strategic Management Journal*, 15(2), 61–83.
Hite, J.M. (2003) 'Patterns of multidimensionality among embedded network ties: a typology of relational embeddedness in emerging entrepreneurial firms', *Strategic Organisation*, 1(1), 9–49.
Holm, B.D., Eriksson, K. and Johanson, J. (1996) 'Business networks and cooperations in international business relationships', *Journal of International Business Studies*, 27(5), 1033–53
Hsu, C.C. and Pereira, A. (2008) 'Internationalisation and performance: the moderating effects of organisational learning', *The International Journal of Management Science*, 36(2), 188–205.
Inkpen, A. and Crossan, M.M. (1995) 'Believing is seeing: joint ventures and organisation learning', *Journal of Management Studies*, 32(5), 595–618.
Jackson, S.E., Brett, J.F., Sessa, V.I., Cooper, D.M., Julin, J.A. and Peyronnin, K. (1991) 'Some differences make a difference: individual dissimilarity and group heterogeneity as correlates of recruitment, promotions and turnover', *Journal of Applied Psychology*, 76(5), 675–89.
Jarillo, J.C. (1988) 'On strategic networks', *Strategic Management Journal*, 9(1), 31–41.
Johanson, J. and Vahlne, J.E. (1977) 'The internationalisation process of the firm – a model of knowledge development and increasing foreign commitments', *Journal of International Business Studies*, 8(1), 23–32.
Jones, M.V. and Coviello, N. (2005) 'Internationalisation: conceptualizing and entrepreneurial process of behaviour in time', *Journal of International Business Studies*, 36(3), 284–303.
Jones, M.V. and Young, S. (2009) 'Does entry mode matter: reviewing current themes and perspectives', in Jones et al. (eds) *Internationalisation, Entrepreneurship and the Smaller Firm* (UK: Edward Elgar Publishing Ltd).
Kale, P., Dyer, J.H. and Singh, H. (2002) 'Alliance capability, stock market response, and long term alliance success: the role of the alliance function', *Strategic Management Journal*, 23(8), 747–67.
Kale, P., Singh, H. and Perlmutter, H. (2000) 'Learning and protection of proprietary assets in strategic alliances: building relational capital', *Strategic Management Journal*, 21(3), 217–37.
Kanter, R. (1994) 'Collaborative advantage: the art of alliances', *Harvard Business Review*, 72(4), 96–108.

Kapasuwan, S. (2006) 'Effects of networks on organisational learning capability and firm performance' paper presented at the *Academy of International Business Annual Conference*, Bejing, China, June 23–6.

Katsikeas, C.S., Leonidou, L. and Morgan, N. (2000) 'Firm level export performance assessment: review, evaluation and development', *Academy of Marketing Science*, 28(4), 493–511.

Katsikeas, C.S., Skarmeas, D. and Bello, D.C. (2009) 'Developing successful trust-based international exchange relationships', *Journal of International Business Studies*, 40(1), 132–55.

Kenny, B. and Sheikh, H. (2000) 'Foreign language use and training: a study of US firms operating in the mid west region of Ireland', *The Journal of Language for International Business*, 11(1), 41–57.

Kogut, B. (1988) 'Joint ventures: theoretical and empirical perspectives', *Strategic Management Journal*, 9(4), 319–22.

Kranenburg, H.V., Pennings, J., Dalzotto, C. and Hagedoorn, J. (2008) 'Innovation through external sourcing activities: an overview of major trends and patterns of telecommunications service providers industry' paper presented at the *Academy of International Business annual conference on Knowledge Development and Exchange in International Business Networks*, Milan, 30 June–2 July.

Landis, R.S., Beal, D.J. and Tesluk, P.E. (2000) 'A comparison of approaches to forming composite measures in structural equations modeling', *Organisational Research Methods*, 3(2), 186–207.

Lane, P.J. and Koka, B.R. (2006) 'The reification of absorptive capacity: a critical review and rejuvenation of the construct', *Academy of Management Review*, 31(4), 833–63.

Lane, P.J. and Lubatkin, M. (1998) 'Relative absorptive capacity and inter-organisational learning', *Strategic Management Journal*, 19(5), 461–77.

Lavie, D. (2007) 'Alliance portfolios and firm performance: a study of value creation and appropriation in the US software industry', *Strategic Management Journal*, 28(12), 1187–212.

Li, J. and Guisinger, S. (1991) 'Comparative business failures of foreign controlled firms in the United States', *Journal of International Business Studies*, 22(2), 209–24.

Li, P.C. and Lin, B.W. (2006) 'Building global logistics competence with Chinese OEM suppliers', *Technology in Society*, 28(3), 333–48.

Lieberman, M.B., Lau, L.J. and Williams, M.D. (1990) 'Firm-level productivity and management influence: a comparison of US and Japanese automobile producers', *Management Science*, 36(10), 1193–215.

Loane, S. and Bell, J. (2006) 'Rapid internationalisation among entrepreneurial firms in Australia, Canada, Ireland and New Zealand – an extension to the network approach', *International Marketing Review*, 23(4), 467–85.

Loane, S. and Bell, J. (2009) 'Clients as hidden resources in rapid internationalisation', in Jones et al. (eds) *Internationalisation, Entrepreneurship and the Smaller Firm* (UK: Edgar Elgar Publishing Ltd).

Loane, S., Bell, J. and Cunningham, I. (2009) ' New wave globals: the dynamic capabilities of digital content firms' paper presented at the *Academy of International Business UK and Ireland Chapter*, 36th Annual Conference, University of Glasgow, Scotland, 1–3 April.

Lorenzoni, G. and Lipparini, A. (1999) 'The leveraging of inter-firm relationships as a distinctive organizational capability: a longitudinal study', *Strategic Management Journal*, 20(4), 317–36.

Loxton, R. and Weerawardena, J. (2006) 'Examining the role of networking capability in small and medium size firm internationalisation' paper presented at *the Academy of International Business Annual Conference*, Bejing, China, 23–6 June.

Lyles, M.A., Sulaiman, M., Barden, J.Q. and Kechik, A. (1999) 'Factors affecting international joint venture performance: a study of Malaysian joint ventures', *Journal of Asian Studies*, 15(2), 1–20.

Madhok, A. (1995) 'Opportunism and trust in joint venture relationships: an exploratory study and model', *Scandinavian Journal of Management*, 11(1), 57–74.

Marshall, G.W., Goebel, D.J and Moncrief, W.C. (2003) 'Hiring for success at the buyer-seller interface', *Journal of Business Research*, 56(4), 247–55.
Mc Evily, B. and Zaheer, A. (1999) 'Bridging ties: a source of heterogeneity in competitive capabilities', *Strategic Management Journal*, 20(12), 1133–56.
Mc Naughton, R.B. and Bell, J. (2001) 'Competing from the periphery: export development through hard business network programmes', *Irish Marketing Review*, 14(1), 43–55.
Mohr, J. and Nevin, J.R. (1990) 'Communication strategies in marketing channels: a theoretical perspective', *Journal of Marketing*, 54(4), 36–51.
Mohr, J. and Spekman, R. (1994) 'Characteristics of partnership success', *Strategic Management Journal*, 15(2), 135–52.
Moller, K. and Svahn, S. (2006) 'Role of knowledge in value creation in business nets', *Journal of Management* Studies, 43(5), 985–1007.
Moller, K. and Törronen, P. (2003) 'Business suppliers' value creation potential: a capability based analysis', *Industrial Marketing Management*, 32(2), 109–18.
Moran, P. (2005) 'Structural versus relational embeddedness: social capital and managerial performance', *Strategic Management Journal*, 26(12), 1129–51.
Mowery, D.C., Oxley, J.E. and Silverman, B.S. (1996) 'Strategic alliances and inter-firm knowledge transfer', *Strategic Management Journal*, 17(2), 77–92.
Nahapiet, G. and Ghoshal, S. (1998) 'Social capital, intellectual capital and the organisation advantage', *Academy of Management Review*, 38(2), 242–66.
Narver, J.C. and Slater, S.F. (1990) 'The effect of a market orientation on business profitability', *Journal of Marketing*, 54(4), 20–35.
Overby, J.W. and Min, S. (2001) 'International supply chain management in an internet environment: a network oriented approach to internationalisation', *International Marketing Review*, 18(4), 392–420.
Penrose, E.T. (1959) *The Theory of the Growth of the Firm* (Oxford: Basil Blackwell).
Ping, R.A. (2007) 'Is there any way to improve average variance extracted in a latent variable?', http://home.at.net/~rpingjr/LowAVE.doc. (accessed 24/10/08).
Podolny, J.M. (2001) 'Networks as the pipes and prisms of the market', *American Journal of Sociology*, 107(1), 33–60.
Powell, W.W. (1990) 'Neither market nor hierarchy: network forms of organisation', *Research in Organisational Behaviour*, 12, 295–336.
Powell, W.W., Kogut, K.W. and Smith-Doerr, L. (1996) 'Inter-organisational collaboration and the locus of innovation: networks of learning', *Administrative Science Quarterly*, 41(1), 116–45.
Prahalad, C.K. and Hamel, G. (1990) 'The core competence of the corporation', *Harvard Business Review*, 68(3), 79–91.
Pruitt, D.G. (1981) *Negotiating Behaviour* (New York: Academic Press).
Reid, S.D. (1983) 'Firm internationalisation, transaction costs and strategic choice', *International Marketing Review*, 1(2), 44–56.
Rindfleisch, A. and Moorman, C. (2001) 'The acquisition and utilization of information in new product alliances: a strength of tie perspective', *Journal of Marketing*, 65(2), 1–19.
Ritter, T. and Gemünden, H.G. (2003) 'Network competence: its impact on innovation success and its antecedents', *Journal of Business Research*, 56(9), 745–755.
Rousseau, D.M., Sitkin, S.B., Burt, R.S. and Camerer, C. (1998) 'Not so different after all: a cross discipline view of trust', *Academy of Management Review*, 23(3), 393–404.
Rowley, T.J. (1997) 'Moving beyond dyadic ties: a network theory of stakeholder influences', *Academy of Management Review*, 22(4), 887–910.
Rowley, T.J., Behrens, D. and Krackhardt, D. (2000) 'Redundant governance structures: an analysis of structural and relational embeddedness in the steel and semiconductor industries', *Strategic Management Journal*, 21(3), 369–86.
Rugman, A. and D'Cruz, J.R. (2000) *Multinationals as Flagship Firms; Regional Business Networks* (New York: Oxford University Press).

Sarkar, M.B., Echambadi, R., Cavusgil, S.T. and Aulakh, P.S. (2001) 'The influence of complementarity, compatibility, and relationship capital on alliance performance', *Journal of the Academy of Marketing Science*, 29(4), 358–73.
Selnes, F. and Sallis, J. (2003) 'Promoting relationship learning', *Journal of Marketing*, 67(3), 80–95.
Shoham, A. (1998) 'Export performance: a conceptualization and empirical assessment', *Journal of International Marketing*, 6(3), 53–73.
Simmonds, P.G. (1990) 'The combined diversification breadth and mode dimensions and the performance of large diversified firms', *Strategic Management Journal*, 11(5), 399–410.
Sinkula, J.M., Baker, W.E. and Noordewier, T.A. (1997) 'A framework for market based organisational learning: linking values, knowledge and behaviour', *Journal of the Academy of Marketing Science*, 25(4), 305–18.
Stuart, T.E. (2000) 'Inter-organisational alliances and the performance of firms: a study of growth and innovation rates in a high-technology industry', *Strategic Management Journal*, 21(8), 791–811.
Sullivan-Mort, G. and Weerawardena, J. (2006) 'Networking capability and international entrepreneurship: how networks function in Australian born global firms', *International Marketing Review*, 23(5), 549–72.
Teece, D.J. (1987) 'Profiting from technological innovation: implications for integration, collaboration, licensing and public policy', in D.J. Teece (ed.) *The Competitive Challenge: Strategies for Industrial Innovation and Renewal*, 185–219 (Cambridge MA: Ballinger).
Teece, D.J. and Pisano, G. (1994) 'The dynamic capabilities of firms: an introduction', *Industrial and Corporate Change*, 3(3), 537–56.
Teece, D.J., Pisano, G. and Shuen, A. (1997) 'Dynamic capabilities and strategic management', *Strategic Management Journal*, 18(7), 341–54.
Tolstoy, D. and Agndal, H. (2010) 'Network resource combinations in international venturing of small biotech firms', *Technovation*, 30(1), 24–36.
Uzzi, B. (1997) 'Social structure and competition in inter-firm networks: the paradox of embeddedness', *Administrative Science Quarterly*, 42(1), 35–67.
Van de Van, A.H. and Engleman, R.M. (2004) 'Event and outcome driven explanations of entrepreneurship', *Journal of Business Venturing*, 19(3), 343–58.
Walter, A., Auer, M. and Ritter, T. (2006) 'The impact of network capabilities and entrepreneurial orientation on university spin off performance', *Journal of Business Venturing*, 21(4), 541–67.
Weerawardena, J. and Loxton, R. (2006) 'Examining the role of networking capability in small and medium size firm internationalisation', paper presented at *the Academy of International Business Annual Conference*, Bejing, China, June 23–6.
Weerawardena, J., Mort, G.S., Liesch, P.W. and Knight, G. (2007) 'Conceptualizing accelerated internationalization in the born global firm: a dynamic capabilities perspective', *Journal of World Business*, 42(3), 294–306.
Werner, S. (2002) 'Recent developments in international management research: a review of 20 top management journals', *Journal of Management*, 28(3), 277–305.
Wernerfelt, B. (1984) 'A resource-based view of the firm', *Strategic Management Journal*, 5(2), 171–80.
Westhead, P., Wright, M. and Ucbasaran, D. (2001) 'Internationalisation of new and small firms: a resource-based view', Journal *of Business Venturing*, 16(4), 333–58.
Wilson, D.T. (1995) 'An integrated model of buyer-seller relationships', *Journal of the Academy of Marketing Science*, 23(4), 335–45.
Wincent, J. (2005) 'Does size matter? A study of firm behaviour and outcomes in strategic SME networks', *Journal of Small Business and Enterprise Development*, 12(3), 437–53.
Woodcock, P.C., Beamish, P.W. and Makino, S. (1994) 'Ownership-based entry mode strategies and international performance', *Journal of International Business Studies*, 25(2), 253–73.

Yli-Renko, H., Autio, E. and Tontti, V. (2002) 'Social capital, knowledge and the international growth of technology based new ventures', *International Business Review*, 11(3), 279–304.

Zaheer, A., McEvily, B. and Perrone, V. (1998) 'Does trust matter? Exploring the effects of inter-organisational and interpersonal trust on performance', *Organisation Science*, 9(2), 141–59.

Zhang, C., Cavusgil, T.S. and Roath, A.S. (2003) 'Manufacturer governance of foreign distributor relationships: do relational norms enhance competitiveness in the export market?', *Journal of International Business Studies*, 34(6), 550–66.

17
The Link between Born Global Growth, Network Evolution and Firm Performance: A Theoretical Framework

Fabian Sepulveda and Mika Gabrielsson

Introduction

Born globals (BGs) typically face liabilities of smallness, newness and foreignness (Alvarez and Barney, 2001; Freeman et al., 2006; Hite and Hesterly, 2001; Knight and Cavusgil, 2004; Sharma and Blomstermo, 2003). To meet such challenges, BGs commonly turn to their networks in pursuit of rapid internationalization and fast growth (Coviello and Munro, 1995; Oviatt and McDougall, 1994). At the same time, a BG's original set of challenges combined with rapid entry into multiple countries suggest the firm's growth is characterized by turbulent change. To this end, entrepreneurship and international business research has shown that newly established firms go through a series of growth stages (Churchill and Lewis, 1983; Gabrielsson et al., 2008; Kazanjian, 1988; Larson and Starr, 1993), and from inception to maturation their needs, challenges and opportunities evolve. As BGs grow, they accumulate resources and develop their knowledge and capabilities (Coviello and Cox, 2006; Gabrielsson et al., 2008; Johanson and Vahlne, 2003) enabling them to take actions they originally were not able to take. Similarly, a BG's sustained reliance on its networks can be expected to evolve – but how? This situation prompts our main research question: how do BG networks evolve as the firm grows?

There is an abundance of research on networks in the literature. Entrepreneurship research has a rich history of network studies, and a number of these discuss how networks evolve through a domestic venture creation process (Greve and Salaff, 2003; Hoang and Antoncic, 2003; Larsson and Starr, 1993). However, their application to BGs is limited because most culminate at firm inception and they are purely domestic in context. Other studies have begun to investigate how networks evolve after venture formation (Coviello, 2006; Coviello and Cox, 2006; Hite and Hesterly, 2001; Zhou et al., 2007). However, these are scarce, typically exclude mature firms, often focus on a single industry and rarely place the network itself as the focus of analysis (Coviello, 2006). Moreover, they commonly overlook the evolution of content (i.e. the type of network exchanges) as

BGs grow. This is problematic because, as networks scholars have proposed, finer-grained research about network content could lead to richer insights on network evolution, international expansion decisions, resource acquisition, new product development (Coviello, 2006) and about a network's link to firm performance (Coviello, 2006; Coviello and Cox, 2006; Hite and Hesterly, 2001; Hoang and Antoncic, 2003). Although BGs are frequently labelled as 'entrepreneurial', little is known about the relation between a BG's entrepreneurial behaviour and its networks, which if explored could yield valuable insights about how opportunistically BGs employ their networks. As a result, extant literature does not clarify whether BGs continue to utilize their networks in the same capacity as when they started operations, or how the structure and content of networks transcend as firms grow. In short, the evolution of BG networks is an area rich with research opportunity. This chapter aims to contribute to this research.

Based on the IMP group's networks approach and what we label the 'strategic networks' view, we analyse four elements of networks and tie them to BG performance: network content, structure, management and centrality. Our discussion leads to the proposal of a theoretical framework of BG network evolution and advances six propositions about the aforementioned network elements and firm performance.

In step with the globalization and regionalization theme of this book, our investigation searched for insights relating to 'regionalization versus globalization' arguments by Rugman (2003) and Rugman and Hodgetts (2001), as well as Buckley's (2009) 'global factory' discussion. On the one hand, Rugman's (2001, 2003) studies seem particularly relevant to the development of BG networks, especially if we were to ask: do BG networks truly develop globally, or simply regionally? Would global networks be relevant if the BG operates regionally and not globally? On the other hand, global networks may be a necessity when creating a 'global factory' (Buckley, 2009), depending on a firm's choices on the ownership (internalize vs. outsource) and location of its operations. Although our investigation focuses on areas other than those posed by the preceding questions, Rugman's and Buckley's arguments offer valuable opportunities for further research in BG network evolution.

This chapter aims to make theoretical contributions to international entrepreneurship studies, networks theory and BG entrepreneurs. Furthermore, the chapter answers calls for specific network research (Coviello, 2006; Coviello and Cox, 2006; Hoang and Antoncic, 2003) and forms the conceptual basis for future empirical studies.

Literature review

The unique nature of BGs has attracted significant academic interest as demonstrated by the increasing number of articles about these firms. Recent BG literature has contributed knowledge in internationalization speed and paths (Knight and Cavusgil, 2004; Madsen and Servais, 1997; Oviatt and McDougall, 1994; Rennie,

1993), knowledge acquisition and learning (Zahra et al., 2000), marketing strategies (Knight et al., 2004; Luostarinen and Gabrielsson, 2006), internationalization risk management (Shrader et al., 2000) and several other areas. Although much of this research has highlighted the importance of BG networks, only a small part has focused on BG networks themselves (Coviello, 2006). As a result, our knowledge about BG networks is still superficial, making it an area with ample research opportunities. In this section, we review academic literature about networks in two parts. First, we explore BG research related to networks, discuss key contributions and identify the gaps that position our study. Second, we discuss more general networks literature and highlight the most relevant issues as they relate to network evolution.

Born global networks

At inception, BGs tend to lack an adequate amount of resources and capabilities necessary for long-term survival and growth (Alvarez and Barney, 2001; Freeman et al., 2006; Knight and Cavusgil, 2004; Sharma and Blomstermo, 2003). To make up for these shortages, BGs rely on their networks for access to resources, knowledge and expertise (Oviatt and McDougall, 1994; Coviello and Cox, 2006; Coviello and Munro, 1995; Freeman et al., 2006). As these firms emerge from inception, they combine their own resources and capabilities with those of network players to better protect their survivability and growth (Håkansson and Snehota, 1995; Kazanjian, 1988). As a result, BGs acquire knowledge and experience and develop their capabilities further (Johanson and Vahlne, 2003; Naphiet and Ghoshal, 1998; Yli-Renko et al., 2002), enabling them to take actions they originally could not. In their growth path, BGs undergo a maturation process in which their networks may continue to play a fundamental role. Consequently, how do the networks themselves evolve as the firm grows from birth to maturity? After an extensive review of the BG literature, ten articles emerge as the most aligned with our research question by emphasizing both BGs and their networks. Table 17.1 provides a high-level overview of these articles' main focus.

There are three main contributions about BG networks that we have identified in our review. First, networks influence a BG's internationalization speed and processes, including market selection and entry mode (Andersson and Wictor, 2003; Coviello and Munro, 1995, 1997; Freeman et al., 2006; Oviatt and McDougall, 2005; Sharma and Blomstermo, 2003). Second, a BG's performance, particularly its growth, is influenced by its networks (Yli-Renko et al., 2002; Zhou et al., 2007). Third, BG networks are dynamic and are characterized by change across several network elements including structure, content, management and centrality (Coviello, 2006; Coviello and Cox, 2006; Coviello and Munro, 1995). While the individual contributions of the articles in Table 17.1 are significant and valuable, there are still other important areas about BGs that necessitate further investigation. One of these is a study of how BG networks evolve as the firm matures. To this end, we have discovered that little is known about the evolution of BG networks – especially as the firms mature. The lack of research is most evident in

Table 17.1 Focus areas of selected born globals literature

Main focus of studies (incorporating BG networks)	Coviello and Munro (1995)	Coviello and Munro (1997)	Yli-Renko et al. (2002)	Andersson and Wictor (2003)	Sharma and Blomstermo (2003)	Oviatt and McDougall (2005)	Coviello (2006)	Coviello and Cox (2006)	Freeman et al. (2006)	Zhou et al. (2007)
International market development	✓									
Internationalization patterns, behaviour and performance		✓		✓	✓	✓			✓	✓
Knowledge and social capital acquisition			✓				✓	✓		
Network evolution										

four particular areas: how a BG's *use* of its networks evolves as it matures; *what* elements of networks change; *how* network elements evolve; and *how* the evolution of these elements relates to the firm's performance.

Our review has revealed two main reasons for this scarcity of studies. First, the main focus of BG research seems to be on internationalization speed and processes (see Table 17.1). Second, of the few studies about BG networks, most tend to focus on single-type firms, and often overlook evolutionary aspects of the firm and its networks. Two notable exceptions are Coviello (2006) and Coviello and Cox (2006); however, as conceded by the authors, these studies are limited to software firms only, omit BGs at mature growth stages, and do not explore the relation between networks and firm performance (for which the authors suggest further research). As a result, the extant literature does not clarify if BGs continue to utilize their networks in the same capacity as when they started operations, or how the structure and content of networks transcend as firms grow. This chapter aims to contribute to this gap and in the process may yield important academic and managerial implications.

Networks approaches

The literature about networks seems to reveal two particular approaches as the most influential: the IMP group's tradition and the 'strategic networks' view. (Möller and Rajala (2007) refer to a wide variety of extant network approaches. However, they also compare two 'groups' of approaches similar to the ones in this chapter: the industrial network approach and the strategic management perspective). Both of these approaches have advanced an understanding of networks on the back of substantial empirical evidence. Although these approaches share the same position in many aspects about networks, they face significant differences in other areas. We discuss both traditions by comparing four well-known network dimensions: network structure, content, management and centrality – their evolution and their link to performance. More specifically, we assess each tradition's view on the underlying nature of network structure, the types of resources accessed and exchanged within networks, if and how networks are managed, how network positioning is enhanced, how networks evolve and how performance is linked to networks. Table 17.2 summarizes our comparison of both network views.

The IMP group's networks approach

In the IMP group's tradition, business networks are considered to be a collection of relationships between a firm's suppliers, buyers (Håkansson and Snehota, 1989, 1995) and may include business intermediaries (Easton, 1992). These relationships are made up of actors who interact with other network individuals through various *activities* that involve a dynamic exchange of resources (Håkansson and Snehota, 1995). The purpose and benefit of these relationships vary according to individual firms, dyads of firms or third party firms that are part of extended networks. There are three key reasons why firms seek network relationships. The first is 'complementarity' between organizations, which facilitates effective acquisition of resources; second is knowledge creation through the combination of existing

Table 17.2 Comparative summary of IMP and strategic networks views

Approach	Network nature and structure	Network content	Network management	Network centrality	Network evolution	Performance
IMP group	Clients, suppliers, and business intermediaries make up networks. Networks provide resource stability, variety and risk/uncertainty management	Characterized by resource 'complementarity', knowledge creation, and capability development	Networks cannot be proactively managed	Actors constantly seek to improve network position	Networks change constantly and change can be exogenous or endogenous	Performance strongly depends on management of dyadic relationships
Strategic networks	Networks can be made up of any interpersonal relationship; they are a source of strategic resources and may constitute a strategic competitive advantage themselves	Networks are a source of strategic resources, knowledge, and capabilities	Networks are to be proactively managed and developed	Centrality results from cumulative and proactive investments into relationships	Networks evolve to meet the changing needs of firms	Firms seek strategic value from networks that directly influences performance

knowledge and skills between firms (Håkansson and Snehota, 1995); and third is exploitation of network access to have a level of influence over other firms' resources in order to reduce uncertainty and improve stability (Easton, 1992). When these three elements are observed over an extended period of time, the evolving nature of networks becomes evident. Business networks are made up of relationships, and because these relationships are in a constant state of evolution, networks also constantly change (Håkansson and Snehota, 1989, 1995). That is because established well-functioning relationships are likely to be exploited for different purposes in different situations and between different subsets of network actors (Håkansson and Snehota, 1989, 1995). To this end, it can be argued that the content, strength and nature of relationships – and hence networks – are constantly changing as those involved interact.

In terms of network management, Håkansson and Snehota (1989) differ substantially from others' views in that they do not believe that networks can be proactively managed. Instead, they propose that the external environment, including networks, is beyond the control of the firm. This has three implications. First, business opportunities cannot be created or enacted, but only 'exploited' by adapting to the environment. Second, the firm must continuously adapt to its environment. Third, managing relationships (and hence networks) is difficult at best. Håkansson and Snehota base these claims on the following argument: reacting in relationships is more important than acting; reacting can only be guided by the historical behaviour of actors; and established organizational routines cannot be planned, which makes managing relationships problematic. Instead, those authors propose that organizational effectiveness is managed by 'framing the context rather than by designing (planning) a future pattern of activities' (p. 198). From this, we can infer that in the IMP group's view, network management is not proactive but rather reactionary or even passive.

On the relation between networks and performance, the IMP group adopts a strong view. Simply put, firm performance depends on its ability to handle network relationships. This dependency is not limited to the firm's economic performance but it also encompasses the firm's productivity, effectiveness competence, innovativeness and strategic mobility (Håkansson and Snehota, 1995). The main argument here is that these firm characteristics are not developed in isolation or within the firm, but rather they happen *in and because* of networks (Easton, 1992).

In terms of the evolution of networks, IMP scholars (Easton, 1992; Håkansson and Snehota, 1995; Halinen et al., 1999; Turnbull et al., 1996) believe it is constant. This is because the underlying relationships that make up networks are in a constant state of adaptation that results from the evolution of activities, actors and bonds. In this gradual, path-dependent, evolutionary process, network ties become stronger and more multiplexed as actor bonds adjust to changing needs; and the web of actors changes as learning and experience are acquired (Håkansson and Snehota, 1995). Network change can be both endogenous and exogenous (Håkansson and Snehota, 1995), and both evolutionary and revolutionary (Halinen et al., 1999) depending on the changing needs of the firm.

The strategic networks approach

In the strategic networks view, network relationships are made up of business, social and personal contacts. More specifically, networks can be created via any link between any individual (Hite and Hesterly, 2001; Jarillo, 1989; Larson and Starr, 1993; Zhou et al., 2007) that provides resources, knowledge or capabilities which influence the operation, direction and performance of the firm. These relationships can be made up of business contacts (clients, suppliers and intermediaries in the value chain), as well as social and personal contacts, including friends, family or ex-colleagues. This is markedly different from the IMP approach in that the IMP group tends to consider networks that are only made up of customers, suppliers or business intermediaries, as previously mentioned.

In terms of content and centrality, the strategic networks approach differs from that of the IMP group's in at least three ways. First, the strategic approach suggests firms seek to extract strategic value out of their networks (Larson and Starr, 1993; Hite and Hesterly, 2001) rather than simply achieve resource 'complementarity' (Håkansson and Snehota, 1995) as the IMP group implies. Second, strategic networks aim to develop competitive advantages for the firm rather than only create new knowledge. Third, both approaches suggest firms wish to improve their network positioning, but in the IMP approach firms do it to reduce uncertainty and improve stability (Easton, 1992), whereas strategic networks firms strive to gain some competitive advantage out of its networks (Gulati et al., 2000; Madhavan et al., 1998).

In the strategic networks approach, networks are to be proactively managed. Network management involves the international exploration, screening and selective use of network relationships (Larson and Starr, 1993). This is because firms – particularly small firms – need to identify the 'right contacts' with the 'right resources' at different stages of growth (Larson and Starr, 1993). In fact, gaining access to key networks is the first entrepreneurial problem (Jarillo, 1989), which suggests a strong inclination to manage networks proactively. To this end, proactive management enables a firm's ability to extract strategic advantages and value from networks and facilitates entrepreneurial action, including innovativeness and opportunity discovery and enactment. As such, networks are strategic resources that managers design and develop over time – that is, they purposefully evolve – in order to achieve their changing objectives (Madhavan et al., 1998).

As with the IMP approach, the strategic networks view also suggests there is a direct link between networks and firm performance. However, this relationship is more intentional in the latter approach in that firms seek strategic value from their networks to achieve superior levels of performance (Gulati et al., 2000; Hite and Hesterly, 2001; Yli-Renko et al., 2002). The relation between networks and performance seems to be moderated by the firm's acquisition and continuous development of competitive advantages – which may only be obtained through network membership – and which facilitate a firm's unique performance (Dyer, 1996; Yli-Renko and Autio, 1998).

The strategic view also asserts that networks evolve. In this respect, networks appear to co-evolve with the resource needs of firms; that is, resource exchanges appear to become more strategic in nature as the firm grows. Where firms may originally rely on networks for basic survival support, they may later occupy a strong network position that makes the network itself a strategic asset (Gulati et al., 2000). However, in terms of more specific network evolution, there appear to be some areas of disagreement within the strategic networks view about the evolution of network elements such as size, density and management. For example, while some authors claim that network structure will decrease in size and gain in strength (Larson and Starr, 1993), others believe that weaker ties will increase with network size (Hite and Hesterly, 2001). The same two studies take contrasting views on the evolution of network management where firms will emerge from an identity-based (passive) to a calculative approach (Hite and Hesterly, 2001) or they will be purely calculative (Larson and Starr, 1993).

Based on our review, we believe that both network views are complementary despite some of their differences. Consequently, our study of BG networks is positioned as follows. BG networks can be made up of any inter-personal relationship including clients, suppliers, business intermediaries, social contacts, friends and family. We make no distinction between personal or business contacts, provided that network actors make some contribution to the firm in terms of resources, knowledge or capabilities. We highlight that not all of an entrepreneur's relationships make up his or her networks, but rather, only those actors who can make an actual contribution to the organization.

Conceptual framework and proposition development

Our conceptual framework is illustrated in Figure 17.1. Briefly, the framework proposes that as a BG grows, its internal resources development and entrepreneurial behaviour influence the evolution of its networks. More specifically, internal resource maturation prompts changes in a BG's network content, structure and centrality. Similarly, a BG's entrepreneurial behaviour influences how it manages network relationships. These developments generate 'network-enabled' benefits that have a positive effect on the firm's performance. More specifically, networks are a source of opportunities and competitive advantages, and are essential in risk management.

The evolution of born global internal resources

As we have mentioned, BGs have an insufficient amount of basic resources, knowledge and capabilities *inter alia* to survive on their own during the early stages. In this respect, *basic resources* refer to assets needed for a firm's basic operation, such as plant, equipment, offices, funds (Coviello and Cox, 2006); *knowledge* refers to internationalization processes, local market knowledge, institutional knowledge, (Sharma and Blomstermo, 2003), know-how (Yli-Renko et al., 2002); and *capabilities* refer to a firm's ability to learn, share and apply new knowledge towards specific firm actions such as organizational planning, R&D, competitive

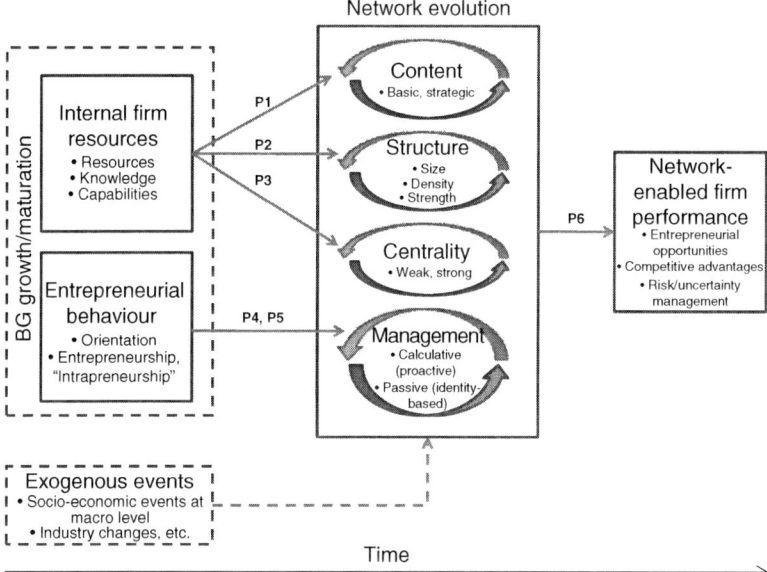

Figure 17.1 Conceptual framework of BG network evolution and proposition development
Note: P1: The maturation of a BG's internal resources shifts the nature of the content it seeks from its networks from basic to strategic.
P2: The evolution of a firm's internal resource needs prompt changes and adaptations in network structure in terms of size, density and strength in order to satisfy those needs.
P3: The maturation of internal resources enhances a BG's network centrality.
P4: The entrepreneurial behaviour of the firm will prompt it to adopt both a passive (identity-based) and calculative approach to network management, although a calculative approach will dominate.
P5: Changes in a BG's entrepreneurial behaviour will influence changes in the management of its networks.

positioning, strategic maneuvering (Gulati et al., 2000). With this understanding of resources, extant studies suggest that in the early stages, BGs typically lack financing (Kazanjian, 1988), organizational resources (Coviello and Cox, 2006), internationalization support (Freeman et al., 2006; Harris and Wheeler, 2005; Oviatt and McDougall, 1994) and other basic resources (Gabrielsson et al., 2008; Kazanjian, 1988; Larson and Starr, 1993) for which they rely on networks. However, these resource needs may evolve as BGs accumulate resources, knowledge and experience.

As a BG develops in its various international markets, it accumulates knowledge and experience from direct operations (Johanson and Vahlne, 2003) and from network partners (Harris and Wheeler, 2005; Yli-Renko et al., 2002). The firm progressively internalizes some of this knowledge (Harris and Wheeler, 2005), develops its internal capabilities (Yli-Renko et al., 2002) and accumulates its own basic resources, while still satisfying remaining needs via networks (Coviello and Cox, 2006). Consequently, by the time BGs become well-established firms, they possess a bank of internal resources (Coviello and Cox, 2006; Gabrielsson et al., 2008), significant operational knowledge (Johanson and Vahlne, 2003) and have likely achieved a reputable level of market acceptance (Hite and Hesterly, 2001).

In other words, a mature firm has the resources, knowledge and experience that enable it to take actions it previously was not able to take. As a result, it could be argued that the content a BG seeks in its networks co-evolves with the firm's maturation. For example, the original need to secure survival-related resources is often replaced by the exploitation of strategic opportunities within networks, such as market positioning (Gabrielsson et al., 2008; Kazanjian, 1988), next generation product development (Kazanjian, 1988) and enhancement of strategic network relationships (Gabrielsson et al., 2008; Larson and Starr, 1993). This evolution of internal resources finds empirical support in studies by Coviello and Cox (2006) and Kazanjian (1988), which demonstrate that the network exchanges (i.e. content) of a newly incepted BG differ from those of a mature BG. That is, a mature BG's network exchanges appear more strategic than those of a newly incepted BG, as we explain next.

The strategic management literature states that for resources or competitive advantages to be 'strategic' they must be rare, valuable, inimitable and difficult to substitute (Barney, 1991). From this resource-based view, network exchanges during a firm's initial stages can arguably be disqualified as strategic, for three reasons. First, because the type of support rendered by the network may not yet constitute or translate into a competitive advantage for the firm. That is because early network exchanges are organizational resources (Coviello, 2006) typically intended to alleviate a BG's liabilities of newness, smallness and foreignness, and those resources may not be rare or inimitable despite their value to the firm. Second, because the new firm's network relationships may not yet accrue to the BG as a competitive advantage since the age/maturity of such relationships tends to be relatively new. Even if the underlying relation between individuals is old and well-established, the relation between the firm and its network – in the capacity of a new business – is as new as the firm itself. At such early stages, most dyadic benefits are yet to be proven, and mutuality, trust and interdependence (Håkansson and Snehota, 1995), typical of well-functioning network relationships, may need further development. Third, a BG's network centrality may not yet be clearly established, possibly inhibiting the firm's influence over network resources (Hite and Hesterly, 2001; Johanson and Mattsson, 1988, 1992). Moreover, if the BG's network includes partnerships with large firms, it may risk being exploited if the relationship is unduly asymmetrical (Alvarez and Barney, 2001). Based on these observations, network exchanges in a new firm's early life are difficult to qualify as strategic because, although they are highly valuable, they seem to be basic, imitable and feasibly substituted.

At the other end of the spectrum, the type of support a mature BG seeks from its networks appears to be of a more strategic nature. In part, this is explained by the BG's accumulation and development of internal resources combined with the emerging challenges typical of a mature firm. For example, a new BG often struggles to find funding, whereas a mature BG seeks sustainable profitability (Churchill and Lewis, 1983); a new BG may be concerned with initial product launch, while a mature BG may be focused on next generation product development (Kazanjian, 1988); a new BG may struggle to break into valuable networks, while a mature BG seeks improved centrality in its established networks (Larson and Starr, 1993); a new BG may be trying to establish a market position, while a mature BG seeks to maintain and strengthen it further (Gabrielsson et al., 2008; Kazanjian, 1988); a new BG often seeks rapid growth, whereas a mature BG strives for sustainable growth (Kazanjian, 1988). These examples help illustrate how a BG's support needs to evolve from basic to 'strategic' as it aims to strengthen something that is rare, valuable, inimitable and difficult to substitute – like market position or a next generation product. Furthermore, the co-creation or joint discovery of entrepreneurial opportunities (Harris and Wheeler, 2005; Hoang and Antoncic, 2003; Zhou et al., 2007) that emerge from novel resource combinations (Håkansson and Snehota, 1995) may influence the strategic nature of network exchanges. Based on the preceding arguments, we make our first proposition:

Proposition 1: *The maturation of a BG's internal resources shifts the nature of the content it seeks from its networks from basic to strategic.*

The evolution of born global networks

In addition to the evolution of network content, networks themselves are in a constant state of change (Håkansson and Snehota, 1995; Halinen et al., 1999). Such changes include size (Coviello, 2006; Greve and Salaff, 2003), tie density and strength (Hite and Hesterly, 2001; Larson and Starr, 1993), and management (Coviello, 2006; Hite and Hesterly, 2001). In this respect, network *size* refers to the total number of network actors that make up the underlying relationships; tie *density* refers to the content 'multiplexity' in relationships, in other words, the total number of resource ties firms have in a single dyad; and *strength* refers to the importance and level of influence any given relationship has on the firm (we address network management in the following section). Many changes across these elements result from network actors adapting to one another, and these changes may be intentional or evolutionary (Håkansson and Snehota, 1995; Halinen et al., 1999), implying that network evolution is largely stimulated by changes in the underlying relationships. On one hand, some network relationships strengthen, develop and become denser with time (Håkansson and Snehota, 1995; Larson and Starr, 1993), and because of this, those relationships constantly adapt to each other based on the evolving requirements of the relationship. In other words, their growing interdependency allows for network actors to jointly modify behaviour, processes and organizational routines in order to maximize the relationship's efficiency and mutual benefits (Håkansson and Snehota, 1995).

On the other hand, while some relationships develop, new ones emerge and old ones decay (Håkansson and Snehota, 1995), which we believe may be related to how well networks satisfy a BG's evolving needs given the firms' rapid internationalization and fast growth. To this end, network support must be timely to avoid losing first-mover advantages and to protect against imitation or substitution. Since the novelty typical of BG products or services is often a competitive advantage, there is a strong need to exploit it rapidly (Gabrielsson et al., 2008), which calls for timely network support. In certain instances, fast growth may prompt a rapid increase in the establishment of new, arm's-length relationships that provide the necessary support (Hite and Hesterly, 2001). At other times, it may trigger the culling of numerous relationships into a few, select, strong ones that offer multiple levels of support (Larson and Starr, 1993). As the BG approaches maturation, it may reach a point where a set of its network relationships limit or restrict further expansion (Gabrielsson et al., 2008; Håkansson and Snehota, 1995; Hoang and Antoncic, 2003). These relationships may include those with the BG's original founders (Churchill and Lewis, 1983) from which it needs to emerge or cut loose. Depending on the firm's level of accumulated resources, break-off may be particularly necessary if a BG's growth has been totally dependent on a relationship with a large MNC which later limits further expansion. This situation implies that BGs must have the 'right' contacts (Gabrielsson et al., 2008; Larson and Starr, 1993) at the right time, and suggests BGs develop, abandon or establish relationships continually in order to meet the rapid and evolving nature of its needs. We emphasize that these adaptations of network structure are prompted by an evolution of firm resources and needs. More specifically, the firm may need to have a certain level of accumulated knowledge, experience and capabilities in order to restructure its networks and achieve higher degrees of independence. To this end, we agree with Halinen et al., (1999) who propose that changes in the network will be both evolutionary and revolutionary in different situations. From the preceding line of argumentation, we make our second proposition:

Proposition 2: *The evolution of a firm's internal resource needs prompts changes and adaptations in network structure in terms of size, density and strength in order to satisfy those needs.*

The accumulation of resources combined with the continued growth and development of network relationships is likely to give a BG greater legitimacy and reputation, making it more attractive to new and more influential network partners (Hite and Hesterly, 2001). This may be particularly true if the firm proactively manages its networks to attract the attention of new network players. Our emphasis here is on the evolution of internal resources in that as a firm grows and accumulates knowledge, capabilities and expertise, its ability to conduct business better and more successfully improves, thus making it more attractive as a partner to other firms. In turn, this situation may improve a BG's network centrality and therefore its ability to influence and control network resources. As a result we propose,

Proposition 3: *The maturation of internal resources enhances a BG's network centrality.*

Entrepreneurial behaviour and networks

Entrepreneurially oriented firms are those that are proactive, innovative, risk-taking (Covin and Slevin, 1991; Lumpkin and Dess, 1996) and have dynamic capabilities (Zucchella and Scabini, 2007). A *proactive* firm has the capacity to anticipate and act on future needs and aggressively pursues opportunities; an *innovative* firm has a tendency to support new ideas, experimentation and new processes; *risk-taking* indicates the will to commit large amounts of resources despite a high potential for failure; and *dynamic capabilities* prompt a firm to adapt, integrate and reconfigure internal and external resources towards changing environments (Covin and Slevin, 1991; Zucchella and Scabini, 2007). Based on this understanding, BGs tend to have a strong entrepreneurial orientation (Knight and Cavusgil, 2004; Lumpkin and Dess, 1996; Oviatt and McDougall, 1994) that seems to have an influence on its actions and strategies, and on the way it manages networks.

Entrepreneurial firms are very proactive in their search for growth (Jarillo, 1989). They creatively overcome resource constraints (Coviello and Munro, 1995, 1997; Freeman et al., 2006), create innovative products and services (Gabrielsson et al., 2008) and continually search for the 'right network contacts' (Larson and Starr, 1993). In addition, BGs often remain alert for entrepreneurial opportunities that may emerge from their networks (Harris and Wheeler, 2005; Hoang and Antoncic, 2003; Zhou et al., 2007). With such a level of 'proactiveness', we believe BGs will be very calculative in their network management, meaning that they will proactively seek out, develop or diminish relationships in order to satisfy the firms' evolving needs and objectives (Hite and Hesterly, 2001). This view is supported in Greve and Salaff (2003), who suggest network contacts are sought and selected based on available resources and commitments, and in Sharma and Blomstermo (2003), who showed that BGs proactively seek network partners to enter new markets. In a related vein, we believe an entrepreneurial BG will proactively manage its networks as it actively seeks to renew its resources, knowledge and capabilities to continually adapt to changing market conditions. This happens because a BG's original innovation may prove fundamental in bringing the firm into the global market, but as competitors emerge, products decline and markets mature, the firm needs to continuously renew its opportunities and competitive advantages in order to grow (Zucchella and Scabini, 2007), let alone survive. A company needs a unique combination of resources and capabilities to profit from a competitive advantage (Barney, 1991; Harms et al., 2009), and entrepreneurship theory asserts that to remain 'unique', this combination needs to be constantly renewed. This contributes to the firm's 'dynamic capabilities'.

In addition, the concept of 'windows of opportunity' suggests there are often waves of limited periods during which the fit between key requirements of a market (i.e. entrepreneurial opportunities) and the particular resources and competencies of a firm competing in that market are at an optimum (Harms et al., 2009). As a result, a BG's entrepreneurial behaviour will determine both its ability to capitalize on those windows of opportunities and the network support it requires to do so. We believe this situation will encourage the firm to adopt a calculative approach to network management. That said, as the organization grows, its approach to network management may shift for a number of reasons: its existing networks may already provide a sufficient level of support for acceptable performance (Larson and Starr, 1993); the firm may already occupy a strong position in its network, reducing the need for calculative network management; or the combination of fast growth and limited human resources may restrict the time and ability of the firm to proactively manage networks. As a result, a BG may shift towards a more passive or 'identity-based' (Hite and Hesterly, 2001) approach in which relationships are path-dependent and evolve naturally with little intentional management. At the same time, networks can also limit a BG's access to new resources, knowledge and capabilities (Gabrielsson et al., 2008; Håkansson and Snehota, 1995; Hoang and Antoncic, 2003) including founding entrepreneurs who may be unwilling to loosen their grip on control (Churchill and Lewis, 1983) at critical growth stages. Under these conditions, we believe that BGs will enact a calculative approach. From this line of argumentation, we agree with Coviello (2006) in that network management will be both calculative and passive; however, we believe a calculative approach will be dominant:

Proposition 4: *The entrepreneurial behaviour of the firm will prompt it to adopt both a passive (identity-based) and calculative approach to network management, although a calculative approach will dominate.*

As a BG matures, its entrepreneurial orientation may evolve, causing changes to the way it manages networks. There are at least three ways entrepreneurial behaviour can change. First, the organizational structure of a BG develops and begins to resemble that of a larger firm. That is, formal structures, processes and governance systems begin to appear, which may introduce levels of bureaucracy and ossification that risk organizational inertia and the loss of dynamic capabilities and entrepreneurial activity (Churchill and Lewis, 1983). Second, the potential departure of the founding entrepreneur(s) may significantly change the firm's entrepreneurial orientation. This exit could be voluntary (planned exit, cash-out, start of new venture and so on) or forced. The latter case is common in organizations where the founding entrepreneurs resist sharing control, turn overly risk-averse, fail to delegate adequately or become complacent (Churchill and Lewis, 1983), hindering the firm's entrepreneurial continuum. Third, the firm may retain a strong entrepreneurial orientation, but as its organizational growth increases its behaviour may evolve from entrepreneurial to 'intrapreneurial' (Zucchella and Scabini, 2007). Clearly, each of these three scenarios could modify the way a firm manages networks as follows. Ossification and organizational inertia may significantly reduce the proactiveness of firms to develop network relationships. The voluntary or forced departure of founding entrepreneurs could potentially cut off significant parts of a BG's networks and may require the fostering of new relationships. An evolution towards intrapreneurship may involve 'localizing' teams to manage networks in different geographic or organizational units, which at a corporate level may largely diversify the way a firm manages its networks. From the preceding argument we propose:

Proposition 5: *Changes in a BG's entrepreneurial behaviour will influence changes in the management of its networks.*

The relation between BGs, networks and firm performance

Throughout this chapter we have discussed how networks provide resources and support to growing BGs. But we have yet to crystallize a link between network benefits and firm performance. For this purpose, we focus our discussion on what we view as three of the most important network-provided benefits besides the general provision of resources. These are access to entrepreneurial opportunities, creation and development of competitive advantages, and management of risk and uncertainty.

Networks are a valuable source of entrepreneurial opportunities (Harris and Wheeler, 2005; Hills et al., 1997; Koller, 1988; Singh, 2000). In a study of 65 entrepreneurs, Koller (1988) found that more than half of them obtained their original business idea from their networks. In a similar study about differences between 'networked' and 'solo' entrepreneurs, Hills et al. (1997) established that networked entrepreneurs found more opportunities than solo entrepreneurs. Furthermore, the opportunities found by networked entrepreneurs were more diverse in that they spanned across industries and were not necessarily related to the entrepreneur's industrial background. From a conceptual point of view, Singh (2000) stresses that entrepreneurship does not happen in a vacuum, and as such, opportunities are both found and developed in the context of networks. Similarly, Håkansson and Snehota (1995) state that network relationships have an effect on innovation in the use of resources, which in turn may lead to the discovery of previously unknown resource combinations and purposes, implying the emergence of new business opportunities. But how do opportunities link to firm performance? In our view, performance depends at least on two factors: first, the possession of a sustainable business opportunity; and second, the ability of the firm to bring it to fruition successfully. To this end, we have argued that networks commonly provide the first element of that combination and, needless to say, the greater number of opportunities, the greater the chances of the firm to commercialize any one of them. But as we have already mentioned, firms must have the ability to develop such opportunities into commercial success. Furthermore, firms need to have the ability to develop such an opportunity in a better way than competitors, so that in the long term they will be able to sustain their success. In short, they need to have competitive advantages – for which networks are also fundamental.

Networks have been shown to be a source of competitive advantages (Gulati et al., 2000). First, networks offer access to privileged information, knowledge and 'social capital' (Naphiet and Ghoshal, 1998; Yli-Renko et al., 2002) that is difficult to obtain in isolation, particularly if a BG seeks membership in local or industrial clusters (Yli-Renko and Autio, 1998). Second, networks offer distinct capabilities like collective learning, resource complementarity, leveraging of dyadic core strengths and access to extended networks (Dyer and Singh, 1998; Foss, 1999; Håkansson and Snehota, 1995; Harris and Wheeler, 2005), which isolated firms do not have. Third, network membership can be a competitive advantage (Gulati et al., 2000) because it restricts other firms from joining and offers benefits from reputational effects and referrals (Inkpen and Tsang, 2005; Naphiet and Ghoshal,

1998). From the preceding argument we can see how network-derived competitive advantages can position the firm for superior performance. To illustrate, consider Dyer's (1996) study, which established that the network-based competitive advantages of Japanese car makers enabled the firms to significantly outperform their American competitors. The study shows how the Japanese companies' competitive advantages emerged from their specialized network of suppliers and specifically linked them to quality, profitability, and other performance measures. In particular, the relationships of 'specialized' supplier networks entailed specific knowledge, required joint capabilities of specialized production, and required network membership. Based on this line of argumentation, we believe there is a clear link between networks, competitive advantages and firm performance.

Networks also facilitate the management of risk and uncertainty (Easton, 1992; Gulati et al., 2000; Zhou et al., 2007). As we have mentioned earlier, BGs not only face the typical risks of a startup (such as liabilities of newness and smallness) but they also face a slew of risks associated with foreign market operations. These risks include difficulties in enforcing international contracts, information asymmetry, geographical distance and assessing capabilities of foreign partners (Majkgård and Sharma, 1998). In this respect, networks help reduce risk and uncertainty by offering internationalization and foreign market knowledge and experience, improving the reliability of supply chains, facilitating foreign sales and marketing channels, and providing many other support functions (Easton, 1992; Hite and Hesterly, 2001; Turnbull et al., 1996). To illustrate the link between risk management and performance, consider a special case in Freeman et al. (2006). In their study of BG alliances, those authors demonstrate how a telecoms company was able to weather an industrial downturn, and managed to survive and prosper. Faced with the bursting of the dot-com bubble at the turn of the millennium, the case firm significantly diversified its product line and was able to survive by selling their new innovations to existing client networks. Clearly, networks are a valuable tool in risk and uncertainty management.

From the preceding discussion, we can see that networks are a source of opportunities and competitive advantages, and are fundamental in the management of risk and uncertainty. Moreover, we believe that these network benefits are resources in their own right, and that as networks evolve it is likely that the number of opportunities increases, competitive advantages strengthen and risk management improves. Regardless of this contention, the link between the three network benefits discussed and firm performance is difficult to dispute. As a result, we advance our last proposition:

Proposition 6: *Networks continually provide a BG with entrepreneurial opportunities, competitive advantages and risk/uncertainty management which are positively related to the firm's performance.*

In this section, we have discussed two main drivers of network evolution: the maturation of internal resources and entrepreneurial behaviour. We acknowledge that there are additional factors that have an influence on the evolution of networks, such as socio-political or macroeconomic events, and we agree that change is both endogenous and exogenous and may be influenced by events outside the control of the firm (Håkansson and Snehota, 1995; Halinen et al., 1999; Madhavan et al., 1998). However, we chose to focus only on internal resources and entrepreneurial behaviour for three main reasons. First, both of these can be either controlled or influenced by managers. In this regard, one of our aims was to contribute a conceptual framework that allows BG managers to pragmatically assess their use of networks at different points in their growth in order to capture as much strategic value as possible. Second, external elements such as socio-political or macroeconomic activity are largely outside the control or influence of management, and therefore provide few venues of immediate action by BG entrepreneurs. Third, they establish the conceptual basis for empirical research that will follow this study about the specific use of networks by growing BGs. We realize there is much value from further research into exogenous network change, but this falls outside our intended scope for this chapter.

Conclusion

Born global firms rely on their networks to overcome liabilities of smallness, newness and foreignness. As these firms grow, they continue to use their networks but appear to do so in different capacities. In part, this is due to the maturation of the firms' internal resources. More specifically, as BGs grow, they accumulate basic resources and develop knowledge and capabilities enabling the firms to take actions they originally were not able to take on their own. As a result, their basic needs, opportunities and challenges evolve and consequently we have proposed that networks also evolve. Taking support from the IMP group's approach and the strategic networks view, our argument is based on three dynamic processes that underlie a BG's growth: a BG's internal resources mature, causing changes in its network needs; a BG's entrepreneurial behaviour influences how it manages network relationships; BG networks adapt to the evolving needs of the firm.

We have also established a link between networks and BG performance. Our argument is based on the contention that networks are a source of entrepreneurial opportunities and competitive advantages, and are fundamental in the management of risk and uncertainty. We stated that these network benefits are resources in their own right, and that as networks evolve it is likely that the number of opportunities increases, competitive advantages strengthen and risk management improves, thus further enhancing the performance of the firm.

From a theoretical perspective, we believe our chapter makes four contributions. (1) It offers insights about the evolution of networks specifically for BG firms, hence addressing a shortage of studies in this area. (2) It establishes a relation between BG growth and the evolution of networks. Consequently, it builds on the studies of Coviello (2006) and Coviello and Cox (2006) by setting up a platform for future empirical studies that may include BGs at full maturity and from industries other than software services. (3) It establishes a link between a BG's networks and its performance, thus extending the work of the IMP group to include BGs. (4) It incorporates an introductory analysis of entrepreneurial behaviour, setting the stage for future studies about BG entrepreneurship. From a managerial point of view, our conceptual framework aims to help BG entrepreneurs extract strategic value from their networks. It may help entrepreneurs assess their use of networks in order to identify *what* network resources are needed, *when* they are needed and *how* they evolve, so they may concentrate their efforts to strategically develop their networks into a competitive advantage.

Our investigation also yielded insights relating to Rugman's (2001, 2003) regionalization versus globalization and Buckley's (2009) global factory arguments. On a preliminary view, our findings seemed to align with the arguments made by Rugman (2001, 2003) and Buckley (2009) in two ways. First, it appears that the development of BG networks most frequently starts domestically (see, e.g. Sharma and Bloomstermo, 2003) and later progresses outward regionally, thus aligning with Rugman's (2001) claim that regionalization is more common than globalization, even when applied to the network development of firms. Second, the international segmentation of a 'global factory's' (Buckley, 2009) operations seems to reinforce the firm's need to develop the necessary foreign networks around each operational segment – particularly to address the information costs and flexibility arguments raised by Buckley (2009). In both cases, empirical studies would be better suited to assess the previous observations, making these areas attractive research opportunities.

Acknowledgments

This research is part of the 'Born Globals – Growth Stages and Survival' cooperation project between the Helsinki School of Economics, the University of Vaasa and six companies. We would like to thank the financiers of the project: the LIITO-program of the Finnish Funding Agency for Technology and Innovation (Tekes), and the partner firms.

References

Alvarez, S.A. and Barney, J.B. (2001) 'How entrepreneurial firms can benefit from alliances with large partners', *Academy Management Executive*, 15(1), 139–48.

Andersson, S. and Wictor, I. (2003) 'Innovative internationalization in new firms: born globals – the Swedish case', *Journal of International Entrepreneurship*, 1(3), 249–76.

Barney, J. (1991) 'Firm resources and sustained competitive advantage', *Journal of Management*, 17(1), 99–120.

Buckley, P.J. (2009) 'The impact of the global factory on economic development', *Journal of World Business*, 44(2), 131–43.

Churchill, N.C. and Lewis, V.L. (1983) 'The five stages of small business growth', *Harvard Business Review*, 61(3), 30–50.

Coviello, N.E. (2006) 'The network dynamics of international new ventures', *Journal of International Business Studies*, 37(5), 713–31.

Coviello, N.E. and Cox, M.P. (2006) 'The resource dynamics of international new venture networks', *Journal of International Entrepreneurship*, 4(2/3), 113–32.

Coviello, N.E. and Munro, H.J. (1995) 'Growing the entrepreneurial firm: networking for international market development', *European Journal of Marketing*, 29(7), 49–61.

Coviello, N.E. and Munro, H.J. (1997) 'Network relationships and the internationalization process of small software firms', *International Business Review*, 6(4), 361–86.

Covin, J. and Slevin, D. (1991) 'A conceptual model of entrepreneurship as firm behavior', *Entrepreneurship Theory and Practice*, 4, 7–25.

Dyer, J.H. (1996) 'Specialized supplier networks as a source of competitive advantage: evidence from the auto industry', *Strategic Management Journal*, 17(4), 271–91.

Dyer, J. and Singh, H. (1998) 'The relational view: cooperative strategy and sources of interorganizational competitive advantage', *Academy of Management Review*, 22(4), 660–79.

Easton, G. (1992) 'Industrial networks: a review' in B. Alexsson and G. Easton (eds) *Industrial Networks: A New View of Reality*, 1–27 (London: Routledge).

Foss, N. (1999) 'Networks, capabilities, and competitive advantage', *Scandinavian Journal of Management*, 15(1), 1–15.

Freeman, S., Edwards, R. and Schroder, B. (2006) 'How smaller born–global firms use networks and alliances to overcome constraints to rapid internationalization', *Journal of International Marketing*, 14(3), 33–63.

Gabrielsson, M., Kirpalani, V.H.M., Dimitratos, P., Solberg, C.A. and Zucchella, A. (2008) 'Born globals: propositions to help advance the theory', *International Business Review*, 17(4), 385–401.

Greve, A. and Salaff, J.W. (2003) 'Social networks and entrepreneurship', *Entrepreneurship Theory and Practice*, 28(1), 1–22.

Gulati, R., Nohria, N. and Zaheer, A. (2000) 'Strategic Networks', *Strategic Management Journal*, 21(3), 203–15.

Halinen, A., Salmi, A. and Havila, V. (1999) 'From dyadic change to changing business networks: an analytical framework', *Journal of Management Studies*, 36(6), 779–94.

Harms, R., Schulz, A., Kraus, S. and Fink, M. (2009) 'The conceptualization of "opportunity" in strategic management research', *International Journal of Entrepreneurial Venturing*, 1(1), 57–71.

Harris, H. and Wheeler, C. (2005) 'Entrepreneurs' relationships for internationalization: functions, origins, and strategies', *International Business Review*, 14(2), 187–207.

Hills, G., Lumpkin, G.T. and Singh, R.P. (1997) 'Opportunity recognition: perceptions and behaviors of entrepreneurs', *Frontiers of Entrepreneurship Research*, 203–18, Babson College, Wellesley, MA.

Hite, J.M. and Hesterly, W.S. (2001) 'The evolution of firm networks: from emergence to early growth of the firm', *Strategic Management Journal*, 22(3), 275–86.

Hoang, H. and Antoncic, B. (2003) 'Network-based research in entrepreneurship: a critical view', *Journal of Business Venturing*, 18(2), 165–87.

Håkansson, H. and Snehota, I. (1989) 'No business is an island: the network concept of business strategy', *Scandinavian Journal of Management*, 5(3), 187–200.

Håkansson, H. and Snehota, I. (1995) *Developing Relationships in Business Networks* (London: Routledge).

Inkpen, A. and Tsang, E. (2005) 'Social capital, networks, and knowledge transfer', *Academy of Management Review*, 30(1), 146–65.

Jarillo, J.C. (1989) 'Entrepreneurship and growth: the strategic use of external resources', *Journal of Business Venturing*, 4(2), 133–47.

Johanson, J. and Mattsson, L.-G. (1988) 'Internationalization in industrial systems-a network approach', in N. Hood and J.-E. Vahlne (eds) *Strategies in Global Competition*, 87–314 (New York: Croom Helm).

Johanson, J. and Mattsson, L.-G. (1992) 'Network positions and strategic action – an analytical framework', in B. Axelsson and G. Easton (eds) *Industrial Networks: A New View of Reality*, 205–17 (London: Routledge).

Johanson, J. and Vahlne J.-E. (2003) 'Business relationship learning and commitment in the internationalization process', *Journal of International Entrepreneurship*, 1(1), 83–101.

Kazanjian, R. (1988) 'Relation of dominant problems to stages of growth in technology-based new ventures', *Academy of Management Journal*, 31(2), 257–79.

Knight, G.A. and Cavusgil, S.T. (2004) 'Innovation, organizational capabilities, and the born-global firm', *Journal of International Business Studies*, 35(2), 124–41.

Knight, G.A., Madsen, T.K. and Servais, P. (2004) 'An inquiry into born-global firms in Europe and the USA', *International Marketing Review*, 21(6), 645–65.
Koller, R.H. (1988) 'On the source of entrepreneurial ideas', *Frontiers of Entrepreneurship Research*, 78–85 (Wellesley, MA: Babson College).
Larson, A. and Starr, J.A. (1993) 'A network model of organization formation', *Entrepreneurship Theory and Practice*, 17(2), 5–15.
Lumpkin, G.T. and Dess, G.G. (1996) 'Clarifying the entrepreneurial orientation construct and linking it to performance', *The Academy of Management Review*, 21(1), 135–72.
Luostarinen, R. and Gabrielsson, M. (2006) 'Globalization and marketing strategies of born globals in SMOPECs', *Thunderbird International Business Review*, 48(6), 773–801.
Madhavan, R., Koka, B. and Prescott, J.E. (1998) 'Networks in transition: how industry events (re)shape inter-firm relationships', *Strategic Management Journal*, 19(5), 439–59.
Madsen, T.K. and Servais, P. (1997) 'The internationalization of born globals: an evolutionary process?', *International Business Review*, 6(6), 561–583.
Majkgård, D. and Sharma, D.D. (1998) 'Client-following and market-seeking strategies in the internationalization of service firms', *Journal of Business to Business Marketing*, 4(3), 1–41.
Möller, K. and Rajala, A. (2007) 'Rise of strategic nets – new modes of value creation', *Industrial Marketing Management*, 36(7), 895–908.
Naphiet, J. and Ghoshal, S. (1998) 'Social capital, intellectual capital and the organizational advantage', *Academy of Management Review*, 23(2), 242–66.
Oviatt, B.M. and McDougall, P.P. (1994) 'Toward a theory of international new ventures', *Journal of International Business Studies*, 25(1), 45–64.
Oviatt, B.M. and McDougall, P.P. (2005) 'Defining international entrepreneurship and modeling the speed of internationalization', *Entrepreneurship Theory and Practice*, 29(5), 537–53.
Rennie, M.W. (1993) 'Global competitiveness: born global', *The McKinsey Quarterly*, 4, 45–52.
Rugman, A. (2003) 'Regional strategy and the demise of globalization', *Journal of International Management*, 9(4), 409–17
Rugman, A. and Hodgetts, R. (2001) 'The end of global strategy', *European Management Journal*, 19(4), 333–43.
Sharma, D.D. and Blomstermo, A. (2003) 'The internationalization process of born globals: a network view', *International Business Review*, 12(6), 739–53.
Shrader, R.C., Oviatt, B.M. and McDougall, P.P. (2000) 'How new ventures exploit trade-offs among international risk factors: lessons for the accelerated internationalization of the 21st century', *The Academy of Management Journal*, 43(6), 1227–47.
Singh, R.P. (2000) *Entrepreneurial Opportunity Recognition through Social Networks* (London: Garland Publishing).
Turnbull, P., Ford, D. and Cunningham, M. (1996) 'Interaction, relationships and networks in business markets: an evolving perspective', *Journal of Business and Industrial Marketing*, 11(3/4), 44–62.
Yli-Renko, H. and Autio, E. (1998) 'The network embeddedness of new technology-based firms: developing a systemic evolution model', *Small Business Economics*, 11(3), 253–67.
Yli-Renko, H., Autio, E. and Tontti, V. (2002) 'Social capital, knowledge, and the international growth of the technology-based new firms', *International Business Review*, 11(3), 279–304.
Zahra, S.A., Ireland, D.R. and Hitt, M.A. (2000) 'International expansion by new venture firms: international diversity, mode of market entry, technological learning and performance', *Academy of Management Journal*, 43(5), 925–50.
Zhou, L., Wu, W.-P. and Luo, X. (2007) 'Internationalization and the performance of born-global SMEs: the mediating role of social networks', *Journal of International Business Studies*, 38(4), 673–90.
Zucchella, A. and Scabini, P. (2007) *International Entrepreneurship: Theoretical Foundations and Practices* (Hampshire, UK: Palgrave MacMillan).

Part VI
International Joint Ventures

18
Conceptual, Operational and Methodological Considerations in Studying the Trust–Performance Relation: A Critical Review of Empirical Research in International Strategic Alliances

Tahir Ali and Jorma Larimo

Introduction

To successfully grow and compete on intra-regional, bi-regional and global level, firms need to adopt cooperative behaviour through strategic alliances. The international business literature has observed the growing importance of strategic alliances (Beamish and Killing, 1997a, 1997b, 1997c; Contractor and Lorange, 2002; Reuer, 2004). International strategic alliances (ISAs) refer to inter-firm cooperative arrangements, whether based on equity or contract, that entail frequent interaction between autonomous firms based in different countries, for achieving the strategic objectives of the partner firms (Contractor and Lorange, 2002; Das and Teng, 2000). There are many types of strategic alliances, including horizontal alliances between competitors, vertical alliances between buyers and suppliers, and diagonal alliances between firms in different industries (Nooteboom, 1999).

In spite of ISAs' popularity, there is a consensus that the majority of these arrangements fail to achieve their set objectives, leading to premature dissolution (Kasuser and Shaw, 2004; Meschi and Riccio, 2008). In response to this unsatisfactory ISA performance, an increasing amount of contemporary research has stressed the importance of creating trust between ISA partners (Kauser and Shaw, 2004; Lin and Wang, 2008; Nielsen, 2007; Robson et al., 2008). The conceptualization and operationalization of trust and ISA performance and their internal links are therefore critical issues in IB research (Robson et al., 2008). Previous reviews have attempted to gain insights into the nature of this link. These include a review of the performance relevance of behavioural attributes in ISAs (Robson et al., 2006); and a review on nature, development, role and outcomes of inter-organizational trust (Zaheer and Harris, 2006). Nevertheless, neither of these reviews deals specifically with the performance effects of trust, and paradoxically lack comprehensive evaluations of the conceptualization and operationalization of trust. Further, they largely ignore the performance measures employed in empirical research on the performance effects of trust. There is a need to acquire a deeper grasp of the limited but growing body of empirical work, to understand and take stock of the current state of the field.

This chapter aims to provide a critical review of empirical research on the trust–performance relation in ISAs. An additional goal is to critically analyse the conceptualization and operationalization of core constructs of trust and performance along with the methodologies used, to direct future research and theory development. By addressing these objectives, the chapter offers a clear contribution to the present stock of knowledge on the performance effects of trust in international strategic alliances. Key aspects of our contribution are noteworthy. First, unlike previous reviews, we focus simultaneously on the conceptualization and operationalization of core constructs of trust and alliance performance along with the methodologies used in studying the trust–performance relation. Second, our critical review covers the previous and current empirical research on the trust–performance relation (1980–2009) to reflect the state of the art in this field of research. Third, to make the study comprehensive, we not only identify the performance effects of unidimensional trust, but also performance effects across different levels and dimensions of trust, geographical location and alliance type.

Characteristics of the reviewed studies

In order to provide a critical review of performance effects of trust, we searched for articles in journal databases (ABI\inform, Science Direct, EbscoHost, Emerald and Jstor) and in edited books (Arino and Reuer, 2006; Bachmann and Zaheer, 2005; Beamish and Killing, 1997a, 1997b, 1997c; Contractor and Lorange, 2002; Reuer, 2004) published between 1980 and 2009. We used the time frame 1980–2009 because the first published study on performance effects of trust in ISAs appeared in early 1980s (Simiar, 1983). This direct search was combined with a snowball approach based on references and citations to find further influential studies, leading to a total of 109 articles. We selected 29 empirical studies for deeper analysis on the basis of the following criteria. The study had to (a) be empirical in nature with analysis based on primary or secondary data; (b) examine the performance effects of trust; (c) exclusively focus on trust (in contrast to the vast number of studies treating trust as a broader part of relational capital); (d) examine trust between organizations as opposed to trust inside an organization; and (e) examine trust in ISAs as opposed to arm's length and full internalizing entry modes. Although all 29 studies meet these selection criteria, they differ considerably in their samples, methodologies and in the conceptualization and operationalization of trust in international cooperative agreements (ICAs) and international joint ventures (IJVs). Table 18.1 provides a summary of these studies' features.

Table 18.1 Sample location, relationship type, industries studied, data collection side, methodology and data analysis methods

Studies	Sample location	RE type	I	Data	Instrument, data collection side	Key informants	Final sample	Analysis method
Simiar (1983)	HMC: Foreign firms (DC) HSC: Iran	IJVs	M	P, C	Personal interviews. Both sides	Top managers (MI)	29	N.I
Mohr and Spekman (1994)	N.I	ICAs	S	P, C	MS (Q) + interviews. Dealers	Owner/managers (SI)	140 (RP 25%)	Multiple regression
Aulakh et al. (1996)	HMC: US HSC: Asia, EU, Central/South America	ICAs	M	P, C	MS (Q). US manufacturers	Upper managers (MI)	181 (RP 39.4%)	Multiple HR
Fey (1996)	HMC: Foreign firms (DC) HSC: Russia	IJVs	M	P, C	MS (Q) + interviews. IJV	General managers (SI)	34	Discriminant analysis
Inkpen and Currall (1997)	HMC: Japan HSC: NA	IJVs	S	P, C	MS (Q) + interviews. North American firms	Senior managers (SI)	35 (RP 28%)	OLS regression
Sako (1998)	HMC: EU, US, Japan HSC: N.I	ICAs	S	P, C	MS (Q). Suppliers from Japan, US, EU	Upper managers (SI)	1415 (675 US, RP 55%; 472 Japan, RP 30%; 268 EU, RP 17%)	CR, Order probit regression
Chen and Boggs (1998)	HMC: Foreign firms (DC) HSC: China	IJVs	N.I	P, C	MS (Q) + interviews. Chinese firms	IJV general managers (SI)	33 (RP 82.5%)	Multiple regression

317

Table 18.1 (Continued)

Studies	Sample location	RE type	I	Data	Instrument, data collection side	Key informants	Final sample	Analysis method
Ramaseshan and Loo (1998)	HMC: N.I HSC: Singapore	ICAs	M	P, C	MS (Q). Singaporean firms	Alliance managers (SI)	164 (RP 32%)	Multiple regression
Jennings et al. (2000)	HMC: US HSC: Australia	IJVs	S	P, L	Interviews (1992; 1995) + archival data. Both firms + IJV	Upper managers (MI)	One IJV	N.I
Lane et al. (2001)	HMC: Foreign firms (DC) HSC: Hungary	IJVs	M	P, L	MS (Q) (1993; 1996) + interviews. Hungarian firms	General managers (SI)	201 in 1993 and surviving 78 in 1996	Multiple regression
Luo (2001)	HMC: Foreign firms (DC) HSC: China	IJVs	N.I	P (for T), SE (for PM), C	MS (Q) + archival data + interviews. Both sides	IJV general managers (SI)	282 (RP 35.25%)	SEM, CR
Luo (2002)	HMC: Foreign firms (DC) HSC: China	IJVs	MF	P (for T), SE (for PM), C	MS (Q) + archival data + interviews. Both sides	IJV general managers (SI)	255 (RP 31.87%)	Multiple HR
Fryxell et al. (2002)	HMC: Japan, Germany, Canada, France HSC: US	IJVs	MF	P, C	MS (Q). Both sides (51 cases) + IJV	Upper managers (MI)	129 (RP 32 %)	SEM, CR
Gill and Butler (2003)	HMC: Japan HSC: UK, Malaysia	IJVs	S	P, C	Interviews. Both sides	Upper managers (MI)	2 IJVs	N.I
Selnes and Sallis (2003)	HMC: Scandinavia HSC: EU	ICAs	S	P, C	MS (Q) + interviews. Both sides	Upper managers (SI)	319 (RP 40%)	SEM, CR

Dyer and Chu (2003)	HMC: US, Japan, Korea HSC: US, Japan, Korea	ICAs	S	P, C	MS (Q) + interviews. Suppliers	Vice Presidents (SI)	344 (101 Japan, RP 68%; 135 US, RP 66%; 108 Korea, RP 55%)	CR, Multiple regression
Jap and Anderson (2003)	N.I	ICAs	M	P, L	MS (Q) + interviews. Both sides	N.I	300	SEM, CR, Multiple regression
Kauser and Shaw (2004)	HMC: UK HSC: US, EU, Japan	ISA (IJVs, ICAs)	S	P, C	MS (Q). UK firms	Managers. (SI)	114 (RP 25.3%)	Multiple regression
Krishnan et al. (2006)	HMC: 21 countries (DC) HSC: India	ISA (IJVs, ICAs)	M	P, C	MS (Q) + archival data + interviews. Indian firms	MDs/CEOs (SI)	126 (RP 18%)	CR, OLS regression
Voss et al. (2006)	HMC: US HSC: Japan	ICAs	M	P, C	Field Survey (Q) + interviews. Both sides	Senior managers (SI)	97 (RP 43%)	OLS regression
Brouthers and Bamossy (2006)	HMC: West Europe HSC: Romania, Hungary	IJVs	M	P, L	Interviews (1994; 1999). Both sides + IJV	MDs (MI)	8	N.I
Ng et al. (2007)	HMC: Hong Kong, US, Japan, Taiwan HSC: China	IJVs	MF	P, C	Field survey (Q). IJV + Chinese companies	Upper managers (SI)	298 IJVs, 178 Chinese parents	Multiple HR

Table 18.1 (Continued)

Studies	Sample location	RE type	I	Data	Instrument, data collection side	Key informants	Final sample	Analysis method
Nielsen (2007)	HMC: Denmark HSC: EU, NA and Asia	ISA (IJVs, ICAs)	MF	P, C	Web survey (Q) + interviews. Danish firms	MDs (SI)	120 (RP 33%)	CR, Multiple regression
Muthusamy et al. (2007)	HMC: US HSC: EU, India, China, Singapore, Malaysia	ISA (IJVs, ICAs)	M	P, C	MS (Q) + archival data + interviews. US firms	Alliance executives (N.I)	144 (RP 25.57%)	CR, Multiple regression
Robson et al. (2008)	HMC: US, Western Europe, Far East HSC: UK	ISA (IJVs, ICAs)	MF	P, C	Personal interviews. UK firms	Directors, managers (SI)	177 (RP 52%)	SEM, CR
Luo (2008)	HMC: US, EU, Japan HSC: China	ISA (IJVs, ICAs)	MF	P, C	MS (Q) + archival data + interviews. Both sides	CEOs (SI)	168	SEM, CR, Multiple HR
Lin and Wang (2008)	HMC: US, UK, Taiwan, Japan, Hong Kong HSC: China	IJVs	M	P, C	Field survey (Q). JV managers (Chinese + Asian + Western)	Top level managers (SI)	500 (China, 219; Western, 132; Asia, 149)	ANCOVA
Kwon (2008)	HMC: US, EU, Japan HSC: Korea	IJVs	N.I	P, C	MS (Q). Korean side	Upper managers (SI)	94 (RP 29.8%)	CR, OLS regression
Wilson and Brennan (2009)	HMC: UK HSC: China	IJVs	M	P, C	Interviews + archival data. UK firms	GMs (SI)	20	Content analysis

Notes: Home country (HMC); host country (HSC); relationship (RE); industry (I); single (S); multiple (M); manufacturing (MF); primary (P); cross-section (C); longitudinal (L); trust (T); performance (PM); secondary (SE); mail survey (MS); questionnaire (Q); single informant (SI); multiple informants (MI); response rate (RP); correlation (CR); hierarchical regression (HR); structural equation modeling (SEM); N.I (no information); North America (NA).

Fieldwork characteristics

Most of the studies disclosed their key countries or regions of ISA operations; only two did not (Jap and Anderson, 2003; Mohr and Spekman, 1994). Thirteen studies (45 per cent) were conducted on DC–DC (developed country–developed country) alliances, with a focus on the three regions of Asia, America and Europe (6 studies), two regions of Asia and America or Asia and Europe (5 studies), and within Europe (Selnes and Sallis, 2003). Fourteen studies (48 per cent) examined DC–LDC (developed country–less developed country) alliances, with focus on China (7), Hungary (2 studies), India, Russia, Romania and Iran (1 study each).

Twelve studies focused on multiple industries; a further eight focused on only one industry (e.g. automotive, computer or pharmaceutical); and six compiled manufacturing sector samples. Concerning the type of the alliance, 15 studies focused on IJVs exclusively, while the remaining 14 used samples that featured ICAs.

Samples, data collection and analysis methods

Study samples ranged from one to 1,415 alliances, with an average sample of 197 cases. Ten studies used a relatively small sample (< 100 cases), whereas in a great majority (19 of 29 studies) the sample size exceeds 100 cases. These constitute relatively large sample sizes, which allow for more sophisticated statistical analysis. However, for the studies that used small samples external validity and generality can be questioned, and conclusions should be regarded as suggestive rather than conclusive.

The data for the studies were collected via mail surveys (6 studies), field surveys (3 studies), mail survey and interviews (13 studies), interviews (6 studies) and web survey (1 study). The response rates for the mail surveys varied from 18 per cent to 82 per cent, with an average response rate of 36 per cent. Further, 25 studies (86 per cent) collected cross-sectional data, and four studies (Brouthers and Bamossy, 2006; Jap and Anderson, 2003; Jennings et al., 2000; Lane et al., 2001) collected data from more than one point in time. In all studies, primary data were collected for trust conceptualization. Given the difficulties associated with objective financial measures of ISA performance, only two studies used secondary data for performance measurement. The data for the studies were collected from one side of the alliance (15 studies), both parent organizations (8 studies), both parent organizations and IJV (3 studies), IJV (2 studies), IJV and one parent organization (one study). Collecting data from both sides not only reduces common method variance caused by single source bias, but also provides more information with which to triangulate the findings.

The statistical methods most commonly used in trust–performance research are multiple regression analysis (8 studies), followed by structural equation modelling (6 studies). These types of analyses are logical for studies looking at the trust–performance relation where trust dimensions can be treated as independent variables and performance as the dependent variable. Other statistical methods used are hierarchical regression analysis (4 studies) to study the effects of moderating variables and different levels of trust, OLS regression analysis (4 studies), ordered probit regression (1 study) and ANCOVA (1 study).

A review of approaches in the conceptualization and operationalization of trust

Trust conceptualization

Trust has long been acknowledged in the disciplines of psychology, sociology, social psychology and economics. Researchers from the various disciplines occupying different turf have extended the conceptualization of trust into the context of strategic alliances. Economists tend to view trust as either calculative or institutional; psychologists commonly frame their assessment of trust in terms of the attributes of trustors and trustees and focus on a host of internal cognitions that those personal attributes yield; and sociologists often find trust in socially embedded properties of relationships between people or institutions (Zucker, 1986). Parkhe (1998) sheds light on the concept of trust and argues that in the context of alliances, trust is seen to have important psychological, sociological and economic properties simultaneously.

These 'inter-disciplinary conceptualization of trust' concerns triggered research efforts to define the term *trust* and operationalize it for empirical work. These efforts mostly focused on developing different dimensions of trust, but a consensual definition remains elusive. Table 18.2 shows that critical components in trust definitions are vulnerability (11 studies), willingness (8 studies), expectations (7 studies) and implicitly expressed 'uncertainty'. These findings confirm the earlier evidence of common elements in trust definitions provided by the reviews of Rousseau et al. (1998) and Li (2007). Li (2007) concludes that the trust literature seems to converge towards two necessary conditions (uncertainty, vulnerability), and two functions (expectations of being trustworthy, willingness to trust) in most trust definitions. Further, there is no consensus on specific dimensions of trust. Table 18.2 validates this abundance. A recent review by Seppanen et al. (2007) also concludes that the number and content of trust dimensions are yet to be agreed upon.

Given the heterogeneity in trust conceptualization, a clear distinction can be made between studies that took a unidimensional approach to the conceptualization of trust (20 of 29 studies), and those (9 of the 29 studies) that treat trust as multi-dimensional. Given the fact that trust is intrinsically complex and multifaceted (Lewicki and Bunker, 1996), research on trust in the context of inter-firm relations has predominantly emphasized expectations regarding others' goodwill (8 studies), reliability (4 studies), competence and integrity (both in 3 studies), calculative (2 studies) and identification (1 study).

Regarding the theoretical roots used in trust–performance empirical work, transaction cost theory (TCE) was used in nine studies, followed by social exchange theory in four. In seven studies, TCE and SET (social exchange theory) were used together. These empirical attempts to combine SET with TCE encourage researchers to grasp the richer, more multi-dimensional nature of trust. Trust has not traditionally been a focal concept in transaction cost economics (Williamson,

Table 18.2 The theoretical approaches, conceptualization, dimensions, levels and operationalization of trust

Studies	TR	Trust conceptualization	TD	TL	Trust operationalization
Simiar (1983)	N.I	N.I	N.I	OL	N.I
Mohr and Spekman (1994)	SET	Belief that a party's word is reliable and that party will fulfil its obligation in an exchange.	N.I	OL	**3 items**: 1. Trust on manufacturer's decisions, 2. Getting fair deal from manufacturer, 3. Harmony relationship with manufacturer.
Aulakh et al. (1996)	TCE	Degree of confidence, the individual partners have on reliability and integrity of each other.	R, I	OL	**3 items**: 1. High levels of trustable relationship, 2. Relationship abide by the terms of the contracting, 3. Sceptical information.
Fey (1996)	N.I	Belief that party A will do what it promised party B and if trust exists, party A's actions will not be taken with disregard for party B.	N.I	OL	Single item.
Inkpen and Currall (1997)	TCE, SET	An individual's behavioural reliance on another person under a condition of risk.	N.I	IL, OL	**18 items**: [15 items for inter-personal trust, and 3 items for inter-organizational trust.]
Sako (1998)	TCE, SET	Expectation that partner will behave in a mutually acceptable manner, including an expectation that neither party will exploit the other's vulnerability.	G, CT, CM	OL	**3 items**: 1. Reliance on customer's help beyond the agreement (goodwill), 2. Helping advice from customer (competence), 3. Everything spelt out in detail in contract (contractual).
Chen and Boggs (1998)	TCE, SET	N.I	N.I	OL	Single item.

Table 18.2 (Continued)

Studies	TR	Trust conceptualization	TD	TL	Trust operationalization
Ramaseshan and Loo (1998)	N.I	Willingness to rely on an exchange partner in whom one has confidence.	R, I	OL	**7 items**: In alliance, our partner: 1. Cannot be trusted, 2. Can be counted on to do what is right, 3. Has high integrity, 4. Is perfectly honest and truthful, 5. Can be completely trusted, 6. Is always faithful, 7. I have great confidence in our partner.
Jennings et al. (2000)	N.I	Mutual confidence that no party to an exchange will behave opportunistically and exploit another's vulnerabilities.	N.I	OL	N.I
Lane et al. (2001)	OLT	Confidence that the other firm will refrain from exploiting your vulnerabilities.	N.I	OL	Single item.
Luo (2001)	TCE, SET	Degree to which boundary spanners from each party are socially bound through having developed inter-personal relations and learning.	IT	IL	**4 items**: Extent of inter-personal relations development: {1. Since the ICV was formed, 2. Before ICV was formed}, and needed personal skills and knowledge provided: {3. To Chinese managers, 4. To foreign managers}.
Luo (2002)	TCE, SET	Psychological state comprising the intention to accept vulnerability based on positive expectations of intentions/behaviour of another.	N.I	IL, OL	**16 items**: {8 items for inter-personal trust, 8 items for inter-organizational trust (developed from Inkpen and Currall, 1997)}.

Fryxell et al. (2002)	TCE	Willingness to make vulnerable to the actions of others under conditions of risk, based on the characteristics/qualities of specific others, groups, or systems.	G	OL	**5 items**: 1. Freely sharing ideas, feelings and hopes about the IJV, 2. Freely talk about difficulties with the venture, and concerns addressed, 3. A sense of loss if the IJV was to be dissolved, 4. Constructively responding to partners' concerns about venture, 5. Considerable emotional investments in working relationship.
Gill and Butler (2003)	N.I	Willingness to compromise, and meeting contractual or verbal promises.	G	OL	N.I
Selnes and Sallis (2003)	OLT	Perceived ability and willingness of the other party to behave in ways that consider the interest of both parties in the relationship.	G	OL	**5 items**: Partner's: {1, Respond with understanding in event of problems, 2. Ability to fulfil contractual agreements, 3. Task competency, 4. Trustworthy, 5. Contact people are trustworthy}.
Dyer and Chu (2003)	TCE	One party's confidence that the other party in the exchange relationship will not exploit its vulnerabilities.	R, F, G	OL	**3 items**: 1. Treating supplier fairly, 2. Automaker's reputation of trustworthiness, 3. Unfairly taking advantage of supplier.
Jap and Anderson (2003)	TCE, RM, AT	Willingness of a party to be vulnerable to the actions of another party based on expectation that the other will perform a particular action important to the trustor, irrespective of the ability to control that other party.	N.I	IL	**5 items**: 1. Promises to each other are reliable, 2. Honesty in dealing with each other, 3. Trusting each other, 4. Going out of way to help each other out, 5. Considering each other's interests when problems arise (developed from Jap, 1999).

325

Table 18.2 (Continued)

Studies	TR	Trust conceptualization	TD	TL	Trust operationalization
Kauser and Shaw (2004)	RDT, TCE	N.I	N.I	OL	**11 items**: {all items are for inter-organization level trust}.
Krishnan et al. (2006)	TCE	Expectation held by one firm that another will not exploit its vulnerabilities when faced with the opportunity to do so.	R, E, G	OL	**5 items**: Foreign partner: {1. Changes facts to get benefit, 2. Does not abide by contract, 3. Provides truthful information beyond the contract, 4. Provides sceptical information, 5. Is sceptical on local partner information (developed from Aulakh et al., 1996)}.
Voss et al. (2006)	SET	N.I	G, CM	OL	**8 items**: {4 items for competence trust, and 4 items for goodwill trust}.
Brouthers and Bamossy (2006)	TCE	N.I	N.I	OL	**5 items**: 1. Trusting local partner, 2. Trusting foreign partner, 3. Trust related interactions affecting on IJV performance, and change in attitude towards trust in 4. Local partner, 5. Foreign partner.
Ng et al. (2007)	TCE	N.I	N.I	OL	**14 items**: {all items are for inter-organization level trust.}
Nielsen (2007)	TCE, RBV	N.I	G	OL	**3 items**: 1. Trust level between alliance partners, 2. Dependence on partner for joint projects 3. Confidence on partner's goodwill.
Muthusamy et al. (2007)	SET	Trustworthiness based on skills, integrity and benevolent attitudes of the partner as perceived by the focal firm.	CM, I, G	OL	**17 items**: {6 items for ability trust, 5 items for benevolence trust and 6 items for integrity trust.}

Robson et al. (2008)	SET, TCE	Willingness to accept vulnerability based on the positive expectations about counterpart's intentions or behaviour.	C, G	OL	**14 items**: {3 items for calculative trust, 4 items for affective trust, 4 items for forbearance, and 3 items for influence acceptance.}
Luo (2008)	JT	Intention to accept vulnerability based on positive expectations of the intentions or behaviour of another.	N.I	IL, OL	**16 items**: {8 items for inter-personal trust, 8 items for inter-organizational trust (developed from Inkpen and Currall, 1997)}.
Lin and Wang (2008)	TCE, SET	Willingness to rely on a partner in whom one has confidence.	N.I	OL	**3 items**: A party's perception of the other party's: 1. Dependability, 2. Reliability, 3. Overall trustworthiness.
Kwon (2008)	SET	N.I	N.I	OL	**3 items**: Both partners believe in each other's: 1. Honesty and truthfulness, 2. Fulfilling the contract, 3. Unification
Wilson and Brennan (2009)	RC	Willingness to rely on JV partner to behave in a mutually acceptable manner.	N.I	OL	N.I

Notes: TR (theoretical roots); SET (social exchange theory); TCE (transaction cost economics); OLT (organization learning theory); RM (relationship marketing); AT (agency theory); RDT (resource dependence theory); RBV (resource-based view); JT (justice theory); TD (trust dimensions); R (reliability); I (integrity); G (goodwill); CT (contractual trust); CM (competence trust); F (fairness); C (calculative); TL (trust level); OL (organizational level); IL (inter-personal level).

1975, 1985). The central premise of transaction cost economics is minimization of transaction costs as performance criteria. The basic rationale behind using transaction cost theory in trust research is that trust potentially reduces transaction costs (Williamson, 1993) and increases benefits by lowering opportunism, uncertainty, bounded rationality and asymmetric information. However, this economic approach to trust overlooks social elements, ethical norms and higher levels of trust, and merely emphasizes calculations (calculative trust). In turn, social exchange theory focuses on developing higher levels of trust in social exchange relationships where one party voluntarily provides a benefit to another, invoking an obligation of the other party to return the favour. Over time, trust between the two parties develops through reliable performance (by reciprocating benefits received from others) and through gradual expansion of exchanges (Blau, 1964). The rationale behind using social exchange theory in trust research is that high levels of trust – that is, goodwill trust, competence trust and integrity trust – develop over time through reciprocity.

These two theories complement each other to grasp a richer, more multidimensional nature of trust. TCE, which minimizes the value of trust to mere calculation, alone may not be adequate to study the effects of higher levels of trust on alliance performance, as a higher level of trust and its development has its roots in social exchange theory. As a result, combining these two theories provides an appropriate theoretical base for the analysis of the impact of multi-dimensional trust on the ISA performance, including the development of trust and its antecedents.

Operationalization of trust

For all the diversity surrounding the conceptualization of trust, its operationalization is more important to the generalizability of the studies. The trust–performance relation depends not only on fully understanding the theoretical mechanisms but also on improving the way core constructs are measured (Robson et al., 2008). The 29 studies use as many measures of trust as they have authors, and this is due to the diverse conceptualizations of trust and differences in the theoretical bases chosen. With three exceptions (Chen and Boggs, 1998; Fey, 1996; Lane et al., 2001), all studies have employed multiple-item measures to operationalize trust. Further, the construct of trust was measured in two ways in our sample of studies: integrated trust measures for a unidimensional trust construct, and separate trust measures for each dimension of trust. Twenty studies developed integrated trust measures for a unidimensional construct of trust, which are narrow in scope to simultaneously tap the pivotal facets of trust. In the remaining nine studies, separate measures for each dimension of trust were developed to capture the complex multifaceted nature of trust.

All studies operationalizing trust as a multi-dimensional construct appeared after 1997, showing evolving interest in the development of separate measures for each dimension of trust. Nevertheless, there is no uniformly accepted operationalization of these dimensions. For example, goodwill trust has been operationalized in terms of feelings and emotions (Fryxell et al., 2002; Nielsen, 2007; Sako, 1998), but it is envisaged as cognitive in other studies (e.g. Selnes and Sallis, 2003). This large number of approaches to trust operationalization restricts the advancement of the literature because it makes hard to compare and contrast the findings from different studies. Further, researchers have developed their own trust measures; no study has completely replicated the trust measures from previous studies. As can be seen in Table 18.2, three studies partially replicated trust measures from previous studies. Krishnan et al. (2006) borrowed two items from Aulakh et al. (1996), and Luo (2002, 2008) borrowed trust items from Inkpen and Currall (1997). To develop a more coherent theory of trust in ISAs, future studies should take a multi-dimensional approach to the conceptualization of trust, develop separate measures for each dimension of trust and borrow the trust measures from previous studies by validating their applicability in the current context for comparisons of results across industries and across countries.

Level of analysis and key informants

The relevance of the distinction between inter-organizational trust measured at an individual level and at an organizational level is an important issue. The work of Zaheer et al. (1998) is paradigmatic in this matter. They assess inter-personal trust and inter-organizational trust as distinct constructs having different consequences. Eighty-three per cent of the studies (24 of the 29) measure trust on an inter-organizational level, seven per cent (2 of the 29) measure trust on an inter-personal level, and three studies measure trust on both inter-personal and inter-organizational levels.

Twenty-one (72 per cent) studies collected data from a single key informant, and six studies (21 per cent) collected data from multiple informants. The use of a single key informant on the topic of inter-personal trust is justifiable, but use of a single key informant on questions of inter-organizational trust is problematic from the point of view of validity. An individual asked to give information about organizational-level issues may respond in terms of personal perceptions, opinions and feelings that could be subjectively considered commonly shared views; in other words, the informant is making a subjective generalization. For inter-organizational trust, therefore, multiple informants should be used, and their competency and experience should be assessed thoroughly (Currall and Inkpen, 2002; Medlin and Quester, 2002). Further, all the studies reviewed in this chapter collected data from upper management for inter-personal and inter-organizational trust, supporting Zaheer et al.'s (2002) finding that trust is more important at the level of upper boundary-spanners than at lower hierarchical levels.

Performance measurement

If a company that is involved in a relationship wants to succeed, besides acknowledging the elements that will contribute to success, it has to know how to measure performance. The 29 studies have used a variety of performance measures.

Subjective measures of performance

In view of the difficulties associated with objective measures of ISA performance, several studies have advocated the use of subjective measures. Table 18.3 summarizes performance measurement used and the performance effects of trust

Table 18.3 Performance measurement and performance effects of trust

Studies	Performance operationalization	Trust–performance relation
Simiar (1983)	IJV performance: {ST: Continuation of IJV}	DR: Trust has direct positive relation with IJV stability
Mohr and Spekman (1994)	Partnership success: {(FP: Dyadic sales) (S: 1. manufacturer's support, 2. Profit)}	DR: Trust is positively related to satisfaction with profit
Aulakh et al. (1996)	Partnership performance: {PPE: 1. Sales growth, 2. Market share}	IR: Increase in asset specificity (moderating variable) positively relates trust to performance, but without asset specificity, trust to performance relation is not significant
Fey (1996)	IJV performance: S {Overall performance of IJV}	DR: Trust has direct positive effect on IJV performance
Inkpen and Currall (1997)	IJV performance: PPE {1. ROI, Market share, 2. ROE, 3. Customer satisfaction, 4. Sales growth, 5. Industry reputation, 6. Reducing operation costs, 7. Cost position in industry, 8. Productivity gains, 9. Access to technology}	IR: Trust has indirect positive relation with IJV performance mediated by forbearance
Sako (1998)	Suppliers' performance: PPE {1. Suppliers' costs, 2. Just-in-time delivery, 3. Joint problem solving}	DR: Goodwill trust has strong positive effect on JIT delivery, and learning and continuous improvement
Chen and Boggs (1998)	IJV performance: {ST: Continuation of IJV for the next 10 years}	DR: Trust has direct positive relation with stability of IJVs
Ramaseshan and Loo (1998)	Alliance performance: PPE {(1. Partner's responsibilities and commitment to alliance, 2. Your firm's responsibilities and commitment to alliance, 3. Alliance productivity, 4. Worthwhile of alliance) and S (Satisfaction with alliance)}	DR: Trust has direct positive effect on ICA performance
Jennings et al. (2000)	IJV performance: {FP: 1. Governance costs, 2. Revenue growth, 3. Profitability, 4. Market value}	DR: Trust has direct positive relation with IJV performance
Lane et al. (2001)	IJV performance: PPE {1. Increasing business volume, 2. Increasing market share, 3. Achieving planned goals, 4. Making profit, 5. Overall IJV performance}	DR: Trust is not related to learning, but is instead positively related to IJV performance

Luo (2001)	IJV performance: {(S: 1. Managing venture, 2. Developing technology, 3. Product design, 4. Quality control, 5. Labour productivity, 6. Marketing, 7. Distribution, 8. Customer service, 9. Cost control, 10. Organisation reputation) and FP (ROI)}	DR: Identification-based trust leads to satisfaction with IJV process performance and return on investment
Luo (2002)	ISA performance: FP (1. ROI, 2. SPA)	IR: Positive trust to performance relation will be stronger with higher market uncertainty, stronger resource interdependency, commensurate risk sharing, greater reciprocal commitment and when alliance is younger
Fryxell et al. (2002)	IJV performances: PPE {1. Return on equity, 2. Operating costs, 3. Production processes, 4. Marketing and sales, 5. Technology and customer services}	IR: Goodwill trust moderates by empowering social control mechanisms to have positive effect on IJV performance; without trust, social controls have the opposite effect
Gill and Butler (2003)	IJV performance: PPE {(1. Profitability, 2. Rates of return, 3. Market share, 4. Sales volume), and ST (Continuation of IJV)}	DR: Trust has direct positive relation with IJV stability for the Japanese. **IR:** Trust has positive indirect relation with IJV stability through dependence for the Malaysian
Selnes and Sallis (2003)	Relationship performance: PPE {1. Lower logistic costs, 2. Increased flexibility in handling unforeseen fluctuations in demand, 3. Better product quality, 4. Synergies in sales and marketing, 5. New product development skills improvement, 6. Efficient use of time and money, 7. Quick response to customers before competitors}	IR: Trust acts as moderator; the positive affect of relationship learning on performance is lower under conditions of high trust than under conditions of low trust
Dyer and Chu (2003)	Buyer's performance: FP {ROA}	DR: Trust has direct positive relation with buyer's profit
Jap and Anderson (2003)	Relationship performances: PPE {[1. Evaluations of the counterpart's performance (4 items), 2. Achievement of competitive advantages (4 items), 3. Joint profit performance (3 items)], and ST [Expectations of relationship continuity (2 items)]}	IR: Trust has significant positive effect on performance when opportunism is low; trust fails to uphold performance under high level of ex-post opportunism

Table 18.3 (Continued)

Studies	Performance operationalization	Trust–performance relation
Kauser and Shaw (2004)	Alliance performance: PPE {[1. Market share, 2. Profitability, 3. Sales growth], and S [1. Relationship satisfaction (9 items), 2. Satisfaction with alliance goals]}	DR: Trust has direct positive relation with ISA performance
Krishnan et al. (2006)	Alliance Satisfaction: S {1. Local partner's satisfaction with overall alliance performance, 2. Foreign partner's satisfaction with overall alliance performance, 3. Achieving alliance goals 4. Local partner's satisfaction with alliance financial performance, 5. Foreign partner's satisfaction with alliance financial performance}	IR: Type of uncertainty moderates the positive relationship between trust and ISA performance, with behavioural uncertainty strengthening, and environmental uncertainty weakening the relation
Voss et al. (2006)	Alliance performance: PPE {1. Penetration of new markets, 2. Commercialization of new technology, 3. Sales revenues, 4. Access to distribution channels, 5. Knowledge of competitors, 6. Competitive advantage gains, 7. Preempting competition}	IR: Exchange of quality information is a significant mediator of the trust to performance relationship
Brouthers and Bamossy (2006)	IJV performance: PPE {1. Achieving goals and objectives of your firm, your partner firm, and key stakeholders, 2. Achieving IJV goals and objectives compared to previous IJV, and compared to other firms in your industry}	DR: Greater trust leads to higher IJV performance
Ng et al. (2007)	IJV performance: PPE {1. Financial achievements (profit, sales in local and foreign markets and market share), and 2. Non-financial achievements (product quality, acquisition of management skills, technology transfer and cooperation)}	DR: Trust leads to both financial and non-financial goals IR: Trust positively (moderates) increases explanatory power of local reliance for financial and non-financial goals

Nielsen (2007)	ISA performance: PPE [1. Relational equity (Marketing, Distribution, Customer service), 2. Financial performance (Sales, Market share, Profitability), 3. Learning, 4. Efficiency (Efficient procedures, Low operation cost)]	DR: Trust is positively related to relational equity, financial performance and efficiency. Further, trust does not affect learning
Muthusamy et al. (2007)	ISA performance: PPE [[1. Perceived alliance performance (5 items)], and ST [Propensity to continue the alliance (5 items)]]	DR: Ability-based trust, and integrity-based trust are positively related to alliance performance and stability, but benevolence-based trust is not significant in the relationship
Robson et al. (2008)	ISA performance: PPE [[1. Effectiveness (3 items), 2. Efficiency (3 items), 3. Responsiveness (4 items)], and FP [1. Sales volume, 2. Profitability]]	IR: 1: Positive trust-performance relation is stronger when alliance size (as moderator) is small
Luo (2008)	ISA performance: PPE [[1. Labour productivity, 2. Quality control, 3. Technology development, 4. Customer service, 5. Managerial efficiency], and FP [ROI]]	DR: Trust stimulates financial performance
Lin and Wang (2008)	IJV satisfaction: S [1. Financial performance, 2. Personal interaction, 3. General relationship]	DR: Trust leads to IJV satisfaction in Chinese-Asian JVs IR: Increase in legalism positively moderates (strengthens) the trust–performance relation for Western managers
Kwon (2008)	IJV performance: PPE [[Achieving JV's strategic objectives], and S [1. Both partners' satisfaction with focal relationship, 2. Both partners are good to each other, 3. Both selecting each other when forming new venture, 4. Both want liquidation]]	DR: Mutual trust has direct positive effect on IJV performance
Wilson and Brennan (2009)	IJV performance: <u>S</u> [1. Informational, 2. Social, 3. Financial]	DR: Trust leads to IJV performance

Notes: Perceived performance effectiveness (PPE); satisfaction (S); financial performance (FP); stability (ST); direct relation (DR); indirect relation (IR).

found in these studies. They have measured subjective performance in the following three ways: perceived performance effectiveness, satisfaction with ISA or partner firm and alliance stability.

Perceived performance effectiveness

The most commonly used and heterogeneous subjective performance measure in the studies is perceived performance effectiveness. This is the extent to which desired private or common ISA goals are achieved (Robson et al., 2008). The assumption underlying this measure is that partners join an ISA to achieve their strategic objectives by complementing each other's goals. When such goals clearly exist, measures such as overall satisfaction with alliance performance may be unable to accurately capture the success of an ISA.

Sixty-two per cent (18 of 29) of the studies have used perceived performance effectiveness as performance measure to cover the various objectives of the ISA parents. These include market share (8 studies), profitability and sales growth (both in 7 studies), sales volume and access to technology (both in 4 studies), efficiency, ROE, and just in time delivery (each in 2 studies), among others.

Although this measure is the most commonly used measure in trust–performance relations in ISAs, a common criticism of parents' different weighing of important goals can be overcome by examining the evaluation of managers from both sides of the ISA, and also by including newly formed organizations in the case of IJVs (Jap and Anderson, 2003; Luo, 2008; Ng et al., 2007; Selnes and Sallis, 2003).

Satisfaction with ISA or partner firm

Satisfaction is an important consequence of inter-firm exchange, and is based on the notion that success is determined, in part, by how well the partnership achieves the performance expectations set by the partners (Anderson and Narus, 1990). Partners' satisfaction with the ISA overall or partner firm performance has been reviewed in eight studies (28 per cent). These studies measure satisfaction in terms of profit (5 studies), general satisfaction with the alliance (Krishnan et al., 2006; Lin and Wang, 2008; Ramaseshan and Loo,1998), market share and sales growth (Kauser and Shaw, 2004), and partner support (Mohr and Spekman, 1994), among others. Further, a common criticism that satisfaction might be differently perceived by respondents can be overcome by simultaneously sampling multiple respondents, including managers from both partners. For example, two studies (Lin and Wang, 2008; Luo, 2001) collected data from both sides, but they did not collect it from multiple informants.

Alliance stability

Another advanced unidimensional concept that has been used to gauge the level of ISA performance is alliance stability. It is a psychological measure of managers' perceptions of the likelihood of continuing cooperation between partners (Chen and Boggs, 1998). The basic assumption of this approach is that intention of continuation is a sign of success and termination is a sign of ISA failure. Although compared to alliance stability as an objective measure (Gill and Butler, 2003; Simiar, 1983), this subjective approach to stability is an advanced measurement technique (Chen and Boggs, 1998; Jap and Anderson 2003; Muthusamy et al., 2007).

Objective measures of performance

Subjective measures of performance – like learning, relational equity, honesty and acquisition of managerial skills – are less likely to be measured objectively, whereas financial outcomes are easily measured objectively. The following section discusses the objective financial outcomes used to assess ISA performance in the studies analysed.

Financial output measures

Researchers have recently become interested in profitability measures (e.g. ROI, ROA), sales performance measures (e.g. sales volume, sales growth), and market performance measures (e.g. market share) as preferred approaches to ISA performance (Dyer and Chu, 2003; Jennings et al., 2000; Luo, 2001, 2002; Mohr and Spekman, 1994; Robson et al., 2008). Financial measures are not only used independently but also used alongside the assessment of satisfaction with ISA performance (Luo, 2001; Mohr and Spekman, 1994), and perceived performance effectiveness (Robson et al., 2008). Research exists that confirms the high correlation of financial measures with assessment of satisfaction with ISA performance (Choi and Beamish, 2004), and with the perceived performance effectiveness (Robson et al., 2008). Such integration increases the validity of these measurements and improves the robustness of the results.

Performance effects of trust

A growing body of research is concentrating on linking trust to performance. The precise form of the performance effects of trust varies considerably. Some researchers emphasize a direct relation; others examine more complex, indirect relations (see Table 18.3). Sixty-six per cent of the studies (19 of 29) find exclusively positive direct effects of trust on performance; 28 per cent (8 of the 29 studies) find indirect positive effects; one study finds an indirect negative effect; and one other finds both positive direct and indirect effects. Further, studies are liable to arrive at a direct positive relation for the trust–performance link when they involve DC–LDC rather than DC–DC, IJVs rather than ICAs, and when trust is measured on an organizational level rather than an inter-personal level (see Table 18.4).

Interestingly, more studies find a direct positive trust–performance relation when trust is measured as unidimensional construct (15/19 studies) than multidimensional (4/9). This may reflect the tendency among contemporary researchers (Fryxell et al., 2002; Voss et al., 2006) to model trust dimensions as a background factor that influences performance indirectly through, or conditions the influence of, another variable.

Table 18.4 Trust to performance relation across ISA geographical location, trust levels and alliance type

Trust	N	Trust–performance relation						ISA geographical location								Level of trust									Alliance type				
		DR			IR			DC-LDC		DC-DC		N.I			OL		IL		OL, IL		IJVs		ICAs	
								DR	IR	DR	IR			DR	IR	DR	IR	DR	IR	DR	IR	DR	IR
		+	0	−	+	0	−	+ 0 −	+ 0 −	+ 0 −	+ 0 −			+ 0 −	+ 0 −	+ 0 −	+ 0 −	+ 0 −	+ 0 −	+ 0 −	+ 0 −	+ 0 −	+ 0 −
Unidimensional trust	20	15	2	5				9 1 3		5 1 1		2		14 1 2		1		1 1 2		10 1	2	5 1 3	
Goodwill trust	8	3	2	3			1	1		3 1 3	1			3 2 3	1		+		+	1	1	2 2 2	1
Competence trust	3	1	2	1				1		2 1				1 2 1		+		+				1 2 1	
Identification trust	1	1						1								1				1				

Notes: 1. N (number of studies); DR (direct relationship); IR (indirect relationship); DC (developed countries); LDC (less developed countries); OL (organisational level); inter-personal level (IL); IJV (international joint venture); ICA (international cooperative alliance); N.I (no information); 0 (not significant).
2. Empty columns are removed.

Direct effects of trust

Research on trust in the context of an ISA has predominantly emphasized the direct positive effects of a unidimensional construct of trust on performance outcomes. These include direct positive effects on alliance stability (Chen and Boggs, 1998; Simiar, 1983); satisfaction with alliance or partner firm performance (Fey, 1996; Lin and Wang, 2008; Mohr and Spekman, 1994; Wilson and Bernnan, 2009); and achievement of financial and non-financial goals (Brouthers and Bamossy, 2006; Kauser and Shaw, 2004; Kwon, 2008; Lane et al., 2001; Ramaseshan and Loo, 1998). Further direct positive effects of trust have been found on objective financial performance (Jennings et al., 2000; Luo, 2008). Given the fact that trust is intrinsically complex and multifaceted (Sako, 1998), this raises the important question of which dimensions of trust affect performance outcomes. In the following section, the positive direct effects of several trust dimensions (goodwill, competence and identification-based trust) on performance are discussed in light of the subject studies.

Goodwill trust

Goodwill trust is the extent to which an exchange partner will look out for another's best interests (Sako, 1998). Variations of goodwill trust include normative trust, benevolence, effect-based trust and relational trust. Sako (1998) found that goodwill trust has a direct effect on learning and continuous improvement. Nielsen (2007) finds that goodwill trust is directly related to relational equity, financial performance and efficiency. Gill and Butler (2003) find that goodwill trust has a direct positive association with the stability of IJVs. The findings of these three studies support the concept of goodwill as a dimension of trust that has a direct relation with performance.

Competence trust

Competence trust refers to whether the other party is capable of doing what it says it will do (Sako, 1998). This form of trust has also been referred to as ability-based trust (Muthusamy et al., 2007). The recent study by Muthusamy et al. (2007) finds that competence trust has a direct positive effect on the achievement of financial goals. Based on the fine-grained findings of this study, future research should further enrich the competence trust link to performance.

Identification-based trust

Identification-based trust refers to the confidence arising from the understanding that full internalization of each other's desires and intentions has been achieved. A shared identity, mutual understanding and friendship are central to identification-based trust (Lewicki and Bunker, 1996). Luo (2001) finds that personal attachment (identification-based trust) has a direct positive association with international cooperative alliance (ICA) process performance and ROI. Additional research that clearly develops the construct of identification-based trust (see, e.g.

McAllister et al., 2006) and explores its relation with performance would be valuable.

Indirect effects of trust

In addition to investigating the direct effects linking trust to performance, researchers have also investigated the more complex indirect relation between trust and performance. They have identified moderating and mediating variables that strengthen or weaken the positive effect of trust on performance. Aulakh et al. (1996) discovered that asset specificity moderates the relation between inter-organisational trust and performance, suggesting a positive trust–performance link when asset specificity increases. Jap and Anderson (2003) find that rising ex-post opportunism decreases the positive effects of inter-personal trust on ISA performance. Krishnan et al. (2006) find that the type of uncertainty (behavioural uncertainty strengthens and environmental uncertainty weakens) moderates the positive trust–performance relation, and Luo (2002) finds that positive trust–performance relation will be strong when market uncertainty, interdependence and reciprocal commitment are high in case of younger than older alliances. Robson et al. (2008) discovered that alliance size moderates the relation between trust and performance, suggesting a stronger positive trust–performance link when alliance size is small than when it is large. Gill and Butler (2003) find that dependence moderates the goodwill trust–performance relation, suggesting a stronger positive link when dependence is more than when it is less.

In addition to moderating variables, researchers have identified the mediating variables of trust–performance relations. Inkpen and Currall (1997) find that trust has an indirect effect on performance mediated by forbearance. Voss et al. (2006) find that competence trust and goodwill trust have an indirect positive effect on performance when mediated by quality of information exchange. Regarding the moderating role of trust, Ng et al. (2007) find that inter-organizational trust increases the explanatory power of the local reliance variable for financial and non-financial goals. Further, Fryxell et al. (2002) find that goodwill trust moderates by empowering the social control to have positive effect on performance.

Finally, although most of the 29 studies indicated the performance enhancing effects of trust, trust does not always result in a positive outcome. Selnes and Sallis's (2003) study focused on a downside of inter-organizational trust in ISAs. They found that positive performance effects of relationship learning level off and eventually diminish under high levels of goodwill trust. Given the fact that most research focuses on the positive outcomes of trust, studying the downside of trust – including the lock-in from unproductive high-trust relationships – is an important avenue for future research.

Conclusions and directions for future research

This chapter provides a critical review of the empirical research on the trust–performance relation in ISAs from 1980–2009 by focusing on the conceptualization and operationalization of trust and ISA performance along with the methodologies used. Our review suggests that while there are positive indirect links (28 per cent) between trust and alliance performance, the direct positive trust–performance link (66 per cent) proves more consistent. The results appear more consistent when taking into consideration the study's context, in terms of ISA geographical location, alliance type and level of trust measurement. *First*, this review suggests that a direct positive trust–performance link is more consistent in DC–LDC alliances than DC–DC alliances, implying that the relative importance of trust varies according to geographical location. Trust can be relied on to directly pay off in LDC alliance settings, but should be applied more cautiously in DC where its effects are indirect. This finding suggests that trust becomes a background factor that influences performance indirectly through other variables (such as forbearance, information exchange, asset specificity, alliance size) in the case of DC–DC alliances.

Second, we find that the trust–performance relation is susceptible to the influence of ISA type. The proportion of studies finding a direct positive trust–performance relation was higher for IJV studies than ICA studies. This finding contradicts that of Robson et al. (2006) that a direct positive trust–performance relation was higher for ICAs than IJVs. The direct importance of trust for IJV performance strongly reinforces observations in the literature concerning the use of IJV for idiosyncratic investments that feature trust when faced with a challenging business opportunity. Higher levels of specific investment in IJVs than ICAs require a higher level of trust in partners, which helps assuage the partner's concerns about performance (Das and Teng, 1998).

Third, we find that the proportion of studies finding a direct positive trust–performance relation was higher in studies of inter-organizational trust than studies of inter-personal trust. This finding supports Zaheer et al. (1998) – that inter-personal trust and inter-organizational trust are distinct constructs, with inter-organizational trust having direct positive effects on alliance performance.

Further, although most of the studies reviewed show a direct positive trust–performance relation, a few studies also discuss when and/or where trust enhances the performance of an alliance (Krishnan et al., 2006; Luo, 2002; Selnes and Sallis, 2003). Conditions posed by contingency factors are crucial in determining whether the positive link between trust and performance will become stronger or weaker in the context of ISAs. Accordingly, more emphasis placed on the contingency view of the trust–performance link will substantially contribute to the trust–performance literature.

However, progress in specifying the trust–performance relation depends not only on emphasis on a contingency perspective, but also on improving the way core constructs are conceptualized and operationalized, and the methodology applied. Although there has been some progress, many unresolved theoretical, conceptual, operational and methodological issues are hindering the development of a cumulative body of research on the trust–performance relation.

We present some suggestions that can enrich trust–performance research by filling important gaps in the literature. On conceptualization; *first*, research on trust in the broad alliance literature is fragmented and lacks cohesion, resulting in a variety of treatments such as unidimensional or multi-dimensional constructs. Future research should focus on using different dimensions of trust to grasp the intrinsically complex and multifaceted nature of the term. This shift in emphasis will help researchers to identify which dimensions of trust affect ISA performance. *Second*, there has been a shift towards combining and integrating theories, especially transaction cost economics and social exchange theory (Chen and Boggs, 1998; Luo, 2002; Robson et al., 2008; Sako, 1998). This is potentially encouraging researchers to grasp the multi-dimensional nature of trust. *Third*, there is an emerging consensus about the two necessary conditions (uncertainty and vulnerability), and functions (expectation and willingness) of trust in most trust definitions (see, e.g. Li, 2007; Rousseau et al., 1998). Thus, as also suggested by Muthusamy et al. (2007), future research should include the referred conditions, functions and dimensions of trust in their trust definition.

On operationalization; *first*, there has been a shift from developing integrated trust operational measures to looking at developing 'separate multiple operational measures' for each dimension of trust. This shift is encouraging a better understanding of the properties of each dimension of trust (see, e.g. Robson et al., 2008). *Second*, there seems to be a tendency for each researcher to develop fresh trust measures, as there are currently no widely accepted operational measures of trust. However, to bring the previous studies' findings into the broader research stream for comparison with the current research findings, trust measures should be borrowed from previous studies, and their validity verified in the topical context. *Third*, there seems to be scholarly interest in identifying whether trust conceptualization, constitution, and its effects are culturally specific or universal (see, e.g. Lin and Wang, 2008; Sako, 1998). To establish this, researchers should borrow trust measures from previous studies and assess whether emerging trust conceptualization, constitution and its effects are unique to one culture, comparable across cultures, overlapping or completely universal. *Fourth*, there has been a shift from single levels of analysis (i.e., inter-personal) to multiple levels (i.e., both inter-personal and inter-organizational) of trust (Inkpen and Currall, 1997; Luo, 2002, 2008). Future research should therefore develop separate measures for each level of trust. *Fifth*, recent research has begun incorporating financial measures of ISA performance (Dyer and Chu, 2003; Luo, 2001, 2002) along with the subjective measures (satisfaction with an ISA or partner firm, and perceived performance effectiveness). Future research should incorporate objective measures of ISA performance along with subjective measures not only to triangulate on the constructs and increase the validity of these measurements, but also to compare the trust impact on objective and subjective variables.

On methodology; *first*, there has been a shift towards collecting data from both sides of the ISA partnership (Ng et al., 2007). This not only reduces common method variance caused by single source bias, but also provides more information with which to triangulate the findings. *Second*, using multiple key informants would appear to enrich the measurement of inter-organizational trust. *Third*, each of the studies analysed here has featured a recommendation to shift the emphasis from a static to a dynamic analysis, inspired by the better evidence offered by longitudinal research when used to investigate how the trust–performance relation unfolds over time.

Beyond this, there are many avenues for future research. Scholars could investigate whether, in a scenario where one partner's trust is abused, trust can be rebuilt, and just what the main antecedents of trust are. Another avenue of research is on the evolution of trust in ISAs (see, e.g. Boersma et al., 2003; Styles and Hersch, 2005). Examination of how evolving inter-partner trust effects ISA performance could be a promising area for upcoming research. Finally, there is evidence (see Gomes-Casseres, 1987; Yan and Zeng, 1999) that many successful joint ventures make structural changes to adapt to changing external environments or the internal strategies of their parent firms. Future research exploring the role of trust in IJV structural stability and instability is therefore warranted.

References

Anderson, J.C. and Narus, J.A. (1990) 'A model of distributor firm and manufacturing firm working partnership', *Journal of Marketing*, 54(1), 42–58.
Arino, A. and Reuer, J.J. (2006) *Strategic Alliances: Governance and Contracts*, 1st edn (Hampshire, England: Macmillan).
Aulakh, P.S., Kotabe, M. and Sahay, A. (1996) 'Trust and performance in cross-border marketing partnerships: a behaviour approach', *Journal of International Business Studies*, 27(5), 1005–32.
Bachmann, R. and Zaheer, A. (2005) *Handbook of Trust Research*, 1st edn (Cheltenham, UK: Edward Elgar).
Beamish, P.M. and Killing, J.P. (1997a) *Cooperative Strategies: North American Perspectives*, 1st edn (San Francisco, CA: New Lexington Press).
Beamish, P.M. and Killing, J.P. (1997b) *Cooperative Strategies: European Perspectives*, 1st edn (San Francisco, CA: New Lexington Press).
Beamish, P.M. and Killing, J.P. (1997c) *Cooperative Strategies: Asian Pacific Perspectives*, 1st edn (San Francisco, CA: New Lexington Press).
Blau, P.M. (1964) *Exchange and Power in Social Life* (New York: Wiley).
Boersma, M.F., Buckley, P.J. and Ghauri, P.N. (2003) 'Trust in international joint venture', *Journal of Business Research*, 56(12), 1031–42.
Brouthers, K.D. and Bamossy, G. (2006) 'Post-formation processes in Eastern and Western European joint ventures', *Journal of Management Studies*, 43(2), 203–29.
Chen, R. and Boggs, D. J. (1998) 'Long-term cooperation prospects in international joint ventures: perspectives of Chinese firms', *Journal of Applied Management Studies*, 7(1), 111–26.
Choi, C.-B. and Beamish, P.W. (2004) 'Split management control and international joint venture performance', *Journal of International Business Studies*, 35(3), 201–15.
Contractor, F.J. and Lorange, P. (2002) *Cooperative Strategies and Alliances*, 1st edn (Oxford: Elsevier Science Ltd).
Currall, S.C. and Inkpen, A.C. (2002) 'A multilevel approach to trust in joint ventures', *Journal of International Business Studies*, 33(3), 479–95.
Das, T.K. and Teng, B.-S. (1998) 'Between trust and confidence: developing confidence in partner cooperation in alliances', *Academy of Management Review*, 23(3), 491–512.
Das, T.K. and Teng, B.-S. (2000) 'Instabilities of strategic alliances: an internal tensions perspective', *Organisation Science*, 11(1), 77–101.
Dyer, J.H. and Chu, W. (2003) 'The role of trustworthiness in reducing transaction costs and improving performance: empirical evidence from United States, Japan, and Korea', *Organisation Science*, 14(1), 57–68.

Fey, C.F. (1996) 'Key success factors for Russian – foreign joint ventures', *The International Executive*, 38(3), 337–57.

Fryxell, G.E., Dooley, R.S. and Vryza, M. (2002) 'After the ink dries: the interaction of trust and control in U.S.-based international joint ventures', *Journal of Management Studies*, 36(6), 865–86.

Gill, J. and Butler, R.J. (2003) 'Managing instability in cross-cultural alliances', *Long Range Planning*, 36(6), 543–63.

Gomes-Casseres, B. (1987) 'Joint venture instability: is it a problem?', *Columbia Journal of World Business*, 22(2), 97–102.

Inkpen, A.C. and Currall, S.C. (1997) 'International joint venture trust', in P.W. Beamish and J.P. Killing (eds) *Cooperative Strategies: North American Perspectives*, 308–34 (Lexington, CA: Lexington press).

Jap, S.D. (1999) 'Pie-expansion efforts: collaboration process in buyer-seller relationships', *Journal of Marketing Research*, 36(4), 461–75.

Jap, S.D. and Anderson, E. (2003) 'Safeguarding interorganisational performance and continuity under ex post opportunism', *Management Science*, 49(12), 1684–701.

Jennings, D.F., Artz, K., Gillin, L.M. and Christodouloy, C. (2000) 'Determinants of trust in global strategic alliances: AMRAD and the Australian biomedical industry', *Competitiveness Review*, 10(1), 25–44.

Kauser, S. and Shaw, V. (2004) 'The influence of behavioural and organisational characteristics on the success of international strategic alliances', *International Marketing Review*, 21(1), 17–52.

Krishnan, R., Martin, X. and Noorderhaven, N.G. (2006) 'When does trust matter to alliance performance?', *Academy of Management Journal*, 49(5), 894–917.

Kwon, Y.-C. (2008) 'Antecedents and consequences of international joint venture partnerships: a social exchange perspective', *International Business Review*, 17(5), 559–73.

Lane, P.J., Salk, J.E. and Lyles, M.A. (2001) 'Absorptive capacity, learning, and performance in international joint ventures', *Strategic Management Journal*, 22(12), 1139–61.

Lewicki, R.J. and Bunker, B.B. (1996) 'Developing and maintaining trust in work relationships', in R.M. Kramer and T.R. Tyler (eds) *Trust in Organisations: Frontiers of Theory and Research*, 114–39 (London: Sage Publications).

Li, P.P. (2007) 'Towards an interdisciplinary conceptualisation of trust: a typological approach', *Management and Organisation Review*, 3(3), 421–45.

Lin, X. and Wang, C.L. (2008) 'Enforcement and performance: the role of ownership, legalism and trust in international joint ventures', *Journal of World Business*, 43(3), 340–51.

Luo, Y. (2001) 'Antecedents and consequences of personal attachment in cross-cultural cooperative ventures', *Administrative Science Quarterly*, 46(2), 177–201.

Luo, Y. (2002) 'Building trust in cross-cultural collaborations: toward a contingency perspective', *Journal of Management*, 28(5), 669–94.

Luo, Y. (2008) 'Procedural fairness and inter-firm cooperation in strategic alliances', *Strategic Management Journal*, 29(1), 27–46.

McAllister, D.J., Lewicki, R.J. and Chaturvedi, S. (2006) 'Trust in developing relationships: from theory to measurement', *66th Annual Academy of Management Conference Chapter*, Atlanta: Georgia.

Medlin, C. and Quester, P. (2002) 'Inter-firm trust: two theoretical dimensions versus a global measure', *18th Annual IMP Conference Chapter*, Perth: Australia.

Meschi, P.-X. and Riccio, E.L. (2008) 'Country risk, national cultural differences between partners and survival of international joint ventures in Brazil', *International Business Review*, 17(3), 250–66.

Mohr, J. and Spekman, R. (1994) 'Characteristics of partnership success: partnership attributes, communication behaviour, and conflict resolution techniques', *Strategic Management Journal*, 15(2), 135–52.

Muthusamy, S.K., White, M. and Carr, A. (2007) 'An examination of the role of social exchanges in alliance performance', *Journal of Management Issues*, 19(1), 53–75.

Ng, P.W.-K., Lau, C.-M. and Nyaw, M.-K. (2007) 'The effects of trust on international joint venture performance in China', *Journal of International Management*, 13(4), 430–48.

Nielsen, B.B. (2007) 'Determining international strategic alliance performance', *International Business Review*, 16(3), 337–61.

Nooteboom, B. (1999) *Inter-Firm Alliances: Analysis and Design*, 1st edn (New York: Routledge).

Parkhe, A. (1998) 'Understanding trust in international alliances', *Journal of World Business*, 33(3), 219–40.

Ramaseshan, B. and Loo, P.C. (1998) 'Factors affecting a partner's perceived effectiveness of strategic business alliance: some Singaporean evidence', *International Business Review*, 7(4), 443–58.

Reuer, J.J. (2004) *Strategic Alliances: Theory and Evidence*, 1st edn (New York: Oxford University Press).

Robson, M.J., Katsikeas, C.S. and Bello, D.C. (2008) 'Drivers and performance outcomes of trust in international strategic alliances: the role of organisational complexity', *Organisation Science*, 19(4), 647–65.

Robson, M.J., Skarmeas, D. and Spyropoulou, S. (2006) 'Behavioural attributes and performance in international strategic alliances', *International Marketing Review*, 23(6), 585–609.

Rousseau, D.M., Sitkin, S.B., Burt, R.S. and Camerer, C. (1998) 'Not so different after all: a cross-discipline view of trust', *Academy of Management Review*, 23(3), 393–404.

Sako, M. (1998) 'Does trust improve business performance?', in C. Lane and R. Bachmann (eds) *Trust Within and Between Organisation*, 88–117 (Oxford: Oxford University Press).

Selnes, F. and Sallis, J. (2003) 'Promoting relationship learning', *Journal of Marketing*, 67(3), 80–95.

Seppanen, R., Blomqvist, K. and Sundqvist, S. (2007) 'Measuring inter-organisational trust – a critical review of the empirical research in 1990–2003', *Industrial Marketing Management*, 36(2), 249–65.

Simiar, F. (1983) 'Major causes of joint-venture failures in the Middle East: the case of Iran', *Management International Review*, 23(1), 58–68.

Styles, C. and Hersch, L. (2005) 'Relationship formation in international joint ventures: insights from Australian-Malaysian international joint venture', *Journal of International Marketing*, 13(3), 105–34.

Voss, K.E., Johnson, J.L., Cullen, J.B., Sakano, T. and Takenouchi, H. (2006) 'Relational exchange in US-Japanese marketing strategic alliances', *International Marketing Review*, 23(6), 610–35.

Williamson, O.E. (1975) *Markets and Hierarchies: Analysis and Antitrust Implications* (New York: Free Press).

Williamson, O.E. (1985) *The Economic Institutions of Capitalism: Firms, Markets, Relational Contracting* (New York: Free Press).

Williamson, O.E. (1993) 'Calculativeness, trust, and economic organisation', *The Journal of Law and Economics*, 36(1), 453–86.

Wilson, J. and Brennan, R. (2009) 'Relational factors in UK-Chinese international joint ventures', *European Business Review*, 21(2), 159–71.

Yan, A. and Zeng, M. (1999) 'International joint venture instability: a critique of previous research, a reconceptualisation, and directions for future research', *Journal of International Business Studies*, 30(2), 397–414.

Zaheer, A. and Harris, J.D. (2006) 'Inter-organisational trust', in O. Shenkar and J.J. Reuer (eds) *Handbook of Strategic Alliances*, 169–97 (Thousand Oaks, CA: Sage).

Zaheer, A., Lofstrom, S. and George, V. P. (2002) 'Interpersonal and interorganisational trust in alliances', in F.J. Contractor and P. Lorange (eds) *Cooperative Strategies and Alliances*, 347–77 (Oxford: Elserier Science Ltd).

Zaheer, A., McEvily, B. and Perrone, V. (1998) 'Does trust matter? Exploring the effects of inter-organisational and interpersonal trust on performance', *Organisation Science*, 9(2), 141–59.

Zucker, L.G. (1986) 'Production of trust: institutional sources of economic structure', in B.M. Staw and L.L. Cummings (eds) *Research in Organisational Behaviour*, 53–111 (Greenwich, CT: JAI Press).

19
Asset Specificity, Asset Opacity and Ownership Structures in Domestic and Cross-Border Joint Ventures

Sougand Golesorkhi and Mo Yamin

Introduction

Inter-firm collaboration, including inter-firm joint ventures, has been researched extensively in the business and management literature (Delios and Beamish, 1999; Hennart and Larimo, 1998; Pan, 1996; Yan and Gray, 1994). In the international business (IB) context, cross-border joint ventures (IJVs) have been highlighted as a key element of internationalization and market development by globalizing enterprises. Whereas early IB literature focused mostly on foreign direct investment, recent literature reflects the increasing regional and global integration in the world economy, highlighting the importance of strategic flexibility as a competitive imperative facing multinational corporations (Buckley and Ghauri, 2004; Rugman and Verbeke, 2004, 2008). Ownership and location flexibility have been particularly emphasized by Buckley and Ghauri (2004) and Buckley (2009). As a consequence, the focus on alliance and joint venture formation has gained increased salience in the IB literature.

The IB literature has focused mainly on the choice between joint ventures (JVs) and other modes of market development; however, limited attention has been paid to share owners within JVs. In this chapter, we utilize the theoretical framework that views JVs' share (in both domestic and cross-border context) as being partially a function of the asset characteristics contributed by JV partners. This chapter develops and tests hypotheses linking the equity ownership structure (i.e. the share of JV equity owned by each partner) of IJVs to the relative specificity and opacity of the assets contributed by JV partners. Our basic argument, which we derive through applying insights from the measurement branch of transaction cost economics, is as follows. JVs are structured, in part, to economize on monitoring costs. Each partner's share of JV capital reflects the monitoring costs associated with measurement (and hence monitoring) costs associated with the asset that each partner contributes. The partner whose assets give rise to greater monitoring costs will own a larger share of the JV capital. In this way JV equity capital share helps to minimize monitoring costs because, in effect, it provides a collateral guarantee function. In this chapter, we focus on the specificity and opacity characteristics of the assets contributed by the JV's partners as these characteristics are shown to be highly correlated with measurement costs.

We extend this basic argument to the cross-border context. *Ceteris paribus*, measurement costs associated with a given level of asset specificity or opacity are likely to be greater in IJVs and therefore the relation between equity capital shares and relative monitoring cost of partners' assets is expected to be stronger than in domestic JVs. We test a hypothesis based on the above arguments for 542 UK-based JVs (the sample includes JVs with both UK–UK partners as well as UK–foreign partners). The literature on organizational choice has been dominated by the choice over alternative modes of market entry; that is, wholly owned subsidiaries over JVs or acquisitions (Delios and Beamish, 1999; Hennart and Reddy, 1997; Slangen and Hennart, 2008). This chapter is potentially an important contribution to knowledge. Although a substantial body of research has also examined the determinants of JV structure, the focus has mostly been on equity versus non-equity JVs, and the determinants of the share of equity capital contributed by each party have not been extensively examined (Folta, 1994; Foss and Robertson, 2000; Garcia Canal, 1996; Reuer and Ragozzino, 2006). Those studies that have examined the distribution of equity in JVs have tended to associate it with contextual conditions (such as the role of cultural and other inter-country differences) external to the JV (Blodgett, 1991; Chadee and Qiu, 2001; Gary and Yan, 1992; Pan, 1996; Yan and Gray, 1994). While these factors are clearly important, what is lacking is a coherent explanation of how the distribution of capital share in the JV may also be influenced by differences in the nature and characteristics of the assets contributed by each partner in the JV. In fact, an important question is how the nature of the assets and the contextual factors such as psychic/regional proximity *interact* in determining the capital share in JVs. In this chapter, we endeavour to shed some light on this question. We do so by first examining the guarantee role of equity capital in all JVs, and then by arguing this guarantee role is more important in IJVs.

Theoretical background: measurement costs and JV structure

Measurement costs in market transactions

In this section, we develop an explanation of the determinants of equity distribution in JVs in terms of 'measurement costs'. Measurement costs are a pervasive feature of transactions and arise due to the performance variability of virtually all goods and services (Akerloff, 1970; Barzel, 1982, 1985; Hart and Moore, 1990). Barzel defines measurement costs as arising from lack of homogeneity such that no two units of the 'same' product or service will perform in an identical way. He argues that differences in the value of various units of the 'same', apparently homogenous, good is the property right of the owner (seller) of the product who may nevertheless choose to put it in the public domain. We may interpret this as the variability in the performance inducing the owner to provide a guarantee to the (buyer) – by allowing the buyer to examine the quality of the good in question. Another influential study in the realm of measurement cost is Akerloff's

(1970) celebrated discussion of the market for 'lemons'. The lemon problem arises due to information asymmetry with regard to quality; buyers cannot *ex ante* know about the quality of the product and may thus refrain from purchasing. The solution to the lemon problem lies in the seller providing a level of guarantee to the buyer relating to the future performance of the product. More generally, the measurement strand of transaction cost economics is committed to a fundamental proposition relating to contractual structure in the presence of performance variability. The proposition states that, in order to maximize the value of an exchange, the party whose contribution has a greater effect on outcome variability should bear more of the variability in the payoff resulting from exchange. 'Bearing the variability' may take different forms depending on the type of exchange or transaction. For example, in market transactions between firms as sellers and households as buyer, the sellers' proactive provision of information relevant to (or guarantee of) future performance of durable products is a common feature of market economies. A similar logic applies to the ownership structuring of JVs.

The guarantee function of equity in JV structure

As Buckley and Casson (1988) have noted, each party in a JV has an inalienable de facto right to pursue his/her own interest at the expense of the other. The governance issue in JVs is therefore rooted in the potential variability in the JV's performance arising primarily from cooperation problems. Under the assumption of self-interest or its stronger form of opportunism, collectively beneficial outcomes fail to arise due to actions motivated by the private benefit to individuals (Camerer and Kenz, 1996; Foss, 2001). Agency theory focuses on how to formulate the best contract in order to govern the relationship between parties (Jensen and Meckling, 1976). However, it is also acknowledged that the information requirement of such contractual agreements may be quite daunting, as the contract would need, in particular, to provide a mutually agreed mechanism for the monitoring of each of the parties' behaviour germane to JV performance. In fact it would seem that an 'optimal' contract in the context of JVs is particularly subject to problems of bounded rationality, asymmetric information and enforcement cost that transaction cost analysis highlights as impediments to complete contracting (Hart, 1995; Williamson, 1979, 1985). As Teece (1992) argues, given that complete *ex ante* contracting is not feasible, the JVs partners' commitment to jointly own the venture in accordance with a negotiated share of the equity capital provides a mechanism for distributing residuals.

We consider that 'negotiated' (whether explicitly or implicitly) shares of the capital invested in the JVs are likely to reflect key characteristics of the assets contributed by each party. The important characteristics of assets in this context are those that give rise to monitoring costs (entailed in 'measuring' the relative contributions of the partners to JV performance). Monitoring costs arise from a combination of information asymmetry and opportunism. The party (A) who contributes an asset which is more easily 'measurable' (in relation to JV performance) is less likely to behave opportunistically, primarily due to the fact that such behaviour is easily detectable (and can be punished). The opposite is likely to be the case for the party (B) whose performance is more difficult to measure (again due to the characteristics of the contributed assets). In this scenario, party (A) would need a credible 'guarantee' that party (B) would not behave opportunistically. Therefore, party (B) should bear the larger proportion of the value of residual claim compared to party (A). This clearly translates to party (B) having a larger share of the equity capital invested in the JVs. This way an optimal JV structure can be obtained that allows for constraining agency hazard through residual claim. In the next section, we develop this argument by linking capital shares of partners to the specificity and opacity of the assets contributed by the JV parties. These characteristics reflect the monitoring and measurement costs.

Two economic elements are critical for understanding ownership: residual control rights and residual rights to income – residual claim (Grossman and Hart, 1986; Hart, 1995; Hart and Moore, 1990). The appropriate allocation of residual control rights suggests mitigating *ex post* contractual problems, while on the other hand appropriately aligning residual claims leads to mitigating *ex ante* contractual problems. In our analysis, both residual control and residual claim (*ex post* and *ex ante* contractual) issues are at the heart of the definition of equity capital ownership. In particular, assignment of the residual income provides the guarantee function of the equity capital.

Partner's asset specificity and opacity and equity shares in JVs

Asset specificity and asset opacity

The characteristics of assets and their implication for organizational governance and performance are rooted in several schools of thought, such as transaction costs and resource-based view of the firm (Ainuddin et al., 2007; Barney, 1991; Luo, 2002; Peteraf, 1993; Tsang, 2000). The specificity and opacity of assets employed in a transaction have a significant impact on the efficiency (transaction costs) of alternative governance structures (Hennart, 1994; Williamson, 1991). Specific assets can be defined as those that have a shadow price higher than their market price or the opportunity cost for their owner (e.g. intangible assets like R&D and brand name). Asset specificity does not raise valuation difficulties or ambiguities per se – the value of the asset can be determined but it will be expected to vary depending on the transactional context (and the partners may have different valuations). By contrast, asset opacity is essentially a consequence of valuation difficulties; following Vicente-Lorente (2001), they are assets that, due either to their nature or the firm's actions, possess a value that cannot be easily determined. Thus, asset opacity arises when information germane to valuation cannot be communicated to outsiders (i.e. tacit knowledge rooted in social complexity, human resource deployment, culture and value). The key difference between asset specificity and asset opacity can be highlighted in the following terms: opacity of assets results from a 'transfer barrier' precluding imitation or substitution (Lippman and Rumelt, 1982; Winter, 1987); whereas specific assets may be transferable, although there may be a diminution of value of a firm's asset when it is used by outsiders.

As already noted, in JVs parties contractually agree to bind their assets for a joint purpose. Consequently, the party who contributes less specific or opaque assets to the JV becomes more dependent on the party contributing the more specific assets than vice versa. The former becomes vulnerable to the performance variability stemming from the specific assets deployed in the JV. In particular, because the costs of the non-performance (e.g. due to lack of sufficient management input) are shared, the party with the specific assets may have an incentive to contribute less effort than if s/he was the sole owner. To alleviate this problem and to facilitate the acquiescence of the party with the non-specific assets to bind his/her resources in the venture, it would be necessary for the owner of the specific asset to own a large share of the capital invested in the JV. Thus;

Hypothesis 1a: *The equity share in JVs is positively related to the relative specificity of the assets the partners contribute to JVs.*

Asset opacity is likely to have a similar consequence. The performance of the venture is likely to be influenced by the presence of opaque assets such as tacit managerial skills and competencies, the existence of private information held by the parties (such as databases, customers' trade secrets) and the prevalence of assets that may be difficult to transfer such as goodwill. The party whose assets are less opaque becomes more dependent on the party contributing opaque assets. Again to alleviate this dependence and to facilitate acquiescence of the party with the non-opaque assets to bind his/her resources in the venture, it would be necessary for the owner of the opaque asset to own a large share of the capital invested in the JV. Thus;

Hypothesis 1b: *The equity share in JVs is positively related to the relative opacity of the assets the partners contribute to JVs.*

Asset specificity and asset opacity in IJV context

We consider that inter-country differences strengthen the guarantee function of equity capital in IJVs. Our reasoning is that the perceived uncertainty/variability associated with a given level of asset specificity will be greater in IJVs and thus the guarantee function of the equity share gains an enhanced significance in such a context. In the domestic context, the JV partners are to some degree embedded in the same socio-cultural, economic and institutional milieu as each other, and as a consequence face relatively few 'search and deliberation' problems (Rangan, 2000) in interpreting the information and clues emanating from their partners' behaviour. By contrast, in the cross-border context greater 'search and deliberation' obstacles will be encountered in interpreting partner behaviour. Studies highlighting the 'liability of foreignness' also speak to similar concerns (Hymer, 1976; Nachum, 2003; Zaheer, 1995). Following Barkema et al. (1996, 1997), IJVs face a 'double-layered acculturation' task in as much as their understanding of partner behaviour is complicated by their relatively poor appreciation of the (foreign market) context of the partner. Such extra barriers to understanding or interpreting partner behaviour and, more importantly, the implications of this for JV performance are rooted in the cultural distance managers perceive with respect to foreign business environments (Evans and Mavondo, 2002; O'Grady and Lane, 1996; Yamin and Sinkovics, 2006). This supports the argument that in JVs between partners of different nationality, the uncertainty perception associated with a given level of asset specificity and opacity is 'magnified' compared to that in domestic JVs. Accordingly, our expectation is that the relation between partners' equity capital share and assets specificity and opacity should be greater when the JV partnership is cross-border. Thus;

Hypothesis 2a: *The relation between equity shares and relative asset specificity is stronger in IJVs.*
Hypothesis 2b: *The relation between equity shares and relative asset opacity is stronger in IJVs.*

Following Rugman (2005), information acquisition and processing by firms regarding a partner is easier if both parties belong to the same region. This is partly because psychic and physical distances between the partners' countries will generally be greater if they are not in the same region. In addition to the distance effect, however, there is a specifically regional effect in terms of 'rules of engagement', which, as Rugman (2005) points out, differ between the triad regions. Inter-regional differences and the distance between the partner countries increase the cost of knowledge acquisition (Eriksson et al., 1997) relating to the 'foreign' partner, thus *ceteris paribus*, partners may acquire less information pertaining to partner behaviour the greater the psychic/physical distance and if the countries are not in the same region. This reasoning supports extending the logic behind H2a and H2b generally with respect to the cultural distance or proximity between the country/regions of JV partners. Thus;

Hypothesis 3a: *In IJVs, the relation between equity shares and relative asset specificity contributed to the JV is affected by the regional proximity between partners in the JV.*
Hypothesis 3b: *In IJVs, the relation between equity shares and relative asset opacity contributed to the JV is affected by the regional proximity between partners in the JV.*

Methodology

Sources of data and sample selection

In this chapter we utilize data capturing the characteristics of the assets that partners contribute to particular JVs to test the hypotheses developed in the previous section. The sample includes JVs formed by only two partners during 1995–2000, from Thomson Financial database. This yielded a sample of 1800 JVs. We consider JVs based only in the UK to control for diverse regulatory and jurisdictional requirements of the countries in which the JV is located. Given the above consideration, as well as the availability of detailed financial data for each party in the JV, the actual number of observations is reduced to 542 JVs. These are formed between UK and foreign partners (in China, Europe and the US) as well as 134 observations for UK–UK partners (regarded as domestic JVs). We segment the foreign partners based on their respective region. Within our sample, we observed three regional categories: US (25 per cent), China (consists of China, Hong Kong, Taiwan and Macau) (30 per cent) and Europe (20 per cent). Public announcements of JVs are obtained using the SDC Platinum JV/JVs database provided by Thomson Financial. This database is the industry standard for information on joint ventures/JVs, M&A and share repurchases on a worldwide basis. Accounting and financial data for each partner is extracted from Thomson Datastream.

Dependent variable

In the specification of our dependent variable we distinguish between minority and majority equity share contributions through the use of a categorical dependant variable, with partners with less (more) than 50 per cent equity shares categorized as minority (majority) contributors, respectively. JVs where partners each contribute 50 per cent equity are categorized as equal contributors (Hu and Chen, 1993; Pan, 1996). Thus using this classification, the dependent variable (Y) assumes a value of 1, reflecting a negotiated equity contribution of less than 50 per cent, $Y = 2$ captures the probabilities of a 50 per cent equity contribution and $Y = 3$ signals an equity contribution of more than 50 per cent.

Independent variables

Explanatory variables

We measure specificity of assets by drawing from previous studies (Brouthers and Brouthers, 2000; Lu and Hebert, 2005; Vicente-Lorente, 2001). They are R&D intensity (ratio of R&D expenses to total sales), specific human capital (ratio of total sales to the total number of employees) and cost of sales (ratio of selling expenses to total sales). The cost of sales is assumed to capture (partially) the costs of promotion and advertising. (Data limitation meant that we were unable to obtain direct advertising costs.) The specific human capital is the turnover per employee and it is used as a measure of the productive efficiency of the firm, with more productive firms postulated to have more specific human capital. These proxies are observable measures for the stock of specific assets that generate economic rent and have an imperfect market. In addition to R&D intensity, in order to capture asset opacity we consider ratio of the firm's intangible assets to its total assets. These intangible assets include non-monetary assets such as trade secrets (e.g. customer lists), copyrights, patents, trademarks and goodwill (Vicente-Lorente, 2001). Asset specificity and opacity are assumed to be the main effects and positively related to the equity capital contribution among JV partners.

Control variables

This section documents the controls we introduce for other relevant firm-level factors that may influence equity contribution. Growth options are capital assets that add value to the firm. This is measured by the ratio of capital expenditure to total assets (Rajan and Zingales, 1995). However, as firms generally engage in R&D to generate future investment and growth options, R&D intensity also serves as an indicator of growth potential. Growth options may also have an industry dimension; JVs may be preferred in high-growth markets, since in these markets the opportunity costs of a delayed entry is high (Brouthers and Brouthers, 2000). We predict a positive relation between equity contribution of the foreign partner and its growth options. The size of the partner firm may also affect the degree of ownership that it takes. Although the empirical evidence on the relation between size and preference for sharing equity is mixed, the traditional argument is that small firms do not have the necessary resources to put much of the capital in the JV (Larimo, 1993). We measure size of the firm by the natural logarithm of its sales (Titman and Wessels, 1988; Tsang and Yip, 2007).

The literature has emphasized that the national origin of the foreign partners may have an impact on the choice of market entry (Kogut and Singh, 1988; Slangen and Van Tulder, 2009). We extend this argument to account for cultural distance between partners in our analysis using Kogut and Singh's (1988) index. They establish an overall index for cultural distance based on Hofstede's work as follows:

$$\text{Cultural distance } j = \sum_{i=j}^{4} \frac{\left\{(I_{ij} - I_{iu})^2 / V_i\right\}}{4} \tag{19.1}$$

where I_{ij} stands for the index for the ith cultural dimension and jth country, V_i is the variance of the index of the ith dimension, u indicates the nation from which the cultural distance is calculated (which is UK in this chapter) and cultural distance j is the cultural distance of the jth country from the UK. China was not in Hofstede's sample. Therefore, the ratings for Taiwan were used as a surrogate measure for China (also see Pan, 1996). In addition, we incorporate dummy variables to control for the partner's industry (Hennart and Larimo, 1998) on the basis of their two-digit SIC codes. We obtain the following industry sectors: manufacturing (32 per cent), transportation, communication and utilities (28 per cent), mineral industry (21 per cent) and construction (19 per cent). (Construction is our base category.)

Interactive terms

Hypotheses 2 and 3 are tested through estimating interactive terms. They are based on multiplying the measures for asset specificity and opacity with foreign partners' regional dummies. In order to know which partner has what kind of equity ownership, three 0–1 dummy variables for the US, Europe and China are created.

Specification of the model

The logistic regression is often used in studies on ownership strategies, and it has been suggested that the equity share contribution is not exactly on a percentage continuum (Chadee and Qiu, 2001; Contractor, 1990; Pan, 1996). A certain percentage difference in the equity ownership has very different strategic implications. For example, the difference between a 25 per cent or 26 per cent equity ownership is obviously not the same as that between a 49 per cent and a 50 per cent equity ownership. The decision on equity ownership is primarily a categorical one, and is often driven by the need of control over the venture. Therefore, the first key decision is whether to go for a minority, a 50 per cent or a majority equity share (Chadee and Qiu, 2001; Pan, 1996). Because of the categorical and ordinal nature of the dependent variable, that is, $y = 1, \ldots, j+1$ and $1 < 2 < 3$, an ordered logit model is more appropriate and takes the following general form:

$$g\left(pr\frac{(Y \leq i)}{X}\right) = a_i + \beta'x \tag{19.2}$$

where $0 \leq i \leq j$, and $\alpha_i, \ldots, \alpha_j$ and j intercept parameters, and β is the vector of slope coefficients.

Discussion of the results

The Pearson correlation coefficients and summary of descriptive statistics are reported in Tables 19.1 and 19.2 respectively. When a large number of interaction terms involving one variable are included in the model, multicollinearity may be a problem. Because some of the correlations among the variables are high, the original variables were rescaled using procedures recommended by Aiken and West (1991). In Table 19.3, column 1 presents results from the ordered-logit model, testing the effect of specificity and opacity on structure of shareholding of all JVs in our sample. Column 2 highlights the interaction results, indicating that the effect of monitoring costs on equity shareholding is stronger in IJVs.

Fit of the model

Table 19.3 reports that estimated ordered logit regressions are statistically significant at 1 per cent level for both models according to the relevant models chi-squared statistic. The model statistics show that the percentage of correctly predicted outcomes ranges from 68 per cent for Model 1 to 70 per cent for Model 2. Overall, the model that includes the interaction terms as well as main effects (Model 2) has a greater explanatory power, at 70 per cent. This suggests the fraction of cases where the actual outcome, the likelihood of the equity capital contribution being more than 50 per cent, particularly in IJVs corresponds to the predictions. It is also noted that the highest value for McFadden's R^2 (0.39) is Model 2, and therefore it is the preferred model. In the light of these results, the regressions appear to have reasonable explanatory and predictive ability.

Effect of specificity and opacity

As expected, the positive relation between asset specificity – measured by specific human capital, R&D intensity and cost of sales – on equity participation indicates that specific assets deployed in the JV are statistically significant in predicting the

Table 19.1 The Pearson correlation matrix for independent variables (n = 542)

	A	B	C	D	E	F	G	H	I	J	K	L	M	N	O	P	Q
A	1	−0.34	−0.05	0.02	−0.14	−0.04**	−0.16	0.07	0.21	0.02	−0.14	0.02	0.35	0.16	−0.01	0.06	0.31
B		1	0.08*	−0.21*	−0.02*	0.19	0.13*	−0.18	−0.19	−0.04	0.03	0.21*	−0.12	0.15	0.02	0.03	0.17*
C			1	−0.03	0.08	0.04	0.30	0.03*	−0.16*	−0.10	−0.01*	−0.15	0.18	0.04*	0.43**	−0.24	−0.11
D				1	−0.07*	−0.02	−0.22	0.09	0.04	0.15**	−0.12	0.16*	−0.04	0.02	−0.18	0.01**	0.05*
E					1	0.09	−0.03*	0.06*	−0.19	−0.04	−0.21	0.11**	0.36	0.01**	−0.09	−0.05	−0.27
F						1	0.01	0.04	0.08	−0.15	0.29	−0.06	−0.66	0.14	−0.01*	0.03	0.02
G							1	0.13	0.03**	0.12	0.06	0.1	0.22**	0.34	0.38	0.12	0.06
H								1	0.09	0.04	0.23**	0.43**	−0.13	0.05	−0.14	0.03	0.25**
I									1	0.07*	0.01	0.02	−0.14*	0.22**	0.23**	0.41	0.02
J										1	0.24	0.15	0.12	−0.17	0.22	−0.31	−0.40
K											1	0.32*	0.18	0.21	−0.33	−0.26*	0.29*
L												1	0.38	−0.18**	0.27*	0.39	0.48
M													1	0.42	−0.22	0.33*	−0.20*
N														1	0.25	0.39	0.38
O															1	0.46	0.32*
P																1	0.36
Q																	1

Notes: A = R&D intensity; B = cost of sales; C = specific human capital; D = intangible assets; E = growth; F = size; G = cultural distance; H = cross-border; I = US*R&D intensity; J = China*R&D intensity; K = Europe*R&D intensity; L = US*specific human capital; M = China*specific human capital; N = Europe*specific human capital; O = US*intangible assets; P = China*intangible assets; Q = Europe*intangible assets. **Correlations significant at 0.01 level (two-tailed). *Correlations significant at 0.05 level (two-tailed).

Table 19.2 Descriptive statistics ($n = 542$)

Variables	Mean	S.D.
A	2.25	0.11
B	1.69	0.24
C	4.49	31.12
D	3.42	1.96
E	2.40	0.73
F	15.69	0.80
Country of origin	**Numbers**	**Percentage**
US: Partners from US	136	25
China: Partners from China (including Hong Kong, Taiwan and Macau)	165	30
Europe: Partners from European countries	107	20
UK	134	25
Sector		
Manufacturing	175	32
Transportation, communication and utilities	151	28
Mineral industry	115	21
Construction	101	19
Ownership share		
Minority: 1–49 per cent	174	32
Equal: 50/50 per cent	166	31
Majority: > 50 per cent	202	37

likelihood of increased equity contribution (majority ownership). These variables in general are significant at 1 per cent to 5 per cent level. The proxy for opacity of assets – the level of intangible assets – also exhibits a positive and significant coefficient at the 5 per cent level, suggesting that the relative opacity of assets contributed to the JV increases the likelihood of a larger equity capital shareholding. These results give support to H1a and H1b and are consistent with previous findings that suggest the level of equity ownership is positively related to the level of a firm's specific assets dedicated to the JV (Delios and Beamish, 1999; Dunning, 2000; Gatignon and Anderson, 1988; Pan, 1996). Our results are also consistent with the Lu and Hebert (2005) finding that partners' increased equity contribution appears to be positively related to the presence of highly proprietary R&D assets. In addition, partners' transferring specific and opaque assets to the JV with 'inadequate' ownership shares might find that the efficient exploitation of their assets is hampered. For example, their assets may be utilized for purposes that are not specified in the agreement or in ways that could be damaging to their interest (Oxley, 1997; Steensma and Lyles, 2000). Thus, a JV structure that assigns to the partner contributing specific or opaque assets a greater share of the equity capital may enhance the performance of the JV.

Regarding H2a and H2b, the cross-border dummy is significant at the 1 per cent level, supporting the view on the effect of specificity and opacity of the assets

Table 19.3 Results of the ordered logit analysis ($n = 542$)

	Model 1		Model 2	
Constant	164.045	(0.188)	−366.078	(0.324)
R&D intensity	58.7784	***(0.007)	59.051	***(0.002)
Cost of sales	33.630	**(0.018)	37.477	**(0.044)
Specific human capital	1.431	***(0.001)	2.213	**(0.016)
Intangible assets	7.097	***(0.005)	5.136	***(0.009)
Growth	15.428	**(0.047)	14.014	**(0.046)
Size	−0.148	(0.318)	−115.202	(0.330)
Cultural distance			−0.301	***(0.002)
Cross-border			1.353	***(0.002)
US			1.96	(0.341)
Europe			−2.731	**(0.023)
China			−7.686	**(0.043)
US*R&D intensity			2.173	(0.632)
Europe*R&D intensity			5.835	**(0.042)
China*R&D intensity			−8.512	***(0.002)
US*Intangible assets			−4.325	**(0.047)
Europe*intangible assets			7.284	**(0.037)
China*intangible assets			−9.004	***(0.001)
US*specific human capital			−6.287	(0.447)
Europe*specific human capital			4.169	(0.125)
China*specific human capital			−12.414	**(0.012)
A. Models statistics:				
Log likelihood function	−57.362		−50.312	
Restricted log likelihood	−87.237		−82.428	
Chi-squared	62.450		70.233	
p-value of chi-squared	0.005		0.002	
Predicted	68%		70%	
McFadden's R^2	0.342		0.390	
B. Contribution of interaction terms:				
Chi square $\chi^2 53.0$ with 9 df ($\rho = 0.002$)				
C. Wald test for industry:				
Industry Wald $\chi^2 2.143$ ($\rho = 0.032$)				

Notes: p values in parentheses; * significant at 10 per cent level, ** significant at 5 per cent level and *** significant at 1 per cent.

and increased level of equity shareholding in cross-border JVs. In addition, a comparison of the full model (Model 2) with the effect of specificity and opacity of assets (Model 1) reveals that when the interactions terms are included the model has a greater interpretive power. Testing separately for the effect of all interaction terms, they account for a substantial amount of variation in equity contribution (chi square $\chi^2_{(9)} = 53 \rho = 0.002$). This underscores the impact of specific and opaque assets on the level of equity contribution in IJVs, and this result supports the view that the perceived uncertainty/variability associated with the dedication of specific and opaque assets is greater in IJVs. This result is consistent with the existing literature (Barkema et al., 1996, 1997; Eriksson et al., 1997) where IJVs entail higher information and knowledge acquisition costs.

Controlling for IJVs, the result also shows that the foreign partner is more likely to have a smaller share of the equity capital as cultural distance increases (Model 2). The cultural distance variable is significant at the 1 per cent level and is negatively signed. This result suggests that the foreign partner faced with 'liability of the foreignness' aims to lower its equity shareholding as cultural distance increases, and it is in accordance with Yamin and Golesorkhi (2010), who found that foreign partners are more likely to acquire minority ownership in IJVs. This is consistent with the literature on mode of market entry, supporting the view that the greater the cultural distance between the country of the investing firm and the country of entry, the more likely a firm will choose a JV (Kogut and Singh, 1988; Larimo, 2003; Slangen and Hennart, 2008). However, we have extended this finding to predict the level of equity shareholding in JVs.

The significance of regional dummies in case of European and Chinese partners at the 5 per cent level (Model 2) highlights that there are significant differences across the three foreign origins in respect to their equity participation. When other factors are held constant, the overall results suggest that on average the Chinese partners hold the lowest share of equity capital, followed by European and US partners. The results of interaction terms give partial support to H3a and H3b. With respect to what leads these partners to have a smaller equity capital shareholding, interactions with all measures of specificity and opacity are significant for R&D intensity, specific human capital and intangible assets in case of Chinese partners. The results show that the Chinese partners are more likely to have a smaller equity capital shareholding based on the level of their R&D intensity, specific human capital and intangible assets deployed in the JV. The interaction of R&D intensity and intangible assets is significant for Chinese partners at the 1 per cent level while the interaction with specific human capital is significant at the 5 per cent level.

In the case of European partners, we find that R&D intensity and intangible assets are significant and have positive signs. This result could support the regional argument by Rugman (2005), whereby information acquisition and processing by a firm regarding a partner is easier if both parties belong to the same region. European partners are from the same region as their JV partner (UK), having the advantage of being more familiar with the cultural and the organizational environment of their partner. In the case of US partners, we only find support for H3a and H3b for interaction with intangible assets. This supports the view that US partners, being outside the region of the JV partner, are faced with additional costs of knowledge and information acquisition when they contribute intangible assets to the JV, therefore opting for a lower level of equity shareholding.

Overall, these results indicate that in IJVs, partners faced with increased 'liability of foreignness' when deploying specific and opaque assets to the JV require guarantees from their respective partners, hence the provision of a smaller equity capital. In this context, higher monitoring and/or measurement costs stem from barriers to understanding and interpreting partners' behaviour (as expressed by Johanson and Vahlne, 2009), and use of assets contributed to the IJV. The literature on country of origin has been predominately concerned with firm organizational mode choice, while we consider the role of equity as a guarantee function (Kogut and

Singh, 1988; Slangen and Hennart, 2008; Slangen and Beugelsdijk, 2010). Studies that have examined the country of origin of partners and their preferred level of equity capital ownership in IJVs have exhibited mixed results. Chadee and Qiu (2001) find that European partners have the lowest equity capital shareholding in their JV with Chinese partners, followed by the US; while Pan (1996) and Hu and Chen (1993) find that partners from Hong Kong have the lowest equity share in their Chinese JVs. However, this chapter provides new insight into determinants of equity capital shareholdings based on partners' asset specificity and/or opacity and monitoring costs in IJVs.

With respect to control variables, the sign for growth is positive, as expected, and significant at the 5 per cent level. The inclusion of the growth variable enables a further analysis to be undertaken of the effects of specific assets on equity contribution. This follows as growth options are also partially captured by our proxy for R&D intensity, therefore similarly signed effects could be expected. The variables capturing the partner firm's size is not significant and negatively signed. One possible explanation is that this variable may also be related to industry characteristics and therefore is captured by its corresponding industry group dummies. The industry dummy variables are jointly significant at the 5 per cent level for the manufacturing and transportation, communication and utilities sectors, based on a Wald test.

Conclusion

Even though previous studies have acknowledged that ownership of equity is related to the perceived need to govern the intra-JVs interdependencies, the influence of the nature of the assets contributed on such interdependence has not been a major plank of previous research. The contribution of this chapter is twofold. First, this chapter provides theoretical argument and empirical evidence on the influence of relative specificity and opacity of the assets contributed by partners on the ownership structure of JVs. Second, our results confirm the insight of previous studies as to the importance of regional differences in structuring of IJVs (Rugman and Verbeke 2004, 2008). Our results indicate that this factor strongly interacts with and reinforces the impact of asset characteristics on JV ownership structure. Our chapter has clear limitations. We have only considered UK-based JVs; our findings cannot necessarily be generalized to JVs based in other countries. Furthermore, due to data constraints we have captured cultural distance rather crudely, largely at the regional level. Capturing regional and psychic differences at the individual country level would have put our findings on a more robust basis.

References

Aiken, L.S. and West, S.G. (1991) *Multiple Regression: Testing and Interpreting Interactions* (Newbury Park, CA: Sage Publications).

Ainuddin, R.A., Beamish, P.W., Hulland, J.S. and Rouse, M.J. (2007) 'Resource attributes and firm performance in international joint ventures', *Journal of World Business*, 42(1), 47–60.

Akerloff, G. (1970) 'The market for lemons: quality, uncertainty and the market mechanism', *Quarterly Journal of Economics*, 84(3), 488–500.

Barkema, H., Bell, J.H. and Pennings, J.M. (1996) 'Foreign entry, cultural barriers, and learning', *Strategic Management Journal*, 17(2), 151–66.

Barkema, H.G., Shenkar, O., Vermeulen, F. and Bell, J.H.J. (1997) 'Working abroad, working with others: how firms learn to operate international joint ventures', *Academy of Management Journal*, 40(2), 426–42.

Barney, J. (1991) 'Firm resources and sustained competitive advantage', *Journal of Management*, 17(1), 99–120.

Barzel, Y. (1982) 'Measurement cost and the organisation of markets', *Journal of Law and Economics*, 25(1), 27–48.

Barzel, Y. (1985) 'Transaction costs: are they just costs', *Journal of Institutional and Theoretical Economics*, 114(1), 4–6.

Blodgett, L.L. (1991) 'Partner contribution as predictors of equity share in international joint ventures', *Journal of International Business Studies*, 21(1), 63–78.

Brouthers, K.D. and Brouthers, L.E. (2000) 'Acquisition or green-field start-ups? Institutional, culture and transaction cost influence', *Strategic Management Journal*, 21(1), 89–97.

Buckley, P. (2009) 'The Impact of the Global Factory on Economic Development', *Journal of World Business*, 44(2), 131–43.

Buckley, P. and Casson, M. (1988) 'The theory of cooperation in international business', in F. Contractor and P. Lorange (eds) *Cooperative Strategies in International Business* (Toronto: Lexington Books).

Buckley, P. and Ghauri, P. (2004) 'Globalisation, economic geography and the strategy of multinational enterprises', *Journal of International Business Studies*, 35(2), 81–98.

Camerer, C. and Kenz, M. (1996) 'Coordination, organisational boundaries and fads in business practices', *Industrial and Corporate Change*, 5(1), 89–112.

Chadee, D.D. and Qiu, F. (2001) 'Foreign ownership of equity joint ventures in China: a pooled cross-section-time series analysis', *Journal of Business Research*, 52(2), 123–33.

Contractor, F.J. (1990) 'Ownership patterns for U.S. joint ventures aboard and the liberalization of foreign government regulations in the 1980s: evidence from the benchmark surveys', *Journal of International Business Studies*, 20(1), 55–73.

Delios, A. and Beamish, P.W. (1999) 'Ownership strategy of Japanese firms: transactional, institutional and experience influences', *Strategic Management Journal*, 20(10), 915–33.

Dunning, J. (2000) 'The eclectic paradigm as an envelope for economic and business theories of MNE activity', *International Business Review*, 9(2), 163–90.

Eriksson, K., Johanson, J., Majkgard, A. and Sharma, D. (1997) 'Experiential knowledge and cost in the internationalization process', *Journal of International Business Studies*, 28(2), 337–59.

Evans, J. and Mavondo, F.T. (2002) 'Psychic distance and organizational performance: an empirical examination of international retailing operations', *Journal of International Business Studies*, 33(3), 515–32.

Folta, T.B. (1994) 'Innovation through quasi-integration: an application of option theory to governance decisions in the biotechnology industry', Unpublished Doctoral Dissertation, Purdue University, West Lafayette, IN.

Foss, N.J. (2001) 'Leadership, beliefs and coordination: an explorative discussion', *Industrial and Corporate Change*, 10(1), 357–88.

Foss, J.N. and Robertson, P. (2000) 'Introduction: resources, technology and strategy', in J.N. Foss and P. Robertson (eds) *Resources, Technology and Strategy: Explorations in the Resource-Based Perspective* (London: Routledge).

Garcia Canal, E. (1996) 'Contractual form in domestic and international strategic JVs', *Organisation Studies*, 17(5), 773–94.

Gary, B. and Yan, A. (1992) 'A negotiations model of joint ventures formation, structure and performance: implications for global management', *Advances in International Comparative Management*, 7(7), 41–75.

Gatignon, H. and Anderson, E. (1988) 'The multinational corporation's degree of control over foreign subsidiaries: an empirical test of a transaction cost explanation', *Journal of Law, Economics and Organisation*, 4(2), 305–36.

Grossman, S.J. and Hart, O.D. (1986) 'The costs and benefits of ownership: a theory of vertical and lateral integration', *Journal of Political Economy*, 94(4), 691–719.

Hart, O. (1995) *Firms, Contracts, and Financial Structure* (New York: Oxford University Press).

Hart, O. and Moore, J. (1990) 'Property rights and the nature of the firm', *Journal of Political Economy*, 98(6), 1119–58.

Hennart, J. (1994) 'The comparative institutional theory of the firm: some implication for corporate strategy', *Journal of Management Studies*, 31(2), 193–207.

Hennart, J.F. and Larimo, J. (1998) 'The impact of culture on the strategy of multinational enterprise: does national origin affects ownership decisions?', *Journal of International Business Studies*, 29(3), 515–38.

Hennart, J.F. and Reddy, S. (1997) 'The choice between mergers/acquisitions and joint ventures: the case of Japanese investors in the United States', *Strategic Management Journal*, 18(1), 1–12.

Hu, M.Y. and Chen, H. (1993) 'Foreign ownership in Chinese joint ventures: a transaction cost analysis', *Journal of Business Research*, 26(2), 149–60.

Hymer, S. (1976) *The International Operations of National Firms* (Cambridge, MA: MIT Press).

Jensen, M.C. and Meckling, W.H. (1976) 'Theory of the firm: managerial behaviour, agency costs and ownership structure', *Journal of Financial Economics*, 3(4), 305–60.

Johanson, J. and Vahlne, J.E. (2009) 'The Uppsala internationalisation process model revisited: from liability of foreignness to liability of outsidership', *Journal of International Business Studies*, 40(9), 1411–31.

Kogut, B. and Singh, H. (1988) 'The effects of national culture on the choice of entry mode', *Journal of International Business Studies*, 19(3), 411–32.

Larimo, J. (1993) 'The ownership arrangement decisions in foreign direct investments: behaviour of Finnish firms in OECD countries', European International Business Academy, Lisbon, Portugal.

Larimo, J. (2003) 'Form of investment by Nordic firms in world markets', *Journal of Business Research*, 56(10), 791–803.

Lippman, S. and Rumelt, R. (1982) 'Uncertain imitability: an analysis of interfirm differences under competition', *Bell Journal of Economics*, 13(2), 418–39.

Lu, J.W. and Hebert, L. (2005) 'Equity control and survival of international joint ventures: a contingency approach', *Journal of Business Research*, 58(6), 736–45.

Luo, Y. (2002) 'Capability exploitation and building in foreign markets: implications for multinational enterprises', *Organisation Science*, 13(1), 48–63.

Nachum, L. (2003) 'Liability of foreignness in global competition? Financial service affiliates in the city of London', *Strategic Management Journal*, 24(12), 1187–208.

O'Grady, S. and Lane, H.W. (1996) 'The psychic distance paradox', *Journal of International Business Studies*, 27(2), 309–33.

Oxley, J. (1997) 'Appropriability hazards and governance in strategic JVs: a transaction cost approach', *Journal of Law, Economics and Organisation*, 13(2), 387–409.

Pan, Y. (1996) 'Influences on foreign equity ownership level in joint ventures in China', *Journal of International Business Studies*, 27(1), 1–26.

Peteraf, M. (1993) 'The cornerstones of competitive advantage: a resource-based view', *Strategic Management Journal*, 14(3), 179–91.

Rajan, R.G. and Zingales, L. (1995) 'What do we know about capital structure? Some evidence from international data', *Journal of Finance*, 50(5), 1421–60.

Rangan, S. (2000) 'The problem of search and deliberation in economic action: when social networks really matter', *Academy of Management Review*, 25(4), 813–28.

Reuer, J.J. and Ragozzino, R. (2006) 'Agency hazards and JV portfolios', *Strategic Management Journal*, 27(1), 27–43.

Rugman, A. (2005) *The Regional Multinationals: MNEs and 'Global' Strategic Management* (Cambridge: Cambridge University Press).

Rugman, A. and Verbeke, A. (2004) 'A perspective on regional and global strategies of multinational enterprises', *Journal of International Business Studies*, 35(1), 3–18.

Rugman, A. and Verbeke, A. (2008) 'The theory and practice of regional strategy: a response to Osegowitsch and Sammartino', *Journal of International Business Studies*, 39(2), 326–32.

Slangen, A.H.L. and Beugelsdijk, S. (2010) 'The impact of institutional hazards on foreign multinational activity: a contingency perspective', *Journal of International Business Studies*, 41(6), 980–95.

Slangen, A.H. and Hennart, J.F. (2008) 'Do multinational really prefer to enter culturally distant countries through greenfields rather than through acquisitions? The role of parent experience and subsidiary autonomy', *Journal of International Business Studies*, 39(3), 472–90.

Slangen, A.H.L. and Van Tulder, R.J.M. (2009) 'Cultural distance, political risk, or governance quality? Towards a more accurate conceptualisation and measurement of external uncertainty in foreign entry mode research', *International Business Review*, 18(3), 276–91.

Steensma, H. and Lyles, M. (2000) 'Explaining IJV survival in a transitional economy through social exchange and knowledge-based perspectives', *Strategic Management Journal*, 21(8), 831–51.

Teece, D. (1992) 'Competition, cooperation and innovation: organisational arrangements for regimes of rapid technological progress', *Journal of Economic Behavior and Organisation*, 18(1), 1–25.

Titman, S. and Wessels, R. (1988) 'The determinants of capital structure choice', *Journal of Finance*, 43(1), 1–19.

Tsang, E.W.K. and Yip, P.S.L. (2007) 'Economic distance and the survival of foreign direct investments', *Academy of Management Journal*, 50(5), 1156–68.

Tsang, W.K. (2000) 'Transaction cost and resource-based explanations of joint ventures: a comparison and synthesis', *Organisation Studies*, 21(1), 215–42.

Vicente-Lorente, J.D. (2001) 'Specificity and opacity resource-based determinants of capital structure: evidence for Spanish manufacturing firms', *Strategic Management Journal*, 22(2), 157–77.

Williamson, O.E. (1979) 'Transaction cost economics: the governance of contractual relations', *Journal of Law and Economics*, 22(2), 233–61.

Williamson, O.E. (1985) *The Economic Institutions of Capitalism: Firms, Markets, Rational Contracting* (New York: Free Press).

Williamson, O.E. (1991) 'Comparative economic organisation: the analysis of discrete structural alternatives', *Administrative Science Quarterly*, 36(2), 269–96.

Winter, S.G. (1987) *Knowledge and Competence as Strategic Assets* (New York: Harper and Row).

Yamin, M. and Golesorkhi, S. (2010) 'Cultural distance and the pattern of equity ownership structure in international joint ventures', *International Business Review*, 19(5), 457–67, doi: 10.1016/j.ibusrev.2009.11.004.

Yamin, M. and Sinkovics, R. (2006) 'Online internationalisation, psychic distance reduction and the virtuality trap', *International Business Review*, 15(4), 339–60.

Yan, A. and Gray, B. (1994) 'Bargaining power, management control, and performance in United States-China joint ventures: a comparative case study', *Academy of Management Journal*, 37(6), 1478–517.

Zaheer, S. (1995) 'Overcoming the liability of foreignness', *Academy of Management Journal*, 38(2), 341–63.

Part VII
Corporate Governance and Organization

20
Economic Organization and Social Solidarity: *Keiretsu* as a Local/Global Concept

Tomoko Oikawa

This chapter argues, first, that to see *keiretsu* only as an economic organization does not provide a complete picture of the term; accordingly, it is necessary to explore the philosophical concept of *keiretsu*. Secondly, it argues that the concept of *keiretsu* is based on the principles of social solidarity that are unique to Japanese society. A third point focuses on conventional socio-economic aspects of *keiretsu* and develops these in terms of the conceptual matrix put forward in the earlier sections. Finally, the principles of *keiretsu* are explored through structural linguistics.

Over the last two decades, a variety of analyses have been carried out on the strength of Japanese firms in comparison with their Western counterparts. A major focus of these studies has been as *keiretsu*. There remain wide-ranging differences in the assessment of both the uniqueness and the universality of *keiretsu*; however, it is commonly seen that most studies dealt with a partial *keiretsu* and explained the rationale behind *keiretsu* based on transaction cost economics. This chapter claims that *keiretsu* organization needs to be grasped conceptually and viewed as an organic whole. For this, socio-economic aspects – Granovetter's view in particular – are of use. This leads to a structuralism viewpoint of *keiretsu*.

The various definitions and terms used for *keiretsu*

Following the collapse of Japan's economic bubble in 1990 and the Asian crisis, the so-called 'dismantlement of Nissan *keiretsu*' (1999) was particularly prominent in the press. Some economists and commentators (Chew, 2001; Cowling and Tomlinson, 2000; Lamming, 2000; Miwa and Ramseyer, 2002; *The Economist*, 25 November 2000; *Business Week*, 15 March 1999; Bremner, Thornton and Kunii, 15 March 1999) predicted that *keiretsu* in general would fade away, following the dissolution of Nissan *Keiretsu*. Others argued that the 'Japanese model' was undergoing a change that would, sooner or later, result from exogenous pressures (Dore, 1998; Whittaker and Kurosawa, 1998). It was also argued (Hosono et al., 2004) that the positive roles of *keiretsu* affiliation and cross-shareholdings had disappeared during the 'lost decade' of the 1990s. On the other hand, there are views that *keiretsu* has still been substantial in Japanese business (Lai, 1999; McGuire and Dow, 2003) and that the vertical *keiretsu* has even been strengthened (Morita and Nakahara, 2004).

Various terms for *keiretsu*

There exist different and diversified aspects of *keiretsu* and, correspondingly, a wide variety of alternative terms are used to describe *keiretsu* (Abegglen and Stalk, 1985; Buckley, 2004; Chowdhury and Geringer, 2001; Dewenter, 2003; Dore, 1998; Dyer, 1996; Nakamura and Odaka, 2003; Orrù et al., 1989; Solis, 2003; Womack et al., 1990). Most studies carried out on *keiretsu* defined it as bank-centred business groups (Dewenter et al., 2001), that is, a horizontal *keiretsu*. In contrast, subcontracting relationships described as vertical *keiretsu* are either limited to those listed on the first section of the Tokyo Stock Exchange (Aoki, 1988; Asanuma, 1990; Gerlach, 1992a, 1992b) or else they are not clearly defined, which is the case in most studies. Broadly, economists share the view that *keiretsu* organization is not intrinsic to Japan. Sociologists stress the importance of seeing cultural factors in *keiretsu*. It is puzzling that in all this rich literature, nowhere has the origin and/or the definition of the concept of *keiretsu* been proposed.

Various definitions of *keiretsu*

Komiya (1990, p. 185) distinguishes *keiretsu* by three different types of groups: (a) ancestral descendants of the three old *zaibatsu* groups, that is, Mitsui, Mitsubishi, and Sumitomo; (b) 'business groups' formed around the Daiichi Kangyo Bank, the Fuyo Group, and the Sanwa Bank; these 'ancestral and business groups' constitute the 'six largest *keiretsu*'; and (c) the industrial groups formed around these giant corporations. These are composed of subsidiaries, allied firms, important customers, subcontractors (primary, secondary, tertiary), wholesalers and retailers. Examples include the Matsushita Group, the Toyota Group, the Hitachi *keiretsu* and the Shin-Nittetsu *keiretsu*.

Most studies on *keiretsu* have focused on (a) or (b) above – the ancestral and bank-centred business groups, as horizontal *keiretsu*; other studies, focusing on (c) which is linked to vertical *keiretsu*, have failed to see it as an organic whole. Instead, they have focused on the supplier–user relationships at the primary tier (Aoki, 1988; Asanuma, 1989; Dyer, 1996, 1997; Dyer and Singh, 1998; Hill, 1995; Tallman, 1991; Williamson, 1991) to show their achievements of high asset specificity and low transaction costs. Most institutionalist economists and sociologists take a similar attitude towards the *keiretsu* organization.

Mainstream economics takes the view that organizational practices in Japan are not culturally unique, but rather rationally or consciously developed (Aoki, 1988, 1990; Dore, 1973; Koike, 1994). Some sociologists (Abegglen and Stalk, 1985; Bhappu, 2000; Dore, 1987, 2000; Gerlach, 1992a, 1992b; Orrù et al., 1989; Sugimoto, 1988) maintain that there is some intrinsic cultural factor in *keiretsu*. Rugman and Collinson (2004) refer to Toyota, which enjoys an amicable long-term relationship with suppliers, sometimes a *keiretsu*-style relationship. More needs to be said, however, to explain *keiretsu* organization as an organic whole.

Imai (1992, pp. 198–230) took an evolutionary view of *keiretsu* starting from *the zaibatsu as corporate networks*, to *postwar business groups* and to *the network industrial organization*. Anthropologists such as Nakane (1973) and Lebra Sugiyama (1992) demonstrated the social order of *keiretsu*. Interestingly, however, even sociologists, who see some cultural factors in *keiretsu*, adopt the definitions of economists.

Komiya (1990, p. 185) stated that the groups in category (c) are not much different in nature from the industrial groups found in other developed countries. He emphasized a number of special characteristics: (1) that large Japanese firms try hard to remain lean; (2) that business relations within a group are based on the mutual (long-term) advantages of the parties involved; over the long term, transactions within the group must conform to the same, or even better, standards in terms of quality and prices as would prevail in transactions with firms outside the group; and (3) that relations between the firms in an industrial group are not based on short-term interests, nor do they always rely on contracts; instead, they are based upon mutual trust cultivated over the years between the members of the firms' top management. Komiya's statement above indicates the possibility that linking business practice with cultural commitment might lead to an in-depth understanding of the concept of *keiretsu*.

Gerlach (1992a, 1992b) carried out the first systematic analysis of *keiretsu*. His emphasis is on a vague distinction between *keiretsu* and non-*keiretsu*. He asks 'then what is the nature of *keiretsu*?', but deals mainly with the economic aspects (1992a, p. 116), suggesting that 'economic efficiency remains only a partial explanation'. He underlined (1992b, p. 15) 'the importance of understanding why these features have evolved in the distinctive form they have in Japan and that *keiretsu* is considered to be the result of a continuing unfolding of overlapping economic, political, and social forces at the national level'. This is a promising recognition of the cultural complexity of *keiretsu*, but Gerlach does not press this point.

Aoki (1988, 1994) refers to *keiretsu* as two types of corporate groupings through stockholding. One type is the so-called former *zaibatsu* corporate or financial group, and the other is the subsidiary grouping, or capital *keiretsu*. In capital *keiretsu* – the focus of this chapter – a dominant parent company combines its own subsidiaries through full or partial stockholding and vertical technological relations. Furthermore, it tends to rely on sub- and/or spin-off subsidiaries to externalize activities performed at the core of its internal organization. Considering a stylized model of the prime manufacturer–supplier relation in the car industry, two types of suppliers are distinguished. In relation to the distinction between suppliers, Aoki (1988) refers to Asanuma (1989). Asanuma (1989) classified suppliers into two parts: (i) parts produced following 'Drawings Supplied (DS)' provided by the enterprise concerned; (ii) parts produced following 'Drawings Approved (DA)' designed by the supplier and approved by the concerned enterprise. Both of them supply parts directly to major car manufacturers. However, there also exists a vast majority of suppliers with less specialized technological expertise, and they supply less crucial components to the primary manufacturer.

Aoki highlighted financial *keiretsu* and capital *keiretsu*. The 'DA parts' supplier and 'DS parts' supplier are included in capital *keiretsu*, which are linked directly to major car manufacturers. They are considered to be the epitome of subcontracting enterprises (Watanabe, 1992), and other less important suppliers with no stockholding are considered to be outside capital *keiretsu*.

Sako (1992) maintains a sociological stance on *keiretsu*; the *keiretsu* group is a self-defined business community bound by virtue of having overlapping and multiple reciprocal ties in shareholding, personnel and trading. Sako (1992) refers to smaller suppliers and subcontractors in Japan as *shitauke* firms, as typically organized into overlapping pyramidal structures of primary, secondary and tertiary suppliers with firm size diminishing as one goes down the hierarchy. Similar to Aoki's aspect (1988), *shitauke* is distinguished here from the hierarchical network of core suppliers and subcontractors such as the Toyota group.

Dore (1998, 2000) sees a specific feature of the Japanese economy as one of Asia's version of capitalism in its distinctiveness – compared with Anglo-Saxon capitalism. Japanese firms are seen more as communities and such characteristics have originated from the egalitarian characteristics of Japanese society. Rugman (2003, 2005) stresses the importance of the realization that regional rather than global strategies are the pivot for multinational enterprises (MNEs). In this context, he refutes the universalist view that there is an emerging global culture of high-living professionals with common values, and claims that instead of 'one language, one thirst, one food, one car', there are strong regional differences in each part of the triad (EU, Asia and the US). His argument confirms the existence of regional differences not only in culture but also in the business strategy of MNEs. These different perspectives indicate that *keiretsu* possesses culturally specific factors, and complicate further the question, 'what is the nature of *keiretsu*?'.

Institutional perspectives: economists and sociologists

Since the 1990s, both economists and sociologists have increasingly underlined institutional and/or cultural aspects of organizations in different ways. The new institutional perspectives on business strategy have emerged among economists and sociologists (Granovetter, 1992, 1994, 1999; Gulati, 1995; Hill, 1995; Jones et al., 1997; Nooteboom, 2000; North, 1990, 1991; Oliver, 1997; Osborn and Hagedoorn, 1997; Scott, 1995; Simon and March, 1993; Williamson, 1991). While 'institutional theories vary among economists and sociologists in their mode of carrier or host and also in their different operating level' (Scott, 1995, pp. 55–7), they are expected to explain 'why strategies of firms in non-Western countries differ from Western counterparts' (Peng, 2002, p. 52). Sociologists emphasize a cognitive conception, cultural carriers, and macro-level focus. The new institutional economists stress a regulative conception, structural carriers, and a micro focus. Hill (1995) and Dyer (1996, 1997) attempted a number of empirical studies focusing on the supplier–user relationship in the case of Japan to examine what conditions can achieve the benefits of high asset specificity and low transaction costs.

Hill (1995) argues that the institutional structure of a nation helps to explain the ability of firms based in that nation to succeed or fail in a competitive global marketplace, and that one important factor underlying the economic success of

Japan is a set of *informal* constraints, the cultural value system. This system helps facilitate cooperation between individuals and encourages them to undertake productivity-enhancing investments in specialization. Dyer (1996, p. 649) defines *keiretsu* as 'hybrid alliances'. He argues that *keiretsu* has resulted in minimizing transaction costs and maximizing transaction values of human asset specificity and information sharing. He suggests (Dyer, 1997, p. 552) that 'a key factor of efficient governance is trust and/or trustworthiness of transactors'. Williamson (1991) highlighted three contributing factors – employment, subcontracting and banking – to the Japanese economy. He noted that the efficacy of each of these depends on distinctive institutional supports, and that the three key factors bear a complementary relation. With regard to subcontracting, he claimed that the logic of economics outweighed the myth that the Japanese had led to a greater propensity to cooperate.

Late in the 1990s, there emerged another aspect of economic organization among some sociologists and economists. They developed a multifaceted view that alliances and networks are evolutionary, multifaceted institutions for cooperation (Gulati, 1995; Jones et al., 1997; Nooteboom, 1999, 2000; Osborn and Hagedoorn, 1997). Some scholars (Bhappu, 2000; Chowdhury and Geringer, 2001; Lai, 1999; Mcguire and Dow, 2003) also remarked on the importance of social embeddedness in understanding *keiretsu*. While these empirical studies highlighted the importance of institutions in relation to *keiretsu*, they still saw *keiretsu* as subject to the control of transaction cost economics.

Granovetter's theory of business groups

Hill (1995) and Dyer (1996, 1997) stressed the importance of institutions, of cultural systems and of trustworthiness. The cultural value system is, however, linked directly to individual actions, and the hybrid alliance of *keiretsu* is explained in terms of its efficiency by the existence of trustworthiness between transactors. It is presumed that new institutional economists have tried to define cultural systems and institutions within the field of transaction cost economics. Thus, a socio-economic viewpoint of the cultural value system, embedded in the economic system and in the hybrid alliance of *keiretsu*, is required in order to achieve its intended linkage. New institutional economics has tried to define even cultural systems and institutions within transaction cost economics, reducing further the recognition of the cultural strength of the concept.

Granovetter (1992, 1994, 1999) argues that it is important to recognize how economic action is constrained and shaped by the structures of social solidarity in which all real economic actors are embedded. Theorists such as Durkheim and Weber pioneered this viewpoint and saw economic action as a subordinate and special case of social action. Granovetter (1992) stressed the contingencies associated with historical background, and of social structure and collective action and their corresponding constraints, and claims that his aim is to find general principles that are valid for all times and places. He maintains that there is a second question parallel to Coase's (1937) question, 'why do firms exist?' (1994, pp. 453–4). He asks, 'why is it that in every known capitalist economy, firms do not conduct business as isolated units, but rather form cooperative relations with other firms, with legal and social boundaries of variable clarity around such relations.' Four answers have been proposed. One is 'resource dependence', which argues that firms are rarely self-sufficient and will typically form alliances or connections with other firms upon which they regularly depend for resources. The other three are (1) the need for 'strategic alliances' among firms – a need said to derive from the changing nature of markets and of consumer demand; (2) the need asserted by Marxist analysts for coalitions of capitalists to form against other societal interests, or of one sector of capitalist firms against others; and (3) the desire of firms to extract 'rents' from the economy or the government through coalitions, over and above those that could be obtained in a properly competitive economy (Granovettor, 1994, p. 454).

All these answers focus on either what motivates economic actors to establish a linkage, or on how their economic outcomes will be improved by such a linkage. Granovetter (1994, p. 454) argues that these answers do not illuminate the likelihood or explain the occurrence of such linkages. Instead, they require a consideration of how economic actors construct their alliances and what the structure of all such connections is in a given economy. From the perspective of Granovetter, the concept of *business groups* (original emphasis) would come into focus: (1) A business group is a collection of firms bound together in some formal and/or informal ways, excluding, on the one hand, a set of firms bound merely by short-term strategic alliances and, on the other, a set of firms legally consolidated into a single one. (2) Within business groups, there are generally personal and operational ties among all the firms. (3) What distinguishes business groups from collections of firms united by, for example, common financial origins, as in American conglomerates, is the existence of social solidarity and social structure among component firms. (4) It thus becomes of interest to what extent the underpinning is clearly identifiable, by such factors as region, political party, ethnicity, kinship or religion. It is important to note that Granovetter distinguished *business groups* which are based on the existence of the principles of social solidarity and social structure from other business groups. Notably, the *keiretsu* in Japan and the *chaebol* in Korea are exemplified. The key issue arises: what are the principles of social solidarity and social structure in the case of *keiretsu*?

Solis (2003) seems to support Granovetter's theory, showing an invisible aspect of *keiretsu*. This study focuses on Japanese production networks abroad and examines the pervasiveness of *keiretsu* ties within them. It was found that even in the absence of *keiretsu* commitments that could constrain purchasing decisions, Japanese electronic production networks overseas remained remarkably closed to outside suppliers. This indicates that *keiretsu* functioned not as tangible ties but as principles. Further, it suggests that *keiretsu* is essentially the principle of social solidarity.

It is widely understood that when the term '*keiretsu*' was used originally, its definition was not clear. However, it first occurred publicly in the '*shitauke-keiretsu ron'sou*' (the argument as to whether there had been change in *shitauke* which developed to systematic subcontracting – *keiretsuka* – with the principal firms) during the 1950s among economists in Japan (based on personal communication with Mitsui Itsutomo, a professor at Yokohama National University in Japan, 8 March 2006). Nakane (1973, p. 102) states that each group is known informally as 'of the line of A' or 'descended from A', and the word *kei*, signifying descent or genealogical relationship, symbolizes the Japanese social system. This indicates that *keiretsu* is the institution at the national level. The principles of *keiretsu*, therefore, should be considered at a national level. In order to explore the principles of *keiretsu*, we use a linguistic approach.

The principles of *keiretsu*: A linguistic approach

> The object is not given in advance of the viewpoint: far from it. Rather, one might say that it is the viewpoint adopted which creates the object. (Saussure, 1983, p. 8)

Structural linguistics originated from Saussure's *Cours de linguistique générale* (1916). Saussure's theory (1916) branched off in Europe and the US. In the US, Sapir (1949) and Whorf (1952) are distinguished as structural linguists, but Chomsky (1957) began to dominate after the late 1950s and 1960s. His approach to the study of language emphasizes an innate set of linguistic principles shared by all humans, known as 'generative grammar' or 'universal grammar'.

As discussed in the previous section, Granovetter (1992) pointed out the contingencies associated with historical background of social structure and collective actions, and their corresponding constraints. This aspect leads to the structural linguistics view. Importantly, the word '*keiretsu*' has its own particular explanation as a common noun of the Japanese language as Nakane (1973) described (as discussed at the end of the previous section). We conjecture that the principles of *keiretsu* represent the core values of social solidarity in Japanese society. Based on these points of view, this section explores how the core values of *keiretsu* are expressed and explained in the Japanese language. First we briefly discuss how language is linked to thoughts and values; then, the Japanese language will be explored in relation to the core values of *keiretsu*. 'The self' in terms of language will be the focal point in this context.

Language and thoughts

Sapir (1949, pp. 68–9) states that language conditions our observation and thinking, which build up the 'real world'. We live in the 'real world' very much at the mercy of the particular language. This position was extended by Whorf (1952, pp. 167–88) who declared 'This study (of language) shows that the forms of a person's thoughts are controlled by inexorable laws of pattern of which he is unconscious... [His] thinking itself is in a language – in English, in Sanskrit, in Chinese. And every language is a vast pattern-system, different from others... [it] channels his reasoning, and builds the house of his consciousness.' We will compare and contrast the Japanese language with English, following Whorf's suggestion, in order to clarify the distinction between the two languages in terms of thoughts and values, and to demonstrate Saussure's axiom that 'it is the viewpoint adopted which creates the object.'

Keiretsu

The word *keiretsu* is a noun in Japanese and is commonly used in Japanese society. *Kei* in Japanese means 'a line, lineage, blood to connect or to be connected' such as a group of interrelated elements, and *retsu* means line or row, or an array of people or things. Thus, *keiretsu* means a type of group consisting of persons connected like a line or a series of things lined up organically (Japanese dictionaries). The use is not limited to business, but is also found in the field of sociology (Lebra Sugiyama, 1992; Nakane, 1973) (e.g. for flower arrangement, tea ceremony, school organization or even just for small private groups).

Thus we suggest that the major aspect of the word *keiretsu* may be an organic relationship of a group of interrelated elements or an array of people. This aspect could even imply that all members of a group in a *keiretsu* relationship would collapse without trust and dependence one upon another. Such an argument refers to individualism and collectivism. As a historical fact the word 'individualism' was imported; there is no root of this word as a concept in Japanese culture. There is also no concept or word for privacy (Kin'daichi, 2002) – a point that confirms the Saussure/Whorf approach to language. Therefore, how the self is viewed in the Japanese language will be the focus in evaluating *keiretsu* as the core values in social solidarity.

Self

Doi (1981) discussed how psychological *dependence* is structured in both personal and social solidarity in Japan. Benedict (1967) pointed out that the shame culture of Japan is contrasted to the sin culture of the West: in Japan, moral values arise from a communal consciousness, and in the West they arise from internal consciousness. Other anthropologists (Cole, 1979; Lebra Sugiyama and Lebra, 1986; Rohlen, 1974; Vogel, 1975) have remarked on the *dependence* peculiar to Japan, seen in a family, a couple and in the workplace.

With regard to the relationship between culture and the self, Markus and Kitayama (1991) contrast America and Asia. In Asian culture the emphasis is on attending to others, fitting in, and harmonious interdependence with them, whereas American culture neither assumes nor values such a connectedness among individuals, who, on the contrary, seek to maintain their independence from others by attending to the self. Here, two construals of the self are distinguished: the *independent construals of the self* in the West (in this context, America) and the *interdependent* in the non-West (Asia). These studies suggest that the relation to the self – which distinguishes Japan from America – indicates distinctive core values of social solidarity. Next we focus on the self in the Japanese language to explore the core values of *keiretsu*.

The Japanese language and self

Analogous to the thoughts of Markus and Kitayama (1991), but focusing on the linguistic aspect of self reference and address, Suzuki (1984) demonstrates the distinction of first and second personal pronouns between the Japanese and English languages, and shows a striking contrast in core values between the two languages. The basic difference is seen in the use of self-reference and address. The Japanese language has no first- and second-person pronouns equivalent to those found in English. Japanese terms of self-reference and address serve to specify and confirm the concrete roles of the speaker and the addressee within a given social context. In English, the speaker designates himself/herself by means of a first-person pronoun and then calls the addressee by a second-person pronoun – *I* and *you*. Thus, the function of first-person pronouns is to designate the user explicitly as the speaker. The meaning of the act of using *I* in English is to express verbally that the one who is speaking at this moment is nobody else but me. In contrast, *self-designation* in Japanese is relative and other-oriented. Other-oriented self-designation is the assimilation of the self, who is the observer, with the other, who is observed, with no clear distinction made between the positions of the two. It can be called 'empathetic identification'. They are accustomed to identifying with, and depending on one another. As Whorf comments, 'every language is a vast pattern-system, different from others.'

English is quite structured compared with the Japanese language, in the way of thinking and expressing logic, concepts and abstraction. In this context, *I* is the axis in the centre of the speaker's own world, restructured through his/her own perception. His/her perceived world should be logical and distinctive from the others because of the fixed and stable dimension of *I*. Such an *I* can be described as independent – individualist, egocentric and autonomous. In this way there should be no room for ambiguity or blurring. By contrast, the Japanese language indicates that Japanese people have no concept of an individual in a Western sense, and what is more they view the self as being immersed with the other, and thus regard an emphatic identification in order to overcome the distinction between the self and the other. Such values of the self symbolize the social solidarity in Japanese society. This may be connected with the essential implication of the term *keiretsu* – trust and dependence – in terms of social solidarity. For Saussure, what counts as 'object' is always dependent on the linguistic framework that creates a 'view' of that which constitutes the world. '*Viewpoint*' and '*object*' for (Saussure) are interdependent.

The Japanese language and society

Personal pronouns are a useful case study. Ohno (1999) comments on social relationships from a linguistic standpoint, as follows (Ohno, 1999, pp. 146–54):

> The use of personal pronouns written in the Japanese original characters, *hiragana and katakana*, corresponds with the physical distance between the speaker and a particular person in conversation. The more distant, the more honorific the word used...honorific words suggest a horizontal relationship in the society. *Kanji*, imported from China, brought the idea of patriarchy to Japan, a vertical relationship between self-designation and addressee.

Table 20.1 Summary of characteristics of the Japanese and English languages regarding self

Japanese	English
No personal pronouns (Suzuki, 1984)	Use of personal pronouns (Suzuki, 1984)
Other-oriented/relative (Suzuki, 1984)	Self-oriented/absolute (Suzuki, 1984)
Trust and dependence (Suzuki, 1984)	Independence/logic (Suzuki, 1984)
Multifaceted (Suzuki, 1984)	Centred (Suzuki, 1984)
Horizontal and vertical relationships/concrete (Inoue, 1993; Ohno, 1999)	Linear/abstract (Suzuki, 1984)
Ambiguity (Kato and Hardy, 1994).	Clarity (Kato and Hardy, 1994)
More psychological (Kin'daichi, 2002)	Less psychological (Kin'daichi, 2002)
No concept of privacy (Kin'daichi, 2002)	Concept of privacy

This insight into the Japanese characters *hiragana*, *katakana* and *kanji* confirms the structural linguistics approach used here. This also shows another aspect of *keiretsu* organization as horizontal and vertical, and helps us to understand the uniqueness in terms of organization. Pronoun use varies markedly between East and West; these differences are summarized in Table 20.1. Business practice using *keiretsu* is an Eastern form and does not easily travel to the West. But it is necessary that business practices everywhere recognize these important cultural divisions – in language, concept and philosophy.

Concluding comments

In this chapter I have attempted to clarify the concept of *keiretsu*. The concept of *business group* proposed by Granovetter was a starting point for this scheme, and led to a linguistic approach to find out the principles of *keiretsu*; in particular the structural linguistics viewpoint as represented by Saussure, Sapir and Whorf. The *keiretsu* is developing and evolving. *Keiretsu* transaction relationships are developing closer information exchanges between enterprises, which has led to increased numbers of enterprises in the network (Japan Small Business Research Institute, 2007). In other words, the *keiretsu* is changing and branching off into more complex relationships. However, the principles of *keiretsu* – the core values of trust and dependence – have not changed. These are essentially the core values in Japanese society.

The findings of this chapter point to further issues to be explored. The study of Rugman (2003; Rugman and Collinson 2004) on regional and global strategies among MNEs, for example, could be situated and supported within the context of structural linguistics. Individualism and collectivism are terms normally used in explaining organizational behaviour. However, these concepts remain to be clarified. They would require the support of structural linguistics. Another potential research topic is that the contrast between structural linguistics of Sassure, Sapir and Whorf-structural linguistics and Chomsky's 'generative grammar' or 'universal grammar' linguistics could be linked to the issues of business strategies among

MNEs. Finally, a further potential topic for future research is the link between Buddhism and *keiretsu* values.

References

Abegglen, J.C. and Stalk, G. (1985) *Kaisha: The Japanese Corporation* (New York: Basic Books).
Aoki, M. (1988) *Information, Incentives, and Bargaining in the Japanese Economy* (Cambridge: Cambridge University Press).
Aoki, M. (1990) 'Towards an economic model of the Japanese firm', *Journal of Economic Literature*, 28(1), 1–27.
Aoki, M. (1994) 'The Japanese firm as a system of attributes: a survey and research agenda', in M. Aoki and R. Dore (eds) *The Japanese Firm, Sources of Competitive Strength* (Oxford: Oxford University Press).
Asanuma, B. (1989) 'Manufacturer-supplier relationships in Japan and the concept of relation-specific skill', *Journal of the Japanese and International Economics*, 3(1), 1–30.
Asanuma, B. (1990) 'Nihon ni okeru meka to sapuraiya tono kankei – kankei tokushugino no gainen no chushutu to teishikika (Manufacturer-supplier relationship in Japan and the concept of relation-specific skill)', *Keizai Ronso* (Economic Review), Kyoto Daigaku Keizaigaku-kai (Kyoto University Economic Society), 145(1/2), 237–40.
Benedict, R. (1967) *The Chrysanthemum and the Sword: Patterns of Japanese Culture* (London: Routledge and Kegan Paul Ltd).
Bhappu, A.D. (2000) 'Note – the Japanese family: an institutional logic for Japanese corporate networks and Japanese management', *Academy of Management Review*, 25(2), 409–15.
Bremner, B., Thornton, E. and Kunii, I.M. (1999) 'Fall of A Keiretsu', *Business Week*, 86–92.
Buckley, P.J. (2004) 'Asian network firms: an analytical framework', *Asia Pacific Business Review*, 10(3/4), 254–71.
Chew, E. (2001) '*Keiretsu* are fading away', *Automotive News Europe*, 6(19), 14–31.
Chomsky, N. (1957) *Syntactic Structures* (The Hague: Mouton).
Chowdhury, S.D. and Geringer, J.M. (2001) 'Institutional ownership, strategic choices and corporate efficiency: evidence from Japan', *Journal of Management Studies*, 38(2), 271–91.
Coase, R. (1937) 'The nature of the firm', *Economica*, 4(16), 386–405.
Cole, R.E. (1979) *Work, Mobility and Participation: A Comparative study of American and Japanese Industry* (Berkeley, CA: University of California Press).
Cowling, K. and Tomlinson, P.R. (2000) 'The Japanese crisis – a case of strategic failure?', *The Economic Journal*, 110(464), 358–81.
Dewenter, K.L. (2003) 'The risk-sharing role of Japanese *keiretsu* business groups: evidence from restructuring in the 1990s', *Japan and World Economy*, 15(3), 261–74.
Dewenter, K.L., Novaes, W. and Pettway, R.H. (2001) 'Visibility versus complexity in business groups: evidence from Japanese keiretsu', *The Journal of Business*, 74(1), 79–100.
Doi, T. (1981) *The Anatomy of Dependence* (Tokyo: Kodansha International).
Dore, R. (1973) *British Factory, Japanese Factory: The Origins of National Diversity in Industrial Relations* (Berkeley, CA: University of California Press).
Dore, R. (1987) *Taking Japan Seriously: A Confucian Perspective of Leading Economic Issues* (London: The Athlone Press).
Dore, R. (1998) 'Asian crisis and the future of the Japanese model', *Cambridge Journal of Economics*, 22(6), 773–87.
Dore, R. (2000) *Stock Market Capitalism: Welfare Capitalism Japan and Germany versus the Anglo-Saxons* (Oxford: Oxford University Press).
Dyer, J.H. (1996) 'Does governance matter? Keiretsu alliances and asset specificity as sources of Japanese competitive advantage', *Organisation Science*, 7(6), 649–66.
Dyer, J.H. (1997) 'Effective interfirm collaboration: how firms minimize transaction costs and maximize transaction value', *Strategic Management Journal*, 18(7), 535–56.

Dyer, J.H. and Singh, H. (1998) 'The relational view: cooperative strategy and sources of interorganizational competitive advance', *Academy of Management Review*, 23(4), 660–79.
Gerlach, M.L. (1992a) 'Twilight of the keiretsu? A critical assessment', *Journal of Japanese Studies*, 18(1), 79–118.
Gerlach, M.L. (1992b) *Alliance Capitalism: The Social Organisation of Japanese Business* (Berkley, CA: University of California Press).
Granovetter, M. (1992) 'Economic institutions as social constructions: a framework for analysis', *Acta Sociologica*, 35(1), 3–11.
Granovetter, M. (1994) 'Business groups', in N.J. Smelsen and R. Swedberg (eds) *The Handbook of Economic Sociology*, 453–75 (Princeton, NJ: Princeton University Press).
Granovetter, M. (1999) 'Coarse encounters and formal models: taking Gibbons seriously', *Administrative Science Quarterly*, 44(2), 158–62.
Gulati, R. (1995) 'Does familiarity breed trust? The implications of repeated ties for contractual choice in alliances', *Academy of Management Journal*, 38(1), 85–112.
Hill, C. (1995) 'National institutional structures, transaction cost economizing and competitive advantage: the case of Japan', *Organisation Science*, 6(1), 119–31.
Hosono, K., Tomiyama, M. and Miyagawa, T. (2004) 'Corporate governance and research and development: evidence from Japan', *Economics of Innovation and New Technology*, 13(2), 141–65.
Imai, K. (1992) 'Japan's corporate networks', in H. Rosovsky and S. Kumon (eds) *The Political Economy of Japan*, 3 (*Cultural and Social Dynamics: 198–230*) (Stanford, CA: Stanford University Press).
Inoue, H. (1993) *Jikasei Bunshōtokuhon* (Homemade writing textbook) (Tokyo: Shin'chosha).
Japan Small Business Research Institute (2007) *White Paper on Small and Medium Enterprises in Japan* (Ministry of Economy, Trade and Industry).
Jones, C., Hesterly, W.S. and Borgatti, S.P. (1997) 'A general theory of network governance: exchange conditions and social mechanisms', *Academy of Management Review*, 22(4), 911–45.
Kato, K. and Hardy, V. (1994) *Eigo shōronbun no kakikata – eigo no lojikku-nihongo no lojikku* (How to write an English short essay – English logic Japanese logic) (Tokyo: Kodansha gendai shinsho).
Kin'daichi, H. (2002) *Nihon'go: shinpan* (Japanese: new edition) I and II (Tokyo: Iwanami shoten).
Koike, K. (1994) 'Learning and incentive systems in Japanese industry', in M. Aoki and R. Dore (eds) *The Japanese Firm, Sources of Competitive Strength* (Oxford: Oxford University Press).
Komiya, R. (1990) *The Japanese Economy: Trade, Industry, and Government* (Tokyo: University of Tokyo Press).
Lai, G.M.-H. (1999) 'Keiretsu and keiretsu business groups', *Journal of World Business*, 34(4), 423–48.
Lamming, R. (2000) 'Japanese supply chain relationships in recession', *Long Range Planning*, 33(6), 757–79.
Lebra Sugiyama, T. (1992) *Japanese Social Organization* (Honolulu, HI: University of Hawaii Press).
Lebra Sugiyama, T. and Lebra, W.P. (1986) *Japanese Culture and Behavior* (Honolulu, HI: University of Hawaii Press).
Markus, H.R. and Kitayama, S. (1991) 'Culture and the self: implications for cognition, emotion, and motivation', *Psychological Review*, 98(2), 224–53.
McGuire, J. and Dow, S. (2003) 'The persistence and implications of Japanese keiretsu organisation', *Journal of International Business Studies*, 34(4), 374–88.
Miwa, Y. and Ramseyer, J.M. (2002) 'The fable of the keiretsu', *Journal of Economics and Management Strategy*, 11(2), 169–224.

Morita, H. and Nakahara, H. (2004) 'Impacts of the information-technology revolution on Japanese manufacturer-supplier relationships', *Journal of the Japanese and International Economies*, 18(3), 390–415.
Nakamura, T. and Odaka, K. (2003) *Volume 3: Economic History of Japan 1914–1955 – A Dual Structure* (London: Oxford University Press).
Nakane, C. (1973) *Japanese Society* (Harmondsworth: Penguin Books).
Nooteboom, B. (1999) 'Voice and exit-based forms of corporate control: Anglo-American, European and Japanese', *Journal of Economic Issues*, 33(4), 845–60.
Nooteboom, B. (2000) 'Network interactions and mutual dependence: a test in the car industry', *Industry and Innovation*, 7(1), 117–45.
North, D.C. (1990) *Institutions, Institutional Change and Economic Performance* (Cambridge: Cambridge University Press).
North, D.C. (1991) 'Institutions', *Journal of Economic Perspectives*, 5(1), 97–112.
Ohno, S. (1999) *Nihongo ren'shū chō* (Practice book of Japanese language) (Tokyo: Iwanami shoten).
Oliver, C. (1997) 'Sustainable competitive advantage: combining institutional and resource-based views', *Strategic Management Journal*, 18(9), 697–713.
Orrù, M., Hamilton, G.G. and Suzuki, M. (1989) 'Patterns of inter-firm control in Japanese business', *Organization Studies*, 10(4), 549–74.
Osborn, R.N. and Hagedoorn, J. (1997) 'The institutionalization and evolutionary dynamics of inter-organisational alliances and networks', *Academy of Management Journal*, 40(2), 261–78.
Peng, M.W. (2002) 'Cultures, institutions, and strategic choices: toward an institutional perspective on business strategy', in M.J. Gannon and K.L. Newman (eds) *The Blackwell Handbook of Cross-Cultural Management*, 52–66 (Oxford and Malden, MA: Blackwell Publisher Ltd).
Rohlen, T.P. (1974) *For Harmony and Strength: Japanese White-collar Organization in Anthropological Perspective* (Berkeley, CA: University of California Press).
Rugman, A.M. (2003) 'Regional strategy and the demise of globalization', *Journal of International Management*, 9(4), 409–17.
Rugman, A.M. (2005) 'A further comment on the myth of globalization', *Journal of International Management*, 11(3), 441–5.
Rugman, A.M. and Collinson, S. (2004) 'The regional nature of the world's automotive sector', *European Management Journal*, 22(5), 471–82.
Sako, M. (1992) *Price, Quality and Trust: Inter-firm Relations in Britain and Japan* (Cambridge: Cambridge University Press).
Sapir, E. (1949) *Culture, Language and Personality* (Berkeley and Los Angeles, CA: University of California Press).
Saussure, F. (1916) *Cours de Linguistique Générale* (Paris: Payot).
Saussure, F. (1983) *Course in General Linguistics* (translated and annotated by Roy Harris) (London: Duckworth).
Scott, W.R. (1995) *Institutions and Organisations* (Thousand Oakes, CA: Sage Publications).
Simon, H.A. and March, J.G. (1993) 'Organisation Revisited', *Industrial and Corporate Change*, 2(3), 299–316.
Solis, M. (2003) 'On the myth of the *keiretsu* network: Japanese electronics in North America', *Business and Politics*, 5(3), 303–33.
Sugimoto, Y. (1998) *An Introduction to Japanese Society* (Cambridge: Cambridge University Press).
Suzuki, T. (1984) *Words in Context: A Japanese Perspective on Language and Culture* (Tokyo and New York: Kodansha International).
Tallman, S.B. (1991) 'Strategic management models and resource-based strategies among MNEs in a host market', *Strategic Management Journal*, 12(1), 69–83.
The Economist (25 November 2000) 'Regrouping', *The Economist*, 74.

Vogel, E.F. (1975) *Modern Japanese Organization and Decision-Making* (Berkeley, CA: University of California Press).
Watanabe, Y. (1992) 'Kokusaika no shinten to kokunai chiikikan bungyokozo no shintenkai (New developments in internationalization and the domestic inter-district division of labour)', *Shoko kin'yu*, July, 4–22.
Whittaker, D.H. and Kurosawa, Y. (1998) 'Japan's crisis: evolution and implications', *Cambridge Journal of Economics*, 22(6), 761–71.
Whorf, B.L. (1952) 'Language, mind, and reality', *Technology Review* 9(3), 167–88.
Williamson, O.E. (1991) 'Calculativeness, trust and economic organisation', *Journal of Law and Economics*, 26(3), 453–86.
Womack, J.P., Jones, D.T. and Roos, D. (1990) *The Machine That Changed the World* (New York: Rowson Associates and Macmillan Publishing Company).

21
Institutional Determinants of Good Corporate Governance: The Case of Nigeria*

Emmanuel Adegbite and Chizu Nakajima

Introduction

Economic globalization has stimulated debate on the similarities and differences between national corporate governance systems (McCahery and Renneboog, 2002). Whilst the equilibrium of evidence appears to be tilted in favour of a convergence towards a focus on shareholder primacy, the literature remains puzzling and contradictory. In an attempt to reconcile the shareholder and stakeholder models of corporate governance, some scholars have talked about 'enlightened shareholder value', 'instrumental stakeholder theory', 'strategic corporate social responsibility' or 'the good firm' (Filatotchev et al., 2007; Jones, 1995; Kay and Silberston, 1995; Parkinson, 1995), as the hybrid model. However, in today's world of corporate, economic and political globalization, how (and to what extent) is corporate governance shaped by firm and national level institutional environments? What are the different institutionalized expressions of corporate governance in varieties of capitalism? Which institutional parameters and arrangements constrain good corporate governance in emerging markets? Given that the spectacles of the influential agency theory do not explain these relations, our aim in this chapter is to conceptualize corporate governance structures and practices as institutionally determined and guided. We show that national corporate governance systems are endogenous responses to certain national and firm-specific institutional environments. This is critical to a better understanding of corporate governance. Specifically, we argue that corporate governance models, especially in developing countries, are inapplicable if they are not institutionally based and explained. In particular, we examine the extent to which certain underlying national conditions, such as the political, economic, legal and social environments as well as firm/industry values, culture, ethics and history, play a determining role in corporate governance.

It must be noted that whilst there have been recent efforts towards the embeddedness framing of governance and opportunism in order to ensure a cross-national accommodating theory of agency (Lubatkin et al., 2005, 2007), in this chapter we take a step beyond the assumptions of the conventional agency theory (as postulated in Jensen and Meckling, 1976, and Fama and Jensen, 1983).

We account for the institutional determinants of good corporate governance in developing countries with a particular reference to one of Africa's most important financial markets – Nigeria. While we focus specifically on this country, our discussions have cross-national theoretical implications. We add to the body of evidence (Aguilera and Jackson, 2003; Aoki, 2000, 2001; Lubatkin et al., 2007) on the burgeoning institutional theory of corporate governance. Palepu et al. (2006) argued that whilst nations may formally adopt corporate governance systems that resemble those elsewhere, the acceptance of the enshrined principles may lag in their institutions. This has significant implications for the convergence debate and can explain the diversity of corporate governance structures and practices around the world – that have persisted despite pressures from globalization. Indeed, corporate governance varies from country to country, and despite the rich descriptions of these different systems that can be found in the literature, there remains a challenging task of conceptualizing this cross-national diversity and of identifying the major factors that would explain these differences (Aguilera and Jackson, 2003).

Institutional theory (Meyer and Rowan, 1977; Zucker, 1987) offers an explanation. It focuses on the deeper and more resilient aspects of social structure, considering the processes by which structures (schemes, rules, norms, and routines) become established as authoritative guidelines for social behaviour (Scott, 2004). It is thus important that corporate governance discussions reflect a broader perspective of institutional domains (Aoki, 2001). The lack of convincing evidence for the convergence of national systems of corporate governance and the reality that corporate governance systems and practices cannot be transplanted across countries without significant misalignment (even in countries considered similar such as the UK and the US) are indications that the agency framework does not fully encapsulate the multi-dimensional complexity and character of the corporate governance phenomenon. Indeed, in the context of developing countries, and Nigeria in particular, where good corporate as well as public governance is imperative to economic survival and growth, it is of the essence to understand the underlying rationale and machinery upon which business conduct and governance structures and practices are developed, nurtured and sustained over time. In this chapter, we provide empirical evidence on how the institutional theoretical frame of corporate governance applies to a particular national context, in this case, Nigeria.

Institutional theory and corporate governance

While economists like Shleifer and Vishny (1997) have considered the principal/agent model to be a supra-national lens for evaluating all corporate governance issues, the model is based on a number of assumptions that may undermine the complexity (Lubatkin et al., 2007) and multi-faceted character of the governance phenomenon. For example, agency theory somewhat presupposes the operation of an efficient and competitive environment, where information asymmetries are minimized and competitive pressures are maximized (Udayasankar et al., 2005). On the other hand, there is increasing scholarly recognition (Aguilera, 2005; Aguilera and Jackson, 2003; Aoki, 2001; Boehmer, 1999; Judge et al., 2008; Leaptrott, 2005; Liu, 2005; Lubatkin et al., 2005, 2007) with regard to the institutional 'embeddedness' of countries' corporate governance systems and key players. Institutional theory emphasizes that organizations should be seen not only as the means by which goods are produced and services are provided, but as social and cultural systems (Judge et al., 2008). It therefore offers a rich view of organizations, arguing that organizations are influenced by normative pressures that can be external or internal (Zucker, 1987). It further inquires as to how social structures are developed, diffused, adopted, adapted, fall into decline, and are disused over space and time (Scott, 2004). Institutional theory refers to the enduring systems of social beliefs and socially organized practices which are associated with diverse functional areas of societal systems such as religion, work, politics, laws and regulations (Judge et al. 2008). One of the keys to understanding organizations and corporate governance systems, therefore, is to study the institutional environments that guide or constrain their legitimacy (Judge et al., 2008).

Certainly comparative corporate governance scholars would agree that the diversity of national corporate governance ideologies, systems and practices is such that one might begin to wonder if we are still discussing the same subject. This diversity has been obscured by the dominance of Anglo-Saxon corporate governance dogmas and theories in the literature. Furthermore, a considerable number of comparative national corporate governance studies have been only descriptive, failing to convincingly account for the differences across countries. Recognizing the institutional effects on corporate governance will therefore enable us to understand why certain governance mechanisms are more effective in some jurisdictions while they do not appear to work in others, and why certain governance challenges are characteristic of some environments. Indeed, in making generalizations about corporate governance systems around the world, scholars need to be cautious, as certain traditional and institutional mechanisms have already created firm bedrocks of informal/self-regulation which makes subsequent regulatory initiatives effective in certain market economies such as that of the UK, while these structures are either not present or are just emerging in most developing economies (Nakajima, 1999). Therefore, in conceptualizing the dynamics of business relationships and corporate governance, especially in developing economies (and in particular, Nigeria), it is important to understand and account for certain firm-level and country-level institutional effects which constitute vibrant forces that shape the behaviour of managers and boards of directors, the level of investors' participation, the role of the state, as well as the degree of effectiveness of regulatory initiatives. Eisenhardt and Graebner (2007), however, argue that the challenge of justifying inductive case research depends on the nature of research questions. In our attempt to extend the literature on the relevance of institutional theory in corporate governance, we follow their advice by framing our research questions within the context of institutionalism in ways that facilitate inductive theory-building using a mix of qualitative data. This has prompted us to 'hang' our research on the question, which firm and national level institutional environments shape corporate governance, especially in developing countries?.

Research design, survey methodology and analysis

This chapter adopts a mix of qualitative research methods including in-depth interviews, focus groups and direct observations. These were used to conduct a survey of corporate governance professionals in academia, in practice and in the Nigerian polity. Part of this included a 2-month period of field work in Nigeria. From the outset, the key contributors to the corporate governance debate, ranging from the academy through practice to regulators, were identified. Exhaustive attempts were then made to contact them via emails and follow-ups with telephone calls, outlining the research agenda. The interview questions were pre-tested to ensure their appropriateness and to ascertain the potential respondents' understanding and proper interpretation. Furthermore, where appropriate, control questions were asked to ensure further validity and reliability of responses. An ethical commitment was also made to treat responses with required confidentiality. Closed and open questions were asked in order to gain a variety of responses drawn from real-life business and personal experiences, free from fear or bias. The average duration of interviews was 60 minutes. Respondents were mainly high-profile individuals, including present and former CEOs, chairmen, board directors, renowned academics, corporate governance consultants and senior officials of the relevant regulatory agencies. Notably these are key stakeholders in the Nigerian corporate governance system. By virtue of their positions, they made rich and in-depth comments on the institutionalized corporate governance phenomenon in the country (see Filatotchev et al., 2007). It should also be noted that one of the authors is a member of the Society for Corporate Governance in Nigeria and maintains close working relationships with relevant stakeholders in the Nigerian corporate governance system. This helped to alleviate some of the challenges relating to access to data and respondents. The snowballing technique (see also, Amaeshi et al., 2006) also proved very helpful in gaining access to these high-calibre respondent(s), until data saturation was reached. In all, there were 26 structured interviews, all face-to-face and recorded. The interviews were subsequently transcribed and analysed.

Since the majority of the interviews were structured, the utilization of focus groups enabled further discussions on corporate governance in Nigeria in a more unstructured way which gave additional insights into the overall picture (see Filatotchev et al., 2007). In order to increase the efficiency of the focus groups and to allow members to expressly discuss the topics of interest without actual or perceived intimidation, the size of the groups was kept deliberately small (see Ewings et al., 2008). Certain degrees of overall representation were achieved with participants drawn from different backgrounds and functions, so as to harness a mix of perspectives. Two separate focus group discussions were held; one had

9 members and the other had 11, totalling 20 respondents. Discussions were also recorded and each of them took an average of 90 minutes.

Furthermore, direct observations of the situation at hand were made in order to complement and validate some of the information collected through interviews and focus group discussions. The annual general meetings (AGMs) of two listed corporations were attended and observed. The authors were not granted permission to record proceedings. Significant note-taking of proceedings and interactions, however, constituted helpful alternatives. These survey techniques altogether allowed for a rich pictorial representation of the complex institutionalized corporate governance system in Nigeria. We further ensured adequate methodological self-consciousness throughout the data collection process to avoid potential bias in data collection and interpretation. We specifically ensured that our functions as researchers and administrators of the data collection process did not interfere or affect the data collected, thus minimizing negative obtrusiveness, and as a result enhancing both the data-gathering and eventual credibility (Harrington, 2002). The total number of respondents for the interviews and focus group discussions is 42. In terms of the professional/disciplinary backgrounds of the experts, a reasonable spread was achieved. The breakdown is summarized in Table 21.1, and Table 21.2 presents summary information on respondents' institutional expertise.

This study lends itself to an analytic induction research method, and the data generated through this mix of qualitative methods were analysed with the Nvivo software. This helped build explanations, which explored links between

Table 21.1 A breakdown of the professional/disciplinary backgrounds of the survey respondents

Background/research field	Number of experts
Economics	4
Business, management	4
Finance and accounting	15
Law	11
Sociology	3
Others (Manufacturing, HRM, Sciences, etc)	5

Table 21.2 A breakdown of survey respondents' institutional expertise

Institutional expertise	Regulatory	Academia	Practice
Regulatory	17	–	–
Academia	–	4	5
Practice	–	–	16

literatures, events, findings and actions in one case and the iterative extension of these to emerging issues (Katz, 2001). The research logic allowed for an in-depth scrutiny of corporate governance in Nigeria. The mixed-methods strategy also compensated for the weaknesses inherent in individual methods. The overall methodology and data collection techniques allowed for a judicious access to numerous corporate governance specialists and experts in Nigeria, with sufficient 'capacity mix', enriching the research data.

Findings and discussion

Institutional framing of corporate governance in Nigeria: an overview

We proceed to examine the Nigerian external and internal institutional environments and their influences on corporate governance. The aim is to explore the complementary relationships of these institutional environments and related practices with good corporate governance. The discussion is presented under two headings. Macro-level environments are those external institutional configurations that profile a firm's corporate governance at the country level, consisting of Nigeria's political, economic, social and legal environments. The micro-level analysis focuses on institutions that are internal to the firm or its industry, consisting of the firm's and industry's values, culture, history and ethics. Industry-level discussions are deliberately not presented as meso-level analyses given the lack of demarcation between the firm-level and industry-level institutional environments of corporate governance, as suggested by the data.

Macro (external) institutions

The political context of corporate governance in Nigeria

Politics shape corporate governance (Fligstein, 1990; Roe, 1994). Following independence, Nigerians (until about a decade ago) have lived predominantly within a political environment characterized by military/tyrannical dictatorship, incessant political turbulence and violence, political assassinations and elections marked by massive vote-rigging. It is therefore not surprising that the past decades of unrest in the Nigerian polity have had serious implications for business conduct and corporate governance. Business requires a conducive political atmosphere to thrive. Indeed, organizations that are impeded by political turmoil and thus unable to function properly are less valuable to investors. Dampening political turmoil, or insulating an organization from its effects, therefore constitutes a strong force in shaping an organization's ownership and its eventual governance (Roe, 2003).

This brings to the fore the need to understand the correlations between a country's polity and corporate governance. Politics affects the firm in many ways, given that it determines the firm's ownership and ability to obtain external finance. It further determines the firm's growth and profit potential, and ultimately how authority is distributed within the firm (Roe, 2003). Indeed, in Nigeria it is generally uncontested that top politicians (directly or indirectly) hold majority stakes in many organizations, which allows them to nominate board members and management. As a result, they are able to stifle the organization to suit their political interests and in other situations use their political powers to benefit the organization. It is also not uncommon for multinationals to compromise their ethical standards in order to do business. A good example is the recent conviction of Siemens for bribing a number of top government officials in Nigeria in order to win telecommunications contracts. However, politically motivated corporate corruption takes different shapes and forms. Unlike Siemens, which seemingly bribed government officials directly, survey evidence suggests that MNCs often pay bribes via 'consultants' who negotiate the deal and win the business or contract. Consultants therefore act as the medium through which the bribes are paid to the corrupt government officials. While commenting on the issue, an interview respondent who is a senior regulatory officer stated that:

> The case of Siemens is an exception; they were not just smart enough, they wanted to do the bribery for themselves, so they got caught.

Traditionally the country's corporate governance system and practices have been riddled with endemic corruption. Indeed, the private sector and corporate governance evolved and continues to evolve in an environment of systemic political corruption. The Cadbury Nigeria Plc (a subsidiary of Cadbury Schweppes) scandal, which led to the sacking of some of the company's senior officials including the CEO, represents another dimension of the political determinants of corporate governance in Nigeria. As an academic/corporate governance consultant observes:

> Corruption in the private sector is largely covered up. Taking the Cadbury scandal for example, if not for some external political interests that were in the matter, shareholders' funds would have been eroded without anyone noticing.

Survey respondents unanimously agree that the private sector is gradually becoming the epitome of corruption in Nigeria. Given that the government traditionally held significant shareholdings in major areas of the economy, despite the considerable efforts to divest them, typical of all Nigerian government-owned ventures, 'people saw/see them as nobody's business'. Therefore, politicians/office holders have traditionally used government-owned companies to fuel political agendas directly or indirectly. Furthermore, given the nature of partisan politics in Nigeria, politicians continuously seek financial support from corporations which further facilitates public-private corrupt dealings before and after elections. According to a former CEO and Chairman of a large Nigerian corporation:

> Following victory at the polls, politicians upon assuming office see themselves as dispensers of favours to individuals, groups or companies who have supported their parties. These supporters get more 'favours', ranging from government contracts, fast-tracking of trade licenses, whilst denying other qualified individuals or companies, especially if they are perceived as oppositions.

The Nigerian polity strives amidst corruption and illegality, thus inhibiting good corporate governance. Large organizations, including multinationals, can triumph and remain competitive only with significant political will and support. It has also become common for corrupt politicians and ex-office holders to become elected as board members, thus hindering good corporate governance – more so as they often bring their entrenched public corruption behaviour into the private sector.

The economic context of corporate governance in Nigeria

While Nigeria's dilemma in harnessing its resource-rich economy into an epitome of globalization is shared by many of the world's developing nations, the efficiency of markets and consumer participation in the economy is strongly limited by the lack of durable networks, stable electricity supply, potable water, efficient telecommunication facilities, as well as safe and efficient roads, railways and ports (Country Focus, 2006). Small and medium enterprises capable of making immense contributions to the economy have thus been stymied by the poor economic infrastructure of the country. Given that corporate governance in a particular country is an endogenous response to firms' economic environment (Mulherin, 2004), developing countries such as Nigeria – with its pervasive but inefficient government controls on economic activities and its imperfect capital markets – automatically inherit a weak corporate governance system (Singh, 2003).

Prior to independence, foreigners, especially the British, owned most of the large businesses operating in Nigeria, but following the prohibition of 100 per cent foreign ownership in sensitive economic areas (such as infrastructure and oil), they had to divest their shareholdings. However, as there were insufficient domestic investible funds available, the Nigerian government and a small number of very wealthy Nigerian politicians ended up buying a majority of the divested shares (Ahunwan, 2002; Akinsanya, 1983; Yerokun, 1992). Consequentially, most large corporations that sprung up were state-owned and state-controlled, and the corporate governance practices that developed were replicas of the corrupt practices of the military and civilian governments that ruled Nigeria thereafter. According to the chairman of a large Nigerian corporation:

> There was no vision for good corporate governance as a means to create long-term value for the firm and its stakeholders as well as to position the country on the path of economic sustainability.

Essentially these corporations served as means for top government officials and their wealthy Nigerian friends to loot shareholders' funds (amongst other corrupt practices), which eventually led to the collapse of a considerable number of the traditional Pan-African corporations. Therefore, for any corporate governance reform in developing economies, particularly Nigeria, to make a reasonable impact, it must, at the very least, understand and reflect the economic situation within which corporate governance structures and practices have evolved.

The social context of corporate governance in Nigeria

While there appeared to be a great deal of optimism in the 1960s about the developmental prospects of the newly independent Nigeria (Ahunwan, 2002), nearly five decades later the country is still optimistically regarded as 'developing'. Candidly stated, Nigeria is undeveloped, lacking adequate social infrastructure and basic amenities. Poverty, high unemployment, armed robbery, bad roads, power shortages – amongst other problems – plague the Nigerian state. The result is a poor quality of life for the majority of the populace, and the consequence of this is a general perception that everyone will have to (and must) fend for himself or herself. This is the underlying cause of the endemic public and private enterprise corruption in the country. According to a senior regulatory officer:

> In Nigeria, there is a general notion that you need to 'take care of yourself'. It doesn't matter if this amounts to corruption.

Furthermore, the lack of adequate social amenities as well as the government's corresponding lackadaisical approach is stimulating the debate on corporate social responsibility in Nigeria. As the vice-chairman of a large Nigerian corporation puts it:

> Looking at social infrastructure, the government has failed its people and as such they look unto corporate bodies to fill in that gap. Indeed multinational corporate bodies can become role models for how things can be done.

More broadly, and almost inevitably, the governance of corporations becomes affected by these infrastructural and social determinants. While the agency theoretical construction concerns the possibility of self-serving behaviours of corporate managers that may not be in alliance with that of shareholders, this problem is seriously aggravated and socio-institutionally accommodated in Nigeria. According to a former governor of the Central Bank of Nigeria:

> The social structure of Nigeria can be described as "a fertile ground for bribery, corruption, idleness and the contrivance of get-rich quick attitude which are antithetical to hard work and discipline". (Ahunwan, 2002, p. 271)

This has serious implications for corporate governance. For example, Nigeria has lost a significant number of banks since the banking industry came into being in the country in 1914, due to bad corporate governance largely facilitated by the corrupt and opportunistic behaviours entrenched in the country's social environment. Again, while business connections can reduce agency conflicts by promoting efficient and informal information transfers, it can also constitute channels for favouritism (Kuhnen, 2009). For example, business connections in Nigeria, especially through personal and family affiliations, interfere with the efficient management and governance of corporations, resulting in serious cases of insider dealing, appointments to corporate directorships based on personal affinities, use of companies' properties for personal purposes by directors, managers and their associates, and leasing/selling personal and associates' properties to the company at exorbitant prices. Indeed, as with many developing countries, a corrupt social mindset has engulfed both public and private enterprise, allowing activities such as drug counterfeiting, environmental degradation, bribery and corruption to become the norm, such that doing things right has become an anomaly (Olebune, 2006).

The legal context of corporate governance in Nigeria

Formal rules are the laws and regulations (North, 1990) that govern behaviour. The legal context within which corporate governance has developed in Nigeria was dictated by English law, which still constitutes a substantial part of Nigerian law. Indeed, having described the political, economic and social operating environments of corporate governance in Nigeria, it is worth noting that Nigeria's mimicking of UK laws following independence meant it failed to address company law problems that were specific to Nigeria's socio-political environment, and also did not tackle the economic and commercial challenges of the country (Okike, 2007). According to an academic respondent: 'What we have in Nigeria is a legal system that could best be described as non-Nigerian.'

Even after successive reform of company law over the years, the legal infrastructure of corporate governance in Nigeria remains fashioned along the Anglo-Saxon model. It is unsurprising, therefore, that this misalignment has allowed governance malfunctions to flourish. Right from the colonial period through independence, and even until the 1990s, there was limited challenge to management's prerogative to run corporations, no efforts directed to external supervision with regard to ensuring transparent disclosure of information, and no substantial intervention in matters of accountability and corporate power administration and relationship (Yakasai, 2001). Nigeria needs a legal system that reflects and tackles the peculiar challenges posed by the institutional environments described above. This system must nonetheless remain competitive in attracting both domestic and foreign investments by not stifling the independent dynamism that underlies modern capitalism. Furthermore, there has been a traditional disregard for the rule of law in Nigeria, although recent government commitments, particularly the setting up of anti-corruption bodies, are creating a general awareness that the law is there to govern and must therefore be allowed to do so. While the current focus of government campaigns appears to concentrate on public office-holders, it is however expected that the trend will proceed to confront some of the deep-rooted and highly complex corruption perpetrated by managers and directors alike, as a result of the laxity in law enforcement. As a senior official of a law enforcement regulatory agency puts it: 'The problem in Nigeria is that of enforcement which is silent except when there is a public outcry.'

Corporate governance laws and regulations should bring an element of morality and conscience into business and limit majority rule in a consistent manner. This can only be achieved by addressing the various institutional impediments to good corporate governance in the laws and the 'codes of conduct' governing corporations and corporate conduct, which are the Companies and Allied Matters Act of 1990, the 2003 Code of Corporate Governance in Nigeria (revised in 2009), the 2006 Central Bank of Nigeria's Code of Corporate Governance for Nigeria Banks and the 2007 Code of Conduct for Shareholders' Associations in Nigeria.

Micro (internal) institutions

Corporate values as determinants of good corporate governance in Nigeria

Corporate values constitute an internal institutional force which guides corporate behaviour. Lencioni (2002) organized corporate values into four categories: (1) core/inherent values which are the cornerstone principles that guide all of a company's actions; (2) aspirational values which are those needed to succeed in the future; (3) permission-to-play values which reflect the minimum permissible behavioural and social standards; (4) accidental values which are those that arise spontaneously without being cultivated by leadership. The overall quality of the values of a corporation is a strong determinant of its corporate leadership and governance beyond the rigours of regulation. The practical implementation of corporate governance codes of conduct cannot be realized solely by a regulatory compliance programme as the latter's relevance and effectiveness in daily business conduct is determined by the moral values of the company (Wieland, 2005).

Thus, good corporate governance is itself a value comprising numerous other values including accountability, transparency, honesty, integrity, responsibility and fairness, amongst others. A senior internal auditor of a large Nigerian corporation observes:

> In Nigeria, as in other developing countries, values such as accountability and honest stewardship are hugely unsynonymous with most corporations.

Corporate Nigeria thus needs to incubate certain essential values and nurture good governance practices and curb corrupt behaviour. While robust regulatory initiatives will undoubtedly help the state of corporate governance in Nigeria, any successful fight against corporate corruption over the long term must, at the very least, inculcate and promote these important values to a point where they become self-sustainable and therefore can themselves generally infer good governance internally. *Accidental values* need to be developed in Nigerian companies to ensure good corporate governance practices in the short term, but these values must become entrenched as *core values* to foster long-term and sustainable good corporate governance practices.

Corporate culture and good corporate governance in Nigeria

Culture is an exceptionally elusive construct (Jahoda 1984) and can be defined as 'the learned, socially acquired traditions and life styles of the members of a society, including their patterned, repetitive way of thinking, feeling and acting' (Harris, 1987, p. 6). Depending on the subject of inquiry, the society in question may be a nation, an ethnic group or an organization (Salacuse, 2003). Corporate governance is itself a culture which is especially influenced by the overall corporate culture, which dictates the behaviour and interaction of key players in a firm-level corporate governance structure.

The corporate culture in Nigeria reflects the country's national culture, which varies across three major tribes – Hausa, Ibo and Yoruba – but nonetheless share major prescriptions with regards to basic business conduct and relationships. Tackling corporate governance problems in Nigeria would mean digging deep to effect a significant change in the cultures of Nigerian corporations that have been sufficiently permeated by societal corruption. No doubt this necessitates a zero-tolerance regulatory policy on corporate corruption, but regulation alone cannot stop corporate misconduct, especially in developing countries. A strong corporate culture that is in alignment with good principles of corporate governance needs to be developed to constitute internal checks and balances. A spirited corporate culture, one with very clear guidelines on expected behaviour (Deal and Kennedy, 1982), could solve some of the corporate governance issues that plague developing countries. For example, Haniffa and Cooke (2002) found empirical evidence suggesting that corporate culture is linked to the range and scope of voluntary disclosure practices. Manipulation of accounts, auditors' compromise, non-transparent disclosure and other fraudulent behaviours will thrive in a company that lacks the cultural strength to internally address them before they result in major scandals. Furthermore, the survey respondents generally suggested that good culture must also permeate the regulatory authorities and the professional bodies who perform the oversight monitoring function of corporate governance.

Path dependency: how corporate history shapes corporate governance in Nigeria

Here we investigate the path dependency (Arthur, 1989, 1990; David, 1985) of historical institutionalism on the governance of Nigerian corporations. David (1985) and Arthur (1989, 1990) maintained that inefficiencies can become institutionalized as industry standards, and may persist for extended periods of time even when they have significant defects. Leibowitz and Margolis (1990) and Leibowitz (1995) have criticized this proposition, arguing that market forces will not tolerate significant inefficiencies (Stack and Gartland, 2003). Applying the theory of historical institutionalism to corporate governance research nevertheless brings another dimension to our understanding of the subject, especially as a continuum. This continuum can be understood as the institutionalization of a set of persuasive ideas that have been successful in describing reality solving problems over long periods of time (Peters et al., 2005). These ideas may be good or bad.

In the context of corporations, traditional practices sustained over a long period may become difficult to change, but continue to be the norm even when better alternatives become available. A major thesis of the historical institutional theory literature is that organizational initiatives as well as policymaking systems tend to be conservative and find ways of defending existing norms and patterns, which later become self-reinforcing institutionalized processes and configurations that are difficult to change (Peters et al., 2005; Pierson, 2000), although they may be subtly modified to adapt to changing conditions. The path-dependency theory can therefore explain why certain corporate governance problems persist over time in some firms, industries and countries, especially after rigorous regulatory measures have been specifically deployed to address them. Indeed, the convergence debate and path dependency premises remain competing hypotheses in our explanation of similarities and diversities of national corporate governance structures and practices.

No doubt firms all over the world should compete for reputation status in institutional fields as corporate audiences rely on the reputations and histories of firms in making investment decisions, career decisions, and product choices (Dowling, 1986; Fombrun and Shanley, 1990). However, as we have indicated earlier, corporations in Nigeria generally have a long history of corrupt behaviour which has been sustained over time and has become somewhat immune to regulatory reforms. Rather, bad corporate governance in Nigeria constantly adapts to increasingly vigorous regulatory measures by changing in style and in the form in which it is perpetrated, thus increasing in complexity and becoming more impervious. According to one academic respondent:

> Managers and directors of typical Nigerian companies, as well as their auditors, have historically benefited hugely from several corporate frauds and seem not to be ready to change but continue to transform and derive more complex means of perpetrating their crime to circumvent the claws of the law.

Ethical climate and corporate governance in Nigeria

Seventy-six per cent of investors in a recent survey would move their investments from a company with which they are invested if they learned that the company is engaged in an unethical albeit legal behaviour, irrespective of the potential high returns (Corporate Board, 2007). Indeed, there is further evidence that corporate stakeholders use ethics as a very important criterion to judge companies (Lewis, 2003). As a response, many companies have implemented ethical programmes (Schlegelmilch and Pollach, 2005) aimed at establishing a good reputation in order to prevent customer churn and labour turnover on the one hand, and to attract new customers and high-calibre employees on the other, which altogether enable them to charge a premium based on their distinguished reputations (Fombrun, 1996). The thesis here is that ethical companies can derive financial benefits, directly or indirectly. Simply put, ethics in the corporate world involves 'ordinary decency', which encompasses integrity, honesty and fairness in the conduct of business (Sternberg, 2000). The science of ethics encompasses a reflective study of what we ought to do, or how we ought to live (Ekennia, 1998); corporate ethics, therefore, relates to choices and judgements made with regard to business conduct (Erondu et al., 2004).

Decades of predominantly military rule meant modern corporate Nigeria developed in an unethical climate, and corruption-riddled business practices were the norm. In the words of a corporate governance consultant:

> Perhaps the first thing that comes to mind for many foreign investors wanting to do business in Nigeria is corruption. They are correct to think that way. Corruption has engulfed Nigeria.

However, while corruption in Nigeria is closely linked with the attitudes of individual Nigerians, such an epidemic would not have flourished if external parties, especially foreigners doing business in the country, had not been beneficiaries of the proceeds of corruption. This further suggests that the subject of business ethics in Nigeria may remain in idealism for a long while. The absence of an ethical climate for business conduct, like the institutional problems discussed earlier, aids the negative conduct of corporate governance. Nevertheless, following the establishment of democracy in the country, Nigeria has made giant strides in reducing (or rather managing) corruption and promoting good business practice, and has since moved from being the world's second-most corrupt nation with a corruption perception index (CPI) score of 1.6 in 2005, to 2.2 in 2007 (Transparency International, 2008).

Summary

In summarizing our findings above, we show in Figure 21.1 two classes of institutional effects on corporate governance: those external to the firm (macro) and those internal (micro). The external institutional environments that profile a firm's corporate governance consist of the country's social, economic, political and legal environments, while those internal to the firm consist of the firm's/industry's values, culture, history and ethics. While this model is neither an extension nor modification of the principal-agent model of Jensen and Meckling, it represents an encompassing framework that provides illumination on certain institutional effects and relationships, thereby encapsulating the complex dynamics and realities of governance in modern-day corporations. It thus constitutes a useful context

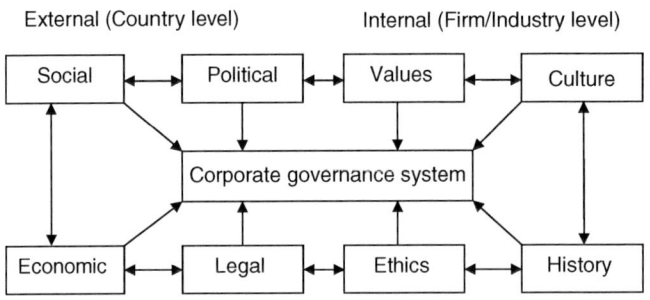

Figure 21.1 Institutional determinants of corporate governance

in which we can analyse corporate governance structures – across diverse countries, cultures, belief systems, traditions, industries, scholarly orientations and disciplines. It specifically adds to the literature on the institutional determinants of corporate governance (Aguilera, 2005; Aguilera and Jackson, 2003; Aoki, 2001; Boehmer, 1999; Judge et al., 2008; Leaptrott, 2005; Liu, 2005; Lubatkin et al., 2005, 2007), with rich insights from a developing-market African economy.

We argue that corporate governance practices do not develop out of vacuity. They are governed by institutions. The format and expression of governance in modern corporations across different countries are a reflection of their institutional environments. Two classes of these have been described, and their interactions with corporate conduct and governance in the case of Nigeria have been analysed. More importantly, these institutions are interdependent; they also influence and interact with one another. Therefore, in conceptualizing corporate governance in developing countries, particularly Nigeria, it is important to note that the overall nature of the country's national and firm-level institutional environments are not complementary with good corporate governance principles, both at the national and corporate/industry levels. These have inhibited the developments of necessary corporate governance infrastructures such as rigorous regulatory enforcement, properly functioning markets, honest and highly regulated auditing and accounting firms as well as vibrant professional bodies. Nigeria requires the institutional enforcement capacity to promote, administer and maintain the principles of corporate governance.

Institutions matter in corporate governance. There is no doubt that corporate governance practices have travelled the world and despite the existence of national corporate governance isomorphism, the reality remains a translation of practices to fit the national institutional settings of a particular country (Aguilera, 2005). As such, despite globalization pressures, corporations continue to be influenced by the institutional environments of their respective countries. Thus, corporate governance models should not be seen in isolation of the rest of the institutional underpinnings of the economy (Guillen, 2000). Indeed, corporate governance does not develop in isolation but reflects the underlying institutions which affect the structures, rights and responsibilities of managers and directors and the ways these are organized in different countries.

Note

* This chapter majorly constitutes a chapter in Adegbite, E. (2010) The determinants of good corporate governance: The case of Nigeria. *Doctoral Thesis* (City University: London).

References

Aguilera, R.V. (2005) 'Corporate governance and director accountability: an institutional comparative perspective', *British Journal of Management*, 16(1), 39–53.

Aguilera, R.V. and Jackson, G. (2003) 'The cross-national diversity of corporate governance: dimensions and determinants', *Academy of Management Review*, 28(3), 447–65.

Ahunwan, B. (2002) 'Corporate governance in Nigeria', *Journal of Business Ethics*, 37(3), 269–87.
Akinsanya, A.A. (1983) 'State strategies towards Nigerian and foreign businesses', in I.W. Zartman (ed.) *The Political Economy of Nigeria* (New York: Preager).
Amaeshi, K.M., Adi, A.B.C., Ogbechie, C. and Amao, O.O. (2006) 'Corporate social responsibility in Nigeria: Western mimicry or indigenous influences?' *Journal of Corporate Citizenship (winter edition)*, 24: 83–99.
Aoki, M. (2000) *Information, Corporate Governance, and Institutional Diversity: Competitiveness in Japan, the USA, and the Transnational Economies* (Oxford: Oxford University Press).
Aoki, M. (2001) *Towards a Comparative Institutional Analysis* (Cambridge, MA: MIT Press).
Arthur, B. (1989) 'Competing technologies, increasing returns, and lock-in by historical events', *Economic Journal*, 99(394), 116–31.
Arthur, B. (1990) 'Positive feedbacks in the economy', *Scientific American*, 262, 92–9.
Boehmer, E. (1999) *Corporate Governance in Germany: Institutional Background and Empirical Results* (Berlin: Humboldt University).
Corporate Board (2007) 'Investors are looking closely at corporate ethics', *Corporate Board*, 28(166), 28–39.
Country Focus (2006) 'Nigeria advances but uncertainties abound', *Market: Africa/Mid-East*, 11(5), 6–7.
David, P. (1985) 'Clio and the economics of QWERTY', *American Economic Review*, 75(2), 332–7.
Deal, T.E. and Kennedy, A.A. (1982) *Corporate Culture* (Reading, MA: Addison-Wesley).
Dowling, G.R. (1986) 'Managing your corporate images', *Industrial Marketing Management*, 15(2), 109–15.
Eisenhardt, K.M. and Graebner, M.E. (2007) 'Theory building from cases: opportunities and challenges', *Academy of Management Journal*, 50(1), 25–32.
Ekennia, O. (1998) *Towards a Virile Economic Revival for Africa* (Owerri: The Pointer).
Erondu, E.A., Sharland, A. and Okpara, J.O. (2004) 'Corporate ethics in Nigeria: a test of the concept of an ethical climate', *Journal of Business Ethics*, 51(4), 349–57.
Ewings, P., Powell, R., Barton, A. and Pritchard, C. (2008) 'Qualitative research methods' (Peninsula Research and Development Support Unit: UK).
Fama, E.F. and Jensen, M.C. (1983) 'Separation of ownership and control', *Journal of Law and Economics*, 26(2), 301–25.
Filatotchev, I., Jackson, G., Gospel, H. and Allcock, D. (2007) *Key Drivers of 'Good' Corporate Governance and the Appropriateness of UK Policy Responses* (The Department of Trade and Industry: London, UK).
Fligstein, N. (1990) *The Transformation of Corporate Control* (Cambridge, MA: Harvard University Press).
Fombrun, C.J. (1996) *Reputation, Realizing Value from the Corporate Image* (Boston, MA: Harvard Business School Press).
Fombrun, C.J. and Shanley, M. (1990) 'What's in a name? Reputation building and corporate strategy', *Academy of Management Journal*, 33(2), 233–58.
Guillen, M.F. (2000) 'Corporate governance and globalization: is there convergence across countries', in T. Clarke (ed.) *Theories of Corporate Governance: The Philosophical Foundations of Corporate Governance* (London and New York: Routledge).
Haniffa, R.M. and Cooke, T.E. (2002) 'Culture, corporate governance and disclosure in Malaysian corporations', *Abacus*, 38(3), 317–49.
Harrington, B. (2002) 'Obtrusiveness as strategy in ethnographic research', *Qualitative Sociology*, 25(1), 49–61.
Harris, M. (1987) *Cultural Anthropology* (New York: Harper and Row).
Jahoda, G. (1984) 'Do we need a concept of culture', *Journal of Cross Cultural Psychology*, 15(2), 139–51.

Jensen, M.C. and. Meckling, W.H. (1976) 'Theory of the firm: managerial behaviour, agency costs and ownership structure?', *Journal of Financial Economics*, 3(4), 305–60.

Jones, T.M. (1995) 'Instrumental stakeholder theory: a synthesis of ethics and economics', *Academy of Management Review*, 20(2), 305–60.

Judge, W.Q., Douglas, T.J. and Kutan, A.M. (2008) 'Institutional antecedents of corporate governance legitimacy', *Journal of Management*, 34(4), 765–85.

Katz, J.K. (2001) 'Analytic induction', in Smelser, N. and Baltes. P.B. (eds) *International Encyclopedia of Social and Behavioral Sciences* (Amsterdam: Elsevier).

Kay, J. and Silberston, A. (1995) 'Corporate governance', *National Institute for Economic and Social Research*, 84, 84–97.

Kuhnen, C.M. (2009) 'Business networks, corporate governance and contracting in the mutual fund industry', *Journal of Finance*, 64(5), 2185–20.

Leaptrott, J. (2005) 'An institutional theory view of the family business', *Family Business Review*, 18(3), 215–28.

Leibowitz, S. (1995) 'Policy and path dependence: From QWERTY to Windows 95', *Regulation*, 18(3), 33–41.

Leibowitz, S. and Margolis, S. (1990) 'The fable of the keys', *Journal of Law and Economics*, 33(1), 1–25.

Lencioni, P.M. (2002) 'Make your values mean something', *Harvard Business Review*, 80(7), 113–7.

Lewis, S. (2003) 'Reputation and corporate responsibility', *Journal of Communication Management*, 7(4), 356–64

Liu, Q. (2005) 'Corporate governance in China: current practices, economic effects, and institutional determinants', *CESifo Economic Studies*, 52(2), 415–53.

Lubatkin, M., Lane, P.J., Collin, S. and Very, P. (2005) 'Origins of corporate governance in the USA, Sweden, and France', *Organization Studies*, 26(6), 867–88.

Lubatkin, M., Lane, P.J., Collin, S. and Very, P. (2007) 'An embeddedness framing of governance and opportunism: towards a crossnationally accommodating theory of agency', *Journal of Organizational Behaviour*, 28(1), 43–58.

McCahery, J. and Renneboog, L. (2002) 'Recent developments in corporate governance', in J. McCahery, P. Moerland, T. Raaijmakers and L. Renneboog (eds) *Corporate Governance Regimes: Convergence and Diversity* (Oxford: Oxford University Press).

Meyer, J.W. and Rowan, B. (1977) 'Institutionalized organizations: formal structure as myth and ceremony', *The American Journal of Sociology*, 83(2), 340–63.

Mulherin, J.H. (2004) 'Corporations, collective action, and corporate governance: one size does not fit all', *Public Choice*, 124(1/2), 179–204.

Nakajima, C. (1999) *Conflicts of Interest and Duty: A Comparative Analysis in Anglo- Japanese Law* (London: Kluwer Law International).

North, D.C. (1990) *Institutions, Institutional Change and Economic Performance* (Cambridge: Cambridge University Press).

Okike, E.N.M. (2007) 'Corporate governance in Nigeria: the status quo', *Corporate Governance: An International Review*, 15(2), 173–93.

Olebune, C. (2006) 'Social entrepreneurship, the Nigerian perspective', *African Events*, available at http://www.africanevents.com/Essay-Olebune-SocEntrprNignPersp.htm, Accessed 10 December 2010.

Palepu, K., Khanna, T. and Kogan, J. (2006) 'Globalization and similarities in corporate governance: a cross-country analysis' *The Review of Economics and Statistics*, 88(1), 69–90.

Parkinson, J. (1995) 'The role of exit and voice in corporate governance', in I. Filatotchev, G. Jackson, H. Gospel and D. Allcock (2007) *Key Drivers of 'Good' Corporate Governance and the Appropriateness of UK Policy Responses* (London: The Department of Trade and Industry).

Peters, B.G., Pierre, J., King, D.S. (2005) 'The politics of path dependency: political conflict in historical institutionalism', *Journal of Politics*, 67(4), 1275–300.

Pierson, P. (2000) 'Increasing returns, path dependence, and the study of politics', *American Political Science Review*, 94(2), 251–68.

Roe, M.J. (1994) *Strong Managers, Weak Owners: The Political Roots of American, Corporate Finance* (Princeton, NJ: Princeton University Press).

Roe, M.J. (2003) *Political Determinants of Corporate Governance: Political Context, Corporate Impact* (Oxford: Oxford University Press).

Salacuse, J.W. (2003) 'Corporate governance, culture and convergence: corporations American style or with a European touch', *European Business Law Review*, 14(5), 471–96.

Schlegelmilch, B.B. and Pollach, I. (2005) 'The perils and opportunities of communicating corporate ethics', *Journal of Marketing Management*, 21(3/4), 267–90.

Scott, W.R. (2004) 'Institutional theory: contributing to a theoretical research program' in K. Smith and M. Hitt (eds) *Great Minds in Management: The Process of Theory Development* (Oxford: Oxford University Press).

Shleifer, A. and Vishny, R.W. (1997) 'A survey of corporate governance', *Journal of Finance*, 52(2), 737–83.

Singh, A. (2003) 'Competition, corporate governance and selection in emerging markets', *Economic Journal*, 113(491), 443–64.

Stack, M. and Gartland, M.P. (2003) 'Path creation, path dependency, and alternative theories of the firm', *Journal of Economic Issues*, 37(2), 487–94.

Sternberg, E. (2000) *Just Business: Business Ethics in Action* (Oxford: Oxford University Press).

Transparency International (2008) *Global Corruption Report 2007*, Transparency International.

Udayasankar, K., Das, S. and Krishnamurti, C. (2005) 'Integrating multiple theories of corporate governance: a multi-country empirical study', *Academy of Management Best Conference Paper*, 01–06.

Wieland, J. (2005) 'Corporate governance, values management, and standards: a European perspective', *Business and Society*, 44(1), 74–93.

Yakasai, G.A. (2001) 'Corporate governance in a Third World country with particular reference to Nigeria', *Corporate Governance: An International Review*, 9(3), 239–40.

Yerokun, O. (1992) 'The changing investment climate through law and policy in Nigeria', in C.O. Okonkwo (ed.) *Contemporary Issues in Nigerian Law* (Lagos: Taiwo Fakoyede).

Zucker, L.G. (1987) 'Institutional theories of organizations', *Annual Review of Sociology*, 13, 443–64.

22
Socially Entrepreneurial Behaviour of Multinational Corporations: Are MNCs 'Social Entrepreneurs'?

Misagh Tasavori and Rudolf R. Sinkovics

Introduction

Multinational corporations (MNCs) have been recognized as the key agents of globalization. Rugman and Verbeke (2004) highlight the fact that most MNCs' sales are within their home region, namely in North America, the European Union and Asia. On the other hand, Dunning and Lundan (2008) emphasize that MNCs are deemed to be not only bringers of economic development but also agents of social well-being, especially in less developed countries. Thus, a growing number of MNCs are altering their strategies to play a substantial role as regional agents to solve social challenges. They are embracing a new approach to corporate social responsibility (CSR) by reformulating their CSR activities. They identify social problems, not as a challenge to be avoided, but as a profitable opportunity that can be seized. Among various social problems, this paper will focus on poverty, which has inspired MNCs' efforts in less developed countries (London and Hart, 2004; Prahalad, 2009). For instance, the bottom of the pyramid (BOP) approach explains the new strategy for implementing social responsibility and poverty reduction as well as making profit. In his seminal book, *The Fortune at the Bottom of the Pyramid*, Prahalad (2004) provides examples of pioneering MNCs in emerging markets that have modified their businesses and processes. As in many emerging fields, most of the examples and case studies about the innovative initiatives of MNCs in offering sustainable solutions to social hurdles are fragmented and there have been few attempts to provide a theoretical explanation. Thus, this research aims to bridge this gap by borrowing the literature from entrepreneurship and social entrepreneurship domains.

The primary contribution of this chapter will be to offer a theoretical clarification of the socially entrepreneurial behaviour of MNCs. Moreover, this conceptual work will contribute to extending the literature of international business and social entrepreneurship (SE) by offering the term 'corporate social entrepreneurship' as a new avenue for learning about MNCs' role as social agents.

Social challenges and commercial firms' responsibilities

While the world is experiencing massive wealth creation, technological innovation and political emancipation, almost two-thirds of the world's population are still deprived of access to basic services and products (World Economic Forum, 2005). The United Nations Development Program has invited all nations of the world to embrace the Millennium Development Goals and address relevant dimensions of global poverty and human development. Historically, non-profit organizations, including non-governmental organizations (NGOs) and civil society organizations, have been deemed responsible for satisfying needs overlooked by governments (Wei-Skillern et al., 2007). Though their endeavours have been fruitful, evidence demonstrates that tackling poverty will not be strikingly successful without the engagement of all agents. This has led to increasing expectations that private sector firms, especially MNCs, offer sustainable solutions for the mitigation of social hurdles such as poverty (Prahalad and Hart, 2002). By harnessing their managerial and financial capabilities, MNCs can offer new products, services, initiatives and business models to solve social problems and promote quality of life in societies. On the other hand, commercial firms and their shareholders may view firms' social responsibility as the supply of the goods and services required by societies at the right price, quality and level of service. Knox and Maklan (2004) argue that demanding that MNCs commit themselves to solving social challenges may be an over-expectation.

These two divergent requirements have made MNCs rethink their approach towards social responsibilities and they have begun to envisage social problems as opportunities to satisfy the development agencies' expectations at the same time as the profitability demands of their shareholders.

Social challenges as an opportunity: a market-based approach

There is increasing agreement among NGOs and MNCs that charity and philanthropic donations will only satisfy the short-term needs of the poor but will not remove the underlying reasons for their poverty. This means that the pressure on corporations to mitigate social hurdles such as poverty will not diminish and they will continue to need to donate considerable amounts of money.

On the other hand, MNCs in developed countries are faced with saturated markets which propel them to look for new opportunities to guarantee their long-term growth and profitability (London and Hart, 2004). The billions of dollars in untapped markets such as the BOP provide a new window of opportunity for MNCs. While the traditional approach to poverty assumed that at the subsistence level people were not able to help themselves and needed charity or public assistance, the new approach views social problems as an opportunity to be addressed by the provision of market-based solutions. Advocates of the latter practice believe that being poor does not necessarily eliminate commerce; instead, the poor can be treated as potential consumers and producers (Hammond et al., 2007). A market-based approach suggests solutions such as producing affordable new products and services and/or incorporating poor people in the MNCs' supply chains (Prahalad, 2009). When corporations view this market as an opportunity, then the potential growth that they can offer their investors will be massive. It has been estimated that growth in developed countries will be around 3 per cent annually, whereas the growth rate in poor countries will be double or three times that rate. Additionally, the number of the low-income population is many times the number of the middle class or rich (Agarwal, 2006).

MNCs' innovative initiatives in addressing social challenges

There is a surging consensus that business is the key driver in mitigating social problems both through the opportunities it creates and the services it provides. MNCs can link rich and poor countries, and transfer capital, knowledge, ideas and values to less developed economies (Meyer, 2004) and employ their global resource base and superior technology for the eradication of poverty (Prahalad and Hart, 2002).

Serving the low-income population is a demanding job even for large corporations, as it requires a new deeper understanding of the consumers' needs and paying capacity. Companies should rethink their current business models and embrace new innovative strategies (London and Hart, 2004). Prahalad (2004) adds that corporations have to revise every step in their supply chains. CEMEX, for example, one of the world's largest cement manufacturers, had to change its distribution strategy and bypass several intermediaries to provide affordable building materials for the low-income population in Mexico. Another example is Hindustan Unilever that has employed a new distribution strategy to serve the poor in India. It has developed a rural network of women who sell detergent products door-to-door in more than 100,000 villages, while raising awareness of the importance of hygiene and nutrition (Subrahmanyan and Gomez-Arias, 2008). Another example by this company is the introduction of a new iodized salt in rural areas of India, to prevent iodine deficiency and mental disorders. It was noticed that in India most of the iodine in salt is lost in the process of storage, transportation and cooking. Since iodized salt prevents iodine deficiency, the company modified its product for this market and developed a proprietary micro-encapsulation technology to stabilize the iodine content in salt (Prahalad, 2004). ITC, a multinational company in India, has provided internet access for low-income farmers to benefit from a variety of information such as weather forecasts, prices of commodities and best practices for farming (Subrahmanyan and Gomez-Arias, 2008).

Theoretical explanation of socially innovative strategies of MNCs

As indicated in the previous two sections, increasing numbers of MNCs are recognizing social challenges as opportunities which can be exploited profitably. However, this necessitates fundamental changes in their business models and strategies for the production and provision of services. The process of the recognition of social opportunities and the innovative exploitation and mobilization of resources is usually the focus of attention in the emerging field of SE. Hence, in the following sections, we review some definitions of SE and unveil the key components of the concept. Then we examine whether MNCs can be considered to be social entrepreneurs.

Review of the SE literature

SE refers to organizations that employ innovative business models to satisfy the basic human needs which have been ignored by existing markets and institutions (Seelosa and Mair, 2005). Although SE has a long heritage among practitioners (Mair and Marti, 2006), it has only a brief scholarly history (Weerawardena and Mort, 2006). Similar to other emerging fields, there is still not much consensus on its definitions (see Table 22.1) and domains (Mair and Marti, 2006; Martin and Osberg, 2007; Peredo and McLean, 2006). Some academics describe SE broadly as the effort of an individual, group, network, organization or alliance of

Table 22.1 Examples of social entrepreneurship definitions

Author(s)	Definition
Dees (1994)	Social enterprises are private organizations dedicated to solving social problems, serving the disadvantaged and providing socially important goods that were not, in their judgement, adequately provided by public agencies or private markets.
Leadbeater (1997)	The use of entrepreneurial behaviour for social ends rather than for profit objectives, or alternatively, that the profits generated from market activities are used for the benefit of a specific disadvantaged group.
Dees (1998)	Social entrepreneurs play the role of change agents in the social sector by: (1) adopting a mission to create and sustain social value (not just private value), (2) recognizing and relentlessly pursuing new opportunities to serve that mission, (3) engaging in a process of continuous innovation, adaptation and learning, (4) acting boldly without being limited by resources currently in hand and (5) exhibiting heightened accountability to the constituencies served and for the outcomes created.
Fowler (2000)	Social entrepreneurship is the creation of viable socio-economic structures, relations, institutions, organizations and practices that yield and sustain social benefits.
Thompson et al. (2000)	Social entrepreneurs are people who realize where there is an opportunity to satisfy some unmet need that the welfare state will not or cannot meet.
Drayton (2002)	A social entrepreneur is a major change agent, one whose core values centre on identifying, addressing and solving societal problems.

Alvord et al. (2004)	Social entrepreneurship creates innovative solutions to immediate social problems and mobilizes the ideas, capacities, resources, and social arrangements required for sustainable transformation.
Haugh (2005)	Social entrepreneurs combine innovation, entrepreneurship and social purpose to be financially sustainable by generating revenue from trading.
Austin et al. (2006)	Social entrepreneurship is an innovative, social value-creating activity that can occur within or across the non-profit, business or government sectors.
Peredo and McLean (2006)	Social entrepreneurship is exercised where some person or group...aim(s) at creating social value...shows a capacity to recognize and take advantage of opportunities...employ innovation...accept an above average degree of risk...and are unusually resourceful...in pursuing their social venture.
Mair and Marti (2006)	Social entrepreneurship is a process of creating value by combining resources in new ways...intended primarily to explore and exploit opportunities to create social value by stimulating social change or meeting social needs.
Light (2006)	Social entrepreneurship is an effort by an individual, group, network, organization, or alliance of organizations that seeks sustainable, large-scale change through pattern-breaking ideas in what governments, non-profits and businesses do to address significant social problems.
Martin and Osberg (2007)	Social entrepreneurship is the: (1) identification of a stable yet unjust equilibrium which excludes, marginalizes or causes suffering to a group which lacks the means to transform the equilibrium, (2) identification of an opportunity and development of a new social value proposition to challenge the equilibrium and (3) the forging of a new, stable equilibrium to alleviate the suffering of the targeted group through the imitation and creation of a stable ecosystem around the new equilibrium to ensure a better future for the group and society.
Massetti (2008)	Social entrepreneurship is making profits by innovation in the face of risk with the involvement of a segment of society and where all or part of the benefits accrue to that same segment of society.
Zahra et al. (2008)	Social entrepreneurship encompasses the activities and processes undertaken to discover, define, and exploit opportunities in order to enhance social wealth by creating new ventures or managing existing organizations in an innovative manner.
Light (2008)	Social entrepreneurship includes efforts to solve intractable social problems through pattern-breaking change.
Bloom and Chatterji (2009)	Individuals who start up and lead new organizations or programmes that are dedicated to mitigating or eliminating a social problem, deploying change strategies that differ from those that have been used to address the problem in the past.

organizations to pursue sustainable, large-scale change, through pattern-breaking ideas in what government, non-profit organizations, and businesses do to solve significant social problems (Light, 2006). It has also been observed that it is the process of exploring and exploiting opportunities and combining resources in new ways to create social value (Mair and Marti, 2006). Fowler (2000) simply explains it as new structures to solve social problems. Similarly, Austin et al. (2006) provide a concise definition by referring to SE as social value-creating activities. To better understand the boundaries of this field, the key concepts in SE definitions have been identified and discussed in the next section.

Key concepts in SE definitions

A review of SE definitions illustrates a variety of approaches towards defining this domain. Some scholars have explained it by unravelling the 'social' and 'entrepreneurial' dimensions (Peredo and McLean, 2006). Others have referred to the level of analysis such as individuals, firms, networks and alliances (Light, 2006). Another group has emphasized the funding strategy in their definitions (Leadbeater, 1997; Massetti, 2008). Built upon the review of the extant SE literature, we classify these common concepts in SE definitions into five main categories: the entrepreneurial dimension, social mission and social value creation, the level of analysis, the context and the funding strategy. Learning about these elements will help us to investigate whether MNCs can be considered as social entrepreneurs.

Entrepreneurial dimension

Several researchers have recognized the entrepreneurial dimension as the essential component of SE (Nicholls, 2008a; Peredo and McLean, 2006). Inheriting entrepreneurship as the core component, SE has incurred a continuous debate over its definition and evolution. Some scholars seek to understand social entrepreneurs by their characteristics. Drayton (2002) states that social entrepreneurs are change agents who are inspired by identifying, addressing and solving societal challenges. Based on their experiences with many social entrepreneurs, Elkington and Hartigan (2008) provide a long list of social entrepreneurs' characteristics.

Another group of researchers define entrepreneurship as a combination of innovative, proactive and risk-taking behaviour (Covin and Slevin, 1989; Miller, 1983). Likewise, some SE researchers have developed their definitions based on key entrepreneurial dimensions such as innovativeness (Alvord et al., 2004; Austin et al., 2006; Zahra et al., 2008).

The third strand of definitions refers to the process of entrepreneurship or what the entrepreneurs do (Gartner, 1988; Kent et al., 1982). In this approach, entrepreneurs identify opportunities and exploit them innovatively. Shane and Venkataraman (2001) define entrepreneurship as 'examination of how, by whom, and with what effect opportunities to create future goods and services are discovered, evaluated and exploited'. Nicholls and Cho (2008) highlight innovation and market orientation as key entrepreneurial dimensions of social entrepreneurs. Similarly, some scholars identify innovation, opportunity creation and recognition as determinant elements in SE (Dees et al., 2004; Thompson, 2002). Zahra et al. (2008) refer to SE as the innovative activities and processes undertaken to discover, define and exploit opportunities to enhance social wealth. Some researchers have highlighted the resource mobilization process. Mair and Marti (2006) define SE as the process of creating value by mobilizing resources in new ways to explore and exploit opportunities to offer social changes or address social needs. Finally, Brooks (2009) indicates that the SE process includes five stages: opportunity recognition, concept development, resource mobilization, launch and venture growth and harvesting the venture.

Social mission and social value creation

Despite the differences in the various definitions, the social dimension has been the common element in all definitions of SE (Brooks, 2009). Nicholls and Cho (2008) distinguish social entrepreneurs from their commercial counterparts by the 'social' element. For social entrepreneurs, the social mission is at the centre of their agenda and has priority over all other organizational objectives (Dees, 1998; Nicholls, 2008a). Dees (1994) emphasizes that social entrepreneurs solve social problems, serve the disadvantaged and offer socially important goods. Though social mission and social value creation have been referred to as the vital components of the SE definition, few researchers have provided an explanation about the realm of this dimension. Those who have defined this term have built their argument on the operation, process, output or context of social mission (Nicholls, 2008a). Nicholls (2008a), for instance, explains that the embracing of the social mission by social entrepreneurs means that they identify unmet social needs or create new social value. Emerson (2003) explains social objectives through their outcomes. He states that social entrepreneurs address social opportunities which are usually the result of dysfunctional systems due to a range of reasons, including a lack of reliable performance information, high transaction costs and a lack of innovation. Smallbone et al. (2001) describes social objectives as providing goods and services which the market or public sector is either unwilling or unable to provide, developing skills and empowering socially excluded people. Bornstein (2004) identifies the primary social challenges addressed by social entrepreneurs as:

- poverty alleviation through empowerment, for example, the microfinance movement
- healthcare, ranging from small-scale ventures to tackling the HIV/AIDS pandemic
- education and training, such as widening participation and the democratization of knowledge transfer
- environmental preservation and sustainable development, such as 'green' energy projects
- community regeneration, such as housing associations

- welfare projects, such as employment for the unemployed or homeless and drug and alcohol abuse projects
- advocacy and campaigning, such as fair trade and human rights promotion.

The most recent definition of social value creation has been provided by Young (2008). He provides a detailed explanation of the dimensions of social value creation. He states that 'social' may be found in everything and the 'value' that social entrepreneurs pursue refers to benefiting people whose urgent needs are not satisfied by other means. He then conceptualizes social value through four elements, namely, social added value, empowerment and social change, social innovation and systemic change. He believes that social added value is a common feature among all the activities of social entrepreneurs. There is a variety of models that create social added value. For example, it could refer to the generation of economic and social benefits in poor communities, or alternatively to combining personal, family and community resources (low-cost resources) to produce new product or offer services that are affordable to all. Young (2008) explains that added value represents additional inputs which enhance the quality of the beneficiaries' lives.

Young's second aspect of SE refers to empowerment and social change. Further to the creation of added social value, social entrepreneurs strive to change the social and economic situations of disadvantaged groups. They create employment opportunities for those who are seen by other parts of society to be taboo, dysfunctional or undeserving. Approaches that alter practices, structures, beliefs and deep-rooted cultural prejudices will be also valuable as they create social change.

Social innovation creates social value by allowing people to achieve more for less, or by solving insoluble problems. Innovation is the result of combining existing elements in a new way. International Development Enterprises' experience in India, for example, has proved how cheap, simple, durable technology, such as water pumps or irrigation design, can transform the lives of poor farmers by allowing them to earn more money from their land.

Finally, systemic change describes the transformation of how things work and is a crucial factor in social value creation. The work of Mohammad Yunus, who introduced microfinance to the people at Grameen Bank, is one of the most successful examples in this area. The system he employed for giving loans to the poor changed the prospects of many Bangladeshi people, and has now become popular in other parts of the world as well.

Level of analysis

The level of analysis has been addressed in a few of the SE definitions. In some of the definitions, social entrepreneurs are limited to 'individuals' looking for new ways to add value (Brinckerhoff, 2001; Thompson et al., 2000). Peredo and McLean (2006) refer to social entrepreneurs as 'persons' or 'groups' who create social value. Light (2006) expands this boundary by mentioning that SE is an effort by an individual, group, network, organization or alliance of organizations.

Context

Another concept which has been employed in some of the SE definitions is the context or sector in which SE can occur. Leadbeater (1997) suggests that SE can be present across all three sectors of society, namely, the public sector adopting business skills, socially affirmative businesses or businesses focusing on social ends and, finally, the voluntary and not-for-profit sector adopting more entrepreneurial approaches (Nicholls, 2008a). In the same vein, Austin et al. (2006) state that SE can occur within or across the non-profit, business and government sectors.

Funding strategy

Funding strategy is another element which has been stated in a number of SE definitions. While early studies of SE shared the assumption that SE is a non-profit sector phenomenon (Dees et al., 2001), some scholars disagree and argue that social entrepreneurs can rely on different sources of funding. As an example, some researchers introduce the concept of the double bottom line and view non-profit organizations that employ income-generating strategies as social enterprises or 'hybrid' organizations (Davis, 1997). In this case, social entrepreneurs earn money and invest the profits to extend their products and/or services. These groups of scholars emphasize that the primary motive of a social entrepreneur's economic mission is to gain 'surplus' rather than 'profit' to ensure the viability of their activities (Fowler, 2000). For example, some non-profit organizations establish an enterprise to support other non-economically viable activities (Fowler, 2000).

Elkington and Hartigan (2008) believe that most social entrepreneurs' business models are closer to those of non-profit organizations because of the immaturity of the markets they address. Nicholls (2008a) suggests a continuum of SE ventures based on their funding strategies (Figure 22.1). At one extreme, voluntary activism is dependent on donated assets and volunteers and, at the other extreme, corporate social innovation represents social ventures within the context of private sector organizations. Moving along the continuum, social entrepreneurs seek greater self-sufficiency through generating income to support their activities.

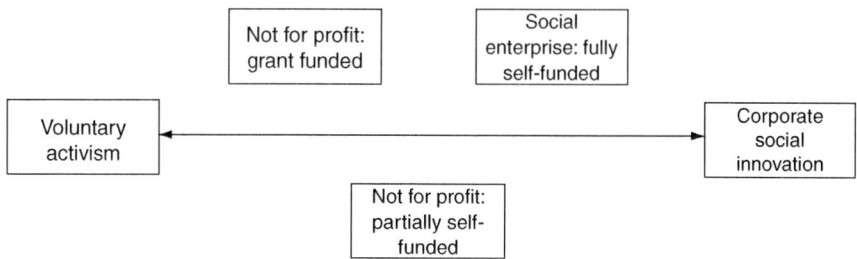

Figure 22.1 Continuum of social entrepreneurship based on funding strategy
Source: Nicholls (2008b).

Reconciling SE definitions

Although SE is widely accepted as a phenomenon, an agreed universal definition of SE is absent. Before proceeding to the question of whether MNCs can be classified as social entrepreneurs, it is crucial to reach an agreement on its definition. For the purpose of this paper, we offer a comprehensive but broad definition which will be beneficial for the development of the early stages of the field (Sharma and Chrisman, 1999). SE refers to "embracing social mission (solving a social problem and offering solutions for the unmet needs of the disadvantaged groups) as the primary mission, employing entrepreneurial activities to achieve the mission and creating social value" (see Figure 22.2).

It is important to highlight the fact that in our definition social mission and social value creation have been differentiated. Since there are social problems in the society, social entrepreneurs choose to play a part as change agents. Hence the main reason behind the establishment of their enterprises will be a social rather than economic mission. Even when they are for profit, they aim to generate a surplus to support their activities (Fowler, 2000). Social value creation will be the outcome of their activities and as Young (2008) has indicated this results in social added value, empowerment and social change, social innovation and systemic change.

Some may claim that social value creation may also be the result of economic activities of organizations. Commercial firms also provide jobs and enhance the lives of a group of people through the employment opportunities that they offer. Though these consequences can be deemed as empowerment, it is important that organizations adopt a social mission and create value for those parts of the society that are deemed as dysfunctional or taboo.

The entrepreneurial dimension is definitely the core concept of SE definitions. Not all organizations that pursue social missions are entrepreneurs. Based on the entrepreneurship literature, they should be innovative, proactive and risk-taking (Covin and Slevin, 1989; Miller, 1983). From the process perspective of the entrepreneurship literature, social entrepreneurs perceive social problems as opportunities and mobilize the required resources innovatively in order to seize them.

In line with Light's (2006) definition, SE may be pursued by individuals, groups, networks, organizations or alliances of organizations in the public or private sector, but it is important that they embrace social missions as the primary goals for their activities. Also, an increasing number of examples confirms that social entrepreneurs may adopt different approaches towards their funding strategies (Nicholls, 2008a).

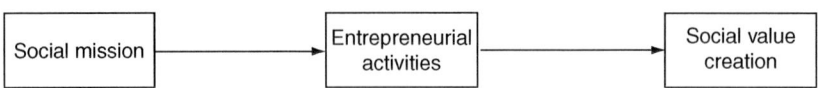

Figure 22.2 Social entrepreneurship definition

Are MNCs social entrepreneurs?

To answer this question, we should examine whether the key concepts of SE are applicable for MNCs' behaviour. The first dimension is the entrepreneurial approach which has been distinguished as an effective instrument towards the mitigation of social problems in the world (Dees, 2001). As previously highlighted, a growing numbers of MNCs are recognizing social challenges as opportunities and mobilizing financial and managerial resources to offer innovative solutions.

Social mission and social value creation have been recognized as the key elements of SE. To investigate the presence of these two concepts in the socially entrepreneurial behaviour of MNCs, we start with social value creation. MNCs offer some social value at the BOP level, which results in poverty reduction. They offer new products and services for deprived and disadvantaged groups who have been neglected by other agents. Commercial banks, for example, offer microfinance to the low-income population who may not otherwise have access to loans. MNCs also empower the poor by modifying their sourcing and supply chain strategies. Nestlé trains poor farmers in good practices for breeding and feeding herds in order that they can enhance milk yields and consequently they have increased the income of these farmers (Subrahmanyan and Gomez-Arias, 2008).

Social mission is the major antecedent in the SE process. Despite the considerable roles of MNCs in solving social challenges in an entrepreneurial manner, the primary aim of MNCs is not the pursuit of a social mission. To this end it may require a new term for describing the socially entrepreneurial behaviour of MNCs.

Corporate SE

Apart from SE scholars, CSR researchers have employed the term corporate social entrepreneurship (CSE) in recent years. Wood (2008) in *The A to Z of Corporate Social Responsibility* refers to CSE and defines it as the creation or development of new products, services or market segments to satisfy social needs, innovation in processes or less harmful technologies, or the identification of business opportunities to earn profit while addressing a social challenge. Similarly, Schwab (2008) in 'Global corporate citizenship' describes CSE as the transformation of socially and environmentally responsible ideas into products and services. Drawing on CSR literature we suggest expanding the SE literature by introducing the concept of CSE to describe socially entrepreneurial behaviour of MNCs. This will be also in accordance with the entrepreneurship domain that distinguishes between entrepreneurship in small- and medium-sized enterprises and large and established organizations by introducing corporate entrepreneurship. CSE refers to "embracing an economic and social mission (solving a social problem and offering solutions for the unmet needs of the disadvantaged groups) as the primary mission; employing corporate entrepreneurial activities to achieve the mission and creating social value" (see Figure 22.3).

When embarking on CSE, a large organization will employ the characteristics of corporate entrepreneurs to offer social enhancement. Therefore, MNCs that alter

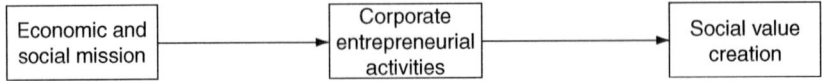

Figure 22.3 Corporate social entrepreneurship definition

their business models innovatively, offer new products and services to ignored segments of the population, such as the poor, and enhance their lives, can be considered corporate social entrepreneurs.

It is noteworthy to clarify that social responsibility related activities can be referred to as SE only when there is an entrepreneurial element. Thus, we believe that the devotion of employees' time to educating poor students, although valuable, cannot be classified as CSE. Similarly, the initiatives of organizations that engage in charitable giving or cause-related branding cannot be categorized as CSE.

Conclusion and future research directions

Rugman and Verbeke (2004) emphasize that IB scholars should take into account the fact that most MNCs' activities are in their home region. This research seeks to explain the new role of MNCs in emerging economies as economic and social engines. Recently, MNCs have begun to recognize social challenges such as poverty as opportunities and have mobilized the required resources to address them. The main contribution of this research relies on highlighting the socially entrepreneurial behaviour of MNCs and examining whether we can offer new insights into the field of international business by incorporating the SE literature. To this end, the definitions of SE have been reviewed and its components have been discussed. In spite of our expectations, the analysis of the extant literature demonstrates that MNCs cannot be deemed social entrepreneurs as they pursue both an economic and social mission. Thus, we have drawn on the CSR literature and suggested CSE to refer to the socially entrepreneurial behaviour of MNCs.

This research is the first building block in the domain of CSE in international business. It will be beneficial that IB scholars further elaborate on the definition of CSE and its underlying concepts. In addition, developing a typology of CSE will highlight a new profitable strategy for MNCs to play a more substantial role in the implementation of their social responsibility. CSE that offers a win-win strategy for addressing social problems have crucial implications for policymakers; it opens a new avenue for the eradication of social problems by utilizing the MNCs' financial and managerial resources. In addition, investigating how MNCs can successfully align a social mission with their economic mission will help to tackle conflicting expectations about their role towards society. We also suggest re-examining the role of NGOs and civil society in persuading MNCs to embrace CSE and access the BOP. Partnerships between MNCs and NGOs at the BOP have brought about innovative business models which invites further studies.

References

Agarwal, R. (2006) 'Business strategies for profitable sales to the poor: how free enterprise can fight poverty', in S.C. Jain and S. Vachani (eds) *Multinational Corporations and Global Poverty Reduction*, 125–41, (Cheltenham: Edward Elgar).

Alvord, S.H., Brown, D.L. and Letts, C.W. (2004) 'Social entrepreneurship and societal transformation: an exploratory study', *Journal of Applied Behavioral Science*, 40(3), 260–83.

Austin, J.E., Stevenson, H. and Wei-Skillern, J. (2006) 'Social and commercial entrepreneurship: same, different, or both?', *Entrepreneurship: Theory and Practice*, 30(1), 1–22.

Bloom, P.N. and Chatterji, A.K. (2009) 'Scaling social entrepreneurial impact', *California Management Review*, 51(3), 114–33.

Bornstein, D. (2004) *How to Change the World: Social Entrepreneurs and the Power of New Ideas*, 1st edn (Oxford: Oxford University Press).

Brinckerhoff, P.C. (2001) 'Why you need to be more entrepreneurial – and how to get started', *Nonprofit World*, 19(6), 12–5.

Brooks, A.C. (2009) *Social Entrepreneurship: A Modern Approach to Social Venture Creation* (Hillsdale, NJ: Pearson Education).

Covin, J.G. and Slevin, D.P. (1989) 'Strategic management of small firms in hostile and benign environments', *Strategic Management Journal*, 10(1), 75–87.

Davis, L. (1997) *The NGO Business Hybrid: Is the Private Sector the Answer?* (Baltimore, MD: Johns Hopkins University).

Dees, J.G. (1994) 'Social enterprise: private initiatives for the common good', *Harvard Business Review*, 76(1), 54–8.

Dees, J.G. (1998) 'The meaning of social entrepreneurship' Research Paper, Duke University's Fuqua School of Business, Center for the Advancement of Social Entrepreneurship.

Dees, J.G. (2001) *The Meaning of Social Entrepreneurship* [Online]: Fuqua School of Business, Duke University. Available: http://www.caseatduke.org/about/whatissocialentrepreneurship/ (March 07, 2009).

Dees, J.G., Anderson, B.B. and Wei-Skillern, J. (2004) 'Scaling social impact', *Stanford Social Innovation Review*, 1(1), 24–32.

Dees, J.G., Emerson, J. and Economy, P. (2001) *Enterprising Non-Profits: A Toolkit for Social Entrepreneurs* (Non-Profit Series) (New York: John Wiley and Sons).

Drayton, W. (2002) 'The citizen sector: becoming as entrepreneurial and competitive as business', *California Management Review*, 44(3), 120–32.

Dunning, J.H. and Lundan, S.M. (2008) *Multinational Enterprises and the Global Economy*, 2nd edn (Cheltenham: Edward Elgar).

Elkington, J. and Hartigan, P. (2008) *The Power of Unreasonable People* (Boston, MA: Harvard Business Press).

Emerson, J. (2003) 'The blended value proposition: integrating social and financial returns', *California Management Review*, 45(4), 35–51.

Fowler, A. (2000) 'NGDOs as a moment in history: beyond aid to social entrepreneurship or civic innovation?', *Third World Quarterly*, 21(4), 637–54.

Gartner, W.B. (1988) 'Who is an entrepreneur? is the wrong question', *American Journal of Small Business*, 12(4), 11–32.

Hammond, A.L., Kramer, W.J., Tran, J., Katz, R. and Walker, C. (2007) *The Next 4 Billion: Market Size and Business Strategy at the Base of the Pyramid* (Washington, D.C.: World Resources Institute, IFC, and the World Bank).

Haugh, H. (2005) 'The role of social enterprise in regional development', *International Journal of Entrepreneurship and Small Business*, 2(4), 346–57.

Kent, C.A., Sexton, D.L. and Vesper, K.H. (1982) *Encyclopaedia of Entrepreneurship* (Englewood Cliffs, NJ: Prentice-Hall).

Knox, S. and Maklan, S. (2004) 'Corporate social responsibility: moving beyond investment towards measuring outcomes', *European Management Journal*, 22(5), 508–16.

Leadbeater, C. (1997) *The Rise of the Social Entrepreneur* (London: Demos).
Light, P.C. (2006) 'Reshaping social entrepreneurship', *Stanford Social Innovation Review*, 4(3), 47–51.
Light, P.C. (2008) *The Search for Social Entrepreneurship* (Washington, D.C.: The Brookings Institution).
London, T. and Hart, S.L. (2004) 'Reinventing strategies for emerging markets: beyond the transnational model', *Journal of International Business Studies*, 35(5), 350–70.
Mair, J. and Marti, I. (2006) 'Social entrepreneurship research: a source of explanation, prediction, and delight', *Journal of World Business*, 41(1), 36–44.
Martin, R.L. and Osberg, S. (2007) 'Social entrepreneurship: the case for a definition', *Stanford Social Innovation Review*, 5(2), 29–39.
Massetti, B.L. (2008) 'The social entrepreneurship matrix as a "tipping point" for economic change', *Emergence: Complexity and Organization*, 10(3), 1–9.
Meyer, K.E. (2004) 'Perspectives on multinational enterprises in emerging economies', *Journal of International Business Studies*, 34(4), 259–77.
Miller, D. (1983) 'The correlates of entrepreneurship in three types of firms', *Management Science*, 29(7), 770–91.
Nicholls, A. (2008a) 'Introduction', in A. Nicholls (ed.) *Social Entrepreneurship: New Models of Sustainable Social Change*, 1–35 (Oxford: Oxford University Press).
Nicholls, A. (ed.) (2008b) *Social Entrepreneurship: New Models of Sustainable Social Change* (Oxford: Oxford University Press).
Nicholls, A. and Cho, A.H. (2008) 'Social entrepreneurship: the structuration of a field', in A. Nicholls (ed.) *Social Entrepreneurship: New Models of Sustainable Social Change*, 99–118 (Oxford: Oxford University Press).
Peredo, A.M. and McLean, M. (2006) 'Social entrepreneurship: a critical review of the concept', *Journal of World Business*, 41(1), 56–65.
Prahalad, C.K. (2004) *The Fortune at the Bottom of the Pyramid: Eradicating Poverty through Profits* (Upper Saddle River, NJ: Wharton School Publishing).
Prahalad, C.K. (2009) *The Fortune at the Bottom of the Pyramid: Eradicating Poverty through Profits*, 5th edn (Upper Saddle River, NJ: Wharton School Publishing).
Prahalad, C.K. and Hart, S.L. (2002) 'The fortune at the bottom of the pyramid,' *Strategy and Business*, 26(1), 54–67.
Rugman, A.M. and Verbeke, A. (2004) 'A perspective on regional and global strategies of multinational enterprises', *Journal of International Business Studies*, 35(1), 3–18.
Schwab, K. (2008) 'Global corporate citizenship', *Foreign Affairs*, 87(1), 107–18.
Seelosa, C. and Mair, J. (2005) 'Social entrepreneurship: creating new business models to serve the poor', *Business Horizons*, 48(3), 241–6.
Shane, S. and Venkataraman, S. (2001) 'Entrepreneurship as a field of research: a response to Zahra and Dess, Singh, and Erikson', *The Academy of Management Review*, 26(1), 13–16.
Sharma, P. and Chrisman, J.J. (1999) 'Toward a reconciliation of the definitional issues in the field of corporate entrepreneurship', *Entrepreneurship: Theory and Practice*, 23(3), 11–27.
Smallbone, D., Evans, M., Ekanem, I. and Butters, S. (2001) 'Researching social enterprise', in *Final Report to the Small Business Service*, London: Centre for Enterprise and Economic Development Research.
Subrahmanyan, S. and Gomez-Arias, J.T. (2008) 'Integrated approach to understanding consumer behavior at bottom of pyramid', *Journal of Consumer Marketing*, 25(7), 402–12.
Thompson, J.L. (2002) 'The world of the social entrepreneur', *The International Journal of Public Sector Management*, 15(4/5), 412–32.
Thompson, J.L., Alvy, G. and Lees, A. (2000) 'Social entrepreneurship – a new look at the people and the potential', *Management Decision*, 38(5), 328–39.
Weerawardena, J. and Sullivan Mort, G. (2006) 'Investigating social entrepreneurship: a multidimensional model', *Journal of World Business*, 41(1), 21–35.

Wei-Skillern, J., Austin, J.E., Leonard, H. and Stevenson, H. (2007) *Entrepreneurship in the Social Sector* (Los Angeles, CA/ London/ New Delhi/ Singapore: Sage Publications, Inc).

Wood, D. (2008) 'Corporate social opportunity', in W. Visser, D. Matten, M. Pohl and N.Tolhurst (eds) *The A to Z of Corporate Social Responsibility: A Complete Reference Guide to Concepts, Codes and Organisations*, 119–20 (New York: John Wiley and Sons).

World Economic Forum (2005) 'Partnering for success: business perspectives on multi-stakeholder partnerships', in Geneva, Switzerland: World Economic Forum.

Young, R. (2008) 'For what it is worth: social value and the future of social entrepreneurship', in A. Nicholls (ed.) *Social Entrepreneurship: New Models of Sustainable Social Change* (Oxford, New York: Oxford University Press).

Zahra, S.A., Gedajlovicb, E., Neubaumc, D.O. and Shulman, J.M. (2008) 'A typology of social entrepreneurs: motives, search processes and ethical challenges', *Journal of Business Venturing*, 24(5), 519–32.

23
'Imported' Management Practices: The Disclosure of Individual Executive Compensation and Firm Performance

Amon Chizema

Introduction

The question of whether executive directors have much impact on organizational outcomes is crucially important to a wide array of research agendas, including studies of executive compensation (Bebchuk and Fried, 2004). For example, research on the pay of executive directors is now a legitimate international business (IB) topic since such remuneration may motivate the strategies of peak-tier decision-makers in a variety of different institutional environments around the world (Buck et al., 2008). Research in this domain mainly seeks to measure the sensitivity of executive pay to share price performance (Tosi et al., 2000) relevant to pay packages supposedly designed to reduce agency problems by better aligning the rewards of shareholders and executives.

Much of the research on executive compensation tends to be about the US and the UK. However, in the last 10 years there has been more research on executive rewards in other markets including Germany (Sanders and Tuschke, 2007) and China (Buck et al., 2008). In Germany, for example, firms are adopting some features of US-style corporate governance (Sanders and Tuschke, 2007) and executive compensation is at the centre of the corporate law reform agenda following pressure from international, globe-spanning discussions over excessive CEO pay packages and management self-dealing.

Beyond CEOs, the extant literature also considers the extent of the public disclosure of executive pay for all individual executive directors in German firms (Werner and Zimmermann, 2006). This research shows that the disclosure of compensation for individual executive directors – a practice common in the US and UK – is a welcome innovation in some German firms but highly contestable in others (Werner and Zimmermann, 2006). Firms that resist this innovation give several justifications, the main one being that disclosure of individual executive compensation does not translate into better firm performance (Chizema, 2008). While these recent studies discuss the determinants of the disclosure or non-disclosure of individual executive pay by German firms (Werner and Zimmerman, 2006), research on the impact of pay disclosure on firm performance is lacking, at least in the context of Germany. This chapter attempts to remedy this omission by examining the impact of disclosing individual executive compensation on firm performance in German firms.

A lot of empirical research in accounting and finance focuses on the operating performance of corporations (Barber and Lyon, 1996). These studies generally assess operating performance following major corporate events or decisions, such as dividend initiation (Healy and Palepu, 1988), stock splits (Asquith et al., 1989) or management buy outs (Kaplan, 1989). The decision to disclose individual executive pay in Germany is certainly a major corporate decision (Werner and Zimmermann, 2006). Indeed, from all the distinguishing governance characteristics of stock market and welfare capitalism, executive pay (including its disclosure) is one of the most important distinctive governance tools available to stakeholders, including shareholders. To our knowledge no studies assess changes in operating performance following a decision to disclose individual executive pay (at least in Germany), and this chapter attempts to fill this lacuna. Shareholder-value practices of this nature are relatively new in Germany and still only some firms disclose individual executive compensation (Chizema, 2008; Werner and Zimmermann, 2006), following a recommendation in the German Code of Corporate Governance. Given the distinct nature of Germany's variety of capitalism (Hall and Soskice, 2001), the choice of this country provides an interesting context in which to analyse the effect of a governance mechanism on firm performance.

The chapter claims three contributions to the theory and practice of international corporate governance. First, by focusing on the adoption of American-style governance practice in Germany – a feature of globalization in the domain of management practices – this chapter extends international corporate governance research. In particular, it shows the extent to which Anglo-American corporate governance elements are diffusing and getting contested in different institutional contexts. Although this chapter focuses on a single country – Germany – as an important laboratory to test theoretical propositions, it is clearly situated within the domain of IB studies, since its focus is on the challenges and effects of adopting a certain governance practice (by firms in one country) that is imported from another governance system – indeed a cross-border activity (Tung and van Witteloostuijn, 2008). As such the chapter adds to the literature on the convergence/divergence of corporate governance systems, by considering a practice that is potentially contestable and illegitimate (Sanders and Tuschke, 2007) in a governance system that is traditionally not known for upholding shareholder supremacy.

Second, the chapter provides evidence on the economic value of disclosure in general and of executive compensation in particular (Buck and Shahrim, 2005; Chizema, 2010). By showing that a close association between the disclosure of individual executive pay and firm performance exists, the contents of this chapter may deflect shareholders' criticisms. Thus, pay disclosure may motivate directors to act in shareholders' interests by improving firm performance.

Third and finally, the chapter demonstrates that the adoption of good management innovations coming from a different corporate governance system may still be resisted by firms. The fact that firms may reject good practices raises the question of whether national corporate governance codes must be voluntary or mandatory. Thus, this research has important implications for policymakers even within regional structures such as the European Union, where work on the harmonization of corporate governance is ongoing.

German corporate governance: convergence or continued divergence?

The literature employs various labels to describe the system of corporate governance in Germany, such as a bank-based system (Vitols, 2004), a relationship-oriented system (Buck and Shahrim, 2005), a network-based or insider system (Cheffins, 2001), a stakeholder system, where employee interests play a predominant role (Dore, 2000), or a coordinated system of corporate governance (Hall and Soskice, 2001).

A large body of research documents the economic logic of the German model of corporate governance (e.g. Casper et al., 1999). They argue that bank-centred financial systems such as the German system are ideally suited to incremental innovations. Arguments in support of this theory also emphasize that national corporate governance systems are path-dependent (Hall and Soskice, 2001), owing to several reasons such as the existence of sunk adaptive costs and the notion of complementarities, where a change in one part requires simultaneous adjustment of the rest of the system. Indeed, institutional theory conventionally puts a strong emphasis on inertia, social embeddedness and path-dependence, since any governance innovations, including executive pay packages and their disclosure, must be socially legitimate in relation to the prevailing regulatory, normative and cognitive influences on firms, and these societal functions must also reconcile with organizational efficiency (Scott, 2001). Such theories therefore support the continued divergence of different governance systems.

However, another growing body of literature cites the inadequacies of the German variety of capitalism, suggesting possible convergence on the US-style of corporate governance (e.g. Hansmann and Kraakman, 2004). Such literature cites the recent adoption of a German code of corporate governance, including reforms of the two-board system, the adoption of equity-based compensation schemes (Fiss and Zajac, 2004; Sanders and Tuschke, 2007) and the disclosure of individual executive compensation (Chizema, 2008; Werner and Zimmermann, 2006). The hostile takeover of Mannesmann AG by Vodafone PLC in 2000 and the successful initial public offering of Deutsche Telekom AG are further evidence of convergence on US-style shareholder capitalism in Germany.

A third set of literature lies between the two extremes, where theory proposes the 'translation' of governance reforms (Buck and Shahrim, 2005) or a negotiated style (Vitols, 2004) of corporate governance. Thus the adoption of illegitimate organizational innovations (Sanders and Tuschke, 2007), inconsistent with existing local institutions (Chizema and Buck, 2006), may face resistance, or at least 'translation' to give the *appearance* of adoption (Buck and Shahrim, 2005). In other words, reforms may result in the hybridization of corporate governance models, where practices common in one national setting diffuse to another, where they undergo adaptation through their recombination with other governance practices (Aguilera and Jackson, 2003). Here, firms select elements of corporate governance from various systems to suit their corporate needs. Indeed, Buck and Shahrim (2005) demonstrate how firms in Germany extend executive stock options (ESOs) to many managers, whereas in the US (where ESOs originate), they remain the preserve of peak-tier executives. Consistent with these arguments on translation and/or negotiation, German firms might adopt US-style executive pay (e.g. stock options) but then choose not to disclose such adoptions publicly.

This tripartite split in the interpretation of corporate governance reform may suggest that the German system is at a crossroad, potentially lying along a clear fault line between stock market and welfare state capitalism (Chizema, 2010; Vitols, 2004). In this regard, the disclosure of individual executive pay is a crucial test case in reform.

Disclosure of individual executive compensation

A regulatory account

Since November 2002, the European Union (EU) has been working on initiatives that emphasize, *inter alia*, the need to have a European-wide regime for executive compensation, basically oriented around the central principles of shareholder approval, and full, individualized disclosure of executive compensation schemes (Bauwhede and Willekens, 2008). Indeed, based on the EU Commission recommendation of 14 December 2004, Member States have the responsibility to ensure that listed companies disclose their directors' remuneration policy to inform shareholders on the levels and form of individual director pay. It also suggests that shareholders should have adequate control over executive pay and share-based remuneration schemes. To implement this recommendation, member states make provisions in their adopted codes of corporate governance that are either voluntary (i.e. suggestions or recommendations) or mandatory.

The German Code of Corporate Governance (KODEX), for example, makes a clear distinction between recommendations and suggestions (Chizema, 2008). First, the code contains legal provisions and the word *'must'* characterize them. The other two categories, *'shall' recommendations* and *'should or can' suggestions*, are not required by law. Consequently, firms can deviate from these rules, but there is an obligation to disclose deviations from *'shall' recommendation*s in the annual statement of conformity in the spirit of *comply or explain*.

The KODEX contains recommendations and suggestions on issues such as the composition and structure of the management and supervisory boards, shareholders and the general meeting, reporting and audit of annual financial statements and the highly contested matter of board remuneration. Section 4.2.4 of the KODEX describes the recommendation on individual disclosure of compensation of board members. Specifically, recommendation 4.2.4 states that 'Compensation of the members of the Management Board shall be reported in the Notes of the

Consolidated Financial Statements subdivided according to fixed, performance-related and long-term incentive components. *The figures shall be individualized.'* This means that annual reports show separately executive compensation for each individual executive director as opposed to the disclosure of an aggregate figure for the whole executive board.

An empirical account

While one academic report indicates a generally high level of compliance with the KODEX that is likely to improve in future (Werder et al., 2005), compliance with recommendations on the disclosure of individualized executive compensation is weak. With reference to provision 4.2.4 of the code, almost all German companies report compensation figures in the notes of Consolidated Financial Statements, but often for the whole board, without the recommended individualization.

Werner and Zimmermann (2006) report that block-holdings, average executive remuneration, book-to-market ratio and the percentage of union representatives in the supervisory board significantly decrease the likelihood of disclosures on individualized compensation figures. They also find that firm size and the presence of takeover activity have a significant positive influence on the disclosure of individual executive compensation. Drawing on neo-institutional theory, Chizema (2008) finds that the power, interests and value commitment of different firm actors determine the decision to disclose or not disclose individual executive compensation. Besides institutional theory, there is a wealth of literature, drawing on agency (Jensen and Meckling, 1976), signalling (Hughes, 1986) and information (Verrecchia, 2001) theories, that advance the economic case for disclosure. However, associations between disclosure compliance with best practice codes and firm performance are inconclusive (Nowak et al., 2006). For example, recommendations of the Cadbury Report supposedly led to positive changes in corporate control through better board supervision (Stiles and Taylor, 1993), an increased likelihood of outside CEO appointment (Dahya and McConnell, 2005), higher sensitivity of CEO turnover to performance (Dahya et al., 2002) and an improvement in the average performance of firms (McKnight and Mira, 2003). On the other hand, Doble (1997) presents mixed evidence of the value-relevance for small- and medium-sized companies. Weir et al. (2002) find only a weak effect of the extent of code compliance in the UK on firm performance, and some German firms argue that the disclosure of individual pay does not bring any economic benefits (Chizema, 2008).

Corporate disclosure in theory, and hypotheses

The disclosure of corporate information (including that of individual executive pay) is central to the field of corporate governance and possible agency problems (Fama and Jensen, 1983), and thus is of interest to shareholders who seek to maximize their returns.

The proposition that corporate governance mechanisms (e.g. incentives, monitoring and disclosure) alter the behaviours of top executives is an important assumption of agency theory (Murphy, 1985). Consequently, such mechanisms may affect firm performance. Indeed, many agency theorists assume that proper governance not only alters the behaviours of top executives (e.g. investment decisions, effort), but that it also has positive effects on firm performance (Jensen and Meckling, 1976).

As part of the agency problem, arguments deriving from information economics theory suggest a significant information asymmetry between outside investors and inside managers. However, managers with detailed knowledge of the firm's operations may reduce this asymmetry by voluntarily disclosing information (in addition to either mandated disclosures or other actions by the firms) to investors in an attempt to influence their decisions about the value of the firm. This voluntarily disclosed information may reduce information asymmetry between managers and investors when it is credible and economically significant. Of course, credibility and the economic significance of information depend on two sets of factors: the type of information and the context of the announcement (Verrecchia, 2001).

However, the theory on corporate voluntary disclosures also primarily aims at identifying the triggers behind firms' incentives to suppress information from investors. The most notable explanations for the withholding of information are the costs (direct and indirect) associated with disclosure (Verrecchia, 2001) and the uncertainty of investors about the endowment of the firms with the information (Dye, 1985). Direct costs associated with disclosure include preparing and disseminating information and various indirect costs include revealing proprietary information to competitors (Darrough and Stoughton, 1990).

Nevertheless, there are benefits deriving from disclosing corporate information. For example, Frankle et al. (1995) suggest that external financing needs motivate managers to disclose more information about their firms' operations and future prospects. For firm managers, there is an incentive to provide more information to a wider outside ownership because that reduces information costs for the investors and hence improves the liquidity of the stock (Verrecchia, 1990). The underlying assumption is that greater disclosure reduces the cost of equity capital, thus enabling companies to raise more capital or to raise the same level of capital at lower cost (Healy and Palepu, 1993), thereby facilitating growth through better performance.

These arguments also draw support from signalling theory that several studies use to address situations replete with information asymmetries between two parties (e.g. Hughes, 1986). Indeed, the act of signalling reduces the information asymmetry between management and investors. For instance, management with more information about their company (e.g. individual executive compensation) could signal the information in order to disclose to equity markets the quality of the firm's management. Thus, firms with high-quality management have an incentive to want to differentiate themselves from lower quality firms by making additional voluntary disclosure. Hughes (1986) suggests that such direct and additional disclosures by firms provide a credible signal about the firm's good intentions and result in attracting a better perception by investors, potential employees and suppliers subsequently translating to better firm performance.

In Germany, the disclosure of executive pay for directors in aggregate proceeds without any contest (Chizema, 2008) and this serves as a minimum disclosure requirement within a regulated environment where firms should explain non-disclosure of individual executive pay in the spirit of 'comply or explain'. This situation provides an opportunity to test the robustness of information asymmetry and signalling theories in a regulated environment because it sets minimum disclosure requirements, while encouraging considerable discretion in disclosing individual executive compensation. Indeed, the KODEX allows such flexibility in the disclosure of individual executive pay, and gives guidance on additional details to achieve full disclosure. In this case, German firms intending to perform better would prefer this flexibility and would disclose individual executive compensation as a signal of their good corporate governance and quality.

From information economics theory, a possible argument is that the decision to voluntarily disclose individual executive compensation by German firms is a result of the assessment of the economic benefits that derive from this additional disclosure. Following this argument, the following hypothesis is made:

Hypothesis 1: *There is a positive relation between the disclosure of individual executive compensation and firm performance.*

Moderator hypotheses

Studies on the diffusion of shareholder value practices drawing from innovation diffusion theory (Rogers, 1995) and insights from resource dependency theory (Pfeffer and Salancik, 1978) show that previous adoption of another practice within the same general policy area may smooth the way for subsequent effective adoptions (Fiss and Zajac, 2004; Sanders and Tuschke, 2007; Tuschke and Sanders, 2003). Such shareholder value practices include the use of more transparent accounting methods such as International Accounting Standard or US GAAP (Tuschke and Sanders, 2003), payment of top executives by stock options and appointment of outside directors. In the case of Germany, Fiss and Zajac (2004) cite changes in the accounting system (from HGB to US GAAP or IAS) as a predictor of change to a market-oriented system of corporate governance that places value on better financial performance. For firms that are already used to reporting their information in an internationally recognized accounting system, disclosing individual executive compensation may be taken as an extra step towards achieving shareholder value. This argument draws support from the view that corporate governance elements are complementary. As such, reforms in one area of the governance system become more effective when they are enhanced by further changes that aim to achieve the same objective. Therefore:

Hypothesis 2: *The relation between the disclosure of individual executive compensation and firm performance is more positive among firms that have a longer history of using IAS or US GAAP standards.*

A number of German firms have securities listed in the US through American Depository Receipts (ADRs) (Sanders and Tuschke, 2007). An ADR is a receipt for the shares of a foreign-based company held by a US bank that entitles the shareholder to all the dividends and capital gains of the underlying stock. ADRs trade similarly to stocks on US exchanges, and provide a way for Americans to invest in foreign-based companies by buying their shares in the US instead of through an overseas exchange. By listing ADRs in the US, German firms submit themselves to scrutiny and compliance by the Securities and Exchange Commission (SEC) with the effect of improving shareholder value and hence better performance. Like the use of IAS or US GAAP, firms with ADRs may have developed a corporate culture that considers the disclosure of more information a necessary tool to achieve better performance. Following this discussion, the following hypothesis can be made:

Hypothesis 3: *The relation between the disclosure of individual executive compensation and firm performance is more positive among firms that have ADRs.*

Haleblian and Finkelstein (1993) suggest that the size of top management teams (TMT) represent an important determinant of firm performance. First, larger management teams have an increased ability to process information, a task that is 'critical to organizational functioning and performance' (Henderson and Fredrickson, 1996, p. 576). Second, larger management teams increase the number of individual judgements that can be used to correct errors that occur during the decision-making process. Third, larger management teams increase the number of potential solutions and range of perspectives that can be applied and considered while evaluating problems (Certo et al., 2006). Indeed, upper echelons theory (Finkelstein and Hambrick, 1990) suggests positive relations between a variety of top management teams' demographics indicators, including size, and firm outcomes. The argument here is that the effectiveness of large top executive teams is likely to be enhanced where there is full disclosure of individual executive remuneration. This is because each board member may seek to display a certain level of performance to justify the disclosed figures. In such circumstances, larger boards are likely to be more beneficial as the collective effort of a larger dedicated group should be better than one given by a smaller management board. Therefore:

Hypothesis 4: *The relation between the disclosure of individual executive compensation and firm performance is more positive among firms that have a larger management board.*

Methodology

Data are collected on the status of listed corporations, that is, firms in the DAX listing, including the DAX 30 (Germany's largest firms in terms of market capitalization), plus the MDAX (representing 70 mid-caps), and the SDAX (50 small-caps), thus providing a potential sample of 150 firms. To provide an impression of typical firms in each category, Table 23.1 shows six examples of DAX, MDAX

Table 23.1 Examples of companies in the DAX 30, MDAX and SDAX listings

DAX 30	MDAX	SDAX
Adidas AG	Atlanta AG	Axel Springer AG
BASF AG	HeidelbergCement AG	BayWa AG
Continental AG	Hugo Boss AG	Dyckerhoff AG
Deutsche Lufthansa AG	Puma AG	Fuchs Petrolub AG
Deutsche Telekom AG	Rheinmettal AG	Gerresheimer AG
ThyssenKrupp AG	SAP AG	MPC AG

and SDAX companies. The modal industrial sector (with the largest number of firms in the sample) is pharmaceuticals and healthcare, followed by industrial manufacturing.

The sample is adjusted by eliminating banks and insurance companies because of their atypical financial structures. Firms not domiciled in Germany are also excluded because they do not fall directly under German regulation. After these adjustments, the actual sample comprises 126 firms drawn from 18 industrial sectors as defined in the Deutsche Börse Group's 'Guide to the Equity Indices' (see http://deutsche-boerse.com).

Dependent variable

Firm performance (PERFM) is measured for each year by return on assets (ROA), which is taken as the ratio of net income to total average assets, expressed as a percentage. ROA has been used in many studies to proxy for firm performance (Bhagat and Black, 2002). Data on ROA is obtained from Datastream International, Thomson and Deutsche Börse. Where data from two sources were not reconcilable, the Investor Relations section of the respective firm was contacted for clarification.

Independent variable

The independent variable in this research is the disclosure of individual executive compensation (DISCLOSE). If a firm disclosed individual figures of executive compensation during the year, the variable was coded 1, and 0 otherwise. Other studies of corporate governance reform in Germany use the same approach (e.g. Chizema, 2008; Fiss and Zajac, 2004; Sanders and Tuschke, 2007) to determine data on disclosure of executive pay. Since German firms apparently announce the disclosure of individual executive pay only at annual general meetings (AGMs), the sources of the independent variable are annual reports and companies' websites.

Moderator variables

The moderator variables in our research are two corporate governance variables associated with a greater transparency environment, namely use of International Accounting Standards (IAS) and ADRs. The third moderating variable is the size of the management board. Larger boards are likely to have a wider variety of skills and expertise that help firms to formulate better decisions, leading to better performance.

IAS is taken as prior adoption of better accounting standards, signalling subsequent compliance with more shareholder value-oriented practices, in this case disclosure of individual compensation for board members. A dummy variable is used coded 1 if a firm adopted IAS or US GAAP before 2002 and 0 for persistent use of German accounting standards (HGB). Data for this variable were collected from firms' annual reports and the Deutsche Börse website at www.deutscheborse.de, and previous research has employed this variable (e.g. Fiss and Zajac, 2004; Sanders and Tuschke, 2007).

ADR is a dummy variable that indicates whether a German firm has securities listed in the US or not; the variable is coded 1 if the firm has an ADR and 0 otherwise. These data were obtained from www.adr.com as well as directly from the American stock exchanges. This information was cross-checked for reliability with companies' annual reports and Form 20-Fs supplied to the US SEC by listed firms. Size of the management board (SIZEMB) represents the number of directors on the company's management board. The SIZEMB has been used in previous studies to represent the collective power or influence of the board members in decision-making (e.g. Franks and Mayer, 2001). These data were sourced from companies' annual reports.

Control variables

Firm size (FIRMSIZ) is the logarithm of total assets, a measure that has been used in several previous studies (e.g. Sherer and Lee, 2002). Data on total assets were obtained from Datastream, and verified by consulting firms' financial reports accessible through their websites. The natural logarithm of a firm's age is used as a proxy for firm experience (FIRMEXP); it has been used in previous research (Ahmadjian and Robbins, 2005; Fernandez and Nieto, 2006) for the same purpose. The Deutsche Börse website was the source for the dates on which firms were established.

Block ownership (BLOCKOWN) is the total percentage of closely held shares in the hands of block-holders. A database derived from Hoppenstedt Aktienführer was the principal source of ownership data of the variables described above (institutional, foreign, dispersed, bank, family and state). These data were verified and complemented by consulting another database, Deutsches AktienInstitut (DAI), and by checking directly from companies' annual reports. Where data were incomplete for some firms, respective investor relations departments were contacted.

Data analysis and results

Table 23.2 provides descriptive statistics (the mean and standard deviation) and the Pearson correlation coefficients between the independent variables. According to our data, the average of firm performance based on ROA is 4.88. In terms of firm characteristics, the average size of the firm based on the logarithm

Table 23.2 Descriptive statistics and correlations

	Mean	SD	1	2	3	4	5	6	7	8
1. PERFM	4.88	8.68	1							
2. FIRMSIZ	6.39	0.95	-0.07^+	1						
3. FIRMEXP	74.60	58.61	-0.08^+	0.03	1					
4. BLOCKOWN	38.55	27.42	0.07	-0.16^{**}	-0.02	1				
5. DISCLOSE	0.45	0.49	0.10^{**}	0.29^{***}	-0.20^*	-0.25	1			
6. IAS	0.51	0.51	-0.11^*	0.24^{**}	-0.06	-0.17	0.38^*	1		
7. ADR	0.24	0.43	0.23	0.22^*	-0.11^*	-0.27	0.02	0.16^{**}	1	
8. SIZEMB	4.24	1.42	0.12^*	0.31^*	0.05	-0.14	0.04	0.14^{**}	0.17^{**}	1

Notes: Standardized regression coefficients $^{***}p < 0.001$; $^{**}p < 0.01$; $^{*}p < 0.05$; $^{+}p < 0.10$; $N = 126$.

of total assets is 6.39, and the average age of the firm, used here as a proxy for experience, is 74.60 years. The data also reveal that average block ownership is 38.55 per cent and that the average management board consists of four directors.

The correlation coefficients are all below 0.4. As a rule of thumb, multicollinearity in regression analysis is considered harmful only when correlations exceed 0.7 (Tabachnick and Fidell, 1996). Additionally, the variance inflation factors (VIFs) for each independent variable were computed and examined. In all cases, the VIFs are below two, far lower than the critical value of ten (Tabachnick and Fidell, 1996), suggesting multicollinearity is not a major problem.

Moreover, some of our hypotheses (H2, H3 and H4) suggest interaction terms composed of the decision to disclose individual executive pay and other variables (IAS, ADR and SIZEMB). To deal with possible multicollinearity between the interaction terms and their components, the interaction term was mean-centred, thus creating the interaction terms by multiplying the relevant mean-centred scales (Aiken and West, 1991). Further tests to ensure the applicability of OLS regression to the data were carried out. For example, using the P-P plot, the data satisfy the assumption of normality of the dependent variable, and scatter graphs suggested a linear relation between the dependent and independent variables. Tests for heteroscedasticity and correlation error terms show the absence of these problems in the data.

Table 23.3 shows the results of the ordinary least squares regression analysis. A hierarchical approach is taken, where control variables are entered first then the focal variable (DISCLOSE), followed by moderator variables and finally including interaction terms. This procedure results in four models.

The overall regression equation in Model 1 is not statistically significant ($F = 1.784$, $p > 0.10$), which suggests that control variables, on their own, do not explain firm performance. The regression equations in Models 2, 3 and 4 are all statistically significant ($F = 2.763$, $p < 0.01$; $F = 5.221$, $p < 0.001$ and $F = 4.944$, $p < 0.001$, respectively). From the control variables, firm size is positively associated with firm performance in Models 2 ($\beta = 0.097$, $p < 0.1$), 3 ($\beta = 0.146$, $p < 0.1$) and 4 ($\beta = 0.155$, $p < 0.01$). Block ownership is also positively associated with firm performance in the three models at ($\beta = 0.095$, $p < 0.1$) in Model 2, ($\beta = 0.112$, $p < 0.01$) in Model 3, and ($\beta = 0.126$, $p < 0.01$) in Model 4. The coefficients of firm experience are all negative but insignificant.

Hypothesis 1 considers the effect of disclosing individual executive compensation on firm performance. As shown in Table 23.3, Hypothesis 1 is supported, as disclosure of individual executive compensation relates positively to firm performance in Model 2 ($\beta = 0.135$, $p < 0.01$), Model 3 ($\beta = 0.254$, $p < 0.001$) and in Model 4 ($\beta = 0.261$, $p < 0.01$). Hypothesis 2 assesses the moderating role of international accounting standards between disclosure of individual executive compensation and firm performance. The interaction between DISCLOSE and IAS is positively associated with ROA in Model 4 ($\beta = 0.324$, $p < 0.001$). Hypothesis 2 is therefore supported, as the beta coefficient of the interaction variable DISCLOSE*IAS is larger than the coefficients of DISCLOSE in Models 2, 3 and 4 at ($\beta = 0.135$, $p < 0.01$) ($\beta = 0.254$, $p < 0.001$) and ($\beta = 0.261$, $p < 0.01$) respectively.

Table 23.3 Results of hierarchical regression analysis on firm performance (ROA)

	Model 1	Model 2	Model 3	Model 4
Constant	6.850***	7.128***	6.126***	5.722***
	(2.275)	(2.137)	(2.219)	(2.298)
FIRMSIZE	0.062	0.097	0.146+	0.155**
	(0.326)	(0.336)	(0.349)	(0.345)
FIRMEXP	−0.078	−0.049	−0.038	−0.057
	(0.005)	(0.005)	(0.005)	(0.005)
BLOCKOWN	0.084	0.095+	0.112*	0.126*
	(0.011)	(0.011)	(0.011)	(0.011)
INDUSTRY	Yes	Yes	Yes	Yes
DISCLOSE		0.135**	0.254***	0.261**
			(0.703)	(1.048)
IAS			0.219**	0.158**
			(0.659)	(0.851)
ADR			(0.057)	0.134
			(0.718)	(1.027)
SIZEMB			0.189***	0.277***
			(0.212)	(0.291)
DISCLOSE*IAS				0.324***
				(0.226)
DISCLOSE*ADR				0.357***
				(1.886)
DISCLOSE*SIZEMB				0.168***
				(0.993)
Adjusted R^2	0.046	0.122	0.175	0.249
F-Statistic	1.784	2.763**	4.944***	5.221***

Notes: Standardized regression coefficients ***$p < 0.001$; **$p < 0.01$; *$p < 0.05$; +$p < 0.10$. Standard errors appear in parentheses. $N = 126$.

Hypothesis 3 assesses the moderating role of ADRs between disclosure of individual executive compensation and firm performance. The interaction between DISCLOSE and ADR is positively associated with ROA in Model 4 ($\beta = 0.357$, $p < 0.001$). These results support Hypothesis 3 since the beta coefficient of the interaction variable DISCLOSE*ADR is larger than the coefficients of DISCLOSE in Models 2, 3 and 4.

Hypothesis 4 assesses the moderating role of the size of the management board between disclosure of individual executive compensation and firm performance. The interaction between DISCLOSE and SIZEMB is positively associated with ROA in Model 4 ($\beta = 0.168$, $p < 0.001$). The coefficient of the interaction variable DISCLOSE*SIZEMB is larger than the coefficient of DISCLOSE in Model 2, but smaller in Models 2 and 3. Thus, these findings partly support the hypothesized idea that the relation between disclosure and firm performance would be strengthened.

Further analysis

Paired sample t-tests for expected and actual performance of firms that disclose individual executive compensation were carried out. The expected performance mirrors 'what could have been' if the firms had chosen not to disclose individual executive pay (see Appendix, below, for a description of the sub-sample and the econometric model used).

Results from this test show a positive and significant difference in ROA between expected and actual performance, of 1.18 ($p < 0.1$, $t = 1.58$). Further tests on the difference between the means of corporate performance in firms that disclosed individual executive pay and the ones that did not before, during, and the year after the event were carried out. Before the event, non-disclosing firms had a better average ROA than firms that went on to disclose (-2.11, $p < 0.05$). Although not significant, results of the event year show that disclosing firms had better ROA averages. The ROA mean difference between non-disclosing and disclosing firms is positive and significant a year after disclosure (1.68, $p < 0.1$).

Discussion and concluding comments

This chapter examines the relation between the disclosure of individual executive compensation and firm performance in German firms. The result in relation to the first hypothesis (Hypothesis 1) is central to our study. The findings from this hypothesis indicate that the disclosure of individual executive pay is significantly associated with firm performance. The result from the moderator hypotheses (Hypotheses 2 and 3) shows that the relation between the disclosure of individual executive compensation and firm performance is more positive among firms that were early adopters of IAS/US GAAP and that have ADRs. Although not the case in one of the models, there is evidence that the association between the disclosure of individual executive compensation and firm performance is stronger in firms with larger management boards.

While the practice of disclosing individual executive compensation has a relatively longer history in the US and UK, in other institutional contexts (including Germany) it may be considered a contestable management innovation. Like several corporate governance mechanisms deriving from shareholder capitalism, the disclosure of corporate information is argued to enhance shareholder value through better firm performance. With this view diffusing across the world, national codes of corporate governance now emphasize Anglo-American governance practices including the disclosure of individual executive compensation. While such changes are fairly obvious at national level through legal and regulatory requirements, a different picture is likely to emerge at firm level, given the intra-organizational dynamics at play. Indeed, a recommendation to disclose individual executive compensation met with resistance in some German firms and yet was taken as a welcome innovation in others. German firms that resist the disclosure of individual executive compensation argue that there is no economic value in disclosing individual executive compensation. Disclosure of executive pay as a total sum for all directors' compensation, they argue, should suffice. On the basis of this contestation, this study tested its main hypothesis that the disclosure of individual executive compensation is positively associated with firm performance. This hypothesis was supported in three models, adding weight to arguments in favour of shareholder-value maximization that emphasize the disclosure of corporate information.

Indeed, contrary to the negative reaction by some German firms, results from further analysis that compares pre-disclosure and post-disclosure performance of disclosing firms generally demonstrate the net benefits of disclosure. As shown in the results, the mean value of the difference between actual and expected performance is positive and significant. Moreover, results from the paired t-test are interesting especially as they show that non-disclosing firms had better performance than firms that went on to disclose the following year. This possibly means that poorly performing firms are the ones that decided to disclose individual executive pay. One interpretation of this behaviour is that poorly performing firms, in search of an approach that improves their performance, are keen to try management innovations. The disclosure of individual executive pay seen as an element of the shareholder-value concept would certainly signal the firm's good intentions, thus likely to generate better performance in the future. On the other hand, firms that were performing well found no incentive to change and preferred to maintain the status quo.

Studies have shown that firms that trade on American stock exchanges through ADRs and use more transparent accounting standards such as IAS are subjected to stricter disclosure requirements and tend to perform better than firms trading only on domestic markets. This chapter has therefore argued that the relation between the disclosure of individual executive compensation and firm performance is determined by whether the firm has ADRs. Results from this hypothesis do support the notion that performance is better in firms that disclose individual executive compensation and have ADRs. The same observation is made for firms that were early users of IAS. These findings lend support to the body of literature that argues for the reduction of information asymmetry and improvement of transparency.

This study is one of the first to examine the effect of disclosing individual executive compensation on firm performance in a stakeholder-oriented governance system where there is concern about the inflow of shareholder-oriented governance practices. Indeed, both IB scholars and policymakers have paid some attention to the impact of rapid globalization of corporate governance practices. In particular, attention has been given to the question of whether corporate governance systems are actually or symbolically converging on the Anglo-American variety of capitalism (Chizema and Kim, 2010; Fiss and Zajac, 2004; Hansmann and Kraakman, 2004). The disclosure of individual executive pay is seen as a contested management practice in the German system of capitalism (Sanders and Tuschke, 2007), but results in this study may give support to those who dismiss symbolism in governance reforms, advocating for real and effective globalization of governance practices. Of course, such optimism needs to be treated with caution. While the results may suggest the arrival of a new governance paradigm in Germany, it is too early to assume the convergence of capitalist systems. Indeed, research on comparative systems tends to highlight the robustness and stability of local institutions (Hall and Soskice, 2001) and the entrenched interests of a wider set of local actors (inter- and intra-organizational) as sources of inertia.

This study has implications at a wide, regional level, for example for the proposed harmonization of corporate governance practices in the EU. While the EU recommends that individual member states ensure that their listed firms disclose individual executive pay in their annual reports, several companies in the member countries do not comply. Part of this delay in implementation may be due to a lack of evidence on the net economic benefits of disclosing individual executive pay.

On another level, this study also shows that not all resistances to innovations are efficient. While some German firms argue that disclosing individual compensation is not worthwhile, results in this study support a different conclusion. Some provisions of codes of corporate governance may need to be made mandatory rather than be left to the choice of the firm on a 'comply or explain' basis, as is the case in many countries, especially with the disclosure of individual executive pay. This chapter is on German firms, which possibly limits its generalization. Further research involving several countries, for example other EU member states, is therefore necessary on this issue of executive pay disclosure and firm performance.

Appendix Sub-sample and econometric model

The sub-sample of firms that disclosed individual executive compensation at any time between 2002 and 2005 was considered. To assess whether a firm performs unusually well or poorly after disclosure, the performance expected in the absence of an event (i.e. disclosing individual executive compensation) is specified, thus providing a benchmark against which sample firms can be compared. Following Barber and Lyon (1996) expected performance is estimated. Expected performance is defined as a firm's past performance plus the change in the industry's performance as shown in the model below:

$$E(P_{it}) = P_{it-1} + \Delta PI_{it} \tag{23.1}$$

where, $E(P_{it})$ is the expected performance, P_{it-1}, is the firm's past performance and ΔPI_{it} is the change in the industry's performance over a period of one year.

Consequently, the abnormal performance of firm i in year t, AP_{it}, is defined as realized performance, P_{it}, less expected performance, $E(P_{it})$:

$$AP_{it} = P_{it} - E(P_{it}), \tag{23.2}$$

where, performance is measured using *ROA*.

To test the null hypothesis, in which mean abnormal performance is equal to zero for a sample of size n, a parametric test statistic is used thus:

$$t = \frac{\overline{AP}}{\sigma(AP_{it})/\sqrt{n}} \tag{23.3}$$

where, $\overline{AP}$ is the average of abnormal performance and $\sigma(AP_{it})$ is the cross-sectional standard deviation of abnormal performance for the sample of n firms.

As an alternative approach, the level of an industry comparison group to measure expected performance (without any pre-event performance matching) is used. To compare performance changes around the disclosure of individual executive compensation a matched sample is constructed as follows: each disclosing firm is matched by size and industry at the year prior to the disclosure with a non-disclosing firm. Specifically, disclosing and non-disclosing firms are matched on the basis of their size as measured by total assets and also based on the same four-SIC industry code. For this sub-sample, data for the one-year period around the event year were collected. This procedure yielded a total 46 disclosing and a similar number for non-disclosing firms.

References

Aguilera, R.V. and Jackson, G. (2003) 'The cross-national diversity of corporate governance: dimensions and determinants', *Academy of Management Review*, 28(3), 447–65.

Ahmadjian, C.L. and Robbins, G.E. (2005) 'A clash of capitalisms: foreign shareholders and corporate restructuring in 1990s Japan', *American Sociological Review*, 70(3), 451–71.

Aiken, L.S. and West, S.G. (1991) *Multiple Regression: Testing And Interpreting Interactions* (Newbury Park, CA: Sage).

Asquith, P., Healy, P. and Palepu, K. (1989) 'Earnings and stock splits', *The Accounting Review*, 64(3), 387–403.

Barber, B.M. and Lyon, J.D. (1996) 'Detecting abnormal operating performance: the empirical power and specification of test statistics', *Journal of Financial Economics*, 41(3), 359–99.

Bauwhede, H.V. and Willekens, M. (2008) 'Disclosure on corporate governance in the European Union', *Corporate Governance: An International Review*, 16(2), 101–15.

Bebchuk, L.A. and Fried, J.M. (2004) *Pay without Performance. The Unfulfilled Promise of Executive Compensation* (Cambridge, MA: Harvard University Press).

Bhagat, S. and Black, B. (2002) 'The non-correlation between board independence and long-term firm performance', *Journal of Corporation Law*, 27(2), 231–74.

Buck, T. and Shahrim, A. (2005) 'The translation of corporate governance changes across national cultures: the case of Germany', *Journal of International Business Studies*, 36(1), 42–61.

Buck, T., Liu, X. and Skovoroda, R. (2008) 'Top executive pay and firm performance in China', *Journal of International Business Studies*, 39(5), 833–50.

Casper, S., Lehrer, M. and Soskice, D. (1999) 'Can high-technology industries prosper in Germany? Institutional frameworks and the evolution of the German software and biotechnology industries', *Industry and Innovation*, 6(1), 5–24.

Certo, S.T., Lester, R.H., Dalton, C.M. and Dalton, D.R. (2006) 'Top management teams, strategy and financial performance: a meta-analytic examination', *Journal of Management Studies*, 43(4), 813–39.

Cheffins, B. (2001) 'The metamorphosis of German Inc: the case of executive pay', *American Journal of Comparative Law*, 49(3), 497–539.

Chizema, A. (2008) 'Institutions and voluntary compliance: the disclosure of individual executive compensation in Germany', *Corporate Governance: An International Review*, 16(4), 359–74.

Chizema, A. (2010) 'Early and late adoption of American-style executive pay in Germany: governance and institutions', *Journal of World Business*, 45(1), 9–18.

Chizema, A. and Buck, T. (2006) 'Neo-institutional theory and institutional change: towards the "Americanization" of German executive pay practice', *International Business Review*, 15(5), 488–504.

Chizema, A. and Kim, J. (2010) 'Outside directors on Korean boards: governance and institutions', *Journal of Management Studies*, 47(1), 109–29.

Dahya, J., and McConnell, J.J. (2005) 'Outside directors and corporate board decisions', *Journal of Corporate Finance*, 11(1/2), 37–60.

Dahya, J., McConnell, J.J. and Travlos, N. (2002) 'The Cadbury committee, corporate performance and management turnover', *Journal of Finance*, 57(1), 461–83.

Darrough, M.N. and Stoughton, N.M. (1990) 'Financial disclosure policy in an entry game', *Journal of Accounting and Economics*, 12(1–3), 219–43.

Doble, M. (1997) 'The impact of the Cadbury code on selection of directors and board composition in UK newly-quoted companies', *Corporate Governance: An International Review*, 5(4), 214–23.

Dore, R. (2000) *Stock Market Capitalism: Welfare Capitalism. Japan and Germany versus the Anglo-Saxons* (Oxford: Oxford University Press).

Dye, R.A. (1985) 'Strategic accounting choice and the effects of alternative financial reporting requirements', *Journal of Accounting Research*, 23(2), 544–74.

Fama, E.F. and Jensen, M.C. (1983) 'Separation of ownership and control', *Journal of Law and Economics*, 26(2), 301–25.

Fernandez, Z. and Nieto, M.J. (2006) 'Impact of ownership on the international involvement of SMEs', *Journal of International Business Studies*, 37(3), 340–51.

Finkelstein, S. and Hambrick, D.C. (1990) 'Top management team tenure and organizational outcomes: the moderating role of managerial discretion', *Administrative Science Quarterly*, 35(3), 484–503.

Fiss, P.C. and Zajac, E.J. (2004) 'The diffusion of ideas over contested terrain: the (non) adoption of a shareholder value orientation among German firms', *Administrative Science Quarterly*, 49(4), 501–34.

Frankle, R., McNichols, M. and Wilson, G.P. (1995) 'Discretionary disclosure and external financing', *The Accounting Review*, 70(1), 135–50.

Franks, J. and Mayer, C. (2001) 'Ownership and control of German corporations', *The Review of Financial Studies*, 14(4), 943–77.

Haleblian, J. and Finkelstein, S. (1993) 'Top management team size, CEO dominance, and firm performance: the moderating roles of environmental turbulence and discretion', *Academy of Management Journal*, 36(4), 844–63.

Hall, P.A. and Soskice, D. (2001) *Varieties of Capitalisms. The Institutional Foundations of Comparative Advantage* (Oxford: Oxford University Press).

Hansmann, H. and Kraakman, R. (2004) 'The end of history for corporate law', in J.N. Gordon and M.J. Roe (eds) *Convergence and Persistence in Corporate Governance* (Cambridge: Cambridge University Press).

Healy, P.M. and Palepu, K.G. (1988) 'Earnings information conveyed by dividend initiations and omissions', *Journal of Financial Economics*, 21(2), 149–76.

Healy, P.M. and Palepu, K.G. (1993) 'The effects of firms' disclosure strategies on stock prices', *Accounting Horizons*, 7(1), 1–11.

Henderson, A.D. and Fredrickson, J.W. (1996) 'Information-processing demands as a determinant of CEO compensation', *Academy of Management Journal*, 39(3), 575–606.

Hughes, P.J. (1986) 'Signaling by direct disclosure under asymmetric information', *Journal of Accounting and Economics*, 8(2), 119–42.

Jensen, M. and Meckling, W. (1976) 'Theory of the firm: managerial behavior, agency costs and ownership structure', *Journal of Financial Economics*, 3(4), 305–60.

Kaplan, S. (1989) 'The effect of management buyouts on operating performance and value', *Journal of Financial Economics*, 24(2), 217–54.

McKnight, P.J. and Mira, S. (2003) 'Corporate governance mechanisms, agency costs and firm performance in UK firms', Working Paper, Cardiff: Cardiff University Business School.

Murphy, K.J. (1985) 'Corporate performance and managerial remuneration: an empirical analysis', *Journal of Accounting and Economics*, 7(1–3), 11–42.
Nowak, E., Rott, R. and Mahr, T.G. (2006) 'The (ir)relevance of disclosure of compliance with corporate governance codes-evidence from the German stock market', Working Paper, University of Lugano, Switzerland.
Pfeffer, J. and Salancik, G. (1978) *The External Control of Organizations* (New York: Harper and Row).
Rogers, E.M. (1995) *Diffusion of Innovations*, 4th edn (New York: Free Press).
Sanders, W.G. and Tuschke, A.C. (2007) 'The adoption of institutionally contested organizational practices: the emergence of stock option pay in Germany', *Academy of Management Journal*, 50(1), 33–56.
Scott, W.R. (2001) *Institutions and Organizations* (Thousand Oaks, CA: Sage Publications).
Sherer, P.D. and Lee, K. (2002) 'Institutional change in large law firms: a resource dependency and institutional perspective', *Academy of Management Journal*, 45(1), 102–19.
Stiles, P. and Taylor, B. (1993) 'Benchmarking corporate governance: an update', *Long Range Planning*, 26(6), 138–9.
Tabachnick, B.G. and Fidell, L.S. (1996) *Using Multivariate Statistics* (New York: Harper Collins).
Tosi, H.L., Werner, S., Katz, J.P. and Gomez-Mejia, L.R. (2000) 'How much does performance matter? A meta-analysis of CEO pay studies', *Journal of Management*, 26(2), 301–39.
Tung, R. and van Witteloostuijn, A. (2008) 'From the editors: what makes a study sufficiently international?', *Journal of International Business Studies*, 39(2), 180–3.
Tuschke, A.C. and Sanders, W.G. (2003) 'Antecedents and consequences of corporate governance reform: the case of Germany', *Strategic Management Journal*, 24(7), 631–49.
Verrecchia, R.E. (1990) 'Information quality and discretionary disclosure', *Journal of Accounting and Economics*, 12(4), 365–80.
Verrecchia, R.E. (2001) 'Essays on disclosure', *Journal of Accounting and Economics*, 32(1), 97–180.
Vitols, S. (2004) 'Negotiated shareholder value: the German variant of an Anglo-American practice', *Competition and Change*, 8(4), 357–74.
Weir, C.M., Laing, D. and McKnight, P.J. (2002) 'Internal and external governance mechanisms: their impact on the performance of large UK public companies', *Journal of Business and Accounting*, 29(5/6), 579–611.
Werder, A., Talaulicar, T. and Kolat, G.L. (2005) 'Compliance with the German corporate governance code: an empirical analysis of the compliance statements by German listed companies', *Corporate Governance: An International Review*, 13(2), 178–87.
Werner, J.R. and Zimmermann, J. (2006) 'Disclosure of individualized executive compensation figures: an empirical analysis of compliance with the German corporate governance code', *Corporate Ownership and Control*, 4(1), 106–12.

Index

Abegglen, J. C., 366
ability-based trust, 337
Abimbola, T., 181
Abrahamson, E., 272
Academy of International Business, 1
accidental values, 389
accountability, 224
Achrol, R. S., 188, 264, 268
adaptability, 56
Adler, N. J., 206, 208, 209
Agarwal, J. P., 82, 83, 84, 89, 118, 399
agency selection, 130
Aggarwal, R., 128
Agmon, T., 128
Agndal, H., 279
agreements
 bilateral investment, 114
 bilateral trade, 40, 45
 Free Trade, 38–9
 regional trade, 39
Aguilera, R. V., 380, 381, 393, 415
Ahmadjian, C. L., 421
Ahunwan, B., 386, 387
Aiken, L. S., 353, 423
Ainuddin, R. A., 348
Aizenman, J., 89
Akaike's information criterion (AIC), 120
Akerloff, G., 346
Akinsanya, A. A., 386
Albaum, G., 183
Albuquerque, R., 84, 89
Alderson, S., 220, 223
Allen, L., 100
alliance, international cooperative, 337
alliance capability, 14
 see also alliance entrepreneurship/capability and foreign market performance, relations between
alliance entrepreneurship, 13–15
 alliance capability, 14
 foreign market performance, 14–15
 see also alliance entrepreneurship/capability and foreign market performance, relations between

alliance entrepreneurship/capability and foreign market performance, relations between, 11–24
 analysis/results, 19–21; measure validation, 19–20; structural model, 20–1
 measures, 18–19; operation of constructs, 18–19; sample, 19
 research methodology, 17–18
 theory/hypothesis, 13–17; alliance entrepreneurship, 13–15; alliance knowledge sharing, barriers to, 15–16; learning orientation, 16–17
alliance knowledge sharing, barriers to, 15–16
alliance stability, 334–5
Altonji, J. G., 237
Alvarez, S. A., 12, 292, 294, 302
Alvord, S. H., 402
Amaeshi, K. M., 382
Amano, R. A., 86
Amber, 277
American Depository Receipts (ADRs), 419, 421
Amit, R., 164, 165, 166, 280
Amoako-Adu, B., 120
Amoateng, K., 120
analyses
 alliance entrepreneurship/capability and foreign market performance, relations between, 19–21
 of corporate governance and organization, 382–4
 internationalization, 131–6
 International Strategic Alliances (ISA), trust-performance study of, 321–2
 level of, 404
 trust, level of, 329
 unit of, 273–4
 of variance, 221
 see also empirical analysis
analysis of variance (ANOVA), 221
Anderson, P., 158, 187, 321, 334, 335, 355
Andersson, U., 48, 50, 56, 58, 59, 294
Andrews, D., 86, 87
Anglo-Saxon corporate governance, 381
Annand, B. N., 12, 14

annual general meetings (AGMs), 383, 420
Antal, J., 235
Antoncic, B., 292, 293, 303, 304, 306
Aoki, M., 366, 367, 368, 380, 381, 393
apparently born globals, 152
architecture, 164
Arino, A., 316
Armstrong, J. S., 149
Arthur, B., 390
Asanuma, B., 366, 367
ASEAN countries (Indonesia, Malaysia, the Philippines and Thailand), 117
Ashkanasy, N., 218
Asia, foreign direct investment in, 27–46
  determinants of, analytical framework on, 34–7
  empirical model, 37–41
  international product fragmentation, 28–30; implications of, 36–7
  international production networks, 30–4; Granger causality tests, 32–4
  results, 41–5
Asian Development Bank, 41
Asquith, P., 413
assertiveness, 229
asset opacity, *see* asset specificity/asset opacity
asset specificity/asset opacity, 348–9
  in IJV, 349–50
Athukorala, P., 27, 28, 31, 35, 44
Audi, R., 224
Augmented Dickey–Fuller (ADF) tests, 119
augmented unit root tests, Dickey–Fuller and Kwiatkowski, 85–6
Aulakh, P. S., 276, 329, 338
Austin, J. E., 402
authenticity, 225
Autio, E., 165, 166, 178, 186, 191, 299, 307
autonomy, 144
average variance extracted (AVE), 20, 274
Axinn, C. N., 163
Ayal, I., 145, 151

Baba, M. L., 205
Bachmann, R., 316
Baden-Fuller, C., 22, 269
Bagozzi, R. P., 153, 274
Baharumshah, A. Z., 120
Bailey, A., 57, 58
Bajo, O., 116
Baker, W. E., 272
Balabanis, G. I., 143, 148
Baldwin, R., 84

Balogun, J., 52, 53, 58, 250
Bamossy, G., 321, 337
Banerjee, A., 86, 130
Barber, B. M., 413, 427
Barkema, H. G., 349, 356
Barney, J. B., 12, 14, 185, 292, 294, 302, 305, 348
Barnlund, D., 228
Baron, M. A., 267
Barringer, B. R., 12
Barry, F., 28
Barsoux, J. L., 216, 217, 227
Bartik, T. J., 130
Bartlett, C. A., 48, 49, 50, 51, 59, 67, 76, 147, 251
Barzel, Y., 346
basic resources, 300
Bass, B. M., 221
Batonda, G., 277
Baumgarten, K. E. E., 234, 235
Baumgartner, H., 152
Bauwhede, H. V., 415
Beamish, P. W., 23, 96, 97, 100, 126, 163, 266, 315, 316, 335, 345, 346, 355
Bebchuk, L. A., 412
Belitz, H., 91
Bell, J., 145, 178, 264, 268, 280
Bénassy-Quéré, A., 35
Benedict, R., 372
Bengtsson, M., 165
Bennett, M. J., 227
Berg, N., 201
Bergström, F., 130
Bernnan, 337
Berry, H., 100
Berthold, N., 82
Beugelsdijk, S., 358
Bhagat, S., 420
Bhappu, A. D., 366, 369
Bhaskar-Shrinivas, 236
bilateral investment agreements (BITs), 114
bilateral trade agreement (BTA), 40, 45
Bilkey, W. J., 177
Bingham, R. D., 130
Bird, S., 234
Birkinshaw, J., 48, 50, 52, 53, 54, 57, 59, 67, 250
Bitner, M. J., 182
Bjerke, B., 177, 180, 186, 189
Björkman, I., 249
Black, J. S., 234, 236, 237, 242, 420
Blanchard, P. N., 235
Blanes, J. V., 132

Blau, P. M., 328
Blesa, A., 185
Blodgett, L. L., 346
Blomqvist, K., 204
Blomstermo, A., 178, 292, 294, 300, 305
Bloodgood, J. M, 178, 191
Bloomstermo, 310
blue ocean strategy, 181
Blundell, R., 131
Boehmer, E., 381, 393
Boersma, M. F., 341
Boggs, D. J., 328, 334, 335, 337, 340
Bok, S., 217
Bolten, J., 216
Bonner, J. M., 267, 268, 269, 278
Booms, B. H., 182
born globals (BGs)
 apparently, 152
 internal resources, 300–3
 networks, 294–6; evolution of, 303–4; firm performance and, link between, 292–310
 truly, 151
Bornstein, D., 403
Borys, B., 269
Boschma, R., 251
bottom of the pyramid (BOP) approach, 397
Boulton, R., 164
Bouquet, C., 50
Bradley, J., 28
Brannick, T., 220
Brazeal, D. V., 281
Bremner, B., 365
Brett, J. M., 207
Brewer, T. L., 126, 130, 136
Brewster, C., 234
BRIC countries (Brazil, Russia, India, and China), 71
Briggs, N. E., 235
Brinckerhoff, P. C., 404
Brinkmann, J., 228
Brislin, R. W., 236
Brock, D. M., 157
Brodbeck, F. C., 218
Brooks, A. C., 403
Brouthers, K. D., 321, 337, 352
Brown, J. R., 18, 216, 217, 221, 252
Bruce, R., 186, 189
Buck, T., 412, 413, 414, 415
Buckley, P. J., 11, 13, 15, 21, 22, 23, 35, 48, 49, 50, 51, 59, 67, 81, 96, 97, 126, 128, 136, 145, 163, 187, 233, 249, 257, 263, 279, 293, 310, 345, 347, 366

Buehler, S., 49
Bundesbank, Deutsche, 82, 83, 87, 88, 89
Bundestag, Deutscher, 82
Bunker, B. B., 322, 337
Bunyaratavej, K., 49
Burgel, O., 178, 179, 276
Burgelman, R. A., 57, 157
Burt, R. S., 268, 271, 272
Business and Finance, 273
business groups
 concept of, 374
 Granovetter's theory of, 369–71
business model
 concept of, 163, 165, 370
 and value chain constructs of international entrepreneurial orientation, 163–74; data collection, 168–9; methodology of, 168–9; Syscon Ltd, 169–73; theoretical discussion, 164–8
business model construct, 164–5
Business Week, 365
Busom, I., 132
Butler, K., 81, 335, 337, 338
Buzzell, R. D., 182, 191
Byram, M., 226, 227

Cadbury Nigeria Plc scandal, 385
Cadbury Report, 416
Cadbury Schweppes, 385
Cadogan, J. W., 147, 150, 151
Calantone, R. J., 18, 190
Caligiuri, P., 235, 240, 241
Calof, J. L., 163, 266
Camerer, C., 347
Campbell, A., 223
Cantwell, J., 50
capabilities, 300
Carson, D., 177, 180, 181
Casper, S., 414
Casrnir, F. L., 216
Casson, M. C., 49, 67, 96, 97, 145, 257, 347
Castells, M., 263
Catholic Church, 225
causality, 119
Cavusgil, T. S., 143, 145, 146, 148, 151, 168, 177, 179, 181, 182, 191, 292, 293, 294, 305
Cedrone, D., 205
Celaya, L., 235
CEMEX, 399
Central Bank of Nigeria, 387
Certo, S. T., 419

ceteris paribus measurements, 346, 350
Chadee, D. D., 346, 352, 353, 358
Chandra, Y., 178, 236
character, 224
Chararbaghi, K., 165
Chaston, I., 180, 183, 184, 188
Cheffins, B., 414
Chen, M., 68, 227, 328, 334, 335, 337, 340, 351, 358
Chesbrough, H., 164
Chetty, S. K., 270, 272, 279
Cheung, Y. W., 120
Chew, E., 365
Chiagouris, L., 177, 180, 189
Chin, W. W., 20, 21
Chizema, A., 412, 413, 414, 415, 418, 420, 426
Cho, A. H., 402, 403
Choi, I., 86, 335
Chomsky, N., 371, 374
Choo, S., 276
Chowdhury, S. D., 366, 369
Chrisman, J. J., 406
Chu, W., 335, 340
Chudoba, K., 207
Churchill, N. C., 292, 302, 304, 306
Ciulla, J., 221
Claeys, T., 129, 130
Clancy, K. J., 180
Clark, B., 216, 227, 265
Coase, R., 369
Cockburn, I., 265
Code of Corporate Governance 2003, 389
Code of Corporate Governance for Nigeria Banks, 389
Code of Corporate Governance for Shareholders' Association, 389
codes of conduct, 388–9
coefficient rho, 134
Cohen, B. I., 114, 251, 269, 271, 272
Cohen, W., 16
Cohendet, P., 13
Cole, R. E., 233, 372
collective orientation-organization, 224
Collinson, E., 180, 183, 366, 374
commercial multinational corporations (MNCs), 398
common method bias, 273–4
communication, 206–7
Companies and Allied Matters Act of 1990, 389
compatibility, 271
competence, 337
 of intercultural ethical leadership, implications for, 226–9; ethical leadership competencies, 227–9; intercultural competencies, 226–7
competitive aggressiveness, 144
Conant, J. S., 146
conflicts, 208
Connaughton, S. L., 201, 206
context, 405
Contractor, F. J., 110, 145, 265, 315, 316, 352
control variables, 237, 351–2, 421
conventional agency theory, 379
Cook, K., 167
Cooke, T. E., 390
Cool, K., 269
coordination, 268–9
core partners, 171
Corporate Board, 391
corporate culture, 389–90
corporate disclosure in theory, and hypothesis, 416–19
 moderator hypothesis, 418–19
corporate governance
 Anglo-Saxon, 381
 German, 414–15
 institutional theory and, 380–2
 macro (external) institutions, 384–9
 micro (internal) institutions, 389–92
 organization and, 363–430; analysis, 382–4; economic organization, and social solidarity, 365–75; imported management practices, 412–28; institutional determinants of, 379–93; multinational corporations (MNCs), socially entrepreneurial behaviour of, 397–408; observations and discussion, 384–92; research design, 382–4; survey methodology, 382–4
 see also Nigeria, corporate governance in
corporate social entrepreneurship (CSE), 407–8
corporate social responsibility (CSR), 397
corporate values, 389
Corrigan, D., 263
corruption perception index (CPI), 392
Costa Dias, M., 131
Country Focus, 386
country specific advantages (CSAs), 67

Coviello, N. E., 145, 146, 177, 178, 179, 190, 279, 281, 292, 293, 294, 296, 300, 301, 302, 303, 305, 306, 309
Covin, J. G., 145, 146, 148, 157, 185, 304, 305, 402, 406
Cowling, K., 365
Cox, M. P., 292, 293, 294, 296, 300, 301, 309
Craig, S. C., 186, 190
Cramton, C. D., 205
Crick, D., 145
Cromie, S., 177
Cronbach, 237
Crossan, M. M., 272
cross-border joint ventures (JV), *see* domestic/cross-border joint ventures (JV)
cross-cultural business ethics, 219–20
cross-cultural leadership, 219
cross-cultural training (CCT), 234
Crowston, K., 277
Cullen, J. B., 276
culture
   corporate, 389–90
   human resources, leadership and, 199–245
   societal, 217–19
   see also human resources, leadership and culture
Currall, S. C., 329, 338, 340
customer lock-in, 169–70
customer value, 169–70
Cyert, R. M., 251
Czinkota, M. R., 183

Dahya, J., 416
Daiichi Kangyo Bank, 366
Dana, L. P., 177, 178
Darroch, J., 180
Darrough, M. N., 417
Das, T. K., 339
Dasgupta, A., 118
data sources, 350–1
   business model and value chain constructs of international entrepreneurial orientation, 168–9
   exports on outward federal direct investment, influence of, 118–19
   German manufacturing industries, persistence of outward FDI from, 87–8
   imported management practices, 421–5

International Strategic Alliances (ISA), trust-performance study of, 321–2
network international performance and telecommunications, convergence of, 273–4
Datastream International, 420, 421
D'Aveni, R. A., 269
David, P., 390
Davis, L., 405
Davison, S. C., 205, 206, 207, 208
DAX 30, 419–20
Day, D. V., 219
DC-LDC (developed country-less developed country), 321, 339
D'Cruz, J. R., 263, 264, 280
Deal, T. E., 390
De Dreu, C. K., 208
Deery, S., 69
Dees, J. G., 403, 405, 407
degree of internationalization (DOI), 147–8
De Hoogh, A. H. B., 216, 221
Delany, E., 48, 50
deliberate strategy, 56–7
Delios, A., 23, 345, 346, 355
Den Hartog, 216, 219, 221
dependence, 372
   Japanese, 372–3
dependent variables, 351, 420
Desai, M. A., 89
Deshpande, S. P., 234
design, 164
Dess, G. G., 143, 144, 146, 148, 157, 158, 185, 304, 305
Deutsch, M., 269
Deutsche Börse Group, 420, 421
Deutsches AktienInstitut (DAI), 421
development mechanisms, 184–7
Dewenter, K. L., 366
Dicken, P., 49
Dickey, D., 85
Dickson, M. W., 216, 219, 221
Dierickx, I., 269
Dimitratos, P., 165, 181
disclosure of individual executive compensation (DISCLOSE), 420, 423
DiStefano, J., 206
distributed partners, 13
Dixit, A., 84
Doble, M., 416
Doh, J. P., 49, 51, 76
Doi, T., 372

domestic/cross-border joint ventures (JV), 345–58
  asset specificity/asset opacity, 348–9; in IJV, context of, 349–50
  methodology, 350–3; data sources, 350–1; dependent variables, 351; independent variables, 351–2; sample selection, 350–1
  results, 353–8; fit of model, 353; specificity/opacity, effect of, 353–8
  theoretical background, 346–8; equity in JV structure, guarantee function of, 347–8; market transactions, measurement costs in, 346–7
Domingo, C., 81
Donaldson, T., 228
Dore, R., 366, 368
Dorfman, P. W., 218
Dörrenbächer, C., 49, 52, 58
double bottom line, 405
Douglas, S. P., 186, 190
Doving, 264
Dow, S., 366, 369
Dowling, G. R., 391
downstream sales partners, 171–2
Doz, Y., 12, 164, 280
Drayton, W., 402
Driffield, N., 98
Dru, J.-M., 180
Duncan, W., 220
Dunfee, T. W., 228
Dunning, J. H., 34, 48, 49, 51, 67, 82, 83, 96, 97, 118, 355, 397
Duran, J. J., 129
Durkheim, 369
Dye, R. A., 417
Dyer, J. H., 267, 271, 299, 307, 308, 335, 340, 366, 368, 369
dynamic capabilities, 305

Earley, P. C., 205, 206, 207, 208, 209, 211
Easton, G., 296, 298, 299, 308
econometric methods, 85–6
economic organization, and social solidarity, 365–75
  business groups, Granovetter's theory of, 369–71
  institutional perspectives, of economists and sociologists, 368–9
  keiretsu', 365–8, 371–4; principles of, linguistic approach to, 371–4; terms for, alternate, 365–8
Economist, The, 365

efficiency-seeking FDI, 35
Eisenhardt, K. M., 16, 52, 168, 169, 252, 258, 259, 264, 280, 381
Ekeledo, I., 144
Ekelund, B. Z., 208
Ekennia, O., 391
Elango, B., 100
Elkington, J., 402, 405
Ellis, P. D., 147, 277
Emerson, J., 167, 403
empirical account, 416
empirical analysis
  Asia, foreign direct investment in, 37–41
  German manufacturing industries, persistence of outward FDI from, 88–91
  internationalization, financial incentives and firm performance in Italy, 131–6; data, 131–2; econometric findings, 134–5; model, 132–4; variables, 132–4
  see also analyses
endorsement of ethical leadership, 220–3
Engleman, R. M., 281
enlightened shareholder value, 379
entrepreneurial behaviour, and networks, 304–5
entrepreneurial dimension, 402–3
entrepreneurial firms, 141–97
  entrepreneurial marketing strategies, 177–92
  international entrepreneurial orientation (IEO): business model and value chain constructs of, 163–74; contingency factors in, 143–59
entrepreneurial marketing, 177, 180–1
entrepreneurial marketing strategies, 177–92
  conceptual framework, 184–90; development and influence mechanisms, 184–7; propositions, 187–90
  dimensions of, in international new venture (INV), 181–4
  literature review and entrepreneurial marketing dimensions, 178–84; entrepreneurial marketing, 180–1; entrepreneurship-marketing interface, 180–1; international entrepreneurship (IO), research on marketing in, 178–80; international new venture (INV), research on marketing in, 178–80
entrepreneurial orientation (EO), 144–5

entrepreneurship/entrepreneurs
  alliance, 13–15
  corporate social, 407–8
  international, 178–80
  networked, 307
  social, 407
  solo, 307
entrepreneurship-marketing interface, 180–1
environmental turbulence, 148–9
equity in joint venture (JV), guarantee function of, 347–8
Erez, M., 206
Ericksson, 270, 272, 356
Eriksson, K., 350
Erondu, E. A., 391
Eschbach, D., 241
ethical climate, 391–2
ethical leadership
  definition of, 220–1
  endorsement of, 220–3
ethical relativism, 216
ethics
  cross-cultural business, 219–20
  ethical climate, 391–2
  intercultural ethical leadership, 216–29; in Germany, 223–6; in Ireland, 223–6
European Central Bank, 88
European Commission, 129
European Union (EU), 415
European Union (EU) Commission, 415
European Values Survey, 220
Evans, M., 350
Ewings, P., 382
executive stock options (ESOs), 415
expatriate adjustment, training programmes for, 233–42
  discussion, 239–41
  duration of, 235
  intensity of, 235–6
  method, 236–7; measurements, 236–7; sample, 236
  results, 237–8
  timing of, 234–5
expected performance, 427
explanatory variables, 351
export performance, in India, 114–16
exports on outward federal direct investment, influence of, 113–23
  data and methodology, 118–19
  India, 114–16; export performance, 114–16; OFDI, overview of, 114

literature review, 116–18
  results, 120–1
external institutions in corporate governance, 384–9

fairness, 224
Fama, E. F., 379, 416
Fantini, A. E., 241
FDI, *see* foreign direct investment (FDI)
Felin, T., 250, 257, 258
Fernandez, Z., 421
Fernandez-Arias, E., 84, 89
Fey, C. F., 337
Fidell, L. S., 21, 423
Filatotchev, I., 379, 382
financial incentives, *see* internationalization, financial incentives and firm performance in Italy
financial output measures, 335
Financial Times, 82
Fink, L. S., 235, 278
Finkelstein, S., 419
Finnish Funding Agency for Technology and Innovation, 310
firm experience (FIRMEXP), 421
firm performance (PERFM), 99, 127–30, 420
  born global (BG) networks and, link between, 292–310
  and born globals (BGs) networks, link between, 292–310; conceptual framework, 300–9; literature review, 293–4; network approaches, 296
  see also internationalization, financial incentives and firm performance in Italy
firms
  entrepreneurial, 141–97
  global, 151–2
  good, 379
  international, 152
  proactive, 304–5
  small and medium-sized entrpreneurial (SME), 11
firm size (FIRMSIZ), 421
firm-specific advantages (FSAs), 67
Firoozi, F., 89
Fiss, P. C., 414, 418, 420, 421, 426
Fletcher, R., 166, 173
flexibility, 224
Fligstein, N., 384
Floren, H., 278

Florkowski, G. W., 239
Floyd, S. W., 49, 52, 54, 55, 57, 58, 250
Floyd and Woodridge's typology, proposed extensions to, 57–8
  downward influences, 57–8
  upward influences, 57
Fogarty, M. P., 220, 225
Fogel, D. S., 239
Folta, T. B., 346
Fombrun, C. J., 391
foreign direct investment (FDI)
  in Asia, 27–46; determinants of, analytical framework on, 34–7; empirical model, 37–41; international product fragmentation, 28–30, 36–7; international production networks, 30–4; results, 41–5
  financial incentives and growth of, 129–30
  see also outward foreign direct investment (OFDI)
foreign market performance, 14–15
  see also alliance entrepreneurship/capability and foreign market performance, relations between
foreign partner, 350
Fornell, C., 20
Forsgren, M., 50
Foss, N. J., 250, 257, 258, 307, 346, 347
Fowler, A., 402, 405, 406
Frankel, J., 89
Frankle, R., 417
Franks, J., 421
Franz, W., 82
Fraser Institute, The, 41
Fratianni, M., 69
Fredrickson, J. W., 419
Freeman, S., 292, 294, 301, 305, 308
Free Trade Agreement (FTA), 38–9
French, R., 216
Frese, M., 218
Fried, J. M., 412
Friedman, V. J., 250, 257
Friesen, P. H., 144, 148
Frost, T., 48
Fryxell, G. E., 277, 328, 335, 338
FUD (fear, uncertainty, doubt), 158
Fujimoto, T., 265
Fujita, M., 49
Fulk, J., 204, 207
Fuller, W., 85
funding strategy, 405

future orientation, 229
Fuyo Group, 366

Gabrielsson, M., 179, 180, 186, 190, 191, 292, 294, 301, 302, 303, 304, 305, 306
Gadde, L. E., 280
Galaskiewicz, J., 265
Gammelgaard, J., 52
Gandhi, Rajiv, 118
Garcia Canal, 346
Gardner, H. K., 205, 206
Gartland, M. P., 390
Gartner, W. B., 402
Garud, R., 16
Garvis, D. M., 144, 148, 149, 157, 159
Gary, B., 346
Gassmann, O., 143, 166, 177, 178, 179, 190
Gatignon, H., 355
Gavetti, G., 251
Gemünden, H. G., 267, 268, 270
gender egalitarianism, 229
general adjustment, 237
generative grammar, 374
George, G., 163, 235
Geppert, M., 49, 52, 58
Gereffi, G., 51
Geringer, J. M., 366, 369
Gerlach, M. L., 366, 367
German Code of Corporate Governance (KODEX), 415–16
German corporate governance, 414–15
German manufacturing industries, persistence of outward FDI from, 81–92
  data, 87–8
  econometric methods, 85–6; unit root tests, augmented Dickey–Fuller and Kwiatkowski, 85–6
  empirical results, 88–91
  history, 82–4
  unit root test, Zivot and Andrews, 86–7
Germany, intercultural ethical leadership in, 223–6
Gerstner, C. R., 219
Gertsen, M. C., 235
Ghauri, P. N., 21, 22, 49, 50, 51, 81, 126, 130, 136, 163, 187, 249, 263, 345
Ghoshal, S., 48, 49, 50, 51, 59, 147, 204, 249, 251, 278, 294, 307
Gibbs, J. L., 205, 206, 211
Gibson, C. B., 204, 205, 206, 207, 208, 211
Giddens, A., 278
Gill, J., 335, 337, 338

Gilmore, A., 177
Gingerich, D., 90
Gini, A., 216, 221
Ginsberg, A., 185
global factory, 263
global firms, 151–2
Global Leadership and Organizational Behavior Effectiveness study (Project GLOBE), 217
global perspectives, *see* regional and global perspectives
global subsidiaries, evolution of, 49–51
Globerman, S., 126, 127, 128
Gluesing, J. C., 206
Glunk, U., 223
Goerzen, A., 96, 97
Golden, B. R., 253
Goldstein, I., 84
Goleman, D., 227
Golesorkhi, S., 357
Gomes-Casseres, B., 341
Gomez-Arias, J. T., 399, 407
González, X., 132
Gooderham, P. N., 264
good firm, 379
goodwill trust, 337
Gopinath, S., 122
Goshal, S., 67, 76
government policy, 74–7
Govindarajan, V., 205, 206, 207, 249, 251, 252
Graebner, M. E., 381
Granger, C. W. J., 119
Granger causality tests, 32–4
Granovetter, M. S., 265, 266, 267, 278, 368, 369, 370, 371
Grant, R. M., 15, 22, 249, 269, 270
Gray, P. H., 250, 252, 345
Grayson, K., 277
Gregersen, H., 237
Greiner, L. E., 186
Greve, A., 292, 303, 305
Griffin, A., 272
Grossman, S. J., 348
Grove, C. L., 233, 234
Grubb, A. R., 204, 207
guarantee function of equity in joint venture (JV), 347–8
Guba, E. G., 254
Gubbi, S. R., 114, 122
Gudykunst, W. B., 217, 235, 240
"Guide to the Equity Indices" (Deutsche Börse Group), 420

Guillen, M. F., 393
Guirdham, M., 216, 217
Guisinger, S., 130, 276
Gulati, R., 264, 265, 266, 267, 269, 272, 299, 300, 301, 307, 308, 368, 369
Gupta, A. K., 205, 206, 207, 218, 249, 251, 252

Haas, M. R., 251
Hackman, J. R., 201
Hagedoorn, J., 168, 368, 369
Hagg, I., 266
Hair, J. F., 242
Håkansson, H., 167, 280, 294, 296, 298, 299, 302, 303, 304, 306, 307, 309
Haleblian, J., 419
Halinen, A., 298, 303, 304, 309
Hall, A., 81, 85, 90, 413, 414, 426
Hallbäck, J., 186
Hambrick, D. C., 206, 209, 419
Hamel, G., 12, 164, 180, 185, 186, 189, 270
Hammond, A. L., 398
Hanges, P. J., 218, 221
Haniffa, R. M., 390
Hansen, M. T., 250, 251, 252
Hansmann, H., 414, 426
Harms, R., 305
Harrigan, K. R., 271
Harrington, B., 383
Harris, H., 234, 301, 303, 307, 315, 389
Harrison, J. S., 12
Hart, S., 57, 279, 346, 347, 348, 397, 398, 399
Hartigan, P., 402, 405
Harveston, P. D., 179
Harwood, G. R., 235
Hatzer, B., 216
Haucaup, J., 49
Hausmann, R., 84, 89
H2b, 158
HCM, *see* home country measures (HCMs)
Healy, P. M., 413, 417
Heatherton, T. F., 153
Hebert, L., 351, 355
Hechanova, R., 237
Heckman, J. J., 130
Heide, J. B., 18, 277
Heimeriks, K. H., 12
Heine, S. J., 217
Helfat, C. E., 264
Helfert, G., 268, 270
Helpman, E., 117

Helsinki School of Economics, University of Vaasa, 310
Henderson, A. D., 265, 419
Hennart, J.-F., 67, 345, 346, 348, 352, 357, 358
Henttonen, K., 204
Herbert, J. F., 281
Hersch, L., 341
Hesketh, B., 235
Hesterly, W. S., 250, 292, 293, 299, 300, 301, 302, 303, 304, 305, 306, 308
high value resellers, 171
Hill, H., 35, 44, 180, 366, 368, 369
Hills, G. E., 177, 178, 180, 183, 307
Hinds, P. J., 204, 205, 206, 208, 209
Hitachi, 366
Hite, J. M., 277, 292, 293, 299, 300, 301, 302, 303, 304, 305, 306, 308
Hoang, H., 292, 293, 303, 304, 306
Hodgetts, R., 81, 293
Hofstede, 352
Holladay, C. L., 235
Holm, U., 50, 272
home country measures (HCMs), 127–30
  rationale for, to promote OFDI, 127–9
honesty, 225
Hood, N., 48
Hornsby, J., 52
Hosono, K., 365
House, R. J., 217
Hoven Stohs, J., 220
Hsu, C. C., 270
Hu, M. Y., 351, 358
Huber, G. P., 253
Huberman, M., 53, 254
Hubert, F., 83, 89, 90
Hughes, P. J., 416, 417
Hulland, J., 19
Hultman, C. M., 177, 180, 186, 189
humane orientation, 229
human resources, leadership and culture, 199–245
  expatriate adjustment, training programmes for, 233–42
  intercultural ethical leadership, 216–29
  transnational teams (TNTs), interpersonal relationships in, 201–12
Hunt, S. D., 189
Hutson, Elaine, 110
Huy, Q. N., 53
hybrid organizations, 405
Hymer, S. H., 50, 97, 349

hypotheses, 13–17
  alliance entrepreneurship/capability and foreign market performance, relations between, 13–17
  alliance knowledge sharing, barriers to, 15–16
  corporate disclosure in theory and, 416–19
  international entrepreneurial orientation (IEO), 144–9
  learning orientation, 16–17
  moderator, 418–19
  research, 265–72
  Sapir-Whorf, 7

IBM, 17
ICT systems, 169
identification-based trust, 337–8
IEO, *see* international entrepreneurial orientation (IEO)
Imai, K., 367
Imaizumi, A., 241
IMP group's network approaches, 296–8
imported management practices, 412–28
  corporate disclosure in theory, and hypothesis, 416–19; moderator hypothesis, 418–19
  data analyses and results, 421–5
  German corporate governance, 414–15
  individual executive compensation, disclosure of, 415–16; empirical account, 416; regulatory account, 415–16
  methodology, 419–21; control variable, 421; dependent variable, 420; independent variable, 420; moderator variable, 420–1
incremental processes, 57–8
independent construals of self, 372
independent variables, 351–2, 420
  control variables, 351–2
  explanatory variables, 351
  interactive terms, 351–2
  specification of model, 352–3
India, 114–16
  export performance, 114–16
  OFDI, overview of, 114
individual executive compensation, disclosure of, 415–16
  empirical account, 416
  regulatory account, 415–16
influence mechanisms, 184–7
informal constraints, 369

information, 56
information and communications technology (ICT), 163
information sharing, 271–2
infrastructure, 39
in-group collectivism, 229
Inkpen, A., 16, 272, 307, 329, 338, 340
innovativeness, 144, 158
innovative value creation, 180
institutional collectivism, 229
institutional perspectives, of economists and sociologists, 368–9
institutional theory, 380–2
instrumental stakeholder theory, 379
intangible assets, 100
intellectual property rights, *see* multinational performance, and intellectual property rights
interaction adjustment, 237
interactive terms, 351–2
intercultural ethical leadership, 216–29
  competence of, implications for, 226–9: ethical leadership competencies, 227–9; intercultural competencies, 226–7
  cross-cultural business ethics, 219–20
  cross-cultural leadership, 219
  ethical leadership: definition of, 220–1; endorsement of, 220–3
  in Germany, 223–6
  in Ireland, 223–6
  societal culture, 217–19
internal institutions in corporate governance, 389–92
International Business Review, 81
international cooperative alliance (ICA), 337
international diversification, 68–74
  international strategy, 71–4
  multinationals, 69–71
  performance, 74
international diversification strategy, 145
international entrepreneurial orientation (IEO), 144–5
  business model and value chain constructs of, 163–74
  contingency factors in, 143–59
  measurement of, 150
  and performance, 146–9; degree of internationalization (DOI), effects of, 147–8; environmental turbulence, effects of, 148–9
international entrepreneurship (IE), 164, 178–80
international financial crisis, 65–6
International Financial Statistics (IFS), 40
international firms, 152
internationalization, 127–30
  degree of, 147–8
  measurement of: scales of, 151; scope of, 151; time of, 151
  pathways and degree of, 145–6
  see also internationalization, financial incentives and firm performance in Italy
internationalization, financial incentives and firm performance in Italy, 126–37
  empirical analysis, 131–6: data, 131–2; econometric findings, 134–5; model, 132–4; variables, 132–4
  firm performance, 127–30
  foreign direct investment (FDI), financial incentives and growth of, 129–30
  home country measures (HCMs), 127–30; rationale for, to promote OFDI, 127–9
  internationalization, 127–30
  methodology, 130–1
international joint ventures (IJV), 313–61
  asset specificity/asset opacity, context of, 349–50
  domestic/cross-border joint ventures (JV), 345–58
  International Strategic Alliances, trust-performance study of, 315–41
International Monetary Fund (IMF), 40
international new venture (INV)
  concept of, 179
  entrepreneurial marketing strategies, dimensions of, 181–4
  research on marketing in, 178–80
International Office Database, 41
international performance, 272
international product fragmentation, 28–30
  definition of, 27
  implications of, 36–7
international production networks, 30–4
  Granger causality tests, 32–4

International Strategic Alliances (ISA)
  satisfaction with, 334
  trust-performance study of, 315–41;
    analysis methods, 321–2; data
    collection, 321–2; fieldwork,
    characteristics of, 321; performance
    measurements, 329–35; reviewed
    studies, characteristics of, 316–20;
    samples, 321–2; trust, 322–38
international strategy, 71–4
interpersonal affect, 208–9
Investment Development Path (IDP), 34
inward foreign direct investment (IFDI), 34
Ireland, intercultural ethical leadership in,
  223–6
ISA, see International Strategic Alliances
  (ISA)
Ishida, J., 129
Italy, internationalization, financial
  incentives and firm performance in,
  126–37
Itsutomo, Mitsui, 371
Ivancic, K., 235

Jackson, S. E., 217, 219, 270, 380, 381, 393,
  415
Jain, S. C., 182, 185, 187
Jambulingam, T., 146, 150
Janssens, M., 207
Jantunen, S., 144
Jap, S. D., 321, 334, 335
Japanese dependence, 372–3
Japanese language, 372–3
  and society, 373–4
Japanese multinational enterprises, fall of,
  69–71
Japan Small Business Research Institute,
  374
Jarillo, J., 48, 267, 278, 299, 305
Jarvenpaa, S. L., 206, 208, 209
Javalgi, R. G., 166
Javidan, P. W., 217
Jaworski, B. J., 18, 150
Jelinek, M., 209
Jemison, D., 269
Jennings, D. F., 321, 335, 337
Jensen, M. C., 347, 379, 392, 416, 417
Jha, R., 118
Johanson, J., 48, 97, 117, 119, 120, 122,
  145, 177, 266, 270, 292, 294, 301, 302,
  357
John, G., 18
Johnson, G., 52, 53, 250

joint venture (JV), guarantee function of
  equity in, 347–8
Jones, M. V., 145, 146, 147, 165, 178, 190,
  235, 281, 368, 369, 379
Jongwanich, J., 28
Jöreskog, K. G., 153
Joshi, V., 114, 115, 208
Jost, T., 83, 89
Journal of International Business Studies, 81
Judge, W. Q., 381, 393
Jungnickel, R., 84
Juselius, K., 119

Kakabadse, A., 220, 223
Kale, P., 12, 23, 264, 267, 269, 271, 280
Kanaya, T., 235
kanji, 373
Kankahalli, A., 208, 211
Kanter, R., 277
Kanungo, R. N., 221
Kapasuwan, S., 264
Kaplan, S., 413
Kasuser, 315
Katsikeas, C. S., 12, 13, 143, 148, 185, 187,
  190, 191, 272, 277
Katz, J. P., 234, 384
Kauser, S., 315, 334, 337
Kay, J., 379
Kazanjian, R., 292, 294, 301, 302, 303
Kealey, D. J., 233, 234
Kearney, C., 119
Kearney, Colm, 1
Keating, M., 217
keiretsu'
  definition of, 365–8
  principles of, linguistic approach to,
    371–4; dependence, 372–3; language,
    371–4; thoughts, 371
  terms for, alternate, 365–8
  see also economic organization, and social
    solidarity
Kelly, L., 180
Kennedy, P., 85, 390
Kenny, B., 267
Kent, C. A., 402
Kenz, M., 347
Keupp, M., 143, 166, 177, 178, 179, 190
Khandwalla, P. N., 184, 185, 187
Khanna, T., 12, 14, 16
Killing, J. P., 315, 316
Kim, D., 11, 86, 181, 183, 188, 190, 216,
  217, 426
Kin'daichi, 372

King, R. G., 119
Kitayama, S., 372
Kittler, M., 205, 206, 234
Klein, H. J., 235
Klimoski, R., 205
Kline, J. M., 130
Klodt, H., 91
Knight, G. A., 11, 143, 145, 146, 147, 148, 151, 168, 178, 179, 181, 292, 294, 305
knowledge, 300
knowledge and networks, 247–312
   born globals (BGs), network, and firm performance, link between, 292–310
   network international performance and telecommunications, convergence of, 263–84
   subsidiary learning, microfoundation for middle manager, 249–60
knowledge creation, 207–8
knowledge redundancy, 271
knowledge search, microfoundation of, 255–6
Knox, S., 398
Knudsen, M. P., 166, 172, 173
Kocak, A., 181
Kock, S., 165
Kogut, B., 15, 16, 249, 257, 266, 352, 357
Kohli, A. K., 18, 150
Koike, K., 366
Koka, B. R., 269
Kokko, A., 126, 127, 136
Koller, R. H., 307
Komiya, R., 366, 367
Kompass Finland, 149
Korhonen, H., 173
Kosonen, M., 164
Kotler, P., 177, 182, 183
KPSS test statistic, 85
Kraakman, R., 414, 426
Kranenburg, H. V., 263
Krapfel, R. E., 167, 168
Krieg, P. C., 180
Krishnan, R., 329, 334, 338, 339
Kropp, F., 144, 181
Krugman, P., 84, 117
Kuhnen, C. M., 387
Kuivalainen, O., 143, 144, 145, 146
Kumar, N., 37, 113, 117, 122, 128, 207, 211
Kunii, I. M., 365
Kurosawa, Y., 365
Kutschker, M., 146
Kwiatkowski, D., 85, 86
Kwon, Y.-C., 337

Laanti, R., 179, 186
Lado, N., 18
LaForge, R. W., 177
Lage-Hidalgo, F., 119
Lai, K. S., 120, 366, 369
Lall, R. B., 118
Lam, L. W., 163
Lamming, R., 365
Landis, R. S., 274
Lane, P. J., 250, 269, 272, 321, 328, 337, 350
language, 371
   Japanese, 372–4
Larcker, D., 20
Larimo, Jorma, 186, 345, 352, 357
Larson, A., 292, 299, 300, 301, 302, 303, 304, 305
Lau, E., 204
Lavie, D., 279
Law 100/1990, 131
law abiding, 225
Lawrence, R. Z., 31
Layes, G., 216
Leadbeater, C., 402, 405
Leadership, *see* human resources, leadership and culture
Leaptrott, J., 381, 393
learning, 269
learning orientation, 16–17
Lee, M. J., 131, 132, 235, 421
Leibowitz, S., 390
Leidner, D. E., 208, 209
Lencioni, P. M., 389
Lenihan, H., 129
Leonidou, L. C., 182, 191
Levchenko, A., 89
level of analysis, 404
Levinson, C., 180
Levinthal, L., 16, 251, 269, 271, 272
Levitt, T., 182
Lewicki, R. J., 322, 337
Lewin, A., 82
Lewis, V. L., 292, 302, 304, 306, 391
Li, L., 96, 97, 98, 100, 145, 147, 271, 272, 276, 322, 340
Li, P. P., 35
liability of foreignness, 349
Lieberman, M. B., 265
Liesch, P. W., 147
Liew, V. K. S., 120
Light, P. C., 402, 404, 406
Likert, R., 52
Lim, S. H., 130
Lin, A. L., 117, 271, 272, 315, 334, 337, 340

Lincoln, Y. S., 254
Lindqvist, J., 179
Lipparini, A., 266, 267
Lippman, S., 348
Lipsey, R., 82, 84
LISREL 8.30, 153, 274
literature reviews
  entrepreneurial marketing strategies, 178–84; entrepreneurial marketing, 180–1; entrepreneurship-marketing interface, 180–1; international entrepreneurship (IO), research on marketing in, 178–80; international new venture (INV), research on marketing in, 178–80
  exports on outward federal direct investment, influence of, 116–18
  multinational performance, and intellectual property rights, 97–8
  social entrepreneurship (SE), 400–2
Little, I. M. D., 114, 115, 153
Liu, X., 81, 116, 118, 381, 393
Loane, S., 178, 179, 264, 280
Löhnert, B., 223, 226
Löhr, A., 219, 220, 226
London, T., 397, 398, 399
Longnecker, C. O., 235
Loo, P. C., 337
Lorange, P., 265, 315, 316
Lord, R. G., 219
Lorenzoni, G., 266, 267
Lou, Y., 126, 129
Lovås, 251, 252
Love, J. H., 119
Loxton, R., 264, 267, 272
Lu, J. W., 100, 126, 351, 355
Lubatkin, M., 269, 272, 379, 380, 381, 393
Lumpkin, G. T., 143, 144, 146, 148, 157, 158, 185, 304, 305
Lundan, M., 97, 397
Luo, X., 329, 334, 335, 337, 338, 339, 340, 348
Luostarinen, R., 177
Lusch, R. F., 18
Lyles, M., 277, 355
Lyon, D. W., 148, 413, 427
Lyostarinen, 294

MacDonald, R., 119
MacKinnon, J., 85
macroeconomics stability, 39
macro institutions in corporate governance, 384–9

Maddala, G., 86
Madden, G., 220
Madhavan, R., 299, 309
Madhok, A., 267
Madsen, T. K., 151, 179, 293
Maeseneire, W., 129, 130
Mahadevan, B., 164
Mahajan, V., 180
Mair, J., 400, 402, 403
Majkgård, D., 308
majority ownership, 355
Maklan, S., 398
Mallampally, P., 84
managed services model, 263
management practices, *see* imported management practices
Manuel, J. A., 206
March, J. G., 22, 251, 368
Margolis, S., 390
Marion, N., 89
market orientation, 185
market transactions, measurement costs in, 346–7
Markman, G. D., 267
Markus, G., 372
Markusen, A., 130
Markusen, J. R., 117, 122
Marschak, J., 130
Marsh, S. J., 12
Marshall, G. W., 267
Marti, I., 400, 402, 403
Martin, J. A., 16, 219, 223, 226, 227, 264, 280, 400
Martinez, J., 48
Martins, P. S., 97, 98, 106, 110
Massetti, B. L., 402
Mathews, J. A., 145
Matsuno, K., 185
Matsushima, N., 129
Matsushita Group, 366
Matthyssens, P., 163
Mattsson, L.-G., 302
Matze, M., 216, 227
Mauborgne, R., 181, 183, 188, 190
Maurice, M., 223
Mauro, P., 89
Mavondo, F. T., 350
maximum likelihood (ML), 153
Maydeu-Olivares, A., 18
Mayer, C., 421
Mazarol, 276
Maznevski, M. L., 204, 206, 207
McAllister, D. J., 338

McAuley, A., 279
McCahery, P., 379
McCarthy, J. E., 182
McConnell, J. J., 416
Mcdonough, 205
McDougall, P. P., 143, 144, 145, 146, 147, 163, 173, 177, 178, 179, 181, 186, 190, 191, 292, 293, 294, 301, 305
McEvily, B., 265
McFadden, 353
McGrath, R. G., 164, 201
McGuire, J., 366
McKnight, P. J., 416
McLean, M., 400, 402, 404
McNaughton, R., 179, 268
MDAX, 419–20
measurements
  alliance entrepreneurship/capability and foreign market performance, relations between, 18–19
  ceteris paribus, 346, 350
  expatriate adjustment, training programmes for, 236–7
  international entrepreneurial orientation (IEO), 150
  of internationalization, 151
  market transactions, costs in, 346–7
Meckling, W. H., 347, 379, 392, 416, 417
Medlin, C., 329
Meister, D. B., 250, 252
Melitz, J. M., 98, 179
Mendenhall, M. E., 201, 209, 234, 236, 240, 242
Mendonca, M., 221
Menon, T., 251, 258
Merz, G. R., 150
Meschi, P.-X., 315
Mesquite, L. F., 15
meta-ethic, 228
methodology/methods
  business model and value chain constructs of international entrepreneurial orientation, 168–9
  corporate governance and organization, 382–4
  domestic/cross-border joint ventures (JV), 350–3; data sources, 350–1; dependent variables, 351; independent variables, 351–2; sample selection, 350–1
  expatriate adjustment, training programmes for, 236–7; measurements, 236–7; sample, 236

imported management practices, 419–21; control variable, 421; dependent variable, 420; independent variable, 420; moderator variable, 420–1
international entrepreneurial orientation (IEO), 149–58; data collection, 149; measurement items, 150–3
internationalization, financial incentives and firm performance in Italy, 130–1
subsidiary learning, microfoundation for middle manager, 252–4; data collection and analysis, 253–4; research design and setting, 252–3
subsidiary middle manager, contribution of, 52–4; case, selection of, 53; data analysis, 53–4; data collection, 53–4; research design, 52–3
Meyer, K. E., 12, 202, 212, 380, 399
micro institutions in corporate governance, 389–92
Microsoft, 17
middle manager, *see* subsidiary middle manager
middle manager entrepreneur, 57
Miles, M., 53, 180, 254
Millennium Development Goals, 398
Miller, D., 144, 148, 185, 202, 212, 253, 402, 406
Milner, C., 28, 36, 37
Min, S., 271
Miner, A. S., 18
Ministry of International Trade and Commerce, 131
Mira, S., 416
Mitsubishi, 366
Mitsui, 366
Miwa, Y., 365
MNE, *see* multinational enterprise (MNE)
moderator hypothesis, 418–19
moderator variable, 420–1
Moen, O., 146, 151, 179
Moffit, R., 130, 177, 180, 189
Mohammed, S., 205
Mohr, J., 268, 321, 334, 335, 337
Möller, K. E., 167, 168, 171, 272, 279, 280, 296
Mom, T., 250
Montero, M., 116, 249, 251
Montoya-Weiss, M. M., 208
Moore, J., 346, 348
Moorman, C., 265, 267, 271
morality, 220
Moran, P., 266, 267

Morgan, N., 189
Morita, H., 366
Morris, S., 118, 177, 178, 180, 181, 183, 185, 187, 188, 189, 191, 233
Morrison, A., 227
Mort, G., 400
Mortensen, M., 204, 205, 206, 208, 209
Mosakowski, E., 204, 205, 206, 208, 209, 211
Mosselman, M., 129
Mowery, D. C., 271
Mudambi, R., 49, 50
Mulherin, J. H., 386
multinational corporations (MNCs)
  commercial, responsibilities of, 398
  social challenges, 398; initiatives for addressing, 399; theoretical explanation of, 399–400; market-based approach, 398–9
  social entrepreneurship (SE), 407; corporate, 407–8; definitions of, 402–6; literature, 400–2
  socially entrepreneurial behaviour of, 397–408
multinational enterprise (MNE)
  developing, rise of, 71
  Japanese, fall of, 69–71
  regional, 64–77; government policy, 74–7; international diversification, 68–74; international financial crisis, 65–6
  as regional networks, 67–8
  subsidiary middle manager, contribution of, 48–60; findings, 54–8; methodology, 52–4; case, selection of, 53; data analysis, 53–4; data collection, 53–4; research design, 52–3; theoretical framework, 49–52
  United States, fall of, 69–71
multinationalisty, 99–100
multinationality-performance (MP) relationship, 98
multinational performance, and intellectual property rights, 96–110
  contributions, 98–105; data, 98–9; descriptive statistics, 101–5; key variables, 99–101; results, 105–7
  literature review, 97–8
  results, 105–7
  robustness, 107–9
multivariate analysis of variance (MANOVA), 221
Munro, H. J., 178, 179, 292, 294, 305
Murnighan, J. K., 204

Murphy, P. E., 220, 224, 417
Murray, G. C., 178, 179, 276
Muthusamy, S. K., 335, 337, 340
Myers, M. B., 147

NACE industrial classification, 87, 90
Nachum, L., 349
Nahapiet, J., 204, 249, 278
Nakahara, H., 366
Nakajima, C., 381
Nakamura, T., 366
Nakane, C., 367, 371, 372
Naphiet, J., 294, 307
Narula, R., 51, 168
Narus, J. A., 334
Narver, J. C., 150, 185, 188, 272
natural resources, 45
Navarra, P., 50
Nayyar, P., 16
Nelson, R. R., 250, 253
Nesse, K., 130
network approaches, 296
  IMP group's, 296–8
  strategic, 299–300
networked entrepreneurs, 307
network industrial organization, 367
network initiation, 268
network international performance and telecommunications, convergence of, 263–84
  capabilities model of, 264–5
  data collection, 273–4
  research hypothesis, 265–72; coordination, 268–9; information sharing, 271–2; international performance, 272; learning, 269; network initiation, 268; network relationships, 266–7; network resources, 270; strength of ties, 265–6; synergy sensitive resources, 271; trust, 267–8
  results, 274–5
  unit of analysis, 273–4; common method bias, 273–4; scale validation, 274
network learning, 269
network operation, 277–8
network relationships, 266–7
network resources, 270, 279
networks
  born globals (BGs), 294–6; evolution of, 303–4; firm performance and, link between, 292–310
  entrepreneurial behaviour and, 304–5

international production, 30–4
  regional, MNE as, 67–8
  strategic, 296
  see also born globals (BGs); knowledge and networks
network size, 303
Nevin, J. R., 268
newly industrialized economies (NIEs), 27
Newman, A., 130
Newton, J., 51
Ng, P. W.-K., 334, 338, 340
Nicholas, S. J., 122
Nicholls, A., 402, 403, 405, 406
Nicholson, N., 241
Nickerson, J. A., 251
Nielsen, B. B., 315, 328, 337
Nieto, M. J., 421
Nigeria, corporate governance in
  corporate culture and, 389–90
  corporate values as determinants of, 389
  economic context of, 386
  ethical climate and, 391–2
  institutional framing of, 384
  legal context of, 388–9
  path dependence and shaping of, 390–1
  social context of, 387–8
  see also corporate governance
Nolan, P., 51
Nonaka, I., 250
non-discriminatory treatment, 224
non-governmental organizations (NGOs), 398
non-tariff barriers, 39
Nooteboom, B., 315, 368, 369
Nordman, E. R., 179
North, D. C., 368, 388
Noteboom, B., 251
Notes of the Consolidated Financial Statements, 416
Nowak, E., 416
Nummela, N., 163
Nunnenkamp, P., 83, 84, 89
Nutt, P. C., 258

object, 373
O'Cass, A., 158
Odaka, K., 366
Oddou, G. R., 239
O'Dwyer, B., 220
OECD, 129
O'Grady, S., 350
Oh, C. H., 69, 71
Ohno, S., 373

Okhuysen, G. A., 258
Okike, E. N. M., 388
Oldham, G. R., 201
Olebune, C., 388
Oliver, C., 368
Oracle, 17
Orbis, 98
Organization, *see* corporate governance
organizational adaptation, achieving, 254–5
original equipment manufacture (OEM), 11
Orrù, M., 366
Osberg, S., 400
Osborn, R. N., 368, 369
Osman-Gani, A. M., 235, 240
outsourcing, 263
outward foreign direct investment (OFDI), 79–139
  exports on, influence of, 113–23
  German manufacturing industries, 81–92
  home country measures for promotion of, 127–9
  India, 114
  internationalization, financial incentives and firm performance in Italy, 126–37
  multinational performance, and intellectual property rights, 96–110
  see also foreign direct investment (FDI)
Overby, J. W., 271
Overton, T. S., 149
Oviatt, B. M., 143, 145, 146, 147, 163, 173, 177, 178, 179, 181, 186, 191, 292, 293, 294, 301, 305
ownership advantage, 97
Oxelheim, L., 130
Oxley, J., 355

Page, A. L., 272
Pain, N., 83, 89, 90, 116
Palamara, G., 179
Palazzo, B., 220, 223, 226
Palepu, K. G., 380, 413, 417
Pan, Y., 345, 346, 351, 352, 353, 355, 358
Panaccio, A., 233
Pangarkar, N., 96, 97
Panteli, N., 205
Pantzalis, C., 100, 101
Pappas, J., 59
Parkhe, A., 322
Parkinson, J., 379
partner categorization, 167

partners
  core, 171
  distributed, 13
  downstream sales, 171–2
  foreign, 350
path dependence, 390–1
Pedersen, T., 67
Peng, M. W., 368
Penrose, E. T., 97, 164, 272
Peredo, A. M., 400, 402, 404
Pereira, A., 270
performance, 74
  expected, 427
  export, in India, 114–16
  firm, 99, 127–30
  foreign market, 14–15
  international, 272
  international diversification, 74
  international entrepreneurial orientation, 146–9
  multinational, and intellectual property rights, 96–110
  network international, and telecommunications, 263–84
  trust, effects of, 335–8
performance effectiveness, 334
performance orientation, 229
Perron, P., 86
Perry, A. C., 277
personal moral code, 225
Peteraf, M., 264, 348
Peters, B. G., 390, 391
Petri, P. A., 117
Petrick, J. A., 221
Pfaffermayr, M., 116, 117, 118
Pfeffer, J., 251, 258, 418
Pickard, J., 234
Piercy, N. F., 173
Pierson, P., 391
Ping, R. A., 274
Pisano, G., 269
Plakoyiannaki, E., 181
Podolny, J. M., 266
Podsiadlowski, A., 201
Polanyi, M., 249
Pollach, I., 391
Porter, M. E., 64
post-arrival training (POAT), 233–5
postwar business groups, 367
Powell, W. W., 267, 269, 272
Power, D. J., 253
power distance, 229
Poynter, T., 48

Pradhan, J., 128
Pradhan, J. P., 113, 114, 115, 118, 122
Prahalad, C. K., 180, 185, 186, 189, 270, 397, 398, 399
pre-departure training (PRDT), 233–5
Prince, Y., 129
privacy, 374
proactive firm, 304–5
proactiveness, 144
production network, *see* international product fragmentation
Profile Direct, 149
propositions, 187–90
Protheroe, D. R., 233, 234
Pruitt, D. G., 267
Puck, J. F., 207, 233, 236
Pugh, D., 54

Qian, G. M., 100, 101
Qiu, F., 346, 352, 353, 358
Quester, P., 329
Quinn, J. F., 221
Quinones, M. A., 235

Ragozzino, R., 346
Rajala, A., 296
Rajan, R. G., 352
Rallet, A., 251
Ramamurti, R., 68
Ramaseshan, B., 337
Ramseyer, J. M., 365
Ranft, A. L., 12
Rangan, S., 31, 183, 349
Rappoport, P., 86
Rauch, A., 143, 185
Razin, A., 84
Read, S., 189
real effective exchange rate (REER), 38
Reddy, S., 346
regional and global perspectives, 9–78
  alliance entrepreneurship/capability and foreign market performance, 11–24
  foreign direct investment (FDI), in Asia, 27–46
  multinational enterprise (MNE): regional, 64–77; subsidiary middle manager in, contribution of, 48–60
regional multinational enterprise (MNE), 64–77
  government policy, 74–7
  international diversification, 68–74
  international financial crisis, 65–6
  regional networks, MNE as, 67–8

regional trade agreements (RTA), 39
regulatory account, 415–16
Reid, S. D., 277
Renneboog, L., 379
Rennie, M. W., 179, 293
research design, 382–4
research hypothesis, 265–72
  coordination, 268–9
  information sharing, 271–2
  international performance, 272
  learning, 269
  network initiation, 268
  network relationships, 266–7
  network resources, 270
  strength of ties, 265–6
  synergy sensitive resources, 271
  trust, 267–8
Resick, J., 216, 219, 221, 223
resources
  basic, 300
  born global (BG) internal, 300–3
  natural, 45
  network, 270, 279
  synergy sensitive, 271
  Syscon Ltd, 172–3
respect, 224
results of studies
  alliance entrepreneurship/capability and foreign market performance, relations between, 19–21
  Asia, foreign direct investment in, 41–5
  domestic/cross-border joint ventures (JV), 353–8; fit of model, 353; specificity/opacity, effect of, 353–8
  expatriate adjustment, training programmes for, 237–8
  exports on outward federal direct investment, influence of, 120–1
  multinational performance, and intellectual property rights, 105–7
  network international performance and telecommunications, convergence of, 274–5
return on assets (ROA), 420
return on investment (ROI), 132
Reuer, J. J., 315, 316, 346
Rialp, J., 166, 178, 179, 190
Riccio, E. L., 315
Ricks, A., 126
Ridderstråle, J., 50
Rifkin, G., 180
Rindfleisch, A., 265, 267, 271
Ripollès, 185

risk-taking, 144, 305
Ritter, T., 267, 268, 270
Robbins, G. E., 421
Roberts, M. J., 84
Robertson, P., 220, 346
Robie, C., 233
Robson, M. J., 11, 13, 315, 328, 334, 335, 338, 339, 340
robustness, 107–9
Roe, M. J., 384
Rogers, E. M., 418
Rohlen, T. P., 372
Romanelli, E., 148
Ronkainen, I. A., 183
Rose, A., 89
Rosen, E., 180
Rosenbloom, R., 164
Rosenkopf, L., 272
Rouleau, L., 53
Rousseau, D. M., 206, 267, 322, 340
Rowan, B., 380
Rowley, T. J., 264, 265, 267
Rugman, A. M., 48, 65, 67, 68, 69, 71, 76, 81, 96, 145, 147, 151, 163, 186, 250, 263, 264, 280, 293, 310, 345, 350, 357, 358, 366, 368, 374, 397, 408
Rumelt, R., 348
Ruokonen, M., 167, 171
Ryans, J. K., 182, 186

Saka-Helmhout, A., 257
Sako, M., 328, 337, 340, 368
Salacuse, J. W., 390
Salaff, J. W., 292, 303, 305
Salancik, G., 418
Sallis, J., 277, 321, 328, 334, 338, 339
Sanders, W. G., 412, 413, 414, 418, 419, 420, 421, 426
Sanwa Bank, 366
SAP, 17
Sapienza, H. J., 191
Sapir, E., 371
Sapir-Whorf hypothesis, 7
Sarkar, M. B., 12, 277
Sarmah, P., 126, 127, 128, 129, 130
Sauber, M. H., 150
Saussure, F., 371, 372, 373
Sauvant, K., 84
Savahn, 168
Scabini, P., 304, 305, 306
scale validation, 274
Schlegelmilch, B. B., 220, 391
Schreiner, M., 12, 14, 18, 23, 216, 217, 227

Schulz, A., 249
Schumpeter, J. A., 180
Schwab, K., 407
Schweiger, D. M., 258
Schwenk, C., 258
Scott, W. R., 186, 189, 368, 380, 381, 414
SDAX, 420
Securities and Exchange Commission (SEC), 419
Seelosa, C., 400
Seifer, D., 234
self, 372
self-designation, 373
self-selection, 130
Selmer, J., 233, 234, 237, 240, 241
Selnes, F., 277, 321, 328, 334, 338, 339
Sephton, P. S., 86
Seppanen, R., 322
Servais, P., 166, 172, 173, 179, 293
Seymour, R. G., 164, 165, 178, 179
Shaffer, M. A., 237
Shahrim, A., 413, 414, 415
Shams, R., 84
Shane, S., 13, 402
Shanley, M., 391
Shapiro, A., 126, 127, 128, 201, 204, 205, 233
shared understanding, 205
Sharma, K., 113, 122, 178, 292, 294, 300, 305, 308, 310, 406
Shaw, E., 180, 183, 315, 334, 337
Sheikh, H., 267
Shepherd, D., 143, 144, 146
Sherer, P. D., 421
Sheth, J. N., 180
Shin-Nittetsu, 366
shitauke group, 368
Shleifer, A., 380
Shoham, A., 274
Shrader, R. C., 178, 179, 294
Shuffler, M., 201, 206
Siddharthan, N., 118
Siggelkow, N., 53
Silberston, A., 379
Simiar, F., 316, 335, 337
Simmonds, P. G., 276
Simon, H. A., 368
Simonin, B. L., 15
Singh, H., 12, 23, 154, 267, 271, 307, 352, 357, 358, 366, 386
Singh, J., 68
Single European Market programme, 83, 90
Sinkovics, R., 48, 50, 254, 350

Sinkula, J. M., 269
Sitkin, S. B., 235
Sivakumar, K., 144
size of the management board (SIZEMB), 421, 424
Skuras, D., 130
Slangen, A. H., 346, 352, 357, 358
Slater, S. F., 150, 185, 272
Slevin, D. P., 145, 148, 185, 304, 305, 402, 406
Slywotzky, A., 164
small and medium-sized entrpreneurial (SME) firms, 11
Smallbone, D., 403
Smart, D. T., 146
Smith, C., 164, 168, 226
Snehota, I., 294, 296, 298, 299, 302, 303, 304, 306, 307, 308
social competence, 267
social entrepreneurship (SE), 407
    corporate, 407–8
    definitions of: key concepts in, 402–5; reconciliation of, 406
    literature, 400–2
    social challenges, 403–4
social exchange theory (SET), 322
socially entrepreneurial behaviour of multinational corporations (MNCs), 397–408
social mission, 403–4
social openness, 224
social solidarity, *see* economic organization, and social solidarity
social value creation, 403–4
societal culture, 217–19
society, Japanese language and, 373–4
Society for Corporate Governance, 382
Solis, M., 366, 370
solo entrepreneurs, 307
Sörbom, D., 153
Sosik, J. J., 228
Soskice, D., 81, 90, 413, 414, 426
Spanish Institute for Foreign Trade, 129
Sparrow, P., 212, 239
specification of model, 352–3
Spekman, R., 321, 334, 335, 337
Spence, M., 145
Spender, J. C., 22, 251, 258, 259
Spletzer, J. R., 237
Stack, M., 390
Stahl, G. K., 201, 205, 208, 234
Stalk, G., 366

Standard of International Trade
    Classification (SITC) data, 28, 41
Starosta, W. J., 227
Starr, J. A., 292, 299, 300, 301, 302, 303,
    304, 305
Steenkamp, J.-B. E. M., 152
Steensma, H., 355
Steidlmeier, P., 221
Steinmann, H., 219, 220, 226
Sternberg, E., 391
Stettes, O., 82
Stiles, P., 416
Stoughton, N. M., 417
Strange, R., 51
strategic contributions by subsidiary middle
    manager, 54–5
strategic corporate social responsibility, 379
strategic influences of subsidiary middle
    manager, 55–7
    downward influences, 56–7
    upward influences, 55–6
strategic network approaches, 299–300
strategic networks, 296
strategies
    blue ocean, 181
    deliberate, 56–7
    entrepreneurial marketing, 177–92
    funding, 405
    international, 71–4
    international diversification, 145
strategy development by subsidiary middle
    manager, 52, 54
strength of ties, 265–6, 303
Structural Equation Modeling (SEM)
    approach, 19
Stuart, T. E., 279
Sturgeon, T., 51
Styles, C., 164, 165, 178, 179
subcontracting, 263
sub-group formation, 204–5
Subrahmanyan, S., 399, 407
subsidiary learning, microfoundation for
    middle manager, 249–60
    methods, 252–4; data collection and
        analysis, 253–4; research design and
        setting, 252–3
    observations, 254–6; knowledge search,
        microfoundation of, 255–6;
        organizational adaptation, achieving,
        254–5; subsidiary level learning,
        outcomes of, 254–5
    theoretical background, 250–2
subsidiary level learning, 254–5

subsidiary middle manager
    in multinational enterprise, contribution
        of, 48–60; findings, 54–8;
        methodology, 52–4; theoretical
        framework, 49–52
    strategic contributions, 54–5
    strategic influences, 55–7; downward
        influences, 56–7; upward influences,
        55–6
    strategy development, 52, 54
    see also subsidiary learning,
        microfoundation for middle manager
Sugimoto, Y., 366
Sugiyama, Lebra, 367, 372
Sullivan, D., 145, 151
Sullivan-Mort, G., 276
Sumitomo, 366
Sutanto, J., 205
Suzuki, M., 372
Svahn, S., 279, 280
Swift, J. S., 235
synergy sensitive resources, 271
Syscon Ltd, 169–73
    capabilities, 172–3
    customer lock-in, 169–70
    customer value, 169–70
    downstream sales partners, 171–2
    key resources, 172–3
    upstream suppliers, 170–1
    value creation, changes in, 172–3
Szulanski, G., 16, 249, 251

Tabachnick, B. G., 21, 423
Taggart, J., 48
Tajfel, H. H., 204
Takeuchi, R., 237
Tallman, S., 96, 97, 145, 366
tariff barriers, 39
Tavares, A., 83
Taylor, P. J., 235, 416
team identity, 204
Teece, D. J., 16, 164, 185, 264, 269, 271,
    347
telecommunications, 279–80
    see also network international
        performance and
        telecommunications, convergence of
Tell, J., 278
Teng, B.-S., 315, 339
Tesar, G., 177
Te Velde, 126, 127, 128, 129, 130, 133,
    136
Thacker, J. W., 235

Theodosiou, M., 182
theories, 13–17
  alliance entrepreneurship/capability and foreign market performance, relations between, 13–17
  alliance knowledge sharing, barriers to, 15–16
  corporate disclosure in, and hypothesis, 416–19
  Granovetter's, of business groups, 369–71
  institutional, 380–2
  instrumental stakeholder, 379
  learning orientation, 16–17
  social exchange, 322
  transaction cost, 322
Thomas Financial, 350
Thompson, J. L., 403, 404
Thornton, E., 365
thoughts, 371
tie density, 303
Tikkanen, H., 164
Timmers, P., 164
Titman, S., 352
Toh, T. S., 235
Tolstoy, D., 279
Tomlinson, P. R., 365
Torbiorn, I., 233, 234
Torre, A., 251
Törrönen, P., 167, 168, 171
Tosi, H. L., 412
Townsend, J. D., 186, 190
Toyota Group, 366
Toyota Stock Exchange, 366
transaction cost theory (TCE), 322
transfer barrier, 348
transnational, virtual teams, see transnational teams (TNTs)
transnational teams (TNTs)
  behavioral aspects, 206–8
  cognitive aspects, 204–6
  interpersonal affect, 208–9
  interpersonal relationships in, 201–12
Transparency International, 392
Treviño, L. K., 216, 217, 221
truly born globals, 151
trust, 205–6, 267–8
  ability-based, 337
  competence, 337
  conceptualization of, 322–8
  direct effects of, 337–8
  goodwill, 337
  identification-based, 337–8
  indirect effects of, 338
  key informants for, 329
  level of analysis for, 329
  operationalisation of, 328–9
  performance effects of, 335–8
Tsai, W., 249
Tsang, E. W. K., 235, 307, 348, 352
Tuckman, B., 208
Tung, R. L., 234, 413
Turnbull, P., 298, 308
Turner, C., 204
Tuschke, A. C., 412, 413, 414, 418, 419, 420, 421, 426
Tushman, M. L., 148, 158, 187
"two waves," concept of, 114
Tybout, J. R., 84
Tzelepis, D., 130

Ubeda, F., 129
Udayasankar, K., 381
Ulrich, P., 220
uncertainty avoidance, 229
UNCTAD data, 118
United Nations Commodity Statistics Database (UNCOMTRADE), 28, 40–1
United Nations Conference on Trade and Development (UNCTAD), 82, 84, 113, 122, 126, 129, 130
United Nations Development Program, 398
United States multinational enterprises, fall of, 69–71
unit of analysis, 273–4
  common method bias, 273–4
  scale validation, 274
unit root tests
  augmented, Dickey–Fuller and Kwiatkowski, 85–6
  Zivot and Andrews, 86–7
universal grammar, 374
University of Vaasa, 310
upstream suppliers, 170–1
Urata, S., 32
Uzzi, B., 265, 266, 267

Vahlne, J. E., 48, 97, 117, 122, 145, 177, 270, 292, 294, 301, 357
value chain, 163
value chain construct, see business model
value-creating transactions interfaces, 166
value creation, 172–3

value creation potential, 167–8
value resellers, 171
values, 389
   accidental, 389
   corporate, 389
   customer, 169–70
   enlightened shareholder, 379
Van de Ven, 281
van Luijk, 219
van Norden, S., 86
Van Tulder, R. J. M., 352
van Wijk, 251, 252, 257
van Wittelosstuijn, 413
variables
   control, 237, 351–2, 421
   dependent, 351, 420
   explanatory, 351
   independent, 351–2, 420
   moderator, 420–1
Varis, J., 171
Vector autoregressive (VAR) representation, 119
Venkataraman, S., 13, 185, 402
Verbeke, A., 48, 67, 68, 69, 81, 145, 147, 163, 186, 250, 345, 358, 397, 408
Vermeulen, F., 205, 211
Vernon, Ray, 48, 74, 97, 116
Verrecchia, R. E., 416, 417
Veugelers, R., 117
Vicente-Lorente, J. D., 348, 351
viewpoint, 373
Vishny, R. W., 380
Viswesvaran, C., 234
Vith, K., 268
Vitols, S., 414, 415
Vogel, E. F., 372
Vogiatzoglou, K., 28
Von Glinow, M. A., 208
Voss, Z. G., 143, 144, 335, 338

Wagner, J., 117
Wakelin, K., 116
Wallsten, S. J., 130
Walsh, J., 69
Walter, A., 264, 267, 268, 272
Wang, C. L., 315, 334, 337, 340
Ward, K., 205, 206, 207
Warner, M., 223
Watanabe, Y., 368
Waxin, M.-F., 233
Weber, C., 235, 369
Weerawardena, J., 158, 264, 267, 272, 276, 400

Weingart, L. R., 208
Weir, C. M., 416
Wei-Skillern, J., 398
Weitzman, E. A., 254
Welch, L., 234
Werner, S., 264, 412, 413, 414
Wernerfelt, B., 14, 185, 188, 270
Wessels, R., 352
West, S. G., 423
Westerlund, M., 166, 353
Westhead, P., 270
Westney, E., 68
Wheeler, C., 301, 303, 307
White, R., 48, 163
Whitley, R. D., 68, 81
Whittaker, D. H., 365
Whorf, B. L., 371, 372
Wictor, I., 294
Wiedersheim-Paul, F., 117, 177
Wieland, J., 389
Wiklund, J., 143, 144, 146
Willekens, M., 415
Williams, C., 48
Williamson, Oliver, 67, 322, 328, 347, 348, 366, 368, 369
Wilson, D. T., 209, 277, 279, 337
Wincent, J., 267, 276
Wind, Y., 180
windows of opportunity, 305
Winter, S. G., 14, 16, 250, 253, 254, 348
Witt, R., 82
Womack, J. P., 366
Wood, D., 407
Woodcock, P. C., 276
Wooldridge, B., 49, 52, 53, 54, 55, 57, 58, 59, 250, 253
work adjustment, 237
World Bank, 40, 97
World Economic Forum, 398
Wright, W., 126, 136

Yakasai, G. A., 388
Yamin, M., 48, 50, 350, 357
Yan, A., 341, 345, 346
Yang, Y., 97, 98, 106, 110
Yeoh, P. L., 12, 151
Yerokun, O., 386
Yi, Y., 153, 274
Yin, R. K., 52, 53, 169, 252, 254
Yip, P. S. L., 187, 352
Yli-Renko, H., 178, 294, 299, 300, 301, 307
Young, S., 83, 130, 281, 404, 406
Yunus, Mohammad, 404

Zaheer, S., 130, 265, 278, 315, 316, 329, 339, 349
Zahra, S. A., 143, 144, 146, 148, 149, 151, 157, 159, 163, 165, 166, 177, 178, 179, 188, 189, 190, 191, 294, 402, 403
zaibatus groups, 366, 367
Zajac, E. J., 414, 418, 420, 421, 426
Zakaria, N., 204
Zander, U., 15, 16, 143, 145, 241, 249, 257
Zeithaml, V. A., 187
Zellmer-Bruhn, M., 207, 211
Zeng, M., 341
Zenger, T. R., 251
Zhang, K. H., 276
Zhao, M. Y., 110
Zhou, L., 292, 294, 299, 303, 308
Zif, J., 145, 151
Zimmermann, A., 212, 239, 242, 412, 413, 414
Zingales, L., 352
Zivot, E., 86, 87
Zollo, M., 14, 16, 254
Zott, C., 164, 165, 166, 280
Zucchella, A., 179, 304, 305, 306
Zucker, L. G., 322, 380, 381